# CONTENTS

# AUTHOR'S NOTE

The storyline of this book focuses on key events in Seventh-day Adventist history from 1844 through 1891. Where additional comments and/or contrasting viewpoints that have been expressed by various authors since that time have been included in the endnotes, and they have been indicated by an asterisk (*) beside the endnote reference number. Chapters 18 through 36 are currently being written and will be published as a second volume, Lord willing, in 2011.

In the rush to print this book before the 2010 General Conference session, a much-needed final edit failed to take place. That fact, along with problems created between two incompatible computer programs, resulted in many formatting errors as well. Despite these shortcomings, nearly 3000 copies have been distributed since the General Conference session. With this second printing much effort has gone into correcting typographical and grammatical errors, formatting mistakes, missing references and confusing chapter organization. Nevertheless, with all the work that has gone into improving the book, it still remains the collective effort of laymen whose expertise is not in the writing, editing, or publishing profession. Any corrections are welcome. It is our prayer that *The Return of the Latter Rain* might play a small part in a renewed interest in the subject of the latter rain and give a credible answer for its long delay.

# The Loud Cry
# and The Latter Rain

## A Crucial Subject
## for Seventh-day Adventists Today

> There is nothing that Satan fears so much as that the people of God shall clear the way by removing every hindrance, so that the Lord can pour out his Spirit upon a languishing church and an impenitent congregation. ... Satan can no more hinder a shower of blessing from descending upon God's people than he can close the windows of heaven that rain cannot come upon the earth.[1]

Perhaps no other subject should receive our close attention as the subject of the Holy Spirit and His relationship to the plan of redemption. We are told that the Holy Spirit was given as a "regenerating agent, and without this the sacrifice of Christ would have been of no avail." Why? Because "sin could be resisted and overcome only through the mighty agency of the Third Person of the Godhead."[2] The Holy Spirit is the representative of Christ Himself, and is "accessible to all."[3] "This promised blessing, claimed by faith, brings all other blessings in its train."[4] This was the subject upon which Christ "dwelt most largely" during his earthly ministry.[5]

During the last 150 years, Seventh-day Adventists have given much attention to the subject of the Holy Spirit. In the *Index to the Writings of E. G. White,* 30 pages of references are listed on the topic of the Holy Spirit. Many Adventist books have been written over the years on the subject, all seeking to present more clearly the work of the Holy Spirit and our need of His indwelling.

The "early rain" and "latter rain" are intimately connected with this topic for they also "represent the work of the Holy Spirit."[6] "The outpouring of the Spirit in the days of the apostles was the beginning of the early, or former, rain, and glorious was the result."[7] The disciples, who only a few days before had all deserted Christ, now boldly testified of Him. The result of the early rain was soon realized; 3,000 were converted in a day and in a short time the world was "turned upside down" (Acts 17:6).

However, those of us living at the close of this earth's history will see a far greater manifestation of the Holy Spirit's power: "The great work of the gospel is not to close with less manifestation of the power of God than marked its opening. The prophecies which were fulfilled in the outpouring of the former rain at the opening of the gospel, are again to be fulfilled in the latter rain at its close."[8]

The early rain also represents the work of the Holy Spirit in conversion and the process of spiritual growth "from one stage to another." The latter rain, ripening earth's harvest, "represents the spiritual grace that prepares the church for the coming of the Son of man." But if the early rain has not done its work "the latter rain can bring no seed to perfection."[9]

The full significance of the latter rain, however, is seen only when placed in its proper setting in Adventist theology. Rather than being just one of a list of beliefs, the latter rain is closely associated with a proper understanding of the cleansing of the sanctuary, end-time judgment and last-day events, all set in the context of the great controversy theme.

The "loud cry" is closely connected with the latter rain, for those who receive the heavenly showers will give the final *message* of God to the world. "It is the latter rain, the refreshing from the presence of the Lord, the loud cry of the third angel" that enables God's people to "speak forth the truth with great power" amidst the most trying circumstances.[10] This "refreshing from the presence of the Lord, will come, to give power to the loud voice of the third angel, and prepare the saints to stand in the period when the seven last plagues shall be poured out."[11]

This "last message of mercy to be given to the world is a revelation of His character of love,"[12]* "the message of Christ's righteousness,"[13] the message of "justification by faith" which is the "third angel's message in verity [truth]."[14]

This message which God "commanded to be given to the world ... is to be proclaimed with a loud voice, and attended with the outpouring of His Spirit in a large measure."[15] We may look forward to the time when "the events of the Day of Pentecost shall be repeated with even greater power than on that occasion. John says, 'I saw another angel come down from heaven, having great power; and the earth was lightened with his glory' [Rev. 18:1]."[16]

One of the greatest reasons for anticipating this outpouring is the prospect of unity among church members as on the day of Pentecost. Yet this unity must take place first—during the early rain experience—before the latter rain can be poured out:

> We have need of divine illumination. ... [God's] transforming grace upon human hearts will lead to unity that has not yet been realized; for all who are assimilated to Christ will be in harmony with one another. The Holy Spirit will create unity. ...

> The Holy Spirit glorifies God by so revealing His character to His people that he becomes the object of their supreme affections, and by making manifest his character in them. They see clearly that there was never any righteousness in the world but his, no excellence in the world but that derived from him. When the Spirit was poured out from on high, the church was flooded with light, but Christ was the source of that light; his name was on every tongue, his love filled every heart. So it will be when the angel that comes down from heaven having great power, shall lighten the whole earth with his glory [Rev. 18:1].[17]

We can easily see why there is nothing that Satan fears more than the outpouring of the latter rain. If ever there was a time when the outpouring of the Holy Spirit was needed, it is now. We should all be personally praying for the early rain experience and for the unity that will be created among us, which will prepare us for the outpouring of the latter rain. It is only in this way that we will have a united voice through which the loud cry can be proclaimed.

### *What About Unity?*

One look at the current condition of our beloved Seventh-day Adventist Church, however, tells us that we are far from unity and perhaps have even entered into a shaking time. On the one hand, some offshoot groups and various independent ministries have organized, calling themselves "historic Adventists" while at the same time calling the organized church "Babylon." Some of these ministries have separated themselves from local churches into small groups or home churches, and recognize no church authority while diverting tithe money away from the denomination. Issues over doctrines, from the subject of the Trinity to timing of the Sabbath according to ancient calendars, from time setting to reinterpretation of last day prophecies, are examples at the core of many a new movement.[18]

On the other hand, and riding the pendulum in the other direction, several churches in North America over the last two decades have separated from the denomination, becoming Adventist Congregational churches. Although some of these churches are church plants, many of them are derived from the splitting of older established churches. Not only has there been a diversion of church members and their monetary support; there has also been an apparent abandoning of many foundational doctrines of the Advent faith. A common denominator amongst many of the Congregationalist churches is a disregard for the Biblical doctrines of 1844, the cleansing of the sanctuary, the investigative judgement, the three angels' messages, and other distinctive Adventist beliefs that are closely connected to an end-time understanding of the message of righteousness by faith.[19]* More recently the church seems to be struggling with the fact, newly made public, that some professors in our universities and colleges (not just La Sierra), are promoting evolutionary theory.[20] The role of Ellen White and the question of her inspiration, as well as the inspiration of the entire Bible, continue to be questioned by some.[21] *Adventist Today*, the voice of the progressive Adventist movement, adds issues to the pot on almost a monthly basis.

While Church membership is swelling toward the 20 million mark on the world wide scale, membership is more static in North America. The reason for such a condition may lie in the fact that amidst the seeming polarization taking place throughout the North American Division, thousands of members within the organized church are faced with a multitude of voices calling for their attention. In his book *The Remnant*, Clifford Goldstein depicts in graphic language some of the terrible sins that exist in our church.[22] It does not require a great deal of investigation to come to the conclusion that all is not well within our ranks. The prospect of unity seems more out of reach than at any other time in Adventist history. Many are expressing the idea that the only hope for survival is to "clear the way" that God might pour out the latter rain upon His "languishing church." But one of the greatest possible hindrances to unity, sadly enough, is over the issue of the latter rain and the loud cry itself, specifically in regard to our Adventist history. Two main views are present in the church today, both claiming the support of Ellen White, although each differing somewhat in their view of her authority and inspiration. Before we proceed, we would do well to take a brief look at these two main views regarding the latter rain and the loud cry, the 1888 era, and other closely connected theological issues.

### *The Loud Cry Came and Was Accepted, The Latter Rain Did Not Come, Therefore No Rejection*[23*]

As we take a look at the first main view, we must realize that although there may not be agreement in every detail among those who hold this view, there are major points of agreement that link them together. This view holds that toward the end of the dark ages God sent the Reformation as a full revelation of the plan of salvation. The significance of 1844, rather than being a change in the ministry of Christ in the heavenly sanctuary, primarily represents the date at which time God raised up an end-time people to share with the world the Reformation gospel along with other Adventist distinctives—such as the Sabbath and state of the dead. When Adventism got sidetracked in the 1870s and 1880s with legalism, God answered by sending a most precious message. According to this view, the "1888 message" is that which was given at Minneapolis in 1888 only. No one knows exactly what was said at Minneapolis but it can be summed up as basic Christianity. This message was the loud cry message; basic Christianity as found in the Reformation teaching of a forensic-only justification by faith—as taught by the holiness preachers—combined with the unique Adventist teaching of the Sabbath, the law and the nonimmortality of the soul. Jones and Waggoner didn't fully grasp this message in 1888, but Ellen White did, thus she could state that we now had the loud cry message.

According to this view, there was an initial rejection of the message at Minneapolis, but it was primarily caused by personality conflicts largely incited by Jones and Waggoner. The majority of Adventists accepted the message as shared at the 1889 campmeetings and the 1889 to 1891 Ministerial Institutes and General Conferences. The repentance of those who initially rejected the message brought about its overall acceptance. Thus, 1888 is seen as a victory rather than a great disappointment. The church's work exploded as it reorganized in 1901 and spread around the world.

This view states that Ellen White supported Jones and Waggoner, but it was for their message of basic Christianity. Much of the interaction Ellen White had with Jones and Waggoner was in seeking to correct their theological errors, as is proven by her statements made at Minneapolis that she did not agree with all they taught. Although she never identified in what areas she disagreed, numerous examples are produced, by those holding this view, when surveying Jones' and Waggoner's theology and comparing it to the Reformation gospel. It is claimed that Ellen White didn't correct them on many of these areas because she never intended to be an authority on theological issues. She sought only to point people back to the Bible.

Those holding this view suggest that one of the principal theological errors Jones taught was that the latter rain had begun by 1892. Jones, it is stated, stirred up such an idea because he believed Anna Rice had been given the prophetic gift in fulfillment of Joel chapter 2, while Ellen White, on the other hand, said that only the loud cry had begun but not the latter rain. Thus, the loud cry and the latter rain, although connected, can be separated. The latter rain is the power given to proclaim the loud cry message. Therefore, the loud cry message began over one hundred years ago and was accepted, but the latter rain never began, partly because of the disunity in the church caused by Jones and Waggoner.

This view states that since the latter rain never began in 1888 there is no need to repent for rejecting it, only to pray for its outpouring in the near future. Therefore, the church has not been wandering in the wilderness waiting for the Lord's return but has been prospering, as corroborated by the presence of

Adventist institutions scattered throughout the world and a membership of over 16 million. Even though we as a people may be partly to blame for the delay of the Lord's second coming, without a doubt most of the responsibility lies in His hands or in world events over which we have no control.

Although *some* of these views on the loud cry and the latter rain date back to the 1890s with some of the participants in the great events of that decade, *many* of these views have been presented more prominently since the early 1930s. Initially this started as a response to A. G. Daniells' book, *Christ Our Righteousness*, and even more so to Taylor Bunch's manuscript—*Forty Years in the Wilderness in Type and Antitype*—comparing the Adventist Church with ancient Israel. D. E. Robinson, A. T. Robinson, and C. McReynolds all wrote papers in early 1931 seeking to defend the Church from what they saw as extreme misrepresentations.[24]* The 1940s produced three other defenses of the church from N. F. Pease, L. H. Christian, and A. W. Spalding, men who likewise felt that charges of a latter rain rejection were an attack on the church.[25]*

Following Robert Wieland's and Donald Short's submission of *1888 Re-examined* in 1950, several more books and documents were published, in which the Church was defended from what was seen as an unwarranted attack in regard to 1888. Many of these books, articles and reports were produced under the auspices of the General Conference, which generally held this view.[26]

In the autumn of 1957, Adventist leadership published *Questions on Doctrine* (*QOD*), as a quasi-official reply to the questions raised by Evangelical Calvinists Walter Martin (young researcher, "specialist" in non-Christian cults, consulting editor of *Eternity* magazine), and Dr. Donald Barnhouse (editor of *Eternity* magazine). The publishing of *QOD* followed several years of discussion between Barnhouse and Martin, and T. E. Unruh (president of the East Pennsylvania Conference), Walter Read (field secretary of the General Conference), Roy Allan Anderson (editor of *Ministry* magazine), and LeRoy Froom (author, editor, teacher and founder of *Ministry* magazine), who were seeking to cast off Adventism's cult status within the Evangelical world.[27]* Following the release of *QOD*, most books published by the church in regard to 1888 took on a new understanding of 1888 history, the 1888 message, and what caused Jones' and Waggoner's downfall at the turn of the century. This became more evident after Desmond Ford's Reformation doctrine challenge at Palmdale in 1976. In the 35 years since then, most publications produced and funded by the church in regard to the loud cry and latter rain in the context of 1888 have continued in this line of understanding.[28]*

The acceptance view espoused since the 1970s and 1980s claims that much of the disunity in the church from the 1890s to the present has been caused primarily through false theology that came directly from Jones' and Waggoner's underlying message immediately after Minneapolis—which was the same theology basic to their understanding of the gospel that led them directly out of the church. According to this view, Jones' and Waggoner's false theology was probably part of their understanding in seed form before Minneapolis but wasn't fully developed until right after the 1888 Conference. Thus, Ellen White could support them for their "1888 message." These theological errors are claimed to be found in Jones' and Waggoner's campmeeting presentations in early 1889. Here, four key heresies were readily expressed: 1) Jones' and Waggoner's denial of the doctrine of original sin (which led them into three other heresies); 2) Christ took the fallen sinful nature of Adam; 3) righteousness by faith included justification and sanctification—instead of being a forensic-only justification by faith; 4) the final generation will develop perfect characters before Christ's return. Proponents of this view claim that these four heresies led Waggoner directly into pantheism and Jones into the holy flesh movement, and the resurgence of these same four heresies today—brought primarily through conservative historic Adventists—is the "Omega" apostasy of which Ellen White warned.

We now turn our attention to the second main view regarding the latter rain and loud cry, the 1888 era, and other closely connected theological issues.

### *The Latter Rain and Loud Cry Came and Were Rejected*[29]*

As we take a look at the second main view, we must realize that although there may not be agreement in every detail among those who hold this view, there are major points of agreement that link them together. This view holds that the Lord sent great light through the Reformers in the 16th century to call the people out of the darkness of papal error; yet that light would continue to grow brighter to the very end of time. The Advent movement, leading to the organization of the Seventh-day Adventist end-time remnant church, is seen as the final repository of that culminating light which must then be taken to the world. The end of the 2300 years in 1844 indicates a change in Christ's priestly ministry in the heavenly sanctuary. Rather than signifying a change in the way a person is saved, the investigative judgment announces the culmination of the plan of salvation —the judgment hour message— which is to help prepare those living for the return of Christ. This understanding is established within the context of the great controversy theme and matured in the setting of the three angels' messages.

According to this view a failure to continue to accept and grow in the advancing light led to a Laodicean state within a decade following the Great Disappointment. Failure to heed heaven's call to repentance through the Laodicean message in the 1850s led to the pharisaism of the 1870s and 1880s. With the church in this condition the Lord sent a special message intended to complete His work of grace in human hearts so the great controversy could be brought to an end. This message, which began in 1888, was the beginning of the latter rain and loud cry. The latter rain and loud cry, although distinct from one another, can never be separated—the latter rain being the *cause* and the loud cry the *effect*. Rather than being just an increase in *volume*, the latter rain brought an increase in *light*, which would enable the loud cry to enlighten the earth with its glory and blanket the earth with an end-time gospel message of God's much more abounding grace.

This view states that the 1888 message was different from the popular Evangelical message of the day. The 1888 message of righteousness by faith is closely connected to distinctive Biblical truths given to Seventh-day Adventists, especially the understanding of the cleansing of the sanctuary which prepares a final generation to stand before God—cleansed from sin in a final demonstration of His grace at the summation of the great controversy. The acceptance of such *light* would be synonymous with the acceptance of the latter rain, which is more than just nebulous *power*, but rather great *authority* in conjunction with the intimate presence of Jesus, through the Holy Spirit. The ability to give the loud cry was contingent on our accepting the message, which then would have lightened the whole earth with its glory as God's people, in perfect unity, shared the good news all over the world. As a result, the harvest would have been ripened and Christ would have soon come to the earth to put a full end to sin and suffering.

This view states that the light the Lord sent was in the form of a message, which in His great mercy He sent through two messengers—A. T. Jones and E. J. Waggoner. Although God began moving on Jones' and Waggoner's hearts in the early 1880s, the most precious message primarily began when brought to the leadership of the church in 1888. The fact that we do not have a transcript of the "1888 message" given at Minneapolis is not considered a problem because the same message was proclaimed in greater detail in the campmeetings and Ministerial Institutes in the years that followed; and under the watchful direction of Ellen White, whom God had called to her post of duty.

According to this second view, the 1888 message that God sent through Jones and Waggoner was a comprehensive teaching of the matchless charms of Christ in the context of righteousness by faith. Although the 1888 message includes many components, *at least* four aspects of the message diverge from the popular Evangelical views and have been surrounded by noticeable conflict.[30]* 1) Because Jones' and Waggoner's understanding of the nature of sin and the nature of man was understood in the context of the great controversy issues, they rejected the Augustinian doctrine of original sin as papal falsehood. They understood that the sacrifice of Christ was for the human race, freeing all from the condemnation of Adam's sin, which gave all people the freedom to choose their destiny even though having received a sinful nature. 2) Jones and Waggoner understood that Christ took upon his sinless divine nature our sinful human nature in order to save man from sin. 3) They understood that righteousness by faith was more than just a legal declaration, but included both justification and sanctification. 4) They understood as part of the great plan of salvation that God would prepare an end-time people in an end-time setting— through His latter rain message—to stand in the righteousness of Christ before a

Holy God, without sin. This final demonstration would validate God's claims in the great controversy against Satan by a display of His power to save from sin—not in sin—accomplished through the ministry of the new covenant in the final cleansing of the sanctuary.[31]*

According to this view, however, the message was not recognized for what it was, by many of the leadership and laity, who claimed to believe in justification by faith already. As a result of their pride and stubbornness, the Holy Spirit was slighted, spurned, and rejected. The rejection of the message did not occur because Jones and Waggoner had offensive personalities, but because of a rising up against the message itself. Although some repented and later accepted the message, others claimed to have repented but kept fighting against the message, while still others appeared to repent but only assented to the message. As a result of the latter rain's rejection during those key years, the church as a whole has been wandering in the wilderness of this world of sin for well over 100 years. Moreover, the only way the latter rain will be poured out in abundance again upon a languishing church is for the membership—leaders and laity alike—to recognize the sins of their fathers, repent individually and as a church body, and recover and proclaim the message the that Lord sent over 120 years ago.

This view claims that Ellen White drew parallels between the Jewish nation and the Seventh-day Adventist Church. Just as the Jews looked forward to the coming of the Messiah but did not recognize Him when He came, so we as a people looked forward to the latter rain but did not recognize its manifestation and scorned Jesus away. Though many Jews still pour out their hearts in prayer at the Wailing Wall begging God to send the long-hoped-for Messiah, their prayers will never be answered, nor *can* they be. Not until they realize the Messiah already came, and with a clear understanding repent of their unbelief, can their prayers be answered. In the same way, we as a people have prayed for the outpouring of the latter rain for over 120 years since 1888. But God cannot answer our prayers until we recognize and admit the sins of our forefathers, including our years of denial ever since. Admitting the truth of our history will save us from perpetuating their mistakes and will lead us to a deep repentance for our own personal unbelief.

This view also claims that Ellen White gave numerous endorsements to Jones and Waggoner and the most precious message of righteousness by faith sent through them. When Jones and Waggoner made mistakes, both being fallible men, Ellen White sought to correct them by giving them specific counsel on where they had erred. As long as they humbly listened to that counsel, they benefited from it. Ellen White warned that Jones and Waggoner might be overthrown by temptation, but if that happened it would not prove their message was faulty. Thus Waggoner's panentheism and Jones' bitterness, and any extremes he exhibited in later years were not caused by the message the Lord sent, but rather by a departure in the later 1890s from that message. Again, panentheism, the holy flesh movement or any other extremes were not the result of a fatal flaw in Jones' and Waggoner's original understanding; rather, their understanding was changed by accepting a parasite of error which often lies close to the truth, and were thereby overcome by temptation. Furthermore, Jones' and Waggoner's error developed after enduring years of opposition and rejection to the true message that God had sent through them.

This second main view in regard to the loud cry and latter rain has been expressed since the 1890s, first by some of the participants in the great events of that decade. However, this view has been presented more prominently since the 1920s, starting with the General Conference President A. G. Daniells in his book *Christ Our Righteousness*. In summarizing the events of 1888 and the nearly 40 years that followed, Daniells stated: "The [1888] message has never been received, nor proclaimed, nor given free course as it should have been in order to convey to the church the measureless blessings that were wrapped within it. The seriousness of exerting such an influence is indicated through the reproofs that were given. These words of reproof and admonition should receive most thoughtful consideration at this time. ... O that we had all listened as we should to both warning and appeal as they came to us in that seemingly strange, yet impressive, way at the Conference of 1888! What uncertainty would have been removed, what wanderings and defeats and losses would have been prevented! What light and blessing and triumph and progress would have come to us!"[32]

Only a few years after Daniells' book was printed, Taylor Bunch, pastor, Bible teacher, and author, produced a pamphlet titled, *Forty Years in the Wilderness in Type and Antitype*, which put forth similar views on the latter rain and loud cry.[33]* In this pamphlet, Bunch presents the parallels between the Seventh-day Adventist Church and the children of Israel in their journey from Egypt to Canaan. With the help of his wife, Taylor Bunch presented the fall and spring weeks-of-prayer at Pacific Union College during the 1930-1931 school year, where he presented the subject matter from his pamphlet.[34] Several years later in 1937, Bunch presented a similar series of 36 sermons at the Battle Creek Tabernacle during the Sabbath afternoon vesper services. These sermons were published in book form under the title *The Exodus and Advent Movement in Type and Antitype*, for "the special accommodation of those who heard them, and also because of requests from ministers and other gospel workers who desire them."[35]*

In his studies, Bunch went into more detail than Daniells. When he came to the Kadesh-Barnea experiences of ancient Israel, Bunch applied it to the 1888 Minneapolis Conference and its aftermath, and the Church's turning back into the wilderness of wandering. Bunch claimed the latter rain had been rejected, and that the issues of 1888 would not go away until brought before the people that they might realize what had really taken place:

> The message of righteousness by faith was preached with power for more than ten years during which time the Minneapolis crisis was kept before the leaders. This message brought the beginning of the latter rain. 'The time of test is just upon us, for the loud cry of the third angel has already begun in the revelation of the righteousness of Christ, the sin-pardoning Redeemer. This is the beginning of the light of the angel whose glory shall fill the whole earth. R.H. Nov. 22, 1892. Why did not the latter rain continue to fall? Because the message that brought it ceased to be preached. It was rejected by many and it soon died out of the experience of the Advent people and the loud cry died with it. It can begin again only when the message that brought it then is revived and accepted. …
>
> Just before the end the Advent people will review their past history and see it in a new light. We must study and understand the antitypes of the two Kadesh-Barnea experiences of ancient Israel and profit by the mistakes of our fathers especially during the 1888 crisis. We must acknowledge and confess

the mistakes of our fathers and see to it that we do not repeat them and thus further delay the final triumph of the Advent Movement. The history of the past must be reviewed and studied in the light of these mistakes and their consequence in a long delay of the coming of Christ.[36]

Donald K. Short and Robert J. Wieland, missionaries in Africa for many years, became perhaps the most well known and prominent supporters of many of these views, after they submitted their manuscript *1888 Reexamined* to the General Conference in 1950. In the 1970s they began to widely publish their views through many books, some through the church's publishing houses, some privately, and later some under the auspices of the 1888 Message Study Committee.[37]* Others have supported many of these viewpoints in various articles and books.[38]

## *The Great Dilemma*

I am a fifth-generation Seventh-day Adventist. My great-great-grandfather attended the 1888 General Conference at Minneapolis and later became president of the Wisconsin Conference for a short time. I do not know whether he was one of the "some" who openly rejected what the Lord in His great mercy sent to this church through Elders Waggoner and Jones. One thing I do know, however, is that each one of these five generations, including my own, has looked forward to the time when the Holy Spirit is poured out.

As we study this subject, we will be faced with the great dilemma of deciding which view of our history is correct. If the Lord did send the beginning of the latter rain and we as a church despised and resisted it, regardless of the potential accusations of causing disunity, should we not seek repentance for ourselves as well as for our church? Otherwise will we not just keep repeating the rejection? On the other hand, if the latter rain never began and therefore we as a church never rejected it, shouldn't we do our best to avoid being distracted or distracting others from the more important work of preaching the Reformation gospel to the world?

As we examine these grand subjects, we should remember that Ellen White was an eyewitness to many of these historical events.[39]* Therefore we must ask ourselves some questions. Did Ellen White see a strong connection between the 1888 message of righteousness by faith and final events taking place at that time? Did she see a connection between the acceptance of that message and Christ's second coming? Did she see a connection between the latter rain and the loud cry? In her description of what was taking place did she separate the latter rain from the loud cry? Could one begin without the other? Could one be accepted without the other? Did Ellen White see the 1893 General Conference as Jones' attempted "latter rain revival," and like Uriah Smith, see it only as "fanaticism" and "excitement?" Did the latter rain really begin? Could it possibly be rejected? Do Ellen White's statements in regard to the latter rain and the loud cry, when looked at in chronological order, express or give us added insights to these questions? To all of these questions and more, we will seek to find answers.[40]*

*The Return of the Latter Rain* began as a simple, yet unique compilation of Ellen White statements on the subject of the latter rain and the loud cry, which she made between the 1840s and the close of her life in 1915. You will find these statements listed throughout the book, with but few exceptions in chronological order. Not all of Ellen White's statements on the latter rain and loud cry are listed, but an extensive summary will be found here. Each chapter progresses chronologically and addresses the relevant issues during that particular time period in regard to the latter rain and loud cry. It should be noted that as the manuscript progressed, more and more background information was added to help give answers to questions raised by the historic events, as well as answers to questions raised by Adventist books that have been published since those events. Context has often been lost sight of when dealing with Adventist history in regard to 1888, at least by some who have entered into this discussion. Consequently, some longer quotations have been included here for the purpose of retaining the full context, which will allow readers to come to more informed conclusions for themselves.

*The Return of the Latter Rain* is the result of a personal study into this important subject. It is based on the original sources including Ellen G. White, A. T. Jones, E. J. Waggoner, and others, thus allowing history to speak for itself.

The writer has attempted to read most of the printed material on this subject to be certain that nothing has been overlooked. I am thankful for the prayers offered and counsel given by many others who have helped in this task. Although I never intended to write a book, this study has been a blessing to my life, and it is shared with the hope that it will be a blessing to others. As is the case with most books, however, not everyone will agree with all the conclusions drawn in this study. Having said that, this writer does not claim infallibility. This is a book in progress. There is much more material to add; not only to future chapters but to the chapters you hold in your hand. This will require more editing and fine-tuning where adjustments are needed.

The driving force behind this study is to understand our history correctly. Ellen White's well-known statement made in 1892 tells us: "We have nothing to fear for the future, except as we shall forget the way the Lord has led us, and *His teaching in our past history*."[41] She also reminds us that the cause of the downfall of Israel was due to forgetting their history:

> The reason why the children of Israel forsook Jehovah was that the generation rose up that had not been instructed concerning the great deliverance from Egypt by the hand of Jesus Christ. Their fathers *had not rehearsed to them the history* of the divine guardianship that had been over the children of Israel *through all their travels in the wilderness*. … The parents neglected the very work that the Lord had charged them to do, and failed to instruct them in regard to *God's purpose* toward his chosen people. They *did not keep before them the fact that idolatry was sin*, and that to worship other gods meant to forsake Jehovah. If parents had fulfilled their duty, we should never have the record of the generation that knew not God, and were therefore given into the hands of the spoilers.[42]

> I was pointed to the work that Moses did just before his death. Calling the children of Israel together, he rehearsed to them their past experience, *their trials, their failures, and the warnings* that had been given them.[43]*

But as we review our history we should remember that it is not for the purpose of finding fault in others—past or present—or for the sake of tearing down, but rather that we might learn from their mistakes and not repeat them. We should note well the words of Kenneth Wood: "As we note the mistakes of our spiritual forebears, we may be filled with anguish and regret. But we cannot change the past. We cannot rewrite history. We can, however, learn from history, and we can set our own hearts and houses in order, giving full opportunity for the Holy Spirit to have His way with us. Only as we today relate rightly to the message of righteousness by faith can we expect the outpouring of the latter rain and the finishing of 'the work.'"[44]

This leads me to the following point. As has always been the case, Satan seeks to derail every reformatory movement through some counterfeit or form of fanaticism.[45] A quick glance through our own Adventist history shows this to be true. Satan sent counterfeits before and after 1888. He sent counterfeits in the early 1920s pointing to 1888, but also calling the church Babylon. This was the case in the 1930s, and 1940s as well. Other forms of fanaticism have been seen since the 1950s, pointing to 1888 and calling people out of the church. All this Satan has done to distract from God's real call to review our history that we might be healed.

Let us make it clear—the church is not Babylon! She will finally heed the call of the "True Witness," and through the Divine remedies make herself ready for the grand wedding. Christ will finally have His bride without spot or wrinkle. Why? Because she will be wearing that spotless robe of Christ's righteousness.

Please keep in mind; that this book is not to be used to tear down the Seventh-day Adventist church; it is not to be used in evangelism to draw people into some offshoot group. It is to be read and prayerfully contemplated by Adventist leaders and educators and interested laymen, for the purpose of seeking a better understanding of our own history.

Finally, we have done our best throughout the pages of this book to follow the excellent advice of George R. Knight: "Let Ellen White speak for herself."[46]

# Introduction Footnotes

1. Ellen G. White, "The Church's Greatest Need," *Review and Herald*, March 22, 1887, p. 177.

2. Ellen G. White, *The Desire of Ages*, (Mountain View, CA Pacific Press Pub. Assn., 1940), p. 671.

3. *Ibid.*, p. 669.

4. *Ibid.*, p. 672.

5. Ellen G. White, *Selected Messages*, book 3 (Washington, DC: Review and Herald Pub. Assn., 1980), p. 156.

6. Ellen G. White, *Testimonies to Ministers and Gospel Workers* (Mountain View, CA.: Pacific Press Pub. Assn., 1923), p. 506, (hereafter *Testimonies to Ministers*).

7. Ellen G. White, *The Acts of the Apostles in Proclamation of the Gospel of Jesus Christ* (Mountain View, CA.: Pacific Press Pub. Assn., 1911), pp. 54, 55, (hereafter *The Acts of the Apostles*).

8. Ellen G. White, *The Great Controversy* (Mountain View, CA.: Pacific Press Pub. Assn., 1911), p. 611.

9. Ellen G. White, *Testimonies to Ministers*, p. 506.

10. Ellen G. White, *Early Writings* (Washington, DC: Review and Herald Pub. Assn., 1945), p. 271.

11. *Ibid.*, p. 86

12. Ellen G. White, *Christ's Object Lessons* (Washington, DC: Review and Herald Pub. Assn., 1941), p. 415. Pastor Jerry Finneman brings out excellent points in the connection between the latter rain and loud cry in his two part series, "The Latter Rain is the Message of Christ and His Righteousness," (*New England Pastor*, Nov./Dec. 2009 and Jan./Feb. 2010).

13. Ellen G. White, *Testimonies for the Church*, vol. 6. (Mountain View, CA Pacific Press Pub. Assn., 1948), p. 19, (hereafter *Testimonies*, vol. 1-9).

14. Ellen G. White, *Selected Messages*, vol. 3 (Washington, DC: Review and Herald Pub. Assn., 1980), p. 372.

15. Ellen G. White, *Testimonies to Ministers*, p. 92.

16. Francis D. Nichol, ed., *Seventh-day Adventist Bible Commentary*, vol. 6 (Washington, DC: Review and Herald Pub. Assn., 1956), p. 1055, (hereafter, *SDA Bible Commentary*).

17. Ellen G. White to Uriah Smith, Letter 25b, Aug. 30, 1892; in *Ellen G. White 1888 Materials* (Washington, DC: The Ellen G. White Estate, 1987), p. 1017, (hereafter *1888 Materials*).

18. See Ty Gibson, *Abandon Ship?: One Man's Struggle to Discover God's Special Purpose for His Church* (Nampa, ID: Pacific Press Pub. Assn., 1997); Allen Barnes, *Detours & Ditches* (Denton, NC: Barnes Printing & Publ., 2005).

19. See Brian Neumann, *Stop: Before it is Too Late* (Delta, BC: Amazing Discoveries, 2005); Thomas Mostert, *Hidden Heresy?: Is Spiritualism Invading Adventist Churches Today?* (Nampa, ID: Pacific Press Pub. Assn., 2005); Samuel Koranteng-Pipim, *Must We Be Silent: Issues Dividing Our Church* (Ann Arbor, MI: Berean Books, 2001), and *Here We Stand: Evaluating New Trends in the Church* (Berrien Springs, MI: Adventists Affirm, 2005). In the *Adventist Review,* November 1997, William G. Johnsson commented on the split into independent congregations of the Damascus church in Maryland, pastored by Richard Fredericks, and the Sunnyside church in Portland, Oregon. Johnsson assured the reader that it is easy to "blow up... to exaggerated dimensions" the Damascus split and that no "imminent threat of fragmentation into independent congregations" faces the church at large. Since the November 1997 publication, however, several churches have joined the ever-increasing number of Seventh-day Adventist Congregational churches. The periodical *Adventist Today,* which to some extent has become the voice of the Adventist congregational movement, listed seven such churches on the front cover of the May - June, 1998 issue titled "The New Congregationalism: What Gives?" Of course much more could be added to this list. Ron Gladden's missioncatalyst.org actively promotes planting more of these churches, and is still active in 2010.

20. www.educatetruth.com

21. Graeme Bradford, *People Are Human (Look what they did to Ellen White)* (Victoria, Australia: Signs Pub. Co., 2006); *More Than a Prophet* (Berrien Springs, MI: Biblical Perspectives, 2006); Desmond and Gillian Ford, *For the Sake of the Gospel: Throw Out the Bathwater, But Keep the Baby* (New York: iUniverse, Inc., 2008); Milton Hook, *Desmond Ford: Reformist Theologian, Gospel Revivalist* (Riverside, CA Adventist Today Foundation, 2008); Gerhard Pfandl, "Ellen G. White and Earth Science," (paper presented at International Faith and Science Conference, Aug. 23-29, 2002); Alden Thompson, "From Sinai to Golgotha," Parts 1-5, *Adventist Review*, Dec. 3-31, 1981.

22. Clifford Goldstein, *The Remnant: Biblical Reality or Wishful Thinking?* (Nampa, ID: Pacific Press Pub. Assn., 1994).

23. Detailed references for the views expressed here will be given throughout the remainder of this book.

24. See: D. E. Robinson to Taylor G. Bunch, Dec. 30, 1930 (see chapter 4, footnote 41); A. T. Robinson, "Did the Seventh-day Adventist Denomination Reject the Doctrine of Righteousness by Faith?" Jan. 30, 1931; C. McReynold, "Experience While at the General Conference in Minneapolis, Minn. in 1888," n.d., 1931; all in *Manuscripts and Memories of Minneapolis 1888* (Boise, ID: Pacific Press Pub. Assn., 1988), pp. 333-342. There is some evidence that some of these men had been working with the SDA Reform Movement, which claimed by this time that 1888 was the starting point from which the church became "Babylon."

25. N. F. Pease, "Justification and Righteousness by Faith in the Seventh-day Adventist Church Before 1900" (Unpublished Master's Thesis, 1945); L. H. Christian, *The Fruitage of Spiritual Gifts* (Washington, DC: Review and Herald Pub. Assn., 1947); A. W. Spalding, *Captains of the Host* (Washington, DC: Review and Herald Pub. Assn., 1949). There is some evidence that some of these men were influenced by, and were reacting to their prior dealings with offshoot groups such as Shepherd's Rod and the Rogers Brothers' movement, both of which pointed to 1888 as the starting point from which the church become "Babylon."

26. General Conference of Seventh-day Adventists, "First General Conference Committee Report," Dec. 4, 1951, in A. L. Hudson, *A Warning and its Reception* (Privately Published., n.d.); General Conference of Seventh-day Adventists, *The Story of Our Church* (Mountain View, CA Pacific Press Pub. Assn., 1956); General Conference of Seventh-day Adventists, "Further Appraisal of the Manuscript '1888 Re-Examined,'" Sept. 1958, in A. L. Hudson, *A Warning and its Reception* (Privately Published., n.d.); A. W. Spalding, *Origin and History of Seventh-day Adventists* (Washington, DC: Review and Herald Pub. Assn., 1962); N. F. Pease, *By Faith Alone* (Mountain View, CA Pacific Press Pub. Assn., 1962); A. V. Olson, *Through Crisis to Victory 1888-1901* (Washington, DC: Review and Herald Pub. Assn., 1966); N. F. Pease, *The Faith That Saves* (Washington, DC: Review and Herald Pub. Assn., 1969); A. L. White, *Ellen G. White: The Lonely Years* (Washington DC: Review and Herald Pub. Assn., 1984).

27. Walter Martin's questions "covered a wide range of Adventist theology, but four areas stuck out in Martin's mind: '(1) that the atonement of Christ was not completed upon the cross; (2) that salvation is the result of grace plus works of the law; (3) that the Lord Jesus Christ was a created being, not from all eternity; (4) and that He partook of man's sinful fallen nature at the incarnation' (*Our Hope*, November 1956, 275)"

(in George R. Knight, *A Search for Identity*, p. 165). Among other issues covered were the sanctuary, 1844, and the inspiration of Ellen White. Notice as well that: "Calvinists reduce their theology to the famous Five Points, all emanating from the core doctrine of their understanding of the sovereignty of God. 1. Total depravity of mankind (all men and women are born sinners). 2. Unconditional election (some are elected to be saved; other are not). 3. Limited atonement (Christ died for only the elect). 4. Irresistible grace (men and women who are elected are given the 'gift' of faith). 5. Perseverance of the saints ('once saved, always saved'). … Calvinism's straitjacket led to 'forensic-only salvation,' which has troubled the Christian church for 400 years. *Forensic Justification* is another term for *penal substitution…* this un-biblical notion has confused the works of grace and the meaning of 'righteousness by faith'" (Herbert E. Douglass, *A Fork in the Road: Question on Doctrine the Historic Adventist Divide of 1957* (Coldwater, MI: Remnant Pub., 2008), pp. 24, 25).

28. Edward Heppenstall, *Is Perfection Possible?* (Mountain View, CA Pacific Press Pub. Assn., 1964); LeRoy E. Froom, *Movement of Destiny* (Washington, DC: Review and Herald Pub. Assn., 1971); Desmond Ford, *The Doctrinal Decline of Dr. E. J. Waggoner: Its Relationship to the Omega Apostasy*, (located at Adventist Heritage Center, Andrews University, Berrien Springs, MI, 1970s); Desmond Ford, "The Relationship Between the Incarnation and Righteousness by Faith," Documents from the Palmdale Conference on Righteousness by Faith (Goodlettsvillle, TN: Jack D. Walker, 1976); Geoffrey J. Paxton, *The Shaking of Adventism: A Documented Account of the Crisis Among Adventist Over the Doctrine of Justification by Faith* (Grand Rapids, MI: Baker Book House, 1977); Edward Heppenstall, *The Man Who Is God: A Study of the Nature of Jesus* (Washington, DC: Review and Herald Pub. Assn., 1977); David P. McMahon, *Ellet Joseph Waggoner: The Myth and the Man* (Fallbrook, CA Verdict Pub., 1979); Robert Brinsmead, *Judged by the Gospel: A Review of Adventism* (Fallbrook, CA Verdict Pub., 1980); Bert Haloviak, "Ellen White and A. T. Jones at Ottawa, 1889: Diverging Paths from Minneapolis," (Archives of the General Conference Seventh-day Adventists, Washington, DC, 1981); Norman R. Gulley, *Christ Our Substitute* (Washington, DC: Review and Herald Pub. Assn., 1982); George R. Knight, *From 1888 to Apostasy: The Case of A. T. Jones* (Washington, DC: Review and Herald Pub. Assn., 1987); Hermut Ott, *Perfect in Christ: Is it Your Job to be Perfect, Or is it Someone Else's?* (Washington, DC: Review and Herald Pub. Assn., 1987); Arthur J. Ferch, Ed., *Towards Righteousness by Faith: 1888 in Retrospect* (New South Wales: South Pacific Division of Seventh-day Adventists, 1989); George Knight, *Angry Saints: The Frightening Possibility of Being Adventist Without Being Christian* (Washington, DC: Review and Herald Pub. Assn., 1989); Eric C. Webster, *Crosscurrents in Adventist Christology* (Berrien Springs, MD: Andrews University Press, 1992); Roy Adams, *The Nature of Christ: Help For a Church Divided Over*

*Perfection* (Hagerstown, MD: Review and Herald Pub. Assn., 1994); Woodrow W. Whidden, *Ellen White on Salvation* (Hagerstown, MD: Review and Herald Pub. Assn., 1995); Woodrow W. Whidden, *Ellen White on the Humanity of Christ* (Hagerstown, MD: Review and Herald Pub. Assn., 1997). George R. Knight, *A User-Friendly Guide to the 1888 Message* (Hagerstown, MD: Review and Herald Pub. Assn., 1998); George R. Knight, *A Search for Identity: The Development of Seventh-day Adventist Beliefs* (Hagerstown, MD: Review and Herald Pub. Assn., 2000); Woodrow W. Whidden, *E. J. Waggoner: From the Physician of Good News to Agent of Division* (Hagerstown, MD: Review and Herald Pub. Assn., 2008); Desmond and Gillian Ford, *For the Sake of the Gospel: Throw Out the Bathwater, But Keep the Baby* (New York: iUniverse, Inc., 2008); Milton Hook, *Desmond Ford: Reformist Theologian, Gospel Revivalist* (Riverside, CA Adventist Today Foundation, 2008). Of all the above writers, LeRoy Froom is the only one who expressed the idea that the latter rain began. He takes the position, however, that the latter rain was accepted.

29. Detailed references for the views expressed here will be given throughout the remainder of this book.

30. See, A. Leroy Moore, *Theology in Crisis* (Corpus Christi, TX: Life Seminars, Inc., 1980); Herbert E. Douglass, *A Fork in the Road: Question on Doctrine the Historic Adventist Divide of 1957* (Coldwater, MI: Remnant Pub., 2008); Dennis E. Priebe, *Face-to-Face With the Real Gospel*, revised edition (Roseville, CA Amazing Facts, 2008).

31. Ellen White summarized this message as: "The Lord in his great mercy sent a most precious message to his people through Elders Waggoner and Jones. This message was to bring more prominently before the world the uplifted Saviour, the sacrifice for the sins of the whole world. It presented justification through faith in the Surety; it invited the people to receive the righteousness of Christ, which is made manifest in obedience to all the commandments of God. Many had lost sight of Jesus. They needed to have their eyes directed to his divine person, his merits, and his changeless love for the human family. All power is given into his hands, that he may dispense rich gifts unto men, imparting the priceless gift of his own righteousness to the helpless human agent. This is the message that God commanded to be given to the world. It is the third angel's message, which is to be proclaimed with a loud voice, and attended with the outpouring of his Spirit in a large measure. ...The uplifted Saviour is to appear... sitting upon the throne, to dispense the priceless covenant blessings. ... Christ is pleading for the church in the heavenly courts above. ... Notwithstanding our unworthiness, we are ever to bear in mind that there is One that can take away sin and save the sinner. ...God gave to His servants a testimony that presented the truth as it is in Jesus, which is the third angel's message, in clear, distinct lines. ...

This... testimony... presents the law and the gospel, binding up the two in a perfect whole. (See Romans 5 and 1 John 3:9 to the close of the chapter)... Neglect this great salvation, kept before you for years, despise this glorious offer of justification through the blood of Christ, and sanctification through the cleansing power of the Holy Spirit, and there remaineth no more sacrifice for sins, but a certain fearful looking for of judgment and fiery indignation" (*Testimonies to Ministers*, pp. 92-98). We will deal more fully with the 1888 message in chapter 4 and appendix A.

32. A. G. Daniells, *Christ Our Righteousness* (Washington, DC: Ministerial Assn. of Seventh-day Adventists, 1926), pp. 47, 69.

33. Various dates are given for Bunch's pamphlet: The Loma Linda Heritage Library lists the publishing date as 1927. George Knight states: "Another book of special importance, although not noted as such at the time, was Taylor G. Bunch's *Forty Years in the Wilderness: In Type and Antitype* (ca. 1928). Apparently Daniells' resurrection of the issues of the 1888 General Conference session had stimulated Bunch to investigate the topic for himself" (*A Search for Identity*, pp. 143-4). L. E. Froom states: "The record would indicate that some forty years after the Minneapolis Conference, and not until then, a serious charge was made of denominational or Conference rejection. This is found in a privately published, undated pamphlet issued in the late 1920s titled: 'The Exodus and the Advent Movement.' The author, a well known pastor, evangelist and Bible teacher, while frequently supporting his points from the Testimonies and the *Review and Herald*, offers no documentary support whatsoever for his bold assertions of rejection. In 1888 he was but a child and could not have been an eyewitness" (L. E. Froom, early draft papers for *Movement of Destiny*, p. 82a, Document File 189m). Arthur White states that "the concept of denominational rejection was introduced in 1930" (A. L. White to L. O. Cook, Feb. 2, 1985).

34. See, *The Advent Review and Sabbath Herald*, March 21, 1931, pp. 24-5

35. Bunch went on to write, "This series is of special value in meeting apostates and divergent movements, and in establishing Seventh-day Adventists in 'the faith which was once delivered unto the saints.'" Unfortunately, others may have seen this work only as an attack against the church and the cause of several offshoot movements.

36. Taylor G. Bunch, *The Exodus and Advent Movements in Type and Antitype* (Privately Published Facsimile, cir. 1937), pp. 107, 168.

37. See: Robert J. Wieland and Donald K. Short, *In Search of the Cross* (Mountain View, CA Pacific Press Pub. Assn., 1967); *The 1888 Message An Introduction* (Washington, DC: Review and Herald, 1980; Revised and Enlarged, 1997); *1888 Re-examined* (Leominster, MA: The EUSEY PRESS Inc., 1987); *Grace On Trial* (Paris, OH: 1888 Message Study Committee, 1988); *Lightened With His Glory* (Paris, OH: Glad Tidings

Pub., 1991); *Made Like. . . His Brethren* (Paris, OH: Glad Tidings Pub., 1991); *Then Shall The Sanctuary Be Cleansed* (Paris, OH: Glad Tidings Pub., 1991); *Corporate Repentance—Plea of the True Witness* (Paris, OH: Glad Tidings Pub., 1992); *Truth on Trial* (Tippecanoe, OH: Privately Published, 1997); *"1888" For Almost Dummies* (Berrien Springs, MI: Glad Tidings Pub., 2007). The "1888 Message Study Committee" describes itself as being "composed of a group of ordained ministers and laymembers who share a common conviction. They see in the 1888 message of Christ's righteousness what Ellen White saw in it—a 'most precious message' that faithfully recovers and revitalizes the 'good news' power that was in the gospel the apostles first preached." Ellen White declared "the 1888 message to be the beginning of the latter rain and the loud cry of Revelation 18." "The Committee functions within the parameters of the church," offering a bimonthly newsletter, books, lectures, and seminars, with the purpose of sharing the good news. "Seminars on the 1888 Message bring revival and spiritual reformation, without extremism or legalism. Results are enduring. The reason for the long delay at last comes into focus" ("The 1888 Message Study Committee: Who, Why?" 1989).

38. C. Mervyn Maxwell, *Tell it to the World: The Story of Seventh-day Adventists* (Mountain View, CA Pacific Press Pub. Assn., 1976); A. Leroy Moore, *Theology in Crisis* (Corpus Christi, TX: Life Seminars, Inc., 1980); Ralph Larson, *The Word Was Made Flesh: One Hundred Years of Seventh-day Adventist Christology 1852-1952* (Cherry Valley, CA The Cherrystone Press, 1986); Arnold V. Wallenkampf, *What Every Adventist Should Know About 1888* (Washington, DC: Review and Herald Pub. Assn., 1988); Jack Sequeira, *Saviour of the World* (Boise, ID: Pacific Press, 1995); Steve Wohlberg, *The 1888 Message for the Year 2000* (Boise, ID: Pacific Press Pub. Assn., 1995); A. Leroy Moore, *Adventism in Conflict: Resolving the Issues that Divide Us* (Hagerstown, MD: Review and Herald Pub. Assn., 1995); Dave Fiedler, *Hindsight: Seventh-day Adventist History in Essays and Extracts* (Harrah, OK: Academy Enterprises, 1996); Herbert E. Douglass, *Messenger of the Lord* (Nampa, ID: Pacific Press, 1998); *Ellen G. White and the Loud Cry* (4th Angel Pub., 2005); Herbert E. Douglass, *A Fork in the Road: Question on Doctrine the Historic Adventist Divide of 1957* (Coldwater, MI: Remnant Pub., 2008). Jean Zurcher, *Touched With Our Feelings* (Review and Herald 1999).

39. We would do well to remember her own words of warning: "The enemy has made his masterly efforts to unsettle the faith of our own people in the Testimonies, and when these errors come in they claim to prove all the positions by the Bible, but they misinterpret the Scripture. ... This is just as Satan designed it should be, and those who have been preparing the way for the people to pay no heed to the warnings and reproofs of the testimonies of the Spirit of God will see that a tide of errors of all kinds will spring into life" (Ellen G. White to W. C. White, Letter 109, Dec 6, 1890; in *1888 Materials*, p. 739).

40. *The Return of the Latter Rain*, vol. 1, covers events from 1844 through 1891. Volume 2 will cover events from 1891 to present. Thus answers to questions regarding 1893 will not be addressed in this volume.

41. Ellen G. White to Brethren of the General Conference, Letter 32, Dec. 19, 1892; in *Testimonies to Ministers*, p. 31.

42. Ellen G. White, "Is the Blood on the Lintel?" *Review and Herald*, May 21, 1895, p. 321, emphasis supplied.

43. Ellen G. White, *Battle Creek Letters*, Nov. 7, 1905, p. 3. It is interesting to note that Korah also gave the children of Israel history lessons, but he perverted their history: "Korah *reviewed the history* of their travels through the wilderness, where they had been brought into strait places, and many had perished because of their murmuring and disobedience. His hearers thought they saw clearly that their troubles might have been prevented if Moses had pursued a different course. They decided that all their disasters were chargeable to him, and that their exclusion from Canaan was in consequence of the mismanagement of Moses and Aaron; that if Korah would be their leader, and would *encourage them by dwelling upon their good deeds, instead of reproving their sins*, they would have a very peaceful, prosperous journey; instead of wandering to and fro in the wilderness, they would proceed directly to the Promised Land" (Ellen G. White, *Patriarchs and Prophets*, p. 397, emphasis supplied, written in 1890).

44. Kenneth H. Wood, "Editor's Viewpoint: F. Y. I.–4," *Review and Herald*, Nov. 18, 1976, p. 2.

45. Ellen G. White, *The Great Controversy*, p. 186, and entire chapter.

46. George R. Knight, *A User-Friendly Guide to the 1888 Message*, p. 166.

ELLEN G. WHITE

# CHAPTER 1

# *The Early Years*

## *Defining, Outlining, and Anticipating the Latter Rain and the Loud Cry*

The year 1844 marked the end of the 2300 years of Daniel 8:14—the Bible's longest time prophecy—and was the culmination of the great Advent Midnight cry. Sadly, the year also marked perhaps the greatest disappointment in the history of the Christian church for those who were anxiously waiting for the Lord's return. After 1844, as many of the disappointed believers continued to study, the Lord revealed more Bible truths, which became the foundational landmark doctrines of the Seventh-day Adventist Church.[1]*

It was during this time, before the denominational name and basic organization were adopted (between 1860 and 1863), that the Lord also revealed truths about the latter rain and the loud cry. Ellen G. Harmon, who married James White in 1846, had been chosen by God as the messenger to the remnant church, and through visions and dreams the Lord revealed what was soon to take place upon the earth.

We begin by looking at some of the earliest statements Ellen White made in regard to the work of the Holy Spirit, the latter rain, and the loud cry. In February of 1845 she was given a vision depicting the end of the 2300 days and Christ entering into His final work in the most holy place—the cleansing of the sanctuary.[2] Ellen White was shown the participation of God's people in the cleansing of the sanctuary and their great need of the Holy Spirit in this process. She was also shown Satan's attempts to deceive and thwart the work taking place there:

> I saw the Father rise... go into the holy of holies within the veil, and sit down. Then Jesus rose up from the throne, and the most of those who were bowed down arose with Him. ... Then He raised His right arm, and we heard His lovely voice saying, "Wait here; I am going to My Father to receive the kingdom; keep your garments spotless, and in a little while I will return from the wedding and receive you to Myself."... He stepped into the chariot and was borne to the holiest, where the Father sat. There I beheld Jesus, a great High Priest, standing before the Father. ... Those who rose up with Jesus would send up their faith to Him in the holiest, and pray, "My Father, give us Thy Spirit." Then Jesus would breathe upon them the Holy Ghost. In that breath was light, power, and much love, joy, and peace.
>
> I turned to look at the company who were still bowed before the throne [holy place]; they did not know that Jesus had left it. Satan appeared to be by the throne, trying to carry on the work of God. I saw them look up to the throne, and pray, "Father, give us Thy Spirit." Satan would then breathe upon them an unholy influence; in it there was light and much power, but no sweet love, joy, and peace. Satan's object was to keep them deceived and to draw back and deceive God's children. I saw one after another leave the company who were praying to Jesus in the Holiest and go and join those before the throne, and they at once received the unholy influence of Satan.[3]*

Several years later Ellen White wrote about the "glories of heaven" that the Lord revealed to her in her girlhood. The light that was to lighten the whole earth with its glory was sent directly from Jesus and was to be manifest through His people. In the years that followed, she would identify this light as the latter rain itself:

> In my very girlhood the Lord saw fit to open before me the glories of heaven. ... I looked to the world as it was in dense darkness. ... and I began to see jets of light like stars dotted all through this darkness; and then I saw another and another added light, and so all through this moral darkness the star-like lights were increasing. And the angel said, "These are they that believe on the Lord Jesus Christ, and are obeying the words of Christ. These are the light of the world. ..." I saw then these little jets of light growing brighter, shining forth from the east and the west, from the north and the south, and lighting the whole world. ...
>
> I saw that the rays of light came directly from Jesus, to form these precious jets of light in the world.[4]

As early as 1850, Ellen White was shown that the latter rain was soon to come with great power, but not all would receive it. Satan was keeping people from the needful preparation:

> You are getting the coming of the Lord too far off. I saw the latter rain was coming as the Midnight Cry and with ten times the power.[5]*

> I saw that many were neglecting the preparation so needful and were looking to the time of "refreshing" and the "latter rain" to fit them to stand in the day of the Lord and to live in His sight. Oh, how many I saw in the time of trouble without a shelter![6]

The latter rain would bring more clearly to view the landmark truths God had revealed after 1844. In the following statement, Ellen White predicted that the latter rain would bring a better understanding of the Sabbath. This was clearly more than what the sixteenth century Reformers understood and taught. It was increased light from the throne of God:

> I saw that we sensed and realized but little of the importance of the Sabbath,... But when the refreshing and latter rain shall come from the presence of the Lord and the glory of His power, we shall know what it is to be fed with the heritage of Jacob and ride upon the high places of the earth. Then shall we see the Sabbath more in its importance and glory.[7]

## Laodicean Condition

But were the early Advent people ready for the latter rain? As early as 1852, Ellen White wrote statements that identified the Advent people as Laodicean, even though they had just separated from other churches:

> Many who profess to be looking for the speedy coming of Christ, are becoming conformed to this world,... They are cold and formal, like the nominal church, that they but a short time since separated from. The words addressed to the Laodicean church, describe their present condition perfectly.[8]

In 1857, Ellen White wrote an article for the *Review* describing what had been recently shown her in vision of the train of events before Christ's second coming. There would be a shaking among God's people caused by those rising up against the straight testimony of the True Witness to the Laodiceans. Those who would enter into a deeper experience with Christ and accept the

Laodicean message would be brought into unity, would be fitted for the final conflict, and would speak forth the truth with power. This was the latter rain and loud cry which would enrage the wicked, causing them to take measures against God's people:

> I asked the meaning of the shaking I had seen. I was shown that it would be caused by the straight testimony called forth by the counsel of the True Witness to the Laodiceans. It will have its effect upon the heart of the receiver of the testimony, and it will lead him to exalt the standard and pour forth the straight truth. This straight testimony, some will not bear. They will rise up against it, and this will cause a shaking among God's people. ...
>
> Said the angel, "List ye!" Soon I heard a voice that sounded like many musical instruments, all sounding in perfect strains, sweet and harmonious. ... It seemed to be so full of mercy, compassion, and elevating, holy joy. ... My attention was then turned to the company I had seen before, who were mightily shaken. ... [T]hey were clothed with an armor from their head to their feet. They moved in exact order, firm like a company of soldiers. ...
>
> I heard those clothed with the armor speak forth the truth in great power. ... The honest who had been held or prevented from hearing the truth, now eagerly laid hold of the truth spoken. All fear of their relatives was gone. ... I asked what had made this great change. An angel answered, "It is the latter rain. The refreshing from the presence of the Lord. The loud cry of the Third Angel. ..."
>
> My attention was turned to the wicked, or unbelievers. They were all astir. The zeal and power with the people of God had aroused and enraged them. ... I saw measures taken against this company, who were having the power and light of God.[9]*

## *The Great Controversy Vision*

During the weekend of March 13 and 14, 1858, James and Ellen White attended meetings at Lovett's Grove, Ohio. On Sunday afternoon, a funeral service was conducted by James in the schoolhouse where the Sabbath meetings had been held. When he had finished speaking to the full house, Ellen arose and feeling urged by the Spirit of the Lord to bear her testimony, began to speak words of comfort to the mourners. While speaking, she was taken off in vision and for two hours through divine revelation the Lord opened before her "the great controversy of the ages between Christ and Satan." Writing about this later, Ellen White stated that although the subject matter was not new, she was now to write it out:

> In the vision at Lovett's Grove, most of the matter which I had seen ten years before concerning the great controversy of the ages between Christ and Satan, was repeated, and I was instructed to write it out. I was shown that while I should have to contend with the powers of darkness, for Satan would make strong efforts to hinder me, yet I must put my trust in God, and angels would not leave me in the conflict.[10]

For nearly five months following her Lovett's Grove experience, Ellen White worked to write the vision and publish it in book form. In early September, 1858, volume 1 of *Spiritual Gifts* was available under the title, *The Great Controversy Between Christ and His Angels, and Satan and His Angels*.[11] Ellen was only thirty years old at the time, but over the next fifty plus years, this small book of just 219 pages would be expanded to a total of 3602 pages as the five-volume Conflict of the Ages Series, with only the fifth and final book bearing the original, all-inclusive title *The Great Controversy*. This all-encompassing theme of the great controversy would become the foundational context in which all Adventist doctrines were understood, including the latter rain and loud cry. This had already been the case before 1858, but it would grow in emphasis throughout the remainder of Ellen White's career:

> The vision at Lovett's Grove, Ohio, on a Sunday afternoon in mid-March, 1858, was one of great importance. In this the theme of the great controversy between Christ and His angels on the one side and Satan and his angels on the other, was seen as one continuous and closely linked chain of events spanning six thousand years. This vision has put Seventh-day Adventists into a unique position with clear-cut views of the working of Providence in the history of our world—a viewpoint quite different from that held by secular historians, who see events of history as the interplay between the actions of men, often seemingly the result of chance or natural developments. In other words, this vision and others of the great conflict of the ages yield a philosophy of history that answers many questions and in prophetic forecast gives the assurance of final victory of good over evil.[12]

In the years after her 1858 vision, Ellen White's ever growing burden was to write what the Lord had shown her (and continued to show her) in regard to the great controversy. Her statements in regard to the loud cry and latter rain would take on new significance as well. In many of her statements, Ellen White would connect Revelation 18, the light that is to lighten the earth with its glory, with both the latter rain and the loud cry. Light would go before and follow the angel of Revelation 18. This light would be sent from heaven to counteract the corruption of the churches since 1844, to help unite God's people in the message, and to prepare them to stand in the time of trouble:

> Then I saw another mighty angel commissioned to descend to earth, and unite his voice with the third angel, and give power and force to his message. Great power and glory were imparted to the angel, and as he descended, the earth was lightened with his glory. The light which went before and followed after this angel, penetrated every where. … [T]his angel… joins in the last great work of the third angel's message, as it swells into a loud cry. … I saw a great light resting upon them, and they united in the message, and fearlessly proclaimed with great power the third angel's message. … I saw that this message will close with power and strength far exceeding the midnight cry.[13]*

> I was pointed down to the time when the third angel's message was closing. The power of God had rested upon his people. They had accomplished their work, and were prepared for the trying hour before them. They had received the latter rain, or refreshing from the presence of the Lord, and the living testimony had been revived. The last great warning had sounded every where, and it had stirred up and enraged the inhabitants of earth, who would not receive the message.[14]

> As the members of the body of Christ approach the period of their last conflict, "the time of Jacob's trouble," they will grow up into Christ, and will partake largely of his Spirit. As the third message swells to a loud cry, and as great power and glory attends the closing work, the faithful people of God will partake of that glory. It is the latter rain which revives and strengthens them to pass through the time of trouble. Their faces will shine with the glory of that light which attends the third angel.[15]

In 1859, Ellen White wrote of the hardness of heart that was keeping the testimony to the Laodiceans from doing its work. Zealous repentance would bring the presence of Jesus and fit the church for the loud cry of the third angel.[16]

This was synonymous with the latter rain. But would "God's people" enter into this work? Many times during the 1860s Ellen White wrote of the condition of the church. An individual work was needed if people were to be prepared to receive the latter rain and loud cry. Following are statements progressing into the late 1860s:

> I was shown that the testimony to the Laodiceans applies to God's people at the present time, and the reason it has not accomplished a greater work is because of the hardness of their hearts. But God has given the message time to do its work. The heart must be purified from sins which have so long shut out Jesus. ... When it was first presented, it led to close examination of heart. Sins were confessed, and the people of God were stirred everywhere. Nearly all believed that this message would end in the loud cry of the third angel. But as they failed to see the powerful work accomplished in a short time, many lost the effect of the message. I saw that this message would not accomplish its work in a few short months. It is designed to arouse the people of God, to discover to them their backslidings, and to lead to zealous repentance, that they may be favored with the presence of Jesus, and be fitted for the loud cry of the third angel. ... If the counsel of the True Witness had been fully heeded, God would have wrought for His people in greater power. ... Those who come up to every point, and stand every test, and overcome, be the price what it may, have heeded the counsel of the True Witness, and they will receive the latter rain, and thus be fitted for translation.[17]

> Ministers and people are unprepared for the time in which they live, and nearly all who profess to believe present truth are unprepared to understand the work of preparation for this time. ... [T]hey are wholly unfitted to receive the latter rain and,... Satan... would cause them to make shipwreck of faith, fastening upon them some pleasing self-deception. They think they are all right when they are all wrong.[18]

> God's people are not prepared for the loud cry of the third angel. They have a work to do for themselves which they should not leave for God to do for them. He has left this work for them to do. It is an individual work; one cannot do it for another.[19]

> I was shown that if God's people make no efforts on their part, but wait for the refreshing to come upon them and remove their wrongs and correct their errors; if they depend upon *that* to cleanse them from filthiness of the flesh and spirit, and fit them to engage in the loud cry of the third angel, they will be found wanting. The refreshing or power of God comes only on those who have

prepared themselves for it by doing the work which God bids them, namely, cleansing themselves from all filthiness of the flesh and spirit, perfecting holiness in the fear of God.[20]

Nothing changed during the 1870s in regard to the promises of God. He was still promising to cleanse men and women from all defilement so that they would be able to recognize and receive the latter rain and proclaim the third angel's message with a loud cry. It was in this way that the loud cry and latter rain itself would play a part in helping church members grow up in character, and prepare them to stand in the final conflict:

> As the members of Christ's body approach the period of their final conflict they will grow up into him, and will possess symmetrical characters. As the message of the third angel swells to a loud cry, great power and glory will attend the closing work. It is the latter rain, which revives and strengthens the people of God to pass through the time of Jacob's trouble referred to by the prophets. The glory of that light which attends the third angel will be reflected upon them. God will preserve his people through that time of peril.[21]

The Lord continued to lay a burden on both James and Ellen White to have her publish more in regard to the Great Controversy, but these were very busy times and Satan was ever ready to bring about delays. The continuing struggle to establish church order took up a good part of the early 1860s. In May, 1863, "the first *official* General Conference session" convened in Battle Creek and "marked the completion of the organizational structure among Seventh-day Adventists."[22] Yet this did not end the growth pains of an advancing movement. The unrest and Civil War taking place in the United States during this time also required time and attention.[23] The dire need of health reform and the newly erected Western Health Reform Institute in Battle Creek, along with the challenges of those who brought in fanaticism, were very wearing on both James and Ellen. They were no strangers to sickness themselves, with James suffering four strokes between 1865 and 1873, which required extra time and attention from Ellen, taking her away from her important writing.[24] She was not only a wife but also a mother, giving birth to their fourth child, John Herbert, in September, 1860. Three months later their young baby would die only to be joined by the eldest son Henry, in December, 1863.[25]

These examples represent only a small sampling of the trials James and Ellen White faced during these years of strenuous labor for God's end time church. Finally in November of 1870, *The Spirit of Prophecy,* volume 1 was published, covering the story of creation down through the reign of Solomon. In 1876, volume 2 was published covering the life and teachings of Christ and His miracles. Volume 3 followed in 1878 covering the remaining story of the life of Christ through to His crucifixion. But the one book which laid so heavily on Ellen White's heart was volume 4, which would become the *Great Controversy.*

The Lord desired that Ellen and James White be free from their other labors so she could spend time in writing more fully the themes of the great controversy. Living in Battle Creek, where James was editor of the *Review,* did not leave them time for this work. Their plan was to leave in the summer of 1881 and head west to California where Ellen could devote more time to writing. James also had a burden on his heart to present more fully the subject of redemption:

> The spring and early summer of 1881 we spent together at our home in Battle Creek. My husband hoped to arrange his business so that we could go to the Pacific coast and devote ourselves to writing. He felt that we had made a mistake in allowing the apparent wants of the cause and the entreaties of our brethren to urge us into active labor in preaching when we should have been writing. My husband desired to present more fully the glorious subject of redemption, and I had long contemplated the preparation of important books. We both felt that while our mental powers were unimpaired we should complete these works—that it was a duty which we owed to ourselves and to the cause of God to rest from the heat of battle, and give to our people the precious light of truth which God had opened to our minds.[26]

> We had designed to devote the coming winter to writing [1881]. My husband had said, "Let us not be turned aside from our purpose. I think we have made a mistake, in allowing the apparent wants of the cause and the earnest entreaties of our brethren to urge us into active labor in preaching when we should have been writing. … I feel assured there is a crisis before us. We should preserve our physical and mental powers for future service. The glorious subject of Redemption should long ago have been more fully presented to the people; but I have allowed myself to be called into the field, to attend campmeetings, and have become so worn that I could not engage in writing."[27]

ORIGINAL PAINTING ENTITLED "THE WAY OF LIFE"

Sometime in the early 1870s, Dr. M. G. Kellogg designed and copyrighted a 19″ by 24″ picture depicting the plan of salvation, giving it the title *The Way of Life*: "The picture bore the subtitle, 'From Paradise Lost to Paradise Restored.' Beginning back at the very gates of Eden, the story of man's fall and his restoration was unfolded pictorially in an allegorical engraving." The picture was accompanied by a descriptive booklet and sold through the *Review and Herald*.[28] James White found the picture to be "a great aid to Adventist evangelists in their efforts to properly present the relationship between the law and the gospel."[29] In 1876, James White decided to improve the picture and to produce a new descriptive brochure, printing 20,000 copies to be sold through the *Review* and the *Signs*.[30] But the overshadowing feature in the picture was the Ten Commandments hanging from the two lower limbs of the giant tree in the center of the picture. Although the cross was present in the picture it did not stand out as prominently as did the law tree.

REVISED PAINTING ENTITLED "CHRIST THE WAY OF LIFE

Four years later James White began another revision of the lithograph, demonstrating a change in emphasis in his understanding by the prominent place the cross obtained in the center of the picture. Writing to his wife in early 1880, James stated: "I have a sketch also of the new picture, Behold the Lamb of God. This differs from the Way of Life in these particulars: The Law Tree is removed. Christ on the cross is made large, and placed in the center."[31] In January of 1881, James went to New York City to see Thomas Morgan, who was said to be the best artist in the world, in hopes of having a steel engraving made of the Way of Life. Further inspired with the potential power of the new picture, James planned next to publish a book to accompany it, enlarging the explanation of the plan of salvation already in print. He planned to entitle it Christ, the Way of Life: From Paradise Lost to Paradise Restored.[32] But the Way of Life picture was not the only example of the changing emphasis in James' life.

### *Preach Christ More* [33]*

In February 1881, James White expressed his desire that Adventist ministers spend more time presenting Christ. But they must themselves have more than just a theory of Christ; there must be "an indwelling Christ." True to his own words, James began to emphasize Christ in all his sermons and in his dealings with others. Such was the result of dwelling on Christ more fully:

> With some there is an unutterable yearning of soul for Christ, and the writer is one of this class. With some of us it has been business, work, and care, giving Christ but little room in the mind and in the affections. With others it has been nearly all theory, dwelling upon the law and the prophets, the nature and destiny of man, and the messages, while destitute, to an alarming degree, of an indwelling Christ. ...

> Our preachers need more encouragement. They should preach Christ more, and they should know more of Him upon whom all our hopes of success here, and of Heaven hereafter, depend.[34]

> Two summers I spent with him [James White] in Colorado. During the last few months... I was with him about eight weeks; so that I have had the best of opportunities to know him thoroughly. ... In our travels together, he often mentioned the mistakes he thought he had made in his life. As we prayed alone together, he would weep over them, and plead for grace to be a true Christian man. He often said to me privately, and also spoke of it over and over in nearly all his sermons this spring and summer, that he felt he must be more tender toward his brethren, more compassionate toward the erring, that he must cultivate more love for Christ and more patience in his trials. ... As all will remember, wherever he preached the past few months, he dwelt largely upon faith in Christ and the boundless love of God.[35]

Through late June and July, 1881, James and Ellen White continued their ministry in Battle Creek. James was still editor-in-chief at the *Review.* Often they went to the grove near their home for a season of prayer. Ellen White later recalled one such occasion:

> While walking to the usual place for prayer, [James] stopped abruptly; his face was very pale, and he said, "A deep solemnity is upon my spirit. I am not discouraged, but I feel that some change is about to take place in affairs that concern myself and you. What if you should not live? Oh, this cannot be! God has a work for you to do. But I hope you will give yourself time to rest, that you

may recover from this enfeebled condition. It continues so long that I feel much anxiety as to the result. I feel a sense of danger, and with it comes an unutterable longing for the special blessing of God, an assurance that all my sins are washed away by the blood of Christ. I confess my errors, and ask your forgiveness for any word or act that has caused you sorrow. There must be nothing to hinder our prayers. Everything must be right between us, and between ourselves and God."

We there in humility of soul confessed to each other our errors, and then made earnest supplication for the mercy and blessing of God. My husband remained bowed some minutes after our prayers had ceased. When he arose, his countenance was cheerful and happy. He praised the Lord, saying he felt the assurance of the love of Christ. …

He then uttered a few words of earnest prayer: "Thou, O God, hast a work to be done in the earth; a work so great that we in our weakness tremble as we contemplate its magnitude. But if thou wilt give us strength, we will take up the work committed to our hands, and carry it forward. We will seek to put self out of sight, and to magnify the power of grace in every word and act of life. A solemn trust is ours. What will be our record in the day of God? I will praise thee, O Lord, for I am wholly thine, and thou art mine."[36]

Not long after this James began to sense the possible effects on the work in Battle Creek if he and Ellen were to leave for the West Coast. Ellen "urged upon him the importance of seeking a field of labor where [they] would be released from the burdens necessarily coming upon us at Battle Creek." In reply James spoke of various matters which required attention before they could leave—duties which someone must do. Then with deep feeling he inquired:

"Where are the men to do this work? Where are those who will have an unselfish interest in our institutions, and who will stand for the right, unaffected by any influence with which they may come in contact?" With tears he expressed his anxiety for our institutions at Battle Creek. Said he: "My life has been given to the up-building of these institutions. It seems like death to leave them. They are as my children, and I cannot separate my interest from them. These institutions are the Lord's instrumentalities to do a specific work. Satan seeks to hinder and defeat every means by which the Lord is working for the salvation of men. If the great adversary can mold these institutions according to the world's standard, his object is gained. It is my greatest anxiety to have the right man in the right place. If those who stand in responsible positions are weak in moral power, and vacillating in principle, inclined to lead toward the world, there are enough who will be led. Evil influences must not prevail. I would rather die than live to see these institutions mismanaged, or turned aside from the purpose for which they were brought into existence."[37]

## *The Death of James White*

James had made up his mind. He would rather die than live to see changes come into Battle Creek into the work for which he had poured out his life and soul. Within days, as he and Ellen headed off together in a carriage for a campmeeting, James became chilled and soon developed a severe sickness. By the end of the week it was evident that unless the Lord healed him, he would pass to the grave. It was there, as Ellen White sat by the side of her dying husband, that the Lord gave her a promise for the future of the work:

> When I sat with the hand of my dying husband in my own, I knew that God was at work. While I sat there on the bed by his side, he in such feverness, it was there, like a clear chain of light presented before me: The workmen are buried, but the work shall go on. *I have workmen that shall take hold of this work.* Fear not; be not discouraged; it shall go forward.
>
> It was there I understood that I was to take the work and a burden stronger than I had ever borne before. It was there that I promised the Lord that I would stand at my post of duty, and I have tried to do it. I do, as far as possible, the work that God has given me to do, *with the understanding that God was to bring an element in this work that we have not had yet.*[38]*

God would raise up others that would bring in an element to the work which they had not had yet. After James' death, Ellen White was at the point of death herself. When she recovered, she sought the Lord's will for her life. In an interesting dream, she received her answer. Her work of writing was of utmost importance; sharing through pen what God had shown her years before and that should be put before the people. She was also shown that more precious jewels of light were to be shared with God's people:

> "Ellen Dreams of James After His Death—A few days since I was pleading with the Lord for light in regard to my duty. In the night I dreamed I was in the carriage, driving, sitting at the right hand. Father [James White] was in the carriage, seated at my left hand. He was very pale, but calm and composed. 'Why Father,'

I exclaimed, 'I am so happy to have you by my side once more! I have felt that half of me was gone. Father, I saw you die; I saw you buried. Has the Lord pitied me and let you come back to me again, and we work together as we used to?'

He looked very sad. He said, 'The Lord knows what is best for you and for me. My work was very dear to me. We have made a mistake. We have responded to urgent invitations of our brethren to attend important meetings. We had not the heart to refuse. ...'

'Now, Ellen, calls will be made as they have been, desiring you to attend important meetings, as has been the case in the past. But lay this matter before God and make no response to the most earnest invitations. Your life hangs as it were upon a thread. You must have quiet rest, freedom from all excitement and from all disagreeable cares. We might have done a great deal for years with our pens, on subjects the people need that we have had light upon and can present before them, which others do not have. Thus you can work when your strength returns, as it will, and you can do far more with your pen than with your voice.'

He looked at me appealingly and said, 'You will not neglect these cautions, will you, Ellen?... We ought to have gone to the Pacific Coast before, and devoted our time and energies to writing. Will you do this now? Will you, as your strength returns, take your pen and write out these things we have so long anticipated, and make haste slowly? There is important matter which the people need. Make this your first business. You will have to speak some to the people, but shun the responsibilities which have borne us down.'

'Well,' said I, 'James, you are always to stay with me now and we will work together.' Said he, 'I stayed in Battle Creek too long. I ought to have gone to California more than one year ago. But I wanted to help the work and institutions at Battle Creek. I have made a mistake. Your heart is tender. You will be inclined to make the same mistakes I have made. Your life can be of use to the cause of God. Oh, those precious subjects the Lord would have had me bring before the people, precious jewels of light!' I awoke. But this dream seemed so real.[39]

After Ellen White recovered following the death of James, she moved to Healdsburg, California, to seek rest and quiet where she could once again take up her work on volume 4, *The Great Controversy*.[40]* Early in August, 1882, Ellen White bought a two-story house on Powell Street which bordered the town. In late August, while in Oakland, she suffered serious illness that lasted several weeks. As she began to recover, she pleaded to be taken to the Health Retreat at St. Helena, but she did not improve there. As the time for the

California camp meeting to be held at Healdsburg drew near, she requested to be taken back to her Healdsburg home. She wished to be strong enough to bear her testimony at the camp meeting. It was her hope, and the hope of her family, that in the environment of the camp meeting she might experience a renewal of life and strength.[41]

Camp meeting opened in early October, 1882, in a grove about half a mile from her home. Although very feeble and hardly able to leave her bed, at noon on the first Sabbath she gave instruction to prepare a place in the large tent where she could hear the speaker. A sofa was arranged for her on the broad speaker's stand, and she was carried into the big tent and placed upon it. Those nearby observed not only her weakness but also the deathly paleness of her face. Recalling the experience some years later, Ellen White said that not only was the large tent full, but "it seemed as if nearly all Healdsburg was present."[42]

## It's a Miracle

J. H. Waggoner, editor of the *Signs of the Time*s, spoke that Sabbath afternoon "on the rise and early work of the message, and its progress and present state."[43] Waggoner also presented signs that showed that the day of God was very near. When he had finished his address, Ellen White turned to Willie and Mrs. Ings, who were at her side, and said, "Will you help me up, and assist me to stand on my feet while I say a few words?" They aided her to the desk. "For five minutes I stood there," she later recalled, "trying to speak, and thinking that it was the last speech I should ever make—my farewell message." With both hands she steadied herself at the pulpit:

> All at once I felt a power come upon me, like a shock of electricity. It passed through my body and up to my head. The people said that they plainly saw the blood mounting to my lips, my ears, my cheeks, my forehead.[44]

Every eye in the audience seemed fixed on her. Mr. Montrose, a businessman from the town, stood to his feet and exclaimed, "We are seeing a miracle performed before our eyes; Mrs. White is healed!" Her voice strengthened, her sentences came clear and full, and she bore a testimony such as the audience had never heard before. J. H. Waggoner filled out the story in his report in the *Signs*:

Her voice and appearance changed, and she spoke for some time with clearness and energy. She then invited those who wished to make a start in the service of God, and those who were far backslidden, to come forward, and a goodly number answered to the call.[45]

Uriah Smith, who was present, reported in the *Review and Herald* that after the miraculous healing "she was able to attend meetings… as usual, and spoke six times with her ordinary strength of voice and clearness of thought."[46] Referring to the experience, Ellen White said, "It was as if one had been raised from the dead. … This sign the people in Healdsburg were to have as a witness for the truth."[47] This event, which seemed to be a turning point in her physical condition, opened the way for a strong ministry. In reporting her two-month illness, she remarked that she had expected it would gradually pass. Instead, she was healed instantaneously:[48]

> For two months my pen has been resting; but I am deeply grateful that I am now able to resume my writing. The Lord has given me an additional evidence of his mercy and loving-kindness by again restoring me to health. By my recent illness I was brought very near to the grave; but the prayers of the Lord's people availed in my behalf. …
>
> When the first Sabbath of the meeting came, I felt that I must be upon the camp-ground, for I might there meet the Divine Healer. … The people saw me in my feebleness, and many remarked that to all appearance I was a candidate for the grave. Nearly all present marked the change which took place in me while I was addressing them. … Divine power has wrought a great work for me, whereof I am glad. I was able to labor every day during the meeting, and several times spoke more than one hour and a half. My whole system was imbued with new strength and vigor. A new tide of emotions, a new and elevated faith, took possession of my soul. …
>
> Before my sickness, I thought that I had faith in the promises of God; yet I find myself surprised at the great change wrought in me, so far exceeding my expectations. I am unworthy of this manifestation of the love of God. I have reason to praise God more earnestly, to walk in greater humility before him, and to love him more fervently than ever before. I am placed under renewed obligation to give to the Lord all that there is of me. I must shed upon others the blessed radiance which he has permitted to shine upon me.[49]

## *A Promise Kept*

There was more than one miracle that took place at the 1882 Healdsburg camp-meeting. Young E. J. Waggoner, son of J. H. Waggoner, at 27 years of age attended the camp-meeting where Ellen White was miraculously healed. E. J. Waggoner was born to Adventist parents in 1855. He grew up in Michigan, and later graduated from Battle Creek College where he also met and married his wife Jessie Moser. Waggoner then left Battle Creek to pursue a medical degree, which he obtained from Long Island College Hospital in Brooklyn, New York, graduating in 1878.[50]* After receiving his M.D. degree, Waggoner returned to work in the Battle Creek Sanitarium until around 1880 when he moved to California. It was here, at the 1882 Healdsburg camp-meeting, that Waggoner had a most remarkable experience.

E. J. WAGGONER

As he sat a little apart from the body of the congregation in the large tent one gloomy Sabbath afternoon, he listened to Ellen White preach "the gospel of His grace" with, as Uriah Smith stated, "extra ordinary strength of voice and clearness of thought."[51]* Waggoner would later describe his experience as being as real as that of Paul's experience on the road to Damascus. This experience would guide him in the study of the Bible for the rest of his life and prepare him for taking that message of divine grace to a church languishing in a Laodicean condition. Clearly, God had kept His promise to Ellen White a year before and was raising up other workers to take the place of James White. He was also placing on their hearts the same burden of presenting Christ in all of the Bible, and giving a fuller view of the plan of salvation and righteousness by faith. Waggoner would write of this experience several times throughout his lifetime:

There are some scenes that are landmarks in my experience, beginning with my first conviction of sin, after the reproof of the Spirit and then the revelation of Christ crucified for me, while you were speaking at the Healdsburg camp-meeting in 1882. That has been a light upon my way, that has guided me in all my study of the Bible, and which has got brighter and brighter.[52]

It was during a talk given by you [Ellen White] twenty-one years ago [1882] that I received the light which has been the great blessing of my life and which so far as I have kept it in view, has guided me in the study of the Bible. Therefore I have always had peculiar evidence of the fact that God has used you for a special work in His cause.[53]

Many years ago, the writer sat in a tent one dismal rainy afternoon, where a servant of the Lord was presenting the *Gospel of His grace*; not a word of the text or texts used, nor of what was said by the speaker, has remained with me, and I have never been conscious of having heard a word; but, in the midst of the discourse an experience came to me that was the turning point in my life. Suddenly a light shone about me, and the tent seemed illumined, as though the sun were shining; I saw Christ crucified for me, and to me was revealed for the first time in my life the fact that God loved me, and that Christ gave Himself for me personally. It was all for me. If I could describe my feelings, they would not be understood by those who have not had a similar experience, and to such no explanation is necessary. I believe that the Bible is the word of God, penned by holy men who wrote as they were moved by the Holy Ghost, and I knew that this light that came to me was a revelation direct from heaven; therefore I knew that in the Bible I should find the message of God's love for individual sinners, and I resolved that the rest of my life should be devoted to finding it there, and making it plain to others. The light that shone upon me that day from the cross of Christ, has been my guide in all my Bible study; wherever I have turned in the Sacred Book, I have found Christ set forth as the power of God, to the salvation of individuals and I have never found anything else.[54]

At that time Christ was set forth before my eyes 'evidently crucified' before me. I was sitting a little apart from the body of the congregation in the large tent at a camp meeting in Healdsburg, one gloomy Sabbath afternoon. … All that has remained with me was what I saw. Suddenly a light shone round me, and the tent was more brilliantly lighted than if the noon-day sun had been shining, and I saw Christ hanging on the cross, crucified for me. In that moment I had my first positive knowledge, which came like an overwhelming flood, that God loved me, and that Christ died for me.

God and I were the only beings I was conscious of in the universe. I knew then, by actual sight, God was in Christ reconciling the world unto Himself; I was the whole world with all its sin. I am sure that Paul's experience on the way to Damascus was no more real than mine. ... I resolved at once that I would study the Bible in light of that revelation, in order that I might help others to see the same truth.[55]*

It was only a short time after this experience that by God's providence Waggoner would meet A. T. Jones and together they would bring a "most precious message" to the church. It was God's intent that when the latter rain message was accepted it would soon go to the entire world with a loud cry.

A. T. Jones was born in 1850, and unlike Waggoner, did not grow up in an Adventist home. He joined the army at age twenty and had served for

A.T. JONES

fourteen months before some Adventist publications fell into his hands.[56] On August 8, 1874, Jones was baptized in Walla Walla, Washington Territory. For weeks he had been "earnestly seeking the Lord," and a few days earlier he had received "bright evidence of sins forgiven."[57] After his conversion and baptism, he immediately joined I. D. Van Horn in evangelistic work and raising up churches in the Northwest. In 1877 he was married to Frances Patton and was ordained as a minister the following year. Unable to attend further training at Battle Creek, Jones had to rely on his love for reading for his education. Early on, he became one of the most well-read defenders of religious liberty.[58]

Only a few months before the Healdsburg camp-meeting, Ellen White penned words which carry significant meaning in light of Jones' and Waggoner's conversion experiences. God would choose men that were taught by God rather than the schools of the day:

> In the last solemn work few great men will be engaged. ... But it may be under a rough and uninviting exterior the pure brightness of a genuine Christian character will be revealed. ...
>
> God will work a work in our day that but few anticipate. He will raise up and exalt among us those who are taught rather by the unction of His Spirit than by the outward training of scientific institutions. ... God will manifest that He is not dependent on learned, self-important mortals.[59]

Ellen White also wrote of the Church's great need for the outpouring of the Holy Spirit to make it's work effective. But what was the condition of God's people? The True Witness was still calling for repentance. Backsliding had become chronic and true revival was needed. Only the quickening power of the Holy Spirit through the gospel would remedy the situation:

> We should pray as earnestly for the descent of the Holy Spirit as the disciples prayed on the day of Pentecost. If they needed it at that time, we need it more today. Moral darkness, like a funeral pall, covers the earth. All manner of false doctrines, heresies, and satanic deceptions are misleading the minds of men. Without the Spirit and power of God it will be in vain that we labor to present the truth.[60]
>
> The Lord has not closed heaven to us, but our own course of continual backsliding has separated us from God. ...
>
> Will you heed the counsel of the True Witness to seek the gold tried in the fire, the white raiment, and the eyesalve? The gold is faith and love, the white raiment is the righteousness of Christ, the eyesalve is that spiritual discernment which will enable you to see the wiles of Satan and shun them, to detect sin and abhor it, to see truth and obey it.[61]

There is altogether too little of the Spirit and power of God in the labor of the watchmen. The Spirit which characterized that wonderful meeting on the Day of Pentecost is waiting to manifest its power upon the men who are now standing between the living and the dead as ambassadors for God. The power which stirred the people so mightily in the 1844 movement will again be revealed. The third angel's message will go forth, not in whispered tones, but with a loud voice.[62]

Nothing but the life-giving influences of the gospel can help the soul. Pray that the mighty energies of the Holy Spirit, with all their quickening, recuperative, and transforming power, may fall like an electric shock on the palsy-stricken soul, causing every nerve to thrill with new life, restoring the whole man from his dead, earthly, sensual state to spiritual soundness. You will thus become partakers of the divine nature, having escaped the corruption that is in the world through lust; and in your souls will be reflected the image of Him by whose stripes you are healed.[63]

God had not given up on His people. He had kept his promise to Ellen White. He was preparing workmen who would bring in "an element in this work that we have not had yet."[64] Workmen who would be able to "preach Christ more," that the "most precious message" of an "in dwelling Christ" so vital for God's people, would be proclaimed. This was in order that the church, and the world, "should know more of Him upon whom all our hopes and success here, and of Heaven hereafter, depend."[65] Heavenly plans were set in place that the "mighty energies of the Holy Spirit" might soon fall upon the church and renew their palsy-stricken souls.

# CHAPTER 1 FOOTNOTES

1.  Ellen White would later summarize these landmarks as the passing of time in 1844 taking in the hope of the second coming, the cleansing of the sanctuary, the three angel's messages, the commandments of God, the faith of Jesus, the seventh-day Sabbath, and the nonimmortality of the wicked. See Ellen G. White, *1888 Materials,* p. 518.

2.  See Arthur L. White, *Ellen G. White: The Early Years*, (Hagerstown, Md.: Review and Herald Pub. Assn., 1985) p. 127, (hereafter *The Early Years)*.

3.  Ellen G. White, *Early Writings,* pp. 55-56, vision of 1845. The last sentence in this statement was in the 1851 edition of *A Sketch of the Christian Experience and Views of Mrs. E. G. White*, but was not retained when published as *Early Writings*, 1882 edition. The original quote can be found in: Broadside #1, "To the Little Remnant Scattered Abroad," April 6, 1846, par. 7. In the book *The Great Controversy* Ellen White stated: "The coming of Christ as our high priest to the most holy place, for the cleansing of the sanctuary, brought to view in Dan. 8:14… is also represented by the coming of the bridegroom to the marriage, described by Christ in the parable of the ten virgins, of Matthew 25. … It is those who by faith follow Jesus in the great work of the atonement, who receive the benefits of his mediation in their behalf; while those who reject the *light* which brings to view this work of ministration, are not benefited thereby" (pp. 426, 430, 1888 edition, emphasis supplied).

4.  Ellen G. White, *Gospel Workers*, pp. 378-379, 1892 ed., and *Selected Messages*, vol. 1 (Washington, D.C.: Review and Herald Pub. Assn., 1958), p. 76, vision seen in her girlhood or late 1840s.

5.  Ellen G. White, *Spalding and Magan Collection of Unpublished Manuscripts*, (Payson, AZ: *Leaves-Of-Autumn* Books, 1985), p. 4, written Sept. 1852. Another rendering of this quote is: "I saw [that] the Latter Rain was coming as suddenly as the midnight cry and with ten times the power" (*The Adventist Apocalypse*, Chapter 4, Par. 1). This rendering seems to be substantiated by what A. T. Jones said at the 1893 General Conference: "Another Testimony that has never been printed says that this [manifestation of the power of God] will come as suddenly as it did in 44, and with 'ten times the power'" ("The Third Angel's Message—No. 7," *General Conference Daily Bulletin*, Feb. 5, 1893, p. 152).

6.  Ellen G. White, *Early Writings*, p. 71. Vision May 14, 1851.

7.  Ellen G. White to Sister Harriet, Letter 3, Aug. 11, 1851; *Selected Messages*, book 3, p. 388.

8.  Ellen G. White, "To the Brethren and Sisters," *Review and Herald*, June 10, 1852, p. 21.

9.  Ellen G. White, "The Future," *Review and Herald*, Dec. 31, 1857, p. 59. Some of the imagery describing the "army" shown Ellen White is similar to that mentioned in Joel chapter 2. Also notice how Ellen White does not separate the latter rain and the loud cry. In the compilation *Last Day Events*, this statement is found under the heading, "The Latter Rain Will Produce the Loud Cry" (Ellen G. White, *Last Day Events* [Nampa, ID: Pacific Press, 1992], pp. 186-187).

10. Ellen G. White, *Life Sketches of Ellen G. White* (Mountain View, Ca.: Pacific Press, 1915), p. 162.

11. This would later be published with other material under the title *Early Writings*.

12. Arthur L. White, *Ellen G. White: The Early Years* (Washington, D.C.: Review and Herald Pub. Assn., 1985), p. 366.

13. Ellen G. White, *Spiritual Gifts*, vol. 1, facsimile reprint (Washington, D.C.: Review and Herald Pub. Assn., 1945), pp. 193-196, written in 1858. The phrase, "light which went before and followed after," is again imagery from Joel 2:3.

14. *Ibid.*, p. 197, written in 1858.

15. Ellen G. White, "The Future," *Review and Herald*, May 27, 1862, p. 202.

16. The fact that the Lord was ready to finish this work in 1859 did not negate the need, however, for the message He sent through Jones and Waggoner in 1888. This was to be the culmination of the Laodicean message that the people might be "favored with the presence of Jesus." The light that is to lighten the whole earth with its glory is the same message for all time.

17. Ellen G. White, *Testimonies*, vol. 1, pp. 186-187, written in 1859.

18. Ellen G. White, *Testimonies*, vol. 1, p. 466, written in 1865.

19. *Ibid.*, p. 486, written in 1865.

20. *Ibid.*, p. 619, emphasis supplied, written in 1867.

21. Ellen G. White, "Jacob and the Angel," *Signs of the Times*, Nov. 27, 1879.

22. Arthur L. White, *Ellen G. White: The Progressive Years* (Hagerstown, MD: Review and Herald Pub. Assn., 1986), p. 33.

23. *Ibid.*, pp. 34-72

24. *Ibid.*, pp. 73-238, 381.

25. *Ibid.*, pp. 70-72; *The Early Years*, pp. 24-31.

26. Ellen G. White, *Life Sketches*, p. 247.

27. Uriah Smith, *Last Sickness and Death of James White* (Battle Creek, MI: Review and Herald Press, 1881), p. 54.

28. The inspiration and helpful input for the research that follows grew out of a phone conversation with Raymond Joseph, in January 2010.

29. LeRoy E. Froom, *Movement of Destiny*, pp. 182-183.

30. A "History of the *Way of Life* Pictures," Shelf Document (Silver Spring, MD: Ellen G. White Estate, n.d.), p. 1.

31. James White, "Way of Life," *Review and Herald*, Dec. 14, 1876, p. 192.

32. James S. White to Ellen G. White, March 31, 1880, in "History of the *Way of Life* Pictures," p. 2.

33. "History of the *Way of Life* Pictures," p. 2. James White's ambition was not fulfilled in his lifetime, however, for he died on August 6, 1881. With the help of her sons, Ellen White undertook to fulfill her husband's plan, and in 1883, a beautiful new steel plate engraving was copyrighted by Ellen White which placed Christ at the center of the plan of salvation (*Ibid.*). By June of 1884, the engraving was available with the accompanying booklet in "Danish, Swedish, German, French, and English languages" ("Christ the Way of Life," *Review and Herald*, June 5, 1884, p. 350. James Edson White featured the picture in his book *The Coming King* (Battle Creek, MI: Review and Herald, 1898), p. 56.

34. James White, "Eastern Tour," *Review & Herald*, Feb. 8, 1881, p. 88.

35. D. M. Canright, "My Remembrance of Elder White," *Review & Herald* Aug. 30, 1881, p. 153.

36. Ellen G. White Manuscript 6, Sept. 1881.

37. Ellen G. White, *Testimonies*, vol. 1, pp. 106-107.

38. Ellen G. White Manuscript 9, "Responding to New Light," Feb. 3, 1890; in *1888 Materials*, p. 540, emphasis supplied. Years later Ellen White would refer to this experience while preaching to those at the 1890 General Conference. She made a direct connection between this promise that God had made and the message that was being presented by Jones and Waggoner, which so many were rejecting. See chapter 13.

39. Ellen G. White to W. C. White, Letter 17, Sept. 12, 1881, pp. 2-4.

40. *Spirit of Prophecy*, Volume 4 would not be finished until October 1884. Nine months later, on July 25, 1885, Ellen White, with her son W. C. White and several others, headed to Europe for a two-year stint, returning in July, 1887. While in Europe she would once again be led to take up her work on a revision and addition to *Volume 4* as she spent time in the land of the Reformation (see: Arthur L. White, *The Lonely Years*, pp. 249, 291, 374). God was preparing this book, *The Great Controversy*, for wide distribution in the United States and around the world. The 1888 edition of *The Great Controversy* was published just in time to meet the Sunday law crisis developing in America. We will pick up this story again in chapter 3.

41. The following paragraph and section are adapted from, Arthur L. White, *The Lonely Years*, pp. 203-205.

42. Ellen G. White, Letter 82, Feb. 28, 1906.

43. J. H. Waggoner, *Signs of the Times*, Oct. 26, 1882.

44. Ellen G. White, Letter 82, Feb. 28, 1906.

45. J. H. Waggoner, *Signs of the Times*, Oct. 26, 1882.

46. Uriah Smith, "Close of the California Campmeeting," *Review and Herald*, Oct. 31, 1882, p. 680.

47. Ellen G. White, Letter 82, Feb. 28, 1906.

48. Arthur L. White, *The Lonely Years*, p. 205.

49. Ellen G. White, "My Health Restored," *Signs of the Times*, Nov. 2, 1882, p. 484.

50. Clinton Wahlen, *Selected Aspects of Ellet J. Waggoner's Eschatology and Their Relation to His Understanding of Righteousness by Faith*, Master's Thesis, Andrews University, July, 1988, p. xiii. Clinton states: "All of the published sources are inaccurate in stating that EJW received his M.D. from Bellevue Medical College, although he apparently took one session of classwork there." See also: Pearl W. Howard to L. E. Froom, Jan. 17, 1962, p. 1 (Document File #236, Ellen G. White Estate, Washington, D. C.).

51. Uriah Smith, "Close of the California Campmeeting," *Review and Herald*, Oct. 31, 1882, p. 680. *The fact that Ellen White was healed on October 7, 1882, and mentions nothing of the "gloomy day"* (possibly rain or fog in that area during the month of October), leads me to believe that Waggoner's experience took place on October 14, 1882, the second Sabbath of the Campmeeting.

52. E. J. Waggoner to Ellen G. White, Oct. 22, 1900.

53. E. J. Waggoner to Ellen G. White, Nov. 3, 1903.

54. E. J. Waggoner, *The Everlasting Covenant* (International Tract Society, 1900), p. V.

55. E. J. Waggoner, "Confession of Faith," May 16, 1916. George R. Knight, commenting on this event, states that "pantheism was an extension of two principles growing out of his 1882 conversion experience." First, Waggoner "had extended his desire to find Christ everywhere in the Bible to everywhere in general." And second, "the root of his problem was his determination to 'study the Bible in the light' of his subjective experience in 1882, rather than evaluating that experience by the Bible" (*A User-Friendly Guide to the 1888 Message*, p. 142). Malcolm Bull and Keith Lockhart join with similar thoughts: "The doctrine of perfection was propagated by some church members such as E. J. Waggoner, whose experience was similar to that of contemporary Americans who attended the camp meetings of the Holiness movement. Waggoner's enthusiasm was grounded in an experience he had at a campmeeting in Healdsburg, California" (*Seeking a Sanctuary: Seventh-day Adventism and the American Dream* [San Francisco: Harper and Row Publishers, 1889], p. 77). One might rightly wonder, in light of the miraculous events of 1882, and the numerous Ellen White endorsements of Waggoner a few years later, how such statements could be made today. Is it correct, as some writers insinuate, that Waggoner had a fatal flaw in his conversion experience, and that the message the Lord sent through him was also flawed because it was based on his experience that day?

56. "Jones, Alonzo T," *SDA Encyclopedia*, vol. 10, p. 832.

57. A. T. Jones, *American Sentinel* (nondenominational), July 1923, p. 3; in George R. Knight, *1888 to Apostasy*, p. 15.

58. Marlene Steinweg, "A. T. Jones: Editor, Author, Preacher," *Lest We Forget*, 4th Quarter, 1997, p. 2.

59. Ellen G. White, *Testimonies*, vol. 5, pp. 80, 82, written June 20, 1882.

60. Ellen G. White, *Testimonies*, vol. 5, p. 158, written in 1882.

61. *Ibid.*, pp. 217, 233, written in 1882.

62. *Ibid.*, p. 252, written in 1885.

63. *Ibid.*, p. 267, written in 1885.

64. Ellen G. White Manuscript 9, "Responding to New Light," Feb. 3, 1890; in *1888 Materials*, p. 540.

65. James White, "Eastern Tour," *Review & Herald*, Feb. 8, 1881, p. 88.

# *The Latter Rain and Loud Cry Soon to Come*

## *Call for Preparation & Warning Lest the Latter Rain be Condemned*

During the 1880s, Ellen White began to express more urgency in her statements concerning the loud cry and latter rain. A real message was coming that would lighten the earth with its glory. She wrote of God's plan to send simple men to do this great work that would create a "religious interest" far exceeding that of the sixteenth century Reformation. The message would be more than just a revival of the evangelical preaching of the day. Ellen White also spoke of the "spurious loud cry" that Satan was sending to try and divert minds from the true message for "this" time. To her, these manifestations were one of the "greatest evidences" the loud cry was on its way:

> In the last solemn work few great men will be engaged. … But it may be under a rough and uninviting exterior the pure brightness of a genuine Christian character will be revealed. …
>
> God will work a work in our day that but few anticipate. He will raise up and exalt among us those who are taught rather by the unction of His Spirit than by the outward training of scientific institutions. … God will manifest that He is not dependent on learned, self-important mortals.[1]
>
> God is raising up a class to give the loud cry of the third angel's message. [Acts 20:30 quoted] It is Satan's object now to get up new theories to divert the mind from the true work and genuine message for this time. He stirs up minds to give false interpretations of Scripture, a spurious loud cry, that the real message may not have its effect when it does come. This is one of the greatest evidences that the loud cry will soon be heard and the earth will be lightened with the glory of God.[2]

The angel who unites in the proclamation of the third message is to lighten the whole earth with his glory. A work of worldwide extent and unwonted power is here brought to view. The Advent movement of 1840-44 was a glorious manifestation of the power of God …in this country there was the greatest religious interest which has been witnessed in any land since the Reformation of the sixteenth century; but these are to be far exceeded by the mighty movement under the loud cry of the third message. The work will be similar to that of the day of Pentecost. … By thousands of voices, all over the earth, the message will be given. Miracles are wrought, the sick are healed, and signs and wonders follow the believers. Satan also works with lying wonders, even bringing down fire from heaven in the sight of men. Thus the inhabitants of the earth are brought to take their stand.[3]

During the summer of 1885, through the evangelistic efforts of E. P. Daniels, a revival began in Healdsburg, California. Deep heart searching and repentance had brought a wonderful manifestation of the Spirit of God, which resulted in love and unity among many members. Some of the older workers (J. H. Waggoner and J. N. Loughborough) stepped in and put a stop to the meetings, branding them a "delusion" and

J.H. WAGGONER

"fanaticism." When Ellen White, who was traveling in Sweden, heard what had happened she sent several letters of warning. The work that had begun at Healdsburg was the very work that every church needed. Yes, Satan would always send a counterfeit, but unless changes were made, while fighting against fanaticism, men would "condemn the work of the latter rain":

J.N. LOUGHBOROUGH

From the letters written I have reason to judge a good work was begun in Healdsburg. Those who felt it was wrong, and condemned it, committed, I believe, one of the greatest errors. ...

Brethren, it is high time that revivals similar to the one that has stirred the church in Healdsburg should come to every Seventh-day Adventist church in our land, else the church will not be prepared to receive the latter rain. A work must be done for the individual members of the church. They will confess one to another. ... And whenever this work begins and wherever it is seen, there will be the working of the power of Satan—envy, jealousy, evil surmising will be in exercise. ...

If there is a true, there will be, most assuredly, a counterfeit. ...

Why I dwell so much on this now is because there will be most remarkable movements of the Spirit of God in the churches, if we are the people of God. And my brethren may arise and in their sense of paring everything done after their style, lay their hand upon God's working and forbid it. I know what I am talking about. ...

We have limited faith and sinful hearts and God cannot work in power for us for if He should...[we] could not distinguish the work of God from the counterfeit.[4]

[I]n reference to the revival at Healdsburg I am not in harmony with your treatment of this matter. That there were fanatical ones who pressed into that work I would not deny. But if you move in the future as you have done in this matter, you may be assured of one thing, you will condemn the work of the latter rain when it shall come. For you will see at that time far greater evidences of fanaticism.

When an effort shall be made in the work of God, Satan will be on the ground to urge himself to notice, but shall it be the work of ministers to stretch out the hand and say, This must go no further, for it is not the work of God? ...

I have not confidence in Elder J. H. Waggoner's judgment in these matters. ... If this is the way you manage when God sends good, be assured the revivals will be rare. When the Spirit of God comes it will be called *fanaticism*, as in the day of Pentecost. ...

God has chosen man to do a certain work. His mental capacities may be weak, but then the evidence is more apparent that God works. His speech may not be eloquent but that is no evidence that he has not a message from God.[5]*

During this same time G. I. Butler, General Conference President, took actions to "restrict the work at the New York camp meeting" because of a lack of funds. Ellen White responded in a similar way as she had to the situation at Healdsburg. Unless a change was made, men would bind up the work of the Holy Spirit:

G.I. BUTLER

> Never take action to narrow and circumscribe the work unless you know that you are moved to do so by the Spirit of the Lord. ... Unless those who can help in New York are aroused to a sense of their duty, they will not recognize the work of God when the loud cry of the third angel shall be heard. When light goes forth to lighten the earth, instead of coming up to the help of the Lord, they will want to bind about His work to meet their narrow ideas. Let me tell you that the Lord will work in this last work in a manner very much out of the common order of things, and in a way that will be contrary to any human planning. There will be those among us who will always want to control the work of God, to dictate even what movements shall be made when the work goes forward under the direction of the angel who joins the third angel in the message to be given to the world. God will use ways and means by which it will be seen that He is taking the reins in His own hands. The workers will be surprised by the simple means that He will use to bring about and perfect His work of righteousness.[6]

## *Preparation Needed*

While Ellen White was writing letters of warning against making moves that would hinder the work of the Holy Spirit, she was also expressing in many letters and articles the great need for preparation in order to receive the latter rain. As described in her earlier writings, this involved the cleansing of the soul temple in connection with Christ's work in the heavenly Sanctuary (Dan. 8:14). When the latter rain came, it would bring light, and those who were prepared and received the light, would proclaim the commandments of God and the testimony of Jesus Christ. This third angel's message was not to be given by debate, but by the deep movings of the Holy Spirit. Notice several Ellen White statements:

> The third angel, flying in the midst of heaven and heralding the commandments of God and the testimony of Jesus, represents our work. The message loses none of its force in the angel's onward flight, for John sees it increasing in strength and power until the whole earth is lightened with its glory. ... *Soon* it will go with a loud voice, and the earth will be lightened with its glory. Are we preparing for this great outpouring of the Spirit of God?[7]

> It is with an earnest longing that I look forward to the time when the events of the day of Pentecost shall be repeated with even greater power than on that occasion. John says, "I saw another angel come down from heaven, having great power; and the earth was lightened with his glory."... Thousands of voices will be imbued with the power to speak forth the wonderful truths of God's word. The stammering tongue will be unloosed, and the timid will be made strong to bear courageous testimony to the truth. May the Lord help his people to cleanse the soul temple from every defilement, and to maintain such a close connection with him that they may be partakers of the latter rain when it shall be poured out.[8]

> When the latter rain comes upon the people of God you must have a preparation to press right on, because those whose vessels are clean, whose hands are free just when that latter rain comes get the *light* that comes from on high and their voices are lifted every one to proclaim the commandments of God and the testimony of Jesus Christ.[9]

> The Lord appoints and sends forth ministers not only to preach, for this is a small part of His work, but to minister, to educate the people not to be fighters but to be examples of piety. ... Some have ...educated themselves as debaters, and the churches under their care show the character of their work. ... The great issue so near at hand will weed out those whom God has not appointed, and He will have a pure, true, sanctified ministry prepared for the latter rain.[10]

> Is this indifference to continue from year to year? Is Satan always to triumph, and Christ to be disappointed in the servants whom he has redeemed at an infinite price? We are looking forward to the time when the latter rain will be poured out, confidently hoping for a better day, when the church shall be endued with power from on high, and thus fitted to do more efficient work for God. But the latter rain will never refresh and invigorate indolent souls, that are not using the power God has already given them.[11]

## *Law in Galatians*

While Ellen White was counseling church leaders and members to prepare for the latter rain, admonishing them to be careful lest moves be made that would hinder the needed work, a controversy arose in Battle Creek. On the surface, the controversy was over the law in Galatians, but it involved much more than that. It was really a controversy over justification by faith; the gospel itself. How did this controversy begin, and what did it involve? The rest of this chapter will be devoted to answering these questions.[12] *

In Galatians 3:19, The apostle Paul wrote of the "added Law," and in verse 24, of the "schoolmaster to bring us unto Christ." To which law did these verses refer; the ceremonial law or moral law—the ten commandments? Adventists pioneers during the 1850s, including James White, J. N. Andrews, Uriah Smith, and Joseph Bates, *had* held that the law Paul referred to in Galatians chapter 3 was the ten commandments. This however, had changed.

Protestant dispensationalists of that day were proclaiming emphatically that men were now living in the New Testament dispensation of grace; using texts such as Galatians 3:19 and 3:24 to *prove* that the ten commandments were done away with altogether. This had brought about a shift in the thinking of many Adventists, who hoped to counter such arguments by explaining that Galatians chapter 3 referred to the ceremonial law. However, in 1854, J. H. Waggoner (father of E. J. Waggoner) published a pamphlet entitled: "The Law of God: An Examination of the Testimony of Both Testaments." When this pamphlet presented the view that the law in Galatians chapter 3 referred to the ten commandments *only*, other Adventists took exception, and a controversy developed.

Several days of meetings were held in Battle Creek in which the position of J. H. Waggoner was, according to Uriah Smith, proven wrong. James and Ellen White attended these meetings, and soon after the meetings convened Ellen White had a vision about the law issue. She immediately wrote to J. H. Waggoner stating his position was not to be pressed to the front. James White, as a result of this vision, withdrew J. H. Waggoner's book from the market.

HEALDSBURG COLLEGE

According to Uriah Smith, J. H. Waggoner repeatedly solicited to have the pamphlet reprinted, but James White replied, "'NOT until you revise your position on the law.'"[13]

The controversy over the law in Galatians remained dormant for almost 30 years until the mid 1880s when A. T. Jones and E. J. Waggoner came on the scene. On October 1, 1883, one year after his campmeeting experience, Waggoner began sharing his newfound faith by teaching Bible classes at Healdsburg College, which had opened on April 11, 1882. Somehow, he

 also found time to pastor the Oakland Seventh-day Adventist church and help his father in editing *The Signs of the Times*. A. T. Jones came to California in 1884, relieving Waggoner of his teaching responsibilities in the fall of 1885 and also helping as assistant editor of the *Signs*.[14] * In addition to his other duties, Jones pastored one of the local churches.[15] * When J. H. Waggoner left for Europe

in 1886, A. T. Jones and E. J. Waggoner became the chief editors of the *Signs,* a position that Jones

held until 1889, and E. J. Waggoner held until 1891, when he was sent to England. Both men also took over as chief editors of the *American Sentinel*, a position Waggoner held until 1890, and Jones held till 1897 when he was placed on the General Conference Executive committee.

Although Jones and Waggoner worked together as editors of the *Signs,* they studied separately, coming to many of the same conclusions. Consequently, in their articles in the *Signs*, their classes at the college, and in their preaching in local churches, their underlying message was the same. Jones describes it this way:

> Each of us pursued his own individual study of the Bible and teaching and preaching. Never in our lives did we spend an hour in study together on any subject or upon all subjects. Yet we were led in perfect agreement in the truths of the Bible all the way. To illustrate: On Sabbath Bro. Waggoner was away from Oakland in a campmeeting, and I preached in his place in Oakland church. My subject was "Righteousness by Faith." The next Sabbath he was home and preached in his own place in Oakland church, and I in San Francisco. Sunday morning when I came into the "Signs" office and began to work, I said to Bro. Bollman, "What did Bro. Waggoner preach on yesterday?" He replied, "The same that you did last Sabbath." I asked him, "What was his text?" He replied, "Same one that you had." I said, "What line did he follow? What illustration?" He replied, "The same that you did."[16]

During the summer of 1884, E. J. Waggoner wrote ten articles on the law and the gospel and their relation to one another. In his September 11, 1884 *Signs* article he dealt more specifically with the law in Galatians and departed from the accepted Adventist position that the law in Galatians chapter 3 referred to the ceremonial law.[17] It was during the 1884-85 school year that E. J. Waggoner began to present the same views at Healdsburg College.[18] Although some were pleased with Waggoner's writing and teaching, others became very concerned. Uriah Smith, Chief Editor of the *Review*, and G. I. Butler, President of the General Conference, were the most outspoken in their concerns.

In the spring of 1885, before Ellen White and W. C. White left for England, E. J. Waggoner talked with W. C. White about the concerns he had regarding his writing for the *Signs* and his teaching at the college. His first concern was about writing articles that "would be in conflict with Eld. Canright's writing."[19] D. M. Canright was one of the most prominent evangelists of the time who had successfully debated many Adventist opponents. He had also written many books including, *The Two Laws* which was first published in 1876. In this book Canright took the same position on the law in Galatians as Uriah Smith and G. I. Butler.

The second concern Waggoner shared with W. C. White was in reference to the controversy regarding the law in Galatians, which his father had been involved in years before. W. C. White expressed his "opinion freely that he [E. J. Waggoner] and the editors of the *Signs* should teach what they believed to be truth" even if it did "conflict with some things written by Eld. Canright and others," but regarding the old controversy, he should "avoid it if possible." W. C. White also advised Waggoner to publish "articles on the subjects he had presented at the college."[20] *
E. J. Waggoner took his advice and continued to present the law and gospel through the pages of the *Signs* and adult Sabbath School quarterly, and in college classes and local campmeetings.

## 1886 General Conference

It was not long before A. T. Jones' and E. J. Waggoner's teaching and writing came under fire. In early 1886, G. I. Butler visited Healdsburg College and was informed that "strenuous efforts" had been made by Jones and Waggoner to "impress upon the minds of theological students" that the "added law" of Galatians was the "moral law of the commandments." Butler expressed great concern over the situation since, in his mind, the issue had been settled years before. Besides, E. J. Waggoner's view was contrary to that of James White, Uriah Smith, D. M. Canright and himself. In a letter to Ellen White, he reminded her that she had received light on the subject years before "to the effect that it [the law in Galatians] related to the remedial system rather than the moral law."[21]

In response to Butler's letter, Ellen White immediately sent off a letter to Jones and Waggoner "protesting against them doing contrary to the light which God had given us in regard to all differences of opinion." This letter, however, would never arrive (and has not been found to this day). Consequently, Jones and Waggoner continued presenting their views.[22]* During the summer, Waggoner even published a nine-part series in the *Signs* specifically on Galatians chapter 3. In these articles, Waggoner took the position in regard to the "schoolmaster" of Galatians 3:24, that "by no possibility can this refer to the ceremonial law."[23]

After reading Waggoner's new series in the *Signs* and having heard nothing from Ellen White personally, Butler once again sent a letter to her, protesting against Waggoner's work. According to Butler, Waggoner was causing a "great debate" by presenting views which "three-fourths of the denomination" did not believe. Butler pressed Ellen White once again to settle the matter, stating that he was "impressed to write a brief comment on the Epistle to the Galatians," and implied that he believed the law referred to in Galatians chapter 3 was the ceremonial law only.[24]

On November 16, 1886, Butler again wrote to Ellen White, telling her that he expected "to call our good *Signs* brethren to an account" at the upcoming General Conference, "for the way they have done in reference to some of the disputed points of our faith; the law in Galatians." This Butler readily did. As soon as the Conference opened on November 18, he gave the delegates his "brief comment" on the Epistle of Galatians in the form of an eighty-five page pamphlet entitled; *The Law in the Book of Galatians: Is It the Moral Law, or Does It Refer to that System of Laws Peculiarly Jewish?* Although not mentioning them by name, the pamphlet was nothing more than a rebuttal written against Jones and Waggoner; taking many shots at them personally, their "minority" views, and their "much vaunted doctrine of justification by faith."[25]

Butler also brought the matter to the attention of the Theological Committee at the General Conference. He wrote several resolutions with the intent to suppress the publication of views contrary to the position "held by a fair majority of our people" unless these views had first been "examined and approved by the leading brethren of experience."[26] All but one of Butler's resolutions were approved by a majority vote of the committee. However, Butler reported all his resolutions in an article in the *Review*, including the resolution that was voted down, which censured Jones and Waggoner for the course they had taken.[27]* As W. C. White would later put it: "There has been a desire on the part of some, that Elds. Waggoner and Jones should be condemned unheard."[28]*

On December 16 Butler again wrote to Ellen White, more emphatically than before. He reminded her that he never received a reply on the issue of the law in Galatians, and that the church had been waiting "for years to hear from [her] on the subject." Again on December 28, Butler wrote to Ellen White mentioning the subject of the *Signs* articles, which in his words, "were opposed to the principles of our faith." The issue was obviously becoming immensely important in his mind as time went on. Perhaps in a final attempt to make Ellen White speak to the matter, Uriah Smith, editor of the *Review*, ran an old article where Ellen White explicitly stated: "Let individual judgment submit to the authority of the church."[29]*

## *Ellen White Responds*

Finally, early in 1887 (and after badgering from Butler for nearly a year), Ellen White wrote once again to Jones and Waggoner and sent copies to Smith and Butler. In her letter she told them *she hadn't read any of the material written by either party* representing the different views on the law in Galatians. She mentioned several times her frustration over not being able to find what she had written years before on the subject.[30]* She felt she had been shown that J. H. Waggoner's "position in regard to the law was incorrect," And now, not being able to find this material, her mind was not "clear" on the issue and she could "not grasp the matter." She expressed her great concern over seeing the "two leading papers in contention." She even stated that Jones and Waggoner were too "self-confident and less cautious than they should be," and that she feared E. J. Waggoner had "cultivated" a love for "discussions and contention" like his father. "Especially at this time should everything like differences be repressed" and unity be sought. Many discourses and articles in the Church papers were "on argumentative subjects" and "were like Cain's offering; Christless." Ellen White was also concerned that those "who are not Bible students" would take a stand on the issue without sufficient study; "yet it may not be truth." If "these things" were to come into a General Conference she would "refuse to attend":

> We have a worldwide message. The commandments of God and the testimonies of Jesus Christ are the burden of our work. To have unity and love for one another is the great work now to be carried on. ...
>
> From the Holy of Holies, there goes on the grand work of instruction. Christ officiates in the sanctuary. We do not follow Him into the sanctuary as we should. There must be a purifying of the soul here upon the earth, in harmony with Christ's cleansing of the sanctuary in heaven. There we shall see more clearly as we are seen. We shall know as we are known.
>
> It is the deep movings of the Spirit of God that is needed to operate upon the heart to mold character. ... The little knowledge imparted might be a hundred fold greater if the mind and character were balanced by the holy enlightenment of the Spirit of God. Altogether too little meekness and humility are brought into the work of searching for the truth as for hidden treasures, and if the truth were taught as it is in Jesus, there would be a hundred fold greater power ...but everything is so mingled with self that the wisdom from above cannot be imparted.[31] *

Ellen White's letter seemed to catch Jones and Waggoner by surprise, but it did serve a good purpose. Jones thanked Ellen White for her letter, stating that he would "try earnestly to profit by the testimony," and that he was "sorry indeed" that he had "any part in anything that would tend to create division or do harm in any way to the cause of God." He also shared his side of the story, giving the background into the controversy over the law in Galatians. He had never heard of the letter sent to them before, nor of the testimony sent to J. H. Waggoner years earlier. He offered gladly to print any light that Ellen White had on the subject in the *Signs*. He also made it plain that he had not allowed the subject to come up in his classes at the College, telling the students that he "would not attempt to say which [view] is right. ...":

> I have told them to look for the gospel of Christ in Galatians, rather than to discuss the law there. ... I thought that if they would keep Christ and the gospel before their minds they would be sure to be on the right side whichever way the question of the law should be finally decided. With Christ before them I could not see how they could possibly go astray. I think however that I have told them that I thought they would find both laws there, and the gospel—justification by faith—underlying the whole of it.[32]

Waggoner expressed similar views. He had not taught in the College since the summer of 1885, therefore he had not been presenting his views to college students. He had never heard of any testimony to his father, nor that Ellen White had ever "spoken on the subject." If he had known that, "the case would have been different." Besides, the views he had taught were "different" from his father's views. He had felt he was helping the advancement of truth but now lamented that he had "been too hasty in putting forth views which could arouse controversy." He had learned a lesson he would not forget:

> I do desire most earnestly that the time may soon come when all our people shall see eye to eye. ... I am truly sorry for the feeling that has existed and does exist between the two offices. I think it is but the simple truth to say that it did not originate here, and that much of what is felt in the east is due to misunderstanding on their part, of the real state of things here, and of the motives of those here; but I do not wish you to consider this as a shirking of blame. I know full well that a feeling of criticism has been allowed to creep in here, as I think in no one more than me. As I now view this spirit of criticism, which springs from the meanest kind of pride, I hate it, and want no more of it. I am determined that henceforth no word of mine, either in public or in private, shall tend to the detraction of any worker in the cause of God.[33]

Not only did Jones and Waggoner search their own hearts and repent, Waggoner lived up to his word of not wanting to detract "any worker in the cause of God." *The Gospel in the Book of Galatians*—Waggoner's seventy-one page response to Butler's pamphlet—although dated February 10, 1887, was not printed until the 1888 General Conference, and only after Ellen White's recommendation for fair play.[34] *

G. I. Butler's response was quite different, however. Having received a copy of the letter to Jones and Waggoner, he "rejoiced," thinking that Ellen White had finally sided with him and Uriah Smith. He hoped that Ellen White would now make a public statement on the added law, because "the added law is either the moral or the ceremonial law systems." Butler opened himself up for later problems by stating that if his position was ever proven wrong he would "have no confidence" in his "own judgement," would not know the "leading of the Spirit," and it would "perfectly unfit [him] for acting any leading part" in the work. Butler let his true feelings toward Waggoner slip out as well. He saw E. J. as inheriting "some of his father's qualities," stating that the "Waggoner stamp appears in all their editorials."[35] *

Butler claimed that contrary to Waggoner publishing his articles in the *Signs*, he had refused to "publish [his own] views on the Law in Galatians in the *Review*," *forgetting* perhaps that he had just published an aggressive article in the March 22 issue.[36] * It did not take long, however, for Butler's rejoicing to be turned to bitter disappointment.

## *1886 in Retrospect*

Before Butler's letter of rejoicing made its way to Ellen White in Switzerland, the Lord opened before her the truth about the events of the previous year. Not only did she have some "impressive dreams," but she had also taken the time to *read* Butler's material, and she was not impressed. She wrote to Butler indicating that perhaps her Testimony to J. H. Waggoner years before, was in regard to making the issue prominent *at that time* (1856), and not in regard to condemning his *position*. Adventists were not to feel that they knew "all the truth the Bible proclaims." If a point could not be supported, they should not be "too proud to yield it." Instead of an admonishment that Waggoner submit his views to those in authority, Ellen White stated that it was now only fair for him to have equal time:

> Now, I do not wish the letters that I have sent to you should be used in a way that you will take it for granted that your ideas are all correct and Dr.

Waggoner's and Elder Jones's are all wrong. ... I think you are too sharp. And then when this is followed by a pamphlet published of your own views, be assured I cannot feel that you are just right at this point to do this unless you give the same liberty to Dr. Waggoner. ... I have had some impressive dreams that have led me to feel that you are not altogether in the light. ... I want to see no Phariseeism among us. The matter now has been brought so fully before the people by yourself as well as Dr. Waggoner, that it must be met fairly and squarely in open discussion. ... You circulated your pamphlet; now it is only fair that Dr. Waggoner should have just as fair a chance as you have had. ... I believe we will have to have far more of the Spirit of God in order to escape the perils of these last days.[37]*

The "impressive dreams" which Ellen White spoke of were set before her in "figures and symbols, but the explanation was given [her] afterwards..."[38]* Thus as time went on, Ellen White's counsel adjusted to the varying circumstances as she understood more definitely what had taken place, and had been revealed to her while she was in Switzerland in 1887. Clearly the Lord was seeking to warn the church of the great dangers that lay ahead. The very light that was to lighten the earth with its glory was ready to be imparted, but the spirit of the Jews was coming into the church. In the latter part of 1888, Ellen White shared what had been revealed to her:

> That conference [1886] was presented to me in the night season. My guide said, "Follow me; I have some things to show you." He led me where I was a spectator of the scenes that transpired at that meeting. I was shown the attitude of some of the ministers, yourself [Butler] in particular, at that meeting, and I can say with you, my brother, it was a terrible conference.

> My guide then had many things to say which left an indelible impression upon my mind. His words were solemn and earnest. He opened before me the condition of the church at Battle Creek. ... [they] needed the "energy of Christ."... A time of trial was before us, and great evils would be the result of the Phariseeism which has in a large degree taken possession of those who occupy important positions in the work of God. ...

> He [then] stretched out his arms toward Dr. Waggoner, and to you, Elder Butler, and said in substance as follows: "Neither have all the light *upon the law*, neither position is perfect."[39]*

During the Conference at Battle Creek [1886], when the question of the law in Galatians was being examined, I was taken to a number of houses, and heard the unchristian remarks and criticisms made by the delegates. Then these words were spoken: "They must have the truth as it is in Jesus, else it will not be a saving truth to them. ..." When finite men shall cease to put themselves in the way ...then God will work in our midst as never before. ... The Jews, in Christ's day, in the exercise of their own spirit, of self-exaltation, brought in rigid rules and exactions, and so took away all chance for God to work upon minds, ... Do not follow in their track. Leave God a chance to do something for those who love him, and do not impose upon them rules and regulations, which, if followed, will leave them destitute of the grace of God as were the hills of Gilboa, without dew or rain.[40]

Two years ago, while in Switzerland, I was addressed in the night season. ... I seemed to be in the Tabernacle at Battle Creek, and my guide gave instructions in regard to many things at the [1886] conference...: "The Spirit of God has not had a controlling influence in this meeting. The spirit that controlled the Pharisees is coming in among this people, who have been greatly favored of God. ... There are but few, even of those who claim to believe it, that comprehend the third angel's message, and yet this is the message for this time. It is present truth. ..."

Said my guide, "There is much light yet to shine forth from the law of God and the gospel of righteousness. This message, understood in its true character, and proclaimed in the Spirit, will lighten the earth with its glory. ... The closing work of the third angel's message will be attended with a power that will send the rays of the Sun of Righteousness into all the highways and byways of life, ..."[41]

Two years ago [1886] Jesus was grieved and bruised in the person of His saints. The rebuke of God is upon everything of the character of harshness, of disrespect, and the want of sympathetic love in brother toward brother. If this lack is seen in the men who are guardians of our conferences, guardians of our institutions, the sin is greater in them than in those who have not been entrusted with so large responsibilities.[42]

The monumental year of 1888, and the Minneapolis General Conference, was rapidly approaching. Truly the Lord was seeking to warn and prepare His church for what lay ahead. In the context of the dreams Ellen White had in Switzerland, she would write very earnestly of Satan's "greatest fear." That fear was that God's people would "clear the way" so He could pour out the latter rain. Satan would seek to hold back this blessing by working from within the church, but he could not stop the latter rain if God's people were ready to receive it:

> A revival of true godliness among us is the greatest and most urgent of all our needs. ... There must be earnest effort to obtain the blessing of the Lord, not because God is not willing to bestow His blessing upon us, but because we are unprepared to receive it. ...
>
> We have far more to fear from within than from without. The hindrances to strength and success are far greater from the church itself than from the world. ... The unbelief indulged, the doubts expressed, the darkness cherished, encourage the presence of evil angels, and open the way for the accomplishment of Satan's devices. ...
>
> There is nothing that Satan fears so much as that the people of God shall clear the way by removing every hindrance, so that the Lord can pour out his Spirit upon a languishing church and an impenitent congregation. If Satan had his way, there would never be another awakening, great or small, to the end of time. But we are not ignorant of his devices. It is possible to resist his power. When the way is prepared for the Spirit of God, the blessing will come. Satan can no more hinder a shower of blessing from descending upon God's people than he can close the windows of heaven that rain cannot come upon the earth. Wicked men and devils cannot hinder the work of God, or shut out his presence from the assemblies of his people, if they will, with subdued, contrite hearts, confess and put away their sins, and in faith claim his promises.[43]

In an earlier sermon, published in *Review* of May 10, 1887, Ellen White expressed the similar thoughts. It was time to get ready for the latter rain; time to prepare for the loud cry:

> My brethren and sisters, let us remember here is the evidence that God will work. You are not to trust in any power but that of the Lord God of Israel. But if you have enmity in your hearts, you cannot expect that God will let his blessing rest upon you. No one will enter the city of God with anything that defiles. We must get ready for the latter rain. The earth is to be lighted with the glory of the third angel,—not a little corner only, but the whole earth. You may think that the work you are doing now is lost; but I tell you it is not lost. When the message shall go with a loud cry, those who hear the truth now will spring to the front and work with mighty power.[44]

Would God's people get ready for the latter rain? Would they be able to stand? We will seek to answer these questions as we take a look at the Minneapolis General Conference in the chapters ahead.

# CHAPTER 2 FOOTNOTES

1.  Ellen G. White, Testimonies, vol. 5, pp. 80, 82, written 1882.

2.  Ellen G. White to Uriah Smith, Letter 20, July 27, 1884; in Manuscript Releases, vol. 9 (Washington, D. C.: Ellen G. White Estate, 1990), p. 27.

3.  Ellen G. White, Spirit of Prophecy, vol. 4 (Battle Creek, MI: Review and Herald Pub. Co., 1884), p. 429, written between 1878 and 1884.

4.  Ellen G. White to W. C. White, Letter 35, Nov. 17, 1885, unpublished.

5.  Ellen G. White to J. N. Loughborough, J. H. Waggoner, E. J. Waggoner, A. T. Jones, Letter 76, April, 1886; in Manuscript Releases, vol. 21, pp. 147-149, emphasis in original.  A. T. Jones and E. J. Waggoner (J. H. Waggoner's son), worked as assistant editors of the Signs of the Times under J. H. Waggoner. Ellen White assumed that E. J. Waggoner would "naturally take his [fathers] view" and thus addressed the letter to him as well.

6.  Ellen G. White to G. I. Butler, Letter 5, Oct. 31, 1885; in Testimonies to Ministers, p. 300.

7.  Ellen G. White, Testimonies, vol. 5, p. 383, emphasis supplied, written in 1886.

8.  Ellen G. White, "Among the Churches of Switzerland," Review and Herald, July 20, 1886, p. 450.

9.  Ellen G. White Manuscript 81, Sept. 21, 1886, "Morning Talk"; in Sermons and Talks, vol. 1, p. 50, emphasis supplied.

10. Ellen G. White to G. I. Butler and S. N. Haskell, Letter 55, Dec. 8, 1886; in Selected Messages, Book 3, p. 385.

11. Ellen G. White, "The Standard of Christian Excellence," The Signs of the Times, Dec. 9, 1886, p. 737.

12. The Law in Galatians was by far not Jones' and Waggoner's primary concern.  This point cannot be overlooked.  They were interested in presenting the everlasting gospel, which in their understanding included a different perspective on the law in Galatians. This became a stumbling block for most of the leading brethren and was at the heart of the controversy at the 1888 Minneapolis General Conference.  Yet, the underlying dispute was over justification by faith.

13. Uriah Smith to W. A. McCutchen, Aug 8, 1901, Manuscripts and Memories, pp. 305-306. See also, G. I. Butler to Ellen G. White, Oct 1, 1888, and Uriah Smith to Ellen G. White, Feb 17, 1890, in Manuscripts and Memories, pp. 85-86, 152-157.

14. Clinton Wahlen, Selected Aspects of Ellet J. Waggoner's Eschatology and Their Relation to His Understanding of Righteousness by Faith, pp. 3-4. See also: R. W. Schwarz, Light Bearers to the Remnant, p. 185; SDA Bible Commentary, vol. 10, p. 707; George R. Knight, From 1888 To Apostasy, p. 22. Schwarz claims Jones came in 1882, the SDA Bible Commentary states May 1885, and Knight claims the summer of 1884. Wahlen's research seems to be the most accurate. E. J. Waggoner's name first appeared in Signs of the Times, May 10, 1883.

15. George Knight states that Jones pastored the Healdsburg church while Jones himself states it was the San Francisco church (Knight, op. cit., p. 22; and A. T. Jones to C. E. Holmes, May 12, 1921; in Manuscripts and Memories, p. 327).

16. A. T. Jones to C. E. Holmes, May 12, 1921; in Manuscripts and Memories, p. 347.

17. E. J. Waggoner, "Under the Law (continued)," The Signs of the Times, Sept. 11, 1884, pp. 553-554.

18. G. I. Butler to Ellen G. White, Oct. 1, 1888; in Manuscripts and Memories, pp. 90-91.

19. W. C. White to Dan T. Jones, April 8, 1890; in Manuscripts and Memories, p. 165.

20. W. C. White to Dan T. Jones, April 8, 1890, and W. C. White to E. J. Waggoner, Jan. 9, 1887; in Manuscripts and Memories, pp. 166, 49. It is interesting to note that W. C. White evidently did not know the extent of the controversy over the law in Galatians, nor all of what E. J. Waggoner had been presenting at the college. W. C. White had counseled Waggoner to write articles on what he had presented at the college, and to write what he thought was truth even if it disagreed with others. But when he was later blamed for being "largely responsible" for Waggoner's articles on the law in Galatians, he could honestly say he "did not remember" advising Waggoner to write "any such articles" (Ibid., p. 49).

21. G. I. Butler to Ellen G. White, June 20, 1886; in Manuscripts and Memories, pp. 18-19.

22. See: Ellen G. White to A. T. Jones and E. J. Waggoner, Feb. 18, 1887; in 1888 Materials, p. 21, and E. J. Waggoner to Ellen G. White, April 1, 1887; in Manuscripts and Memories, p. 71. Not only did Ellen White's letter never arrive but the Testimony she had written to J. H. Waggoner years before could not be located; a fact that is true to this very day. On the other hand, W. C. White's letter to E. J. Waggoner did arrive. In his letter, W. C. White quoted from Butler's June 20 letter to his mother—that Waggoner had "vigorously" taught his views at the college—and then simply stated: "I wish our brethren might give this matter a thorough, candid explanation, and

agree on some common ground" (W. C. White to E. J. Waggoner, Aug. 15, 1886; in Manuscripts and Memories, p. 20). See also Chapter 3, footnote 26.

23. E. J. Waggoner, "Comments on Galatians 3. No. 9," The Signs of the Times, Sept. 2, 1886, p. 534.

24. G. I. Butler to Ellen G. White, Aug. 23, 1886; in Manuscripts and Memories, pp. 21-23.

25. G. I. Butler to Ellen G. White, Nov. 16, 1886; in Manuscripts and Memories, p. 30; and G. I. Butler, The Law in the Book of Galatians (Battle Creek, MI.: Review and Herald Pub. House, 1886), p. 78.

26. "General Conference Proceedings," Review and Herald, Dec. 14, 1886, p. 779; and The Seventh-Day Adventist Year Book, 1887 (Battle Creek, Mich.: Review and Herald Pub. House, 1887), pp. 45-46.

27. G. I. Butler to Ellen G. White, Dec. 16, 1886; in Manuscripts and Memories, pp. 42-43. Those committee members in favor of Jones and Waggoner's position were S. N. Haskell, B. L. Whitney, M. C. Wilcox, and E. J. Waggoner. Those committee members opposed: G. I. Butler, D. M. Canright, W. Covert, J. H. Morrison and Uriah Smith. Butler felt that all the resolutions should have passed.

28. W. C. White to Dan T. Jones, April 8, 1890; in Manuscripts and Memories, p. 166. W. C. White wrote of another possible cause of prejudice against E. J. Waggoner: "[T]he present unfortunate position of his father [J. H. Waggoner] will make it very easy for prejudice to arise and interfere with a candid hearing" (W. C. White to C. H. Jones, Aug. 24, 1886; in Manuscripts and Memories, p. 26). J. H. Waggoner was involved in an inappropriate friendship with a married woman, which Ellen White called, "secret sin." Ellen White had seen this in vision and sent several letters to J. H. Waggoner, one via G. I. Butler (Ellen G. White to G. I. Butler, Letter 51, Aug. 6, 1886; in Manuscript Releases, vol. 21, pp. 378-387). Butler responded by coming down hard on J. H. Waggoner, not giving him "a chance for his life," and deciding "how much feeling the erring one should manifest to be pardoned." Butler had J. H. Waggoner removed from his position as editor of the Signs and revoked his newly appointed assignment to Europe. Ellen White had a second vision "which showed [J. H. Waggoner] restored with the blessing of God resting upon him," but he was not "brought to this position" by the help of Butler. As a result of this situation Ellen White had "about come to the conclusion" that when a grievous sin was presented to her that others knew nothing about, she would say nothing but labor personally for them herself. She declared: "I am now becoming convicted that I have made a mistake in specifying wrong existing in my brethren. Many ... will take these wrongs and deal so severely with the wrongdoer that he will have no courage or hope to set himself right. ... Hereafter I must exercise more caution. I will not trust my brethren to deal with souls, if God will forgive me where I have erred" (Ellen G. White to G. I. Butler, Letter 42, April 13, and Letter 16, April 21, 1887).

29. Ellen G. White, "The Unity of the Church," Review and Herald, Jan. 25, 1887, p. 49. This same article was first published in the Feb. 19, 1880 Review, and run a second time, June 16, 1885. It is also found in Testimonies, vol. 4, pp. 16-20. The idea of submitting to the judgment of the brethren had also been expressed in a Testimony written to William L. Raymond in 1884 (Testimonies, vol. 5, p. 293). See also Chapter 5, footnote 23.

30. This fact, along with the fact that she had already sent Jones and Waggoner one letter (which they never received), could explain the long delay in her writing again on the subject.

31. Ellen G. White to A. T. Jones and E. J. Waggoner, Letter 37, Feb. 18, 1887; in 1888 Materials pp. 26-31. In his book on 1888 message, Steve Wohlberg dedicates an entire chapter to this letter; chapter 22, "The Forgotten Manuscript That Shaped Minneapolis." From this encounter "both E. J. Waggoner and A. T. Jones experienced the practical application of the Laodicean message, and this prepared them to give the third angel's message." Making that experience practical for us, Wohlberg states: "These experiences are extremely important for us. ... We must understand the message, and also be messengers prepared to give that message. That February 18, 1887, letter is for us. It is for you" (The 1888 Message for the Year 2000, pp. 123, 132). A. Leroy Moore describes this situation as caused by Jones' and Waggoner's "violation of the principles of the priesthood of believers." In order "to proclaim Christ our righteousness with power, Waggoner and Jones had to set self aside and humble themselves in a personal focus upon Christ and His atoning sacrifice." But Moore also suggests that even with the repentance of Waggoner and Jones "permanent damage had already resulted," and "would long bear its evil fruit." The "heavy mortgage payments the controversy [caused by Waggoner and Jones], imposed upon the church have yet to be met" (Adventism in Conflict, pp. 93-95). But as Ellen White soon found out, there was much more to the story than what Butler had been sharing. It was the background and the context, both before and after this letter was written, that shaped the events of 1888. Thus, her letter can be rightly understood only when read in the context of what God revealed to her after it was written, and in the context of the calling that Waggoner had received in 1882, and Jones before the Minneapolis conference. God was preparing Jones and Waggoner for their special mission, and this letter served a purpose. But He also had a hand over the first letter Ellen White sent, which never arrived, and in Ellen White not being able to find her earlier Testimony. We must also remember that Ellen White herself never referred back to this situation, nor did she ever place the blame for the rebellion at Minneapolis on Jones and Waggoner!

32. A. T. Jones to Ellen G. White, March 13, 1887; in Manuscripts and Memories, pp. 66-67.

33. E. J. Waggoner to Ellen G. White, April 1, 1887; in Manuscripts and Memories, pp. 71-72.

34. The added "Explanatory Note" in Waggoner's response demonstrates he had taken Ellen White's refroof to heart: "The delay of nearly two years has given ample time to carefully review the subject again and again, and to avoid any appearance of heated controversy. ... It should also be stated that this little book is not published for general circulation. It is designed only for those in whose hands Elder Butler's pamphlet on Galatians was placed. ... That this letter may tend to allay controversy, to help to bring the household of God into the unity of faith ... is the only desire of the writer" (E. J. Waggoner, The Gospel in the Book of Galatians [Oakland, Cal.: 1888], p. 1).

35. G. I. Butler to Ellen G. White, March 31, 1887; Manuscripts and Memories, pp. 68-70. The reader would do well to read both A. T. Jones' and E. J. Waggoner's letters to Ellen White, and compare their spirit with the spirit manifest throughout Butler's letter.

36. *Ibid.*, and G. I. Butler, "Laws Which Are 'Contrary to us,' A 'Yoke of Bondage,' and 'Not Good,'" Review and Herald, March 22, 1887, pp. 182-184. It is interesting to note that this was the same issue of the Review that Ellen White's "The Church's Great Need," was also published. See also Chapter 4, footnote 3.

37. Ellen G. White to G. I. Butler, Letter 13, April 5, 1887; in 1888 Materials, pp. 32-37 Butler's response to Ellen White's letter was one of profound disappointment and anger. It was not until the 1888 General Conference that he wrote to her blaming her for the sickness he had suffered for over eighteen months, due in part to her April 5, 1887 letter to himself and Smith..

38. Ellen G. White Manuscript 24, Dec. 1888, "Looking Back at Minneapolis"; in 1888 Materials, p. 223. Ellen White's counsel to Jones and Waggoner in her letter of February 18, must be read and understood in light of what the Lord revealed to her in her "impressive dreams." The letter served its purpose in confronting Jones and Waggoner with what was in their own hearts and warning them against publishing points of controversy for all to see. But as soon as the Lord revealed to Ellen White the bigger picture of what was taking place, her counsel took on a new direction. Although not ideal, Jones and Waggoner must now be heard even if it meant publishing differences of opinions.

39. Ellen G. White to G. I. Butler, Letter 21, Oct. 14, 1888; in 1888 Materials, pp. 92-93, emphasis supplied. Some have used this statement as a blank check to condemn different aspects of Jones' and Waggoner's teachings they disagree with; the nature of Christ being the primary one (see, George Knight, A User-Friendly Guide to the 1888 Message, pp. 73, 75). However, it is clear from the background presented here that "neither [Butler or Waggoner] had all the light upon the law" because neither had accepted both the ceremonial and moral law as that which was referred to in Galatians 3. Both Butler and Waggoner had singled out only one of the laws as being the correct view, and it was this that Ellen White was referred to in her dream. The position that Galatians 3 referred to both laws was later confirmed by Ellen White (Ellen G. White to Uriah Smith, Letter 96, June 6, 1896; 1888 Materials, p. 1575).

40. Ellen G. White to G. I. Butler, Letter 21a, Oct. 15, 1888; in 1888 Materials, pp. 113-115.

41. Ellen G. White Manuscript 15, Nov. 1888, "To Brethren Assembled at General Conference"; in 1888 Materials, pp. 165-166.

42. Ellen G. White Manuscript 21, Nov. 1888, "Distressing Experiences of 1888"; in 1888 Materials, pp. 179-180.

43. Ellen G. White, "The Church's Great Need," Review and Herald, March, 22, 1887, pp. 177-178.

44. Ellen G. White, "Importance of Trust in God," Sermon, Sept 18, 1886, Review and Herald, May 10, 1887, p. 290.

# *How Shall We Stand?*

## *Measuring the Temple of God and Those Who Worship Therein*

The 1880s were a solemn time in which to be living, not only because of what was happening in the world, but because of what was happening in the church, "the temple of God."[1]* In light of the solemnity of the hour, Ellen White wrote many letters from Europe, counseling and warning the brethren in America. She also directed much of her attention and energies to her literary work. It was her intention to finish revising volume 1 of the *Spirit of Prophecy* series, which would later become *Patriarchs and Prophets*. However, her attention was soon turned to volume 4 of the *Spirit of Prophecy* series, now titled *The Great Controversy*. New plates were needed for the reprinting of the book, and being in the midst of Reformation history in Europe, it seemed a perfect time for its enlargement. By the time she was finished, more than two hundred pages were added to the book, including some new statements on the latter rain:

> As the "former rain" was given, in the outpouring of the Holy Spirit at the opening of the gospel, to cause the upspringing of the precious seed, so the "latter rain" will be given at its close, for the ripening of the harvest. [Hosea 6:3, Joel 2:23, Acts 2:17, 21 quoted].
>
> The great work of the gospel is not to close with less manifestation of the power of God than marked its opening. … Here are "the times of refreshing" to which the apostle Peter looked forward when he said, "Repent ye therefore, and be converted, that your sins may be blotted out [in the investigative Judgment], when the times of refreshing shall come from the presence of the Lord; and he shall send Jesus [Acts 3:19, 20]."[2]*

Before returning home to America in 1887, Ellen White sent a copy of the enlarged manuscript of volume 4 to Jones and Waggoner requesting that they "give careful criticism to the corrections, and to the whole matter." This opportunity may very well have given them added insights into the issue of religious liberty in which Jones, especially, would soon find himself engulfed as he would almost single-handedly take on Senator H. W. Blair's national Sunday law bill. Unfortunately, because of the controversy surrounding Jones and Waggoner which soon erupted, many would be denied the opportunity of reading the *Great Controversy*, at least for a time.[3]*

### *1888 Conference Approaching*

Several events took place during the spring and summer of 1888 that would have an effect on the Minneapolis Ministerial Institute and General

W.C. White

Conference held in October. Early in 1888, W. C. White corresponded with Elder Butler about the Institute to precede the General Conference, and "proposed four or five lines of work; among which were the duties of church officers, new and advanced measures for carrying the message, the study of Bible doctrines, our religious liberty work, and one or two other lines." In one of his letters of response, Butler wrote about the upcoming Institute, and "gave a list of the subjects which he said he supposed would come up for consideration." Among these subjects "he named prominently the Ten Kingdoms, and the Law in Gal[atians]."[4]

In June, W. C. White met with other California ministers and workers from the *Signs* and Pacific Press, including Jones and Waggoner, for a few days of Bible study at "Camp Necessity," in the mountains east of Oakland. Some time was spent reviewing the subjects of the Ten Kingdoms and the Law in Galatians, including Butler's pamphlet that had been distributed at the 1886 General Conference, and Waggoner's response to it, which had not yet been printed. W. C. White explains Waggoner's question in regard to his response:

> At the close of our study, Eld. Waggoner asked us if it would be right for him to publish his MSS [manuscript] and at the next Gen. Conf. place them in the hands of the delegates, as Eld. Butler had his. We thought this would be right, and encouraged him to have five hundred copies printed.[5]*

Because W. C. White thought the matter had been settled regarding the subjects to be discussed at the upcoming Institute and General Conference in October, he mentioned his correspondence with Butler to both Jones and Waggoner at the Bible studies held at Camp Necessity. But when Jones and Waggoner arrived in Minneapolis *ready* to present their subjects, Butler had "forgotten" his letter to W. C. White. It wasn't long before the rumor was spread around that the subjects of discussion where a "surprise" to the men in Battle Creek and were being "pressed" by the men from California.[6]

In September, just prior to the Minneapolis Ministerial Institute and General Conference, a campmeeting was also held in Oakland, California. Unlike the Bible studies held a few months earlier where ministers and workers had all studied together, a bitter spirit of opposition arose against Jones and Waggoner. W. C. White later described the situation:

> At the Cal[ifornia] C[amp] M[eeting] a very bitter spirit was manifested by some toward Elds. Waggoner and Jones, instigated partly, I presume, by the personalities in Eld. Butler's pamphlet; and arising partly from an old family grudge against Eld. Waggoner Senior. We had a ministers' Council in which almost every utterance of these brethren bearing directly or remotely on the Gal. question was criticized. But the brethren who opposed their teachings would neither consent to a fair examination of the subject nor would they let it alone. They preferred the piecemeal picking process, which I dislike so much.[7]

During this same time period, Ellen White wrote of the great need amongst Adventists to search the scriptures for themselves, not only that they might know the truth, but that they might practice it. On August 5, she sent a circular letter to the "Brethren who shall assemble in General Conference." She wasted no time stating the importance of the upcoming meeting, nor of the great dangers facing the church:

> We are impressed that this gathering will be the most important meeting you have ever attended. This should be a period of earnestly seeking the Lord, and humbling your hearts before Him.
>
> All selfish ambition should be laid aside, and you should plead with God for his Spirit to descend upon you as it came upon the disciples who were assembled together upon the day of Pentecost. ...
>
> My brethren, you are Christ's soldiers, making aggressive warfare against Satan and his host; but it is grievous to the Spirit of God for you to be surmising evil of one another, and letting the imagination of your hearts be controlled by the power of the great accuser.[8]

But in order for this latter rain outpouring of the Holy Spirit to take place, as it had "upon the day of Pentecost," there had to be unity among the brethren. This would be accomplished when they searched the Bible together and lived up to the light revealed to them:

> I hope you will regard this [upcoming Conference] as a most precious opportunity to pray and to counsel together. ... Truth can lose nothing by close investigation. Let the word of God speak for itself. ...
>
> It has been shown me that there are many of our ministers who take things for granted, and know not for themselves, by close, critical study of the scriptures whether they are believing truth or error. ... [They] are willing others should search the scriptures for them; and they take the truth from their lips as a positive fact. ... Let every soul now be divested of envy, of jealousy, of evil surmising, and bring their hearts into close connection with God. ...
>
> Our people individually must understand Bible truth more thoroughly, for they certainly will be called before councils. ...
>
> It is one thing to give assent to the truth, and another thing, through close examination as Bible students, to know what is truth. We have been apprised

of our dangers…and now is the time to take special pains to prepare ourselves to meet the temptations and the emergencies which are just before us. If souls neglect to bring the truth into their life, and be sanctified through the truth, that they may be able to give a reason of the hope that is within them, with meekness and fear, they will be swept away by some of the manifold errors and heresies, and will lose their souls. … Many, many will be lost because they have not studied their Bibles upon their knees, with earnest prayer to God that the entrance of the word of God might give light to their understanding. …

We are not to set our stakes, and then interpret everything to reach this set point.[9]

God was seeking to prepare those who would attend the General Conference for the great blessings He had in store. Yet within a month after this counsel was sent, Ellen White sank into a state of "discouragement" which she felt she would "never rise above." What caused this depression that lasted for over two weeks? Since her time in Europe, the Lord had been laying burdens upon her, not only for individual cases, but for the Church in general. She "felt remorse" and "lost her desire to live" for not being able to arouse her "brethren and sisters to see and sense the great loss they were sustaining in not opening their hearts to receive the bright beams of the Sun of Righteousness."[10] Her "courage was gone" and she hoped no one would pray for her recovery:

I had been instructed in regard to many evils that had been coming in among us while I was in Europe…I had also been told that the testimony God had given me would not be received. … Satan had been at work east of the Rocky Mountains as well as west, to make of none effect the messages of reproof and warning, as well as the lessons of Christ, and the messages of consolation. The evil one was determined to cut off the light which God had for his people. … A strong, firm, resistance was manifested by many against anything that should interfere with their own personal ideas. … This laid upon me the heaviest burdens I could possibly bear.[11]

Ellen White was not only concerned with worldly business practices that were coming into the church, but she was particularly concerned with the "want of love and the want of compassion one for another":

> I have been awake night after night with [such] a sense of agony for the people of God, that the sweat would roll off from me. Some things fearfully impressive were presented to me. ... I saw there different names and characters and sins that were written down. There were sins of every description—selfishness, envy, pride, jealousy, evil-surmising, hypocrisy and licentiousness, hatred and murder in the heart, because of this envy and jealousy. These sins were right among the ministers and people. Page after page was turned. ... And a voice said [that] the time had come when the work in heaven is all activity for the inhabitants of this world. The time had come when the temple and its worshipers had to be measured. ... This is what I saw...and it was there I sunk under the burden.[12]

The Lord still had a work for Ellen White to do. He raised her up in answer to a "special season of prayer" and required her to "walk out by faith against all appearances." She was "strengthened" to make the trip to the campmeeting in Oakland and to give her testimony there. She was "urged by the Spirit of God to make strong appeals" to the brethren who would attend the General Conference. She "urged them to humble themselves before God and receive the assurance of his grace, to be baptized with the Holy Ghost, that they might be in a condition to impart light." The "influence of the Spirit of God came into the meeting," hearts were broken and confessions made. Unfortunately, not all was well at the camp meeting. Ellen White was unaware of the Ministers' Council held during the camp meeting where, according to W. C. White, Jones and Waggoner received the "piecemeal picking process." She was also unaware that W. M. Healey, a minister from California, had sent a letter to G. I. Butler warning him of a plot from the West Coast that would undermine the landmarks of the faith. Later Ellen White would comment:

> Little did I think, when making these solemn appeals, that a letter had gone forth from one present at that meeting stating things he thought were true but were not true and which preceded us and built up a wall of difficulty, placing men prepared to fight everything those who crossed the Rocky Mountains should introduce. ...

> Satan used his influence to have that letter do a work which will prove to the loss of souls. ... [I] asked Eld. Butler if Bro. [Healey] did not write to him certain things. He said he did. I asked if he would let me see the letter. I wanted

to know what testimony was given to create such a state of things as we met at Minneapolis. He said he burned the letter, but the impress had made an indelible impression on his mind and on the minds of others. ...[13]*

Thus the stage was set for the coming General Conference. How would the people of God "stand in the time of the latter rain?" This was the question, as we shall soon see, that was not only on the heart of Ellen White, but on the heart of all heaven.

## *Minneapolis 1888*

On October 10, the Ministerial Institute began and continued for seven days. The General Conference followed and lasted until November 4. Attendees numbered perhaps as many as 500, including 96 delegates representing 27,000 church members around the world.[14] Ellen White, who so recently had been brought back from the brink of death, arrived on time for the opening meetings. During the duration of the meetings, Ellen White would speak "nearly twenty times" to those gathered in the newly built Seventh-day Adventist Church in Minneapolis. Unfortunately, only eleven presentations are now extant.[15]*

In his editorial report of the opening of the Institute, Uriah Smith listed the subjects that had been proposed for discussion: "a historical view of the ten kingdoms, the divinity of Christ, the healing of the deadly wound, justification by faith, how far we should go in trying to use the wisdom of the serpent, and predestination. Other subjects will doubtless be introduced."[16]

It did not take long for Ellen White to express the monumental importance of these meetings, which was based on what she had been shown since her time in Europe. God's church had "far more to fear from within than from without" in hindering the outpouring of the latter rain. Satan's greatest fear was that God's people clear the way for the baptism of the Holy Spirit, which God was ready to pour out.[17] On Thursday, October 11, Ellen White gave the morning talk. She had "discerned at the very commencement" of the Institute a "spirit which burdened" her.[18] Would those assembled study as true Bible believers and receive the Holy Spirit?

Now as we have assembled here we want to make the most of our time. ... but we too often let [opportunities] slip away, and we do not realize that benefit from them which we should. ...

If ever we needed the Holy Ghost to be with us, if we ever needed to preach in the demonstration of the Spirit, it is at this very time. ...

The baptism of the Holy Ghost will come upon us at this very meeting if we will have it so. Search for truth as for hidden treasures. ...

Let us commence right here in this meeting and not wait till the meeting is half through. We want the Spirit of God here now; we need it, and we want it to be revealed in our characters.[19]

In the months and years ahead, Ellen White would refer several times to the baptism of the Holy Spirit that fell upon the Disciples at Pentecost, and that God longed to impart at Minneapolis. This "baptism of the Holy Spirit" was just another term for the "latter rain":

What we need is the baptism of the Holy Spirit. Without this, we are no more fitted to go forth to the world than were the disciples after the crucifixion of their Lord. Jesus knew their destitution, and told them to tarry in Jerusalem until they should be endowed with power from on high.[20]

Today you are to have your vessel purified that it may be ready for the heavenly dew, ready for the showers of the latter rain; for the latter rain will come, and the blessing of God will fill every soul that is purified from every defilement. It is our work today to yield our souls to Christ, that we may be fitted for the time of refreshing from the presence of the Lord—fitted for the baptism of the Holy Spirit.[21]

We are to pray for the impartation of the Spirit as the remedy for sin-sick souls. The church needs to be converted, and why should we not prostrate ourselves at the throne of grace, as representatives of the church, and from a broken heart and contrite spirit make earnest supplication that the Holy Spirit shall be poured out upon us from on high?...

Just before he left them, Christ gave his disciples the promise, "Ye shall receive power, after that the Holy Ghost is come upon you:..."

The disciples returned to Jerusalem...and they waited, preparing themselves... until the baptism of the Holy Spirit came."[22]

On Friday night, October 12, "at the commencement of the Sabbath," the delegates gathered once again at the church in Minneapolis, to hear Elder Farnsworth speak. He preached "a most gloomy discourse telling of the great wickedness and corruption in our midst and dwelling upon the apostasies among us and there was no light, no good cheer, no spiritual encouragement in this discourse. There was a general gloom diffused among the delegates to the conference."[23]*

On Sabbath afternoon, October 13, Ellen White was given a "testimony calculated to encourage." She spoke on the "importance of dwelling upon the love of God much more" and letting "gloomy pictures alone." She heartily exclaimed: "Do not talk of the iniquity and wickedness that are in the world, but elevate your minds and talk of your Saviour." She admonished her listeners that "while we may have to bear plain testimony to separate from sin and iniquity, we do not want to be hammering upon that string forever." The effect of her sermon "was most happy" for both "believers and unbelievers bore testimony that the Lord had blessed them."[24]*

On Sunday and Monday, October 14 and 15, Ellen White spent time responding to a thirty-nine page letter she received from G. I. Butler the previous Friday.[25]* In his letter, Butler mentioned that he had been on his sick bed many times in the past eighteen months from "nervous exhaustion," which he blamed on Ellen White's April 5, 1887 letter to him, where she cautioned he and Smith over their treatment of Jones and Waggoner. Now Butler felt he would never recover until he expressed his "feelings fully." He went into great detail rehearsing his chief concern to Ellen White; the whole history of the Law in Galatians controversy from his point of view, dating back to the 1850s. As far as he could see, there were "simply two views" on the added law; his view being the ceremonial law and Waggoner's being the ten commandments. He described Jones and Waggoner as "young fledglings" who were causing problems all over the country. They were "breaking down" the people's faith in the work of the church and opening the door for "old positions of faith" to be discarded. Their work would not only lead to the loss of "confidence" in the "testimonies themselves," it would lead to the loss of souls who would "give up the truth because of this."[26]*

Butler then mentioned a letter he had just received a few weeks before, from "two prominent members of the State Conference Committee of one of the Northern Pacific Conferences," stating that if Jones' and Waggoner's views were to be taught at Healdsburg College "their young men…would be sent elsewhere." Butler pushed the point home, telling Ellen White: "the way this matter has been conducted will tend to seriously affect the prosperity of your Healdsburg College."[27]

Ellen White viewed the letter as "a most curious production of accusations and charges" against her, but she could calmly write: "these things do not move me. I believe it was my duty to come [here]."[28] In her letters she reminded Butler of the history of the controversy over the Law in Galatians from the point of view given her from heaven, including the "terrible conference" of 1886. She reminded him that her heavenly guide had warned of the trial just before them and of the great evils that would result from the "Phariseeism" that had "taken possession" of those who occupied "important positions in the work of God." She pointed out that trying to control God's work would result in hindering it:

> The spirit and influence of the ministers generally who have come to this meeting [1888] is to discard light. …

> The spirit which has prevailed…is not of Christ. … Let there be no such oppression of conscience as is revealed in these meetings. …

> From this night's work there will arise false imaginings, cruel and unjust misunderstandings, that will work like leaven in every church, and close hearts to the striving of the Spirit of God. … [T]he influence of this meeting will be as far-reaching as eternity. …

> Those who have marked out a certain course in which the light must come will fail to receive it, for God works in His own appointed way.[29]*

> The Lord has presented before me that men in responsible positions are standing directly in the way of the workings of God upon his people, because they think that the work must be done and the blessing must come in a certain way they have marked out. …

> I have not the least hesitancy in saying that a spirit has been brought into this meeting, not of seeking to obtain light, but to stand barricading the way, lest a ray should come into the hearts and minds of the people, through some other channel than that which you had decided to be the proper one.[30]

Ellen White not only wrote her reply to G. I. Butler that Monday morning, October 15, being just two days before the General Conference started. It is very likely she once again expressed her concerns in a discourse to the delegates.[31]* She spoke of the "solemn burdens" she had carried since returning from Europe; how Jesus had described the condition of God's people when He told her that "the time had come when the temple and its worshipers had to be measured." She could honestly exclaim: "I feel horribly afraid to come into our conference." Coming to the close of her talk, Ellen White made a solemn appeal:

> It is high time that we were awake out of sleep, that we seek the Lord with all the heart, and I know He will be found of us. I know that all heaven is at our command. Just as soon as we love God with all our hearts and our neighbor as ourselves, God will work through us. *How shall we stand in the time of the latter rain?* Who expects to have a part in the first resurrection? You who have been cherishing sin and iniquity in the heart? You will fail in that day.[32]*

Heaven was waiting to pour out the latter rain through a most precious message, while the very people that were to receive it were asleep in iniquity and sin, and cherishing a spirit of strife.

## *Spirit of Strife at the Institute*

Much of the contentious spirit Ellen White wrote about, which was coming into the meetings, had to do with a minor issue—the controversy over the ten horns. Back in 1884, the General Conference had commissioned A. T. Jones to "write a series of articles gathered from history on points that showed the fulfillment of prophecy."[33] This led Jones to a more in-depth study of the book of Daniel, and while examining the commonly held Adventist view on the ten kingdoms of Daniel 7 as printed in Uriah Smith's *Daniel and the Revelation*, he found that one kingdom had been identified incorrectly. Jones wrote to Smith twice, asking him to send evidence for the historical view and requesting that he examine the recently discovered evidence. Smith did not reply to Jones' first letter and when he finally responded to his second letter, he claimed he had a lack of time for the task. As a result Jones published his views in the *Signs of the Times* without Smith being able to critique them, and sent him a copy in October of 1886.

Uriah Smith responded irately, telling Jones that he would have to counterattack through the *Review* since Jones had scattered his views "broadcast through the paper." Smith was very fearful that thousands of Adventist opponents would "instantly notice the change" in a doctrine held for forty years and claim that, if given enough time, Adventists would acknowledge they were "mistaken on everything."[34] Jones responded by stating that the real battle for truth lay ahead. Soon, because of the Sunday crisis, "every point" of Adventist doctrine and beliefs would be "analyzed and challenged...by the greatest in the land." Thus, when the three angel's messages were being given, Adventists would need a "better reason" for their faith in Bible prophecy "than that 'it has been preached for forty years.'"[35]

To Jones' credit, W. C. White, after listening to Jones' position, spent some time in the summer of 1888 studying into the subject of the ten horns and came to the conclusion that "Eld. Jones had more historical evidence for his position than Eld. Smith."[36] This, however, made little difference, and as the subject was taken up at the 1888 Institute, a very hostile spirit emerged.

Just prior to the 1888 Institute, Butler had labeled Jones a troublemaker for bringing up an interpretation "contrary to the long-established faith of our people taken forty years ago."[37] During the Institute itself, Jones received an ever-increasing amount of criticism and false accusations leveled at him, and on Monday, October 15, the situation came to a head during the ten o'clock meeting. Smith declared it "utterly unnecessary" to look into the issue of the ten horns that tended only to evil. He said the old view had "stood the test for 40 years," and Jones was "tearing up old truth." He said that he, for one, "was not going to sit calmly by and see the foundation stones of our message taken out with ruthless hands." Smith did not stop here; he continued speaking falsely by stating that he "was laboring at a disadvantage because he did not know the issue was coming up." With a bit of irony, he then added that some "seem to have known and brought in libraries of source materials."[38]

Finally, on Wednesday, at the close of the Institute prior to the General Conference proper, Smith tried to force a vote to decide the issue of the ten horns. Waggoner blocked this vote suggesting it not be "settled until it had been thoroughly investigated."[39] Despite the blocked vote, Smith claimed victory for his view in his *Review* editorial claiming: "the sentiment of the delegates appeared…to be overwhelmingly on the side of established principals of interpretation, and the old view. Whether or not this will make any difference with those who are urging the new position, remains to be seen."[40] What Smith failed to mention was that the delegates had voted that "all should study the question faithfully during the year." W. C. White saw Smith's editorial as deceptive, and publicly announced that it "was calculated to mislead the people."[41]

It is understandable that after more than two years of misrepresentation and false accusations, Jones and Waggoner might seek to defend themselves. On Tuesday, October 16, Jones again took up the subject of the ten horns and replied to Smith "in no uncertain terms." He told everyone why he had come with "libraries" of books. He discussed the letters that had passed between Smith, Waggoner and himself, proving that the topic of discussion was no surprise. To underscore his point he admonished the delegates "not to blame him for what Uriah Smith said he didn't know." Ellen White was present at the meeting and, being aware of the significance of what was taking place, cautioned Jones saying: "not so sharp, Brother Jones, not so sharp."[42]*

Ellen White knew that a spirit that would reject "light" was controlling the brethren. Any misstep by Jones or Waggoner would only give the brethren an excuse to continue in their rebellious course. Jones' statement was such a minor component in comparison to the whole controversy taking place that Ellen White never mentioned this incident in any of her writings; neither is there any written report from the 1888 Ministerial Institute that mentions Jones' statement. W. C. White, who took notes of this very meeting, recorded Jones' explanation of his research since 1884 and why he "came prepared with libraries." But he did not record Jones' suppositious statement or Ellen White's presumed admonishment.[43]*

## *The Great Need*

Before the week was over, Ellen White spoke several more times to those gathered in Minneapolis. She knew they were "losing a great deal of the blessing" that they might have received from the Institute, and it would "be an eternal loss." They were "not to be satisfied" with their "own righteousness, and content without the deep movings of the Spirit of God":

> Brethren and sisters, there is great need at this time of humbling ourselves before God, that the Holy Spirit may come upon us. …

> May God help us that his Spirit may be made manifest among us. We should not wait until we go home to obtain the blessing of Heaven. … Those who have been long in the work have been far too content to wait for the showers of the latter rain to revive them.[44]

But in order to be revived by the latter rain, God's people needed a "right relation with Him." There could be no holding onto "doubt and unbelief" or the enemy would "keep the control" of their minds which "always results in a great loss." This Satan was seeking to do at the very time in which God was measuring His temple:

> Christ is here this morning; angels are here, and they are measuring the temple of God and those who worship therein. The history of this meeting will be carried up to God; for a record of every meeting is made; the spirit manifested, the words spoken, and the actions performed, are noted in the books of heaven. Everything is transferred to the records as faithfully as are our features to the polished plate of the artist.[45]*

Ellen White spoke of "measuring the temple of God, and those who worship therein." She used terminology from Revelation 11 and Ezekiel 40-42, as well as the very words spoken to her in the dreams she had during the previous summer.[46] Not only were individuals being measured, the Church was corporately being measured. We must ask ourselves what measurement heaven recorded during those solemn meetings? Were God's people ready to stand?

The Ministerial Institute ended and the General Conference began. Would its record be any different? We will seek to answer this question in the next chapter.

# CHAPTER 3 FOOTNOTES

1.  In 1886 Ellen White wrote: "Have you, dear youth, your lamps trimmed and burning? The work is going on in the heavenly court. In vision on the Isle of Patmos John said: 'And there was given me a reed like unto a rod, and the angel stood, saying, Arise and measure the *temple of God*, and the altar, and them that worship therein.' This solemn work is to be done *upon the earth*. Look and see how stands your *measurement of character* as compared with God's standard of righteousness, his holy law. The worshipers are to pass under the measuring line of God. Who will bear the test? Christ says, 'I know thy works.'. . . How many are purifying their souls by obeying the truth? How many are now in this time wholly on the Lord's side?" (*Youth Instructor*, "The Watching Time," Aug. 25, 1886, emphasis supplied). Ten years later Ellen White would write once again about the temple of God at the heart of the work: "Very much needed to be done that the heart of the work might be kept pure. Much care was necessary to keep the machinery oiled, by the grace of God, so as to run without friction. ... If the power of Satan can come into the *very temple of God*, and manipulate things as he pleases, the time of preparation will be prolonged" (Ellen G. White to O. A. Olsen, Letter 83, May 22, 1896, in *1888 Materials*, pp. 1524, 1525, emphasis supplied).

2.  Ellen G. White, *The Great Controversy* (Battle Creek, MI: Review and Herald Pub. Co., 1888), p. 611. The words in bracket, "[in the investigative Judgment]," are in the original and clearly show the connection of the latter rain with the cleansing of the Sanctuary. These words are not present in the 1911 edition.

3.  W. C. White to C. H. Jones, May 18, 1887. Ellen White finished her work on *The Great Controversy* in May of 1888. Plates were soon made, and thousands of books printed. But the books sat "dead" in the publishing houses and were given little attention. See: chapter 7, and *Return of the Latter Rain*, vol. 2, chapter 18.

4.  W. C. White to Dan T. Jones, April 8, 1890; in *Manuscripts and Memories*, p. 169.

5.  *Ibid.*, pp. 167-168. "Camp Necessity" was the name given by W. C. White for the location of the Bible studies held on June 25 and 26, 1888. His notes from these meetings can be found in, *Manuscripts and Memories*, pp. 414-419, 429-440. In his letter to Dan Jones, April 8, 1890, W. C. White states that the meetings took place in "the first of July, 1888," but this was written nearly two years after the fact and without his "letter book" in hand (*Ibid.*, pp. 167, 169).

6. *Ibid.*

7. *Ibid.*, p. 170.

8. Ellen G. White to Brethren Who Shall Assemble in General Conference, Letter 20, Aug. 5, 1888; in *1888 Materials*, pp. 38, 40.

9. *Ibid.*, pp. 38-41, 44.

10. Ellen G. White Manuscript 21, Nov. 1888; in *1888 Materials*, p. 177.

11. Ellen G. White Manuscript 2, Sept. 2, 1888, "Engaging in Worldly Speculation"; in *1888 Materials*, pp. 47, 49.

12. Ellen G. White Manuscript 26, Oct. 1888, "Remarks After Reading an Article"; in *1888 Materials*, pp. 157-158.

13. Ellen G. White Manuscript 2, Sept. 2, 1888; in *1888 Materials*, pp. 47-56. As a result of this letter written by W. M. Healey, the idea of a "California conspiracy" was born. More than ten years later Ellen White wrote to W. M. Healey declaring that, "these letters resulted in retarding the work of God for years, and brought severe and taxing labor upon me… This experience has left its impress for time and for eternity" (Letter 116, Aug. 21, 1901; in *1888 Materials*, pp. 1759-1760).

14. See: Roger Coon, "Minneapolis/1888: The 'Forgotten' Issue," Transcript of Loma Linda University Lecture, Oct. 23-25, 1988, p. 7.

15. Ellen G. White to Mary White, Letter 82, Nov. 4, 1888; in *1888 Materials*, p. 182. Much of the information on the train of events at Minneapolis can be found in R. D. Hottel's diary and W. C. White's notes taken at the conference (*Manuscripts and Memories*, pp. 441-518). The most concise summary of the train of events at Minneapolis is found in Clinton Wahlen's *Selected Aspects of Ellet J. Waggoner's Eschatology and Their Relation to His Understanding of Righteousness by Faith, 1882-1895*, Master's Thesis, Andrews University, July, 1988, pp. 71-77. See also: Paul E. Penno, *Calvary at Sinai: The Law and the Covenants in Seventh-Day Adventist History*, Master's Thesis, Andrews University, 2001; and Ron Graybill, "Elder Hottel Goes to the General Conference," *Ministry*, February 1988, pp. 19-21.

16. Uriah Smith, *Review and Herald*, Oct. 16, 1888, p. 648; in *Manuscripts and Memories*, p. 399.

17. Ellen G. White, "The Churches Great Need," *Review and Herald*, March 22, 1887, p.177.

18. Ellen G. White Manuscript 24, Dec. 1888; in *1888 Materials*, p. 206.

19. Ellen G. White Manuscript 6, Oct. 11, 1888, "Morning Talk"; in *1888 Materials*, pp. 69, 72, 73.

20. Ellen G. White, "How to Meet a Controverted Point of Doctrine," Morning Talk, Jan. 29, 1890, *Review and Herald*, Feb. 18, 1890; in *1888 Materials*, p. 534.

21. Ellen G. White, "It is not for You to Know the Times and the Seasons," Sermon, Sept. 5, 1891, *Review and Herald*, March 22, 1892; in *1888 Materials*, p. 959.

22. Ellen G. White to S. N. Haskell, Letter 38, May 30, 1896; in *1888 Materials*, pp. 1540, 1541.

23. Ellen G. White to Mary White, Letter 81, Oct. 9, 1888; in *1888 Materials*, p. 68. W. C. White took notes of Farnsworth's talk and gives us an idea of its content: "When Christ shall come shall He find faith on the earth? ... False prophets shall arise. The love of many shall wax cold. ... Is it iniquity among us? ... Our people come up to C.M. to get warmed up ... then they go home and cool off. ... They grow harder? ... Iniquity abounds. ... During the (two?) years 13 or 14 members have left us. They have not only left the truth but some have gone into iniquity and nastiness too horrible to be told. ... How would you feel to hold C[amp] M[eeting] when in radius of 50 miles there are 1,000 to 1,500 Sabbathkeepers and only 300 attend?" ("Notes Made by W. C. White at the Minneapolis Meetings. 1888," p. 2; in *Manuscripts and Memories*, p. 472).

24. Ellen G. White to Mary White, Letter 81, Oct. 9, 1888; and Manuscript 7, Oct. 13, 1888, "Sabbath Afternoon Talk"; in *1888 Materials*, pp. 67, 68, 74-84. In the "Diary of R. Dewitt Hottel," mention is made of Ellen White speaking Sabbath afternoon, but no details are given on her topics (*Manuscripts and Memories*, p. 505).

25. One cannot appreciate Butler's stored up feelings (which kept him from the 1888 conference), nor the history of the Law in Galatians controversy, without reading this entire letter (G. I. Butler to Ellen G. White, Oct. 1, 1888; in *Manuscripts and Memories*, pp. 77-118).

26. *Ibid.*, pp. 78, 100, 89. Butler most likely felt justified in this prediction because of the apostasy of D. M. Canright following the 1886 General Conference controversy over the law in Galatians. In 1882, Canright had revised his book *The Two Laws* (first published in 1876), expanding the section on Galatians from six to twenty–four pages in order to strengthen the view that the epistle dealt with

the ceremonial law. It was concern over views like these that led Waggoner to
question W. C. White in 1885 about editorial policies when there were differences
of opinion. W. C. White suggested they "should teach what they believed to
be truth, [even] if it did conflict with some things written by Eld. Canright
and others" (W. C. White to Dan T. Jones, April 8, 1890; in *Manuscripts and
Memories*, p. 166). In 1886, Canright's book was reprinted by the denomination
and served as a welcome addition to Butler's arsenal. Waggoner responded with
his nine part series in the *Signs*, "Comments on Galatians 3," during the summer
of 1886. Butler, according to Ellen White, encouraged Canright "in giving lessons
to the students in the [Battle Creek] college, and in pouring into the *Review* such a
mass of matter as though he were bishop of the Methodist Church." Ellen White
was shown that Canright's views on the law were "such a mixed up concern,"
and she "advised his books to be suppressed." In fact, she stated, "I would burn
every copy in the fire before one should be given out to our people." Canright
and Butler were allies on the "theological committee," and opposed Waggoner at
the 1886 General Conference. It was here that Canright's doubts about his and
Butler's view cemented his conviction that Galatians was indeed speaking of the
moral law as Waggoner had said. However, because Canright retained Butler's
view of "under the law," he dropped both the perpetuity of the law and Adventism
altogether, becoming one of its foremost critics. Ellen White, rather than seeing
this as the fruit of Waggoner's teaching, blamed Smith and Butler (Ellen G. White
to G. I. Butler and Uriah Smith, Letter 13, 1887; in *1888 Materials*, pp. 33-34).

27. G. I. Butler to Ellen G. White, Oct. 1, 1888; in *Manuscripts and Memories*, pp.
    90-91.

28. Ellen G. White to Mary White, Letter 81, Oct. 9, 1888; in *1888 Materials*, p. 66.

29. Ellen G. White to G. I. Butler, Letter 21, Oct. 14, 1888; in *1888 Materials*, pp.
    86, 94-95. On page 85 of the *Ellen G. White 1888 Materials*, the White Estate
    has devoted the entire page for a footnote that seeks to lessen the impact and
    importance of Ellen White's letter to Butler. The footnote suggests that "Butler
    did not remain in a state of darkness," and that by 1902 he had "profited from the
    experience." Nothing is said, however, about Butler's comment in 1910 "that he
    never could see light in their special messages, and that he had never taken [Jones'
    and Waggoner's] position" (A. G. Daniells to W. C. White, Jan. 21, 1910; in
    *Manuscripts and Memories*, p. 325). But regardless of where Butler stood at the
    time of his death, we must ask ourselves if the *result of the actions taken by him
    and others* at the Minneapolis conference is of insignificant consequence today,
    over 120 years later. See also Chapter 7, footnote 3.

30. Ellen G. White to G. I. Butler, Letter 21a, Oct. 15, 1888; in *1888 Materials*, pp. 113, 116.

31. There is some evidence that the remarks made by Ellen White, found in Manuscript 26, Oct. 1888, may have been made Friday, October 12, instead of Monday, October 15. See, *1888 Materials*, p. 66.

32. Ellen G. White Manuscript 26, Oct. 1888; in *1888 Materials*, p. 162. Years later, Ellen White would write without any reservation: "The Lord has raised up Brother Jones and Brother Waggoner to proclaim a message to the world to prepare a people *to stand in the day of God*" (Ellen G. White Manuscript 61, 1893; in *1888 Materials*, p. 1814, emphasis supplied).

33. A. T. Jones to Uriah Smith, Dec. 6, 1886.

34. Uriah Smith to A. T. Jones, Nov. 8, 1886.

35. A. T. Jones to Uriah Smith, Dec. 3, 1886.

36. W. C. White to Dan T. Jones, April 8, 1890; in *Manuscripts and Memories*, p. 168.

37. G. I. Butler to Ellen G. White, Oct. 1, 1888; in *Manuscripts and Memories*, p. 102.

38. W. C. White, "Notes Made at the Minneapolis Meetings 1888," Oct. 15, 1888, pp. 27, 29; in *Manuscripts and Memories*, p. 420; and Ron Graybill, "Elder Hottel Goes to the General Conference," *Ministry*, February 1988, pp. 19-21.

39. "Talk of a Prophecy," Minneapolis *Tribune*, Oct. 18, 1888, p. 5; in *Manuscripts and Memories*, p. 549.

40. Uriah Smith, "The Conference," *Review and Herald*, Oct. 23, 1888, p. 664; in *Manuscripts and Memories*, p. 400.

41. W. C. White to J. H. Waggoner, Feb. 27, 1889; in *Manuscripts and Memories*, p. 136.

42. Signed report of "Interview with J. S. Washburn, at Hagerstown, Md., June 4, 1950," conducted by Robert J. Wieland, p. 1 (This is taken from a copy of the original "Interview" and differs from the paging of the apparently retyped copy on record in Document File 242, at the Center for Adventist Research, James White Library, Andrews University); Ron Graybill, "Elder Hottel Goes to the General Conference," *Ministry*, February 1988, pp. 19-21.

43.  "Notes of W. C. White Taken at Minneapolis," Oct. 16, 1888; in *Manuscripts and Memories*, p. 422.  Unfortunately, this one statement made by Jones has been used for over 100 years to try to excuse the rejection he and Waggoner received at Minneapolis.  A. T. Robinson perhaps started this when, 42 years after Minneapolis (and with Jones' later bitterness and defection still on his mind), wrote of this incident as a "concrete illustration" that would "justify the attitude" of the leading men against Jones and Waggoner.  Robinson, without giving context, describes Smith as having presented in his "characteristic modesty," and Jones responding in his "characteristic style."  He then quotes Jones' statement, 42 years after it was spoken, as: "'Elder Smith has told you he does not know anything about this matter.  I do, and I don't want anyone to blame me for what he does not know" ("Did the Seventh-day Adventist Denomination reject the Doctrine of Righteousness by Faith?" Jan. 30, 1931; in *Manuscripts and Memories* 336-337).  Young L. H. Christian turned 17 while attending the Minneapolis Conference with his parents in 1888.  Nearly 60 years later (and most likely having been influenced by Robinson's report), Christian wrote of the incident between Smith and Jones, but not as an eyewitness account.  He also describes Smith as a "modest but well-informed man" and Jones as "rugged and boastful."  According to Christian, Jones exact statement was: "'The difficulty with Brother Smith is that he does not know who the ten kingdoms are and yet argues for the Huns while I know and can prove my position.'"  Christian claims that Ellen White "severely reprimanded Elder Jones for his disrespect to an older pioneer in the advent movement."  But Christian's recollection is highly suspect.  He misrepresents the Minneapolis conference as a "glorious victory," siding with the veteran preacher E. W. Farnsworth—who declared "that justification by faith was not a new teaching,"—and J. H. Morrison "an honored minister" who "feared the extreme views of Dr. Waggoner."  Christian casts blame on Jones and Waggoner even suggesting that Ellen White did not support them (*The Fruitage of Spiritual Gifts* [1947], pp. 229-230).  A. W. Spalding, not present at Minneapolis, quotes Robinson's statement, likewise adding his own comments.  Uriah Smith "was a modest man, unobtrusive, retiring," while Jones "was aggressive, and at times obstreperous, and he gave just cause for resentment" (*Captains of the Host* [1949], p. 593).  N. F. Pease quotes Robinson's statement of Jones and concludes: "The men who promoted the doctrine of justification by faith … did not always present their views in a discreet, tactful way.  This unfortunate situation developed a spirit of prejudice against the men that in many minds obscured the real issues" (*By Faith Alone* [1962], p. 131).  A. V. Olson quotes from A. W. Spalding's quote of Robinson's statement about Jones, declaring that "some felt that the manners

and language of one of the young speakers were objectionable" (*Through Crisis to Victory 1888-1901* [1966], p. 44). R. W. Schwarz quotes Robinson and says that Jones' "rash statement" left an "impact on many delegates" and "set the pot of controversy boiling before the really significant theological presentation began" (*Light Bearers to the Remnant*, [1979], p. 188). The script written for the Canadian Union College Heritage Players takes much license in quoting A. T. Jones as follows: "'I am certainly happy to comment on the horns. Elder Smith has just admitted to us that he is not really an authority on the ten horns. I want to assure you that I have given this subject a great deal of study, and I can make up for Elder Smith's ignorance'" ("The News From Minneapolis 1888," *Playing Our Past* [North American Division Office of Education, 1989], p. 126). But perhaps the greatest misrepresentation of A. T. Jones is found in the only biography written about him. George R. Knight begins chapter 3 by quoting Robinson's statement and then proclaims that "such harsh words and pompous attitudes provided part of the backdrop for the conflict that characterized the 1888 General Conference session" (*From 1888 to Apostasy* [1987], p. 35). In response to a critique of his book by Dennis Hokama, George Knight makes a very revealing statement: "I will have to confess to Hokama that I must have failed to communicate effectively. I was doing my best to demonstrate that Jones was aberrant from beginning to end. In the late 1880s and early 1890s this is demonstrated by his harshness and failure to demonstrate Christian courtesy"
("A Spark in the Dark: A Reply to a Sermonette Masquerading as a Critique, George Knight answers Dennis Hokama," *Adventist Currents*, April 1988, p. 43). Knight mentions this situation in other books with similar comments (*Angry Saints*, [1989], pp. 32, 65; *A User-Friendly Guide to the 1888 Message* [1998], pp. 28, 53-54). One can only wonder though, at the reliability of books written under such a stated agenda. J. S. Washburn, who was present at Minneapolis, also mentions this incident 62 years later, but deals with it fairly ("Interview," *op. cit.*). See also Chapter 4, footnote 41, for the wider context of Robinson's statement made in 1931. Interestingly enough, just eight months after this incident at Minneapolis, Ellen White, while addressing her audience in regard to Uriah Smith's most recent *Review* article, made a comment similar to Jones': "'Well,' you say, 'What does Brother Smith's piece in the *Review* mean?' He doesn't know what he is talking about; he sees trees as men walking" (Manuscript 5, June 19, 1889, "Sermon Given at Rome NY"; in *1888 Materials*, p. 348). We must remember, however, that she was being led by God to counteract the rejection of the message sent from heaven.

44. Ellen G. White, "The Need of Advancement," Morning Talk, Oct. 18, 1888, *Review and Herald*, Oct. 8, 1889, p. 625, 626; in *1888 Materials*, pp. 117-118.

45. Ellen G. White, "Have Light in Yourselves," Morning Talk, Oct. 19, 1888, *The Signs of the Times*, Nov. 11, 1889, p. 674; in *1888 Materials*, p. 120. Years later Ellen White would write about an "impressive dream" she had where believers were measured in regard to receiving the Holy Spirit: "During the night of the first Sabbath of the Newcastle meeting, I seemed to be in meeting, presenting the necessity and importance of our receiving the Spirit. ... They must receive the Spirit before they could fully understand Christ's lessons. ... In my dream a sentinel stood at the door of an important building, and asked every one who came for entrance, '*Have ye received the Holy Ghost*?' *A measuring-line was in his hand*, and only very, very few were admitted into the building. 'Your size as a human being is nothing,' he said. 'But if you have reached the full stature of a man in Christ Jesus, according to the knowledge you have had, you will receive an appointment to sit with Christ at the marriage supper of the Lamb; and through the eternal ages, you will never cease to learn of the blessings granted in the banquet prepared for you'" (*Review and Herald*, April 11, 1899, "An Impressive Dream," p. 225, emphasis supplied).

46. Ellen G. White Manuscript 26, Oct. 1888; in *1888 Materials*, p. 157

# CHAPTER 4

# "*Most Precious Message*"

## *Response of the Leading Brethren to the Holy Spirit and Advancing Light*

### 1888 CONFERENCE

The 1888 General Conference began on Wednesday, October 17, at 9:30 a.m. The controversy that had overshadowed the Ministerial Institute did little to set a good tone for the General Conference. Unfortunately, this was only the beginning.

As Jones and Waggoner arrived at the church that opening day, their attention was drawn to a large blackboard positioned up front with two opposing propositions written upon it. The one read: *"Resolved*—That the Law in Galatians Is the Ceremonial Law"—with J. H. Morrison's name affixed. The second read: *"Resolved*—That the Law in Galatians Is the Moral Law"—with a blank space for E. J. Waggoner to sign. Waggoner refused to sign it, saying he had not come to debate. Furthermore, his point was that we do not get righteousness by the law, but by faith—irrespective of whether it be the moral or ceremonial law.[1]

Waggoner had begun his series of at least nine presentations on the relationship of the law to the righteousness of Christ just two days prior, and to him the issue was much larger than of which law the book of Galatians was speaking. Only after he had given the first six presentations on righteousness by faith did he take up the issue of Galatians more specifically, and even then he discussed it in a righteousness by faith context.[2]

It would become obvious that the controversy surrounding 1888 pertained to more than the law in Galatians. Although the central issue was righteousness by faith and its relation to other Bible truths, there was a close connection with many other subjects including religious liberty, church organization, education, publishing, and medical missionary work. We will look more specifically at some of the teachings of Jones and Waggoner in the pages ahead, but before we move on we would do well to summarize the "1888 Message."

## *The 1888 Message*

First, we need to realize that the "message" the Lord sent through Jones and Waggoner was not confined to the year 1888 and the Minneapolis General Conference. To the contrary, as we shall see in the chapters ahead, that message was presented during the 1888 General Conference to a great extent and proclaimed well into the decade that followed. Second, we need to realize that although we do not have an exact transcript of what Jones and Waggoner presented at Minneapolis, we are able to reconstruct a fair and accurate concept of what they taught before, during and after the conference.[3]*

Both Jones and Waggoner were prolific writers of books and articles for the church papers. We know from their writings what they taught before the Conference, including Waggoner's *The Gospel in Galatians*, written in 1887, which was given to the delegates attending the 1888 Conference.

JESSIE WAGGONER

We also know from their writings what they taught after the Conference, including Waggoner's *Christ and His Righteousness*, published in 1890, which was based on shorthand notes taken by Jessie F. Moser-Waggoner of E. J. Waggoner's presentations at the 1888 General Conference.[4]*

We also have available more than 1800 pages of Ellen White's correspondence, manuscripts, and sermons regarding the Minneapolis episode as found in the four volumes of *The Ellen G. White 1888 Materials*. Added to that is *Manuscripts and Memories of Minneapolis*; nearly 600 pages of letters from various participants regarding the 1888 meetings. Included in this collection are copies of denominational and newspaper reports, such as the 1888 *General Conference Daily Bulletin*, R. Dewitt Hottel's diary and two W. C. White notebooks containing notes written during meetings.[5]*

As we take a look at what Jones and Waggoner taught, we need to remember first and foremost that they presented Bible doctrines from the Bible itself.[6] Ellen White confirmed them in their approach, stating that "the Bible must be our standard for every doctrine and preaching,"[7] for "it alone can give a correct knowledge of God's will."[8] Besides, "the Bible and the Bible alone, laid up in the heart and blessed by the Spirit of God, can make man right and keep him right."[9] Ellen White realized that the Bible was not stagnant but a "progressive book"[10] from which "glorious truths" were to be "laid open before the followers of Christ."[11] These "Bible truths connected with the great plan of redemption" would be "continually unfolding, expanding, and developing" for it was "Divine, like its Author."[12]*

These Bible truths that Jones and Waggoner were presenting were in line with the distinct Adventist landmarks. Ellen White confirmed seven landmarks in the context of the 1888 message as: "the passing of the time in 1844... the cleansing of the sanctuary transpiring in heaven, and having decided relation to God's people upon the earth, [also] the first and second angels' messages and the third, unfurling the banner on which was inscribed, 'The commandments of God and the faith of Jesus.'. . . The light of the Sabbath of the fourth commandment [and] the nonimmortality of the wicked." Ellen White suggested that Jones and Waggoner had given these landmarks a "fresh impetus."[13] They presented them in a different context—as "truth as it is in Jesus."[14]* In particular, they presented the gospel—"justification by faith and the righteousness of Christ"—or the faith of Jesus *landmark*, in relation to the law, or hand to hand with the commandments of God *landmark*. This, Ellen White said, is the "third angel's message."[15]

Seventh–day Adventists had proclaimed "the commandments of God," but they had not proclaimed "the faith of Jesus" as of equal importance. It had been "talked about but not understood." It had been "overlooked and treated in an indifferent, careless manner," and had not occupied the prominent position God had intended.[16] The law of God is powerless without the "faith of Jesus," for that faith "comprehends more than is generally supposed."[17] Thus, the real issue at Minneapolis was over the plan of salvation itself.

Toward the end of the General Conference, Waggoner wrote that one of the principal subjects being discussed was "the law and the gospel in their various relations, coming under the general head of justification by faith."[18] Years later Ellen White wrote what is perhaps the most well-known statement regarding the 1888 Message. Here we find a trustworthy summary of the more specific aspects of that precious message:

> The Lord in his great mercy sent a most precious message to his people through Elders Waggoner and Jones. This message was to bring more prominently before the world the uplifted Saviour, the sacrifice for the sins of the whole world. It

presented justification through faith in the Surety; it invited the people to receive the righteousness of Christ, which is made manifest in obedience to all the commandments of God. Many had lost sight of Jesus. They needed to have their eyes directed to his divine person, his merits, and his changeless love for the human family. All power is given into his hands, that he may dispense rich gifts unto men, imparting the priceless gift of his own righteousness to the helpless human agent. This is the message that God commanded to be given to the world. It is the third angel's message, which is to be proclaimed with a loud voice, and attended with the outpouring of his Spirit in a large measure.

The uplifted Saviour is to appear… sitting upon the throne, to dispense the priceless covenant blessings. … Christ is pleading for the church in the heavenly courts above. …

Notwithstanding our unworthiness, we are ever to bear in mind that there is One that can take away sin and save the sinner. …

God gave to His servants a testimony that presented the truth as it is in Jesus, which is the third angel's message, in clear, distinct lines. …

This… testimony… presents the law and the gospel, binding up the two in a perfect whole. (See Romans 5 and 1 John 3:9 to the close of the chapter). …

This is the very work which the Lord designs that the message He has given His servant shall perform in the heart and mind of every human agent. It is the perpetual life of the church to love God supremely and to love others as they love themselves. …

Neglect this great salvation, kept before you for years, despise this glorious offer of justification through the blood of Christ, and sanctification through the cleansing power of the Holy Spirit, and there remaineth no more sacrifice for sins, but a certain fearful looking for of judgment and fiery indignation.[19]

The heart of this message was the "uplifted Saviour," both in His divine and human nature. It presented the Saviour as one with "changeless love" who has taken the initiative to save the whole "human family." His "sacrifice for the sins of the whole world" accomplished something for every human being, and if not despised and neglected would lead to "justification through faith in the Surety." Those who exercised this genuine faith would "receive the righteousness of Christ" which is "manifest in obedience to all the commandments of God." This would be accomplished by the "priceless covenant blessings," not of the old covenant, but of the new, wherein the law is written on the heart. Thus mankind need no longer be in bondage to sin, for Christ condemned sin in the flesh and can "take away sin and save the sinner." Sanctification, therefore, is none other than continually experiencing justification by faith and is clearly a part of righteousness by faith.

Now a new motivation takes the place of fear of punishment and hope of reward, for to "love God supremely and to love others as they love themselves" is the highest motivation. In short, this is "the truth as it is in Jesus, which is the third angel's message," joining the Biblical idea of righteousness by faith with the unique truth of the cleansing of the heavenly sanctuary. One who ever bears in mind this good news will find it easier to be saved than to be lost.

It was this very message that was to be "proclaimed with a loud voice"— the loud cry—"and attended with the outpouring of his Spirit in a large measure"—the latter rain.[20] But how was this message received? We return now to the 1888 General Conference.

### *Votes and Resolutions*

As Waggoner's presentations continued during the first week of the Conference, prejudice and opposition only increased. On Thursday morning, October 18, he presented the subject of "justification by faith in Christ." He said that "liberty in Christ was always freedom from sin, and that separation from Christ to some other means of justification always brought bondage." Both he and Ellen White appealed to the brethren, "old and young, to seek God, put away all spirit of prejudice and opposition, and strive to come into the unity of faith."[21]

On Friday, October 19, Waggoner compared the book of Romans with the book of Galatians with the purpose of showing that "the real

URIAH SMITH

point of controversy [in Paul's day] was justification by faith in Christ." He also said that the "covenant and promises to Abraham are the covenant and promises to us." The implication suggested that the same controversy that rocked the church in Paul's day was once again taking place.[22]* Butler believed that an overemphasis on the gospel threatened the law, while Waggoner believed both the law and the gospel were threatened by a legalistic approach. As one of the delegates put it: "the issue was righteousness by faith vs. righteousness by works."[23]

Uriah Smith had an opportunity to speak later in the day and voiced his opinion that "Romans had no reference to Galatians." He also felt there was "danger in Waggoner's position."[24]

On Sabbath, Ellen White spoke to those assembled about making progress in the Christian life. She mentioned the excuses people would make for not overcoming sin in their lives, but that Christ had come to set men free. His sacrifice was sufficient to bring victory; "He comes in and imputes to me His righteousness in His perfect obedience." She stated that when meetings were held and the truth was "being impressed on minds, Satan presents the difficulties." She spoke of the "state of unbelief" held by the Jews when Christ was on earth and during the time of Elijah. God's people had been so "hardhearted" they would not be "impressed with truth," nor were they "susceptible to the influences of the Spirit of God." Ellen White then brought the application home to the leaders before her:

> Here I want to tell you what a terrible thing it is if God gives light, and it is impressed on your heart and spirit, for you to do as they did. God will withdraw His Spirit unless His truth is accepted. …
>
> The human race is accepted in the Beloved. His long human arm encircles the race, while with His divine arm He grasps the throne of the Infinite, and He opens to man all of heaven. The gates are ajar today. Christ is in the heavenly sanctuary and your prayers can go up to the Father. Christ says, if I go away, I will send you the Comforter, and when we have the Holy Spirit we have everything. …
>
> Then we must enter by faith into the sanctuary with Him, we must commence the work in the sanctuary of our souls. We are to cleanse ourselves from all defilement.[25]

As Ellen White presented, she felt that "the Spirit of the Lord was resting not only upon [her] but upon the people." Many bore testimony after the meeting that it was the happiest day of their lives. She knew that the "presence of the Lord Jesus was in the assembly" to bless the people, and that this "special revealing of the Spirit of God was for a purpose; to quell the doubts, to roll back the tide of unbelief which had been admitted into hearts and minds concerning Sister White and the work the Lord had given her to do."[26]* Would this "season of refreshing" turn the tide?

Sunday morning Ellen White gave a short devotional talk; her subject was "A Chosen People." She spoke of the "high standard" to which God had called His people and that the only way this could be obtained was by taking their eyes off the world and placing them on "heavenly things." It is "only by the light shining from the cross of Calvary… that we can understand anything of the wonderful theme of redemption." Speaking of the law, and echoing what Waggoner had been saying earlier in the session, Ellen White indicated that the moral law pointed us to Christ:

> Our work is to show forth the praises of Him who hath called us out of darkness into His marvelous light. How are we to do this? By showing to the world that we are a commandment-keeping people, walking in harmony with God's law. By never losing sight of His goodness and love, and by making everything in our lives subordinate to the claims of His Word. Thus we shall be representatives of Christ, showing forth in our lives a transcript of His character.
>
> "But," one says, "I thought the commandments were a yoke of bondage." It is those only who break the law that find it a yoke of bondage. To those who keep the law it is life and joy and peace and happiness. The law is a mirror, into which we may look and discern the defects in our characters. Should we not be grateful that God has provided a means whereby we may discover our shortcomings?
>
> There is no power in the law to save or to pardon the transgressor. What, then, does it do? It brings the repentant sinner to Christ. Paul declares, "I… have taught you publicly, and from house to house, testifying to the Jews, and also to the Greeks, repentance toward God and faith toward our Lord Jesus Christ" (Acts 20:20, 21). Why did he preach repentance? Because the law of God had been transgressed. Those who have broken the law must

repent. Why did he preach faith in Christ? Because Christ is the One who has redeemed sinners from the penalty of the law. The law points to the remedy for sin—repentance toward God and faith in Christ. Do you wonder that Satan wants to get rid of the law?[27]*

During the afternoon meeting on educational interests, a resolution was proposed to the effect that: "nothing be taught in our school at Battle Creek contrary to what has been taught in the past, or approved by the General Conference Committee." This proposal was made by the brethren to try to stop Jones and Waggoner from presenting at the General Conference doctrines they had taught in the past, as well as preventing them from presenting new ideas in the future.[28]* G. I. Butler had a part in this for he had spread the report that the parents of several students from Healdsburg College would send their children elsewhere as long as Jones' and Waggoner's views were being taught there.[29] The proposal also aimed to prevent Jones from introducing his views to students at Battle Creek College, where it had been planned he would begin teaching the first of the year.[30]

Ellen White was present at the meeting and asked for a rereading of the proposal. She then asked whether such a resolution had ever been proposed or voted on before. Silence was the response. She pressed the point by asking Uriah Smith, the secretary, whether he knew of such a resolution considered at any time, at any previous meeting. Smith seemed uncertain. Ellen White then pointed out the "'danger of binding about the Lord's work.'" The Lord had revealed to her that it was wrong and dangerous, and she admonished the brethren to "'refrain from voting it.'" W. C. White saw it as a "craze for orthodoxy," so he fought against it hard with his mother and finally "killed it dead."[31] Describing the incident later, Ellen White made it clear why it was so dangerous to vote in such a way:

> I stated that I was a stock holder and I could not let the resolution pass, that there was to be special light for God's people as they neared the closing scenes of this earth's history. Another angel was to come from heaven with a message and the whole earth was to be lightened with his glory. It would be impossible for us to state just how this additional light would come. It might come in a very unexpected manner, in a way that would not agree with the ideas that many have conceived. It is not at all unlikely, or contrary to the

ways and works of God to send light to His people in unexpected ways. Would it be right that every avenue should be closed in our school so that the students could not have the benefit of this light? The resolution was not called for.[32]

Unfortunately, Ellen White's advice did little to stop the sequence of events. Even after she had stated "things clearly," R. A. Underwood "urged that the resolution should be carried into effect."[33] So it was, that with the words from Ellen White's lips still ringing in their ears, a vote was taken; one man voting for the resolution with both hands.[34]* Although the resolution did not pass, this event made one thing clear. Even with the Spirit-filled Sabbath meeting only one day behind them, many of the brethren had lost confidence in Ellen White and her testimonies: "Just as soon as they saw that Sister White did not agree with all their ideas and harmonize with the propositions and resolutions to be voted upon… the evidence they had received had as little weight with some as did the words spoken by Christ in the synagogue to the Nazarenes."[35]

That evening, Ellen White poured out her counsel in a public discourse. She spoke of the need to receive the new "manna fresh from heaven" and the need for "Christlike love" which was so lacking at the Conference. She spoke out against the "jesting and joking," "evil speaking," and "making a mock" of their brethren. Using wording from Revelation 5, she once again spoke out against the attempt made earlier to pass the suggested resolution; it was time "when through God's messengers the scroll is being unrolled to the world":

> The time has come when through God's messengers the scroll is being unrolled to the world. Instructors in our schools should never be bound about by being told that they are to teach only what has been taught hitherto. Away with such restrictions. There is a God to give the message His people shall speak. … The gospel must be fulfilled in accordance with the messages God sends. That which God gives His servants to speak today would not perhaps have been present truth twenty years ago, but it is God's message for this time. …
>
> God is presenting to the minds of men divinely appointed precious gems of truth, appropriate for our time. God has rescued these truths from the companionship of error, and has placed them in their proper framework. … [36]*
>
> Those who have not been sinking the shaft deeper and still deeper into the mine of truth will see no beauty in the precious things presented at this conference. When the will is once set in stubborn opposition to the light given,

it is difficult to yield, even under the convincing evidence which has been in this conference. … Jesus Christ has been in every sleeping room where you have been entertained. How many prayers went up to heaven from these rooms?…

We do well to remember that Christ is the light of the world, and that fresh beams of light are constantly reflected from the Source of all light. …

There was a time when Israel could not prevail against their enemies. This was because of Achan's sin. God declared, "Neither will I be with you any more, except ye destroy the accursed thing from among you." God is the same today. If defiling sins are cherished by those who claim to believe the truth, the displeasure of God rests upon the church, and He will not remove it until the members do all in their power to show their hatred for sin, and their determination to cast it out of the church. God is displeased with those who call evil good and good evil. If jealousy, evil surmising, and evil-speaking are allowed to have a place in the church, that church is under the frown of God. It will be spiritually unhealthy until it is cleansed from these sins, for till then God cannot reveal His power to strengthen and elevate His people and give them victory. …

Oh, how much we all need the baptism of the Holy Ghost.[37]

Although Ellen White was not fully aware of the extent this evil speaking had gone, she had seen enough already to speak out against it. There had been considerable heckling of Waggoner during his presentations. Though Waggoner was short in stature, he could be plainly heard. However, someone called out tauntingly: "We can't see you." There was marked "antagonism by some," and a few even "turned their heads away when Waggoner was seen approaching." All of this was meant to hurt Jones and Waggoner, and it did.[38]

G. I. Butler had been sending messages "over the wires from Battle Creek" telling the brethren to stand by the landmarks, and admonishing them "to bring the people to a decision" on the controverted points under discussion.[39] As Ellen White saw the spirit manifested against Jones and Waggoner, which "seemed to be contagious," her heart was deeply pained. She and W. C. White tried "most earnestly" to have the "ministering brethren" meet in an unoccupied room to pray together, yet this did not succeed "but two or three times." As Ellen White would soon discover, however, there was even more going on behind the scenes.[40]*

Finally, early Monday morning, Ellen White wrote out the matter so that her words "would not be misstated" and presented them in the evening, before quite a number of the "leading responsible men." She told them that she had "heard for the first time the views of Elder E. J. Waggoner," and that she was inexpressibly grateful to God for she "knew it was the message for [that] time." "*All through* the presentation of his views," E. J. Waggoner had presented in a "right spirit, a Christlike spirit." Unlike those opposed to his teachings, Waggoner had "taken a straightforward course, *not involving personalities*, to thrust anyone or to ridicule anyone. He had conducted the subject as a Christian gentleman should, in a kind and courteous manner," not using a "debating style." Ellen White stated that "this was acknowledged to be the case [even] by those who were holding opposite views."[41]*

Ellen White regretted that a much larger number were not present for her talk, for some "began to see things in a different light" after she shared. After speaking for a time she had opportunity to answer some questions which she wrote about later:

> Questions were asked at that time. "Sister White, do you think that the Lord has any new and increased light for us as a people?" I answered, "Most assuredly. I do not only think so, I but can speak understandingly. I know that there is precious truth to be unfolded to us if we are the people that are to stand in the day of God's preparation."

> Then the question was asked whether I thought the matter better drop where it was, after Brother Waggoner had stated his views of the law in Galatians. I said, "By no means. We want all on both sides of the question." But I stated that the spirit I had seen manifested at the meeting was unreasonable. …

> The remark was made, "If our views of Galatians are not correct, then we have not the third angel's message, and our position goes by the board; there is nothing to our faith." I said, "Brethren, here is the very thing I have been telling you. This statement is not true. It is an extravagant, exaggerated statement. If it is made in the discussion of this question I shall feel it my duty to set this matter before all that are assembled, and whether they hear or forbear, tell them the statement is incorrect. … There has been a spirit of Pharisaism coming in among us which I shall lift my voice against wherever it may be revealed. …"

Again, a brother said, "Perhaps you think nothing should be said on the other side of the question." My son Willie and I spoke decidedly that we would not have the matter end here by any means, but we desired that they should bring out all the evidence on both sides of the question for all we wanted was the truth, Bible truth, to be brought before the people.[42]

Early the next morning, on Tuesday, October 23, a meeting was called that neither Ellen White nor her son was invited to attend. Statements were made that "Sister White was opposed to the other side of the question being discussed!" Someone sitting in on the meeting went quickly to W. C. White and told him what was taking place and advised him to come in. When he arrived, a "very mournful presentation of the case" was being presented "which created great sympathy for the brethren" who thought they were "crippled and not allowed a chance to set forth their ideas." W. C. White presented the subject "in the correct light," and spoke in behalf of his mother, "who was just as desirous… to hear all that was to be said on the other side of the question." He informed the brethren that "she had spoken thus decidedly in the council of the ministers the night before."

Later that morning, J. H. Morrison, President of the Iowa Conference and a polished debater, was to speak to the other side of the issue. He had been chosen by the General Conference brethren to refute Waggoner's view and defend the traditional majority view of the law in Galatians. Just before Morrison got up to speak in front of the "mixed congregation" in the packed church in Minneapolis, R. M. Kilgore asked for recognition so he might speak. He "spoke in decided, unqualified language," stating "over and over again, that he greatly deplored the introduction of this question" on the "law in Galatians" and "righteousness by faith" when Elder Butler "was sick and could not be present to manage the matter." With "emphasis he stated that it was a cowardly thing" to deal with the matter when the one "best prepared to handle" the issue was "not present."[43] Kilgore claimed that there had "never been an opportunity" like that given to E. J. Waggoner, who was being allowed to present his new views.[44] Then Kilgore made a motion that the "discussion on the subject of Righteousness by Faith" be stopped until Butler could be present.[45]*

Uriah Smith followed immediately, making "remarks of the same order," which were "all calculated to create sympathy" for their position.[46] Speaking as he would for years to come, Smith claimed that "3/4 of what Bro. W. presents I fully agree to,"[47] and he could have really enjoyed the presentations of Waggoner "first rate"[48] if it had not been for something down yonder still to come, which he deemed erroneous.[49] At this, Ellen White who was seated on the platform, arose to her feet and when recognized said: "'Brethren, this is the Lord's work. Does the Lord want His work to wait for Elder Butler? The Lord wants His work to go forward and not wait for any man.'" To this there was no reply.[50]*

Ellen White was "surprised" and "astonished" by what she heard that morning. Language could not "express the burden and distress" of her soul. The "future experience" of the Adventist church had been set before her while in Europe, "in figures and symbols, but the explanation" had later been given her and she recognized these things being fulfilled before her eyes. She had "not one doubt or question in regard to the matter," for she "knew the light which had been presented" by Jones and Waggoner "in clear and distinct lines." But there was one thing she did question: "for the first time I began to think it might be *we* did not hold the correct view after all upon the law in Galatians, for the truth required no such spirit to sustain it."[51]

This was not the end of the push to officially vote on the subject of the law in Galatians, and righteousness by faith, which was the underlying issue. Ellen White stated that she and W. C. White "had to watch at every point lest there should be moves made, resolutions passed, that would prove detrimental to the future work." Satan seemed to have power to hinder her work in a "wonderful degree," and yet she could say: "I tremble to think what would have been in this meeting if we had not been here."[52]* Toward the end of the Conference, Ellen White once again spoke against settling the matter by a vote:

> There are some who desire to have a decision made at once as to what is the correct view on the point under discussion. As this would please Elder B[utler], it is advised that this question be settled at once. But are minds prepared for such a decision? I could not sanction this course. ... While under so much excitement as now exists, they are not prepared to make safe decisions. ...

> The messages coming from your president at Battle Creek are calculated to stir you up to make hasty decisions and to take decided positions; but I warn you against doing this. You are not now calm; there are many who do not know what they believe. It is perilous to make decisions upon any controverted point without dispassionately considering all sides of the question. Excited feelings will lead to rash movements. ...
>
> It is not wise for one of these young men to commit himself to a decision at this meeting, where opposition, rather than investigation, is the order of the day.[53]

A year later, Ellen White spoke of the danger these resolutions posed to the "work of God" had they been passed: "One year ago [1888] resolutions were brought into the Conference for adoption that, had they all been accepted, would have bound about the work of God. Some resolutions were urged by young, inexperienced ones, that never should have received the consent of the Conference. ... If some resolutions that were accepted had not been proposed, it would have been better, for those who presented them were in darkness and not in the light."[54]

At the 1893 General Conference Session, A. T. Jones spoke about the solemn events of 1888, when "three direct efforts" were made, by those claiming to stand by the landmarks, to vote down the message sent of God. The reason these efforts were not successful was because the angel of the Lord, speaking through Ellen White, said: "'do not do it:'"

> Some of those who stood so openly against that [message of the righteousness of Christ] at that time [the Minneapolis meeting], and voted with uplifted hand against it and since that time I have heard say "amen" to statements that were as openly and decidedly papal as the papal church itself can state them. ...
>
> Whether the creed is drawn up in actual writing, or whether it is somebody's idea that they want to pass off by a vote in a General Conference, it makes no difference. ... And there are people here who remember a time—four years ago; and a place—Minneapolis—when three direct efforts were made to get such a thing as that fastened upon the third angel's message, by a vote in a General Conference. What somebody believed—set that up as the landmarks, and then vote to stand by the landmarks, whether you know what the landmarks are or not; and then go ahead and agree to keep the commandments of God, and a lot of other things that you are going to do,

and that was to be passed off as justification by faith. Were we not told at that time that the angel of God said, "Do not take that step; you do not know what is in that"? "I can't take time to tell you what is in that, but the angel has said, Do not do it." The papacy was in it. That was what the Lord was trying to tell us, get us to understand.[55]*

So it was that the Lord used Ellen White almost single-handedly to block an official rejection, by vote, of that message which He had sent to the Seventh-day Adventist church more than one hundred years ago. This was the very message that was to be "proclaimed with a loud voice and attended with the outpouring of [God's] Spirit in a large measure"—the loud cry and latter rain.[56] The only reason these votes were not *recorded* is that Ellen White wisely forbade it. Clearly, the delegates intended to pass such a vote of rejection, even though it was not mentioned in the *Review and Herald* or the *General Conference Daily Bulletin*.[57]*

As a result of such a stance on her part, however, the brethren "lost confidence in Sister White." She "did not agree with all their ideas and harmonize with the propositions and resolutions to be voted." She spoke out against their "treatment of… A. T. Jones and E. J. Waggoner." She claimed to have "heard for the first time" the views of Jones and Waggoner and could "respond with all [her] heart." Because of all this the brethren thought she had "been influenced" and had "changed," and therefore they "did not believe" her.[58] Sadly, the very ones who were claiming that the message of Jones and Waggoner would "break down confidence" in the testimonies,[59] were themselves making "of none effect the testimonies of the Spirit of God."[60] When Ellen White realized the condition of things in Minneapolis that Tuesday in October of 1888, she purposed to leave, but the Lord had more work for her to do. She was to stand by her post.

# CHAPTER 4 FOOTNOTES

1. Norval F. Pease, "The Truth as it is in Jesus: The 1888 General Conference Session," *Adventist Heritage*, pp. 5-6.

2. See: Ron Graybill, "Elder Hottel goes to General Conference," *Ministry*, February 1988, pp. 19-21; Clinton Wahlen, "What Did E. J. Waggoner Say at Minneapolis?" *Adventist Heritage*, Winter, 1988, pp. 22-37 (this article is taken from Wahlen's Master's Thesis; see footnote 5); L. E. Froom, *Movement of Destiny*, p. 243.

3. Some have tried to suggest that the "most precious message" was that which was delivered in 1888 only; suggesting that even "for Ellen White the 1888 message is the message of 1888 rather than the message of 1893 or 1895" (George R. Knight, *A User-Friendly Guide to the 1888 Message*, pp. 165-166). According to Roy Adams the fact that we don't have an exact transcript of their presentations at Minneapolis is "'one of the best things that happened to the 1888 message.'" And furthermore, we "cannot be sure about what precisely was included in Ellen White's endorsement" of Jones and Waggoner (*The Nature of Christ*, p. 31-32). The conclusion we are being asked to draw from these statements is that Ellen White's commendations were only for what Jones and Waggoner presented at Minneapolis, a message of which we cannot be sure. The reality, however, is that we are not left without plenty of good evidence.

4. L. E. Froom is the primary expositor of the idea that Waggoner's 1888 messages were taken down in shorthand, having obtained letters from Jessie F. Moser-Waggoner that state such. According to Froom, Jessie's shorthand notes of E. J. Waggoner's studies were edited and printed in book form. Froom includes *The Gospel in Creation* (1893-1894), and *The Glad Tidings* (1900), with the list of books that came from these transcribed notes (Jessie Waggoner to L. E. Froom, April 16, 1930; in *Movement of Destiny*, pp. 189, 200-201). We must remember, however, that although Waggoner's basic understanding of Galatians and Romans, the covenants, the human and divine nature of Christ, and the underlying theme of his understanding of righteousness by faith did not substantially change, by 1900 some of the details of these subjects were definitely affected by his panentheistic ideas. Thus, it is not entirely correct to state that his later books reflect the *exact* concepts that he presented at Minneapolis. We must also remember as well, that Froom's primary thesis

in *Movement of Destiny* was seeking to prove that one of Waggoner's *main* themes at Minneapolis was in regard to Christ's divine attributes (*Ibid.*). Jessie F. Moser-Waggoner, E. J. Waggoner's wife, was Corresponding Secretary for the International Sabbath School Association and in attendance at the 1888 General Conference. In addition to taking down E. J. Waggoner's presentations in shorthand, she also gave an informal talk on Tuesday, October 23; "How to Study the Lesson" (*General Conference Daily Bulletin*, Oct. 24, 1888 p. 2-3; in *Manuscripts and Memories*, p. 373-374).

5. The best summaries of the train of events, and of the content of Waggoner's message at Minneapolis itself, can be found in: Clinton Wahlen, *Selected Aspects of Ellet J. Waggoner's Eschatology and Their Relation to His Understanding of Righteousness by Faith, 1882-1895*; and Paul E. Penno, *Calvary at Sinai: The Law and the Covenants in Seventh-Day Adventist History*. George Knight states that "*Manuscripts and Memories* contains only a small percentage of the existing documents that throw light on the meetings" (*A User-Friendly Guide to the 1888 Message*, p. 53). Perhaps more should be released.

6. Ellen G. White Manuscript 9, Oct. 24, 1888, "Morning Talk," and Manuscript 22, Oct. 1889, "Diary Entries"; in *1888 Materials*, pp. 153, 463.

7. Ellen G. White, "To Brethren Who Shall Assemble in General Conference," Letter 20, Aug. 5, 1888; in *1888 Materials*, p. 44.

8. Ellen G. White to G. I. Butler, Letter 21, Oct. 14, 1888; in *1888 Materials*, p. 93.

9. Ellen G. White to G. I. Butler and Wife, Letter 18, Dec. 11, 1888; in *1888 Materials*, p. 194.

10. Ellen G. White Manuscript 16, Jan. 1889, "The Discernment of Truth"; in *1888 Materials*, p. 259.

11. Ellen G. White to H. Miller, Letter 5, June 2, 1889; in *1888 Materials*, p. 333.

12. Ellen G. White Manuscript 27, Sept. 13, 1889; in *1888 Materials*, p. 434. Unfortunately, those who opposed Jones and Waggoner did so based on their understanding of Bible truths which they felt needed to be defended. Ellen White saw that men could have "misunderstandings not only of the testimonies, but of the Bible itself," which led them to the "denouncing of others and passing judgment upon their brethren." This, she claimed, was due to the "spirit of Phariseeism" that had come into the church (*1888 Materials*, p. 312). Men who had trained themselves as debaters were in "continual danger of handling the Word of God deceitfully." They would "change the

meaning of God's word" by quoting "half a sentence" to make it "conform to their preconceived ideas" (*1888 Materials*, pp. 167, 573). George Knight does a good job of describing Ellen White's appeal for more Bible study and her support of Jones and Waggoner in this regard (*A User-Friendly Guide to the 1888 Message*, pp. 60-62). However, he condemns those who accept their Bible-based message, claiming it is reading "the Bible through the eyes of Jones and Waggoner" which is a "perilous mistake." Besides, Knight continues, Ellen White "upheld both men because they were leading Adventism back to Christ and the Bible, not because they had the final word on theology or even had a theology with which she fully agreed" (*Ibid.*, pp. 79, 179). We must agree that Jones and Waggoner were not infallible. But why would God send a most "precious message" leading Adventists back to Christ and the Bible, if at the same time the messengers He sent had perilous theological problems with which Ellen White disagreed? This was the very cry of those who opposed Jones and Waggoner over 120 years ago. They didn't oppose Jones and Waggoner because they were leading Adventism back to "Christ and the Bible;" they claimed to already believe in all that. They rejected "light sent of God, because it [did] not coincide with their ideas" (*1888 Materials*, p. 226).

13. Ellen G. White Manuscript 13, n.d. 1889, "Standing by the Landmarks"; in *1888 Materials*, p. 518.

14. Ellen White used the term "truth as it is in Jesus" many times to describe the 1888 message. Forty-two times the term is mentioned in the *1888 Materials*. See the following examples: pp. 267, 566, 1120, 1126, 1338, 1547.

15. Ellen G. White Manuscript 24, Dec. 1888; in *1888 Materials*, pp. 211, 217.

16. *Ibid.*, pp. 217, 212.

17. Ellen G. White Manuscript 30, June 1889; in *1888 Materials*, pp. 375, 367.

18. E. J. Waggoner, "Editorial Correspondence," *Signs of the Times*, Nov. 2, 1888, p. 662; in *Manuscripts and Memories*, p. 413.

19. Ellen G. White to O. A. Olsen, Letter 57, May 1, 1895; in *Testimonies to Ministers*, pp. 92-98.

20. *Ibid.* For a more detailed look at ten of the particular truths of the 1888 message see Appendix A.

21. *General Conference Daily Bulletin*, Oct. 19, 1888, p. 2; in *Manuscripts and Memories*, p. 359.

22. *General Conference Daily Bulletin*, Oct. 21, 1888, p. 1; in *Manuscripts and Memories*, p. 361. Paul Penno correctly states: "It cannot be stressed enough. E. J. Waggoner's message of righteousness by faith was constructed in connection with this understanding of the law and the covenants. To misunderstand, discount or reject any aspect of this trio would be to distort the 1888 message. The law in Galatians may never be a landmark, but it was crucial for understanding God's plan of salvation for the ages" (*Calvary at Sinai*, p. 114).

23. L. E. Froom, *Movement of Destiny*, p. 255.

24. Ron Graybill, "Elder Hottel goes to General Conference," *Ministry*, February 1988, p. 20; and *Manuscripts and Memories*, p. 424.

25. Ellen G. White Manuscript 8, Oct. 20, 1888, "Sabbath Talk"; in *1888 Materials*, pp. 124-125, 127.

26. Ellen G. White Manuscript 24, Dec. 1888; in *1888 Materials*, p 207. Ellen White stated that her "heart was made glad as I heard the testimonies borne after the discourse on Sabbath. These testimonies made no reference to the speaker, but to the light and truth" (Manuscript 8a, Oct. 21, 1888, "Talk to Ministers"; in *1888 Materials*, p. 143).

27. Ellen G. White Manuscript 17, Oct. 21, 1888; in *1888 Materials*, pp. 123-131. It is comments like these that show Ellen White supported Waggoner's presentations on the "law and the gospel." For a summary of Waggoner's nine-part series see: Paul Penno, *Calvary at Sinai*, pp. 106-114.

28. L. E. Froom, *Movement of Destiny*, pp. 253-254. One could rightly wonder if this resolution was not suggested in part because Ellen White was clearly speaking in terms that favored Waggoner's positions.

29. G. I Butler to Ellen G. White, Oct. 1, 1888: in *Manuscripts and Memories*, p. 91.

30. W. C. White to Mary White, Nov. 24, 1888; in *Manuscripts and Memories*, p. 127; and L. E. Froom, *Movement of Destiny*, pp. 253-254.

31. *Ibid.*, and W. C. White to Mary White, Nov. 3, 1888; in *Manuscripts and Memories*, p. 123.

32. Ellen G. White to R. A. Underwood, Letter 22, Jan. 18, 1889; in *1888 Materials*, p. 239.

33. *Ibid.*

34. L. E. Froom, *Movement of Destiny*, p. 254. This proposed resolution was not mentioned in the *General Conference Bulletin* or the *Review and Herald*.

Thus they cannot be relied upon to determine if a vote was ever taken. When Ellen White protested against such a resolution, there were other reasons why she "could not at that time present before the Conference, because they were not prepared for it" (Manuscript 5, 1890, "Results of Studying Harmful Textbooks"; in *Manuscript Releases*, vol. 19, p. 74). If such an action were taken, it would imply that nothing but truth had heretofore been taught in the classrooms of Battle Creek College, but such had not been the case. Four years earlier G. I. Butler himself had taught error and wrong sentiments in regard to "differences in degrees" of inspiration in the Scriptures. He had even published a series of ten articles in the *Review* (Jan. 15 through June 3, 1884), which pronounced judgement on God's Word "selecting some things as inspired and discrediting others as uninspired." Ellen White was shown the infidelity and skepticism that would result, even in treating the testimonies in the "same way" (Ellen G. White to R. A. Underwood, Letter 22, Jan. 18, 1889; in *1888 Materials*, pp. 238-239).

35. Ellen G. White Manuscript 24, Dec. 1888; in *1888 Materials*, p. 207.

36. For many years the idea has been put forth that the 1888 message was no different than that of the Reformers—just basic Christianity. L. H. Christian stated: "What was the teaching of righteousness by faith which became the mainspring of the great [1888] Adventist revival, as taught and emphasized by Mrs. White and others? It was the same doctrine that Luther, Wesley, and other servants of God had been teaching" (*The Fruitage of Spiritual Gifts* [1947], p. 239). A. W. Spalding commented: "The greatest event of the eighties [1880s] in the experience of the Seventh-day Adventists was the recovery, or the restatement and new consciousness, of their faith in the basic doctrine of Christianity" (*Captains of the Host* [1949] p. 583). A. L. White declared: "The evaluation of the message of righteousness by faith as presented in 1888 as a message more mature and developed, and more practical than had been preached by the pioneers of the message or even by the apostle Paul, was without support and far from accurate" (*A Further Appraisal of the Manuscript "1888 Re-examined"* [General Conference Report, 1958] p. 2). N. F. Pease claimed: "Where was the doctrine of justification by faith to be found in 1888 and the preceding years? In the creeds of the Protestant churches of the day. ... The same churches which were rejecting the advent message and the law of God were holding, at least in form, the doctrine of justification by faith" (*By Faith Alone* [1962], pp. 138-139). Leroy Froom, key player in *Questions on Doctrine*, and driving force behind meetings with Calvinists Barnhouse and Martin, had this to say: "We have not been too well aware of these paralleling spiritual movements—

of organizations and men out side the Advent Movement—*having the same general burden and emphasis, and arising at about the same time.* ... The impulse manifestly came from the same Source. And in timing, Righteousness by Faith centered in the year 1888. For example, the renowned Keswick Conferences of Britain were founded to 'promote practical holiness.'. . . Some fifty men could easily be listed in the closing decades of the nineteenth and the opening decades of the twentieth centuries ... all giving this general emphasis" (*Movement of Destiny* [1971], pp. 319, 320; emphasis original). Desmond Ford has been adamant on this point: "[Question:] Some have affirmed that the theology of preachers E. J. Waggoner and A. T. Jones of the nineteenth century was an advance upon Reformation theology. Do you agree? ... [Answer:] Preachers Waggoner and Jones at the famous Minneapolis Conference of 1888 had the first gleamings of the light which irradiated the Roman world in the first century, Europe in the sixteenth, ... Unfortunately, neither man was clear on other important points such as the distinction between justification and sanctification" (Australian *Signs of the Times*, Feb. 1978, p. 30). Robert Brinsmead follows the same line of thought: "At special periods in our history the gospel has struggled to break through to the Adventist community. The year 1888 marked such a period. ... Waggoner had light on justification for the Adventist community. But better material on justification by faith could be found among Protestant scholars of his day" (*Judge by the Gospel: A Review of Adventism* [1980], pp. 14-15). David McMahon echoes the same thoughts: "E. J. Waggoner had not fully recovered the Protestant message of justification by faith by 1886. Much less had he recovered Paul's message of justification. ... If God used Waggoner to bring light on the gospel to the church, then God was not shining the full blaze of even the imperfect Reformation light on the Adventist community. Those who compare Waggoner's early gropings after the gospel with the clear doctrine of justification propounded by the best nineteenth-century Protestant scholars will be startled" (*The Myth and the Man* [1979], p. 63). George Knight has pushed this same point of view in many of his books: "*The genius of their 1888 message was that they had combined the two halves of Revelations 14:12. They not only taught the commandments of God, but they preached the doctrine of faith that the holiness preachers had proclaimed. Thus, from Ellen White's perspective, the importance of the 1888 message was not some special Adventist doctrine of justification by faith developed by Jones and Waggoner. Rather, it was the reuniting of Adventism with basic Christian beliefs on salvation*" (*A User-Friendly Guide to the 1888 Message* [1998], pp. 108-109; emphasis original). While the earlier authors mentioned above seemed to take their stance primarily from the motivation of defending the church from the allegation that the message was rejected, the latter authors seem to take their stance primarily because of their push for a Calvinistic Reformation or Evangelical gospel. Others, however, have recognized the 1888 message as something more: "The profound uniting [of law and grace] … was [Ellen White's] remarkable contribution to the 1888 crisis over salvation by faith. Further, her messages clearly demonstrate that this 'precious message' was not a mere recovery of a sixteenth-century emphasis, nor a borrowing of a nineteenth-century Methodist accent. … In the 1888 emphasis, linkage was further made between the results of a personal application of salvation by faith and the closing work of Christ in the Most Holy Place. … The 1888 'revelation of the righteousness of Christ' was only the 'beginning of the light of the angel whose glory shall fill the whole earth' (Rev. 18:4)" (Herbert E. Douglass, *Messenger of the Lord*, [1998], pp. 197, 198). Again, Douglass counters claims by modern church historians when he states: "The other rewrite has been the concurrent reluctance to review the theological detour that occurred [since the 1950s], when denominational publications and academic classrooms opined that the key contribution of the 1888 General Conference was to recognize that Adventists had finally recovered the so-called emphasis of the Protestant Reformers regarding 'righteousness by faith.' Nothing could be farther from the truth! This line of reasoning, wherever taught or preached, poisons any genuine study of that remarkable conference. Further, it has locked the door on what Ellen White called 'a most precious message'—a message that would prepare a people for translation. Some day that door will be unlocked" (*A Fork in the Road*, [Coldwater, MI: Remnant Publications, Inc., 2008], p. 85). Clinton Wahlen responds to David McMahon's claims that Waggoner's theology was nothing more than an attempt to resurrect the Reformation gospel (as interpreted by modern followers): "In addition, attempts to trace EJW's theology to Reformation figures like Luther is also without tangible support" (*op. sit.*, p. 63). Robert Wieland & Donald Short expressed similar thoughts in regard to the 1888 message: "Righteousness by faith since 1844 is 'the third angel's message in verity.' Thus it is greater than what the reformers taught and the popular churches understand today. It is a message of abounding grace consistent with the unique Adventist truth of the cleansing of the heavenly sanctuary, a work contingent on the full cleansing of the hearts of God's people on earth" (*1888 Re-Examined*, [1987], p. iv). Ellen White had expressed this clearly before the Minneapolis Conference, in her newest edition of *The Great Controversy*: "There was a present truth in the days of Luther,—a truth at that time of special importance; there is a present truth for the church today. ... But truth is no more desired by the majority today than it was by the papists who opposed Luther" (pp. 143-144, 1888 ed.). While it is true that the Disciples, and the Reformers of the 16th century, laid the foundation upon which the 1888 message stood, the Advent message itself—presenting the second coming and judgment hour message—was a message that Paul and the Reformers "did not preach" (*Ibid.*, p. 356). But the Advent message was not only to bring forth truths that had never been preached before, it was God's purpose that "great truths that have lain unheeded and unseen since the day of Pentecost, are to shine from God's word in their native purity" (Ellen G. White, *Fundamentals of Christian Education*, p. 473). Thus the 1888 message was made up of both "present truth"—that which Paul and the Reformers did not preach, and which God had not sent even "twenty years" earlier—and "rescued" truth; that which had been unheeded and unseen since the day of Pentecost. Both these aspects of the 1888 message were founded *upon* the message of the Reformers but entailed much more. The sad fact of the matter is that those who rejected the present truth message the Lord sent through Jones and Waggoner were also rejecting foundational truths that Paul and the Reformers taught, as are those today who are seeking to take us back to a distorted Reformation gospel.

37. Ellen G. White Manuscript 8a, Oct. 21, 1888; in *1888 Materials*, pp. 133-144.

38. L. E. Froom, *Movement of Destiny*, pp. 244, 245, 260; quotes from F. H. Westphal, W. H. Edwards, and Jessie Moser-Waggoner.

39. Ellen G. White Manuscript 13, 1889; in *1888 Materials*, p. 516.

40. Ellen G. White Manuscript 24, Dec. 1888; in *1888 Materials*, p. 218, emphasis supplied. G. B. Starr recalls one such session of prayer at Minneapolis: "Sister White called a large company of ministers together for a season of special prayer. Uniting with others, Sister White, herself, prayed earnestly for the blessing of God upon the conference. In the midst of her prayer, she suddenly stopped for a short period of possibly one-minute; then, completing the broken sentence, finished her prayer. Not one of us who were present and heard her prayer, and noted the break in it, was aware that anything special had happened. But later, Elder W. C. White informed me that it took her six weeks to write out what she had seen in those sixty seconds. The Spirit of God had flashed, in rapid precession, the life and work of many of the ministers kneeling about her. She saw them in their homes, the spirit they manifested, as Christians. She saw them in the sacred desk and heard their manner of presenting the precious truths of the message for this time"

(G. B. Starr, "*Fifty Years With One of God's Seers*," unpublished manuscript, Ellen G. White Estates Doc. File #496, p. 150-152).

41. Ellen G. White Manuscript 24, Dec. 1888; in *1888 Materials*, 219-222, emphasis supplied. In complete contrast to Ellen White's description of Waggoner's conduct at the meetings, Woodrow Whidden offers the following from his research: "Willie White would later recall (in 1930, 42 years after the session) that 'the pomposity and egotism' of Jones and Waggoner 'seemed out of place in such young men' at the Minneapolis gathering. His is the harshest assessment recorded. ... While some *reportedly* heckled [Waggoner] for his short stature, we have *no record* that he made any retaliatory retorts or exhibited any of *his possible unflattering personality traits* as a *decisive feature* in his public presentations" (*E. J. Waggoner*, p. 105, emphasis supplied). Thus Willie's statements in regard to Waggoner's conduct are pitted against Ellen White's inspired statements as of almost equal import. To Whidden's credit, he seems to recognize the contrast: "Ellen White's observations regarding Waggoner's conduct, stated publicly at the Minneapolis session itself seems to better reflect his overall demeanor and conduct" (*Ibid.*). George Knight, whom Whidden sites as the source of his quotes, states under the heading of "personality conflicts," that "the younger men didn't help matters any. As W. C. White (a participant in the conference) put it: 'the pomposity and egotism' of Jones and Waggoner 'seemed out of place in such young men,' and did much to develop prejudice and feeling against them. Jones, he noted, was especially pompous" (*From 1888 to Apostasy*, p. 33). But what should we do when faced with such differing views between Ellen White and her son Willie White? Should they be taken as of equal authority? That said, there is just one major problem with this quoted evidence. *Willie White never wrote such a letter*. This letter was written by D. E. Robinson, who was born in 1879, was not present at the Minneapolis conference, and wrote to Taylor Bunch while on staff and doing indexing at the White Estates in 1930. Bunch had just finished the fall week-of-prayer at Pacific Union College, where he had compared the Advent movement to ancient Israel's Egypt to Canaan travels. In the course of these meetings, he had compared Israel's Kadesh-Barnea experience to Adventists' 1888 experience, attributing the "long delay of the coming of Christ" to the rejection He received in 1888, and the rejection of the beginning of the latter rain (*The Exodus and Advent Movements*, pp. 107, 168). Robinson took offense to Bunch's comparison and sought to defend the church from what he saw as unwarranted attacks that would only lead to more offshoot groups. It is this episode that also sparked written responses from A. T. Robinson (D. E. Robinson's father), and C. McReynolds (*Manuscripts*

*and Memories*, pp. 136-142; see also Chapter 3, footnote 40). A copy of D. E. Robinson's original letter can be found in Document File #371 at the Ellen White Estate, in Silver Spring, MD. At some point, Robinson's letter was retyped, one paragraph being removed which clarified him as the writer, and A. L. White's name was penciled in. A. L. White's name was then erased and replaced with W. C. White's name, in what appears to be A. L. White's hand writing. The original copy of this *retyped* letter is found in Document File #331, and is the copy published in *Manuscripts and Memories*, pp. 333-335, and attributed to W. C. White (Tim Poirier from the White Estates verified these findings). It seems that this letter falsely attributed to W. C. White, did not surface until it appeared as "Appendix D" in *Thirteen Crisis Years: 1888-1901*, in 1981. This book was a reprint of A. V. Olson's book, *Through Crisis to Victory: 1888-1901*, first published in 1966. But A. V. Olson died in 1963, three years before his book was published, at which time it came under the sponsorship of the Ellen G. White Estate Board, with A. L. White as Secretary. The 1981 reprint was published under the same auspices. In Appendix D, Arthur White makes the claim that W. C. White wrote the letter to deal with "the unsupported conjecture from the pen and lips of one [Taylor Bunch] who was at the time [of the Minneapolis Conference] a child of three," and who had presented "such a distortion of history and such a forecast" (*Thirteen Crisis Years*, p. 331). The missing paragraph from D. E. Robinson's original letter was his 6th paragraph which states: "I have been reading through all the manuscripts and letters that are here on file that pertain to the experiences of the Minneapolis meeting in 1888. Last Sabbath afternoon, by happy chance, Elder W. C. White, Elder C. McReynolds, and my father were together, and I had the privilege of hearing them give their recollections of the meeting and of what followed. From what I have read, and their story, I should reconstruct that meeting something as follows." Although we should not attribute any malicious intent on the part of D. E. Robinson, or even A. L. White—perhaps both thinking to defend the church from what they thought were false accusations—we should realize that only the father of lies could weave this web into what it has become today, thereby distorting what really took place in 1888. This writer would suggest that Satan hates our 1888 history today as much as he hated the possibilities that God intended would take place back then. It is true that both leading men were probably influenced by Jones' and Waggoner's fall in their later years, but this gives no license for what appears to have been underhandedly written about Jones' and Waggoner's personalities. More details of the situation mentioned above will be discussed in a later chapter.

42. Ellen G. White Manuscript 24, Dec. 1888; in *1888 Materials*, pp. 221-222.

43. *Ibid.*

44. W. C. White, "Notes Taken at Minneapolis"; in *Manuscripts and Memories*, p. 424.

45. R. T. Nash to General Conference of SDA, June 25, 1955, "The Minneapolis Conference: And the Issues Concerning the Presentation of the Message of Righteousness by Faith: An Eyewitness Account"; in *Manuscripts and Memories*, p. 354, hereafter "An Eyewitness Account." It appears that R. T. Nash later published this letter with some changes, in pamphlet form under the title: *"An Eyewitness Report of the 1888 General Conference at Minneapolis* (Highland CA: Privately Publ., 1955), hereafter "An Eyewitness Report."

46. Ellen G. White Manuscript 24, Dec. 1888; in *1888 Materials*, p. 221

47. W. C. White, "Notes Taken at Minneapolis"; in *Manuscripts and Memories*, p. 424.

48. Uriah Smith to Ellen G. White, Feb. 17, 1889; in *Manuscripts and Memories*, p. 154.

49. A. T. Jones to Brother Holmes, May 12, 1921; in *Manuscripts and Memories*, p. 329.

50. R. T. Nash, "An Eyewitness Account," Jun 25, 1955; in *Manuscripts and Memories*, p. 354. Ellen White was concerned that Butler had special union only with those who considered his work and his "way of doing it all right." But "many who [were] far more acceptable" he looked upon "with suspicion" because they did not feel "obliged to receive their impressions and ideas from human beings [who] act only as they act, talk only as they talk, think only as they think and, in fact, make themselves little less than machines" (*1888 Materials*, pp. 89-90). Lowliness and humility of mind had departed from Butler: "He thinks his position gives him such power that his voice is infallible" (*Ibid.*, p. 183). Thus Ellen White warned: "We should not consider that either Elder Butler or Elder Smith are the guardians of the doctrines for Seventh-day Adventists, and that no one may dare to express an idea that differs from theirs" (*Ibid.*, p. 188). "It is because men have been encouraged to look to one man to think for them, to be conscience for them, that they are now so inefficient, and unable to stand at their post of duty as faithful sentinels for God" (*Ibid.*, p. 974). Butler felt Ellen White's counsel, which seemed so contrary to what she had said before, was the cause of his illness

(see also Chapter 5, footnote 23). It also led to his resignation as president of the denomination before the end of the Conference and Uriah Smith's resignation from his position as General Conference secretary soon thereafter ("General Conference Committee Minutes," Nov. 16, 1888).

51. Ellen G. White Manuscript 24, Dec. 1888; in *1888 Materials*, pp. 221-223, emphasis supplied.

52. Ellen G. White to Mary White, Letter 82, Nov. 4, 1888; in *1888 Materials*, pp. 182, 184. Another resolution that was passed contrary to Ellen White's counsel was in regard to canvassing, or colporteuring as we call it today. On November 1, 1888, R. A. Underwood made a motion that a person should be required to have a "practical experience in the canvassing field" before being "encouraged to enter the Bible work or the ministry." Ellen White opposed such an "absolute rule," but notwithstanding all she had to say against the resolution, "it was carried." Because this resolution passed it was recorded in the *Review and Herald* under the minutes for Nov. 2, 1888 (*Manuscripts and Memories*, p. 409; *1888 Materials*, pp. 239-240). More than a year later, Ellen White was still speaking against it: "The resolution passed at Minneapolis, requiring young men to canvass before they were granted a license to preach was wrong" (General Conference Committee Minutes," Ninth Meeting, July 16, 1890). Interestingly, this "same requirement is still on the policy books in 1988" even though "in practice it is not applied consistently" (Roger Coon, Transcript of Loma Linda University Lecture, Oct. 23-25, 1988, "Minneapolis/1888: The 'Forgotten' Issue," p. 16).

53. Ellen G. White Manuscript 15, Nov., 1888; in *1888 Materials*, pp. 164, 165, 170.

54. Ellen G. White Manuscript 6, Nov. 4, 1889, "Issues at the Gen. Con. of 1889"; in *1888 Materials*, p. 472.

55. A. T. Jones, "The Third Angel's Message No. 11" and "The Third Angel's Message No. 12," *General Conference Daily Bulletin*, Feb. 13, 14, 1893, pp. 244, 265. Several years later, A. T. Jones again spoke of these attempted votes: "At Minneapolis, in 1888, the General Conference 'administration' did its very best to have the denomination committed by a vote of the General Conference to the covenant of 'Obey and Live,' to righteousness by works" (*God's Everlasting Covenant* [n.p. 1907], p. 31).

56. Ellen G. White, *Testimonies to Ministers*, p. 92.

57. There are at least six modern published denials of a vote being taken. Arthur White, while representing the Board of Trustees of the Ellen G. White Estate,

wrote in a "Historical Forward" that "no action was taken on the Biblical questions discussed" at Minneapolis (*Testimonies to Ministers* [1962], p. xxiv). A. V. Olsen states resolutely: "Unfortunately, the impression exists in some minds today that the General Conference session in 1888 officially rejected the message of righteousness by faith presented to it. This is a serious mistake. No action whatever was taken by vote of the delegates to accept it or to reject it. Its acceptance or rejection by the people present at the session was an individual matter" (*Through Crisis to Victory* [1966], p. 36). N. F. Pease echoes the thought: "Some have maintained that the 'denomination' rejected righteousness by faith in 1888. In the first place, no official action was taken on the subject; and more important, righteousness by faith in Christ is accepted or rejected by *individuals*, not groups" (*The Faith that Saves* [1969], p. 41, emphasis original). L. E. Froom states emphatically: "No vote was taken by the delegate leadership, at Minneapolis, rejecting the teaching of Righteousness by Faith. Indeed, no Conference vote of any kind was taken on the issue." Froom even uses a "dictated personal statement" from R. A. Underwood—the very man involved in seeking to pass resolutions at the 1888 Conference—to prove that "no vote for or against Righteousness by Faith was ever taken" (*Movement of Destiny* [1971], pp. 370, 256). A. L. White asserts: "As to establishing positions, no official action was taken in regard to theological questions discussed. The uniform witness concerning the attitude toward the matter of righteousness by faith was that there were mixed reactions. ... The concept that the General Conference, and thus the denomination, rejected the message of righteousness by faith in 1888 is without foundation and was not projected until forty years after" (*The Lonely Years* [1984], pp. 395, 396). But Taylor Bunch, "forty years after," didn't say that the "denomination" rejected the message, he spoke of the leaders and the effect their rejection had on the church at large: "The message of righteousness by faith was preached with power for more than ten years during which time the Minneapolis crisis was kept before the *leaders*. This *message brought the beginning of the latter rain. ... Why did not the latter rain continue to fall? ... It was rejected by many* and it soon died out of the experience of the Advent people and the loud cry died with it. ... Just before the end, the Advent people will review their past history and see it in a new light. ... We must acknowledge and confess the mistakes of our fathers and see to it that we do not repeat them and thus further delay the final triumph of the Advent movement" (*The Exodus and Advent Movements* [1928, 1937], pp. 107, 168, emphasis supplied). Norman R. Gulley has also expressed his views on the Minneapolis meetings, stating: "There was no official action taken by the GC to reject the messages about

Christ and His righteousness" ("The 1888 'MOVEMENT' Understood Within its Historical Context," [unpublished paper, 1998). But Leroy Moore puts such claims in their proper context: "Nor did the church ever take an *official* action against the Minneapolis message. But one may be technically correct and yet very wrong. ... Corporate rejection of truth always precedes any vote and is no less real even if a vote is prevented, as at Minneapolis by Ellen White's insistence and W. C. White's vigilance (*Adventism in Conflict* [Hagerstown, MD: Review and Herald Pub. Assn.], p. 86, emphasis supplied). Thankfully, George Knight admits that votes were attempted and blocked (*A User-Friendly Guide to the 1888 Message*, pp. 54, 56, 58, 139). Yet one could rightly wonder how the leading brethren could attempt to pass a vote against the message and at the same time be credited by Knight for accepting the same message (*Ibid.*, pp. 119, 139, 147). For more Ellen White statements on "resolutions," see: *1888 Materials*, pp. 114, 182, 238-240, 258, 302, 581, 941, 954, 1186, 1403, 1410, 1435, 1583, 1584, 1601, 1617.

58. Ellen G. White to W. M. Healy, Letter 7, Dec. 9, 1888, and Manuscript 24, Dec. 1888; in *1888 Materials*, pp. 186, and 207, 217, 224.

59. G. I. Butler to Ellen G. White, Oct. 1, 1888; in *Manuscripts and Memories*, p. 89.

60. Ellen G. White Manuscript 24, Dec. 1888; in *1888 Materials*, p. 224.

# Stand by Your Post

## Ellen G. White Raised Up
## to Defend God's Messengers

R.M. KILGORE

Directly following R. M. Kilgore's and Uriah Smith's attempt to stop all discussion on the subject of the law in Galatians and righteousness by faith that Tuesday morning, October 23, 1888, J. H. Morrison presented his first of at least seven presentations. His opening comments were similar to those made by Kilgore and Smith. He maintained that Adventists had "always believed in and taught 'Justification by Faith,' and are children of the free woman." He "contended the subject had been overstressed" at the Conference, and he was "fearful that the law might lose the important place that belonged to it."[1] He "opposed" the discussion of the subject "because no one" was present who had given it "special study," yet he was "glad to defend the truth."[2]* According to A. T. Jones, what Morrison presented "was righteousness by anything and everything else than faith."[3]

An opportunity was given for both Jones and Waggoner to respond, and when the time came they stood up front, "side by side with open Bibles," alternating in the reading of sixteen Bible passages, primarily from the book of Romans and Galatians.

J.H. MORRISON

This was their only answer, and without a word of comment, they took their seats. During the entire time of the readings "there was a hushed stillness over the vast assembly." The Bible spoke for itself.[4]*

Taking in all that had occurred during the meetings to that point, Ellen White felt she had done all that she could to present the light the Lord had given her. She purposed to "quietly withdraw from the meeting" and go to Kansas City, where she had been invited to conduct meetings. She was "afraid to be in such gatherings" lest she be "leavened with the prevailing spirit" by those whose hearts were "padlocked by prejudice and unbelief." She spent "many hours that night" in prayer. The issue over the law in Galatians was a "mere mote," and she would say "amen" to whichever way was "in accordance with a 'Thus saith the Lord.'"[5]

God heard her prayer, and in a "dream or vision of the night" a person of tall, commanding appearance brought her a message and revealed that it was God's will for her to stand at her "post of duty." He reminded her that the Lord had raised her up from her sick bed in Healdsburg and had strengthened her to come all the way to Minneapolis, stating: "'for this work the Lord has raised you up.'"[6] Then "point by point" like a "flash of lightning" the messenger revealed many things to her, much of which, at least at that time, she had "no liberty to write."[7]

The messenger conducted Ellen White to the homes where the brethren were lodging. All these men had an "opportunity to place themselves on the side of truth by receiving the Holy Spirit, which was sent by God in such a rich current of love and mercy." But "the manifestations of the Holy Spirit were attributed to fanaticism."[8] Thus "evil angels" had entered their rooms "because they closed the door to the Spirit of Christ and would not listen to His voice." "Sarcastic remarks were passed from one to another, ridiculing their brethren."[9]

In one home there was "not a vocal prayer offered" for two weeks.[10] There was "lightness, trifling, jesting, [and] joking." All of the "envy, jealousy, evil speaking, evil surmising, [and] judging one another," was considered to be "a special gift given of God in discernment."[11] They felt "Sister White had changed"[12] and was under the influence of Jones and Waggoner who "were not reliable." The brethren said "they did not believe [Ellen White] told the truth when she stated that she had not had conversation with W. C. White, Elder Waggoner, or Elder Jones." The "testimonies of the Spirit of God were freely commented upon," but they "thought and said worse things of Brethren Jones and Waggoner"[13]

The messenger plainly told Ellen White: "'Satan has blinded their eyes and perverted their judgment; and unless every soul shall repent of this their sin, this unsanctified independence that is doing insult to the Spirit of God, they will walk in darkness. ... They would not that God would manifest His Spirit and His power; for they have a spirit of mockery and disgust at My word.'" As a result "not one of the company who cherished the spirit manifested at that meeting would again have clear light to discern the preciousness of the truth sent them from heaven until they humbled their pride and confessed."[14]

The messenger informed Ellen White that the brethren were "ridiculing those whom God had raised up to do a special work."[15] Jones and Waggoner had "presented precious light to the people, but prejudice and unbelief, jealousy and evil-surmising barred the door of their hearts." A "satanic spirit took control and moved with power upon the human hearts that had been opened to doubts and to bitterness, wrath and hatred," and they ended up fighting "against light and truth which the Lord had for this time for His people."[16]

This satanic spirit, which brought "about this state of things...was no sudden work." It "had been gathering strength for years."[17] The messenger told Ellen White: "'it is not you they are despising, but the messengers and the message I send to My people.'"[18] She was told that the brethren would not heed her testimony, and that comparatively, she would "'stand almost alone.'" The promise was given her, however, that God himself would be her helper and would sustain her.[19]

As the Lord revealed to Ellen White what was taking place at Minneapolis, she began to realize just how far the rebellion had gone. She was reminded by God of at least eight other events in the history of the world to which a comparison could be made:

(1) The guide which accompanied me gave me the information of the spiritual standing before God of these men, who were passing judgment upon their brethren. ... Envy, jealousy, evil speaking, evil surmising, judging one another, has been considered a special gift given of God in discernment, when it savors more of the spirit of the *great accuser* who accused the brethren before God day and night.[20]

I have been taken down through the *first rebellion*, and I saw the workings of Satan and I know something about this matter that God has opened before me, and should not I be alarmed?[21]

(2) I had been...shown the lives, the character and history of *the patriarchs and prophets* who had come to the people with a message from God, and Satan would start some evil report, or get up some difference of opinion or turn the interest in some other channel, that the people should be deprived of the good the Lord had to bestow upon them. And now in this case [at Minneapolis] a firm, decided, obstinate spirit was taking possession of hearts, and those who had known of the grace of God and had felt His converting power upon their hearts once, were deluded, infatuated, working under a deception all through that meeting.[22]

(3) When I purposed to leave Minneapolis, the angel of the Lord stood by me and said: "Not so; God has a work for you to do in this place. The people are acting over the rebellion of *Korah, Dathan, and Abiram*. I have placed you in your proper position, which those who are not in the light will not acknowledge; they will not heed your testimony; but I will be with you; My grace and power shall sustain you."[23]*

(4) I heard the jesting, the sarcastic remarks in regard to the messengers and the message—that doctrine that differed from their ideas of truth; and I was told there was a witness in every room as surely as the witness was in *Belshazzar's palace* at that festival, mingled with the praise of idols and of wine. The angel on that occasion traced the characters over against the walls of the palace; so there was a witness writing in the books of heaven the unkind speeches of those who knew not what manner of spirit they were of.[24]

(5) As the *Jews* refused the light of the world, so many of those who claim to believe the present truth will refuse light which the Lord will send to His people.[25]

Said my guide, "this is written in the books as against Jesus Christ. ... This spirit bears...the semblance to...the spirit that actuated the *Jews* to form a confederacy to doubt, to criticize and become spies upon

Christ, the world's Redeemer. ... " I was then informed that at this time it would be useless to make any decision as to positions on doctrinal points, as to what is truth, or to expect any spirit of fair investigation, because there was a confederacy formed to allow of no change of ideas on any point or position they had received any more than did the *Jews*.[26]

Thus it was in the betrayal, trial, and crucifixion of Jesus—all this had passed before me point by point.[27]

(6) We may be led on by the enemy to take a position against the truth...and in the spirit of the Jews, we shall resist the light which God sends. ... The most terrible thing that could come to us as a people is the fatal deception that was the ruin of *Chorasin and Bethsaida*.[28]

(7) Their base passions were stirred and it was a precious opportunity to them to show the mob spirit. ... I could but have a vivid picture in my mind from day to day of the way *reformers* were treated, how slight difference of opinion seemed to create a frenzy of feeling. ... All this was prevailing in that meeting.[29]

The suspicion and jealousy, the evil surmisings, the resistance of the Spirit of God that was appealing to them, were more after the order in which the *Reformers* had been treated.[30]

When the *papists* were in controversy with men who took their stand on the Bible for proof of doctrines they considered it a matter that only death could settle. I could see a similar spirit cherished in the hearts of our brethren. ... [31]

(8) That night the angel of the Lord stood by my bed and said to me many things. ... I was commanded to stand at my post of duty; that there was a spirit coming in taking possession of the churches, that if permitted would separate them from God as verily as *the churches* who refused light that God sent them in messages of warning and of light that they might advance in regard to His second coming to our world [in 1844].[32]

As reformers they had come out of the *denominational churches*, but they now act a part similar to that which the *churches* acted. We hoped that there would not be the necessity for another coming out.[33]*

The Lord revealed all of these things to Ellen White as she was on the verge of leaving Minneapolis. The revelation was almost too much for her:

After hearing what I did my heart sank within me. ... I thought of the future crisis, and feelings that I can never put into words for a little time overcame me. "But take heed to yourselves: for they shall deliver you up to councils; and in the synagogues ye shall be beaten: and ye shall be brought before rulers and kings for my sake, for a testimony against them. ... Now the brother shall betray the brother to death, and the father the son; and children shall rise up against their parents, and shall cause them to be put to death" Mark 13:9, 12.[34]

It was a terrible fact that the very presence of Jesus in the outpouring of the Holy Spirit which Ellen White had spoken of for years was being turned away. But God had not given up; there was still hope: "'Spiritual pride and self–confidence will close the door that *Jesus and His Holy Spirit's power* shall not be admitted. They shall *have another chance* to be undeceived, and to repent, confess their sins, and come to Christ and be converted that He shall heal them.'"[35] Although there was little hope that the Holy Spirit could be poured out at Minneapolis, the Lord was not finished with His people, and Ellen White arose with new strength to meet the challenge.

## *A Call to Repentance*

Later that same morning, October 24, Ellen White attended the ministers meeting. She had some "plain things to say" which she "dared not withhold." She recognized the "spiritual darkness" upon the people and that they were being "moved with a power from beneath." She wondered "what pages of history were being made by the recording angel" for the spirit of the leading brethren had "nearly leavened the lump." As she stood before her brethren, her soul was "pressed with anguish." In fact, what she had to say to them brought "greater anguish" to her than it did to those she addressed. Through the grace of Christ, she "experienced a divine compelling power to stand" before her brethren, "hoping and praying that the Lord would open the blind eyes."[36] She was "compelled to speak plainly, and lay before them the dangers of resisting the Spirit of God."[37]

Ellen White reminded the brethren that no confessions had taken place, thus the Spirit of God was still being shut away from the people. She rebuked those who were complaining that her prayers and talk ran in the same "channel with Dr. Waggoner," and that he "was running" the meetings. She maintained that she had not taken a position on the law in Galatians; that she had not talked with anyone on the subject; and that she could not take her position on either side until she had "studied the question." She even suggested it was providential that she had lost the manuscript from years before because God's purpose was that they "go to the Bible and get the Scripture evidence":

> Now our meeting is drawing to a close, and not one confession has been made; there has not been a single break so as to let the Spirit of God in. Now I was saying what was the use of our assembling here together and for our ministering brethren to come in if they are here only to shut out the Spirit of God from the people?...

> Had Brother Kilgore been walking closely with God he never would have walked onto the ground as he did yesterday and made the statement he did in regard to the investigation that is going on. That is, they [Jones and Waggoner] must not bring in any new light or present any new argument notwithstanding they have been constantly handling the Word of God for years, yet they [the leading brethren] are not prepared to give a reason of the hope they have because one man [Butler] is not here. Have we not all been looking into this subject? I never was more alarmed than at the present time. ...

> When I have been made to pass over the history of the Jewish nation and have seen where they stumbled because they did not walk in the light, I have been led to realize where we as a people would be led if we refuse the light God would give us. Eyes have ye but ye see not; ears, but ye hear not. Now, brethren, light has come to us and we want to be where we can grasp it, and God will lead us out one by one to Him. I see your danger and I want to warn you. ...

> Now, brethren, we want the truth as it is in Jesus. But when anything shall come in to shut down the gate that the waves of truth shall not come in, you will hear my voice wherever it is...because God has given me light and I mean to let it shine. And I have seen that precious souls who would have embraced the truth have been turned away from it because of the manner in which the truth has been handled, because Jesus was not in it. And this is what I have been pleading with you for all the time—we want Jesus. What is the reason the Spirit of God does not come into our meetings? Is it because we have built a barrier around us? I speak decidedly because I want you to realize where you are standing. I want our young men to take a position, not because someone else takes it, but because they understand the truth for themselves.[38]

Ellen White knew that the Holy Spirit was being turned away from the meetings and from the people. Just as the Jewish leaders had turned the people away from the message Jesus brought, so those at Minneapolis were turning the people away from the "truth as it is in Jesus."

No sooner had Ellen White poured out her heart to the delegates than J. H. Morrison presented again on the law in Galatians. Ellen White had stated that she had not taken a stand on the Galatians issue, that she would not settle the matter herself, and had called everyone to deeper Bible study. Yet Morrison quoted several statements from her pen, written previous to the Conference, trying to prove Ellen White supported his point of view, that Galatians chapter 3 was dealing only with the ceremonial law. In the minds of those who held the ceremonial law view, this was proof that they themselves not only had *Spirit of Prophecy* support, but that Jones and Waggoner were speaking contrary to its established doctrine. This also proved, in the leading brethren's minds, that Ellen White had changed, being influenced by Jones, Waggoner and her own son W. C. White.[39]*

Morrison read several quotations from *Sketches From the Life of Paul*, where Ellen White described how the Galatians clung to the ceremonial law as an outward form while at the same time disregarding the moral law:

> The apostle urged upon the Galatians…to leave the false guides by whom they had been misled, and to return to the faith which they had received. … Their religion consisted in a round of ceremonies. …

> To substitute the external forms of religion for holiness of heart and life, is still as pleasing to the unrenewed nature as in the days of the apostles. For this reason, false teachers abound, and the people listen eagerly to their delusive doctrines. … In apostolic times [Satan] led the Jews to exalt the ceremonial law, and reject Christ; at the present day he induces many professed Christians…to cast contempt upon the moral law. … It is the duty of every faithful servant of God, to firmly and decidedly withstand these perverters of the faith, and to fearlessly expose their errors by the word of truth. …

> He [Paul] describes the visit which he made to Jerusalem to secure a settlement…as to whether the Gentiles should submit to circumcision and keep the ceremonial law. …

Thus the emissaries of Judaism…induced them to return to the observance of the ceremonial law as essential to salvation. Faith in Christ, and obedience to the law of ten commandments, were regarded as of minor importance.[40]

Morrison seems to have been confident that he had proved from the writings of Ellen White that the issue in Galatians chapter 3 was *solely* over the ceremonial law; that only the adherence to the ceremonial law, after the death of Christ, had led the Galatians into bondage. He questioned whether the moral law could really be abolished when it was the ceremonial law that was done away with. The insinuation seems to be that Jones' and Waggoner's "new view"—that the law spoken of in Galatians chapter 3 was the moral law—was casting contempt on the ten commandments, and it was his duty, as it was the duty of Paul, "to expose their errors."

Morrison finished his presentation by quoting from *Sketches* page 68, where Ellen White wrote of the yoke of bondage mentioned in Acts 15:10 and Galatians 5:1. With this, Morrison could likely think he was putting the final nail in the coffin of Jones' and Waggoner's theology: "This yoke was not the law of ten commandments, as those who oppose the binding claim of the law assert; but Peter referred to the law of ceremonies, which was made null and void by the crucifixion of Christ."[41]

These Ellen White statements seemed very convincing to Morrison, and he would refer to them several times in the days ahead. Ellen White, on the other hand, was not impressed or convinced by Morrison's presentations. She would "hear E. J. W[aggoner] all the way through, but would get up and go out before Morrison would finish his rebuttal."[42] It was at this point in time that she could honestly state: "I began to think it might be *we* did not hold correct views after all upon the law in Galatians."[43]

As soon as Morrison's final presentation was given, and before the General Conference ended, he returned home to Iowa, telling J. S. Washburn in a private conversation: "They are going to try to force me to acknowledge that I am wrong. So I am leaving."[44]

On Thursday morning, October 25, Ellen White spoke once again to the ministers present, recalling the incidents from the previous days. She "went for

Smith and Bro. K[ilgore]," for the part they played in the attempt to put a stop to the discussion underway. Unfortunately, her remarks made that morning—and remarks made at meetings at least five other times before the close of the General Conference—were either never taken down, or are not extant today.[45]

Uriah Smith, reporting for the *Review* gave a hint of what took place at these morning meetings, though not revealing the great struggle that was taking place: "Among the most interesting and important meetings are the early morning devotional meetings. The exhortations of Sr. White have been most cheering, as she has presented the love of Christ and his willingness to help. *That He is waiting to pour out of his spirit upon his people in abundant measure.*"[46]* One thing is certain; Ellen White's underlying theme was that God wanted to pour out the Holy Spirit in latter rain proportions.

On Sabbath, Ellen White spoke once again. Following the example of Jones and Waggoner, she did not speak "extemporaneously as usual, but principally by reading from Galatians, Ephesians, Colossians, and other Epistles. This was evidently to counter the contention of some that Sister White was under the influence of Jones and Waggoner. So she just read from Scripture, which could not be gainsaid." Even this, however, was misconstrued by a few of the brethren. One man stated: "Mrs. White is in the dark, and does not speak with liberty."[47] Another man, joining in the questioning of the Testimonies, even claimed: "Sister White doesn't understand her own testimonies." But all of this questioning of the Testimonies was because the "brethren did not agree with them."[48]

## *A Call to Deeper Study*

With only a few days left of the Conference, Ellen White pleaded once more with the brethren. She called upon all to study the word of God more deeply, especially in regard to the themes under discussion. She warned once again that without such study the younger brethren, especially, should make no decision. She reminded her listeners of the warnings God had given her regarding dangers confronting the church at that time. "The spirit that controlled the Pharisees" was coming among the people of God, and a "debating spirit" was taking "the place of the Spirit of God." She mentioned J. H. Morrison as one who was a "debater."[49]* Reminding her listeners of the mistakes made by the Jews, Ellen White implored them not to reject light sent from heaven:

> It will grieve the Spirit of God if you close your understanding to the light which God sends you. ...

> Said my guide, "There is much light yet to shine forth from the law of God and the gospel of righteousness. This message, understood in its true character, and proclaimed in the Spirit, will lighten the earth with its glory. ... The closing work of the third angel's message will be attended with a power that will send the rays of the Sun of Righteousness into all the highways and byways of life. ... "

> But Satan will so work upon the unconsecrated elements of the human mind that many will not accept the light in God's appointed way. ...

> I entreat you, close not the door of the heart for fear some ray of light shall come to you. You need greater light. ... If you do not see light yourselves, you will close the door; if you can you will prevent the rays of light from coming to the people. ...

> I have been shown that Jesus will reveal to us precious old truths in a new light, if we are ready to receive them; but they must be received in the very way in which the Lord shall choose to send them. ... Let no one quench the Spirit of God by wresting the Scriptures...and let no one pursue an unfair course, keep in the dark, not willing to open their ears to hear and yet free to comment and quibble and sow their doubts of that which they will not candidly take time to hear. ...

> When the Jews took the first step in the rejection of Christ, they took a dangerous step. When afterward evidence accumulated that Jesus of Nazareth was the Messiah, they were too proud to acknowledge that they had erred. So with the people of our day who reject the truth. They do not take time to investigate candidly, with earnest prayer, the evidences of the truth, and they oppose that which they do not understand. Just like the Jews, they take it for granted they have all the truth, and feel a sort of contempt for anyone who should suppose they had more correct ideas than themselves of what is truth. All the evidence produced they decide shall not weigh a straw with them, and they tell others that the doctrine is not true, and afterward, when they see as light [the] evidence they were so forward to condemn, they have too much pride to say "I was wrong"; they still cherish doubt and unbelief, and are too proud to acknowledge their convictions. Because of this, they take steps that lead to results of which they have never dreamed.[50]*

In words of prophetic significance, Ellen White foretold the inevitable result of not appreciating the light sent from heaven and instead cherishing the spirit manifest at Minneapolis. Unless recognized, the light would become a continual stumbling block in the future:

> No one must be permitted to close the avenues whereby the light of truth shall come to the people. As soon as this shall be attempted God's Spirit will be quenched, for that Spirit is constantly at work to give fresh and increased light to His people through His Word. …
>
> We may be led on by the enemy to take a position against the truth, because it does not come in a way to suit us; and in the spirit of the deceived Jews, we shall resist light which God sends; and that light, instead of being the blessing which heaven meant it to be to us, to advance us in spirituality and in the knowledge of God, will become a stumbling block, over which we shall be constantly falling. …
>
> Unless there is most earnest seeking of the Lord, unless there is zealous work of repentance, darkness will come upon minds, and the darkness will be in proportion to the light which has not been appreciated. Unless there is less of self, and far more of the Holy Spirit to take control of the minds and hearts of men who have stood in the foremost rank, there will be a failure on their part to walk out in harmony with the opening providence of God; they will question and quibble over any light that the Lord may send, and will turn away from the teachings of Christ, confiding in themselves, and trusting in their supposed knowledge of what is truth. As the Jews refused the light of the world, so many of those who claim to believe the present truth will refuse light which the Lord will send to His people. …
>
> In this conference we are sowing seeds that will yield a harvest, and the results will be as enduring as eternity. …
>
> I hope none will go from this meeting repeating the false statements that have been circulated here, or carrying with them the spirit which has been here manifested. It has not been of Christ; it has come from another source.[51]

## *Ellen White's Position on the Law in Galatians*

There is another important issue, which Ellen White spoke of in this, her last recorded talk at Minneapolis; her view of Waggoner's presentations up to that point in time. In this discourse she stated that some things Waggoner presented "do not harmonize with the understanding I have had of this subject," and "some interpretations of Scripture given by Waggoner I do not regard as correct." But before we draw a conclusion regarding these oft-repeated statements, we need to read them in their context. What was Ellen White referring to when she said these things, and how should her statements be understood?

> Dr. Waggoner has spoken to us in a straightforward manner. There is precious light in what he has said. Some things presented *in reference to the law in Galatians, if I fully understand his position, do not harmonize with the understanding I have had of this subject*; but truth will lose nothing by investigation, therefore I plead for Christ's sake that you come to the living Oracles, and with prayer and humiliation seek God. ...

> I would have humility of mind, and be willing to be instructed as a child. The Lord has been pleased to give me great light, yet I know that He leads other minds, and opens to them the mysteries of His Word, and I want to receive every ray of light that God shall send me, though it should come through the humblest of His servants.

> Of one thing I am certain, as Christians you have no right to entertain feelings of enmity, unkindness, and prejudice toward Dr. Waggoner, who has presented his views in a plain, straightforward manner, as a Christian should. If he is in error, you should...seek to show him from the Word of God where he is out of harmony with its teachings. ...

> *Some interpretations of Scripture given by Dr. Waggoner I do not regard as correct*. But I believe him to be perfectly honest in his views, and I would respect his feelings and treat him as a Christian gentleman. I have no reason to think that he is not as much esteemed of God as are any of my brethren, and I shall regard him as a Christian brother, so long as there is no evidence that he is unworthy. The fact that he honestly holds some views of Scripture differing from yours or mine is no reason why we should treat him as an offender, or as a dangerous man, and make him the subject of unjust criticism. ...

> There are some who desire to have a decision made at once as to what is the correct view on the point under discussion. ...

> I know it would be dangerous to denounce Dr. Waggoner's position as wholly erroneous. This would please the enemy. I see the beauty of truth in the presentation of the righteousness of Christ in relation to the law as the doctor has placed it before us. You say, many of you, it is light and truth. Yet you have

not presented it in this light heretofore. Is it not possible that through earnest, prayerful searching of the Scriptures he has seen still greater light on some points? That which has been presented harmonizes perfectly with the light which God has been pleased to give me during all the years of my experience. …

Even if the position which we have held upon the two laws is truth, the Spirit of truth will not countenance any such measures to defend it as many of you would take. The spirit that attends the truth should be such as will represent the Author of truth.[52]

When quoted in their proper context, it should be clearly seen that Ellen White's comments above were not meant as a blanket statement regarding Waggoner's teachings on righteousness by faith, but rather referred to *some* of his views on the law in Galatians, *if she fully understood his position*. Ellen White was not writing a blank check for the brethren to use in discarding whatever they did not agree with in Waggoner's presentations. Much to her concern, they were already doing this. The law in Galatians chapter 3—the *added law* and the *schoolmaster to bring us unto Christ*—had been the controversial issue all along, and Ellen White had not yet taken her position on the matter.

Regardless of the view Ellen White had held in the past in regard to the law in Galatians, her view had been shaped by the light she received in 1856, when she was led to counsel J. H. Waggoner, who was then presenting on the topic. But that Testimony written to J. H. Waggoner could not be found. Nor could Ellen White remember *what she had been shown*. When she first heard from Butler in 1886 that Jones and Waggoner were speaking and writing on the subject of the law in Galatians, and that a controversy had arisen, she immediately sent counsel in regard to all differences of opinion, *but the letter never arrived.* In her second letter to them in early 1887, she told them that she had seen years before that J. H. Waggoner's views "were not correct." But the matter did "not lie clear and distinct" in her mind, nor could she "grasp the matter" at that time.[53]

Only a few weeks later, and after she had "some impressive dreams," Ellen White had written to Butler stating: "I am troubled; for the life of me I cannot remember that which I have been shown in reference to the two laws. I cannot remember what the caution and warning referred to were that were given to

Elder [J. H.] Waggoner. It may be that it was a caution not to make his idea prominent at that time, for there was great danger of disunion."[54]

Early at the 1888 General Conference, Ellen White included herself with the brethren by stating that Jones and Waggoner "may differ with us." In the same discourse, she related that her "guide" had informed her back in 1887 that "'neither [Butler or Waggoner] have all the light upon the law; neither position is perfect.'"[55]

Later in the Conference, she could honestly state that she "had not taken any position yet" and was "not prepared to take a position" on either side until she had "studied the question." This was in contrast to J. H. Morrison and the brethren, who wanted to settle the issue then and there, believing that Ellen White had been influenced by Jones and Waggoner and taken their position. It was at that point Ellen White indicated that losing the manuscript was providential, for God wanted the brethren to go to the Bible "and get the Scripture evidence" for their position.[56]

When a move was made to try to put a stop to the discussions on Galatians, Ellen White had attested: "For the first time I began to think it might be *we* did not hold correct views after all upon the law in Galatians, for the truth required no such spirit to sustain it."[57] Just a few days after the Conference was over, Ellen White stated once again that her views had "not changed." But, she added: "if *we* have had the truth upon this subject our brethren have failed to be sanctified through it."[58]

Several months later, she repeated that she had "no different position," but added, "light will not come till as a people we are in a different condition spiritually."[59] Many times Ellen White made it clear that the issue was not a "burden" to her; that it was not a "landmark" doctrine and was not to be made a "test" question.[60] However, as she saw the spirit of Minneapolis continuing against Jones and Waggoner in 1890, she boldly proclaimed to the leadership: "I am afraid of you and I am afraid of your interpretation of any scripture which has revealed itself in such an unchristlike spirit."[61] "God deliver me from your ideas of the law in Galatians, if the receiving of these ideas would make me so unchristian in my spirit."[62]

It was not until eight years after the 1888 Conference that Ellen White fully revealed what the Lord had shown her; that the law in Galatians chapter 3 referred to *both* the moral *and* ceremonial laws.[63]

Thus, it is clear that Ellen White's statements in her November sermon given at the 1888 Conference are not what some have made them out to be.[64]* Her statements expressing questions with Waggoner's teachings were made specifically in regard to the issue of the law in Galatians. All of Waggoner's points in regard to the law in Galatians did not harmonize with Ellen White's understanding, *if she understood him correctly*. She added, however, that she knew the Lord was leading other minds, and "opens to them the mysteries of His Word." She, for one, was "willing to be instructed" even if it came "through the humblest of His servants," Waggoner and Jones.[65]

Again, when she made the comment that "some interpretations of Scripture given by Dr. Waggoner I do not regard as correct," the context was the law in Galatians. Only a few moments later she exclaimed: "I see the beauty of truth in the presentation of the righteousness of Christ in relation to the law as the doctor has placed it before us. ... That which has been presented *harmonizes perfectly* with the light which God has been pleased to give me." She chided many of the brethren for saying, "it is light and truth," and yet never themselves presenting the truth in the same way before.[66]*

Just a few days prior to Ellen White's last recorded message at the Minneapolis Conference, W. C. White had written a letter to his wife. In his letter he substantiated the fact that Ellen White supported Waggoner in "much" of what he taught while the brethren, on the other hand, felt that Waggoner's teachings disagreed with the Testimonies. The brethren felt that W. C. White had pushed Waggoner's views and had misled and influenced his mother to take a new and faulty position. This accusation, W. C. White wrote, he could prove "to be false":

> Mother has done lots of hard work. She is some discouraged just now, for it is a dark time. Much that Dr. W. teaches is in line with what she has seen in vision, and she has spoken repeatedly against the "Spirit of Pharisaism" that would crush him down, and condemn all he says as erroneous. Some then take it that she endorses all his views, and [torn here] part of his teaching disagrees

with [torn here] and with her Testimonies, they say? [torn here] my endeavor to push Dr. W.'s views [torn here] [mis]led her as to the real issue and [influenced her] to take a position contrary to her [feelings].

I could prove all this to be false. [I] may sometime have an opportunity [torn here] Jonah that has brought on the storm in the minds of many, will have [torn here] results to answer for. I am decidedly unpopular, and I am not sorry.[67]*

Today, we must be careful how we use statements from Ellen White, W. C. White, or anyone else, in deciding whether Jones' and Waggoner's teachings are contrary to the Testimonies. Otherwise, we may build a faulty foundation from which we judge the two messengers and the message the Lord gave them, and will unwittingly fall into the same camp as the brethren who opposed them at Minneapolis over 100 years ago. Having said this, we must admit that Jones and Waggoner were not infallible, but neither is any other human being, including, according to herself, Ellen White.[68] The Lord did send a most precious message through Jones and Waggoner from whom, Ellen White said, she was willing to learn.[69] When Jones or Waggoner needed to be corrected, the Lord, through Ellen White, was always very specific in the correction. Ellen White never wrote "blank checks" that others might use as an excuse to condemn whatever they did not want to believe in the teachings of Jones and Waggoner.

## *Looking Back at Minneapolis*

Sunday, November 4, 1888, marked the end of the Minneapolis General Conference Session. Ellen White had given her last discourse on Sabbath, the day before. Jones, Waggoner and Ellen White headed to Battle Creek, while all the other delegates scattered to their respective fields. What was the outcome and result of the Minneapolis meeting? What lasting effect would it have on the Seventh-day Adventist church? The delegates carried away very different impressions. Some felt that it was one of the most profitable meetings that they had ever attended, while others felt that it was the most unfortunate conference ever held. Some, who had left the Conference early, spread highly colored and discouraging reports in Battle Creek and other places around the country.

The day the Conference ended, Ellen White looked back on the experience with hopeful expectations stating: "We believe that this meeting will result in great good. We know not the future, but we feel that Jesus stands at the helm and we shall not be shipwrecked." She added, however: "We have had the hardest and most incomprehensible tug of war we have ever had among our people."[70]

As Ellen White reflected more on her experience at Minneapolis in the days that followed, she became increasingly concerned as she continued to see the same spirit manifest by the brethren. As God showed her the seriousness of what had taken place at the Conference, she became more distraught at the prospects. Minneapolis had been the "saddest experience" of her life. The Saviour had been disappointed as verily by the attitudes and spiritual blindness manifested by the brethren "as when Christ was in His human form in the world."[71] Not only was the treatment she received at Minneapolis discouraging to her, it was "dishonoring to God and grievous to His Spirit."[72] Heaven saw their conduct as open "rebellion" and an "insult to the Spirit of God."

Jones and Waggoner had also been mistreated, both in public and in private. Men had picked flaws in the "messengers and in the message" and had likewise "grieved the Spirit of God." This treatment was "registered…in the books of heaven as done to Jesus Christ in the person of His saints."[73]

In her first recorded talk at Minneapolis, Ellen White had told the delegates that they could expect the outpouring of the Holy Spirit: "The baptism of the Holy Ghost will come upon us at this very meeting if we will have it so."[74] But, just as in the days of the Jews, by their questioning and unbelief the "Spirit of God was quenched,"[75] so at Minneapolis, "even the outpouring of the Spirit of God [was] treated with contempt."[76] The course pursued there "was cruelty to the Spirit of God."[77] Alas, "all assembled in that meeting had an opportunity to place themselves on the side of truth by receiving the Holy Spirit, which was sent by God in such a rich current of love and mercy. … [But] the manifestations of the Holy Spirit were attributed to fanaticism."[78]* In what might be one of her most sobering statements regarding 1888,

Ellen White quoted Zechariah 13:6 and applied it to what took place at Minneapolis: "Christ was wounded in the house of His friends."[79]*

The aftermath of the 1888 Conference would truly be as far reaching as eternity. But just as Jesus did not "prematurely disclose to the Jews the result of their prejudice and unbelief," so He did not then disclose the results of what had taken place at Minneapolis; that would be revealed as time went on.[80] The history of that meeting had "passed into eternity with its burden of record," and "when the judgment shall sit and the books shall be opened there will be found registered a history that many who were at that meeting will not be pleased to meet."[81]

Was the rebellion at Minneapolis really that bad? Was the Holy Spirit in latter rain power really turned away? Was the message presented there really rejected by more than just a few? And weren't there great revivals that followed the Minneapolis Conference? We will take a look at these questions in the chapters ahead.

## CHAPTER 5 FOOTNOTES

1. R. T. Nash, "An Eyewitness Account," June 25, 1955; in *Manuscripts and Memories*, pp. 352-353; and Paul Penno, *Calvary at Sinai*, p. 108.

2. W. C. White, "Notes Made at the Minneapolis Meetings 1888," Oct. 23, 1888, p. 57; in *Manuscripts and Memories*, p. 424. Kilgore, Smith, and Morrison made their statements while Ellen White was sitting on the platform in front of everyone. They felt it was more important to have G. I. Butler with them than it was to hear the words of the prophet (R. T. Nash, *op. cit.*, p. 354; and Ellen G. White Manuscript 24, Dec. 1888; in *1888 Materials*, p. 221).

3. A. T. Jones to C. E. Holmes, May 12, 1921; in *Manuscripts and Memories*, p. 328.

4. R. T. Nash, *op. cit.*, pp. 353-354. Nash lists the sixteen texts alternately read as follows: Dr. Waggoner read Jeremiah 23:5-7; Elder Jones read Eph. 2:4-8; Waggoner Gal. 2:16-21; Jones Rom. 11:1-33; Waggoner Rom. 1:14-17; Jones Rom. 2:12-29; Waggoner Gal. 3, entire chap; Jones Rom. 3, entire chap; Waggoner Gal. 5:16; Jones Rom. 9:7-33; Waggoner Gal. 2, entire chap; Jones Rom. 4:1-11; Waggoner Rom. 5, entire chap; Jones Rom. 1:15-17; Waggoner Rom. 8:14-39; Jones 1 John 5:1-4.

5. Ellen G. White Manuscript 24, Dec. 1888, and Manuscript 21, Nov. 1888; in *1888 Materials*, pp. 225, 181, 229, 223.

6. Ellen G. White to Dear Brethren, Letter 85, April 1889; in *1888 Materials*, pp. 277-279.

7. Ellen G. White to Children of the Household, Letter 14, May 12, 1889; in *1888 Materials*, pp. 309-311.

8. Ellen G. White to O. A. Olsen, Letter 81, May 31, 1896; in *1888 Materials*, p. 1565.

9. Ellen G. White to Dear Brethren, Letter 85, April 1889; in *1888 Materials*, pp. 277-278.

10. Ellen G. White to J. Fargo, Letter 50, May 2, 1889; in *1888 Materials*, pp. 297-299.

11. Ellen G. White to Children of the Household, Letter 14, May 12, 1889; in *1888 Materials*, p. 312.

12. Ellen G. White Manuscript 24, Dec. 1888; in *1888 Materials*, p. 218.

13. Ellen G. White to Children, Letter 14, May 12, 1889; in *1888 Materials*, pp. 316, 323.

14. Ellen G. White to F. E. Belden and wife, Letter 2a, Nov. 5, 1889; in *1888 Materials*, pp. 1068, 1067.

15. Ellen G. White to Brethren, Letter 85, April 1889; in *1888 Materials*, p. 279.

16. Ellen G. White to Children of the Household, Letter 14, May 12, 1889; in *1888 Materials*, pp. 309, 315-316.

17. Ellen G. White Manuscript 24, Dec. 1888, and Ellen G. White to J. Fargo, Letter 50, May 2, 1889; in *1888 Materials*, pp. 224, 297.

18. Ellen G. White to F. E. Belden and wife, Letter 2a, Nov. 5, 1889; in *1888 Materials*, p. 1068.

19. Ellen G. White to Brethren, Letter 85, April 1889; in *1888 Materials*, p. 277.

20. Ellen G. White to "Dear Children of the Household," Letter 14, May 12, 1889; in *1888 Materials*, p. 312, emphasis supplied.

21. Ellen G. White Manuscript 9, Oct. 24, 1888, "Morning Talk"; in *1888 Materials*, p. 151, emphasis supplied.

22. Ellen G. White to "Dear Children of the Household," Letter 14, May 12, 1889; in *1888 Materials*, p. 309, emphasis supplied.

23. Ellen G. White to Frank & Hattie Belden, Letter 2a, Nov. 5, 1892; in *1888 Materials*,

pp. 1068-1069, emphasis supplied. Ellen White's likening of the rebellion of Korah Dathan, and Abiram, to that of the leading brethren at Minneapolis, was difficult for them to swallow. They could likely see how the counsel applied to others, but not to themselves. One of the hardest things for them to deal with at the Conference, was the *perception* that Ellen White had changed and that the Testimonies could no longer be trusted. A few years earlier, William L. Raymond, a young minister serving in the Northwest, presented doctrinal teachings not in accord with those held by the body of believers. When church leaders did not readily accept his teachings, he began treating them with disrespect, showing disregard for the authority of the church, from the local conference administration and to the General Conference brethren. So many church members joined with him that the conference presidents of the two local fields felt despised, ignored and powerless. This situation all came to a head in the summer of 1884 when Ellen White attended camp meetings in the Northwest. She not only sat with a council of the leading brethren and examined Raymond's teachings, but she also wrote a Testimony dealing specifically with his situation. Raymond was "not correct in all points of doctrine," yet, Ellen White stated: "he obstinately maintains his erroneous positions," his heart being "defiled with bitterness, wrath, envy, jealousy, and evil surmising." His work in leading the people to question and reject the "leaders in this work" and the "testimonies that God has been giving to His people," was "exactly similar to that of Korah, Dathan, and Abiram." It was similar to the "work of jealousy and evil surmising that [Satan] commenced in heaven." And "a similar work" to that of the Jews who "were ever acting as spies on [Jesus] track." In what appeared to be the main thrust of her testimony, Ellen White condemned Raymond because he had "not conformed to the Bible rule and conferred with the leading brethren ... God has not passed His people by and chosen one solitary man here and another there as the only ones worthy to be entrusted with His truth. He does not give one man new light contrary to the established faith of the body ... The only safety for any of us is in receiving no new doctrine, no new interpretation of the Scripture, without first submitting it to brethren of experience ... If they see no light in it, yield to their judgment; for 'in the multitude of counselors there is safety.'" Ellen White then warned of what lay ahead for the "remnant people of God." Satan would be "more determined and decisive in his efforts to overthrow them. Men and women will arise professing to have some new light or some new revelation whose tendency is to unsettle faith in the old landmarks" (*Testimonies for the Church*, vol. 5, pp. 289-295; See also, Author L. White, *The Lonely Years*, pp. 250-259). When Jones and Waggoner came on the scene only a few years later and presented ideas that were perceived as going against the established doctrines, Butler and Smith felt confident that they should submit to the "brethren of experience." But when Ellen White stood in defense of Jones and Waggoner and compared the work of the leading brethren to the same rebellious spirit she had condemned in the work of William Raymond, it was more than they could handle. They felt their views were infallible (See also Chapter 4, footnote 50). The context of Ellen White's counsel to Raymond is very important. First given in 1884, it was not applied to Jones and Waggoner when it was published in *Testimonies*, volume 5, in the year 1889. Butler and Smith felt it applied to Jones and Waggoner, but they received the rebuke of God, failing to see other balancing counsel: "Some charged [Luther] with acting hastily and from impulse. Others accused him of presumption, declaring that he was not directed of God, but was acting from pride and forwardness. 'Who does not know,' he responded, 'that one can seldom advance a new idea without having some appearance of pride, and without being accused of exciting quarrels? Why were Christ and all the martyrs put to death?—Because they appeared proud despisers of the wisdom of the times in which they lived, and because they brought forward new truths without having first consulted the oracles of the old opinions'" (*Great Controversy*, p. 130, 1888 ed.).

24. Ellen G. White Manuscript 13, 1889; in *1888 Materials* p. 517, emphasis supplied.

25. Ellen G. White Manuscript 15, Nov. 1888, "Dear Brethren Assembled at General Conference"; in *1888 Materials*, p. 174, emphasis supplied.

26. Ellen G. White to [Brethren], Letter 85, April 1889; in *1888 Materials*, p. 278, emphasis supplied.

27. Ellen G. White to "Dear Children of the Household," Letter 14, May 12, 1889; in *1888 Materials*, p. 309, emphasis supplied.

28. Ellen G. White, Manuscript 15, Nov. 1888, "Dear Brethren Assembled at General Conference"; in *1888 Materials*, p. 172, emphasis supplied.

29. Ellen G. White to "Dear Children of the Household," Letter 14, May 12, 1889; in *1888 Materials*, p. 309, emphasis supplied.

30. Ellen G. White Manuscript 30, June 1889, "Experiences Following the Minneapolis Conference"; in *1888 Materials*, p. 353, emphasis supplied.

31. Ellen G. White Manuscript 13, 1889; in *1888 Materials* p. 517, emphasis supplied.

32. Ellen G. White to Br. Fargo, Letter 50, May 2, 1889; in *1888 Materials*, p. 296, emphasis supplied.

33. Ellen G. White Manuscript 30, June 1889, "Experiences Following the Minneapolis Conference"; in *1888 Materials*, pp. 356-357, emphasis supplied. Ellen White wondered if there would be "another coming out" like that in 1844. According to the Ellen G. White Estate, this appears to be the "only known statement" of its kind from her pen (Ellen G. White, *Last Day Events* [Boise, ID: Pacific Press Pub. Assn., 1992], p. 48 fn3). Although we don't know how wide this Manuscript was circulated, we do know that at least one other person who was present at Minneapolis remembered

Ellen White's concern. F. H. Westphal, some 43 years later, remembered that Ellen White "had almost lost confidence in humanity and the Lord seemed to be on the point of taking the blessing, of carrying the message [of righteousness by faith] to the world, out of the hands of our people and raising up others to do the work. I do not know if she had reference only to the leaders or the entire people." But then "Sister White cried with brokenness of heart not to do this, and the Lord revealed to her that this work would not be permitted to go down into death and unbelief, that He would watch over it, and that our movement would continue to the end, and that those who would stand by it would be on safe ground" (F. H. Westphal to W. C. White, June 29, 1932; Ellen G. White Document File # 189; and L. E. Froom to W. C. White, April 29, 1932; *Manuscripts and Memories*, p. 343). *Sadly*, the response to Westphal's accurate recollection was one of disapproval: "I think Elder Westphal's memory… is not correct … [M]y memory does not grasp any statement about the Lord turning to other people. I think this is an inference and I would not dare use it and I advise you not to use it … I think we should be very cautious about making statements from memory to what Sister White has said" (W. C. White to L. E. Froom, May 11, 1932; in *Manuscripts and Memories*, pp. 344, 345).

34. Ellen G. White to Children, Letter 14, May 12, 1889; in *1888 Materials*, p. 311.

35. Ellen G. White to Brethren, Letter 85, April 1889; in *1888 Materials*, p. 277, emphasis supplied.

36. Ellen G. White Manuscript 24, Dec. 1888; in *1888 Materials*, p. 225.

37. Ellen G. White Manuscript 37, n.d. 1890, "Light in God's Word"; in *1888 Materials*, p. 829.

38. Ellen G. White Manuscript 9, Oct. 24, 1888, "Morning Talk"; in *1888 Materials*, pp. 151-153.

39. J. H. Morrison told J. S. Washburn at the Minneapolis meetings that Jones and Waggoner had influenced Ellen White while riding on the train together coming from California. Washburn's initial response was: "She's no prophet, if she will be persuaded by men to follow them. We don't really have a prophet!" ("Interview with J. S. Washburn, at Hagerstown, Md., June 4, 1950," p. 1). This is just one example of the effect Morrison's words had on others.

40. Ellen G. White, *Sketches From the Life of Paul*, (Oakland, Cal.: Pacific Press Pub. Assn., 1883), pp. 192-193, 188. See: W. C. White, "Notes Made at the Minneapolis Meetings 1888," Oct. 24, 1888, p. 63; in *Manuscripts and Memories*, p. 425.

41. Ellen G. White, *Sketches From the Life of Paul*, p. 68; and *Manuscripts and Memories*, p. 426.

42. "Interview with J. S. Washburn, at Hagerstown, Md., June 4, 1950," p. 1.

43. Ellen G. White Manuscript 24, Dec. 1888; in *1888 Materials*, p. 221, emphasis supplied.

44. "Interview with J. S. Washburn, at Hagerstown, Md., June 4, 1950," p. 1.

45. See: "Diary of R. Dewitt Hottel," Oct. 25 to Nov. 4, 1888; in *Manuscripts and Memories*, p. 508-512. At least one other Ellen White talk was recorded, however. See footnote 50.

*46.* *General Conference Daily Bulletin*, Oct. 26, 1888; *Manuscripts and Memories*, p. 382 emphasis supplied. The *Daily Bulletin* at that time was published "as *Review and Herald Extras*... by the General Conference at place of session." Uriah Smith was editor at the time (*Seventh-day Adventist Encyclopedia*, vol. 10 [Hagerstown, Md.: Review and Herald Pub. Assn., 1976], p. 498).

47. L. E. Froom, *Movement of Destiny*, p. 250.

48. Ellen G. White Manuscript 2, March 16, 1890; in *1888 Materials*, p. 641.

49. Morrison had "studied infidel books... to meet opponents in arguments" (*1888 Materials*, p. 601). Ellen White warned that he would bring in "dissensions and bickerings," and unless overcome he would "make shipwreck of faith as did Elder Canright" (p. 168). A few days earlier, Ellen White stated that she had seen "an angel of God inquiring of these men who have educated themselves as debaters" (p. 141). G. B. Starr tells of this event years later. He was with J. H. Morrison and two other ministers in the "tent at Oskaloosa, Iowa." A stranger "entered the tent door," one of "the finest looking men" he had ever seen. He was "over six feet tall" and "had such a kindly expression on his face." He went directly to Morrison and asked about the tent meetings and what Seventh-day Adventists believed. "At first [Morrison] replied to the questions in a kindly spirit but soon assumed a debating, controversial attitude ... After about an hour's such conversation, the stranger arose in all his dignity, and addressing [Morrison] said, 'You are no minister of Jesus Christ; you are a controversialist, sir.' Instead of [Morrison] realizing that he had been properly rebuked, he instead chuckled and laughed, and said, 'Oh, you can't meet the argument.'" The stranger made no reference to Morrison's comment but repeated himself. This happened twice. When G. B. Starr told Ellen White of this event she replied: "'Why, Brother Starr, that was an angel of God ... Why I gave that message to that brother at the Minneapolis Conference, and told him that the Lord had sent an angel to rebuke him for his controversial manner of labor'" (G. B. Starr, *"Fifty Years With One of God's Seers,"* unpublished manuscript, Ellen G. White Estates Doc. File #496, p. 150-152). This may explain why Ellen White would get up and leave when Morrison spoke. It also explains what Jones and Waggoner were up against.

50. Ellen G. White Manuscript 15, Nov. 1888; in *1888 Materials*, pp. 163, 166-167, 169-170. This talk by Ellen White, given sometime between Thursday, November 1, and Sabbath, November 3, represents her last recorded talk of the Conference.

51. *Ibid.*, pp. 171-175.

52. Ellen G. White Manuscript 15, Nov. 1888; in *1888 Materials*, pp. 163-165, emphasis supplied.

53. Ellen G. White to E. J. Waggoner and A. T. Jones, Letter 37, Feb. 18, 1887; in *1888 Materials*, pp. 21, 23. See also Ellen G. White to G. I. Butler and Uriah Smith, Letter 13, April 5, 1887; in *1888 Materials*, p. 32.

54. *Ibid.*, pp. 32, 33.

55. Ellen G. White to G. I. Butler, Letter 21, Oct. 14, 1888; in *1888 Materials*, pp. 88, 93.

56. Ellen G. White Manuscript 9, Oct. 24, 1888; in *1888 Materials*, pp. 152, 153.

57. Ellen G. White Manuscript 24, Dec. 1888, in *1888 Materials*, p. 221, emphasis supplied.

58. Ellen G. White to W. H. Healey, Letter 7, Dec. 9, 1888; in *1888 Materials*, pp. 186, 189, emphasis supplied.

59. Ellen G. White to J. H. Morrison, Letter 49, April 4, 1889; in *1888 Materials*, p. 275.

60. Ellen G. White to Uriah Smith, Letter 59, March 8, 1890; and Manuscript 55, n.d. 1890; and Ellen G. White to C. P. Bollman, Letter 179, Nov. 19, 1902; in *1888 Materials*, pp. 604, 841, 1796.

61. Ellen G. White to W. C. White, Letter 83, March 13, 1890; in *1888 Materials*, p. 631.

62. Ellen G. White Manuscript 55, n.d. 1890, "Peril in Trusting to Wisdom of Men"; in *1888 Materials*, p. 841.

63. Ellen G. White to Uriah Smith, Letter 96, June 6, 1896; in *1888 Materials*, p. 1575.

64. Fragments of sentences taken from Ellen White's discourse are often quoted as blank checks to discredit what Jones and Waggoner presented at Minneapolis (and in the years that followed), and to undermine the bountiful support they received from Ellen White. A. V. Olson saught a balanced approach when he stated: "It can be seen that some details in Elder Waggoner's studies Mrs. White did not then approve, but she concurred with and endorsed his emphasis on the great theme of righteousness by faith as presented by him at the conference (*Through Crisis to Victory* [1966], p. 55). But others have used these statements to discredit Jones and Waggoner and promote their own Evangelical views. Desmond Ford claims: "Waggoner and Jones saw clearly the 'gift' nature of righteousness but in some other areas they erred doctrinally as subsequent E. G. White statements make clear. At no time did E. G. White endorse all the positions of Waggoner and Jones. (See *Crisis and Victory [sic]*, A. W. Olsen, p. 294)" ("The Relationship Between the Incarnation and Righteousness by Faith," Documents from the Palmdale Conference on Righteousness by Faith [Goodlettsvillle, TN: Jack D. Walker, 1976], p. 40). George Knight also refers to limited portions of Ellen White's

discourse in an attempt to prove his case: "The extent of her endorsement of Jones and Waggoner is an important issue. Some interpreters have treated it as kind of a blank check in doctrinal matters. That is a dangerous position, since Ellen White's major concerns in connection with 1888 were related to experiential Christianity rather than doctrine. It was on doctrinal issues that she tended to disagree with them—even during the Minneapolis Conference. She freely told the assembled delegates on November 1, 1888, that 'some interpretations of Scripture, given by Dr. Waggoner, I do not regard as correct.' In spite of that, however, she continued to support his work without mentioning where she felt he was wrong … Despite such delimitations, people began to treat Jones and Waggoner's pronouncements as if they possessed divine authority" (*From 1888 to Apostasy* [1987] p. 72). Roy Adams echoes these claims: "Moreover, we have explicit evidence that Ellen White's endorsement of Jones's and Waggoner's messages was not completely without equivocation. 'She freely told the assembled delegates on November 1, 1888, that "some interpretations of Scriptures, given by Dr. Waggoner, I do not regard as correct."' (*From 1888 to Apostasy*, p. 72)" (*The Nature of Christ* [1994], p. 32). At least 14 times throughout the pages of *A User–Friendly Guide to the 1888 Message*, George Knight seeks to lead his readers to question the message of Jones and Waggoner by pointing to Ellen White's "disagreements" with them. We are told that Ellen White "repeatedly asserted that she didn't agree with all of their teachings." That "she never approved of everything in [their] writings… anymore than she did in the works of… Luther, Miller, and Smith." Ellen White "didn't even accept all they were teaching at Minneapolis." She "had not even agreed with all their theology or scriptural interpretations related to the issue at the 1888 meetings" (pp. 69, 72, 166, 141: see also 55, 73, 76, 79, 163, 165, 179, 180). However, based on the same isolated Ellen White statements listed above, Knight suggests that "Ellen White never indicated on what points she disagreed with Waggoner" (*Ibid.*, p. 74). But this leaves to conjecture what exactly it was that Ellen White "didn't agree with." And it is often applied, by those pushing for an Evangelical Reformationist gospel, to topics such as original sin, the nature of Christ, the part sanctification plays in righteousness by faith, and end-time perfection. But we must read all that Ellen White said, as when she stated so emphatically: "When Brother Waggoner brought out these ideas in Minneapolis, it was the first clear teaching on this subject from any human lips I had heard … They [the brethren] cannot see it because they have never had it presented to them as I have. And when another [Waggoner] presented it, every fiber of my heart said, Amen" (*1888 Materials*, p. 349). Perhaps we should let Ellen White answer her own question: "Has God raised up these men to proclaim the truth? I say, yes, God has sent men to bring us the truth that we should not have had unless God had sent somebody to bring it to us" (*Ibid.*, p. 608). R. T. Nash, who was present at the 1888 Conference, offers an account that strongly contradicts Knight's assessment of Ellen White's statements in regard to the teaching of Jones and Waggoner. Nash states simply: "From Mrs. E. G. White's attitude and words at that time it was plain she stood *one hundred percent* with Elders Jones and Waggoner *in the message they were presenting at that General Conference meeting*" ("An Eyewitness Report," p. 6, emphasis supplied. See also *Manuscripts and Memories*, p. 355). We would not deny the fact that both Jones and Waggoner were fallible men who made mistakes and that they were "overthrown by the temptations" years later. But we would stress the importance of reading Ellen White's statements made at the 1888 General Conference in their proper context.

65. Ellen G. White Manuscript 15, Nov. 1888; in *1888 Materials*, p. 163.

66. *Ibid.*, pp. 164-165, emphasis supplied. Ellen White did affirm two of E. J. Waggoner's key points at Minneapolis, although she did not base them on Galatians: First, that the ten commandments are a yoke of bondage to those "who break the law;" second, that "there is no power in the law to save or to pardon the transgressor ... It brings the repentant sinner to Christ" (Manuscript 17, Oct. 21, 1888, "Sermon"; in *1888 Materials*, p. 130).

67. W. C. White to Mary White, Oct. 27, 1888; in *Manuscripts and Memories*, p. 120, quoted verbatim. George Knight, after quoting the two isolated statements from Ellen White's November sermon that we have just mentioned above, quotes from this letter written by W. C. White, to try to substantiate the fact that Ellen White disagreed with much Jones and Waggoner taught. But Knight, misquoting W. C. White's letter, states: "W. C. White substantiates his mother's position. He wrote to his wife from Minneapolis that 'much that Dr. W. teaches is in line with what' his mother had 'seen in vision.' That had led some to jump to the conclusion 'that she endorses all his views, an[d that no] part of his teaching disagrees wi[th Mother] and with her Testimonies ... I could prove all this to be f[alse]'" (*A User-Friendly Guide to the 1888 Message*, p. 74, quoted verbatim). Knight leads one to believe that W. C. White was telling Mary that some thought his mother was supporting all of Jones' and Waggoner's views, but he could "prove all that to be false." However, it was the brethren—the ones who had the "Spirit of Phariseeism"—who said that Waggoner's views disagreed with Ellen White's Testimonies, not W. C. White. It was the brethren who were saying that W. C. White had influenced his mother to accept what Waggoner was saying, and *to this* W. C. White said: "I could prove all this to be false." What literary license is there that allows for misusing, misquoting, and misrepresenting historical evidence in order to try to prove that the most precious message sent through Jones and Waggoner cannot be trusted today? We should be careful that we do not partake of the same spirit of Phariseeism that tried to "crush... down and condemn all" that Jones and Waggoner said over 120 years ago. After lifting out of context statements from Ellen White's November 1888 sermon and misquoting W. C. White's letter to Mary White, Knight

immediately lists, as a "sample," seven items of difference between Ellen White's understanding and that of Jones and Waggoner (*Ibid*. pp. 74-77). But has Knight used the same literary license when writing about these differences? We will take a closer look at each of these seven differences in the pages ahead.

68. Ellen G. White, "Open the Heart to Light," Morning Talk, Feb. 6, 1890, *Review and Herald*, March 25, 1890; and Manuscript 56, Feb. 7, 1890, "Lessons From the Vine"; in *1888 Materials*, pp. 547, 565.

69. Ellen G. White Manuscript 15, Nov. 1888; in *1888 Materials*, p. 163.

70. Ellen G. White to Mary White, Letter 82, Nov. 4, 1888; in *1888 Materials*, p. 182.

71. Ellen G. White Manuscript 21, Nov. 1888; in *1888 Materials*, pp. 179, 177.

72. Ellen G. White to R. A. Underwood, Letter 3, Jan. 26, 1889; in *1888 Materials*, p. 255.

73. Ellen G. White to Children, Letter 14, May 12, 1889; and Ellen G. White Manuscript 30, June, 1889; in *1888 Materials*, pp. 314, 368, 323.

74. Ellen G. White Manuscript 6, Oct. 11, 1888; in *1888 Materials*, p. 72.

75. Ellen G. White Manuscript 24, Dec. 1888; in *1888 Materials*, p. 208.

76. Ellen G. White Letter 14, May 12, 1889; in *1888 Materials*, p. 320.

77. Ellen G. White Manuscript 30, June, 1889; in *1888 Materials*, p. 360.

78. Ellen G. White to O. A. Olsen, Letter 81, May 31, 1896; in *1888 Materials*, p. 1565. The specific context of this letter is addressing meetings held in1894, but the counsel applies to the Minneapolis meetings as well.

79. Ellen G. White to J. Fargo, Letter 50, May 2, 1889; in *1888 Materials*, p. 296. This appears to be the first time Ellen White quoted Zechariah 13:6. Chapter 12 and 13 of Zechariah, addresses the time when a "fountain" of cleansing and forgiveness will be opened for God's people (13:1). The question will finally be asked: "What are these wounds in thine hands?" And the answer will come; "those with which I was wounded in the house of my friends" (13:6). The result of such a realization draws the attention of God's people (leadership and laity alike) to the One whom they have pierced, and true sorrow and repentance takes place. Then, as on the day of Pentecost, the prophecy will be fulfilled: "'He that is feeble... shall be as David; and the house of David... as the angel of the Lord.' Zechariah 12:8" (Ellen G. White, *Acts of the Apostles*, p. 48).

80. Ellen G. White, *Desire of Ages*, p. 165.

81. Ellen G. White to Brethren in the Ministry, Letter 67, Sept. 17, 1890; in *1888 Materials*, p. 706.

# CHAPTER 6

# *Three Responses*

## *Accepting, Assenting, or Rejecting*
## *—What were the Consequences?*

One of the greatest points of controversy that still surrounds the 1888 General Conference session is whether or not the message the Lord sent over 120 years ago was accepted by those gathered in Minneapolis, and as a result heralded to the world. As N. F. Pease put it: "If a person studies the records of those years looking for evidence of acceptance, he can find such evidence. On the other hand, one who looks for evidence of rejection can also find what he seeks."[1] So what do we do with this apparently contradictory evidence? Was Minneapolis a great victory, or was the Holy Spirit turned away and Christ's coming delayed? Does the Laodicean message still apply to us today, and does it have implications in regard to 1888? Did the Church have a fair chance to consider the message unopposed, or was it resisted by the leading brethren and in a large degree kept from our people, and therefore "in a great degree kept away from the world"?[2] Although these questions will be addressed more fully throughout the remainder of this book, we will take an initial look in this chapter.

Ever since the 1888 experience, there has been a tendency among us as a people to credit ourselves with accepting and experiencing the message of righteousness by faith. Since the 1920s, however, when this acceptance idea began to be questioned by some of the leading brethren, there has been a *more* determined effort through the writings of various leaders and church historians, to portray the acceptance theory. Thus, Minneapolis is portrayed as a "glorious victory." It was the "beginning of a great spiritual awakening" among Adventists that was due to the "after effect of the great Minneapolis revival."[3]

It was the "greatest event of the [eighteen] eighties" when "the church was aroused by the revival message of justification by faith."[4] We have been asked to believe that "the rank and file of Seventh-day Adventist workers and laity accepted the presentations at Minneapolis and were blessed."[5]

As was noted earlier, much of the blame for the opposition to Jones and Waggoner at Minneapolis has been attributed to their problematic "personalities."[6]* We are told that it was only "certain leading men there [who] resisted the teaching" of righteousness by faith.[7] "The dissention was largely a conflict of personalities, caused not by irreconcilable differences in doctrine, but by selfishness, pride, and hardness of heart."[8] And, it is stated, "we perceive that it was the rancors aroused by personalities, much more than the differences in beliefs, which caused the difficulty." "From the one side Waggoner was regarded as a conceited upstart, and Jones as a barbarian." It is claimed that Jones and Waggoner were "the progressives, shouting 'Christ is all'... they gave evidence that they were not wholly sanctified." They "failed to show humility and love which righteousness by faith imparts." Furthermore, the "extreme teaching of Jones and Waggoner is observable still" today. Jones, it is asserted, "was aggressive, and at times obstreperous, and he gave just cause for resentment."[9] He was an "angular man, with a loping gait and uncouth posturings and gestures." Not only that but he was "naturally abrupt" and "cultivated singularity of speech."[10] Waggoner, on the other hand, "loved contention" and along with Jones, "presented truth which disallowed the Holy Spirit to bring a convicting, converting presence in the meetings."[11]

As a church we have educated our young people to believe that "Ellen White did not take sides" in the conflict. Her "sermons had supported the views of Jones and Waggoner on righteousness by faith, but she took no stand with them . ... Though the Minneapolis Conference seemed depressing and alarming, it turned out to be a great victory for the church . ... A new experience came to the leaders, and the church made rapid progress in all branches of the work at home and abroad as there was a realization of the proper emphasis which must be given to righteousness by faith."[12] Overall, it is declared, "the thirteen years between Minneapolis, 1888, and the General

Conference session of 1901 were… a period over which Providence could spell out the word *victory*."[13]

In response to more agitation about 1888 in the 1950s, there has been on the part of some an even greater tendency to proclaim that "the denomination as a whole, and its leadership in particular, *did not reject* the message and provisions of Righteousness by Faith in and following 1888." Authors have told us that "the 'some' who rejected turns out to be less than twenty out of more than ninety [delegates]—less than one quarter … *most* of those twenty made confessions, hence ceased being 'rejectors' and thus becoming *accepters*."[14] Although there is a willingness to admit that some fought against the message at first, the question is asked: "Does this mean that the church as a whole, or even its leadership, rejected the 1888 message? Not at all. Some rejected it—a vocal minority."[15] After all, we are told, "contemporary records yield no suggestion of denominational rejection."[16] "'Light' was 'despised by some,' not all . …. [I]t is false to state categorically that 'the Seventh-day Adventist Church rejected the 1888 message.'"[17]

"The denomination," we are assured, "had received the loud cry message in 1888." Waggoner, Jones and Ellen White were in "unity of opinion on the fact that the church had accepted the 1888 message of righteousness by faith," on at least "the intellectual level." Jones and Waggoner, it is maintained, "were anything but rejected by the post-1888 administration . …. The most serious fallacy for the [rejection] theory is that there [is] no such thing as corporate or denominational rejection."[18]* And besides, it is declared, "eventually most of those who opposed the message changed their attitude and accepted the message . …. To understand what happened at Minneapolis is important because some people today claim that the church rejected the message of Minneapolis and call for corporate repentance . …. Minneapolis 1888 was a turning point in the history of the Seventh-day Adventist Church. Through Waggoner and Jones, supported by Ellen White, the church was saved from an incomplete understanding of the gospel."[19]

After more than 120 years since the Minneapolis Conference, we must ask ourselves if the message sent by the Lord was really fully accepted in 1888, and if so, by whom? What did the participants in that great event have to say themselves about the matter? Is accepting the message on the "intellectual level" a genuine acceptance? And, perhaps most importantly, if that message was accepted, regardless of the numbers in each group, why are we still here waiting for the Lord to return?

## *Three Responses to the Message*

Perhaps the statement that is most often referred to when attempting to prove the acceptance theory is one made by A. T. Jones at the 1893 General Conference Session: "By 1893 Jones claimed that 'some there accepted it; others rejected it entirely,' while 'others tried to stand half way between' (1893 GCB 185)."[20] This partial statement, from one of Jones' sermons, has been used to define three responses to the 1888 message. While on one hand, it has been suggested that "it is not possible to establish... the relative number in each of the three groups," very decided opinions have been expressed as to their makeup. The idea has been freely published that "less than one quarter" really *rejected* the message outright and, of those who did so, most repented after a few short years. Thus, the idea is given that only a small percentage— around 10 to 15 percent—*rejected* the message at first, many of whom repented and became supporters.[21]

It has also been expressed that the rest of the brethren, who did not *reject* the message, either wholeheartedly accepted it or were undecided until becoming strong supporters. Thus the claim that both these groups can be classed together as accepting the message: "[Ellen White], her son, and Jones and Waggoner all agreed that the church had largely accepted the message on at least the intellectual level."[22]

Other statements often referred to, in seeking to establish the overall response to the message, are those statements made by Ellen White in which she uses the word "some" to identify those who were opposing the message. The conclusion expressed is the same; that the "some" who rejected or opposed the message represented only a small percentage. But did Ellen White clarify her statements and did any of the other *participants* give and indication as to the makeup of these three groups? Can we know for a fact today if that message was ever fully accepted?

First, we must remember that it was primarily the leadership of the church that gathered at Minneapolis; whose response would to a significant degree be replicated throughout the denomination. This point is substantiated by G. I. Butler, who two years before the 1888 General Conference, told Ellen White that the views Jones and Waggoner were presenting were "views not believed by two–thirds or three–fourths of the denomination." In a long letter written just prior to the 1888 Conference, Butler explains why this was the case: The "position held by the *majority* of our ministers" was contrary to Jones' and Waggoner's position.[23]

It would only make sense that those ministers holding Butler's position were the ones who opposed the message of Jones and Waggoner. J. S. Washburn, who was at Minneapolis, supported this conclusion, stating that "three-fourths of the workers stood against the new light."[24]

A.G. DANIELLS

A. G. Daniells agreed that the message was rejected by the majority: "The message has never been received, nor proclaimed, nor given free course as it should have been . . . . The division and conflict which arose among the *leaders* because of the opposition to the message of righteousness in Christ, produced a very unfavorable reaction. The *rank and file* of the people were confused, and did not know what to do."[25] Likewise, R. T. Nash who attended the Minneapolis meetings maintained this view as well: "Many who attended the meetings at that conference know of what took place at that conference meeting. When Christ was lifted up as the only hope of the church, and of all men, the speakers met an *[sic] united opposition from nearly all the senior ministers*. They tried to put a stop to this teaching by Elders Waggoner and Jones."[26]

C. McReynolds recalled that "the spirit of debate and controversy *ran high* and… the conference closed with a dark shadow over *many* minds . … I am sorry for any one who was at the Conference in Minneapolis in 1888 who does not recognize that there was *opposition and rejection* of the Message that the Lord sent to His people at that time."[27] Taylor G. Bunch expressed the same view: "According to some who attended the Minneapolis

C.C. McReynolds

meeting *fully two thirds* of those present either opposed the message of righteousness by faith or were afraid of it."[28] A. T. Jones himself defined the proportion of those who initially rejected the message at Minneapolis: "I cannot now name anyone who *definitely and openly accepted there* the truth of righteousness by faith."[29]

Taylor G. Bunch

While it is true that several times Ellen White used the word "some" to describe the group of leaders who actively rejected the message, she clarifies her meaning as well. For example, in 1890 she stated that "*some* who ought to have stood in the clear light on this subject [justification by faith] were working on the enemy's side of the question." In the very next paragraph, she clarifies her statement, exclaiming that the position of Jones and Waggoner "is seen to be wrong by *very many,* and they cry, 'Danger, fanaticism,' when there is no heresy and fanaticism."[30]

Writing about the conditions in the church right before the 1888 General Conference, Ellen White made it clear that "a strong, firm, resistance was manifested by *many* against anything that should interfere with their own personal ideas, their own course of action . … *[N]ot many* were standing in a position before God where they could discern their own soul's needs."[31]

During the conference itself, she expressed her concern that "the spirit and influence of the ministers *generally* who have come to this meeting is to discard light."[32] She realized that there were "*many ministers* who [had] *never* been converted."[33] She told the delegates plainly: "From the light that God has given me, I can say that *not half* of those who profess to believe the present truth have a thorough understanding of the Third Angel's Message."[34]

Ellen White's statements were not based on her own personal assessment of the Conference. A messenger from heaven had told her that "'there are *but few*, even of those who claim to believe it, that comprehend the third angel's message.'" Thus she could echo to those gathered at the meetings: "But *how few* take up this message in its true bearing, and present it to the people in its power! With *many* it has but little force." She had pleaded with the young leaders not to commit themselves to a vote in a Conference "where opposition, rather than investigation, [was] the *order of the day*."[35]* She could see that "envy, evil surmisings, jealousies [had] been working like leaven until the *whole lump* seemed to be leavened."[36] Just following the Conference, she stated similar thoughts: "What pages of history were being made by the recording angel! The leaven had indeed done its sharp work, and *nearly leavened the lump*."[37]

When speaking of the way her testimony had been rejected at Minneapolis, Ellen White again spoke of a majority: "I told them plainly [that] the position and work God gave me at that conference was disregarded by *nearly all*. Rebellion was *popular*." A heavenly messenger had told her that she would "stand *almost alone*."[38] When afterwards she bore her testimony in Battle Creek, the response was the same: "There was *not one* of my brethren who had the moral courage to stand by my side and take back or confess that they had pursued a wrong course and misjudged their brethren and misjudged me."[39] It was not just a few leaders who were doing a work to "unsettle the faith of the people of God," it was "Elders Butler, Farnsworth, Smith and *numerous others*."[40] Thus, as a result of opposition, Ellen White could plainly state: "There is not *one in one hundred* who understands for himself the Bible truth on this subject [the plan of salvation] that is so necessary to our present and eternal welfare."[41]

## *Mental Assent the Same as Rejection*

As mentioned previously, much has been made of Jones' statements in regard to the three different responses to the 1888 message. *A User–Friendly Guide to the 1888 Message* suggests that in seeking to find the answer as to whether or not the message was accepted, we should "let the proponents of the message give their own opinion."[42] This is excellent advice. Rather than decide on our own that those who "tried to stand half way between" and accepted the message only on an "intellectual level" were in fact *accepters of the message*," we should allow the proponents of the message to give their own opinion. The fact is that Jones clarified his own often misused statement as to which side the "intellectual" accepters were really on:

> I know that some there accepted it; others rejected it entirely . ... Others tried to stand half way between, and get it that way; but that is not the way it is to be had, brethren, that is not the way it is received. They thought to take a middle course... they were willing to go whichever way the tide turned at the last; whichever way the body turned they were willing to go . ... [They] would speak favorably of it when everything was that way; but when in the fierceness of this spirit—this spirit described there as the persecuting spirit—when that spirit would rise up in its fierceness and make war upon the message of righteousness by faith, instead of standing nobly, in the fear of God, and declaring in the face of that attack, 'it is the truth of God, and I believe it in my soul,' they would begin to yield and in an apologetic way, offer excuses for those who were preaching it.[43]

> [W]hen it was presented four years ago, and all along since, some accepted it just as it was given, and were glad of the news that God had righteousness that would pass the judgment . ... Others would not have anything to do with it at all but rejected the whole thing. Others seemed to take a middle position. They did not fully accept it, neither did they openly reject it. They thought to... go along with the crowd, if the crowd went that way. And that is the way they hoped to receive the righteousness of Christ and the message of the righteousness of God. Others deliberately discounted the message about fifty percent, and counted *that* the righteousness of God. And so, all the way between open and free deliberate surrender and acceptance of it, to open, deliberate, and positive rejection of it—all the way between—the compromisers have been scattered ever since; and those who have taken that compromising position are no better prepared tonight to discern what is the message of the righteousness of Christ than they were four years ago.[44]

Beyond a doubt, Jones saw those who tried to "stand half way between" as "compromisers" who in the end were no different than those who openly rejected the message of justification by faith. Waggoner himself spoke about the claim that everyone believed in justification by faith, stating several years later: "We say we believe in justification by faith. Of course we do. Why, we all believe that, now. But do we? Oh, we have that written down, and we would resent any imputation of our disbelief in it . ... [But] what use for me to say, I believe in the Lord Jesus Christ, when I am doing exactly contrary to what he says?... What is the use for me to say I believe in justification by faith, when I am not letting righteousness and its fruits manifest themselves in my life? Here is the trouble with a good deal of our conception of justification by faith."[45]

Ellen White was even more emphatic that there was little difference between those who openly rejected the light and those who made a mere assent. She had warned the delegates at Minneapolis, that "a *mere assent* to... this truth will not save us . ... We are losing a great deal of the blessing we might have at this meeting because we do not take *advance steps* in the Christian life."[46] She also stated what the result would be: "Some will turn away from light and others will come to a *standstill* in spiritual growth."[47] Again she told them plainly: "If you are not advancing you are *retrograding*."[48]

Many of the delegates admitted that what Waggoner and Jones were presenting was "light and truth," yet they had not presented it in the same light before.[49] This led Ellen White to conclude: "There is a *larger number* who profess to believe the truth for this time, who are represented [in the Bible] as hearing the sayings of Christ and doing them not, *than of those* who diligently hear and are doers of His words."[50] The "faith of Jesus" had been "overlooked and treated in an indifferent careless manner . ... But *very few* had responded except by *assent* to the testimonies borne upon this subject."[51]

A mere mental assent to the message presented by Jones and Waggoner also resulted in the Testimonies of Ellen White being treated with almost total disregard: "In *many* hearts the messages I bear find no response. In *some* hearts they arouse a determined resistance, like... that... of the Jews."[52] Yet, she declared:

> Decided opposition would have done me less harm. A lack of faith in the messages God has given me to bear of the order represented is decided unbelief to all intents and purposes ... and *many* give a *bare assent* to truth when they are not sanctified through the truth. They do not represent Christ . ... So effectually does this delusion take possession of heart and mind that the sharp arrows of the Lord fail to penetrate the armor of self righteousness in which they are encased . ... This is the class our Saviour found most difficult to arouse . ... Thus it is with *many* in this generation.[53]*

It should be clear that a mental assent to the truth is little better, if not worse, than open rebellion. Much more evidence could be given on this point.[54]* Notwithstanding, if we classify those who *assented* to the message presented by Jones and Waggoner as *accepters* of the message, are we not misrepresenting what really took place in our church's history? According to Ellen White, those who assented to the truth were in the same camp with those who openly rebelled. Therefore, when we allow Ellen White to speak for herself, it is clear that the majority of those in leadership positions rejected the 1888 message *at* Minneapolis.[55]* How much would that change in the days that followed?

The same morning the Lord revealed to Ellen White what was really taking place in Minneapolis, He also charged her not to leave, but to stand by her post. Being faithful to that charge, she declared to the leading brethren later that morning: "If the ministers will not receive the light, *I want to give the people a chance; perhaps they may receive it.*"[56] The showers from heaven would not be shut off without first giving the people a chance to receive the message sent from heaven. The time had come for the message to go to the people, and what would be the result? We will find out in the following chapters.

LOCATION OF THE 1888
MINNEAPOLIS GENERAL CONFERENCE

# CHAPTER 6 FOOTNOTES

1. N. F. Pease, *The Faith That Saves*, p. 43.

2. Ellen G. White to Uriah Smith, Letter 96, June 6, 1896; *1888 Materials*, p. 1575.

3. L. H. Christian, *The Fruitage of Spiritual Gifts*, pp. 219, 237, 245.

4. A. W. Spalding, *Captains of the Host*, pp. 583, 602.

5. "A Further Appraisal of the Manuscript '1888 Re-examined,'" (Takoma Park, Washington, D.C.: General Conference 1958) p. 11

6. The conclusion that the opposition was largely due to Jones' and Waggoner's personalities, however, has been based largely on statements made by men who were not at the 1888 Conference and have quoted from one another for support. Once one author has projected a statement, another author picks it up and soon a complete circle of authority is established. For example, in 1945, N. F. Pease quoted from A. T. Robinson's 1931 unpublished manuscript—"Did the Seventh-day Adventist Denomination Reject the Doctrine of Righteousness by Faith" (*Manuscripts and Memories*, pp. 336-337; see also Chapter 3, footnote 43)—in regard to the controversy at Minneapolis. Pease then states that "this unfortunate situation developed a sprit of prejudice against the men that in many minds obscured the real issues involved" ("Justification and Righteousness by Faith in the Seventh-day Adventist Church Before 1900," p. 52). In 1949, A. W. Spalding not only quoted from A. T. Robinson, but also stated his indebtedness to N. F. Pease's 1945 doctoral thesis "for reference to several authorities, as well as for general inspiration" for his book (*Captains of the Host*, pp. 690-691, 602). Spalding had much to say about Jones and Waggoner's personalities: "The conflict, indeed, involved personalities quite as much as preaching. Jones, and especially Waggoner, were young men. ... Jones was aggressive, and at times obstreperous, and he gave just cause for resentment. ... Many others vacillated, torn between previously held views plus personal pique at the messengers. ... The conservatives ... branded the new teachers [Jones and Waggoner] as radical, subversive, undisciplined" (*Ibid.*, pp. 592, 593). Subsequently, in 1962, Pease published his thesis and quoted largely from Spalding when giving a personality sketch of Jones and Waggoner: "In 1949 was published a volume on denominational history by Arthur W. Spalding. ... Regarding Jones and Waggoner he says: '. ... Jones was a towering, angular man, with a loping gait and uncouth posturings and gestures. ... Not only was he naturally abrupt, but he cultivated singularity of speech and manner'" (*By Faith Alone*, pp. 208, 209). In 1966, A. V. Olson quotes Spalding in a footnote that gives additional descriptions of

the personalities of Jones and Waggoner: "'The conflict,' wrote Arthur W. Spalding, '. . . involved personalities quite as much as preaching. Jones, and ... Waggoner ... were resented by not a few of the older men. ... Jones was aggressive, and at times obstreperous, and gave just cause for resentment, in his forceful presentations.'" (*From Crisis to Victory*, p. 44). Included in Olson's book is "Appendix B" where A. L. White, in portraying the personalities of Jones and Waggoner, picks up the same passage used by Pease and Olson as found originally in Spalding: "'Jones was a towering, angular man, ... he was naturally abrupt. ...'" (*Ibid*. 303). In his second book, published in 1969, Pease refers back to Olson's book regarding the 1888 session in general and particularly in reference to the outcome of the session as interpreted by Olson (*The Faith That Saves*, pp. 34-41). In 1971, L. E. Froom quotes Pease's thesis as well as his later published book, *By Faith Alone*, for authoritative support (*The Movement of Destiny*, pp. 608-610, 760). Froom also cites and quotes Spalding (*Ibid*. 239, 260, 605), and refers to Olson, vouching for his "accurate and dependable portrayal of that special period" (*Ibid*. 76, 610-612). In his biography of Waggoner, David P. McMahon refers to Pease, Spalding, Olson and Froom several times to support his views (*The Myth and the Man* 7, 9, 12, 13, 23, 26, 76, 86). In his biography of Jones, George Knight quotes Spalding in regard to Jones' personality (*From 1888 to Apostasy*, p. 16). In chapter 2 of his book, Roy Adams belittles Jones and Waggoner and their supposed 1888 message, quoting no less than 12 times from George Knight's *From 1888 to Apostasy* as his main source of evidence. Not once does Adams quote from Ellen White in this chapter except as stated by Knight (*The Nature of Christ*, pp. 29-36). If all of the above sounds confusing, it should! Does this kind of circuitous research in regard to the personalities of Jones and Waggoner leave something to be desired? Does a statement become accurate and authoritative because one author makes a statement and others pick it up and repeat it? And where in all of this research are the supportive statements from Ellen White, claiming that the personalities of Jones and Waggoner were to blame for the rejection of their message?

7.  "A Further Appraisal of the Manuscript '1888 Re-examined,'" p. 11.

8.  General Conference of Seventh-day Adventists, *The Story of Our Church*, p. 247.

9.  A. W. Spalding, *Captains of the Host*, pp. 599, 593, 601, 592.

10. N. F. Pease, *By Faith Alone*, pp. 208, 209.

11. Norman R. Gulley, "The 1888 'MOVEMENT' Understood Within its Historical Context," pp. 1, 2.

12. General Conference of Seventh-day Adventists, *The Story of Our Church*, pp. 246, 247.

13. A. V. Olson, *Through Crisis to Victory* 1888-1901, p. 7.

14. LeRoy E. Froom, *Movement of Destiny*, pp. 370, 369.

15. Marjorie Lewis Lloyd, *Too Slow Getting Off* (Washington, D. C.: Review and Herald, 1973) p. 19.

16. A. L. White, *The Lonely Years*, p. 396.

17. Steve Wohlberg, *The 1888 Message for the Year 2000*, pp. 22, 108.

18. George R. Knight, *A User–Friendly Guide to the 1888 Message*, pp. 115, 147, 182, 148-150 (all italics in the original). In regards to the charge of "denominational rejection," Robert Wieland and Donald Short stated in response: "[We] have never declared that 'the denomination' rejected the beginning of the latter rain. [We] have only cited Ellen White evidence that *the leadership* rejected it, and 'in a great degree' kept it away from the church at large so that 'the denomination' never had a proper chance to accept it (cf. 1 *SM* 234,235)" (*1888 Re-examined*, p. 173).

19. Gerhard Pfandl, "Minneapolis, 1888: An Adventist Watershed," *Adventist World— NAD*, Jan. 2010, p. 39.

20. George R. Knight, *A User-Friendly Guide to the 1888 Message*, p. 145.

21. LeRoy E. Froom, *Movement of Destiny*, p. 369.

22. *Ibid.*; and George R. Knight, A User–Friendly Guide, p. 182; A. V. Olson, Through Crisis to Victory, p. 38; A. L. White, The Lonely Years, p. 396.

23. G. I. Butler to Ellen G. White, Aug. 23, 1886, and Oct. 1, 1888; in *Manuscripts and Memories*, p. 21, 98, emphasis supplied.

24. "Interview with J. S. Washburn, at Hagerstown, Md., June 4, 1950," p. 2.

25. A. G. Daniells, *Christ Our Righteousness*, pp. 47, 50-51, emphasis supplied.

26. R. T. Nash, *An Eyewitness Report*, p. 4, emphasis supplied. See also *Manuscripts and Memories*, p. 352.

27. C. McReynolds, "Experience While at the General Conference in Minneapolis, Minn. in 1888," Document File 189; in *Manuscripts and Memories*, pp. 341, 342, emphasis supplied.

28. Taylor G. Bunch, *The Exodus and Advent Movements*, p. 90, emphasis supplied.

29. A. T. Jones to C. E. Holmes, May 12, 1921; in *Manuscripts and Memories*, p. 328, emphasis supplied.

30. Ellen G. White to O. A. Olsen, Letter 116, Aug. 27, 1890; in *1888 Materials*, p. 703, emphasis supplied.

31. Ellen G. White Manuscript 2, Sept. 7, 1888; in *1888 Materials*, pp. 49, 50, emphasis supplied.

32. Ellen G. White to G. I. Butler, Letter 21, Oct. 14, 1888; in *1888 Materials*, p. 86, emphasis supplied.

33. Ellen G. White, "Morning Talk," Oct. 18, 1888, *Review and Herald*, Oct. 8, 1889; in *1888 Materials*, p. 117, emphasis supplied.

34. Ellen G. White, "Morning Talk," Oct. 19, 1888, *Signs of the Times*, Nov. 11, 1889; in *1888 Materials*, p. 120, emphasis supplied.

35. Ellen G. White Manuscript 15, Nov. 1888; in *1888 Materials*, pp. 165-166, emphasis supplied. It would seem that the assessment of a messenger from heaven would carry more weight than any other human assessment of our true condition.

36. Ellen G. White to Mary White, Letter 82, Nov. 4, 1888; in *1888 Materials*, p. 183, emphasis supplied.

37. Ellen G. White Manuscript 24, Dec. 1888; in *1888 Materials*, p. 225, emphasis supplied.

38. Ellen G. White to Children, Letter 14, May 12, 1889; in *1888 Materials*, pp. 315, 316, emphasis supplied.

39. Ellen G. White to J. Fargo, Letter 50, May 2, 1889; in *1888 Materials*, p. 297, emphasis supplied.

40. Ellen G. White to O. A. Olsen, Letter 20, Oct. 7, 1890; in *1888 Materials*, p. 717, emphasis supplied.

41. Ellen G. White, "Camp-Meeting at Rome, N. Y." *Review and Herald*, Sept. 3, 1889, emphasis supplied.

42. George R. Knight, *A User-Friendly Guide to the 1888 Message*, p. 145.

43. A. T. Jones, "Third Angel's Message No. 9," *General Conference Daily Bulletin*, Feb. 7, 1893, p. 185.

44. A. T. Jones, "Third Angel's Message No. 11," *General Conference Daily Bulletin*, Feb. 13, 1893, pp. 243-244.

45. E. J. Waggoner, "Organization Talks," *The Daily Bulletin*, Feb. 26, 1899, p. 86.

46. Ellen G. White, "Morning Talk," Oct. 18, 1888, *Review and Herald*, Oct. 8, 1889; in *1888 Materials*, p. 117, emphasis supplied.

47. Ellen G. White to G. I Butler, Letter 21, Oct. 14, 1888; in *1888 Materials*, p. 95, emphasis supplied.

48. Ellen G. White Manuscript 8, Oct. 20, 1888; in *1888 Materials*, p. 124, emphasis supplied.

49. Ellen G. White Manuscript 15, Nov. 1888; in *1888 Materials*, p. 164, emphasis supplied.

50. Ellen G. White Manuscript 21, Nov. 1888; in *1888 Materials*, p. 181, emphasis supplied.

51. Ellen G. White Manuscript 24, Dec. 1888; in *1888 Materials*, p. 212, emphasis supplied.

52. Ellen G. White Manuscript 22, "Diary Entries," Jan/Feb. 1890; in *1888 Materials*, p. 579, emphasis supplied.

53. Ellen G. White to Uriah Smith, Letter 40, Dec. 31, 1890; in *1888 Materials*, pp. 795-796, emphasis supplied. To make the mistake of the Jews is a fatal mistake: "The greatest deception of the human mind in Christ's day was that a *mere assent* to the truth constitutes righteousness. In all human experience a *theoretical knowledge* of the truth has been proved to be insufficient for the saving of the soul. ... He who desires to know the truth must be willing to accept all that it reveals. ... To be wavering and halfhearted in allegiance to truth is to choose the darkness of error and satanic delusion" (Ellen G. White, *Desire of Ages*, pp. 309, 312-313). And truth must be practiced: "But truth is not truth to those who do not practice it. Truth is only truth to you when you live it in daily life, showing the world what those people must be who are at last saved" (Ellen G. White, *General Conference Bulletin*, April 3, 1901, p. 24).

54. During the summer of 1882, Ellen White wrote a Testimony of appeal while in Healdsburg, California, requesting it be read at all the campmeetings in the area. In her appeal, she admonished Church members to have a real connection with Christ, not just an assent: "There is a wide difference between a pretended union and a real connection with Christ by faith. A *profession* of the truth places men in the church, but this does not prove that they have a *vital connection* with the living Vine. A rule is given by which the true disciple may be distinguished from those who claim to follow Christ but have not faith in Him. The one class are fruit bearing, the other, fruitless" (*Testimonies*, vol. 5, pp. 228-229, emphasis supplied). Only a few months before the Minneapolis Conference, Ellen White delineated the difference between one's profession and ones true condition: "Spiritual death has come upon the people that should be manifesting life and zeal, purity and consecration, by the most earnest devotion to the cause of truth. The facts concerning the *real condition* of the professed people of God, speak more loudly than *their profession*, and make it evident that some power has cut the cable that anchored them to the Eternal Rock, and that they are drifting away to sea, without chart or compass. What is to be done? The True Witness points out the only remedy" ("How Do We Stand?" *Review and Herald*, July 24, 1888, emphasis supplied).

55. Although it is very clear that a majority rejected the message at Minneapolis, it might be well for us to remember that while only a minority of the angels in heaven (one third) rebelled and followed Satan, this universe is still dealing with the results of that rebellion.

56. Ellen G. White Manuscript 9, "Morning Talk," Oct. 24, 1888; in *1888 Materials*, p. 151, emphasis supplied.

# CHAPTER 7

# *Return to Battle Creek*

## *The Religious Liberty Crisis in America and in the Church*

Many revivals occurred following the Minneapolis General Conference as the message sent from heaven was presented to the people. Nevertheless, continued opposition to Jones and Waggoner and Ellen White greatly hindered the work and finally turned back the abundant outpouring of the Holy Spirit. J. H. Morrison and some of the other delegates to the Conference left early and returned to Battle Creek with "high colored reports" of a "discouraging character."[1] They reported that A. T. Jones "was a crank, and it seemed as though it would break their hearts to have the people think otherwise." Many believed in the "infallibility doctrine of the Battle Creek authors" Uriah Smith, G. I. Butler, and others, and could not see the possibility of these men being on the wrong side of the controversy.[2]

Upon returning to Battle Creek, Ellen White learned of the many reports that had been brought back from Minneapolis leading the people to believe that "'Sister White must be a changed woman'" and that her testimony had "'changed in its character.'" Speaking to the people in a meeting at Battle Creek, she was given opportunity to make her "position plain, but not a word of response came from the men who should have stood with [her]. ... Not one ventured to say, 'I am with you, Sister White. I will stand by you.'" Although "several shook hands" with her following the meeting and were relieved to hear "the truth of the matter," there were "quite a number who held fast their evil surmisings and clung to the distorted representations made. ... It seemed to be their preference to believe the false reports."[3]* After an absence from Battle Creek, Ellen White would customarily speak at the Tabernacle on her first Sabbath back in town. This she was invited to do, but because "the impressions were so strong" that she had changed, two church elders, brothers Amadon and Sisley, came on Sabbath morning inquiring as to what she planned to speak upon. Ellen White well understood the intent of the question and rebuked the elders, asking as well that A. T. Jones be given a chance to speak "the message given him of God":

> "Brethren, you leave that matter with the Lord and Sister White, for neither the Lord nor Sister White will need to be dictated to by the brethren as to what subject she will bring before them. I am at home in Battle Creek... and we ask not permission to take the desk in the tabernacle. I take it as my rightful position accorded me of God. But there is Brother Jones, who cannot feel as I do, and who will wait an invitation from you. You should do your duty in regard to this matter and open the way before him."

> The elders stated they did not feel free to invite him to speak until they had consulted Brother Smith to know whether he would sanction it, for Elder Smith was older than they. I said, "Then do this at once, for time is precious and there is a message to come to this people and the Lord requires you to open the way."[4]

After nearly a week with no invitation for Jones to speak to the people, Ellen White sent for the elders of the church to ask the reason for the delay. "Prescott, Amadon, and Sicily [*sic*] brought a united testimony" that brother Smith had "'decided it would not be best to ask [Jones] because he took strong positions, and carried the subject of national reform too far.'" Smith felt that "Jones was rather extravagant in his expressions, and took an extreme view, and he hardly thought it best to ask him to speak." Upon hearing their response, Ellen White "felt deeply stirred with indignation at the persistent efforts to close the door to every ray of heaven's light." She bore "a very plain testimony" for about fifteen minutes, and it was "pointed and earnest as [she] had ever made in [her] life." "She told them her mind quite fully about that sort of planning":[5]*

> I answered, Well, if Elder Smith takes that position God will surely remove him out of the way, for God has not given him the authority to say what shall come into the tabernacle from our own people and what shall not. But if he holds that position we will secure a hall in the city and the words God has given Bro. Jones to speak the people shall have them.[6]

> I told them a little of how matters had been carried [on] at Minneapolis, and stated the position I had taken, that Pharisaism had been at work leavening the camp here at Battle Creek, and the Seventh-day Adventist churches were affected. ...
>
> [S]piritual weakness and blindness were upon the people who had been blessed with great light and precious opportunities and privileges. As reformers they had come out of the denominational churches, but they now act a part similar to that which the churches acted [in 1844]. We hoped that there would not be the necessity for another coming out.[7]

As if trying to keep Jones out of the Tabernacle were not enough, "arrangements were made to shut him out of the school for fear something should come in that would be at variance with what [had] been taught." In April of 1888, the General Conference Committee had suggested the appointment of A. T. Jones to teach at Battle Creek College,[8] "and although he came East with the expectation of teaching in the College, it looked as though there was to be no place given him." When the resolution to restrict what could be taught at the College failed to pass at the Minneapolis Conference, the school Board of Trustees, led by Uriah Smith, realized "they had taken no formal action about having A. T. [Jones] teach." Thus, "they voted to employ U. Smith and F. D. Starr to teach the Biblical course" instead.

Not long after, however, the General Conference Committee suggested that F. D. Starr go to Indiana because they were "in a great straight for a man," and once again advised the College to "have a talk with Jones" since he had come east by their advice. A special committee of three, made up of G. I. Butler, Uriah Smith, and W. W. Prescott (President of the Battle Creek College), had a "long conference with Eld. Jones," and what a conference it was. The committee insisted that he assure them "in a very positive manner that if he should be employed to assist in the Lectures he would not knowingly teach any opinions contrary to those which the Board desired to be taught."[9] What they had failed to pass by resolution at Minneapolis, they now imposed upon Jones directly.

Ellen White was incensed at such actions. A short time later, she asked if all the attempts to keep Jones out of the school and the Tabernacle were "inspired by the Spirit of God?" Her answer: "Certainly there was not the spirit of inspiration upon you from God, but from another source." This situation led her to muse: "How few comprehend or try to ascertain the mysteries of the rejection of the Jews and the calling of the Gentiles."[10]

## *Religious Liberty*

Ellen White's fifteen-minute talk with the Elders of the Tabernacle was not without results. Brother Amadon "stirred around, and gave out appointments for Sabbath, & Sunday evenings," so Jones could speak at the Tabernacle. According to W. C. White, Jones spoke on religious liberty and "did real well." Several prominent citizens were there, including a Judge Graves, and Ed. Nichols, who were "much pleased." Jones' presentations were printed in the Battle Creek *Daily Journal* and "2300 of the Journals" were given out.[11] Because of the interest created, Jones was allowed to continue his presentations at the Tabernacle. While leaders in the Church spoke derogatorily of Jones' message and his style of presentation, a worldly paper praised him for both. The Battle Creek *Daily Journal* described his third meeting as such:

> The very large and deeply attentive audiences which have attended these lectures are as indicative of the great interest taken in them by our citizens, as they are complimentary of the able and eloquent manner in which the subject has been presented. Mr. Jones in his third lecture spoke over two hours, holding his audience in breathless attention throughout.[12]

The following week, Jones accompanied Ellen White to Porterville, Michigan, where meetings were held November 22 through 27. Ellen White had been invited by Brother Van Horn and was happy to attend hoping that by her presence the prejudice against Jones and Waggoner would be removed. During the morning meetings "when only our brethren were present," Ellen White spoke very plainly about the Minneapolis Conference, "stating the light the Lord had been pleased to give [her] in warnings and reproof for His people." She warned the brethren of the danger of becoming "dwarfs in spiritual things" because they were placing their trust "upon one man"—G. I. Butler. The men were separating themselves from God, by giving homage to human beings. Ellen White also spoke of the atmosphere that had surrounded them by their laughing, jesting, and joking.[13]

A. T. Jones gave three discourses at Porterville similar to the ones presented at Battle Creek, "two of which related to our nation, with the impending issues relating to church and state, and the warning—the third angel's message—that must be given to our people." Although I. D. Van Horn reported in the *Review* that there was "no manifestation of levity or lightness" and that Ellen White's testimony each day, "evidently dictated by the Spirit of God, added much to the interest and power of the meeting,"[14] her assessment was much different. Speaking in latter rain language, she stated plainly that their course at Minneapolis "was cruelty to the Spirit of God" and "begged them to stop just where they were." She had hoped that the Porterville meetings would make a difference, "but the position of Elder Butler and Elder Smith influenced them to make no change but stand where they did. No confession was made. The blessed meeting closed. Many were strengthened, but doubt and darkness enveloped some closer than before. The dew and showers of grace from heaven which softened many hearts did not wet their souls."[15]

Ellen White had a good reason to be concerned. Throughout the 1880s, Sunday legislation and persecution for Sunday law violation had grown in strength and scope, but now, at a time when Seventh-day Adventists should be keenly interested in such topics, many were busy quibbling over doctrines and ignoring the religious liberty issues at stake.

Between 1885 and 1887, nearly twenty Sabbath keepers in Arkansas alone had been charged with Sunday desecration and fined up to $500 each. In 1887, the Prohibition Party and the Women's Christian Temperance Union sided with the National Reform Association in its drive to establish Sunday laws as a means of improving American morality. In early 1888 the well-known Roman Catholic Cardinal James Gibbons joined forces with many Protestants in endorsing a petition to Congress on behalf of national Sunday legislation. This Sunday movement peaked on May 21, 1888, when Senator H. W. Blair introduced a bill into the United States Senate to promote the observance of "the Lord's day… as a day of religious worship." Only a few days later, Blair submitted a proposal to amend the United States Constitution and Christianize the nation's public school system. This was the first such legislation to go before Congress since the establishment of the Advent movement in the 1840s.[16]

Amidst these monumental movements, which were seen as fulfillments of Bible prophecy, one of the greatest controversies in the history of the Adventist church had taken place in Minneapolis. There, "the manifestations of the Holy Spirit," which would prepare a people to stand during such times, "were attributed to fanaticism."[17] Ellen White had spoken pointedly at the Conference: "Because the ideas of some are not exactly in accordance with their own on every point of doctrine… the great question of the nation's religious liberty, now involving so much, is to many a matter of little consequence."[18] Seeing the opposition against Jones and Waggoner as a result of the Minneapolis controversy greatly disturbed Ellen White as well. Because both men were so actively involved in the Church's religious liberty work, prejudice against them would likely spill over into this important work.

Both Jones and Waggoner were co-editors of the *American Sentinel* (the Church's monthly religious liberty magazine that began in 1886), and were presumably the most active and well-versed writers and teachers on the subject. Both men had been asked to read over Ellen White's new edition of the *Great Controversy* to "give careful criticism and corrections" before its printing in 1888.[19]*

Not only that, but Jones' preaching on the subject received a good response from "prominent citizens" when he presented at the Tabernacle. As the first Adventist to stand before the United States Senate (testifying before the Committee on Education and Labor against the Blair Sunday Bill on December 13, 1888), his efforts were just as praiseworthy. Although Jones was basically self-educated, having never had the opportunity to attend an Adventist school as a student, his defense of freedom of conscience and religious liberty before the Senate was impressive. The arguments he presented were similar to those shared at the Tabernacle, but during the ninety minutes he was allowed to speak, he was interrupted by the Chairman alone (Senator Blair), one hundred and sixty-nine times. Yet the Lord gave Jones words to speak, and the legislation died with the expiration of the fiftieth Congress.[20]*

## *Week of Prayer Revival*

Only two days after Jones' appearance before the U. S. Senate, he returned to Battle Creek to participate with Ellen White in Week of Prayer meetings, which were scheduled from December 15 to 22. Prior to the Week of Prayer, Ellen White gave warnings from the pulpit of the Tabernacle and through the pages of the *Review* of the "approaching crisis." She lamented that it had not been "in the order of God that light" had been kept from the people; "the very present truth which they needed" for that time. The outpouring of the Spirit of God, which was to prepare them for such a crisis, was being held at bay, which was to prepare them for such a crisis. She understood the lack of readiness on the part of the people of God, and that many had "sat in calm expectation of this event" for years. It was a time for "action, not for indolence and spiritual stupor":

> A great crisis awaits the people of God. Very soon our nation will attempt to enforce upon all, the observance of the first day of the week as a sacred day. … [T]here must be, among God's commandment-keeping people, more spirituality and a deeper consecration to God. …

> Unless you arise to a higher, holier attitude in your religious life you will not be ready for the appearing of our Lord. … As great light has been given them, God expects proportionate zeal, devotion, and faithfulness upon the part of his people. But there will be proportionate darkness, unbelief, and blindness as the truth is not appreciated and acted upon. …

> If our people continue in the listless attitude in which they have been, God cannot pour upon them his Spirit. They are unprepared to cooperate with him. They do not realize the threatened danger, and are not awake to the situation. …

> The third angel's message comprehends more than many suppose. What interpretation do they give to the passage which says an angel descended from heaven, and the earth was lightened with his glory? This is not a time when we can be excused for inactivity. …

> The people need to be aroused in regard to the dangers of the present time. The watchmen are asleep. We are years behind.[21]*

In a sermon delivered at Battle Creek on December 8, Ellen White pleaded with the people to "get ready for the week of prayer by humbling [their] hearts before God." She warned that they were "drawing near the close of probation" and there was a great work to do for God. The time had come when the people's attention was to be called "to the sanctuary in heaven." She exclaimed that God was "working for his people" that they "would not be left in darkness." He would have their eyes anointed that they might "discern between the workings of the powers of darkness and the movings of the Spirit of God."[22]

In an article printed for the Week of Prayer, Ellen White wrote of the coming crisis and told the people plainly: "We have been asleep, and our lamps are going out. ... The Laodicean message is applicable to the people of God at this time. They are saying, 'I am rich, and increased with goods, and have need of nothing.'" She warned the brethren of the "grievous sin" of Pharisaism that had come into their midst which was leading them to feel "that we are righteous, and all our acts are meritorious, when we are far from cherishing the right spirit toward God or toward our brethren." In their resistance to the message brought by Jones and Waggoner, they had been "making a man an offender for a word."[23]

As the Week of Prayer began, Ellen White tried to arouse the attention of the brethren to what their true feelings were in regard to Jones and Waggoner and their work being done for religious liberty. Regardless of their claims, their actions spoke louder than words. The warnings in the *American Sentinel* had not influenced the people as they should have, because there had not been a united recommendation by those in leadership positions. As a result, the church was "far behind in making preparations for the work," and as a result, God's blessings had "been withdrawn":

> Much might have been done with the *Sentinel*, if counter-influences had not been at work to hinder it. Even though nothing may be said against it, actions reveal the indifference that is felt in regard to it. ...
>
> The *Sentinel* has been, in God's order, one of the voices sounding the alarm, that the people might hear, and realize their danger, and do the work required at the present time. ... The voice of the True Witness has been heard in reproof, but has not been obeyed. ...

Let every worker for God comprehend the situation, and place the *Sentinel* before our churches, explaining its contents, and urging home the warnings and facts it contains. ... Let not unsanctified feelings lead anyone to resist the appeals of the Spirit of God.

The word of God is not silent in regard to this momentous time, and it will be understood by all who do not resist his Spirit. ...The Lord's messages of light have been before us for years, but there have been influences working indirectly to make of no effect the warnings coming through the *Sentinel* and the "Testimonies," and through other instrumentalities which the Lord sends to his people. Stand not in the way of this light.[24]

J.O. CORLISS

Such appeals, delivered through the pages of the *Review*, along with messages given during the Week of Prayer, began to produce results. Ellen White, A. T. Jones and J. O. Corliss "labored earnestly, speaking at the sanitarium in the early morning, and at the office chapel... and at the tabernacle." Jones spoke on the current issue of the religious amendment, but according to Ellen White, the "principal topic dwelt upon was justification by faith, and this truth came as meat in due season upon the people of God. The living oracles of God were presented in new and precious light." The message given was "not alone the commandments of God—a part of the third angel's message—but [also] the faith of Jesus, which comprehends more than is generally supposed." Thus Ellen White could joyfully proclaim: "The truth as it is in Jesus, accompanied by divine energy, has been brought before the people, and we have reason to praise God."[25]*

The message of righteousness by faith was recognized as having greater significance because it was presented in the context of religious liberty and freedom of conscience, the very foundation upon which God's government is based. The "Holy Spirit" revealed the "deep significance" of these truths as they were related to "new and startling movements in the development of the Religious Amendment to the Constitution." This gave the meetings "more than usual interest as the application of prophecy was plainly made" to their own time.[26]

The message borne "had a wonderful effect on those that heard it. There were many not of our faith who were deeply stirred with the importance of doing something and doing it now, in the struggle for religious freedom." Ellen White could candidly proclaim: "God has sent messengers [Jones and Waggoner] who have studied their Bibles to find what is truth, and studied the movements of those who are acting their part in fulfilling prophecy in bringing about the religious amendment. ... And shall no voice be raised of direct warning to arouse the churches to their danger?" She saw the time was soon coming when those not of our faith would, as a result of this message, "come to the front, gird themselves with the whole armor of God, and exalt [His] law, adhere to the faith of Jesus, and maintain the cause of religious liberty."[27]*

BATTLE CREEK SANITARIUM

Because of the interest created by the Week of Prayer meetings, even among visitors and patients at the Sanitarium, the meetings were continued a fourth week. Writing a short time later about the experience, Ellen White expressed joy at the sight of heaven's light shining upon the people, and the positive results:

Many have sought the Lord with confession of sins and contrition of soul. ... Those who have hitherto been almost destitute of faith have discerned its simplicity, and have been enabled to lay hold of the promises of God. ... [T]heir faith was directed to Christ, our Righteousness. ...

Meetings were held in the College which were intensely interesting. The Spirit of the Lord wrought upon hearts, and there was a precious work done in the conversion of souls. There has been no excitement felt or manifested. The work has been accomplished by the deep movings of the Spirit of God. ... As one after another

BATTLE CREEK COLLEGE

of these students of Battle Creek College, hitherto ignorant of the truth and of the saving grace of God, espoused the cause of Christ, what joy was there in the heavenly courts... and gratitude to God [was] expressed by the workers. ...

Meetings were held in the ... Sanitarium Hospital. ... There were many whose minds had been clouded with doubt, but the light received from the explanation of Scripture encouraged their faith, while the truth was revealed to their minds and hearts in a light in which they had never before seen it. They... realized something of how dishonoring to their Maker was their unbelief. ... [W]e deeply regretted that [the meetings] could not have been longer continued. ...

Meetings were held with the workers of the publishing house. ... Many good testimonies were borne, and it made my heart glad to see those who had been connected with the publishing work for a period of thirty years, rejoice as young converts rejoice in their first love. They expressed their gladness and gratitude of heart for the sermons that had been preached by Bro. A. T. Jones; they saw the truth, goodness, mercy, and love of God as they never before had seen it. They humbled their hearts, confessed their sins, and removed everything that had separated their souls from God, and the Lord had put a new song into their mouth, even praises unto his name. ... O, how we long to have every soul come out into the liberty of the sons of God! Will any of these who have tasted of the Bread of Life ever loathe the manna that has been so sweet to their souls at these meetings?[28]

W.W.PRESCOTT

It was thus that the "blessings of that Week of Prayer extended through the church. Confessions were made. Those who had robbed God in tithes and offerings confessed their wrong and made restitution, and many were blessed of God who had never felt that God had forgiven their sins. All these precious fruits evidenced the work of God."[29] Even some that had so recently been fighting against the messengers God had sent began to recognize their sin. During one of the Week of Prayer meetings, W. W. Prescott arose to give a testimony. He "attempted to speak, but his heart was too full. There he stood five minutes in complete silence, weeping. When he did speak he said, 'I am glad to be a Christian.' He made very pointed remarks. His heart seemed to be broken by the Spirit of the Lord."[30]

Seeing the President of the College in such a state of contrition had an affect on others. Ellen White "invited those who had not accepted the truth, and those who had not the evidence of their acceptance with God, to come forward. It seemed that the whole company were on the move." That night "many more bore precious testimonies that the Lord had forgiven their sins and given them a new heart. The words of truth spoken by Elder Jones had been blessed to their souls."[31]

One of the brethren who had been personally present during the Week of Prayer, described Jones' consecrated labors during the meetings: "Bro. A. T. Jones has been doing most of the preaching. I wish you could have heard some of his sermons. ... Some of his sermons are as good, I think, as I ever heard. They are all new too. He is original in his preaching and in his practical preaching seems very tender and deeply feels all he says."[32] It is no wonder that Ellen White declared: "God... has given these men [Jones and Waggoner] a work to do, and a message to bear which is present truth for this time. ... [W]herever this message comes its fruits are good."[33]

## *Grieved the Spirit of God*

It would be nice if we could end this chapter here, but history does not allow us to do so. Even though many people in Battle Creek were receiving blessings from heaven through the labors of Jones and Waggoner, opposition was still running high. Ellen White could rejoice that "at last an opening was made for Brother Jones, but it was not pleasant to fight every inch for any privileges and advantages to bring the truth before the people." As the Week of Prayer began, Ellen White "longed to hear those who had considered it a virtue to brace themselves against light and evidence, acknowledge the movings of the Spirit of God, cast away their unbelief, and come to the light." She knew that "unless they did this their path would become darker, for light unconfessed and unacknowledged and unimproved becomes darkness to those who refuse it." The longer they waited to acknowledge the light which they had scorned, the harder it would be "for them to go back and gather up the rays. ... The first step taken in the path of unbelief and rejection of light is a dangerous thing":

> There was precious truth and light presented before the people, but hearts that were obdurate received no blessing. They could not rejoice in the light which, if accepted, would have brought freedom and peace and strength and courage and joy to their souls. ...[34]* God was at work, but those who had been pursuing a course of their own devising... felt more confirmed and determined to resist. What shall we name this element? It is rebellion, as in the days of Israel. ...

> The Lord wrought in our midst, but some did not receive the blessing. They had been privileged to hear the most faithful preaching of the gospel, and had listened to the message God had given His servants to give them, with their hearts padlocked. They did not turn unto the Lord... but used all their powers to pick some flaws in the messengers and in the message, and they grieved the Spirit of God. ...
>
> A woe is pronounced upon all such unbelief and criticism as was revealed in Minneapolis and as was revealed in Battle Creek. ... Evidence at every step that God was at work has not changed the manifest attitude of those who in the very beginning pursued a course of unbelief which was an offense to God. With this barrier they themselves had erected, they—like the Jews—were seeking something to strengthen their unbelief and make it appear they were right. ...
>
> Stand out of the way, Brethren. Do not interpose yourselves between God and His work. If you have no burden of the message yourselves, then prepare the way for those who have the burden of the message. ...
>
> Satan is doing his utmost to have those who believe present truth deceived... that those who have accepted unpopular truth, who have had great light and great privileges, shall have the spirit that will pervade the world. Even if it is in a less degree, yet it is the same principle that when it has a controlling power over minds, leads to certain results. ... The result is the same as with the Jews—fatal hardness of heart.[35]

At the very heart of the work in Battle Creek, there was opposition to heaven-sent light.[36]* Instead of the brethren preparing the way for the loud cry and latter rain, they were interposing themselves between God and His work. The very spirit which leads worldly men to pass laws that restrict liberty of conscience, was also active in the Seventh-day Adventist Church. Unless something changed, the result would be fatal hardness of heart.

We can be thankful that even though the Spirit of God was grieved at Minneapolis, and at Battle Creek, the Lord did not give up on His church. Unbelief, criticism and resistance were prevalent among the leading brethren, yet the people scattered across the country must have a chance to hear the most precious message. We will take a look at the results of hearing and receiving that message in the next chapters.

# Chapter 7 Footnotes

1. W. C. White to O. A. Olsen, Nov. 27, 1888; in *Manuscripts and Memories*, p. 129.

2. W. C. White to J. H. Waggoner, Feb. 27, 1889; in *Manuscripts and Memories*, p. 136.

3. Ellen G. White Manuscript 30, June 1889, "Experience Following Minneapolis Conference"; in *1888 Materials*, pp. 354-355. A footnote was added to Manuscript Release No. 1216 as found in *1888 Materials*, page 354, that seeks to lessen Ellen White's description of the impact of this event. It would seem that the reader is encouraged, rather than taking Ellen White's word for it, to read portions of A. V. Olson's *Through Crisis to Victory: 1888-1901*, whose title speaks for itself. It must be remembered, however, that A. V. Olson died in 1963, three years before his book was published, at which time it came under the sponsorship of the Ellen G. White Estate Board, with A. L. White as Secretary.

4. *Ibid.*, pp. 355-356.

5. See: Ellen G. White to R. A. Underwood, Letter 22, Jan. 18, 1889, and Manuscript 30, June, 1889, and Ellen G. White to Uriah Smith, Letter 20, Jan. 6, 1891; in *1888 Materials*, pp. 241, 356, 847. See also: W. C. White to Mary White, Nov. 24, 1888; in *Manuscripts and Memories*, p. 127. This is a perfect example of those who were fighting against Jones because they felt he was an extremist when it came to national reform or religious liberty issues, and of Ellen White's unquestionable support. Similar accusations are leveled against Jones today by those who claim he was an extremist in every area of the religious liberty work. But Ellen White did not support Smith's accusations in 1888, nor would it seem she would support those today who misrepresent all his work as bad.

6. Ellen G. White to Uriah Smith, Letter 20, Jan. 6, 1891; in *1888 Materials*, pp. 847, 848.

7. Ellen G. White Manuscript 30, June, 1889; in *1888 Materials*, pp. 356-357.

8. "Minutes of the General Conference Committee," Fifteenth Meeting, April 5, 1888.

9. W. C. White to Mary White, Nov. 24, 1888; in *Manuscripts and Memories*, pp. 126-127; and "Battle Creek College Board Minutes," Nov. 22, 25, 1888.

10. Ellen G. White Manuscript 16, Jan. 1889; in *1888 Materials*, p. 259.

11. W. C. White to Mary White, Nov. 24, 1888; in *Manuscripts and Memories*, p. 127.

12. Battle Creek *Daily Journal*, Dec. 11, 1888, p. 3.

13. Ellen G. White Manuscript 30, June, 1889; in *1888 Materials*, pp. 357-359.

14. I. D. Van Horn, "The Michigan State Meeting," *Review and Herald Extra*, Dec. 11, 1888, p. 780.

15. Ellen G. White Manuscript 30, June, 1889; in *1888 Materials*, p. 360.

16. For background information on these events see: A. T. Jones, *The Sentinel Library*, Sept. 15, 1889; W. A. Blakely, *American State Papers Bearing on Sunday Legislation*, (Washington, D. C.: The Religious Liberty Association, 1911); Eric Syme, *A History of SDA Church-State Relations in the United States* (Mountain View, CA.: Pacific Press, 1973).

17. Ellen G. White to O. A. Olsen, Letter 81, May 31, 1896; in *1888 Materials*, p. 1565.

18. Ellen G. White Manuscript 24, Dec. 1888; in *1888 Materials*, p. 210.

19. W. C. White to C. H. Jones, May 18, 1887; in A. L. White, *The Lonely Years*, p. 438. It is likely that Jones or Waggoner wrote notes regarding current events in religious liberty which were included in the appendix of the 1888 edition of *The Great Controversy*. On page 565, Ellen White states that "Catholicism is gaining ground upon every side." A footnote refers the reader to the appendix for added information. On page 573, Ellen White states that "in the movements now in progress in the United States to secure for the institutions and usages of the church the support of the State, Protestants are following in the steps of the papists." Again the reader is referred to the appendix for added information that was not found in *Spirit of Prophecy*, Vol. 4, 1884 edition. According to the White Estate, Jones or Waggoner most likely wrote these appendix notes. Both notes were removed in the 1911 edition, probably because they no longer represented current events. The point is that the 1888 edition of *The Great Controversy* was produced for that very time (1888), to alert its readers to what was taking place in the United States and around the world. Ellen White was confident enough in the work of Jones and Waggoner that she allowed their input to be added to the appendix. It is also a fact that God was sending a most precious message to prepare the Church to share the same message with the world. Sadly, the 1888 edition of the *Great Controversy* ended up sitting idle in the Review and Herald storehouse for nearly two years, primarily as the result of the opposition to the message and the messengers.

20. See: *The Sentinel Library*, Sept. 15, 1889. Is it possible that we Adventists do not realize our indebtedness to God for sending A. T. Jones to the defense of the church, as well as to the nation, in regard to religious liberty? One cannot appreciate Jones' work for religious liberty, however, without first reading his works, many of which have been reprinted (primarily by ministries independent of the organized church). Renewed interest has been developing, however. *Liberty* magazine recently reprinted one of Jones' talks along these lines entitled, "What is Patriotism in the United States," and mailed it to their subscriber list. "Each year NARLA [The North American Religious Liberty Association] presents the A. T. Jones Medal to one of its own who exemplifies the best of Jones' contribution to the field of religious liberty. This includes [a] willingness to speak truth [with] power, applying his or her talents to the practical business of researching, writing, speaking and organizing in the advance of liberty, and displaying through action a dedication to the gospel principle of religious liberty" (http://religiousliberty.info/article.php?id=11, March 10, 2010).

21. Ellen G. White, "The Approaching Crisis," *Review and Herald Extra*, Dec. 11, 1888, p. 4. In *A User-Friendly Guide to the 1888 Message*, George Knight presents the idea that "Seventh-day Adventists did not miss the prophetic significance of the Blair bills." That the "high emotional pitch of the participants at the 1888 General Conference" was largely due to "the fact that Adventists felt … that they already faced the end of time." Thus "it is not difficult to see why some of the Adventist leaders reacted violently and emotionally" to what Jones and Waggoner were presenting (pp. 32-33). Ellen White, however, offers a more balanced perspective. Many Adventists may have been aware intellectually of the events taking place, but the watchmen were "asleep," "unprepared," and did "not realize the threatened danger" (*op. sit.*, p. 4).

22. Ellen G. White, "David's Prayer," Sermon, Dec. 8, 1888, *Review and Herald*, Dec. 18, 1888, pp. 786-787.

23. Ellen G. White, "Our Duties and Obligations," *Review and Herald*, Dec. 18, 1888, pp. 794-795.

24. Ellen G. White, "The American Sentinel and Its Mission," *Review and Herald*, Dec. 18, 1888, p. 791.

25. Ellen G. White, "Revival Work in the Battle Creek Church," *Review and Herald*, Feb. 12, 1889, pp. 106-107. The "1888 message" presented by Jones and Waggoner, was very closely connected with the subject of religious liberty and the work of the Holy Spirit preparing a people to stand in the day of God. The fact that Sunday laws were closer to being enacted than at any other time in American history was a powerful and compelling evidence that God had begun to pour out the latter rain—the message of Christ our righteousness— and that the loud cry was about to go forth with unprecedented power.

26. *Ibid*.

27. Ellen G. White Manuscript 30, June 1889; in *1888 Materials*, pp. 378-379. We must not forget that the great adversary has worked for nearly 1500 years through the Papal church to not only do away with the law of God, but also to trample on the faith of Jesus, augmented by taking away liberty of conscience: "The papacy is well adapted to meet the wants of all these. It is prepared for two classes of mankind, embracing nearly the whole world—those who would be saved by their merits, and those who would be saved in their sins. Here is the secret of its power." The Catholic church has also "anathematized 'those who assert the liberty of conscience and of religious worship,' also 'all such as maintain that the church may not employ force'" (Ellen G. White, *Great Controversy*, pp. 572, 564). The three angels' messages counter such falsehood by proclaiming the commandments of God and the faith of Jesus, and by preserving liberty of conscience for all, of which the Sabbath is a sign.

28. Ellen G. White, "Revival Work in the Battle Creek Church," *Review and Herald*, Feb. 12, 1889, pp. 106-107.

29. Ellen G. White Manuscript 30, June 30, 1889; in *1888 Materials*, p. 367.

30. Ellen G. White Manuscript 25, "Diary," Dec. 1888; in Arthur L. White, *The Lonely Years*, p. 421.

31. *Ibid.*

32. Dan T. Jones to J. W. Watt, Jan. 1, 1889. This description of A. T. Jones is unlike many of those given by modern historians. See Chapter 6, footnote 6.

33. Ellen G. White Manuscript 24, Nov. 1888; in *1888 Materials*, p. 228.

34. This description is almost identical to what Ellen White described in *Early Writings* when the people followed Christ into the most holy place and said: "'My Father, give us Thy Spirit.' Then Jesus would breathe upon them the Holy Ghost. In that breath was light, power, and much love, joy, and peace" (p. 55).

35. Ellen G. White Manuscript 30, June 30, 1889; in *1888 Materials*, pp. 366-369, 378-379, 381.

36. There were other factors in Battle Creek that kept some of the people from hearing and receiving the message presented. A Christmas program had been planned involving many of the young children, dressed in costumes. Ellen White expressed her concern in her diary notes for December 24: "There was much arrangement made in the sanitarium, and a large number were not present [at the Week of Prayer meetings] because of this" (*Manuscript* 25, Dec. 1888, unpublished). Ellen White communicated her concern over the great amount of "time and labor" that was spent in preparation for the program: "While these painstaking efforts were being made to get up the performances, meetings were being held of the deepest interest which should have engaged the attention, and which called for the presence of every soul lest they should lose something of the message the Master had sent to them." Sensing the prophetic time in which they were living, and the present truth message being given, Ellen White urged the teachers to discern the light so they might pass it on to the children: "Oh, let the teachers in the Sabbath school be thoroughly imbued with the spirit of the message for this time, carrying that message into all their labor. ... Labor to save them [children], point them to Jesus who so loved them that He gave His life for them. Repeat to them the precious assurance which God Himself has given to them (Ex. 34:6-7 quoted). ... The Light of the world is shining upon us that we might absorb the divine rays and let this light shine upon others. ... It grieves the heart of Jesus that so many refuse the offers of His mercy and matchless love. ... While the awful guilt and grievous character of sin shall be urged home upon the soul, at the same time the mercy and compassion of God should be clearly presented in Christ giving His life for the sins of the world, thus revealing a love that is measureless. ... Jesus must be presented in simplicity to the children as a sin-pardoning Saviour offering within the veil the blood of His atonement. ... Tell them it is in vain to think they can make themselves better and promise to amend, for this will not remove one spot or stain of sin, but the way to obtain a sense of sin and true repentance is to cast themselves just as they are upon the declared mercy and revealed love of God" (Letter 5, Dec. 26, 1888; *Manuscript Releases*, vol. 19, pp. 300-305).

# CHAPTER 8

# *The 1889 Revivals –1*

## *Revival and Reformation the Result of Accepting the Most Precious Message*

"Time is precious and there is a message to come to this people."[1] So said Ellen White to the elders of the Battle Creek church who had come to question her in December of 1888, about whether to allow Jones to preach in the Tabernacle. With Ellen White's persistence, not only was Jones allowed to speak at the Tabernacle, but also, by arrangement of the General Conference Committee (of which W. C. White was chairman), Jones was able to teach classes at Battle Creek College.

Following the December Week of Prayer meetings held in Battle Creek, Ellen White, A. T. Jones and E. J. Waggoner took the precious message to the churches around the country throughout the coming year. Three Ministerial Institutes were held during the following spring and summer. Jones and Waggoner as the main presenters spoke at several campmeetings during the remainder of the summer along with Ellen White. It was not without a struggle, however, that meetings of one kind or another were held in the local conferences, yet God still sought to pour out the Holy Spirit on His languishing church. The results of all these meetings were published in the *Review* and must be read to be fully appreciated. The General Conference session, held in late October, climaxed the years' activities.

As we take a closer look at these Institutes and campmeetings, we will also need to pay particular attention to the messages given by Jones and Waggoner. Some modern historians have suggested that Jones' and Waggoner's 1888 message began to dramatically change immediately after they left Minneapolis from what they claim is the Reformation gospel—as is understood today by many Evangelicals—to a Roman Catholic view of righteousness by faith.[2]*

## *South Lancaster, Massachusetts*

Meetings in South Lancaster were held January 11 to 22, and according to Ellen White, "the fruits were good." The church was "filled with those who had come to receive benefit from the meetings." Not only were many delegates from the northeastern states present at the meetings, but some new converts also attended. A. T. Jones "labored most earnestly for the people," speaking two and sometimes three times a day. Ellen White said of the power attending the meetings: "We had the same spirit and power that attended the first and second angel's messages. … Earnest discourses have been given in the power and Spirit of God by His servants, in regard to the hope set before us in the gospel. The love of Jesus and the righteousness of Christ have been presented, and they are so plainly seen the mind grasps them by faith. … Oh, this is meat in due season from first to last!"[3] During the meetings, Ellen White had felt burdened lest those gathered there "close their hearts to some of the precious rays of heaven's light" that God was sending them:

> There are many who seem to feel that they have a great work to do themselves before they can come to Christ for his salvation. They seem to think that Jesus will come in at the very last of their struggle, and give them help by putting the finishing touch to their lifework. It seems difficult for them to understand that Christ is a complete Saviour, and able to save to the uttermost all that come unto God by him.[4]

As the message of present truth was presented, however, hearts were melted: "We felt the necessity of presenting Christ as a Saviour who was not afar off, but nigh at hand. … There were many, even among the ministers, who saw the truth as it is in Jesus in a light in which they had never before viewed it. They saw the Saviour as a sin-pardoning Saviour, and the truth as the sanctifier of the soul." As a result many were "convicted in the light of the law as transgressors." They realized that they "had been trusting in their own righteousness," which they now saw "as filthy rags in comparison with the righteousness of Christ." Ellen White described the joy in heaven over such an event:

All through the meetings, as the people sought to draw nearer to God, they brought forth works meet for repentance, by confessing one to another where they had wronged each other by word or act. ...

The very message the Lord has sent to the people of this time was presented in the discourses. ...

Both students and teachers have shared largely in the blessing of God. The deep movings of the Spirit of God have been felt upon almost every heart. The general testimony was borne by those who attended the meeting that they had obtained an experience beyond anything they had known before. ...

I have never seen a revival work go forward with such thoroughness, and yet remain so free from all undue excitement. There was no urging or inviting. The people were not called forward, but there was a solemn realization that Christ came not to call the righteous, but sinners, to repentance. ... We seemed to breathe in the very atmosphere of heaven. Angels were indeed hovering around. ... The Lord had visited his people. And there was joy in heaven among the angels over the repentant sinners that had come back to the Father.[5]

The last Sabbath the meetings were held, A. T. Jones spoke with "great power" during the morning meeting, and Ellen White spoke with "great freedom" in the afternoon. It was a "most precious Sabbath" to their souls:

We felt we were breathing in the heavenly atmosphere, and Christ was indeed found of all those who sought for Him. This is indeed a wonderful outpouring of the Spirit of God, testifying to us what the Lord is willing to do for His people who will believe in Jesus for themselves.[6]

A year later, Ellen White reminded the brethren during a Ministerial Institute what had taken place at South Lancaster. Again she compared it with the power that attended the message in 1844:

Those who were at South Lancaster last winter know that the church and the school were moved upon by the Spirit of God. Nearly every student was swept in by the heavenly current, and living testimonies were given that were not surpassed even by the testimonies of 1844 before the disappointment. Many learned at South Lancaster what it meant to surrender their hearts to God— what it meant to be converted.[7]

Such were the results of the "outpouring of the Spirit of God" upon His people— results that would have taken place to a much greater extent among the leaders at Minneapolis if rebellion had not occured. Looking back a short time later on the experience at South Lancaster and other meetings held during the year, Ellen White recalled the privilege of working with Jones and Waggoner. Unlike the modern characterizations that have been attributed to them during this time of their labors, she described how God's hand was at work:

> I have traveled from place to place, attending meetings where the message of the righteousness of Christ was preached. I considered it a privilege to stand by the side of my brethren [Jones and Waggoner], and give my testimony with the message for the time; and I saw that the power of God attended the message wherever it was spoken. You could not make the people believe in South Lancaster that it was not a message of light that came to them. The people confessed their sins, and appropriated the righteousness of Christ. God has set His hand to do this work.[8]

## *Chicago, Illinois*

At the end of March, Jones traveled to Chicago to meet Ellen White for two weeks of meetings. Unlike the meetings in Lancaster where the people readily accepted the beautiful message, most of those present in Chicago were ministers. And "it was a week before there was a break in the meetings. But, like a wave of glory, the blessings of God swept over." Those attending were "pointed to the lamb of God that taketh away the sin of the world." The "deep movings of the Spirit of God" were felt and like everywhere else the message was presented, it "led to the confession of sin and the putting away of iniquity."[9] Ellen White described these meetings as follows:

> Elder A. T. Jones has labored faithfully to instruct those assembled, and in breaking to their souls the Bread of Life. We have felt sorry that not only every Seventh-day Adventist church but every church, whatever their faith and doctrines, could not have the precious light of truth as it has been so clearly presented. I know it would have been a rich feast to very many souls not of our faith to see the plan of salvation so clearly and simply defined. ...

> We have been earnestly and steadily at work to encourage faith in our brethren. This seemed to be as difficult as to teach a child to take its first steps alone. ... The Holy Spirit has been convicting the hearts of men and women.[10]

We feel deeply grateful for the blessing of God that has come into the meeting here… oh, how hard it was to educate the people to look away from themselves to Jesus and to His righteousness. …

My heart rejoiced as I heard the people acknowledge that they were obtaining an education in faith which they had never had before. … Their souls were free, their sins forgiven, the love of Jesus was in their heart… [making] evident the work of the Holy Spirit and grace of Christ in the soul. The Sabbath came to us as a joy, a blessing. We hailed the Sabbath with grateful hearts as the best Sabbath we had ever enjoyed. …[11]*

Now that the enlightenment of the Spirit of God has come, all seem to be learning fast. … More real good could now be accomplished in one day than in one full week before. … All regret that they have been so long ignorant of what constituted true religion… that it was true religion to depend entirely upon Christ's righteousness, and not upon works of merit.[12]

There were no "outbursts of fanaticism, but rather the peace and joy that [were] born of heaven." Among those who made confessions of sin were some that had stood opposed to the message at Minneapolis. Having now seen the results of the "deep movings of the Spirit of God" on the hearts of new converts, they began to realize some of what they had lost at the General Conference. Even Brother Kilgore saw "the mistakes he made at Minneapolis," weeping and rejoicing over his new experience. Writing about his experience in the *Review* he expressed gratitude for the meetings: "The labors of Sister White and Elder Jones were highly appreciated by our brethren. The clear and forcible elucidation of the truth of justification by faith, as set forth by Brother Jones, was truly meat in due season." Even with the confessions made, however, Ellen White knew that "a far greater number" should have been at the meetings where "Brother Jones [had] patiently instructed the people."[13]*

As the meetings in Chicago came to a close in early April, it was obvious to Ellen White that this message needed to be presented at the large campmeetings during the summer. She had been invited to go to Kansas in May, in order to attend three weeks of workers' meetings followed by a one-week campmeeting. Following the Kansas meetings, she was to attend a campmeeting in Williamsport, Pennsylvania. In a letter to her son, W. C.

White, she expressed her concern that those members in Iowa were going to miss out on the blessing if she was tied up so long in one place, and yet she had received no invitation from Iowa leaders. Why? Brothers Morrison and Nicola had "run the [Iowa] conference" until there was "but little life and soul in it":

> Willie, I am in distress for the poor sheep in Iowa. What have they done that they must be left unvisited? The sin of the shepherd should not be visited upon the sheep. I am pained at heart to think of those who are laboring for the churches in Iowa. Could not the camp meetings be arranged so that Brother A. T. Jones could go with me to Iowa? We could go without the waiting for these blind shepherds to signify their wishes to have us come. You know I told you that the people gave an invitation by a rising vote for me to attend the Iowa camp meeting. I will go if it can be arranged so that Brother Jones can accompany me. ...[14]*

> I think that Elder A. T. Jones should attend our large camp meetings, and give to our people and to outsiders as well the precious subject of faith and the righteousness of Christ. There is a flood of light in this subject, and if he goes to the canvassers' meetings only, how can the light come before the largest number? You cannot expect that any of the canvassers can present this matter in the light in which he presents it.[15]* I think that it is robbing the churches of the light and the message for the present time for him not to attend the camp meetings.

> Let the outsiders understand that we preach the gospel as well as the law, and they will feast upon these truths, and many will take their stand for the truth.[16]

## Ottawa, Kansas

Traveling from Battle Creek on May 6, Ellen White headed for the Ottawa, Kansas, campground where workers' meetings were already in progress. Her desire that A. T. Jones be able to speak had been granted, but she was not even on the grounds "over the first night" before her eyes were opened to "the true condition of things. The leaven of Minneapolis was brought from Iowa and its work was being carried on to make of none effect the labors of Eld. A. T. Jones" and herself.[17] "Several of the brethren came on the ground prepared to oppose the views which Elder Jones was presenting."[18] It was the "enemy of Christ and all righteousness" that had inspired these men to come "equipped to leaven the camp with the very same spirit that was so prominent" at the General Conference.[19]

The "atmosphere was oppressive" and Ellen White's "heart was in so weak a condition that it was difficult for [her] to speak to the people." Her "continual prayer to God" was that he would give her strength mentally, physically and spiritually so she could be a blessing to the people. The "powerful agencies continually at work to oppose those who are sent with messages of warning, reproof, or encouragement" were present there, and the people who "should grow strong by accepting light" would "become weak by refusing it."[20]

The next day, Wednesday, May 8, Ellen White attended the early morning meeting and "bore a decided testimony and entreated all present not to act over Minneapolis, and not to be like those Paul describes in Hebrews 4:2." She "entreated them to humble their hearts before God and put away their sins by repentance and confession, and receive the messages God sends them through His delegated servants." The following morning, she felt she needed to speak to the matter again and be "more explicit." This time she cut straight to the heart:

> I was led out to speak more freely in regard to the conference held in Minneapolis, and the spirit that our brethren brought to that Conference. I felt that it was not enough to longer deal in general terms uttering truths which might be assented to, but that would not cut deep in the fleshy tables of the heart. The work to be done demanded something more than smooth words, for God would put His rebuke upon anything and everything savoring of the same kind of spirit and influence that was brought into Minneapolis—doubts, cavilings, playing upon words, turning aside from the close reproofs of the Spirit of God, and regarding them as idle fables and ridiculing and misrepresenting and quibbling upon words.[21]

Ellen White described what had taken place at Minneapolis, how the men had come "under a delusion, with false impressions upon their minds." She told them that "Jones and Waggoner had presented precious light to the people, but prejudice and unbelief" had barred the hearts "that nothing from this source should find entrance." She related how she was about to leave the Conference when a "messenger" had come and told her to stand by her post. He had taken her to the rooms and shown her what was being said against her, and Jones and Waggoner. She related how "like a flash of lightning" all this had been shown her and how it compared to the treatment of God's people throughout the history of the great controversy. She told how Phariseeism had come into the church, how her work at the Conference had been "disregarded by nearly all," that "rebellion was popular," and that their "course was an insult to the Spirit of God."[22]

Ellen White's straight talk was not without effect. Brother Hall, the President of the Kansas conference, stood to his feet and publicly stated that what Ellen White had said was correct. His "'confidence in the testimonies'" was confirmed for he was in "'one of the very rooms she mentioned.'" He had made the mistake of putting "'implicit confidence'" in the "'ministering brethren,'" looking up to them and trusting what they said.[23]* Brother McReynolds also "bore testimony that the description given by Sister White was true to the letter." He had confessed to Ellen White personally, and now he did so publicly. Unfortunately, the meeting had to close before it "could go any farther."[24]

Ellen White was exhausted. At times she "was greatly depressed in spirit" and would "struggle with weakness" until she stood before the people and was given strength to speak.[25] That Thursday afternoon she spoke again, and those who had come for a blessing were blessed, but those "who were watching to find somebody to pick flaws in, whose hearts were barricaded with unbelief, thought Sister White did not talk with much spirit."[26] Rumors had been afloat since Minneapolis that "'Sister White confessed that in some of her remarks at that meeting she had been in error and had manifested a wrong spirit.'" Her strong statements that morning had shaken some people's confidence in her as well, including J. S. Washburn.[27]

## *J. S. Washburn*

J. S. Washburn was an ordained minister from Iowa, just 26 years of age. He had been at the Minneapolis Conference, and according to his own account, was with the "three-fourths of the workers" who stood against the new light." He had gone to the Minneapolis meeting "prejudiced in favor of the 'old' view of the 'law'" in Galatians and was "in favor of Morrison and Butler." He felt that Jones and Waggoner were "undermining the faith," but he "couldn't understand how such a bad man as ATJ[ones]" could pray like he did. Washburn "said to himself, 'He prays as though he knows the Lord.'"[28]

Washburn was associated with J. H. Morrison, who was not only outspoken against Waggoner at Minneapolis, but also "in his belittling the Spirit of Prophecy." When both he and Morrison had approached Ellen White at Minneapolis, "she would give no counsel, [and] said, 'Brethren, my counsel has no weight in Iowa!'" Later, Washburn "decided to go to her alone" and her "simple answer" to his question seemed to relieve his mind somewhat. J. H. Morrison, however, decided to leave the Minneapolis Conference early, telling Washburn privately: "'they are going to try and force me to acknowledge that I am wrong. So I am leaving.'"[29]

J.S. WASHBURN

During the winter of 1889 Washburn struggled with doubt and discouragement: "'We don't have a prophet! She can't be one [if] those two men [Jones and Waggoner] influence her like that,' he reasoned to himself." Even his evangelistic meetings fell flat. He "lost his crowd" and baptized only four or five from his meetings. Thus his "doubts returned strongly." One night he knelt outside and "prayed desperately." He "reasoned out that if this people keep the commandments of God, they must also have the Spirit of Prophecy. But they couldn't have the latter if the prophet was swayed by two young men to go their way. ... 'If there be a God, let me believe,' he prayed." This was the depth to which Washburn fell after Minneapolis.[30]

Washburn happened to ride on the same train with A. T. Jones on their way to the Kansas meetings. Even though Washburn had "doubts about ATJ being 'straight'" and felt he was "wrong along with EJW[aggoner]," he was much impressed by Jones' recent "victory at Washington" regarding the Blair Sunday

Bill. Having an interest in law and politics himself, Washburn "introduced himself to ATJ somewhat fearfully, [but] found the latter very friendly and kind." Washburn "learned to like him, went up with him to [the Kansas] meeting, spent a week-end with him, [and] went up and down the river with him, talking a great deal."[31]

All seemed to be going well for Washburn at the Kansas meetings until Ellen White arrived and presented at the early morning meetings stating: "'We don't want any of that Minneapolis spirit to come down here. If J. H. M[orrison] and Henry Nicola don't repent and are converted, they'll never be saved!'" Washburn was "shocked to hear her talk so bluntly of their Iowa leaders. 'She's wrong!'" he thought. Washburn was "upset again, and the old doubts returned" with the "Minneapolis spirit." He determined to have a visit with Ellen White and settle the matter once and for all.[32]

Ellen White responded kindly and invited him for a visit. Washburn poured out his concern to Ellen White. He told her that "he had always believed that she was a prophet, but was disturbed about the Minneapolis episode." He thought that Uriah Smith and Morrison "were right." To this Ellen White responded: "'Do you know why J. H. M[orrison] left the Conference early?'" Then she told Washburn "just what J. H. M. had told [him] and the revelation of her apparently superhuman knowledge of that private confidential conversation" between Morrison and himself frightened him. He realized that here was one who had secrets revealed to her:

> EGW told him of her guide in Europe, who had strethced [*sic*] his hands out, and said "There are mistakes being made on both sides in this controversy." Then EGW added that the "law in Galatians" is not the real issue of the conference. The real issue was Righteousness by faith!… "EJW can teach righteousness by faith more clearly than I can," said EGW. "Why, Sister White," [Washburn] said, "do you mean to say that E. J. Waggoner can teach it better than you can, with all your experience?" EGW replied, "Yes, the Lord has given him special light on that question. I have been wanting to bring it out (more clearly), but I could not have brought it out as clearly as he did. But when He did bring it out at Minneapolis, I recognized it."[33]*

Washburn then asked Ellen White whether she was infallible. Her answer: "'of course not… I am just a weak erring human being.'" This led Washburn to ask how he could trust what she wrote or said was "from the Lord." To this Ellen White made "no immediate reply" for what seemed about "five full minutes." Washburn was embarrassed, but when her answer came it "settled him forever as to the Spirit of Prophecy":

> "I haven't had a vision in several years. (Her open visions ceased after the early years, but later had night visions). But I never dare to speak or to write as a testimony unless I know that the Holy Spirit controls my mind."[34]

Washburn went away from his interview with Ellen White "a different man, settled in his confidence in this movement and in its divine guidance through the Spirit of Prophecy."[35*]

## A Breakthrough Finally Comes

Friday morning, May 10, at the Ottawa campground, Ellen White spoke once again "before the people assembled, in reference to Minneapolis and the way [the] brethren treated the servants who the Lord sent to them with the messages of truth." As a result of her talk, "several bore testimony in regard to their experience at the meeting at Minneapolis." And yet, she stated, "we did not seem to break through."

On Sabbath morning A. T. Jones presented the sermon, "Seek ye first the kingdom of God and His righteousness." Although he had already presented twenty times during the course of the campmeeting, he had dwelt largely on the issue of religious liberty. Now, on Sabbath morning, he started a series on the "subject of justification by faith and many received it as light and truth."[36] Jones presented to the hundreds gathered that it was the righteousness of God that they needed, "nothing else will avail":

> We must know, however, where to seek for it and how, because we often seek for it in the wrong places; for instance, as many do, in the law of God, and through keeping it. ... The righteousness of God is in His law, but it is not revealed to men by the law, Rom. 1:16-17, the righteousness of God is revealed in the gospel to men, and not in the law. ...
>
> Galatians 2:21; if "righteousness come by the law then Christ is dead in vain," our own righteousness is all, then, we can get out of the law, and that the righteousness of God can come only by Jesus Christ. What is our righteousness?

Isaiah 64:6. Our righteousness is as filthy rags. We have all sinned and come short of the glory of God. What is sin? When Israel came out of Egypt, they knew not God. ... To make them understand their condition and what sin was ... He took a word meaning "missed the mark.". . . Then the more righteousness of the law a man has the worse he is off—the more ragged is he. ...

It is Christ's obedience that avails and not ours that brings righteousness to us. Well then let us stop trying to do the will of God in our own strength. Stop it all. Put it away from you forever. Let Christ's obedience do it all for you and gain the strength to pull the bow so that you can hit the mark. ...[37]

Although Jones spoke to the fact that the righteousness man needed had to come from Christ and not the law, he in no way belittled the law or the keeping of the commandments. He made it clear that the reason Christ came to earth as an "infant instead of a man" was that he might meet "all the temptations a child meets and never" sin. So it is that "any child can stand in His place and resist in His strength":

Now if righteousness is the gift of God, and comes by the gospel, then what is the use of the law?... In the fact that the law demands perfection lies the hope of all mankind, because if it could overlook a sin to a single degree, no one could ever be free from sin, as the law would never make that sin known, and it could never be forgiven, by which alone man can be saved. The day is coming when the law will have revealed the last sin and we will stand perfect before Him and be saved with an eternal salvation. The perfection of the law of God is that it will show us all our sins, and then a perfect Saviour stands ready to take them all away. When God makes known all our sins it is not to condemn us, but to save us, so it is a token of His love for us.[38]

Ellen White recorded in the *Review* her joy at hearing Jones' sermon presented to the people who were not used to hearing such good news:

At the Kansas meeting my prayer to God was, that the power of the enemy might be broken, and that the people who had been in darkness might open their hearts and minds to the message that God should send them. ... Our good and gracious Lord has been presented before the people clothed in the attributes of Satan. ... Many have been living in an atmosphere of doubt, and it seems almost impossible for them to lay hold on the hope set before them in the gospel of Christ. ...

On Sabbath, truths were presented that were new to the majority of the congregation. Things new and old were brought forth from the treasure-house of God's word. Truths were revealed which the people were scarcely able to comprehend and appropriate. Light flashed from the oracles of God in relation to the law and the gospel, in relation to the fact that Christ is our righteousness, which seemed to souls who were hungry for truth, as light too precious to be received. ... The Lord presented the truth... in clear lines, revealing the fact that Christ alone is the source of all hope and salvation. "In him was life; and the life was the light of men. ... And the Word was made flesh, and dwelt among us. ..."

We thank the Lord with all the heart that we have precious light to present before the people, and we rejoice that we have a message for this time which is present truth.[39]

Not all went well, however: "There were many testimonies borne, testifying that they appreciated the light and truth presented to them. But it seemed difficult for those who had been dwelling in an atmosphere of doubt, to take the position of learners. They would quibble at little points that were of no consequence. The leaven that has wrought in Iowa Conference, was in our midst." Sunday morning, Ellen White bore a "clear, sharp testimony," speaking "in regard to the Christless wicked surmisings and misrepresentations that had been made in Minneapolis." She spoke against the "sin of our doubts and unbelief; that in every congregation Satan had his agents right among us through whom he could work."[40]*

The enemy is at work with those who have placed themselves in doubt and unbelief; and they are not satisfied only to be there themselves, but all the time they are strengthening others in the same line. ... From the light God has given me, there never was any new light that came from heaven but that Satan could find something in it to pick at. And so it is with some of the people of today—they will pick at little things. They want light, but there comes along the enemy just as he did to the men of Nazareth, and although the Spirit of God told them that Jesus was the anointed one... they remained in doubt and unbelief. ...

Now, there has not been any improvement made in human nature since that time. Human nature is human nature still. ...

Now brethren I want to tell you, when the Spirit of God comes into our midst, it will strike the minds that are ready to receive it. But if their minds are not open to receive it, they are all ready to pass judgment upon the messenger and the words spoken. … This is the way it was at Minneapolis.

It is because I know the very same spirit is here, and that we should not give place to it for a moment. … I want to ask you if you are satisfied with your coldness, your unbelief, your backslidings. Have you not had enough of it? If not the devil will give you all you desire. …

We see that we are in no better condition than the Jewish people. …

Christ, when talking to the people of His time, told them that they had blinded their eyes and closed their ears. … Light had been given them, but they would not receive it. Darkness was upon them, and they would come and pick the little flaws, and draw the minds of the people away from the solemn truth that was for them. Now, how will it be with us?… We want to know whether we will have the rich blessing of the Lord resting upon us, and we realize that He sheds His rich light and glory upon us. This is my prayer.[41]

Following the morning meeting, and with her mind still stirred with the events of the past months, Ellen White started a letter to her children. Reflecting on Minneapolis, where "rebellion was popular" and "an insult to the Spirit of God," she told of those who had come to the Kansas meetings "with the very same spirit that was so prominent at Minneapolis." She wrote of the Sabbath sermon presented by A. T. Jones that was "light and truth" to many, but to those "dwelling in an atmosphere of doubt" it was only something to "quibble at." Then, as if writing directly to the doubting brethren, Ellen White questioned: "Think ye not that the heavenly Watcher sees your unbelief and opposition? Think ye not your ridiculing, scoffing words are never to appear before you again? Even the outpouring of the Spirit of God you have treated with contempt, and have passed your unsanctified judgment upon; and when the messages have come to you that you must be converted to God, how you have misunderstood and perverted the meaning of these words."[42]

Thankfully, there was some good news to share as well. At the close of Ellen White's Sunday morning talk, there "was a break in the meeting." Brother Porter, a minister from Iowa, arose to his feet to speak. He had not attended the Minneapolis Conference but had come to the Kansas meeting "'in complete darkness'" and with a "'combative spirit.'" Now he could joyfully say: "'I am converted. I see the light.'" Every point which had been clouded with darkness "'was clear as Eld. A. T. Jones has presented it.'"

After Porter spoke "young Washburn arose and talked quite lengthily. He said when at Minneapolis he was one who thought Sister White's testimony could not be truth when she stated she had had in California no conversation with A. T. Jones and E. J. Waggoner." Washburn boldly told all those gathered there before him: "'I confess this to my shame. I have confessed it to Sister White and I confess it to God. I repent of this everlastingly.'"[43]* Others also arose and gave their testimonies:

> The labors of the Sabbath were not in vain. On Sunday morning there was decided evidence that the Spirit of God was working great changes in the moral and spiritual condition of those assembled. ... precious testimonies were borne by those who had long been in darkness. One brother spoke of the struggle that he had experienced before he could receive the good news that Christ is our righteousness. ...

> One of our young ministering brethren said that he had enjoyed more of the blessing and love of God during that meeting than in all his life before. Another stated that the trials, perplexities, and conflicts which he had endured in his mind had been of such a character that he had been tempted to give up everything... and with tears confessed what relief and blessing had come to his soul. At every social meeting, many testimonies were borne as to the peace, comfort, and joy the people had found in receiving light.[44]

Thus it was with great struggle, as meetings of one kind or another were held across the country, that God sought to pour out the Holy Spirit on His languishing church. Many received great blessings from the meetings, while others continued their persistent rebellion. We will continue our survey of these meetings in the next chapter.

# CHAPTER 8 FOOTNOTES

1.  Ellen G. White Manuscript 30, June 30, 1889; in *1888 Materials*, p. 356.

2.  The idea has been presented for nearly sixty years—since the publication of *Question on Doctrines* in the 1950s—that Jones' and Waggoner's "1888 message" was the same as the Evangelical Reformation gospel. Furthermore, it has been asserted that their message *changed* to a Roman Catholic version of righteousness by faith soon after they left Minneapolis. The stated causes for this change resulted from: their supposed *new* (post 1888) view on the human nature of Christ, their rejection of the Original Sin doctrine, their inclusion of sanctification with justification in righteousness by faith, and their belief in the perfection of an end-time generation. All of which is *said* to have led directly to the "holy-flesh movement" and the "Alpha apostasy." Likewise, any reemphasis of Jones' and Waggoner's so called *false* post-1888 message today (which includes the above four points), is stated to be none other than the "Omega apostasy." Desmond Ford, Robert D. Brinsmead, David P. McMahon, Milton R. Hook, Bert Haloviak, Roy Adams, Woodrow W. Whidden, and George R. Knight, along with others, have promoted or are promoting this view in varying degrees. We will document these appraisements throughout the remainder of this book as we examine our history, including Ellen White's inspired observations, to ascertain if their assertion is correct.

3.  *Ibid.*, and Ellen G. White, "Meetings at South Lancaster, Mass," *Review and Herald*, March 5, 1889, in *1888 Materials*, pp. 371-372, 267.

4.  Ellen G. White, *Review and Herald*, March 5, 1889, in *1888 Materials*, p. 267.

5.  *Ibid.*, pp. 267-268.

6.  Ellen G. White, Manuscript 17, "Diary," Jan. 1889; in A. L. White, *The Lonely Years*, p. 427.

7.  Ellen G. White, "Draw Nigh to God," Morning Talk, Feb. 5, 1890, *Review and Herald*, March 4, 1890;

8.  Ellen G. White, "The Present Message," Morning Talk, Feb. 4, 1890, *Review and Herald*, March 18, 1890; in *1888 Materials*, p. 545.

9.  *Ibid.*, see also A. L. White, *The Lonely Years*, p. 428.

10. Ellen G. White to My Dear Brethren, Letter 85, April, 1889; in *1888 Materials*, pp. 280-283.

11. In 1851 Ellen White wrote: "When the refreshing and latter rain shall come from the presence of the Lord and the glory of His power, we shall ... see the Sabbath more in its importance and glory" (Ellen G. White to Sister Harriet, Letter 3, Aug. 11, 1851; in *Selected Messages*, book 3, p. 388). Once again this is positive evidence that by 1888 that glory was already beginning to shine.

12. Ellen G. White to W. C. White, Letter 1, April 7, 1889; in *1888 Materials*, pp. 286-289.

13. *Ibid.*, pp. 289-291; see also, A. L. White, *The Lonely Years*, p. 429. Once again, Ellen White's characterization of Jones as "patiently" instructing the people, is a far cry from some of the labels that have been placed upon him today. We would not deny that Jones struggled with harshness at times, but some have read back into the 1888 through mid 1890s period Jones' post 1900 bitterness toward the church, which not only discredits his earlier calling as a messenger of God, but also the message he was given.

14. It should be noted that although rejecting the message at Minneapolis was a *personal* sin for Morrison and Nicola, the fact that they were in *leadership positions* caused the whole conference to suffer as a result of their choices. Even though the people "gave an invitation by a rising vote" for Ellen White to attend their campmeeting, in the end she was unable to attend because the leadership waited too long to invite her. How true is Ellen White's statement: "The Jews perished as a nation because they were drawn from the truth of the Bible by their rulers, priests, and elders" (Ellen G. White, *Gospel Workers*, pp. 128-129, 1892 ed., and *Testimonies to Ministers*, p. 109). We will take a deeper look at this subject in the pages ahead.

15. The fact that the canvassers could not present the message in the light that A. T. Jones was presenting it should help us understand that this was a special message sent from God—a flood of light—sent from heaven. But this was more than just a reemphasis of the Reformation gospel as taught by the holiness preachers of the day, and the reinterpretation of the Reformation gospel made so popular by many Evangelicals in our day. See also, Chapter 9, footnote 5.

16. Ellen G. White to W. C. White, Letter 1, April 7, 1889; in *1888 Materials*, pp. 290-293.

17. Ellen G. White to J. Fargo, Letter 50, May 2, 1889; in *1888 Materials*, p. 298.

18. W. C. White to L. R. Conradi, June 26, 1889; in *Manuscripts and Memories*, p. 145.

19. Ellen G. White to Children, Letter 14, May 12, 1889; in *1888 Materials*, p. 307. See also "Campmeeting at Ottawa, Kansas," *Review and Herald*, July 23, 1889; in *1888 Materials*, p. 386.

20. *Ibid.*, p. 386

21. Ellen G. White to Children, Letter 14, May 12, 1889; in *1888 Materials*, pp. 307-308.

22. *Ibid.*, pp. 308-316.

23. In sharing this experience of the Kansas meetings with Brother Fargo—a delegate from the Michigan conference—Ellen White related how dangerous it had been at Minneapolis to put implicit trust in man: "There was poor Brother Ostrander that went to that meeting, unbalanced in mind, little less than [an] insane man. His brethren were in so great blindness they were so wrought up over the law in Galatians, they had no sense to discern his true condition and the question was gravely asked me by the committee who visited me, for my counsel of Bro. Ostrander. Would not he be one whose name should be put on the paper as one to run for the presidency of General Conference? This man was even dangerous in his home in his insanity before he left home, for his wife has told me in regard to it. But this man was fully in the confidence of Elder Butler and in his weak condition strong impressions from this man were made on his mind. As Brother Butler stated, my best and most experienced ministering brethren [including Ostrander] could tell him their hearts were nearly broken at the positions Sister White took at the General Conference" (Ellen G. White to J. Fargo, Letter 50, May 2, 1889; in *1888 Materials*, p. 300).

24. Ellen G. White to J. Fargo, Letter 50, May 2, 1889; in *1888 Materials*, pp. 298-299.

25. Ellen G. White "Campmeeting at Ottawa, Kansas," *Review and Herald*, July 23, 1889; in *1888 Materials*, p. 386.

26. Ellen G. White to Children, Letter 14, May 12, 1889; in *1888 Materials*, p. 317.

27. Ellen G. White, "Unfounded Reports," May, 1889; in *Testimonies*, vol. 5, p. 693, and *1888 Materials*, p. 327.

28. "Interview with J. S. Washburn, at Hagerstown, Md., June 4, 1950," p. 1.

29. *Ibid.*

30. *Ibid.*, pp. 1, 2.

31. *Ibid.*
32. *Ibid.*

33. *Ibid.*, pp. 1, 2. Although Washburn's visit with Ellen White was reported in this interview that took place 61 years later, the accuracy of Washburn's recollection is supported by several facts. His description of the vision Ellen White had while in Europe is the same as that found in her private letter to G. I. Butler which was not

published until after Washburn's death (Letter 21, Oct. 14, 1888; *1888 Materials*, p. 93). Washburn's observation that "three-fourths" stood against the light is supported by Butler's private letter to Ellen White (Aug. 23, 1886; *Manuscripts and Memories*, p. 21). Washburn's description of the train of events at the Kansas meetings, including Ellen White's strong statements that Thursday morning May 9, her interview with Washburn Thursday afternoon, and even A. T. Jones' Sabbath sermon title on May 11 (which helped to turn Washburn around), fits perfectly with Ellen White's and W. C. White's own description of these events (See: *1888 Materials*, pp. 302-325; *Manuscripts and Memories*, pp. 138-146). Washburn's description of Ellen White's comments in regard to Waggoner—"'EJW can teach righteousness by faith more clearly than I can, … the Lord has given him special light on that question. … But when he did bring it out at Minneapolis, I recognized it'" ("Interview," p. 2)— are substantiated by other of her recorded statements. For instance, her statement made at the Rome campmeeting June 19, 1889 (only a few weeks after her interview with Washburn): "I have had the question asked, 'What do you think of this light that these men are presenting?['] Why, I have been presenting it to you for the last 45 years—the matchless charms of Christ. This is what I have been trying to present before your minds. When Brother Waggoner brought out these ideas in Minneapolis, it was the first clear teaching on this subject from any human lips I had heard, excepting the conversations between myself and my husband. I have said to myself, It is because God has presented it to me in vision that I see it so clearly, and they cannot see it because they have never had it presented to them as I have. And when another presented it, every fiber of my heart said, Amen" (*1888 Materials*, p. 349). Chances are Washburn was not at this campmeeting, and the transcript of Ellen White's sermon was not published until after his death. Modern historians, however, have strongly disagreed with Ellen White's assessment of Jones and Waggoner and their message. Responding to the suggestion to republish Jones and Waggoner's writings, N. F. Pease suggested: "It is not an overstatement to say that there was nothing said by Waggoner and Jones but that [Ellen White] said better" (*The Faith that Saves*, p. 53). But this creates a serious problem. Why did the Lord send Jones and Waggoner when there was a living prophet already present unless they had a message to give? Why did Ellen White support them, even at the expense of her own reputation as a prophet or messenger of God, unless they were sent with a message from heaven?

34. "Interview with J. S. Washburn, at Hagerstown, Md., June 4, 1950," pp. 2-3.

35. *Ibid.* Washburn recalled his experience at the Kansas meetings in several of his letters to Ellen White in the years that followed: "I was in Ottawa, Kansas, last May attending the Institute there and I was most deeply impressed by the sermons

of Eld. A. T. Jones on the righteousness of Christ and by the talks I had with you" (J. S. Washburn to Ellen G. White, April 17, 1890; *Manuscripts and Memories*, p. 174). "Your gentle kindness with me and patient answering of my questions settled my faith, I trust, forever. After the Minneapolis Conference I was in great trouble, doubt and almost gone to Atheism, but the precious light on Righteousness by Faith by Brother Jones and your talks and especially the long talks I had ALONE with you, settled my wavering faith and fastened it firmly to the Rock of Ages" (J. S. Washburn to Ellen G. White, Dec. 17, 1896, emphasis in original). Once again, this substantiates the accuracy of Washburn's 1950 interview.

36. Ellen G. White to Children, Letter 14, May 12, 1889; *1888 Material*, p. 317.

37. A. T. Jones, "Sabbath Morning Sermon," May, 11, 1889, The Topeka *Daily Capital*, May 14, 1889; in "The 1889 Camp Meeting Sermons" (St. Maries, Id.: LMN Publ. International, n.d.), pp. 30-31.

38. *Ibid.*

39. Ellen G. White "Campmeeting at Ottawa, Kansas," *Review and Herald*, July 23, 1889; in *1888 Materials*, pp. 386-387.

40. Ellen G. White to Children, Letter 14, May 12, 1889, and Ellen G. White to J. Fargo, Letter 50, May 2, 1889; in *1888 Materials*, pp. 317, 299, 318. We will take another look at the opposition to the Kansas meetings in the next chapter.

41. Ellen G. White Manuscript 2, "Picking Flaws," Morning Talk, May 12, 1889; in *1888 Materials*, pp. 302-306.

42. Ellen G. White to Children, Letter 14, May 12, 1889; in *1888 Materials*, pp. 307, 314, 317, 320.

43. *Ibid.* and Ellen G. White to J. Fargo, Letter 50, May 2, 1890; in *1888 Materials*, pp. 307, 299-300. Washburn's conversion experience at the Kansas campmeeting had a profound effect upon his ministry. In 1891 he traveled to England to take up the work there, where he was joined by E. J. Waggoner in 1892, and great were the results. See: David Marshall, "J. S. Washburn: Unsung Hero," *Review and Herald*, Jan. 26, 1989, pp. 16-17.

44. Ellen G. White "Campmeeting at Ottawa, Kansas," *Review and Herald*, July 23, 1889; in *1888 Materials*, p. 387.

# The 1889 Revivals –2

## Arise and Shine for Thy Light Has Come

After Ellen White's Sunday morning talk at the Kansas campmeeting in May of 1889, a break finally came. Many bore testimony of the great blessings they received and of their newfound experience. That same afternoon, Ellen White attended a meeting where, "after Brother Jones had spoken upon faith, there were many [more] free testimonies borne. As many as six and eight were on their feet at a time, and they seemed like starved sheep who were feeding upon meat in due season." Writing of the events of the day to her children, Ellen White expressed her joy and innermost desire: "I pray that this good work may go on and that Zion may arise, because her light has come and the glory of the Lord has risen upon her. Let the individual members of the church humble themselves before God, and accept the message which will bring healing to her bruises and wounds."[1]* Ellen White recognized that the Lord had visited His people with the very light that would heal them and enable them to arise and shine forth to the world around them.

The response to the message sent through Jones and Waggoner was varied. While many of the people were receiving a great blessing and a new religious experience that they had never known before, others saw the message as dangerous heresy. What is interesting to note, however, is that not all agreed on what heresy it was that Jones and Waggoner were supposedly teaching. Ellen White was joyful because she recognized the message they were presenting as a complete message of both law and the gospel combined, which had powerful results.[2]* But of those who opposed the message, some went away thinking Jones and Waggoner did away with the law in favor of an antinomianism or cheap grace, while others felt that they were undermining the gospel, teaching some kind of perfectionism.[3]*

## *Opposition from Both Sides*

Both G. I. Butler and Uriah Smith felt Jones was belittling the law and wrote rebuttals to his campmeetings sermons in the *Review*. In the May 14 issue of the *Review*, Butler wrote on Romans chapter 7 and 8, and titled his article; "The Righteousness of the Law Fulfilled By Us." In contrast to Jones' sermons, where he described one aspect of sin as missing the mark, Butler emphasized that the moral law was given "to show what God regards as right, everything which violates its sacred principles is wrong,—*is sin*. ... 'Sin is the transgression of the law.' 1 John 3:4." Toward the end of his article Butler summarized his concerns:

> If there is any one thing in which the third angel's message is designed to correct the teachings of this age more than another, it is upon this very point,— the necessity of obedience to the law of God. "Here are they that *keep the commandments of God*, and the faith of Jesus." Rev. 14:12. ... There is a sentiment prevailing almost everywhere, and it comes in most pleasing guises, and is made to sound most plausible, that it is not necessary to obey these commandments, or that they *cannot* be obeyed in this world. An easy way of religion is taught. "Only believe in Christ, and you are all right." The heart is not examined; the conscience is dormant; there is little sense of the guilt of sin, little thoroughness in studying the demands of God's law, little self–examination, little abhorrence of sin. Jesus does it all. It is one of the most dangerous heresies in the world. ...
>
> Multitudes are calling themselves Christians today, claiming Christ has done the work for them, who know nothing of his pardoning love, because they have never felt the sinfulness of sin, and make no thorough work of repentance. The work is wholly superficial. So these hide under the shadow of Christ, as they suppose, while really carrying their sins along with them. Thus they make Christ a minister of sin. ...
>
> It will be a sad day for us as a people, if we ever discard the light God has given us relative to our duty to keep, in spirit and in letter, the moral law of God.[4]*

Butler wrote eloquently defending the law against the apparent attacks of Jones, while at the same time he himself was disregarding counsel from the Lord's servant, Ellen White. Smith's rebuttal came in a June 11 article titled, "Our Righteousness." Uriah Smith was more abrasive than Butler, suggesting that the current teaching—by inference that of Jones and Waggoner—was leading down the same path as the "bitter opposers of our cause," who were doing away with the law. He even made a thrust toward Ellen White, stating that anyone "acquainted with Bro. White can imagine about how long it would take him to demolish such an objection":

> Some of our correspondents are beginning to drop remarks leaning very suspiciously toward the view that any attempt on our part to keep the commandments, is simply an attempt to make ourselves better, which we can never do; that it is an attempt to be righteous, which is simply to cover ourselves with filthy rags. ... Just how much they intend to express, we are unable to determine; but it seems to us that they are unconsciously turning their steps toward a position held by a class of bitter opposers of our cause and work, and who draw largely on this line of thought for their material. ...

> Perfect obedience to it [the law] will develop perfect righteousness, and that is the only way any one can attain to righteousness. ... Christ comes in and closes up the gulf between us and God by providing a sacrifice to cancel past sin... [and] to bring us back into harmony with the law. ... Here is where our Methodist friend made a mistake... not perceiving that the whole object of Christ's work for us is to bring us back to the law, that its righteousness may be fulfilled in us by our obedience to it. ...

> [W]e are not to rest on the stool of do-nothing, as a mass of inertia in the hands of the Redeemer. ...

> But it is asked, if a man undertakes to keep the law in his own strength and work out his own righteousness, can he do it? Is he not clothing himself with filthy rags? To what class of people such a query would apply, we do not know. We do know, however, that there is not a Seventh-day Adventist in the land who has not been taught better than to suppose that in his own strength he could keep the commandments. ... We doubt if even the Pharisees rested their self-righteousness on the perfection of their personal obedience to the ten commandments. ...

> There is a righteousness we must have, in order to see the kingdom of heaven, which is called "our righteousness;" and this righteousness comes from being in harmony with the law of God. ... And "our righteousness" cannot in this case be filthy rags.[5]*

Others, besides Butler and Smith, felt the same way about the Ottawa, Kansas meetings. However, before we look at more complaints, we need to take a close look at what was most likely the sermon that brought so much criticism. On Friday, May 17, 1889, Jones finished his series on righteousness by faith in a sermon titled, "Keeping the Commandments." Because so much has been made of Jones' comments, both in 1889 and today, we will include his sermon in its entirety as printed in the Topeka *Daily Capital*:[6]*

> 2 Corinthians 5:17. We have seen how we are brought into Christ and how this says if any man is brought into Christ he is a new creature. Gal. 6:15; 5:6, nothing avails but this and faith that works by love of God, being made a new creature by faith. Romans 5:1, 2, 5; 1 John 5:3—then keeping the commandments comes in after we are new creatures, so then we must be made good, be made righteous, before we can do good or do righteousness; 1 Corinthians 7:19— that is the aim set before us in Christ Jesus. Ephesians 2:8-10. We are created unto good works; made new creatures in him, his righteousness counting for our unrighteousness. The good works God's creatures are created in Christ to do are the good works we could not do before. So a new creature will aim constantly to keep the commandments.

> James 2:1, 9. We do not have the faith of Christ with the transgression of the law. Christ did not come to set us free for that, because if we turn from a single point of the law our faith will not avail. But our intent is accepted and ignorant sins are forgiven, yet willful refusal to accept points of truth presented will cause us to lose all the righteousness we ever had. This explains the fast growing evil in the popular churches of today. Years ago the churches were religious—even when the third angel's message started they were accepted of God but when they refused to comply with the requirements of the message, then they lost all the righteousness they had and have had to invent all manner of means by which to keep the congregations together, by entertainments. This is the philosophy of the degeneration of the churches.

> James 2:14. No more does faith profit unless it is kept alive by these works. God has provided, Num. 18, let us show our faith by our works. Faith is the anchor that holds the craft in the right place to work and the storms beat us nearer home. Verses 21, 23. Abraham was counted righteous when he believed and without works, the other righteousness came in twenty-five years after, so he was not counted righteous by works, that scripture was spoken when he believed and more than twenty-five years after James says the scripture was fulfilled. If he had refused to offer Isaac, his former righteousness would have disappeared, so the obedience of his faith completed his righteousness that he had by faith. Then our keeping of the commandments is not to become

righteous, but because we are righteous. Romans 8:26 shows that we can not even pray aright, but the spirit does it for us, so our prayers are acceptable only through the intercession of Christ and the merits of his blood.

Rev. 8:3, 4. Here is the intercession in the sanctuary making intercession for us and God looks upon Christ, his wounds and his sacrifice and accepts them. Christ was perfect before he came to earth, and his absence makes our prayers acceptable, God imputing his prayer for us to us. How is his righteousness imputed to us? Are our acts righteous as far as they go and is his righteousness applied to finish out the work? No. Christ's righteousness starts at the beginning and makes the action what it ought to be.

Romans 1:16. Is not our faith greater than when we came here? Do we not see more of his righteousness than we did? How is it we have more faith and see more of his righteousness? Why our faith has grown. So it is day by day. We came daily for greater supply of faith. And we finally have so much of Christ's divine nature in us that we can draw the bow strongly enough to hit the mark, and then we will be keeping the commandments of God. Then is it not Christ's work from the beginning and all his divine power? Where, then, do our works come in? Nowhere. Why then do we strive so hard to keep the commandments, if it avails not? It is only by faith in Christ that we can say we are Christians. It is only through being one with him that we can be Christians, and only through Christ within us that we keep the commandments—it being all by faith in Christ that we do and say these things.

When the day comes that we actually keep the commandments of God, we will never die, because keeping the commandments is righteousness, and righteousness and life are inseparable—so, "Here are they that keep the commandments of God and faith of Jesus," and what is the result? These people are translated. Life, then, and keeping the commandments go together. If we die now, Christ's righteousness will be imputed to us and we will be raised, but those who live to the end are made sinless before he comes, having so much of Christ's being in them that they "hit the mark" every time, and stand blameless without an intercessor, because Christ leaves the sanctuary sometime before he comes to earth.

Now some say, "I will live better; I will try to build myself up into that place where God can accept me." If a child tries to do something to build up himself that you may think more of him, and falls, you say it was selfishness and pride, and serves him right; but if a child tries to do something simply to please you, even though bunglingly done, you commend him and praise him. So with us, if we strive to please our God, no matter how bunglingly we do it, he is so glad to put Christ's righteousness upon us and all heaven rejoices over it. How often a child tries to help mother and she lets it go on, although mother has to do it all over again—yet she delights in the effort of the child to please her. Now like as a father pitieth his children so the Lord pitieth them that fear him.

So then we can say with David: "I delight to do thy law, oh, my God." Why? Because the love of God was shed abroad in his heart. Now let me read a few texts about pleasing God: Hebrews 11:6. The aim of faith is to please God, because he is so good. Romans 8:8. Again 2 Cor. 5:14. The love of Christ draws us and we get that love through faith. But can we love God if we cannot keep the commandments of God? No. We can do neither until we become new creatures. 1 John 3:21-22. Now let us read Col. 1:9-10. We should be able to walk pleasingly before him. 1 Thess. 4:1. This then is the root and motive in keeping the commandments—to please God, and not to make ourselves righteous. God makes and keeps us righteous and then we keep the commandment to please God who has done so much for us. As then it is the power of Christ through which we keep the commandments now, and it will be his power through which we shall live forever in the new earth. His name to us is what? Jeremiah says it is "the Lord our Righteousness." Jer. 23:5-6.[7]*

DAN JONES

O.A. OLSEN

Dan Jones, who often opposed Jones and Waggoner, wrote to O. A. Olsen the following Spring complaining that he had to meet with "badly discouraged" ministers in the Kansas conference. "They had got the impression that there were new views coming out that unsettled the old positions we have held, and they were not certain that the new positions were correct. … [They] had got the idea some way that the doctrine of justification by faith practically did away with the law."[8]*

While some of the brethren felt that the law was being done away with by Jones' and Waggoner's teaching on justification by faith, others felt that "exaggerated ideas" on the subject were being taught in regard to overcoming sin. Dan Jones reported to O. A. Olsen, in regard to the same meetings, that some ministers were "under a cloud and going into discouragement. This arose from exaggerated ideas they had received of what our brethren taught on the subject of justification by faith; they had got the idea that the position is now taken that we should stand in a position where we do not sin, that all sin should be put away entirely, and that if we are not in that position we are not converted, etc."[9] The fact that both Jones and Waggoner were teaching that Christ had come to this earth, taking upon His sinless nature our sinful nature, and overcoming sin in our flesh that we might overcome as well, was to some very upsetting. But how did Ellen White see these two responses to their message? Did she suggest that Jones and Waggoner were causing confusion by doing away with the law or teaching perfectionism?[10]*

## *Ellen White's Response*

While Uriah Smith, G. I. Butler, Dan Jones and others were blaming Jones and Waggoner for teaching two opposite extremes in regard to justification by faith, Ellen White, who had been personally present at the campmeetings, saw the real cause for the confusion. She pointedly told Uriah Smith some time later, that "the many and confused ideas in regard to Christ's righteousness and justification by faith are the result of the position *you* have taken toward the man and the message sent of God."[11] In a talk given a few months after the 1889 campmeetings, Ellen White stated that "the danger has been presented to me again and again of entertaining, as a people, false ideas of justification by faith. I have been shown for years that Satan would work in a special manner to confuse the mind on this point." She didn't blame this on Jones and Waggoner, however, but on those who had presented largely on the law of God, "almost destitute of the knowledge of Jesus Christ and His relation to the law as was the offering of Cain. … Many have been kept from the faith because of the mixed, confused ideas of salvation, because the ministers have worked in a wrong manner to reach hearts."[12]

But Ellen White also gave warning to those who felt the present message was calling for too high a standard and that it was not possible for Christ to have taken upon himself man's fallen nature:

The trials of the children of Israel, and their attitude just before the first coming of Christ, have been presented before me again and again to illustrate the position of the people of God in their experience before the second coming of Christ. How the enemy sought every occasion to take control of the minds of the Jews, and to-day he is seeking to blind the minds of God's servants, that they may not be able to discern precious truth. …

Christ came to the world to meet these false accusations, and to reveal the Father. We cannot conceive of the humiliation He endured in taking our nature upon himself. …

The Jews had been looking for the advent of the Messiah, but they had thought He must come in all the glory that will attend his second appearing. Because He did not come with all the majesty of a king, they utterly refused Him. But it was not simply because He did not come in splendor that they refused Him. It was because He was the embodiment of purity, and they were impure. … Such a character in the midst of degradation and evil, was out of harmony with their desires, and He was abused and despised. …

Letters have been coming to me, affirming that Christ could not have had the same nature as man, for if he had, he would have fallen under similar temptations. If he did not have man's nature, he could not be our example. If he was not a partaker of our nature, he could not have been tempted as man has been.[13]*

Two years later Ellen White would repeat these same thoughts. Christ did not have an advantage over mankind when it comes to facing temptation. But grace and power is given to all who receive Him, as He is by faith:

We need not place the obedience of Christ by itself as something for which He was particularly adapted, by His particular divine nature, for He stood before God as man's representative and tempted as man's substitute and surety. If Christ had a special power which it is not the privilege of man to have, Satan would have made capital of this matter. The work of Christ was to take from the claims of Satan his control of man, and he could do this only in the way that He came—a man, tempted as a man, rendering the obedience of a man. …

Bear in mind that Christ's overcoming and obedience is that of a true human being. In our conclusions, we make many mistakes because of our erroneous views of the human nature of our Lord. When we give, to His human nature, a power that it is not possible for man to have in his conflicts with Satan, we destroy the completeness of His humanity. His imputed grace and power He gives to all who receive Him by faith. The obedience of Christ to His Father was the same obedience that is required of man.[14]

## *Williamsport, Pennsylvania*

With some difficulty because of recent flooding, Ellen White and A. T. Jones traveled from Kansas to Pennsylvania for a campmeeting held June 5-11, 1889. E. J. Waggoner joined them from California to help with the meetings which were "eagerly welcomed" by the people.[15]* The Minneapolis spirit of unbelief had come into the Kansas meetings, but at Williamsport, the people "did not seem to possess a spirit of unbelief and resistance to the message the Lord had sent them." Ellen White described the positive results of the meetings a few months later in a *Review* article:

> Our meetings were well attended, and in the early morning meeting, so many were desirous of bearing testimony, that it was difficult to close the meeting at the appointed time. ... The Lord has worked for his people, and they have received the light with joy as meat in due season. Their souls have craved spiritual food, and they have been supplied. ...
>
> [A]s the precious message of present truth was spoken to the people by Brn. Jones and Waggoner, the people saw new beauty in the third angel's message, and they were greatly encouraged. They testified to the fact they had never before attended meetings where they had received so much instruction and such precious light. ... They felt that they now understood better how to win souls to Christ. ...
>
> In every meeting which we attend, we find many who do not understand the simplicity of faith. ... They need to have Christ set forth before them. They need to have courage and hope and faith presented to them. They ask for bread, and shall they receive a stone? Shall the youth in our ranks say, "No man careth for my soul"? Shall we not give light to the souls that are groping in darkness?[16]

In the same *Review* article, Ellen White addressed more specifically the present truth message that Jones and Waggoner were sharing. It was the third angel's message, the grand message of justification by faith, proclaimed with the law of God. It was the message of the Lord our righteousness:

> There are grand truths, long hidden under the rubbish of error, that are to be revealed to the people. The doctrine of justification by faith has been lost sight of by many who have professed to believe the third angel's message. The Holiness people have gone to great extremes on this point. With great zeal

they have taught, "Only believe in Christ, and be saved; but away with the law of God." This is not the teaching of the word of God. There is no foundation for such a faith. This is not precious gems of truth that God has given to his people for this time. This doctrine misleads honest souls. …

God has raised up men to meet the necessity of this time who will cry aloud and spare not, who will lift up their voice like a trumpet, and show my people their transgressions and the house of Jacob their sins. Their work is not only to proclaim the law, but to preach the truth for this time, the Lord our righteousness.[17]*

The message that Jones and Waggoner were presenting placed the commandments of God and the faith of Jesus in their proper framework, and wonderful were the results. Ellen White made it clear that the doctrine of justification by faith had been lost sight of in the Adventist church, as leaders and members depended on a mere legalistic form of religion. The third angel's message that Adventism was to proclaim to the world was not a message of salvation by works. Neither was it the liberal perversion of the reformation doctrine of justification by faith which the holiness preachers taught. The Adventist message was the third angel's message in verity—the law and the gospel combined—which went beyond the message the Reformers taught. It was the message of righteousness by faith built on the foundation of the Reformation, but taught in the context of the final judgement and the cleansing of the heavenly sanctuary.[18]*

In the 1888 edition of *The Great Controversy*, Ellen White wrote about the Reformation and "the great doctrine of justification by faith, so clearly taught by Luther."[19]* But she also stated in the same book, that "the Reformation did not, as many suppose, end with Luther. It is to be continued to the close of this world's history. Luther had a great work to do in reflecting to others the light which God had permitted to shine upon him; yet he did not receive all the light which was to be given to the world. From that time to this, new light has been continually shining upon the Scriptures, and new truths have been constantly unfolding."[20]* There was a "present truth in the days of Luther,—a truth at that time of special importance," but, Ellen White exclaimed, "there is a present truth for the church today."[21]*

In Ellen White's article about the Williamsport campmeeting, she described the great blessings received by those who accepted the present truth messages on righteousness by faith, and then turned her attention to those who were still wavering over whether to accept the message. She warned those in Battle Creek, who themselves were sinning against great light, that it was time for them to choose between Baal and the Lord:

> The Spirit of God is now withdrawing from the people of the earth. ...
>
> The terrible destruction of life and property at Johnstown and Williamsport... call for most serious reflection. ... But we are not to think... [they] were more deserving of punishment than are other cities. ... There are those who are living under the very shadow of our institutions, who are sinning against greater light than were the people of Johnstown... and they will more certainly fall under the wrath of God's retributive judgments. ...
>
> The curse of Meroz will be upon those who do not now come up to the help of the Lord against the mighty. Well may the question be asked in the spirit of Elijah. "How long halt ye between two opinions? If the Lord be God, follow him; but if Baal, then follow him."
>
> All heaven is interested in the work that is going on upon the earth. But there are those who see no necessity for a special work at this time. While God is working to arouse the people, they seek to turn aside the message of warning, reproof, and entreaty. Their influence tends to quiet the fears of the people, and to prevent them from awaking to the solemnity of this time. ... If they do not change their course... the same reward will be apportioned to them as to those who are at enmity and in open rebellion against God.[22]

Ellen White wrote to H. W. Miller, a minister from the Michigan conference, just prior to the Williamsport campmeeting, stating that "some of our leading brethren" have "intercepted themselves between the light and the people." She told Miller that she "had repeatedly presented before [him] and others that there would come a shaking time." In view of the continued rejection of the outpouring of the Spirit of God, she could state unabashedly "we are now entering upon that time."[23]*

## *Rome, New York*

From Williamsport the campmeeting speakers traveled to New York, where the Rome campmeeting ran from June 11 to 18. Ellen White felt "anxious that the grace of Christ should come upon our brethren." Her hopes were not disappointed: "The Lord sent them special messages of mercy and encouragement." Once again she recognized the message for what it was:

> The Lord would have his church arise and shine; for the brightness of the light of God has shone upon his people in the message of present truth. If all will heed the precious words given them from the Great Teacher through his delegated servants, there will be an awakening throughout our ranks, and spiritual vigor will be imparted to the church. We should all desire to know the truth as it is in Jesus. …

> I felt anxious that the light of heaven might shine upon the people of God in this Conference, that they might zealously repent of their sins. … We felt thankful to our Heavenly Father that his message of hope and courage and faith could come before our brethren and sisters in New York, and we deeply regretted that there were not many others present to share the important instruction that was given. …

> As the servants of the Lord brought forth things new and old from the treasure-house of his word, hope came to the hearts of these old soldiers in the truth. They knew that the message was what they needed, and felt that it came from God. …

> There is great need that Christ should be preached as the only hope and salvation. When the doctrine of justification by faith was presented at the Rome meeting, it came to many as water comes to the thirsty traveler. The thought that the righteousness of Christ is imputed to us, not because of any merit on our part, but as a free gift from God, seemed a precious thought. The enemy of man and God is not willing that this truth should be clearly presented; for he knows that if the people receive it fully, his power will be broken. If he can control minds so that doubt and unbelief and darkness shall compose the experience of those who claim to be the children of God, he can overcome them with temptation.[24]

The very message that was shining upon them was the "glory of the Lord" spoken of in Isaiah 60:1; truths both "new and old." If accepted, it would bring an "awakening throughout" the church. Satan did not want this message "clearly presented," for he knew that if the "people receive it fully, his power will be broken." Thus he set out to "control minds" with "doubt and unbelief" that he might "overcome them with temptation." The most effective way he could do this was through those in leadership positions.[25]

During the campmeeting in Rome, Ellen White responded to Smith's June 11 *Review* article, writing him a personal letter. She had been awakened in the night and saw the case of Smith as most discouraging:

> I saw you walked upon the path that almost imperceptibly diverged from the right way. A noble personage stood beside me and said, "Uriah Smith is not on the brink of a precipice but he is in the path that will shortly bring him to the brink and if he is not warned now it will soon be too late. He can now retrace his steps. He is walking like a blind man into the prepared net of the enemy but he feels no danger because light is becoming darkness to him and darkness light. ..."

> This morning I have read your article in [the] *Review.* Now there was no call whatever for you to write as you did. You place Elder Jones in a false position just as Elder Morrison and Nicola and yourself and others placed him in at Minneapolis.[26]*

## *Christ and the Law*

Church members at the Rome campmeeting, where both Jones and Waggoner were preaching, read Uriah Smith's June 11 article in the *Review*. On the last day of the meetings, Ellen White took opportunity to set things straight. In her sermon "Christ and the Law," she explained how Christ revealed to the Jewish people, "old light in new settings" in regard to the law. But the "moment He does that, there arises a resistance against that light. ... It was not as they had taught it. ... [T]heir thoughts were that He did not make the law as prominent as they had done. ... They saw trees as men walking." Ellen White then drew a comparison, asking her listeners how they would the respond to heaven's light?

> What is God going to do for His people—leave them with no new light? "Ye are," says He, "the light of the world." Then we are to get more light from the throne of God, and have an increase of light. Now, we do not tell you in the message that has been given to you here and in other places that it is a grand new light, but it is the old light brought up and placed in new settings. ...[27]*

Just prior to the coming of the Son of man, there is and has been for years a determination on the part of the enemy to cast his hellish shadow right between man and his Saviour. And why? So that he shall not distinguish that it is a whole Saviour, a complete sacrifice that has been made for him. Then he tells them that they are not to keep the law, for in keeping that law man would be united with the divine power, and Satan would be defeated. ... Notwithstanding man was encompassed with the infirmities of humanity he might become a partaker of the divine nature, having escaped the corruption that is in the world through lust. Now here is the redemption.[28]*

If you could see what Christ is, one that can save to the uttermost all that come unto God by Him, then you would have that faith that works. But must works come first? No, it is faith first. And how? The cross of Christ is lifted up between heaven and earth. ...

"Then," says one, "you cannot be accepted unless you repent." Well, who leads us to repentance? Who is drawing us?... Christ is drawing us. Angels of God are in this world, at work upon human minds, and the man is drawn to the One who uplifts him, and the One who uplifts Him draws him to repentance. It is no work of his own; there is nothing that he can do that is of any value at all except to believe. ...

This is the victory—even your faith, feelings, and good works? Is that it? No; "This is the victory... even your faith". ... We are not following cunningly devised fables, no indeed; but we have been revealing Christ our righteousness.[29]

Ellen White told her hearers that a "self–sufficiency" had been coming in among them. She read the message to the Laodicean church, stating that it was "applicable to us." She then defined the remedies for the Laodicean condition as that found in the very message that God had been pleased to send them:

Now what is the difficulty? "Tried in the fire." Christ had such love for us that He could go through all that trying of the crucifixion, and come off conqueror. And the white raiment, what is that? Christ's righteousness. "Anoint thine eyes with eyesalve"—spiritual discernment, that you may discern between true righteousness and self-righteousness. Now here is the work. The heavenly merchantman is passing up and down before you saying: "Buy of Me. Here are heavenly goods; buy of Me." "Will you do it? It is 'Me' you are to buy of." There is no other source in heaven from which we may receive liberty and life but through Jesus Christ our righteousness.

Then He says, "Be zealous therefore, and repent." That message is to us. We want the brethren and sisters in this conference to take hold of this message, and see the light that has been brought to us in new settings.

God has opened to us our strength, and we need to know something about it and be prepared for the time of trouble such as never was since there was a nation. But here is our strength, Christ our righteousness.[30]

As Ellen White came to the end of her talk, she responded to Smith's article in the *Review.* She described him in the same condition as that of the Jews. She defended Jones and Waggoner, and her husband, against Smith's misrepresentations. She made it clear that she was in full support of the message being given and that it was not contrary to what she had "been trying to present" before their minds. Speaking to the congregation in no uncertain terms, she identified the message for what it was; their "light" had come:

Brethren, do not let any of you be thrown off the track. "Well," you say, "What does Brother Smith's piece in the *Review* mean?" He doesn't know what he is talking about; he sees trees as men walking. … [H]e takes those [texts] that have been placed in false settings and he binds them in a bundle as though we were discarding the claims of God's law, when it is no such thing. It is impossible for us to exalt the law of Jehovah unless we take hold of the righteousness of Jesus Christ.

My husband understood this matter of the law, and we have talked night after night until neither of us would sleep. And it is the very principles the people are striving for. They want to know that Christ accepts them as soon as they come to Him. …

I have had the question asked, "What do you think of this light that these men are presenting?" Why, I have been presenting it to you for the last 45 years—the matchless charms of Christ.[31]* This is what I have been trying to present before your minds. When Brother Waggoner brought out these ideas in Minneapolis, it was the first clear teaching on this subject from any human lips I had heard, excepting the conversations between myself and my husband. I have said to myself, It is because God has presented it to me in vision that I see it so clearly, and they cannot see it because they have never had it presented to them as I have. And when another presented it, every fiber of my heart said, Amen. …

I ask you in the name of Jesus Christ of Nazareth to arise and shine, for thy light has come. … Now, you have had light here, and what are you going to do about it?… How I long to see the tidal wave pouring over the people! And I know it can be, for God gave us all heaven in one gift, and every one of us can accept the light, every ray of it, and then we can be the light of the world.[32]

Smith's response was anything but repentance. He wrote a second article in the *Review* entitled "Our Righteousness Again." He stated that his first article seemed "to have been misapprehended by some," and he wrote again "in hope of making it so plain that none can misunderstand it." His stance, however, didn't change. He was concerned that "in exalting the faith side of this question, which is all right in itself,… many have come to think that the [law] is obsolete and the other [obedience] of no consequence."[33]

## *Looking Back*

Several weeks later Ellen White wrote of the campmeeting at Rome. She encouraged those who had "received" light to let it "shine in the various churches of which they" were members, for if they neglect to communicate the light, they would "be left in darkness." She warned those who were criticizing the message that had "divine credentials" that Satan was not only trying to make void the law of God, he was also seeking to trample on the "faith of Christ as our righteousness." If the "present message," which brought with it divine power, was not valued, "false theories" would take minds captive and Christ and His righteousness would be "dropped out of the experience" and Satan would "overcome [them] with his temptations":

> The present message—justification by faith—is a message from God; it bears the divine credentials, for its fruit is unto holiness. Some who greatly need the precious truth that was presented before them, we fear did not receive its benefit… they have suffered great loss. …
>
> It is perilous to the soul to hesitate, question, and criticize divine light. Satan will present his temptations until the light will appear as darkness, and many will reject the very truth that would have proved the saving of their souls. Those who walk in its rays will find it growing brighter and brighter unto the perfect day. …
>
> It has been necessary to exalt the great standard of righteousness, but in doing this, many have neglected to preach the faith of Jesus. If we would have the spirit and power of the third angel's message, we must present the law and the gospel together, for they go hand in hand. As a power from beneath is stirring up the children of disobedience to make void the law of God, and to trample upon the faith of Christ as our righteousness, a power from above is moving upon the hearts of those who are loyal to exalt the law, and to lift up Jesus as

a complete Saviour. Unless divine power is brought into the experience of the people of God, false theories and erroneous ideas will take minds captive, Christ and his righteousness will be dropped out of the experience of many, and their faith will be without power or life. ... [I]f they do not zealously repent, they will be among those who are represented by the Laodiceans, who will be spewed out of the mouth of God. ...

Our present position is interesting and perilous. The danger of refusing light from heaven should make us watchful unto prayer, lest we should any of us have an evil heart of unbelief. When the Lamb of God was crucified on Calvary, the death knell of Satan was sounded; and if the enemy of truth and righteousness can obliterate from the mind the thought that it is necessary to depend upon the righteousness of Christ for salvation, he will do it. If Satan can succeed in leading man to place value upon his own works as works of merit and righteousness, he knows that he can overcome him by his temptations, and make him his victim and prey.[34]*

## *Message Silenced?*

After the Rome campmeeting Ellen White returned to Battle Creek "worn and exhausted." She had to "refrain from speaking for a time" until her health improved.[35] It was during this time that she wrote "Experience following the 1888 Minneapolis Conference." She summarized the events following the General Conference, including some of the revival meetings that took place in the early spring, and sadly, the opposition that still remained strong. Using language from Isaiah 58, she described the interest of the universe in seeing "how many faithful servants are bearing the sins of the people on their hearts and afflicting their souls; how many are colaborers with Jesus Christ to become repairers of the breach... and restorers of the paths." It was not just the Sabbath that needed restoration, but the "path of faith and righteousness."[36]

In late June, Ellen White traveled to Wexford, Michigan, for another campmeeting held June 25 through July 2. Once again the "Spirit of the Lord was manifestly at work," but many refused to be benefited by it. On July 23, Ellen White sent a forty-one page letter to "Elders Madison and Howard Miller," both ministers in the Michigan conference. She rebuked them and others for not recognizing the movings of the Spirit, and for being

"ever ready to question and cavil." Some had an "unfortunate experience…
at Minneapolis." Others, in their present condition, would be "a hindrance in
any meeting or counsel" just like the unfaithful spies, who had "no trouble
in seeing and presenting obstacles that appeared insurmountable in the way
of the advancement of the people of God." She told them that "the Lord
has committed to us a message full of interest, that is as far reaching in its
influence as eternity. We have tidings to give to the people which should
bring joy to their souls." She told them that it was not for them "to choose
the channel through which the light shall come. The Lord desires to heal the
wounds of His sheep and lambs, through the heavenly balm of the truth that
Christ is our righteousness." Their actions were similar to that of the Jews; they
were rejecting Christ "in the person of his messengers." Yet they were "less
excusable than were the Jews; for we have before us their example":

> It is a grievous sin in the sight of God for men to place themselves
> between the people and the message that he would have come to them
> (as some of our brethren have been doing). There are some who like the
> Jews, are doing their utmost to make the message of God of none effect.
> Let these doubting, questioning ones either receive the light of the truth
> for this time, or let them stand out of the way, that others may have an
> opportunity of receiving the truth. …
>
> Those who live just prior to the second appearing of Christ, may expect
> a large measure of His Holy Spirit; but if they do not watch and pray, they
> will go over the same ground of refusing the message of mercy, as the Jews
> did in the time of Christ (If God has ever spoken by me, some of our leading
> men are going over the same ground). If they turn away from the light, they
> will fail to meet the high and holy claims of God, they will fail to fulfill the
> sacred responsibility that he has entrusted to them.
>
> The character and prospects of the people of God are similar to those of
> the Jews, who could not enter in because of unbelief. Self-sufficiency, self-
> importance, and spiritual pride separate them from God.[37*]

Ellen White recognized that the brethren were following in the footsteps of
the Jews. Many were looking "to their leaders" and asking: "'If this message
that Brother A. T. Jones has been giving to the church is the truth, why is it that
Brother Smith and Brother Butler have not received it?'" A "similar guilt" to
that which was incurred by the Jews was upon those leading brethren who were

despising the message and messengers, and yet, Ellen White stated: "Their unbelief is no reason for others to do the same." Coming to the close of her letter to Madison and Miller, Ellen White gave a final caution and plea:

> There are many who have heard the message for this time and have seen its results, and they cannot but acknowledge that the work is good, but from fear that some will take extreme positions, and that fanaticism may arise in our ranks, they have permitted their imagination to create many obstacles to hinder the advance of the work, and they have presented these difficulties to others, expatiating on the dangers of accepting the doctrine. They have sought to counteract the influence of the message of truth. Suppose they should succeed in these efforts, what would be the result? The message to arouse a lukewarm church should cease, and the testimony exalting the righteousness of Christ would be silenced. ...
>
> The character, the motives and purposes of the workmen whom God has sent, have been, and will continue to be, misrepresented. ...
>
> The end is right upon us; and is it reasonable to think that there is no message to make ready a people to stand in the day of God's preparation?... Is the third angel's message to go out in darkness, or to lighten the whole earth with its glory? Is the light of God's Spirit to be quenched, and the church to be left as destitute of the grace of Christ as the hills of Gilboa were of dew and rain?[38]

Ellen White, and Jones and Waggoner, all attended several more campmeetings before the 1889 General Conference in late October, and the results were the same. Many people found a new experience as they heard the message presented, but many of the leading brethren, although claiming to believe in the message presented, continued to fight against what they perceived were flaws in the message and the messengers. Some years later, A. T. Jones summarized the events of the summer of 1889:

> Then when camp meeting time came we all three visited the camp meetings with the message of righteousness by faith and religious liberty: sometimes all three of us being in the same meeting. This turned the tide with the people, and apparently with most of the leading men. But this latter was only apparent: it was never real, for all the time in the General Conference Committee and amongst others there was a secret antagonism always carried on."[39] *

Were Jones' observations correct? We will look into his claims in the chapters ahead.

# CHAPTER 9 FOOTNOTES

1. Ellen G. White to Children, Letter 14, May 12, 1889; in *1888 Materials*, p. 325. "Arise, because her light has come and the glory of the Lord has risen upon her. . . ," is a quote from Isaiah 60. The *SDA Bible Commentary* describes these verses as the "symbol of the divine presence," the very presence of Jesus, that will "be proclaimed with such power that the whole earth will be ablaze with the light of truth (Rev. 18:1)" (vol. 4, p. 313, "Isaiah 60:1"). Thus, these verses are seen as connected with the fourth angel of Revelation 18 that will lighten the earth with its glory during the loud cry and latter rain. Ellen White's statement in her letter written at the Kansas meetings is the first of many statements she made applying Isaiah 60:1 (present tense) to the church of her day, who were hearing the most precious message sent from heaven: "Those who wait for the Bridegroom's coming are to say to the people, 'Behold your God.' The last rays of merciful light, the last message of mercy to be given to the world, is a revelation of His character of love. ... 'Arise, Shine; for thy light is come, and the glory of the Lord is risen upon thee.' Isa. 60:1. To those who go out to meet the Bridegroom is this message given" (*Christ's Object Lessons*, pp. 415, 420).

2. In Ellen White's well-known statement—"The Lord in His great mercy sent a most precious message to His people through Elders Waggoner and Jones"—she describes the message as "the law and the gospel, binding up the two in a perfect whole" (*Testimonies to Ministers*, pp. 91, 94). She knew that "the law and the gospel, blended, will convict of sin" and "in no discourse are they to be divorced." Why? "The one is the complement of the other. The law without faith in the gospel of Christ cannot save the transgressor of law. The gospel without the law is inefficient and powerless. ... The two blended—the gospel of Christ and the law of God—produce the love and faith unfeigned" (*1888 Materials*, pp. 892, 783). Ellen White witnessed this "love and faith unfeigned" among those who accepted the message presented at the summer meetings.

3. Jesus received a similar response. According to the conservative Pharisees, Jesus was far too liberal for their liking, as He didn't have enough respect for the law. But according to the liberal Sadducees, Jesus was far too conservative because He gave no excuse for sin, however small. Although the Pharisees and Sadducees hated one another, they did have one thing in common: they hated Jesus even more, hated the message He proclaimed, and united in His crucifixion.

4. G. I. Butler, "The Righteousness of the Law Fulfilled by Us," *Review and Herald*, May 14, 1889, pp. 313-314. George Knight suggests that "G. I. Butler... also attacked Jones's teachings at Ottawa, Kansas, and other places" in this *Review* article (*From 1888 to Apostasy*, p. 55). Although Butler was technically correct on many points in his article, Ellen White saw him as one working "in a wrong manner to reach hearts" (see footnote 12). Both Jones and Waggoner denied the Augustinian concept of Original Sin, but they wrote about different aspects of the sin problem besides the biblical definition found in John 3:4 (Leroy Moore, *Theology in Crisis*, p. 294; Clinton Wahlen, "Selected Aspects of Ellet J. Waggoner's Eschatology," pp. 10, 115).

5. Uriah Smith, "Our Righteousness," *Review and Herald*, June 11, 1889, p. 376.

6. Between May 5and 20, Jones presented three series of lectures at the Ottawa, Kansas campmeeting, giving 14 lectures on religious liberty, 13 on church government, and 5 on justification by faith. Jones then left with his wife and headed to the Williamsport campmeeting (The Topeka *Daily Capital*, May 22, 1889). This final sermon was attributed to W. C. White in the *Daily Capital*. George Knight suggests that "it is clearly ATJ's sermon. It is his style and it is part of the series of sermons that he presented on righteousness by faith" (*1888 to Apostasy*, p. 263, fn 20). Nevertheless, there are several other facts to consider. A notice in the *Review* stated that "arrangements will be made with newspapers during each [lecture] for a fair report," and that "the General Conference has assigned a competent [stenographic] reporter especially for this work" (*Review and Herald*, April 9, 1889, p 240). Bert Haloviak reveals, however, that there was a "class offered on shorthand reporting" during the campmeeting, and "'nearly all carried tablets, pencils and full notes of all class exercises and reports of sermons and lectures' were thus taken. It was obvious that through this means that the *Capital* was able to report full transcriptions of the major meetings" ("From Righteousness to Holy Flesh: Judgement at Minneapolis," chap. 9, p. 14). O. A Olsen did fill in for Jones earlier in the week because of "Elder Jones needing rest" (*Daily Capital*, May 17, 1889). It is possible that W. C. White could have done the same. It seems improbable that the two men could be mixed up, but whether W. C. White or A. T. Jones gave this sermon, the outcome is still the same. Jones likely gave the sermon so we will address the issues as if he did.

7. A. T. Jones, "Keeping the Commandments," May, 20, 1889, The Topeka *Daily Capital*, May 20, 1889; in "The 1889 Camp Meeting Sermons" (St. Maries, Id.: LMN Publ. International, n.d.), pp. 30-31. Again, this is Jones' sermon in its entirety, as it appeared in the Topeka *Daily Capital*. It should be clear that transcription represents only a summary of his sermon, and not a word for word replication. There is no

way to tell how much the stenographers transcribing affected the meaning of Jones' sermon, while at the same time they were learning their trade (see footnote 6). Thus it would behoove us not to try and build an entire case for or against Jones' theology based on comments he made in this one sermon.

8.   Dan T. Jones to O. A. Olsen, April 27, 1890, archives of the General Conference of Seventh-day Adventists. George Knight sides with Smith, Butler, Dan Jones and others, stating the following about A. T. Jones' sermon: "His use of language certainly left him open to such misinterpretation. After all, he had remarked at the 1889 Kansas meetings: 'Where…do our works come in? Nowhere.' He interspersed such statements throughout his sermons" (*1888 to Apostasy*, p. 55, verbatim quote). Knight summarizes by declaring that "Adventists misunderstood [Jones] on the relation of the law to salvation" because "he was an extremist who had never mastered the Christian virtue of temperance" (*Ibid.*, p. 55). But is the reader able to understand the true intent of Jones' words as quoted by Knight, when only a partial sentence is quoted with ellipses added in? It is clear, *when read in context*, that Jones was referring to the *merit* of our works: "Where then do our works come in? Nowhere." The word "then" being removed by Knight would refer the reader back to Jones' previous clarifying statements. Only a few sentences later Jones clarifies again by stating that it is "only through Christ within us that we keep the commandments." I would also challenge any reader to find where Jones "interspersed such statements *throughout* his sermons," as has been suggested. Those who condemned Jones in his day were "ever ready to question and cavil" and to condemn for a word. The same is true today. Jones' sermon stands on its own merit, but let us consider briefly four points: 1. These sermons were taken down in shorthand by several "reporters," many of which were learning the trade. This left room for human error and personal biases, as the transcribed sermon was very likely a composite from several novice reporters (see footnote 6). It is also obvious from the choppiness of the transcribed sermons that they were not taken down word for word; only the main thoughts were recorded. Many who were finding fault with Jones most likely read his sermons as reported in the *Daily Capital*, and were not present to hear him speak. This would include Uriah Smith. How easy it was to pick out a word here or there to condemn? 2. As will be noted later, many of the accusations that were being made by Smith, Butler, Dan Jones and others turned out to be false (see footnote 26). But the old adage is true: "A lie gets halfway around the world before the truth has a chance to get its pants on" (Winston Churchill). Some of the same lies started in Jones' day are still circulated today. 3. The challenge for both Jones and Waggoner when dealing with the legalism that was prevalent in the church at the time was to present the faith of Jesus aspect of the gospel without overstatements. If they were not perfect in this matter or if people took their statements to an extreme, it should not discredit the

wonderful work they were doing. James White wrote of a similar challenge Ellen White faced in dealing with health reform: "She makes strong appeals to the people, which a few feel deeply…and go to extremes. Then to save the cause from ruin… she is obliged to come out with reproofs for extremists…but the influence of both the extremes and the reproofs are terrible. … Here is the difficulty: What she may say to caution the prompt, zealous, incautious ones, is taken by the tardy as an excuse to remain too far behind" ("The Spirit of Prophecy and Health Reform," *Review and Herald*, March 17, 1868). W. C. White recognized the same problem: "I should infer that what mother writes intended to move the latter [indifferent group] from their dullness and indifference, is taken by the former [extremist group] and used as a club to belabor their brethren; and that what is written to the former class to save them from extreme and inconsiderate positions is taken by the latter class as an excuse for their self-confidence and indifference" (W. C. White to A. O. Tait, Sept. 2, 1895). 4. There is no evidence that Ellen White ever censured Jones for his sermons delivered at Ottawa, Kansas. When she did counsel him later for extreme statements he had made, it was primarily from the standpoint of sparing him from those who were looking to hang him for a word and the confusion, that would result in distracting from the true message he was giving.

9. Dan T. Jones to O. A. Olsen, April 21, 1890, archives of the General Conference of Seventh-day Adventists.

10. Some side today with those who felt that Jones and Waggoner were teaching perfectionism in 1889. Desmond Ford has been a prominent proponent of this idea: "From time to time, messages emphasizing Jesus have come to Seventh-day Adventists. It happened in 1888 through Waggoner and Jones, though their views tended to perfectionism [endnote 1]. Waggoner and Jones did not understand righteousness by faith with the clarity of Luther or Calvin. … Sadly, both Waggoner and Jones quickly lost their way, both morally and theologically" (*For the Sake of the Gospel* [2008], pp. 2, 219). Ford also recommends other resources that support his theological views: "The best book on Waggoner is by David P. McMahon and is entitled *Ellet Joseph Waggoner: the Myth and the Man*. … I would also strongly recommend Woodrow W. Whidden's book *Ellen White on Salvation*. If this book were well known among us, our key heresies would die" (*Ibid.*, p. 85). Robert Brinsmead had similar thoughts: "At special periods in our history the gospel has struggled to break through to the Adventist community. The year 1888 marked such a period. But even here we must keep a proper perspective. As McMahon's book, *Ellet Joseph Waggoner: The Myth and the Man*, has shown, Waggoner had light on justification for the Adventist community. But better material on justification by faith could be found among Protestant scholars of his day." (*Judge by the Gospel: A Review of Adventism* [1980], pp. 14-15). David McMahon doesn't mince words

in his thoughts on Waggoner, and Jones: "But other statements made in 1886 [by Waggoner] lean toward perfectionism. … How disappointing! Waggoner takes us to the very borders of the Promised Land and then turns us back into the old-covenant wilderness." "Unfortunately, between 1889 and 1891 Waggoner moved in this direction [pantheism] with his extreme view of sanctification. These views could have been avoided if he had preserved the distinction between righteousness by faith alone and sanctification." "Waggoner's theology between 1889 and 1891 was a theology of transition. Although not at first abandoning forensic justification, he moved to a concept of 'effective' justification. … Along with the Roman Catholic concept of effective justification, Waggoner developed such supportive concepts as the sinful human nature of Christ, the mystical atonement, sanctification by faith alone, and the law as an exhaustive expression of God's righteousness. Both church history and the history of theology clearly demonstrate that these are pantheistic premises" (*The Myth and the Man* [1979], pp. 44-45, 112-115). One year after the Glacier View meetings with Desmond Ford, Bert Haloviak from the General Conference Archives, drafted his concepts on Jones' meetings at Ottawa, Kansas: "It is apparent that both Jones and Waggoner already in 1888 had aspects to their message that would later develop into full-scale fanaticism and apostasy. While the ingredients of this twist are evidenced in Jones' first [Ottawa] sermon on righteousness (as well as Waggoner's), it became even more apparent by his concluding sermons. … While both Jones and Waggoner stressed righteousness as a free gift, they seemed to consider that gift as an infused righteousness and seemed to believe that this infused righteousness was necessary to sustain God's people through the time of trouble and the future period when they believed Christ would no longer mediate for His people in the heavenly sanctuary." "'Keeping the commandments,' Jones asserted, 'comes in after we are new creatures, so then we must be made good, be made righteous, before we can do good or do righteousness.'… Jones seems to be saying: our faith responds to God's love and motivates us to desire to keep his law; He accepts our desire and infuses His righteousness. … This theology would grow… and would be confronted by Ellen White a decade and a half later during the *Living Temple* crisis" ("Ellen White and A. T. Jones at Ottawa, 1889: Diverging Paths from Minneapolis," [unpublished manuscript, 1981], pp. 15-16, 20-22). But Jones and Waggoner never used the word "infused," other than speaking of the Catholic church's aberrant doctrine. When Jones and Waggoner used the word "imputed" and "accounted," Haloviak states they really meant "infused" (*Ibid.*, p. 18). After quoting from one of Ellen White's glowing endorsements made at Ottawa, Haloviak postulates: "It seems clear that Mrs. White is reacting to Jones' stress upon righteousness as an unmerited gift, rather than that part of his theology that would later be mislabeled righteousness by faith by those espousing holy flesh or *Living Temple* sentiments" (*Ibid.*, p. 17).

Woodrow Whidden received inspiration from Haloviak's manuscript in writing his biography on Waggoner. It seems that almost from page one, seeds are planted seeking to lead the reader to the same conclusions stated above: "Was Waggoner here [in 1888] confusing the work of justification with that of sanctification? These questions will most certainly be one of the key themes that will occupy us in our ongoing survey of Waggoner's theological developments. ... Quite obviously for Waggoner the justified sinner is 'made righteous and just'. ... but that such a declaration also somehow '*make*' the believer righteousness [*sic*] has a bit of an odd ring to it. ... Was he conflating justification and sanctification...?" [Webster's definition of "conflating" is: "The combining of two variant texts into a new one."]. Whidden continues: "What often makes him hard to grasp is the way that he used the language of justification (imputation or being accounted as righteous) to effectively encompass a lot of what we normally ascribe to the work of sanctification. And thus it is often tough to tease out Waggoner's meaning." "Undoubtedly, the most significant and portentous theological trend of the early post-Minneapolis period... was on Waggoner's early 1889 emphasis on the indwelling Christ. ... [I]t would become the source for almost all of the errant theological and practical paths that Waggoner would tread for the balance of his life" (*E. J. Waggoner*, pp. 85, 69-71, 199, 210). George Knight draws from the same authors declaring that Jones' "expressions on Christian holiness misled others" and his teachings "became a major root for the spread of sinless perfectionism among Seventh-day Adventists. ... There is, for example, a fairly direct line from Jones in the post-Minneapolis period to the holy flesh movement in Indiana in 1900. ... [M]any of its holy flesh ideas were extensions of his teachings on righteousness by faith. ... beginning at least as early as 1889..." (*From 1888 to Apostasy,* pp. 56-57). Jeff Reich suggests that "Mr Haloviak of the SDA archives in Washington helped Dr. Knight with some of his research. In fact, the whole idea of Jones teaching holy flesh from 18[89] onward seems to be almost lifted out of some of Haloviak's unpublished documents" (*From 1888 to apostasy: A Critique*, [St. Maries, ID: LMN, 1988], p.10, see also pp. 4-6). There is one major problem with the above scenario presented by all these modern writers: Where in the writings of Ellen White—who was an eyewitness at the Ottawa, Kansas, campmeeting—do we find support for such accusations? Do these accusations line up with Ellen White's assessment, or with the assessment of those who were fighting against the message over 120 years ago? Do we have better perception of what took place there in Kansas than what God gave to Ellen White? How can the results of the 1889 campmeetings be used today as proof that the 1888 message was accepted, while at the same time they are used as proof that the message had a fatal flaw which led to cheap grace on the one hand, and to holy flesh fanaticism and pantheism on the other?

11. Ellen G. White to Uriah Smith, Letter 24, Sept. 19, 1892; in *1888 Materials*, p. 1053, emphasis supplied.

12. Ellen G. White Manuscript 36, "Danger of False Ideas of Justification by Faith," n.d. 1890; in *1888 Materials*, pp. 810-811.

13. Ellen G. White, "How to Meet a Controverted Point of Doctrine," Morning Talk, Jan. 18, 1890, *Review and Herald*, Feb. 18, 1890; in *1888 Materials*, p. 533. For more on this topic see Chapter 11.

14. Ellen G. White Manuscript 1, Nov. 15, 1892; in *Manuscript Releases*, pp. 340-341.

15. Waggoner had just come from California where he was serving as senior editor of the *Signs of the Times*. On April 17, 1889, Waggoner received a "cable dispatch" that his father, J. H. Waggoner, had died in Basel, Switzerland, where he was editor of the French edition of the *Signs of the Times* (*Signs of the Times*, Apr. 22, 1889, p. 256). Only a few weeks later, on May 20, his nine-month-old boy, Ernest Eugene, died from whooping cough. Waggoner had left "only a few days before…on his journey East to fill important engagements, and so will never have the pleasure of beholding the face of his loved one again in this life" ("Obituary," *Signs of the Times*, June 3, 1889, p. 334). Waggoner's return East was for the purpose of visiting his mother, who had just returned from Europe, participating in some of the Eastern campmeetings, and completing a "course of study in Hebrew" at Chatauqua, which he had "been pursuing for several years" (*Signs of the Times*, May 27, 1889, p. 320). His wife and children back in California, who had already lost so much, were fearful he had been lost in the Johnstown and Williamsport flood until they finally received his letter "all soiled and ink-blurred from the water" (Pearl Waggoner Howard, "Biographical Sketch and Background," Document File 236, E. G. White Research Center, Andrews University, Berrien Springs, Michigan, p. 4). It was amidst these disheartening events that Waggoner continued to share the good news of the gospel to those within and without the church, many of whom had no idea of the costs to him.

16. Ellen G. White, "Camp-Meeting at Williamsport, PA.," *Review and Herald*, Aug. 13, 1889, pp. 513-514.

17. Ellen G. White, "Camp-Meeting at Williamsport, PA.," *Review and Herald*, Aug. 13, 1889, pp. 513-514.

18. George Knight refers to Ellen White's Williamsport article several times to try to prove the message that Jones and Waggoner presented was a mix of Adventist distinctive doctrines with the teaching of the holiness preachers: "*The genius of [Jones' and Waggoner's] 1888 message was that they had combined the two*

*halves of Revelation 14:12. They not only taught the commandments of God but they preached the doctrine of faith that the holiness preachers had proclaimed. Thus, from Ellen White's perspective, the importance of the 1888 message was not some special Adventist doctrine of justification by faith developed by Jones and Waggoner. Rather, it was the reuniting of Adventism with basic Christian beliefs on salvation.* ... [J]ustification by faith (an evangelical belief that Adventists have not been able to improve upon)." Knight continues: "Thus Waggoner and Mrs. White were in harmony on the fact that the doctrine of justification by faith he set forth, far from being some new understanding of justification, was the belief in justification neglected by Adventists but quite in harmony with the teaching of Paul, Luther, Wesley and the nineteenth-century holiness preachers. ... The two men had brought together the great truths of Adventism centering on the commandments of God and the great truth of evangelical Christianity centering on salvation by faith in Jesus. ..." A few pages later, Knight states: "In essence, Mrs. White was claiming that Seventh-day Adventists at last had a complete understanding of the third angel's message. ...That is, they had united those aspects of Adventist theology that were distinctively Adventist to the great theme of justification by faith that, as Ellen White put it, was being taught by the holiness preachers (RH, Aug. 13, 1889). The result was that Adventists since 1888 had finally been in a position to present the third angel's message in all of its fullness and balance" (*A User-Friendly Guide to the 1888 Message*, pp.108, 110, 113, emphasis original). But did Ellen White mean what Knight has claimed? She clarifies her statement often quoted by Knight, stating: "The Holiness people have gone to great extremes on this point. With great zeal they have taught, 'Only believe in Christ, and be saved; but away with the law of God.' This is not the teaching of the word of God. There is no foundation for such a faith. This is not precious gems of truth that God has given to his people for this time. This doctrine misleads honest souls" ("Camp-Meeting at Williamsport, PA.," *Review and Herald*, Aug. 13, 1889, pp. 513-514). Knight also seeks to substantiate his position—that Jones and Waggoner's message was in part the teachings of the holiness preachers—by quoting from E. J. Waggoner himself, where he stated in 1887 in his book *The Gospel in Galatians* (p. 70), that his teachings were simply "'a step nearer the faith of the great Reformers from the days of Paul to the days of Luther and Wesley" (*A User-Friendly Guide to the 1888 Message*, p. 110). But Waggoner was defending himself against G. I. Butler's charges that his much "vaunted doctrine of justification by faith" was contrary to scripture and doing away with Adventist doctrines of the law in favor of the liberal holiness movement doctrines. Waggoner's very next sentence reads: "It would be a step closer to the heart of the Third Angel's Message'" (*The Gospel in Galatians*, p. 70). *The third angel's message, which Seventh-day Adventists have been called to preach to the world, is not and never has been, a combination of*

*Adventist legalism (as was being taught by Butler and Smith) combined with the false view of justification by faith that the evangelical holiness preachers were teaching.* The third angel's message was sent directly from the heavenly sanctuary where Christ's work is taking place, not from the holiness preachers who had rejected the first and second angel's messages in 1844 (see Ellen G. White, *Early Writings*, pp. 55-6, 237, 254). This is not to say that the message that Adventists are to take to the world has no connection to the message of the Reformers: their message is in fact built on that foundation, but it is a message that God intends will shine forth in its fullest glory, free from long standing erroneous beliefs. Kenneth H. Wood clearly stated this thought: "In our opinion the 1888 message was distinctive, and included far more than Luther's gospel of 'justification by faith.' It had a strong eschatological emphasis. It was designed to prepare a people for translation at the second coming of Christ. It called attention to the heavenly sanctuary. It emphasized the humanity of Christ, and declared Jesus to be not only our Saviour but our Example—One who lived the life of faith and showed us how to live that same kind of life" ("Editor's Viewpoint," *Review and Herald*, Nov. 18. 1976, p. 2). Herbert E. Douglass agrees: "[Ellen White's] messages clearly demonstrated that this 'most precious message' was not a mere recovery of a sixteenth-century emphasis, nor a borrowing of a nineteenth-century Methodist accent, such as represented by Hannah Whitall Smith's *The Christian's Secret of a Happy Life*" (*Messenger of the Lord*, p. 197). Clinton Wahlen supports this view: "While EJW accepted the fundamental principles of the Reformation, including justification by faith and the Bible as the final authority for Christians, he viewed 'the Third Angel's Message' (which of course, included his own teachings) as an advance beyond the days of the Reformation" ("What Did E. J. Waggoner Say at Minneapolis?" *Adventist Heritage*, Winter 1988, p. 36). Strangely enough, the same author who claims Jones' and Waggoner's message endorsed by Ellen White was only the combination of Adventist law keeping with the "doctrine of faith" of the holiness preachers, also claims that their 1888 message led people directly into the "holy flesh movement." It is claimed that many of the "holy flesh ideas were extensions of [Jones'] teaching on righteousness by faith…he had preached at least as early as 1889" at the Kansas meetings (George R. Knight, *From 1888 to Apostasy*, p. 57). One might rightly ask why Ellen White spoke in favor of Jones' preaching at the Kansas meetings, and against those who were rejecting it, instead of warning the people that it would lead to the holy flesh movement. Not all Adventists authors, however, see the most precious message that way.

19. Ellen G. White, *The Great Controversy*, (1888 ed.), p. 253. Ellen White later described Luther as one of the Reformers whose work laid the foundation of God's temple. Yet, she never wrote that his work represented the entire building: "The enemy of righteousness left nothing undone in his effort to stop the work committed

to the Lord's builders. ... Workers were raised up who ably defended the faith once delivered to the saints. ... Like the apostles, many of them fell at their post, but the building of the temple went steadily forward. ... The Waldenses, John Wycliffe, Huss and Jerome, Martin Luther and Zwingli, Cranmer, Latimer, and Knox, the Huguenots, John and Charles Wesley, and a host of others brought to the foundation material that will endure throughout eternity. And in later years those who have so nobly endeavored to promote the circulation of God's word, and those who by their service in heathen lands have prepared the way for the proclamation of the last great message—these also have helped to rear the structure. Through the ages that have passed since the days of the apostles, the building of God's temple has never ceased. We may look back through the centuries and see the living stones of which it is composed gleaming like jets of light through the darkness of error and superstition. Throughout eternity these precious jewels will shine with increasing luster, testifying to the power of the truth of God" (*Acts of the Apostles*, p. 598-599).

20. Ellen G. White, *The Great Controversy*, (1888 ed.), pp. 148-149. Ellen White also quoted the Puritan Pilgrim, John Robinson, in his assessment of the church of his day: "'I cannot sufficiently bewail the condition of the reformed churches, who are come to a period in religion, and will go no farther than the instruments of their reformation. The Lutherans cannot be drawn to go any farther than what Luther saw, and the Calvinists, you see, stick fast where they were left by that great man of God, who yet saw not all things. This is a misery much to be lamented; for though they were burning and shining lights in their time, yet they penetrated not into the whole counsel of God, but were they now living, would be as willing to embrace further light as that which they first received'" (*Ibid.*, pp. 291-292). As wonderful as was the work done by Luther and Calvin, even their understanding of the foundational doctrine of justification by faith was affected by their misunderstanding of Original Sin and the will of man: "Unfortunately, Luther followed Augustine rather than Paul in his teaching of predestination, freedom of the will, and kindred doctrines. ... The middle of the sixteenth century found, therefore, two dominant Protestant schools of thought in Europe—Lutheranism and Calvinism. Both were serving to emancipate thousands from the bondage of mediaeval Catholicism, and both were defending valiantly certain scriptural doctrines. Both systems, however, possessed glaring weaknesses. ... Within Protestant ranks there arose those who were unwilling to go all the way with the two major reformers. Even Melanchthon, Luther's close friend and co-laborer, held to freedom of will, and avoided Luther's extremes regarding good works. ... In these principles can be seen, not only Wesley's insistence on justification by faith alone as taught by Luther, but another teaching with which neither Luther nor Calvin would have agreed; this is Wesley's cardinal doctrine of freedom of choice" (Norval F. Pease, "Justification and Righteousness by Faith in

the Seventh-day Adventist Church Before 1900," pp. 17, 19, 22, 26). Thus, the most precious message that the Lord sent through Jones and Waggoner, although built on the foundation laid by the Reformers, was to rise above all the papal errors that had come into the church during the dark ages.

21. *Ibid.*, p. 143. Over 50 times the word "present truth" is used in the *1888 Materials* collection, many times in reference to the message God was sending through Jones and Waggoner: "That which God gives His servants to speak today would not perhaps have been present truth twenty years ago, but it is God's message for this time" (p. 133). "God will ever give them to know He has given these men [A. T. Jones and E. J. Waggoner] a work to do, and a message to bear which is present truth for this time. They knew that wherever this message comes its fruits are good" (p. 228). "I have felt pained at heart to read letters from you that evidences that you are filled with doubts and unbelief still in the very message that I know to be present truth for the people of God for this time" (p. 274). See also pp. 120, 174, 267, 286, 365, 387, 429, 436, 502, 518, 917, 1710, 1796.

22. Ellen G. White, "Camp-Meeting at Williamsport, PA.," *Review and Herald*, Aug. 13, 1889, pp. 513-514.

23. Ellen G. White to H. Miller, Letter 5, June 2, 1889; in *1888 Materials*, p. 331. Years before, Ellen White wrote this about the shaking: "I asked the meaning of the shaking I had seen. I was shown that it would be caused by the straight testimony called forth by the counsel of the True Witness to the Laodiceans. It will have its effect upon the heart of the receiver of the testimony, and it will lead him to exalt the standard and pour forth the straight truth. This straight testimony, some will not bear. They will rise up against it, and this will cause a shaking among God's people. … My attention was then turned to the company I had seen before mightily shaken. … I heard those clothed with the armor speak forth the truth in great power. … I asked what had made this great change. An angel answered, 'It is the latter rain. The refreshing from the presence of the Lord. The loud cry of the Third Angel'" (*Review and Herald*, Dec. 31, 1857; in *Testimonies*, vol. 1, pp. 182-183). In 1892, Ellen White told Uriah Smith plainly: "The message which the messengers have been proclaiming is the message to the Laodicean church. … The message given us by A. T. Jones, and E. J. Waggoner is the message of God to the Laodicean church, and woe be unto anyone who professes to believe the truth and yet does not reflect to others the God-given rays" (*1888 Materials*, pp. 1051, 1052).

24. Ellen G. White, "Camp-Meeting at Rome, N. Y." *Review and Herald*, Sept. 3, 1889, pp. 545-546.

25. *Ibid.*

26. Ellen G. White to Uriah Smith, Letter 55, June 14, 1889; in *1888 Materials*, p. 336. Unfortunately the rest of this letter is not extant. Ellen White wrote Smith a second letter in September, showing what power a man in leadership can have over the people: "Again the matter has been presented to me in the night season. I was shown that you have been setting yourself in opposition to the Spirit and work of God. ... Light and truth which I know to be thus, you declare to be darkness and error. ... You have had the privilege of accepting the light, which has been light and precious truth and meat in due season to the hungry, starving flock of God; but you would not acknowledge it as light, as truth, as food. If you could prevent it from coming to the people of God you would do so. ... You are passing over the very same ground as the rejectors of Jesus Christ passed over. ... Poor deluded souls will be led to think that because Elder Smith does not accept the light and the message which has come to his people, light which is the very message for this time, that it must be error and delusion" (Ellen G. White to Uriah Smith, Letter 87, Sept. 1889; in *1888 Materials*, pp. 437-438). Ellen White wrote to Smith again in early 1890, but that letter is not extant. Smith responded on Feb. 17, 1890. Going all the way back to the Minneapolis Conference, he explained his view of the whole situation. He felt that Jones' and Waggoner's views were "contrary to the Scriptures" and "contrary to what [Ellen White] had previously seen." Smith claimed that the views they brought to the conference "nearly ruined" it. He claimed that "we could all agree to" Waggoner's discourses on righteousness by faith, but they paved the way for his erroneous view on the law in Galatians. Smith claimed that Jones was making rash statements; such as, "'I have got the truth and you will have to come to the same position in the end.'" Smith had also been *told* that Jones and Waggoner were supporting strange new interpretations on Revelation contrary to what Adventists had "long taught," which did away with the 1260 year prophecy. He was also upset that "because I ventured a word of caution on some of these points [in the *Review*], I am held up in public as one who is shooting in the dark, and does not know what he is opposing" (Uriah Smith to Ellen G. White, Feb. 17, 1890; in *Manuscripts and Memories*, p. 152-157). After receiving Smith's letter, Ellen White wrote to Jones the very next day. She told him she had started a letter to him before in regard to his making statements that might "confuse minds," and then "a capital is made out of it." She told him of the letter she had just received from Smith with the statements he claimed Jones had made (Ellen G. White to A. T. Jones, Letter 55, Feb. 17, 1890; unpublished, remainder of letter is not extant). On March 7, Jones responded to Ellen White in a letter (see *1888 Materials*, p. 592), and the next morning, March 8, Ellen White wrote back to Smith. Why? Because that very morning the Lord had revealed to her the influence that he was having on other people: "You have refused my testimonies... you labored to make them of none effect as did Korah, Dathan

and Abiram. ... You have strengthened the hands and minds of such men as Larson, Porter, Dan Jones, Eldridge and Morrison and Nicola and a vast number through them.  All quote you, and the enemy of righteousness looks on pleased" (Ellen G. White to Uriah Smith, Letter 59, in *1888 Materials*, p. 599).  A few days later, in a meeting with many of the brethren, Jones and Waggoner were able to share their side of the story (Ellen G. White to W. C. White, Letter 83, March 13, 1888; in *1888 Materials*, p. 627).  Here it was shown that Smith had falsely accused Jones of making rash statements.  Ellen White confronted Smith on this a short time later: "You responded to my letter of appeal by writing me a letter accusing Elder Jones of tearing up the pillars of our faith.  Was this truth?  The meetings of the ministers held in the office when these matters were investigated revealed that you accused him *wrongfully*" (Ellen G. White to Uriah Smith, Letter 73, Nov. 25, 1888; in *1888 Materials*, p. 734, emphasis supplied).

27.  Some have suggested, based on a few Ellen White statements, that what Jones and Waggoner were presenting was not new light; that we really have nothing to gain from looking into the message they brought to the church long ago.  Ellen White did say, "I call it not new light" (*1888 Materials*, p. 140); "This was no new light" (p. 211); "The Lord has shown me the light which shines upon our people is no new light" (p. 463); and "a message which is not a new truth, but the very same that Paul taught, that Christ himself taught" (p. 432).  George Knight quotes these statements and suggests that "the only way one can claim that the 1888 perspective on righteousness by faith is somehow unique to Adventism is to deny totally the plain words of...Ellen White" (*A User-Friendly Guide to the 1888 Message*, pp. 85-86).  But is this what Ellen White meant when she made her statements?  Did she make other clarifying statements?  A summary look through the *Ellen G. White 1888 Materials* will give us an idea.  First, we need to understand that Ellen White made these above mentioned statements in the context of answering those whom, like in the days of Christ's first advent, opposed the message as something *strange* and *new*.  She was trying to impress the brethren's minds that this was not some *new* truth absent from the Word of God, nor that which was replacing the foundational doctrines of the church.  But she did see something very special about Jones' and Waggoner's message, if we will only let her speak.  She clarifies her statement—"a message which is not new truth, but the very same message that Paul taught, that Christ Himself taught"—a few paragraphs later by stating: "but the truth will be continually *unfolding, expanding,* and *developing,* for it is Divine, like its Author" (*1888 Materials*, pp. 432, 434, emphasis supplied).  At Minneapolis she answered the question, "'Do you think that the Lord has any new and increased light for us as a people?'  I answered, 'Most assuredly.  I do not only think so, I but can speak understandingly'"(p. 219).  She felt it was "only reasonable that we should

expect something of the revealings of greater light to the people" (p. 279). Jones and Waggoner "presented precious light" (p. 309), things "new and old…from…God's word" (p. 386), "precious gems of truth in new settings" (p. 518). She asked; has God "not additional truth to reveal to His people?" Her answer was yes, "the ministers of God should be able to bring forth from the treasure house of His Word things new and old" (p. 510). Would God leave His people "with no new light?" Her answer was no, "we are to get more light from the throne of God, and have an increase of light" (p. 341). She stated resolutely: "Do not think that you have caught all the rays of light, and that there is no increased illumination to come to our world" (p. 674). But, she would add, "light must come through the agents whom God shall choose" (p. 507). "Increased light will shine upon all the grand truths of prophecy, and they will be seen in freshness and brilliancy because the bright beams of the Sun of Righteousness will illuminate the whole" (p. 514). She reminded her listeners that they had a part to play: "The truth is advancing truth and we must walk in increasing light" (p. 547). Those who "maintain their consecration, they will see increased light, and the light will continue to grow brighter and brighter unto the perfect day" (p. 671). "God will give additional light, and old truths will be recovered, and replaced in the frame-work of truth" (p. 765). It was "Jesus Christ who had the power of rescuing the truths from the rubbish, and again giving them to the world with more than their original freshness and power" (p. 525). And "when Christ in His work of redemption is seen to be the great central truth of the system of truth, a new light is shed upon all the events of the past and the future. They are seen in a new relation, and possess a new and deeper significance" (p. 807). Ellen White also had a warning to give: "The great error with churches in all ages has been to reach a certain point in their understanding of bible truth and there stop. … [They] say, 'We have all-sufficient light. We need not more.'. . . God's people in these last days are not to choose darkness rather than light. They are to look for light, to expect light. The light will continue to shine from the Word of God. … in brighter and still brighter rays, and reveal more and more distinctly the truth as it is in Jesus" (pp. 826-827). "[T]hose who are half-hearted… pride themselves on their great caution in receiving 'new light,' as they term it. But their failure to receive the light is caused by their spiritual blindness" (p. 1077). Well might Ellen White ask: "What plans have you that new light may be infused through the ranks of God's people?" (p. 534). So today we are to believe the promise: "Great truths that have lain unheeded and unseen since the day of Pentecost, are to shine from God's word in their native purity" (FE 473). In William Miller's dream, described in *Early Writings*, pp. 81-83, we find much of the imagery that Ellen White was using throughout this time period to describe the treasures that God was revealing, the new framework in which they were being presented, and the rubbish of selfish resistance that needed to be swept aside.

28. Satan seeks to cast his shadow over two central truths of Jesus' sacrifice for the salvation of all men: First, that Christ was a whole Saviour, made like unto His brethren. Second, that His sacrifice was complete; thus He is able to keep you from falling. These truths refute the two great errors that take in almost the whole world— those who would be saved by their merits, and those who would be saved in their sins. See footnote 34.

29. Ellen G. White Manuscript 5, "Christ and the Law," Sermon, June 19, 1889; in *1888 Materials*, pp. 341-345.

30. *Ibid.*, pp. 346-347.

31. Some have used this Ellen White statement to try to prove that *everything* the Lord sent through Jones and Waggoner was already found in the writings of Ellen White—even before 1888—and therefore, all we really need is Ellen White's books (George R. Knight, *A User-Friendly Guide to the 1888 Message*, pp. 68-9, 108). Norval Pease, responding to the query as to why the writings of Waggoner and Jones themselves should not be republished, stated: "It is not an overstatement to that there is nothing said by Waggoner and Jones but that [Ellen White] said better" (*The Faith That Saves* [1969], p. 53). But, as Clinton Wahlen points out: "Pease seemed to hint at another reason" Jones' and Waggoner's writings haven't been republished, "namely, that it might tarnish the evangelical image church leaders had sought so diligently to cultivate during the past two decades [1950s and 1960s]. 'Adventism, rightly understood,' he said, 'is evangelical to the core'" ("Selected Aspects of Ellet J. Waggoner's Eschatology," p. xxiii). Of course another point of the argument by Knight, Pease, and many others, is to marginalize the significance of the message sent through Jones and Waggoner. Yes, it is true that Ellen White wrote during the Minneapolis Conference: "This was not new light to me for it had come to me from higher authority for the last forty-four years, and I have presented it to our people by pen and voice in the testimonies of His Spirit. ... Has not this subject been presented in the testimonies again and again?" (*1888 Materials*, pp. 212, 217). But these statements were made to defend against the accusation that she had changed or that she had been influenced by Jones and Waggoner and was supporting new heresy. Somehow, the brethren saw a difference in the message of Jones and Waggoner and the one she had been giving for 45 years. Only a few days prior, she stated distinctly: "I would have humility of mind, and be willing to be instructed as a child. The Lord has been pleased to give me great light, yet I know that He leads other minds, and opens to them the mysteries of His Word, and I want to receive every ray of light that God shall send me, though it should come through the humblest of His servants" (*Ibid.*, p. 163). It was the message she "had been trying to present" for 45 years, and Waggoner was the first to clearly present it

publicly—to which "every fiber of [her] heart said Amen" (*Ibid.*, pp. 348, 349). It is interesting to note that many who see little importance in Jones' and Waggoner's message inexplicably refer to all of the books Ellen White wrote after Minneapolis as proof the message was accepted (Norval Pease, *op. cit.*, p. 46; George Knight, *A User-Friendly Guide to the 1888 Message*, pp. 68-9; L. E. Froom, *Movement of Destiny*, p. 444). We would not question Ellen White's prophetic calling or the authority given her by God in doctrinal matters. Nor would we deny the fact that those who read Ellen White's inspired books will be greatly blessed. If the truths and counsel there presented are accepted by faith and acted upon, they will lead the reader into a saving relationship with Christ and into the kingdom. But we also would not deny what Ellen White herself said: "The Lord has raised up Brother Jones and Brother Waggoner to *proclaim a message to the world to prepare a people to stand* in the day of God." And of that message she said: "God has sent men to bring us the truth that *we should not have had unless God had sent somebody to bring it to us.* God has let me have a light of what His Spirit is, and therefore I accept it, and I no more dare to lift my hand against these persons, because it would be against Jesus Christ, who is to be recognized in His messengers" (*1888 Materials*, pp. 1814, 608, emphasis supplied). Whatever truth the Lord sent through Jones and Waggoner was only building on the foundation already laid, but heaven still identified their message with the beginning of the loud cry and latter rain.

32. Ellen G. White Manuscript 5, "Christ and the Law," Sermon, June 19, 1889; in *1888 Materials*, pp. 348-349.

33. Uriah Smith, "Our Righteousness Again," *Review and Herald*, July 2, 1889.

34. Ellen G. White, "Camp-Meeting at Rome, N. Y." *Review and Herald*, Sept. 3, 1889, pp. 545-546. Ellen White emphasized the fact that when Satan can lead man to look to his own merits he has no power over temptation: "Nearly every false religion has been based on the same principle—that man can depend upon his own efforts for salvation" (*PP* 73). "The principle that man can save himself by his own works, lay at the foundation of every heathen religion; it had now become the principle of the Jewish religion. Satan had implanted this principle. Wherever it is held, men have no barrier against sin" (*The Desire of Ages*, p. 35). "The papacy is well adapted to meet the wants of...two classes of mankind, embracing nearly the whole world—those who would be saved by their merits, and those who would be saved in their sins. Here is the secret of its power" (*The Great Controversy*, p. 572).

35. Ellen G. White Manuscript 25, "Resume of Travels and Labors," n.d. 1889; in A. L. White, *The Lonely Years*, p. 418.

36. Ellen G. White Manuscript 30, June 1889; in *1888 Materials*, p. 363.

37. Ellen G. White to Madison and Miller, Letter 4, July 23, 1889; in *1888 Materials*, pp. 388, 391, 392, 406-407. If it is true that "the prospects of the people of God are similar to those of the Jews, who could not enter in because of unbelief," then is it possible that we are wandering in the wilderness of this world of sin because we have rebelled against God and followed in the footsteps of "unfaithful spies"?

38. *Ibid.*, pp. 417-419, 421-423.

39. A. T. Jones to C. E. Holmes, May 12, 1921; in *Manuscript and Memories*, p. 329. In response to this statement by A. T. Jones, George Knight suggests: "Of course, how much of that antagonism concerned righteousness by faith and how much involved other issues, such as the law in Galatians and Jones's *personality*, is impossible to determine. ... [Jones] lacked an experiential application of his own teachings" (*A User-Friendly Guide to the 1888 Message*, pp. 149, 150).

ote number 16 was inadvertently attached to the end of footnote
. White Manuscript 6, Nov. 4, 1889; in 1888 Materials, pp. 485-
s the footnote numbering is off by one for footnotes numbered
tnote number 16 is actually footnote number 17, and so on.
s inconvenience.

# and Plans for Consolidation

The campmeetings during the year of 1889 had made considerable impact in the lives of those who attended. Many people were blessed by the message presented by Jones and Waggoner. Ellen White in sermons and letters indicated that great light had come upon God's people and it was time for them to "arise and shine," for the earth was to be lightened with Christ's glory. Around this time, F. H. Westphal returned to his home in Wisconsin, "and told the church that the Latter Rain had started."[1]

As the time for the General Conference approached, Ellen White was hopeful that a change had been made and that there would be a stark difference from the Conference at Minneapolis. On October 18, the Conference began in Battle Creek and continued until November 11. As Ellen White contemplated the purpose for the gathering at the beginning of the Conference, she greatly desired that the Sabbath "be a most precious day to our souls." Recognizing they were living "amid the perils of the last days," she perceived that God would "not sanction sectarianism or a legal religion, which is so prevalent even among those who claim to believe present truth. Christ and His righteousness is our only hope." During the first weekend of meetings, many bore "testimony of the blessings received during the past year, of the blessed light they had received and cherished, which was justification through faith." This led Ellen White to declare that the "Spirit of the Lord was in our midst."[2]

As the meetings progressed, Ellen White was given strength to bear a pointed testimony to all those that gathered there. The "Holy Spirit" was breathed upon her as she pleaded with God that the "ministering brethren might be endowed with power from on high to carry the solemn message to all parts of the world." Many more testimonies were given relating to the experiences of the past year. All who shared felt their experience had been "of a more spiritual character than they have had before since embracing the truth. The light of justification through faith, and that the righteousness of Christ must become our righteousness, else we cannot possibly keep the law of God, is the testimony of all who speak, and the fruit is peace, courage, joy, and harmony."[3]

On Sunday, October 27, Ellen White attended the eight o'clock meeting where "Elder Jones presented the Bible evidence of justification by faith." Afterwards Ellen White spoke to the people in regard "to coming to the light and walking in the light lest darkness come upon them." Not all were embracing the light, and thus she gave a word of warning:

> Some who will gossip over the Bible subject of justification by faith, and cavil and question and throw out their objections, do not know what they are talking about. They do not know that they are placing themselves as bodies of darkness to intercept the bright rays of light which God has determined shall come to His people. And they will come; the third angel's message is to go forth with power, filling the earth with its glory. And what is man that he can work against God? He may choose the darkness, he may love the darkness and be left enshrouded in darkness; but the message is to go forward in power, even if some refuse to advance with it.[4]

The next morning, Ellen White spoke "with great plainness in reference to some who were attending the meeting but had given no evidence they were partakers of the Spirit and power of God in the meeting. They did not seem to discern where God was at work." She called upon those who had been "working contrary to God for one year in a marked manner" against the "special, marked light." She warned that "the darkness of every individual [would] be in proportion to his unbelief and his resistance and contempt of the light which God graciously sends." Later that morning Ellen White attended the meeting conducted by Elder Jones:

There were a large number present and he presented the subject of justification by faith in a plain, distinct manner, in such marked simplicity that no one need to be in darkness, unless he has in him a decided heart of unbelief, to resist the workings of the Spirit of God. Many were fed and others seem to be amazed, as though they did not know what justification by faith really meant. Certainly the lines of truth were laid out in a distinct manner. I was glad to hear this testimony. I bore a testimony that that which I heard was the truth, and those who would walk out upon the light given would be on the Lord's side.[5]

The following morning, Ellen White wrote out the experiences of the meetings thus far. She expressed great joy from seeing people who had not yet heard the message "taking it in." Yet, they were living in ominous times:

We are having most excellent meetings. The spirit that was in the meeting at Minneapolis is not here. All moves off in harmony. There is a large attendance of delegates. Our five o'clock morning meeting is well attended, and the meetings good. All the testimonies to which I have listened have been of an elevating character. They say that the past year has been the best of their life; the light shining forth from the word of God has been clear and distinct—justification by faith, Christ our righteousness. The experiences have been very interesting. ...

At eight o'clock Bro. Jones speaks upon the subject of justification by faith, and great interest is manifested. There is a growth in faith and in the knowledge of our Lord and Saviour Jesus Christ. There are quite a number who have not had an opportunity to hear upon this subject before but they are taking it in, and are being fed with large morsels from the Lord's table. The universal testimony from those who have spoken has been that this message of light and truth which has come to our people is just the truth for this time and wherever they go among the churches, light, and relief, and the blessing of God is sure to come in. ...

We may expect at any time new and startling claims from Satan through his agents, and shall not the people of God be wide awake, shall they not become strong in the strength of the mighty one? Wise in the wisdom of God? A crisis has arrived in the government of God in which something great and decisive must be done. The delay will not be prolonged. The wrath of God will not be long withheld, justice is only to speak the word and in a moment what confusion there will be. ...

> Oh for the baptism of the Holy Spirit to come upon the workers that they may represent Jesus Christ in all their labors.[6]

That same morning, Ellen White sent a letter to Mary White expressing the same sentiments. She told her they were "having good meetings. There seems to be no dissension." She wrote of the testimonies shared by ministers who had been blessed by the "light that came to them at Minneapolis and during the past year" and noted that "success has attended their labors during the past year as never before." Ellen White told Mary that "thus far, not one voice of opposition is heard. Unity seems to prevail." She did add, however, "at the same time there are a number who apparently stand where they did at Minneapolis. Oh, that God would work mightily for His people and scatter the clouds of darkness and let the sunlight of His glory in."[7]* Although there were great blessings poured out at the morning meetings "the very ones who most need the influence of these meetings have not been present." Opposition was still strong.[8]

One of those who still stood where they did at Minneapolis was Uriah Smith. The October 29 edition of the *Daily Bulletin* printed his Sabbath sermon in which he addressed the "history and future work of Seventh-day Adventists." He mentioned the fact that in the early work "our ministers went forth with the two great weapons of the message—the commandments of God, and the faith of Jesus. They preached in a way to produce a thorough and permanent reformation of life." Smith implicated Jones and Waggoner when he asserted that Adventist "did not adopt the methods of modern [Protestant] revivalists, and content themselves with merely giving their hearers a taste of honey and the sight of a rainbow; but they wove into their work some flashes from Sinai, to arouse the conscience, and strike the scales from blind eyes."[9] Clearly, Uriah Smith had not heeded Ellen White's counsel to him the summer before.

## *Religious Liberty*

Other issues at the 1889 General Conference were of great concern to Ellen White, including Sunday legislation in the United States and the Church's work for religious liberty. Three years earlier, in response to the ever-increasing agitation for Sunday legislation, the Church began publishing the *American Sentinel* with J. H. Waggoner as editor. A. T. Jones and E. J. Waggoner took over the position as co-editors in 1887. The General Conference also appointed a Religious Liberty committee, with A. T. Jones serving as president. The purpose of this committee was to get more public exposure to the issue of religious liberty through press releases, public speaking engagements, and circulation of petitions against Sunday proposals. The committee also encouraged church members to become actively involved in the religious liberty cause and provided legal aid for those Seventh-day Adventists indicted for Sunday labor.[10]*

BATTLE CREEK TABERNACLE

At the 1888 General Conference in Minneapolis, and in the Battle Creek Tabernacle the following December, A. T. Jones had lectured on religious liberty, with both of his lecture series being widely distributed. Shortly thereafter Jones had stood before the Senate Committee on Education and Labor and spoken against the Blair Sunday Bill. February 22, 1889, found Jones once again before the Senate Committee, this time to testify against Blair's proposed Constitutional amendment that would Christianize the nation's public school system. Thankfully for Seventh-day Adventists, as well as the whole nation, both Blair bills died with the fifty-first congress.[11]*

With Jones actively at the center of the petition campaign, nearly 500,000 signatures were obtained by October 1889, requesting Congress "pass no bill in regard to the observance of the Sabbath, or Lord's day, or any other religious or ecclesiastical institution." Jones saw the petition drive as more than just trying to defeat Sunday legislation, but "to spread the third angel's message, and to warn everybody against the making of the image of the beast," for "in explaining to others the object of the petition, they are, in fact, making them acquainted with the third angel's message."[12]

Even though Jones was perhaps the most active Adventist Minister in the area of religious liberty, some did not appreciate his zeal. In July of 1889, at the Battle Creek Tabernacle, the Religious Liberty Committee had been reorganized and enlarged to 110 members and was renamed the National Religious Liberty Association (NRLA). A. T. Jones was replaced as president by Captain Eldridge: both he and vice-president Dan Jones were strong opposers of Jones and Waggoner. Jones and Waggoner were placed on the editorial committee of the NRLA.

Now, at the 1889 General Conference, and under Eldridge's leadership, the NRLA *formed* and *passed* its by-laws, some of which were similar to the resolutions which had failed to pass at Minneapolis in 1888. Two of the by-laws were: "No literature shall be published or circulated under the name of this Society by any of its officers or members until it has been indorsed by the Executive Committee of the Association. … All matter for publication in newspapers shall be subject to the inspection and approval of the President and at least a majority of the Editorial Committee, before it is sent out by the Secretary, provided, that in the absence of the editorial quorum, the President and first Vice President may act as members of the Editorial Committee."[13]

This NRLA executive committee was also entertaining questions in regard to Sunday legislation, such as what to do for Sabbath keepers in the Southern states who were enduring persecution for working on Sunday. Some of the brethren were "anxious that a resolution shall be passed by the General Conference advising our Sabbathkeeping brethren liable to imprisonment and fines, to refrain from labor" on Sunday. This resolution did not pass even though some pushed for its immediate acceptance.[14]

### Ellen White's Response

On November 4, Ellen White responded to the delegates who "seemed anxious that a resolution shall be passed." Without mincing words, she told them that "such resolutions should not be placed before this Conference, requiring their action." She reminded them that if the disciples had gathered for ten days earnestly praying for the descent of the Holy Spirit, they would need "twenty" days before venturing to "write out a decision for the people on this point. Much earnest prayer and nothing less than the descent of the Holy Ghost would settle these questions." Ellen White warned that there was always "danger of going to extremes." If a decision was made "that our people not labor on Sunday" the brethren in the Southern states would "appear to harmonize with the Sunday law" and there would be a "bowing to an idol god by those who claim to be Sabbathkeepers, there will be a yielding of principles until all is lost." If Adventists rested "on the first day of the week in order to avoid arrests," Ellen White mused, "would this be showing that we stand in right relation to God's holy law?"[15]*

Ellen White saw danger on both sides of the issue if a resolution were passed. She warned the brethren not to "get in the place of God before the people. Enough of this kind of work has been done. Let God work on human minds. … Leave God something to do. … Lift no burdens from God's people that He would have them to bear. … Do not cast burdens upon any class that He would have them released from." She told them not to let "anyone make any proud boast either by precept or example to show that he is defying the laws of the land. Make no resolutions as to what a person in different States may do, or may not do." While men must be careful not to bow the knee to the false Sabbath "there should be no just occasion to our enemies to charge us with being lawless. … We should not feel it enjoined upon us to irritate our neighbors who idolize Sunday by making determined efforts to bring labor on that day before them purposely to exhibit an independence."[16]

While Ellen White urged the brethren not to pass resolutions in regard to Sabbathkeepers' duties toward Sunday laws, she also urged that it "was time for God's people to work as never before." Speaking to those at the General Conference, she declared that "there are many who are at ease, who are, as it were, asleep." Despite their understanding of prophecy regarding "the enforcement of Sunday observance," they "sit down in calm expectation of the event, comforting themselves with the thought that God will protect His people in the day of trouble. But God will not save us if we make no effort to do the work He has committed to our charge." A message was to be given the world:

We should diligently study the Word of God, and pray in faith that God will restrain the powers of darkness, for as yet the message has gone to comparatively few, and the world is to be lightened with its glory. The present truth—the commandments of God and the faith of Jesus—has not yet been sounded as it must be. …

While you have been allowing your minds to be diverted from the very work that God would have you do, and have been doing that which He has not called you to do, Satan has exulted. … You have neglected the testimonies that the Lord in mercy sent to incline your feet in the right path. Some of you have utterly refused these words of warning. …

I felt that if I was permitted to stand before you again I must have the presence of God with me as Moses had when he led the children of Israel through the wilderness. … I would show them that unless they were imbued with the Spirit of God they could do no good in their work. Their coldness, their lukewarmness, was an offense to God. They must walk in Christ's light or Satan would put his blinder before their eyes and they would call light darkness and darkness light. …

Light must come to the people through agents whom God shall choose, who will give the note of warning, that none may be in ignorance of the purposes of God or the devices of Satan. At the great heart of the work Satan will use his hellish arts to the utmost. He will seek in every possible way to interpose himself between the people and God, and shut away the light that God would have come to His children. …

The Lord Jesus has been coming near to us in this conference. I thank God for the heartbreaking I have seen in the ministers' prayer meetings. … But for some reason, the very ones who most need the influence of these meetings have not been present. The very ones who most need to drink at the fountain of life, who ought to stand in the forefront in our ranks, have not received the power that God has been willing to bestow upon them. The future will tell the results of failing to improve these precious morning meetings. …

Those who would now help souls… must themselves have on the whole armor of Christ's righteousness; for we can never lead the people to an experience of which we are not partakers. Those who have not tasted of the rich blessing of God will make little of the blessings that others have received. The light which God is giving to His people may be slighted, refused, rejected, but it is thus treated at great peril to men's souls. Brethren, God is working for us, and I feel deeply in earnest that not one ray of heaven-sent light may be regarded with indifference. God's communication to man is to be appreciated and cherished. If we do not appreciate the light of heaven, it will be our condemnation; our position will be similar to that of the Jews when they rejected the Lord of life and glory.[17]*

## *Plans for Consolidation*

R.A. UNDERWOOD

Another issue at the Conference concerned the future of the Publishing Association and its relationship to the Church. On October 21, the Association's vice-president, C. Eldridge, concluded his opening report with an appeal: "The importance of the publishing work demands your most earnest attention at this time. You should make a thorough study of the existing relations between the association and

E.W. FARNSWORTH

the denomination, and lay such plans as will best advance the general work." After his presentation Eldridge appointed a Nominations Committee with E. W. Farnsworth as chair, and a Resolutions Committee, with R. A. Underwood as chair; both men opposers of Jones and Waggoner.[18]

On October 27, General Conference President O. A. Olsen gave an address on "some important matters that ought to receive the attention of this body." He spoke of the publishing work and the need for a new organization that would "bind together the different denominational institutions and interests." He asked, "why should not our various denominational enterprises be managed by boards, elected by the General Conference? We acknowledge the General Conference to be the highest authority recognized by God on the earth. ...

"Our publishing interests and our book business are of the greatest importance. Should not these properly be under one managing board?... [W]e do feel that this body should not adjourn before some attention is given to this matter."[19]

Attention was quickly given to Olsen's advice, and on the 4th of November, R. A. Underwood presented a resolution, "that we favor the present efforts to secure the consolidation of the various publishing interests of the denomination." Remarkably, "this resolution was adopted without discussion, and the Association adjourned."[20]

At a meeting the next day, R. A. Underwood presented the report "on the consolidation of denominational interests." The report was adopted that very day and reads as follows:

> 1. That steps be taken at once to form a corporation for the purpose of taking entire control of all our publishing interests, thus bring the work under one general management.
>
> 2. That the officers of this Association be a board of twenty-one trustees... with the power to organize themselves by electing a president. ...
>
> 5. That the Stockholders of the Review and Herald Publishing House and the Pacific Press Publishing Company take into consideration the advisability of turning over all their interests to this new organization... that steps be taken as soon as possible to bring about this result.
>
> The object of this new organization shall be:
>
> 1. To hold the title of all our denominational publishing houses and the equipments thereof.
>
> 2. To own, publish, and control the sale of all denominational books, tracts, and periodicals.
>
> 3. To secure, as far as possible, by purchase or otherwise, the plates and copyrights of all denominational books now published by our different publishing houses, or that may be written in the future. ...
>
> 5. To appoint editors and managers, to take a general supervision of the work of the various offices.
>
> In view of the fact that it may take some time to bring about, in full, this much-to-be desired result, and in order to move in that direction as far and as fast as possible, we recommend that at the first, the association assume control

of all denominational publications and periodicals now published in the foreign languages… with a view to assuming entire control of all our publishing interests.

In order that no time may be lost, your Committee would further recommend that a standing Committee of twenty-one be elected by the General Conference at its present session to take this whole question into consideration, with power to act. …

Your committee would further recommend that a similar organization be effected for the purpose of controlling all our educational interests, and owning the property—thus bringing them under one general management. Also, another to control our health institutions.[21]

That very day the Nominating Committee reported that a committee of twenty-one had been elected to "plan for the consolidation of the publishing interests." Dan Jones was elected chair of the committee. Six meetings were held over the next few days and plans were laid for the accomplishment of their goals.[22]*

During this same time the delegates officially approved a plan to divide North America into six divisions, assigning a member of the General Conference Executive Committee to give special attention and supervision to each. The Conference's Plans Committee also recommended replacing separate organizations—such as the Sabbath School Association, Health and Temperance Association, Tract and Missionary Society, and the Educational Society—with a secretary in each conference who would promote that particular line of work. This individual would be a member of the General Conference Committee as well. After three days of discussion, and with the delegates divided on the wisdom of such a plan, the Plans Committee requested that its recommendation be withdrawn, and the conference voted to strike out the entire discussion from its records.[23]*

Dispite the failure of this resolution, advances were made in passing other resolutions that had failed to pass during the 1888 General Conference. Those who had been seeking to silence the message and the messengers were gaining greater control of the church organization, which would affect the direction of the entire church. Based on Ellen White's initial reports, the 1889 Conference has been looked upon as a great turning point; but we might rightly ask, in which direction?

## *A Warning of What Lay Ahead*

Ellen White had seen great revivals taking place across the country as a result of the message presented by Jones, Waggoner, and herself, and yet she had grave cause for concern. Opposition still ran high among many brethren in leading positions. On October 31, 1889, Ellen White had an interview with "Brethren Nicola and Morrison," and it "was not pleasant." They still did not see their true condition or that "their spirit at Minneapolis was not the spirit of Jesus Christ." They justified "their course in everything":

> I had no satisfaction whatever in this interview. If the flock of God is entrusted to such men, may the Lord pity His poor, poor people, the sheep of His pasture, and enlighten them and save them from being molded by the spirit and influence of these men of dark unbelief.
>
> After they left I felt that there had been a funeral in the house. My heart was as heavy as lead. Oh, what a work of death can individual influence exert upon souls who are starving for the light of life and do not know where to go for the knowledge they should have! The table loaded with the manna of heaven is set before them, but they will not eat it.[24]

These men were leaders in the work, men that were deciding the direction the church would take, and yet men that were turning away from the light sent from heaven. Before the close of the Conference, Ellen White gave a warning of the danger that lay ahead because of the plans that were being speedily laid for the control of the work, and this under the guidance of those who were in opposition to the message sent of God:

> To The General Conference: Dear Brethren—I have presented before you matters which the Lord has shown me, and I have a warning to give to this body now assembled in Battle Creek. You are in danger from the fact that plans may be formed, ways may be devised, propositions may be followed that mean, not success, but defeat. I dare not let this Conference close, and those assembled return to their homes, without bidding you to consider carefully every proposition that has been presented. Look well to every plan that has been proposed, and give not your Yea and Amen hastily, as I have heard from the lips of some men whose understanding is beclouded, and they know not what is the character of the sentiments and propositions they are saying Amen to. Be not carried away with proposals that appear innocent, when their end is disaster and a forfeiture of the favor of God. …

Let not men exalt themselves, and seek to carry through their ideas without the cooperation and sanction of the people of God. Your strong spirit, your loud, contemptuous speeches are out of harmony with Christ and his ways. ... God has seen you smiting with the fist of wickedness. You must bear the divine credentials before you make decided movements to shape the working of God's cause. ... But He despises your fierce spirit, he is grieved with the hardness of your heart. ...

I know that a work must be done for the people, or many will not be prepared to receive the light of the angel sent down from heaven to lighten the whole earth with his glory. Do not think that you will be found as vessels unto honor in the time of the latter rain, to receive the glory of God, if you are lifting up your souls unto vanity, speaking perverse things, in secret cherishing roots of bitterness brought from the conference at Minneapolis. The frown of God will certainly be upon every soul who cherishes and nurtures these roots of dissension, and possesses a spirit so unlike the Spirit of Christ.[25]

As her address came to an end, Ellen White made a prediction of what the end result would be if they failed to come into the unity of the faith. Signs were being fulfilled all around them, both in the world and in the church, telling them that Jesus was longing to come. Her words ought to cause us to tremble as we find ourselves living over 120 years after these statements were made:

There has been a departure from God among us, and the zealous work of repentance and return to our first love essential to restoration to God and regeneration of heart has not yet been done. Infidelity to God has been making its inroads in our ranks; for it is the fashion to depart from Christ, and give place to skepticism. The cry of the heart has been, "We will not have this man to reign over us." Baal, Baal, is the choice. The religion of many among us will be the religion of apostate Israel, because they love their own way, and forsake the way of the Lord. The true religion, the only religion of the Bible, that teaches forgiveness through the merits of a crucified and risen Saviour, that advocates righteousness by the faith of the Son of God, has been slighted, spoken against, ridiculed. It has been denounced as leading to enthusiasm and fanaticism.[26]* Take it back while it is not too late for wrongs to be righted; for you have sinned against God. ... What kind of a future is before us, if we shall fail to come into the unity of the faith?

When we are united in the unity for which Christ prayed, this long controversy which has been kept up through Satanic agency, will end, and we shall not see men framing plans after the order of the world, because they have not spiritual eyesight to discern spiritual things. ...

> Let us not longer bow down to the idol of men's opinions, no longer be slaves to any shameful lust, no longer bring a polluted offering to the Lord, a sin-stained soul, which is represented by the offerings of the Moabites and Amorites.
>
> O, shall not repentance take the place of unbelief and rebellion. Or shall this state of impenitence and blindness continue until it shall be said unto us, as to the cities that spurned the offered mercies of Christ in the days of his ministry, 'Woe unto thee, Chorazin! Woe unto thee, Bethsaida!…[27]*

Realizing what was taking place at the headquarters of the church, Ellen White warned that if nothing changed, Baal worship would be the choice. It would be a direct result of rejecting the very message God had sent from heaven—the result of calling light darkness and darkness light. Ellen White knew that Baal worship took in much more then just bowing down to carved idols. Multitudes with "no outward shrine" have a "wrong conception of God and His attributes, and are as truly serving a false god as were the worshipers of Baal."[28] The message that Jones and Waggoner were presenting was one of total dependence on the righteousness of Christ. Baal worship was a "wavering between dependence upon the righteousness of Christ, and dependence upon your own righteousness."[29] Thus Baal worship was self-worship; the result of making an idol out of man's opinions. Ellen White warned that Baal worship would be the result of the plans being laid for the operation of the church organization that were after the world's order and not after God's order: "the very course men will take who are now in office."[30]

In the months ahead Ellen White would have much to say about the plans that had been laid at the 1889 General Conference. Rather than being the turning point for good, they resulted in a confederacy being formed to stand between the people and the message sent from heaven. Well might she say; "The men in responsible positions have disappointed Jesus. They have refused precious blessings. … The knowledge they should receive of God that they might be a light and blessing to others, they refuse to accept, and thus become channels of darkness. The Spirit of God is grieved."[31] Several months later, Ellen White said that God had "a blessing for us" at the 1889 General Conference, but sadly, "there was no reception."[32]*

## *Ministerial Institute*

Plans were made at the 1889 Conference to hold a Bible-school for ministers held in Battle Creek from November 6 through March 25, 1890. This 20 week Bible-school, which was to be entirely separate from the College, grew out of the Ministerial Institute held from January 17 to March 28, 1889, where A. T. Jones had been lead instructor. The new program endeavored to avoid "long courses" that Ellen White had said were not necessary when workers were so urgently needed in the field. W. W. Prescott was elected principal and given the task of drawing up the curriculum for the intensive course in which he, Uriah Smith, A. T. Jones and E. J. Waggoner would be the main instructors.

Prescott announced that this 20 week intensive program was equivalent to a two year program with a "four studies" course each year. Classes were to include: Ancient History, Bible Doctrines, Civil Government, Greek or Hebrew, Church Government, Logic, Evidences of Christianity, and Church History, among others.[33] Classes for laymen were also held in conjunction with the school for ministers, some of the early morning meetings being combined. The program grew to 157 students in regular attendance, but attendance at the combined meetings swelled to over 300.[34]

Ellen White was still in Battle Creek during the Ministerial Institute, although she certainly had not planned to remain away from home for so long when she left California to go to the 1888 General Conference in Minneapolis. Although she was not scheduled to teach any classes, she became actively involved, especially during the last two months of the Institute. Traveling to various conferences and general meetings in nearby churches also kept her very busy. Furthermore, she prepared books for publication, including *Testimony* No. 33, much of which related to the Minneapolis episode, and *Testimonies for the Church* Vol. 5, which was comprised of *Testimony* numbers 31 through 33. She then began working on expanding *Spirit of Prophecy* Volume 1, which would become *Patriarchs and Prophets*, and started her work on the *Life of Christ*, which would eventually be published in 1898 under the title, *The Desire of Ages*.

While Ellen White's work definitely kept her busy, the most laborious task was constantly battling those in leadership positions. That battle was soon to reach even greater proportions: as Waggoner began to present on the subject of the nature of Christ, and the subject of the two covenants at the Ministerial Institute. Another time of crisis had come.

# CHAPTER 10 FOOTNOTES

1. F. H. Westphal to L. E. Froom, April 28, 1930; in *Movement of Destiny*, p. 262.

2. Ellen G. White Manuscript 22, "Diary," Oct. 1889; in *1888 Materials*, pp. 453 454.

3. *Ibid.*, p. 461.

4. *Ibid.*, p. 463.

5. *Ibid.*, p. 465.

6. Ellen G. White Manuscript 10, "The Excellence of Christ," Oct. 1889; in *1888 Materials*, pp. 447-448.

7. Ellen G. White to Mary White, Letter 76, Oct. 29, 1889; in *1888 Materials*, p. 450. Some have quoted Ellen White's Manuscript 10, 1889, and her Letter 76, to Mary White, to try and prove that the revivals of 1889 brought an end, for the most part, to the opposition to the most precious message through Elders Waggoner and Jones. A. V. Olsen states: "The Spirit of contention that characterized the session in Minneapolis was absent at the 1889 meetings in Battle Creek. A spirit of harmony prevailed throughout the meetings. ... [T]he interval between ... 1888 and 1889... yielded 'the peaceable fruit of righteousness'" (*From Crisis to Victory*, pp. 62-63). See also, George R. Knight, *From 1888 to Apostasy*, p. 66; *A User-Friendly Guide to the 1888 Message*, p. 120. But there has been a failure to mention the rest of Ellen White's statements regarding the meeting, which we will look at in the latter part of this chapter.

8. Ellen G. White Manuscript 18, "Religious Liberty," Dec. 1889; in *1888 Materials*, p. 512.

9. Uriah Smith, *General Conference Daily Bulletin*, Oct. 29, 1889, p. 104.

10. See: Eric Syme, *A History of SDA Church-State Relations*, pp. 34-35; A. W. Spalding, *Origin and History of the Seventh-day Adventists*, Vol. 2 (Washington, D. C.: Review and Herald, 1962) p. 254. The stated principles of the General Conference committee were: "We believe in supporting the civil government, and submitting to its authority. We deny the right of any civil government to legislate on religious questions. We believe it is the right, and should be the privilege, of every man to worship according to the dictates of his own conscience. We also believe it to be our duty to use every lawful and honorable means to prevent religious legislation by the civil government; that we and our fellow citizens may enjoy the inestimable blessings of both civil and religious liberty" (*SDA Bible Commentary*, vol. 10, p. 1198).

11. See: W. A. Blakely, *American State Papers Bearing on Sunday Legislation* (1911) p. 366. Jones' 1888 General Conference sermons on religious liberty were finally published in 1889, after some editing, under the title; *Civil Government and Religion, or Christianity and the American Constitution.* His testimonies before the Senate Committee were published under the titles; *The National Sunday Law*, and *Religion and the Public Schools* (both reprinted by LMN Pub. Int.). Senator Blair later characterized Jones as "'a man whom I shall always remember with respect on account of his great ability and the evident sincerity with which he presented his views to the committee'" (in *From 1888 to Apostasy*, p. 76).

12. "Petitions to Congress, Etc." *General Conference Daily Bulletin*, Oct. 18, 1889, p. 7; A. T. Jones, "Circulate the Petitions," *Review and Herald*, March 19, 1889, p. 184.

13. "National Religious Liberty Association," *General Conference Daily Bulletin*, Nov. 5, 1889, p. 148.

14. Ellen G. White Manuscript 6, "Issues at the General Conference of 1889," Nov. 4, 1889; in *1888 Materials*, p. 471.

15. George Knight ridicules Jones for taking a similar stand at the 1893 General Conference, calling it "Jones's rigid inflexibility." Knight suggests that Jones was encouraging people to keep breaking the Sunday law until they brought on the death penalty. Knight lists this as one of seven of the "several teachings out of harmony" with Ellen White's views, suggesting that Ellen White "vigorously objected to his determined stand" (*From 1888 to Apostasy*, p. 83; *A User-Friendly Guide to the 1888 Message*, pp. 74-75). Jones' full statement at the 1893 Conference reads: "The man who compromises with Sunday laws to the extent that he will stop work and observe Sunday because the law says so, while still thinking that he is keeping the Sabbath, has put Satan above Christ" ("The Third Angel's Message—No. 6," *General Conference Daily Bulletin*, Feb. 2-4, 1893, p. 125). Jones' statement about the death penalty (to which Knight refers), was based on Rev. 13:15—"as many as would not worship the image of the beast should be killed"—and Jones was only suggesting that "the penalty of death is in every Sunday law" even though at "the first step," it is "not there in words" (*Ibid.* p. 126). Ellen White's counsel in 1895 to A. T. Jones (to which Knight refers), must be considered in its proper context as well. A meeting with Ellen White and several of the leading brethren took place in Armadale, Australia, on November 20, 1895, "to consider some questions arising from the discussions of our brethren regarding religious liberty work. The position recently taken by some of our brethren indicated that there was a necessity for a more thorough understanding of the principles which govern our work." Ellen White was quick to express her primary concern: "My mind has been much troubled over the positions which some of our brethren are liable to take in regard to the work done

among the colored people in the Southern States.  There is one point that I wish to lay before those who work in the Southern field.  Among the colored people, they will have to labor in different lines from those followed in the North." Because of the prejudice among the "white people" they were not to "encourage the colored people to work on Sunday." Ellen White stated that "at present Sunday-keeping is not the test," and first the "truth must be presented more fully before the people as a witness." Her wise counsel was that "while laboring to introduce the truth, we must accommodate ourselves as much as possible to the field, and the circumstances of those for whom we labor…  Therefore it will not do for those who labor among the colored people to preach the truth as boldly and openly as they would be free to do in other places." Yet as she shared with the brethren in Armadale her inspired counsel, she also gave clarifying statements that are in line with her counsel given at the 1889 General Conference: "What I have said about this should not be understood as referring to the action of old Sabbath-keepers who understand the truth.  They must move as the Lord shall direct them" ("Interview re Work Among The Colored People," Manuscript 22a, Nov. 20, 1895; Spalding and Magan Collection (1985), pp. 19-21).  The day following her meeting with the brethren, Ellen White sent a letter to A. T. Jones expressing the same themes: "Dear Brother: Yesterday extracts were read from letters from your pen in reference to our brethren in the Southern field.  This subject is a very delicate one to handle, and I would not have anything to say upon it if I did not feel that I dare not withhold light that has been given me." She counseled Jones to "never encourage the spirit of defiance and resistance, even if they are placed in the chain-gang…  Our policy is, Do not make prominent the objectionable features of our faith, which strike most decidedly against the customs and practises [sic] of the people, until the Lord shall give the people a fair chance to know that we are believers in Christ, and in his preexistence." She reminded Jones that "our work is to study to weed out of all our discourses everything that savors of retaliation and defiance and making a drive against churches and individuals, because this is not Christ's way and method.  He did not pronounce scathing rebukes against those who knew not the truth, but against those whom God had made the depositaries of sacred responsibilities, a people chosen and favored with every temporal and spiritual advantage, and yet bearing no fruit." She admonished Jones to "let nothing be done to increase prejudice, but everything possible to make prejudice less, by letting in light, the bright rays of the Sun of Righteousness, amid the moral darkness." In closing Ellen White expressed one other motivation for writing him: "Dear brother, I am your friend, and I would stand in perfect harmony with you. *I do not want those who have closed the door of their hearts to light to have any occasion to feel that they are right in criticizing you and Brother [E. J.] Waggoner and Brother [W. W.] Prescott.* I have a great desire that you shall show Christlike wisdom in every movement" (Letter 35, Nov. 21, 1895, emphasis supplied; located in "A Study of Principles—No. 6," *Review and Herald*, April 13, 1911, pp. 5-6; and *Manuscript Releases*, vol. 11, p. 33). In contrast to Ellen White, it seems that some today seek every possible occasion to criticize both Jones and Waggoner, rewriting history, if necessary, to do so. Ellen G. White Manuscript 6, Nov. 4, 1889; in *1888 Materials*, pp. 485-486, 480, 493.

16. Ellen G. White Manuscript 18, "Address in Regard to the Sunday Movement," Dec. 1888; in *1888 Materials*, pp. 502-512. The first page of this manuscript is missing. The date assigned is Dec. 1889, although it was cataloged as MS 18, 1888. From Ellen White's statements in the manuscript it would seem that it was an address given to the brethren at the 1889 General Conference sometime in late October or early November.

17. "Seventh-Day Adventist Publishing Association," *General Conference Daily Bulletin*, Oct. 22, 1889, pp. 35, 37.

18. "An Address by President Olsen," *General Conference Daily Bulletin*, Oct. 28, 1889, pp. 95-96.

19. "National Religious Liberty Association," *General Conference Daily Bulletin*, Nov. 5, 1889, p. 148.

20. "General Conference Proceedings: Eighteenth Meeting," *General Conference Daily Bulletin*, Nov. 6, 1889, p. 149.

21. "Meetings of the Committee on Consolidation of Publishing Interests," *General Conference Daily Bulletin*, Nov. 22, 1889, p. 158-159. S. N. Haskell, W. W. Prescott, and J. H. Kellogg were listed as elected committee members in the original report. Their names were later removed with no explanation given. Of the twenty-one members finally chosen, many were very outspoken in their opposition to Jones and Waggoner: Uriah Smith, A. R. Henry, C. Eldridge, R. A. Underwood, E. W. Farnsworth, D. T. Jones, R. M. Kilgore, J. H. Morrison, and F. E. Belden. Others on the committee were likely also opposed to Jones and Waggoner, even though they may not have expressed it as openly.

22. R. W. Schwarz, *Light Bearers to the Remnant* (Boise, Id.: Pacific Press, 1979) p. 271. The General Conference committee members elected over the six districts were: A. T. Robinson, R. M. Kilgore, O. A. Olsen, E. W. Farnsworth, E. H. Gates, and R. A. Underwood ("General Conference Proceedings," *General Conference Daily Bulletin*, Nov. 6, 1889, p. 155).

23. Ellen G. White Manuscript 22, "Diary," Oct. 1889; in *1888 Materials*, p. 468.

24. Ellen G. White to The General Conference," Letter 24, Oct. 1889; in *1888 Materials*, pp. 439-442.

25. A year later, after Ellen White had her Salamanca vision, she wrote that Baal worship would be the religion of a "sorrowful number among us." She added that "fanaticism and atheism" were the result of the "suspicions and jealousies" created against the message: "The true religion, the only religion of the Bible, that teaches forgiveness only through the merits of a crucified and risen Saviour, that advocates righteousness by the faith of the Son of God, has been slighted, spoken against, ridiculed, and *rejected.*" (*1888 Materials*, pp. 948, 955, emphasis supplied).

26. Ellen G. White to The General Conference," Letter 24, Oct. 1889; in *1888 Materials*, pp. 444-445. "Baal" simply means, "lord." Thus Baal worship is worshiping a false idea of Christ. In Jeremiah chapters 2 and 3, Israel is spoken of as having "gone after Baal," and yet saying, "'I have not sinned'" (2:23, 35). As a result God says: "Therefore the showers have been withheld, and there has been no latter rain. You have had a harlot's forehead; You refuse to be ashamed'" (3:3). This is the same assessment given by the True Witness who says His people do not recognize the shame of their nakedness (Rev. 3:17). Just as Elijah stood on Mt. Carmel against the prophets of Baal only 100 years after Solomon's reign, bringing the people to a decision, so we stand today, over 120 years after the Lord visited His church with a most precious message. Malachi tells us that before the second coming "Elijah the prophet" will come, and turn the hearts of the children to their fathers (which could also mean the children looking back to the history of their fathers). Ellen White intimates that the "Elijah message" is the message that began in 1888 (*Review and Herald*, Feb. 18, 1890). When Christ's bride finally appreciates Him for what He is and what He has done, she will overcome as He overcame—by His faith. She will no longer call Him "Master" or "Baal"—serving Him out of fear or with mere form—but will call Him "My Husband"—serving Him from a heart of full of love and appreciation (Hosea 2:16). It will then be said that "His wife has made herself ready" (Rev. 19:7).

27. Ellen G. White, "The Spirit and Power of Elias," *Review and Herald*, Nov. 6, 1913; in *Prophets and Kings*, p. 177.

28. Ellen G. White, "Living Channels of Light," *Review and Herald*, May 27, 1890; in *1888 Materials*, p. 673.

29. Ellen G. White Manuscript 40, 1890, "Vision at Salamanca," March 1891; in *1888 Materials*, p. 944.

30. Ellen G. White Manuscript 13, "Standing by the Landmarks," n.d. 1889, in *1888 Materials*, p. 519.

31. Ellen G. White Manuscript 2, "Sermon," March 16, 1890; in *1888 Materials*, p. 640. For more information on the topic of consolidation see: "Confederation and Consolidation: Seventh-day Adventist History and the Counsels of the Spirit of Prophecy," (E. G. White Estate, 1968). This pamphlet was reprinted by Pacific Press Pub. Assn. in 1983, just prior to a decision made as to its future. Some were desirous that its printing operation be merged with Review and Herald Publishing Association. Thankfully, a decision was made that the Publishing houses remain separate.

32. W. W. Prescott, "Announcement for 1889-90 Bible School for Ministers, p. 8; in Gilbert M. Valentine, *William Warren Prescott: Seventh-day Adventist Educator*, 1982 Dissertation (Ann Arbor, MI: UMI, 1997), p. 125.

33. "Bible School For Ministers," *General Conference Daily Bulletin*, Oct. 18, 1889, p. 6; Gilbert M. Valentine, *The Shaping of Adventism: The Case of W. W. Prescott* (Berrien Springs, MI.: Andrews University Press, 1992) p. 50; D. T. Jones, "The Work in Battle Creek," *Review and Herald*, April 1, 1890, pp. 205; A. V. Olson, *From Crisis to Victory*, pp. 66-70.

# CHAPTER 11

# *The Righteousness of Christ*
## *"By Beholding We Become Changed"*

Although there has been controversy over the nature of Christ in the Seventh-day Adventist Church, primarily since the 1950s, the roots of that controversy originated over 120 years ago. In this chapter we will take an initial look at Jones' and Waggoner's understanding of the nature of Christ (both His divine and human nature), to see if this subject was part of the "1888 message" which they presented long ago. The fact that Jones' and Waggoner's view on the human nature of Christ was the same view as generally held by the Church from its inception explains why there was not a *major* controversy concerning the subject at that time. However, we should not assume that it was a non-issue. Because Jones' and Waggoner's view on the nature of Christ was an integral part of the message of justification by faith and the righteousness of Christ, opposers to their message found points on which to criticize them before the 1888 Conference, and to an even greater extent at the 1890 Ministerial Institute.

In one of his classes at the Institute, Waggoner presented a verse by verse study of Isaiah's prophecies, emphasizing the nature and work of Christ.[1] This was not a new subject for Waggoner, as he had presented his views on the nature of Christ even before the 1888 Conference. Just like his views on the law in Galatians and the two covenants, Waggoner's views on the nature of Christ (both His divine and human nature) were much more than a side issue; they were a creedal tenets to be argued about in circles of higher learning. Waggoner understood the nature of Christ to be closely connected with the "righteousness of Christ;" the very foundation upon which the doctrine of righteousness by faith was built. In fact, for both Jones and Waggoner, righteousness by faith was in reality only a practical application of justification by faith, sanctification by faith, the covenants, and the law in Galatians; all of which were founded on their understanding of the nature of man, the nature of sin, and the nature of Christ. This understanding, with the truth of the cleansing of the Sanctuary in an end-time setting, is what made the most precious message the "third angel's message in verity."[2]*

## *The Divinity of Christ*

Before we take a look at Jones' and Waggoner's views on the Divinity of Christ, we need to understand the position of many of the Church's key founders up to that time. Two of the principal founders of the Seventh-day Adventist Church, Joseph Bates and James White, were originally members of the Christian Connexion, which rejected the doctrine of the Trinity. James White was an ordained minister of that Church. When he and Bates joined the Advent Movement, they continued to hold the anti-Trinitarian view which they had learned in the Christian Connexion Church." But it wasn't just James White and Joseph Bates; "other prominent Adventists who spoke out against the Trinity were J. N. Loughborough, R. F. Cottrell, J. N. Andrews, and Uriah Smith."[3]* Many of these men held Arian or Semi-Arian views of Christ. Classic definitions of these views are:

> Arianism: A teaching which arose in the fourth century AD in Alexandria. Named after its most prominent representative Arius, a presbyter of Alexandria. It denied that Jesus Christ was of the same substance (Gk. *homoousios*) as the Father and reduced the Son to the rank of a creature, though pre-existent before the world. Arianism was condemned at the Council of Nicaea (AD 325).

> Semi-Arianism: Semi-Arians attempted a compromise between the orthodox and Arian position on the nature of Christ. They rejected the Arian view that Christ was created and had a different nature from God (*anomoisos* – dissimilar), but neither did they accept the Nicene Creed which stated that Christ was "of one substance (*homoousios*) with the Father." Semi-Arians taught that Christ was similar (*homoios*) to the Father, or of like substance (*homoiousios*), but still subordinate.[4]

Uriah Smith is perhaps one of the foremost known supporters of an Arian view of Christ. In 1865, for example, he wrote that Christ was "the first created being, dating his existence far back before any other created being or thing."⁵* Although Smith's and many other church founders' ideas would move toward a more orthodox understanding of the Godhead in the late 1890s, this was a prominent view at the time and the environment in which Waggoner was brought up.

Shortly after his 1882 vision of the cross of Christ Waggoner began to see the significance of presenting Christ as One equal with God. He saw that a correct view of Christ plays a significant role, not just in one's understanding of the Godhead, but also in one's understanding of the plan of salvation and the righteousness of Christ that man must obtain by faith:

> [T]o consider Christ continually and intelligently, just as He is, will transform one into a perfect Christian, for "by beholding we become changed."… This "lifting up" of Jesus, while it has primary reference to His crucifixion, embraces more than the mere historical fact; it means that Christ must be "lifted up" by all who believe in Him, as the crucified Redeemer, whose grace and glory are sufficient to supply the world's greatest need; it means that He should be "lifted up" in all His exceeding loveliness and power as "God with us," that *His Divine attractiveness may thus draw all unto Him*. See John 12:32.⁶

> Our object in this investigation is to set forth Christ's rightful position of equality with the Father, *in order that His power to redeem may be the better appreciated.*⁷

Ellen White also expressed similar thoughts in regard to a correct understanding of the divinity of Christ. In the *Spirit of Prophecy*, vol. 4 (1884), and the later expanded *Great Controversy* (1888 ed.), Ellen White mentioned the dangers in denying the divinity of Christ and the effects it had on a person's understanding of the plan of salvation:

> Another dangerous error, is the doctrine that denies the divinity of Christ, claiming that he had no existence before his advent to this world. … It cannot be entertained without the most unwarranted wresting of the Scriptures. It not only lowers man's conceptions of the work of redemption, but undermines faith in the Bible as a revelation from God. … None who hold this error can have a true conception of the character or the mission of Christ, or of the great plan of God for man's redemption.⁸*

In 1884, Waggoner mentioned Christ's exalted position as God Himself in several *Signs of the Times* articles. He urged that Christ deserves equal reverence and that He partakes of the Father's attributes, including life in Himself, and that He is rightfully called "Lord." Because so much has been made of Waggoner's views of Christ, we will look at many of his statements:

If there is but one that is good, viz., God, and Christ is good, then *Christ must be God*. And this agrees with what the prophet had said of Christ: "For unto us a child is born, unto us a son is given; and the government shall be upon his shoulder: and his name shall be called Wonderful, Counselor, The mighty God, The everlasting Father, The Prince of Peace." Isa. 9:6. …

The Father and the Son are one. John 10:30. Both are worthy of worship. … We are not called upon to explain the mystery of godliness, nor expected to understand it, but Christ has explained to us how he and the Father are one. … This oneness, then, is that of two distinct individuals having the *same thoughts*, the *same purposes*, the *same attributes*. The Father and the Son were one in creating the earth, and one in the devising and carrying out of the plan of salvation.[9]

It is that God only hath immortality. … That is an attribute of God alone. "But," says one, "is not Christ immortal? and do we not read of the angels that they cannot die?" Yes; and we turn to John 5:26 and read Christ's words: "For as the Father hath life in himself; so hath he given to the Son to have life in himself." Christ, then, being the only begotten Son of God, *partakes of his attributes*, and *has life in himself*. That is, he is able to impart life to others.[10]

In our further investigation of this subject, we shall understand that the word "Lord" is *applied both to the Father and the Son*, and that even though we find it in various places applied specifically to one of them, the act predicated of that one is the act of the other also. … From John 5:23 we learn "that all men should honor the Son, even as they honor the Father." Wherever, then, we find an act enjoined by the Father, we know that the performance of that act honors the Son also, and that the neglecting of it is as much an insult to the Son as to the Father. Disobedience to the Father dishonors Christ.[11]

[John 3:16 quoted] What do we learn from this verse? 1. That God's love for the world was so great as to cause him to send his Son for their rescue. We can judge something of God's love for his Son, when we remember that Christ was the brightest of the Father's glory, "and the express image of his person," that he was "heir of all things," the one by whom the worlds were made (Heb. 1:2, 3); and that "in him dwelleth all the fullness of the Godhead bodily." Col. 2:9. God is infinite in all his attributes and therefore his love for his Son was infinite. And since he gave his Son for the world, we know how great was his love for the world. It was infinite.[12]

It is not surprising that Waggoner brought these same concepts into his presentations on righteousness by faith at Minneapolis. An article in the *Review* prior to the 1888 Conference included "the divinity of Christ" as one of the "subjects proposed to be considered."[13] This subject was of growing interest to Waggoner and one of which he would often write and speak. W. C. White recorded one of Waggoner's presentations where he openly declared: "We believe in [the] Divinity of Christ. He created all things in Heaven and the Earth."[14]

Waggoner continued to proclaim Christ's divinity in the years that followed the Minneapolis conference. In a six-part series in the *Signs* he wrote specifically on the divinity of Christ in response to a book issued by the Methodists on the Sabbath question. Before Waggoner responded to the questions raised on the Sabbath, he addressed "a line of thought suggested by a sentence in the preface. Speaking of those who observe the seventh day as the Sabbath... the Doctor [M. C. Briggs] says: 'One only regrets... their... denial of Christ's divinity.'" For an entire six articles, from which we will quote only a portion, Waggoner sought to show that idea as wholly false:

> But when the Doctor [M. C. Briggs] states that Seventh-day Adventists deny the divinity of Christ, we know that he writes recklessly. We are fully persuaded in our own mind that he knows better; but be that as it may, the statement has been made so often by men who professed to know whereof they were speaking, that many have come to believe it; and for their sakes, as well as for the benefit of those who may now have given the subject any thought, we propose to set forth the truth. We have no theory to bolster up, and so, instead of stating propositions, we shall simply quote the word of God, and accept what it says. ...

> John 1:1... From it we learn that *Christ is God*. That text alone, if we had no other, is sufficient to establish the divinity of Christ, for the word "divinity" means, "the nature or essence of God." *We believe in the divinity of Christ*, because the Bible says that *Christ is God*. ...

> The writer to the Hebrews, speaking of Christ's superiority to the angels, says that it is because "he hath by inheritance a more excellent name than they." Heb. 1:3. What name is it that he has by inheritance? It is, "The mighty God." As the only begotten Son of God, he has that name by right.[15]*

> Then what did he mean by saying, "Why callest thou me good? there is none good but one, that is God"? He meant to impress upon the young man's mind the fact that the one whom he was addressing as Master was not a mere man, as one of the rabbis, but that he was God. He claimed for himself absolute goodness, and since there is none good but God, he thereby *identified himself with God.*

And with this we may connect the statement of the apostle Paul, that "in him dwelleth all the fullness of the Godhead bodily." Col. 2:9. ...

"In the year that king Uzziah died I saw also the Lord sitting upon a throne, high and lifted up... Then said I, Woe is me! for I am undone; because I am a man of unclean lips, and I dwell in the midst of a people of unclean lips; for mine eyes have seen the King, the Lord of hosts." Isa. 6:1-5. We should not know to whom this refers, if our Saviour himself had not, in John 12:40, 41, quoted Isaiah's words in the tenth verse of this chapter, and applied them to himself. From these texts we have proof not only that the inspired writers call *Jesus the divine Son of God, but that Jesus himself claimed to be God.*[16]

As Son of God, he must partake of the *nature of God.* "As the Father hath life in himself, so hath he given to the Son to have life in himself." John 5:26. Life and immortality are imparted to the faithful followers of God, but Christ alone shares with the Father the power to impart life. He has "life in himself," that is, *he is able to perpetuate his own existence.* ...

That Christ is divine is shown by the fact that he receives worship. Angels have always refused to receive worship and adoration. But we read of the Father, that "when he bringeth in the first begotten into the world, he saith, And let all the angels of God worship him." Heb. 1:6. ...

If Christ were not God, this would be idolatry. ... It matters not what the position of a creature may be, whether a beast, a man, or an angel, worship of it is strictly forbidden. Only God may be worshiped, and since Christ may be worshiped, Christ is God. So say the Scriptures of truth. ...

In arguing the perfect equality of the Father and the Son, and the fact that Christ is in very nature God. ... *He is of the substance of the Father, so that in his very nature he is God*; and since that is so "it pleased the Father that in him should all fullness dwell." Col. 1:19.[17]

We come to notice some of the works which Christ does as God, and in this we shall find additional proof of his divinity. ...

The first way in which God is revealed to us as demanding honor, is as Creator. ... Now since Christ is to be honored by all, just as they honor the Father, it follows that he is to be honored as Creator; and so, according to Paul's words to the Romans, the visible creation affords proof of the "eternal power and Godhead" of Christ. ...

Col. 1:15-17. ... From the words, "the first-born of every creature," some have argued that Christ himself is a created being. But that is not only a hasty conclusion, but one directly opposed to the text itself. ... In him creation had its beginning, as stated in Rev. 3:14. Creation existed in him, in embryo, as it were; "for it pleased the Father that in him should all fullness dwell." Col. 1:19. No language could more perfectly show the *pre-existence and the creative power of Christ*, than does the language of Col. 1:15-17. ...

Let no one, therefore, say that in exalting Christ we are in danger of lowering our ideas of God. That is impossible, for the more exalted ideas we have of Christ, the more exalted must be our ideas of the Father.[18]

Since all must honor the Son even as they honor the Father, they must honor him not only as Creator, *but as Lawgiver*. ... Only the power that makes the laws can provide for their execution. We shall now proceed to give proof that *the law was given by Christ, even as it is his righteousness*. ...

Christ was the leader of the children of Israel from Egypt to Canaan. ... Now in 1 Cor. 10:9 Paul tells plainly against whom they were murmuring. He says: "Neither let us tempt Christ, as some of them also tempted, and were destroyed of serpents." So it was Christ who, with the name of God, was leading Israel, and it was against him that they murmured.

Heb. 3:5-11 also teaches the same thing very plainly. One has only to read it with care to see that Christ is the one whose voice the Holy Ghost warns us not to reject as did the fathers who tempted him forty years in the wilderness. ...

Since Christ was the leader of ancient Israel from Egypt to Canaan, it follows that *Christ was the Angel of the Lord* who appeared to Moses in the burning bush, and said: "I am the God of thy father, the God of Abraham, the God of Isaac, and the God of Jacob. And Moses hid his face. ..." Ex. 3:6-8.

If any should object to this most natural conclusion, on the ground that the one here speaking calls himself "I AM THAT I AM," the self-existent One-Jehovah-we have only to remind him that the Father hath given to the Son to have life in himself (John 5:26), that Christ asserted the same thing of himself when he said, "Before Abraham was, I am" (John 8:5, 6); for which supposed blasphemy the Jews attempted to stone him; and that by the prophet he is most plainly called Jehovah, in the following passage: "Behold, the days come, saith the Lord, that I will raise unto David a righteous Branch,... and this is his name whereby he shall be called, THE LORD OUR RIGHTEOUSNESS;" literally, "*Jehovah our righteousness*." Jer. 23:5, 6. ...

Ex. 20:1-3. This scripture positively identifies the leader of the children of Israel from Egypt, as the giver of the law from Sinai. If it is said that in the transaction we cannot separate the Father and the Son, we reply that that is just the point we are making. The Father and the Son cannot be separated in any transaction, for they are one. But just as the Son was the one by whom all things were created, so was he the one who declared to the people the law of Jehovah. Thus he is the divine Word. The Son declares the will of the Father, which is also his own will.[19]*

So we have proved in general and in particular that Christ is the Lawgiver for all mankind. We must honor him, therefore, as Creator, and as Lawgiver, and now, lastly, as Redeemer. And in this we come to the comforting, encouraging part of all that has gone before. ...

It is *our God that is our Redeemer*. What a pledge this affords of the faithfulness of the "exceeding great and precious promises" of the gospel. The great law of the universe was broken by the inhabitants of this little planet, and *the Lawgiver gave himself to redeem these rebels.* ...

And if the Lawgiver gave himself for us, to redeem us from the transgression of his own law, what greater assurance could we ask that he will save to the uttermost all who come to him?[20]

In 1890, Waggoner expanded on these articles and published his book *Christ and His Righteousness*. Throughout several chapters, just as in his 1889 articles, he dealt specifically with the divinity of Christ. His stated purpose was clear: "Our object in this investigation is to set forth Christ's rightful position of equality with the Father, in order that His power to redeem may be the better appreciated."[21] We note only a few paragraphs here:

To Christ is committed the highest prerogative, that of judging. He must receive the same honor that is due to God and for the reason that *He is God*. The beloved disciple bears this witness, "In the beginning was the Word, and the Word was with God, and the Word was God." John 1:1. That this Divine Word is none other than Jesus Christ is shown by verse 14: "And the Word was made flesh and dwelt among us (and we beheld His glory, the glory as of the Only-begotten of the Father), full of grace and truth."[22]

In many places in the Bible *Christ is called God*. The Psalmist says, "The mighty God, even the *Lord [Jehovah]*, hath spoken, and called the earth from the rising of the sun unto the going down thereof. ... And the heavens shall declare His righteousness; for God is judge Himself." Ps. 50:1-6. That this passage has reference to Christ may be known 1) by the fact already learned, that all judgment is committed to the Son, and 2) by the fact that it is at the second coming of Christ that He sends His angels to gather together His elect from the four winds. Matt. 24:31.[23]

When He comes it will be as "the mighty God.". . . These are not simply the words of Isaiah; they are the words of the Spirit of God. . . . This name was not given to Christ in consequence of some great achievement, but it is His by right of inheritance. Speaking of the power and greatness of Christ, the writer to the Hebrews says that He is made so much better than the angels, because "He hath by inheritance obtained a more excellent name than they." Heb. 1:4. . . . Christ is the "express image" of the Father's person. Heb. 1:3. As the Son of the self-existent God, *He has by nature all the attributes of Deity.*[24]

And, finally, we have the inspired words of the apostle Paul concerning Jesus Christ, that "it pleased the Father that in Him should all fullness dwell." Col. 1:19. What this fullness is which dwells in Christ, we learn from the next chapter, where we are told that "in him dwelleth all the fullness of the Godhead bodily." Col. 2:9. This is most absolute and unequivocal testimony to the fact *that Christ possesses by nature all the attributes of Divinity.* The fact of the Divinity of Christ will also appear very distinctly as we proceed to consider.[25]

Heb. 1:8-10. Here we find the Father addressing the Son as God, and saying to Him, Thou hast laid the foundations of the earth, and the heavens are the work of Thy hands. When the Father Himself gives this honor to the Son, what is man, that he should withhold it? With this we may well leave the direct testimony concerning the *Divinity of Christ and the fact that He is the Creator of all things.*[26]

Is Christ a Created Being? Before passing to some of the practical lessons that are to be learned from these truths, we must dwell for a few moments upon an opinion that is honestly held by many who would not for any consideration willingly dishonor Christ, but who, through that opinion, do actually deny His Divinity. It is the idea that Christ is a created being, who, through the good pleasure of God, was elevated to His present lofty position. *No one who holds this view can possibly have any just conception of the exalted position which Christ really occupies.*

The view in question is built upon a misconception of a single text, Rev. 3:14:. . . And so the statement that He is the beginning or head of the creation of God means that in Him creation had its beginning; that, as He Himself says, He is Alpha and Omega, the beginning and the end, the first and the last.[27]

Christ "is in the bosom of the Father" *being by nature of the very substance of God and having life in Himself.* He is properly called *Jehovah, the self-existent* One and is thus styled in Jer. 23:56, where it is said that the righteous Branch, who shall execute judgment and justice in the earth, shall be known by the name of Jehovah-tsidekenu—THE LORD, OUR RIGHTEOUSNESS.[28]

Although some readers may feel we have gone laboriously too far in presenting Waggoner's views on the divinity of Christ, in light of those who have accused Waggoner of being an Arian and believing that "Christ was a created god," we wish to make this subject absolutely clear.[29] No further comment is needed; Waggoner's articles speak for themselves.

## *Ellen White's Response*

In a letter to Jones and Waggoner written a year and a half before Minneapolis, Ellen White expressed the need for the Church to recognize the great humiliation of Christ by understanding not only how far down He came—in the likeness of sinful flesh—but understanding from how high He had come—the position of Creator God. During the next three years she would express these same ideas over and over again, in the context of the most precious message that was then being given:

> "Let this mind be in you, which was also in Christ Jesus." Fill the mind with the great humiliation of Christ, and then contemplate His divine character, His majesty and glory of the Highest, and His disrobing Himself of these and clothing His divinity with humanity. Then we can see a self-denial, a self-sacrifice, that was the marvel of angels. … Then look beneath the disguise, and whom do we see?—Divinity, the Eternal Son of God, just as mighty, just as infinitely gifted with all the resources of power, and He was found in fashion as a man.[30]

> Christ condescended to assume human nature, but the dwarfed powers of man were unable through ignorance to comprehend or distinguish the divine. Jesus was not spared the necessity of defining and defending His divine nature, because the minds of men were so thoroughly human they could not discern the divine beneath the assumption of humanity. In order to make His lessons forceful, He was compelled, when these impressions hindered His usefulness, to refer to His mysterious and divine character, leading their minds into a train of thought that was favorable to the transforming power of truth.[31]

> We need a power to come upon us now and stir us up to diligence and earnest faith. Then, baptized with the Holy Spirit, we shall have Christ formed within, the hope of glory. Then we will exhibit Christ as the divine object of our faith

and our love. We will talk of Christ, we will pray to Christ and about Christ. We will praise His holy name. We will present before the people His miracles, His self-denial, His self-sacrifice, His sufferings, and His crucifixion, His resurrection and triumphant ascension. These are the inspiring themes of the gospel, to awaken love and intense fervor in every heart.[32]

The popular doctrines of this age cannot correctly represent Jesus. Our Saviour represented the Father. He rolled away the thick darkness from the throne of God, the hellish shadow which Satan had cast to hide God from sight and from knowledge. Christ reveals the throne of God and reveals to the world the Father as light and love. His clothing his divinity with humanity brings that love in clear evidence of light that humanity can comprehend it. ... Why not by faith take hold of the divine nature. It is our privilege. All things shall be done for him that believeth.[33]

In Christ, divinity and humanity were combined. Divinity was not degraded to humanity; divinity held its place, but humanity by being united to divinity, withstood the fiercest test of temptation in the wilderness. ... Man may become a partaker of the divine nature; not a soul lives who may not summon the aid of Heaven in temptation and trial. Christ came to reveal the Source of his power, that man might never rely on his unaided human capabilities.[34]

As Ellen White heard the message of Christ being proclaimed, she could only rejoice. In 1890, speaking of the very heart of the message Jones and Waggoner were sharing, Ellen White stated that the "messages bearing the divine credentials have been presented to God's people... the fullness of the Godhead in Jesus Christ has been set forth among us with beauty and loveliness."[35] Several years later when summarizing the 1888 message the Lord sent, she wrote of this very subject as being one of the essential parts of that precious message:

The Lord in His great mercy sent a most precious message to His people through Elders Waggoner and Jones. ... Many had lost sight of Jesus. They needed to have their eyes directed to His divine person, His merits, and His changeless love for the human family. All power is given into His hands, that He may dispense rich gifts unto men, imparting the priceless gift of His own righteousness to the helpless human agent. This is the message that God commanded to be given to the world. It is the third angel's message, which is to be proclaimed with a loud voice, and attended with the outpouring of His Spirit in a large measure.[36]

## *The Only Begotten Son*

As Waggoner advanced beyond the Church's common understanding of the divine nature of Christ, with its Arian and Semi-Arian views, there were a few times that he expressed his thoughts in less advanced terms than in later years, when Ellen White's clarifying statements would play a more definitive role. One such statement is found in his 1889 series in the *Signs* and the other in his expanded book on the same topic in *Christ and His Righteousness*, published in early 1890. Waggoner never repeated either of these statements in his later publications:

> Some have difficulty in reconciling Christ's statement in John 14:28, "My Father is greater than I," with the idea that he is God, and is entitled to worship. Some, indeed, dwell upon that text alone as sufficient to overthrow the idea of Christ's divinity; but if that were allowed, it would only prove a contradiction in the Bible, and even in Christ's own speech, for it is most positively declared, as we have seen, that he is divine. There are two facts which are amply sufficient to account for Christ's statement recorded in John 14:28. One is that Christ is the Son of God. While both are of the same nature, *the Father is first in point of time. He is also greater in that He had no beginning, while Christ's personality had a beginning.* Then, too, the statement is emphatically true in view of the position which Christ had assumed. He "emptied himself, taking the form of a servant, being made in the likeness of men." Phil. 2:7, Revised Version. He was "made a little lower than the angels, for the suffering of death." Heb. 2:9. In order to redeem men, He had to come where they were. He did not lay aside his divinity, but He laid aside His glory, and veiled His divinity with humanity. So his statement, "My Father is greater than I," is perfectly consistent with the claim, made by himself as well as by all who wrote of him, that He was and is God.[37]

> The Scriptures declare that Christ is "the only begotten son of God." *He is begotten, not created. As to when He was begotten, it is not for us to inquire, nor could our minds grasp it if we were told.* The prophet Micah tells us all that we can know about it in these words, "But thou, Bethlehem Ephratah, though thou be little among the thousands of Judah, yet out of thee shall He come forth unto Me that is to be ruler in Israel; whose goings forth have been from of old, from the days of eternity." Micah 5:2, margin. *There was a time when Christ proceeded forth and came from God, from the bosom of the Father (John 8:42; 1:18), but that time was so far back in the days of eternity that to finite comprehension it is practically without beginning.*[38]

Neither of these statements brought a rebuke from Ellen White. And why should they? By classic definition Waggoner was neither Arian nor Semi-Arian.[39] He was already advancing the concepts of the Godhead beyond what many of the Church's founders had understood, and he was doing so without the aid of Ellen White's later clarifying statements. Notice the recognition of this fact by modern writers:

> Waggoner's was thus the first competent attempt to deal with the larger, overall view of Christ as all the *fullness* of the Godhead was the all-sufficient basis and provision of Righteousness by Faith for us.

> Unfortunately for Dr. Waggoner, Ellen White had not, at this time, yet made most of her strongest declarations on the eternal pre-existence and complete Deity of Christ. In 1888 Waggoner was pioneering without the benefit of her many later statements.[40]

> The question of the divinity of Jesus was on the agenda for the 1888 Conference. On this occasion... Ellet J. Waggoner, refuted the last semi-Arian arguments remaining in the church, and ultimately laid the biblical foundation needed to establish the full and complete divinity of Jesus Christ. ...

> Together they [Jones and Waggoner] made their mark in the history of the Adventist Church with their presentations on justification by faith. For Waggoner, the subject could be understood only through the lens of Christology. ...

> At the time several leaders of the church still cherished semi-Arian, or adoptionist, concepts concerning the divine nature of Christ; hence the significance of the question raised by Waggoner as he took on the problem: "Is Christ God?"

> Waggoner's insistence that Christ was by nature of the same substance as God and possessed life in Himself was no doubt a novelty in the eyes of some of the delegates at the Minneapolis session. His position on the divine nature of Christ was probably part of the reason for the opposition by many of the delegates to his message of justification by faith.

> Waggoner's contribution on this point, as on that concerning the human nature of Christ was decisive. Froom recognizes it readily: "In 1888 Waggoner was pioneering without the benefit of her [Ellen White] many later statements, not only on Christ's eternal preexistence but on His individual self-existence and His infinity, equality, and omnipotence."

> Ellen White herself expressed it after hearing Waggoner: "The fullness of the Godhead in Jesus Christ has been set forth among us with beauty and loveliness."

For her, it demonstrated that God was at work among them. Waggoner's interpretation was, for the most part, the theological demonstration of what she had always believed and stated in her writings up to that time.[41]

By the spring of 1890, Waggoner appears to have moved yet further beyond his previous concepts stating: "Through the mediation and atonement of Jesus Christ, who, *being God from eternity*, became incarnate, and by his death upon the cross became a sacrifice for sin, made expiation for it, and, having risen from the grave, ascended into heaven, and there sitteth on the right hand of the Father to make intercession for his people. The whole character and value of such a religion consists altogether in being, as it claims to be, a supernatural plan of salvation from sin."[42] It would be another eight years before Ellen White would make her well-known statement: "In Christ is life, original, unborrowed, underived. 'He that hath the Son hath life.' 1 John 5:12. The divinity of Christ is the believer's assurance of eternal life."[43] How sad that today some have completely misrepresented Waggoner on this issue.[44]*

## *Human Nature of Christ*

Not only did Jones and Waggoner lift up Christ in His divine nature, they lifted Him up by showing the depths to which He came in order to redeem man.[45]* In 1884, Waggoner established his views on the human nature of Christ in several articles in the *Signs*. He described Christ as taking "upon Himself our nature (Heb. 2:16, 17); and on Him was laid 'the iniquity of us all' (Isa. 53:6). In order to save us, He had to come where we were, or, in other words, He had to take the position of a lost sinner."[46] Waggoner made it clear that "He was made in all things 'like unto his brethren'; and that means not simply as to the outward, physical frame, but that He bore sin, just as we do."[47] He explained that Jesus "had to put Himself in the exact condition of those whom He would save." It was in this respect that "He bore the sins of the world as though they were His own." The position Christ took is best described as being "made under the law" (Gal. 4:4). Waggoner believed that Christ was not only subject to the moral law, but that He was by His own choice made subject to the condemnation of the law, as any sinner would be "on account of having violated the law." This did not make Christ a sinner, for "the sins that He bore were not His own, but ours."[48]

In 1886, Waggoner again expressed his interpretation of the phrase "under the law" in a series of articles on the book of Galatians: "It has been abundantly proved that 'under the law' indicates, in general, a state of sin and consequently of condemnation."[49] Waggoner's articles brought a response from G. I. Butler in his book *The Law in the Book of Galatians*. Because Butler was defending the idea that Galatians 4:4 spoke only of the ceremonial law to which Christ submitted Himself, he condemned Waggoner's view of "under the law" as "most absurd."[50]* In early 1887, Waggoner responded to Butler's book with *The Gospel in the Book of Galatians*. Speaking directly to the point of Christ being "under the law" Waggoner showed the connection with His human nature:

> These texts [Gal. 4:4, John 1:1, 14, Phil. 2:5-7, Heb. 2:9] show that Christ took upon himself man's nature, and that as a consequence he was subject to death. He came into the world on purpose to die; and so from the beginning of His earthly life He was in the same condition that the men are in whom He died to save.

> Now read Rom. 1:3: The gospel of God, "concerning his Son Jesus Christ our Lord, which *was made* of the seed of David according to the flesh." What was the nature of David, "according to the flesh"? Sinful, flesh was it not? David says: "Behold, I was shapen in iniquity; and in sin did my mother conceive me." Ps. 51:5 Don't start in horrified astonishment; I am not implying that Christ was a sinner. ...[51]*

> One of the most encouraging things in the Bible is the knowledge that Christ took on Him the nature of man; to know that His ancestors according to the flesh were sinners. When we read the record of the lives of the ancestors of Christ, and see that they had all the weaknesses and passions that we have, we find that no man has any right to excuse his sinful acts on the ground of heredity. If Christ had not been made *in all things* like unto His brethren, then His sinless life would be no encouragement to us.[52]*

This response of Waggoner's, written in 1887, was not published until just before the 1888 Conference. During the summer of 1888, while attending a retreat in the mountains east of Oakland, Jones and Waggoner "spent a few days in Bible study" with "as many of the California ministers" as could attend. W. C. White noted that one day was spent looking over "Eld. Butler's law in Galatians and other topics bearing on that question, at the close of which Eld. Waggoner read some MS which he had prepared in answer to Eld. Butler's pamphlet. ... At the close of our study, Eld. Waggoner asked us if it would be right for him to publish his MS and at the next Gen. Conf. [1888] place them in the hands of the delegates, as Eld. Butler had his. We thought this would be right, and encouraged him to have five hundred copies printed."[53]

W. C. White took notes of Waggoner's presentation at this June 26 meeting. According to White's notes, Waggoner spent most of his time dealing with the different viewpoints that he and Butler had on the subject of Christ being "under the law."[54] This was the very point in which Waggoner had clearly expressed his views on the human nature of Christ in his response to Butler, as quoted above.

Not only did Waggoner distribute his published response to all the delegates at the 1888 Conference; he also spoke on the topic of the human nature of Christ. Although it was not the central point of his presentations, it was the foundation of his understanding of justification by faith and the righteousness of Christ.

W. C. White took the same notebook he had used at the June 26 retreat to the Minneapolis Conference, where he recorded Waggoner's October 17 lecture on the subject and definition of "under the law."[55] Waggoner's presentations were also taken down in shorthand by his wife, and shortly after arriving home in Oakland in early 1889, they became the basis for a series of articles published in the *Signs*. These articles, which dealt with both the divine and human nature of Christ, were later included in his book published in 1890, which he appropriately titled: *Christ and His Righteousness*.[56] Before we consider these articles, however, we need to read what Ellen White had to say on the topic.

### A Sadly Neglected Subject

Just prior to the 1888 conference, Ellen White wrote an article for the *Review* titled, "The Work of the Minister," in which she encouraged ministers to avoid public controversy over minor issues, "strivings about words to no profit." She admonished that "opinions upon subjects that are not of real importance… should not be brought to the front, and urged publicly, but should, if held by any, be done quietly and without controversy." The mysteries of the Bible would not all be "fully comprehended until Christ" returned. And because there is "much that human minds can never harmonize" on, it is far better to keep "all minor differences concealed, rather than bring them forth to become subjects of contention." In the "great testing truths… of redemption, the soon-coming of Christ, and the commandments of God" could be found "enough food for thought… to take up the entire attention." Moreover, Christ's condescension to save fallen man was another subject that Ellen White felt should be largely dwelt upon:

> What is the work of the minister of the gospel? It is to rightly divide the word of truth; not to invent a new gospel, but to rightly divide the gospel already committed to them. … There are subjects that are sadly neglected, that should be largely dwelt upon. The burden of our message should be the mission and life of Jesus Christ. Let there be a dwelling upon the humiliation, self-denial, meekness, and lowliness of Christ, that proud and selfish hearts may see the difference between themselves and the Pattern, and may be humbled. Show to your hearers Jesus in his condescension to save fallen man. Show them that He who was their *surety had to take human nature*, and carry it through the darkness and the fearfulness of the malediction of his Father, because of man's transgression of his law; for the Saviour was found in fashion as a man. Describe, if human language can, the humiliation of the Son of God, and think not that you have reached the climax, when you see him exchanging the throne of light and glory which he had with the Father, *for humanity*. He came forth from heaven to earth; and while on earth, he bore the curse of God as surety for the fallen race.[57]

Literally dozens of times throughout her writings, Ellen White makes it clear that for Christ to be man's surety, He had to take man's fallen nature: "It was necessary that Christ should take upon Him our nature, in order to prove the falsity of Satan's statement. … Therefore Christ became man's representative and *surety*."[58] "Man's substitute and *surety* must have man's nature, a connection with the human family whom he was to represent, and, as God's ambassador, He must partake of the divine nature, have a connection with the Infinite."[59] Furthermore, it was Christ in human flesh that lived a life of righteousness to which man might now be a partaker: "We must center our hopes of heaven upon Christ alone, because he is our substitute and *surety*. … The best efforts that man in his own strength can make are valueless to meet the holy and just law that he has transgressed; but through faith in Christ he may claim the *righteousness of the Son of God* as all-sufficient. Christ satisfied the demands of the law in His human nature. … Genuine faith appropriates the *righteousness of Christ*, and the sinner is made an overcomer with Christ."[60] "Divinity took the nature of humanity, and for what purpose? That through the *righteousness of Christ* humanity might partake of the divine nature."[61]

As Ellen White saw it, Christ's human nature was central to the plan of salvation and the restoration of man. Thus, as she wrote to the church in September 1888, rather than seeing the subject of the human nature of Christ as "not of real importance," she saw it as a subject "sadly neglected."[62] It was not just a side issue, it was part of the "gospel already committed to them." It is no wonder then, that when Ellen White heard Waggoner's presentations at the Minneapolis meetings "every fiber of [her] heart said, Amen."[63]

Later she would plainly state that "the loud cry of the third angel has already begun in the revelation of the *righteousness of Christ*. … This is the beginning of the light of the angel whose glory shall fill the whole earth."[64] When she wrote her well-known statement in 1895 of the "most precious message sent through Elders Waggoner and Jones," she included in the description their teaching in the context of the nature of Christ, both His divine and human nature: "This message was to bring more prominently before the world the uplifted Saviour, the sacrifice for the sins of the whole world. It presented justification by faith in the *Surety*; it invited the people to receive the *righteousness of Christ*, which is made manifest in obedience to all the commandments of God. Many had lost sight of Jesus. They needed to have their eyes directed to His *divine person*."[65]

But not all would hear what Waggoner had to say at the Minneapolis Conference. Many had excuses that would make it hard for them to accept the message sent from God. On October 20, 1888, just three days after Waggoner's presentation on Christ being under the law—the very topic that on prior occasions Waggoner had used to present on the human nature of Christ—Ellen White spoke to the delegates about "Advancing in Christian Experience":

Now, what we want to present is how you may advance in the divine life. We hear many excuses: I cannot live up to this or that. What do you mean by this or that? Do you mean that it was an imperfect sacrifice that was made for the fallen race upon Calvary, that there is not sufficient grace and power granted us that we may work away from our own natural defects and tendencies, that it was not a whole Saviour that was given us? or do you mean to cast reproach upon God? Well, you say, it was Adam's sin. You say I am not guilty of that, and I am not responsible for his guilt and fall. Here all these natural tendencies are in me, and I am not to blame if I act out these natural tendencies. Who is to blame? Is God? Why did Satan have this power over human nature? These are accusations against the God of heaven, and He will give you an opportunity, if you want, of finally bringing your accusations against Him. Then He will bring His accusations against you when you are brought into His court of judgment.

How is it that He is pleading, "I know all the evil and temptations with which you are beset, and I sent My Son Jesus Christ to your world to reveal to you My power, My mightiness; to reveal to you that I am God, and that I will give you help in order to lift you from the power of the enemy, and give you a chance that you might win back the moral image of God."…

God accepts Christ, our substitute. He took human nature upon Himself and fought the battles that human nature is engaged in. He is connected with the divine and was to fight the battles with Satan.[66]

It is a simple fact that Ellen White had to confront a mind-set that was trying to find an excuse for falling under temptation. Her answer to such a stance was that Christ was "a whole Saviour," that He knew "all the evil and temptations" with which human nature had to deal "and fought the battles that human nature is engaged in." It was this truth that made it possible for man to overcome. The brethren did not have a clear picture of Christ as their substitute and *surety*, and the message of Jones and Waggoner went to the very heart of the issue, exposing their ignorance. It is because of this fact that many of the brethren responded negatively to their message. Believing that Christ could not have had the same nature as man, else He would have fallen under temptation, would easily lead a person to protest that Waggoner was bringing Christ down too far. Unfortunately, Waggoner's initial response to such claims only made matters worse. Some would use his initial response as an excuse to continue their rejection of the most precious message.

## *"Christ Could Not Sin"*

Waggoner's articles in the *Signs* that were printed shortly after arriving home from the Minneapolis conference covered both the divine and human nature of Christ. His article published January 21 was titled, "God Manifest in the Flesh." Here Waggoner stated that "a little thought will be sufficient to show anybody that if Christ took upon Himself the likeness of man, in order that He might suffer death, it must have been sinful man that He was made like, for it is only sin that causes death." He went on to state that "a brief glance at the ancestry and posterity of David will show that the line from which Christ sprung, as to his human nature, was such as would tend to concentrate all the weaknesses of humanity." Waggoner admitted that "it is impossible for us to understand how this could be, and it is worse than useless for us to speculate about it. All we can do is to accept the facts as they are presented in the Bible."[67]* These facts he presented clearly:

> Moreover, the fact that Christ took upon himself the flesh, not of a sinless being, but of sinful man, that is, that the flesh which he assumed had all the weaknesses and sinful tendencies to which fallen human nature is subject, is shown by the very words upon which this article is based. He was "made of the seed of David according to the flesh." David had all the passions of human nature. …

> If he was made in all things like unto his brethren, then he must have suffered all the infirmities and passions of his brethren. Only so could he be able to help them. So he had to become a man, not only that he might die, but that he might be able to sympathize with and succor those who suffer the fierce temptations which Satan brings through the weakness of the flesh. …

> That Christ should be born under the law was a necessary consequence of his being born of a woman, taking on him the nature of Abraham, being made of the seed of David, in the likeness of sinful flesh. Human nature is sinful, and the law of God condemns all sin. Not that men are born into the world directly condemned by the law, for in infancy they have no knowledge of right and wrong, and are incapable of doing either, but they are born with sinful tendencies, owning to the sins of their ancestors. And when Christ came into the world, he came subject to all the conditions to which other children are subject.[68]

As Waggoner came to the close of his article, he addressed the fears that people might have that he was bringing Christ down too far. With the controversy at Minneapolis still fresh in his mind, he was very likely trying to cover himself against any accusations that he was making Christ out to be a sinner in need of a Saviour Himself:

> Some may though, while reading this article thus far, [think] that we are depreciating the character of Jesus, by bringing him down to the level of sinful man. On the contrary, we are simply exalting the "divine power" of our blessed Saviour, who himself voluntarily descended to the level of sinful man, in order that he might exalt man to his own spotless purity, which he retained under the most adverse circumstances. "God was in Christ," and *hence he could not sin*. His humanity only veiled his divine nature, which was more than able to successfully resist the sinful passions of the flesh. There was in his whole life a struggle. The flesh, moved upon by the enemy of all unrighteousness, would tend to sin, yet his divine nature never for a moment harbored an evil desire, nor did his divine power for a moment waver. Having suffered in the flesh all that men can possibly suffer, he returned to the throne of the Father, as spotless as when he left the courts of glory. When he laid in the tomb, under the power of death, "it was impossible that he should be holden of it," because it had been *impossible for the divine nature which dwelt in him to sin*.
>
> "Well," some will say, "I don't see any comfort in this for me; *it wasn't possible that the Son of God should sin*, but I haven't any such power." Why not? You can have it if you want it. The same power which enabled him to resist every temptation presented through the flesh, while he was "compassed with infirmity," can enable us to do the same. *Christ could not sin*, because he was the manifestation of God.[69]\*

Thus, Waggoner tried to cover himself against false accusations in regard to the human nature of Christ. He reasoned that he wasn't bringing Christ down too far because Christ couldn't sin on account of His divine nature and this same power was now readily available to man also.

### *Ellen White Settles the Matter*

One year later, as Waggoner presented from the book of Isaiah on the topic of the nature of Christ to students attending the 1890 Ministerial Institute held in Battle Creek, he expressed the same idea; "'that Christ could not have sinned, that it was impossible, etc.'"[70] There is a possibility, however, that Waggoner was once again presenting the topic in a way that would protect him from false accusations that he was bringing Christ down too far. Many felt that Christ could not have had the same nature as man, as Waggoner was presenting, or He would have fallen under similar temptations. As Waggoner's presentations on Isaiah came to a close in late January, criticism was once again coming from the brethren in regard to his teachings. Not only were there questions in regard to the classes he was teaching at the Ministerial Institute; there were also questions in regard to the new Sabbath School lesson quarterly dealing with the two covenants, which he had written. Because of this new controversy, some of the brethren were staying away from the Ministerial School, and even from the Sabbath School class. It did not take long however, for Ellen White to respond.

When Ellen White saw what was taking place, she was not at all pleased. On January 17 she sent a letter to Brethren Ballenger (a minister and Review and Herald employee) and Leon Smith (assistant editor of the *Review*, and son of Uriah Smith), warning them of the path they were heading down. There was a correct way to deal with "differences of opinion." Staying away from the meetings was not one of them, for there was a "great need in searching the Scriptures" together:

> Why do you pursue the course you do in keeping away from meetings whose points of truth are investigated?...
>
> The position that you take is very similar to that of the Scribes and Pharisees, constantly criticizing but refusing to come to the light. If you have truth, tell it; if your brethren have truth, be humble and honest before God and say it is truth. ...
>
> If the ideas presented before the Ministerial Institute are erroneous, come to the front like men and present candidly your Bible evidence. ... Do not stand in the position you do as leaders in the Sabbath-school and resisting the light or views and ideas presented by men whom I know to be agents whom the Lord is using. You [*sic*] making of non effect as far as you can their words, and not coming yourself to the light like Christians come to the word to investigate it together with humble hearts, not to investigate the Bible to bring it to your ideas, but bring your ideas to the Bible. ...
>
> You have the example of the Jews how they treated everything that did not harmonize with their opinions of doctrines. ... The Priests and Rulers sent men claiming to be just men for the purpose of catching Him in His words or that

something would drop from His lips that would justify them in their prejudice…
that they could interpret as they choose to present to the people in their own
way and make Christ appear as a deceiver, a heretic. These Jews were not doing
God's work, but the work of the enemy of all righteousness. When I see men
passing over the same ground, I recognize it, and I am worried and distressed. …

Are we Christians or bigots? I say in the fear of God, search the Scriptures.
The interpretation of some portions of Scripture may not be truth in all points,
but let in all the light you can upon these points. …

You will in attending the ministerial school gain new ideas. You will by
digging in the mines of truth be rewarded. …[71]

Even though Ellen White suggested in her letter to Ballenger and Smith
that "the interpretation of some portions of Scripture may not be truth in all
points," she fully supported the presentations of Jones and Waggoner—men
whom she knew to be agents "the Lord is using."[72]

A few days latter, Ellen White addressed the same issues in a morning talk
delivered at the Ministerial Institute. Dan Jones reported that after Waggoner
presented his ideas "that Christ could not have sinned… Sister White came
out a few mornings later and said that Christ could have been overcome
by temptation, and if it were not so he could not be our example and a
consolation to us."[73] Thus, as Ellen White spoke before the entire assembly
gathered in Battle Creek, she attempted to clear up the matter as to whether or
not Christ took human nature like that of man after the Fall and whether or not
it was possible for Him to sin.

First, Ellen White expressed her great concern that they as a people did
not understand the time in which they lived. Her mind was repeatedly taken
back to the Jews and their treatment of Christ: "The trials of the children
of Israel, and their attitude just before the first coming of Christ, have been
presented before me again and again to illustrate the position of the people
of God in their experience before the second coming of Christ." For several
miniutes she spoke of the "humiliation [Christ] endured in taking our nature
upon Himself," and how the Jewish leaders persecuted Him at every step as
a result. She spoke of how they were not able to accept Christ "because He
did not come with all the majesty of a king," but rather as a common man. It

was not only this that caused them to "refuse Him. It was because He was the embodiment of purity, and they were impure." At this point Ellen White spoke to the issue of Christ's nature and the possibility of His yielding to temptation. Waggoner had not brought Christ down too low; no, Christ had come down even lower. It was possible for Him to yield to sin:

> The Son of God was assaulted at every step by the powers of darkness. After his baptism he was driven of the Spirit into the wilderness, and suffered temptation for forty days. Letters have been coming in to me, affirming that Christ could not have had the same nature as man, for if He had, He would have fallen under similar temptations. [But,] if He did not have man's nature, He could not be our example. If He was not a partaker of our nature, He could not have been tempted as man has been. If it were not possible for Him to yield to temptation, He could not be our helper. It was a solemn reality that Christ came to fight the battles as man, in man's behalf. His temptation and victory tell us that humanity must copy the Pattern; man must become a partaker of the divine nature.
>
> In Christ, divinity and humanity were combined. Divinity was not degraded to humanity; divinity held its place, but humanity by being united to divinity, withstood the fiercest test of temptation in the wilderness. ... The plan of God, devised for the salvation of man, provided that Christ should know hunger, and poverty, and every phase of man's experience. He withstood the temptation, through the power that man may command. ... [T]here is not a man or woman who may not have access to the same help through faith in God.[74]

To those who were opposing the teachings of Waggoner, Ellen White's statement made it clear that indeed, Christ had taken upon His sinless nature the same sinful nature as fallen man.[75]* Her statement also removed any excuse for opposition to Waggoner's position because of his teaching that Christ could not sin. Rather than being a rebuke to Waggoner for teaching a great heresy, it was a kind correction, encouraging him not to be apologetic for his view which was actually limiting the risk which God took in sending His Son in the likeness of sinful flesh.

As Ellen White continued her morning talk, she turned to those who were still opposing the messengers and the message. She spoke of John the Baptist, who was not "sent to the school of the prophets and rabbis... that he might not be influenced by their spirit and teaching." The "Lord gave him his message" and he "did not ask if he might proclaim this message." Ellen

White quoted Isaiah 40:3-5—"Prepare ye the way of the Lord"—and stated: "This is the very message that must be given to our people." And yet, the people were unprepared:[76]*

> The Holy Spirit is wanting in our work. Nothing frightens me more than to see the spirit of variance manifested by our brethren. ... I feel like fleeing from the place lest I receive the mold of those who cannot candidly investigate the doctrines of the Bible. ... What we need is the baptism of the Holy Spirit. Without this, we are no more fitted to go forth to the world than were the disciples after the crucifixion of their Lord. ... Every teacher must be a learner, that his eyes may be anointed to see the evidences of the advancing truth of God. The beams of the Sun of Righteousness must shine into his own heart if he would impart light to others. ...

> When the Spirit of God rests upon you, there will be no feeling of envy or jealousy in examining another's position; there will be no spirit of accusation and criticism, such Satan as inspired in the hearts of the Jewish leaders against Christ. ...

> The Jews tried to stop the proclamation of the message that had been predicted in the word of God; but prophecy must be fulfilled. The Lord says, "Behold, I send you Elijah the prophet, before the coming of the great and dreadful day of the Lord." Somebody is to come in the spirit and power of Elijah, and when he appears, men may say, "You are too earnest, you do not interpret the Scriptures in the proper way. Let me tell you how to teach your message.". ... If you continue to find fault, to have a spirit of variance, you will never know the truth. ...

> There are many among us who are prejudiced against the doctrines that are now being discussed. They will not come to hear, they will not calmly investigate, but they put forth their objections in the dark. They are perfectly satisfied with their position [Rev. 3:17-19 quoted]. This scripture applies to those who live under the sound of the message, but who will not come to hear it. How do you know but that the Lord is giving fresh evidences of his truth, placing it in a new setting, that the way of the Lord may be prepared? What plans have you been laying that new light may be infused through the ranks of God's people? What evidence have you that God has not sent light to his children?[77]

This incident gave encouragement to Waggoner and Jones to keep presenting the message of justification by faith and the righteousness of Christ, which was founded on their understanding of the nature of Christ. Never again would Waggoner limit the risk that Christ took in coming to save the race. Unlike many of the brethren, who continued to oppose the most precious message even after numerous rebukes from the pen of Ellen White, Waggoner readily accepted her admonition. When he published his book, appropriately titled *Christ and His Righteousness*, which included his January 21, 1889, article from the *Signs*, Waggoner again clearly presented his views on the divine and human nature of Christ, but he removed his statements that "Christ could not sin."[78]* This is truly the sign of a humble messenger.[79]*

Dan Jones on the other hand saw this incident as confirmation that Jones and Waggoner's message could not be trusted, that Ellen White did not endorse specifically what they were teaching. This led him to conclude that "the matter of doctrine was not the important point," only that men would "accept the doctrine of justification by faith." Of course, to this he could state: "I believe."[80] Ellen White saw things rather differently. As we will see in the chapters ahead, she told Dan Jones that he was not walking in the light, but rather in the "sparks of [his] own kindling."[81]*

It should be clear from historical records, contrary to the writings of some modern historians, that the nature of Christ was part of Jones' and Waggoner's 1888 message.[82]* It was an integral part of the doctrine of justification by faith and the righteousness of Christ as presented before, during, and after the 1888 Conference. The subject of the nature of Christ became more prominent in their presentations in the years that followed, partly because of the continued opposition to that message. Ellen White explained this just a few months after the 1890 Ministerial Institute:

> The spirit of resistance that has been exhibited in presenting the righteousness of Christ as our only hope has grieved the Spirit of God, and the result of this opposition has required the delivery of this matter the more earnestly and decidedly, causing deeper searching into the subject and calling out an array of arguments that the messenger himself did not know was so firm, so full, so thorough upon this subject of justification by faith and the righteousness of Christ as our only hope. ...

> Their [Jones' and Waggoner's] position is seen to be wrong by very many, and they cry, "Danger, fanaticism," when there is no heresy and fanaticism.[83]

Amidst opposition, Jones and Waggoner presented their message. This opposition peaked once again when Waggoner announced he would drop the study of Isaiah and present on the topic of the two covenants.

# CHAPTER 11 FOOTNOTES

1. S. A. Wittier to O. A. Olsen, Jan. 22, 1890; Dan Jones to M. Larson, Jan. 2, 1890.

2. Ellen G. White, "Repentance the Gift of God," *Review and Herald*, April 1, 1890. Jean Zurcher makes the valid point that "Ellet J. Waggoner was the first Adventist theologian to present a systematic Christology, both as it relates to the divinity and humanity of Jesus Christ. … For Waggoner, the subject [justification by faith] could be understood only through the lens of Christology" (*Touched With Our Feelings*, pp. 34-35). The fact remains the same today; the nature of Christ is more than just a side issue, it is intimately connected with the truth of justification by faith. "[T]he church . . . suffers today from a regrettable state of confusion in regard to Christology. The inevitable result is that the same confusion now appears in relation to the doctrine of justification by faith" (*Ibid.*, p. 305). Woodrow Whidden, although taking a different view, recognizes the close connection between the nature of Christ and justification by faith. In his book, *Ellen White on Salvation*, he devotes an entire chapter to the nature of Christ, stating emphatically: "In fact, for us to understand her [Ellen White's] doctrine of salvation, it is absolutely necessary to take into consideration her Christology" (p. 57).

3. Gerhard Pfandl, "The Doctrine of the Trinity Among Adventists," Silver Springs, MD: Biblical Research Institute, 1999, p. 1. It is of interest to note where Ellen White stood in regard to the positions of the early pioneers. Jerry Moon summarizes: "This research has shown that: (1) Ellen White agreed with *some aspects, but not with every aspect* of the antitrinitarian views of other early Adventists. (2) Ellen White's view *did* change— she was raised trinitarian, came to doubt some aspects of the trinitarianism she was raised on, and eventually came to a *different* trinitarian view from the traditional one. (3) There is a basic harmony between Ellen White's earliest statements and her latest ones. Even on internal evidence, there is no reason to question the validity of her later, more trinitarian writings. They are completely consistent with the trajectory of her developing understanding of the Godhead, and there is every evidence that they represent her own thought. In her earliest writings she differed from *some aspects* of traditional trinitarianism and in her latest writings she still strongly opposed *some aspects* of the traditional doctrine of the Trinity. (4) It appears, therefore, that the trinitarian teaching of Ellen White's later writings is *not* the same doctrine that the early Adventists rejected. Rather, her writings describe two contrasting forms of trinitarian belief, one of which she always opposed, and another that she eventually endorsed" ("The Quest for a Biblical Trinity: Ellen White's 'Heavenly Trio' Compared to the Traditional Doctrine," *Journal of the Adventist Theological Society*, 17/1 Spring 2006, pp. 141-142).

4.  Gerhard Pfandl, "The Doctrine of the Trinity Among Adventists," Silver Springs, MD: Biblical Research Institute, 1999, p. 1.

5.  Uriah Smith, *Thoughts on Revelation*, (Battle Creek, MI: Review and Herald, 1865), p. 59. George Knight, in quoting Smith, misapplies the definition of semi-Arian which he uses to distort Waggoner's position: "Smith not only denied the personhood of the Holy Spirit but also had a semi-Arian view of Christ. In 1865, for example, he wrote that Christ was 'the first created being, dating his existence far back before any other created being or thing.' . . . Here at least was a theological point on which the opponents at Minneapolis could agree. E. J. Waggoner's position on the eternity of Christ was essentially that of Smith" (*A Search for Identity*, p. 112). By strict definition Uriah Smith was an Arian. Waggoner never taught that Christ was a *created* Being. In fact, he wrote about the falsehood of such an idea.

6.  E. J. Waggoner, *Christ and His Righteousness*, (Oakland, CA: Pacific Press Pub. Co., 1890), pp. 5-6, emphasis supplied.

7.  *Ibid.*, p. 19, emphasis supplied.

8.  Ellen G. White, *Great Controversy*, 1888 ed., p. 524. Ellen White seems to be describing a belief that is a variant of the Arian view. Notice: "There were quite a number of the First-day Adventists present. They are believers in the age to come, and disbelievers in the pre-existence of Christ before He came to our world. ... Some deny the divinity of Christ, and refuse to believe His pre-existence before the world was made" (Manuscript 53, "Diary," Dec. 1890; in *1888 Materials*, p. 784).

9.  E. J. Waggoner, "An Important Question," *Signs of the Times*, June, 19, 1884, p. 377.

10. E. J. Waggoner, "Immortality," *Signs of the Times*, Sept. 4, 1884, p. 538.

11. E. J. Waggoner, "The Lord's Day," *Signs of the Times*, Nov. 27, 1884, p. 713.

12. E. J. Waggoner, "Which is Evangelical?," *Signs of the Times*, Nov. 12, 1885, p. 681.

13. "The General Conference Institute," *Review and Herald*, Oct. 16, 1888, p. 648.

14. W. C. White, "Notes Made at the Minneapolis Meetings 1888," Oct. 15, 1888; in *Manuscripts and Memories*, p. 421.

15. E. J. Waggoner, "The Divinity of Christ," *Signs of the Times*, March 25, 1889, p. 182, emphasis supplied. The articles should be read in their entirety to gain the full impact of what Waggoner is stating.

16. E. J. Waggoner, "The Divinity of Christ," *Signs of the Times*, April 1, 1889, p. 196, emphasis supplied.

17. E. J. Waggoner, "The Divinity of Christ," *Signs of the Times*, April 8, 1889, p. 214, emphasis supplied.

18. E. J. Waggoner, "The Divinity of Christ," *Signs of the Times*, April 15, 1889, p. 230, emphasis supplied.

19. E. J. Waggoner, "The Divinity of Christ," *Signs of the Times*, April 22, 1889, p. 247, emphasis supplied. It is interesting to note that Ellen White made no mention of Christ being the lawgiver on Sinai in *Spirit of Prophecy* vol. 1 (1870), but in its revision, *Patriarchs and Prophets* (1890), a year after Waggoner's series, she added this concept: "Christ was not only the leader of the Hebrews in the wilderness—the Angel in whom was the name of Jehovah, and who, veiled in the cloudy pillar, went before the host—but it was He who gave the law to Israel. Amid the awful glory of Sinai, Christ declared in the hearing of all the people the ten precepts of His Father's law. It was He who gave to Moses the law engraved upon the tables of stone" (p. 366).

20. E. J. Waggoner, "The Divinity of Christ," *Signs of the Times*, May 6, 1889, p. 262, emphasis supplied.

21. E. J. Waggoner, *Christ and His Righteousness*, p. 19.

22. *Ibid.*, pp. 8-9, emphasis supplied.

23. *Ibid.*, p. 10.

24. *Ibid.*, pp. 11-12.

25. *Ibid.*, pp. 15-16, emphasis supplied.

26. *Ibid.*, pp. 18-19, emphasis supplied.

27. *Ibid.*, pp. 19-21, emphasis supplied.

28. *Ibid.*, pp. 23-24, emphasis supplied.

29. See footnote 44.

30. Ellen G. White to E. J. Waggoner and A. T. Jones, Letter 37, Feb. 18, 1887; in *1888 Materials*, pp. 28, 29.

31. Ellen G. White Manuscript 16, "The Discernment of Truth," Jan. 1889; in *1888 Materials*, p. 260.

32. Ellen G. White Manuscript 27, "Counsel to Ministers," Sept. 13, 1889; in *1888 Materials*, p. 432.

33. Ellen G. White Manuscript 10, "The Excellence of Christ," Oct. 1889; in *1888 Materials*, pp. 448-449.

34. Ellen G. White, "Morning Talk, Jan. 29, 1890," *Review and Herald*, Feb. 18, 1890, p. 97; in *1888 Materials*, p. 533.

35. Ellen G. White, "Living Channels of Light," *Review and Herald*, May 27, 1890, p. 321; in *1888 Materials*, p. 673.

36. Ellen G. White to O. A. Olsen, Letter 57, May 1, 1895; in *1888 Materials*, p. 1336.

37. E. J. Waggoner, "The Divinity of Christ," *Signs of the Times*, April 8, 1889, p. 214, emphasis supplied. These articles were picked up by other papers, being printed in Australia's *Bible Echoes*, Oct. 1, 1889, and England's *Present Truth*, Dec. 18, 1890, but Waggoner never wrote these ideas in new articles or books.

38. E. J. Waggoner, *Christ and His Righteousness*, p. 21, emphasis supplied.

39. Eric Webster observes correctly: "For Waggoner Christ was divine and pre-existent, but, at least according to his views in 1889, not fully eternal. *In this one connection Waggoner shows affinity with the semi-Arian position.* ... Waggoner has a high view of the deity of Christ. He gives scriptural evidence of the fact that Christ is God. ... For Waggoner Christ was not a created being but was begotten of the Father. He makes a clear distinction between being created and being begotten. ... He indicates that Christ is of the 'very substance and nature of God' and that 'He possesses immortality in His own right, and can confer immortality upon others'" (*Crosscurrents in Adventist Christology*, pp. 177-179, emphasis supplied).

40. LeRoy E. Froom, *Movement of Destiny*, p 296.

41. J. R. Zurcher, *Touched With Our Feelings*, pp. 34-37.

42. E. J. Waggoner, "A Movement to Unite Church and State," *American Sentinel*, March 27, 1890, p. 100, emphasis supplied. Eric Webster makes reference to a similar statement made in *Glad Tidings*, that this "could be an advancement on his 1890 position" (*Crosscurrents*, p. 198).

43. Ellen G. White, *Desire of Ages*, p. 530. Ellen White's view was not an "opposite position" to Waggoner's earlier stated view as George Knight declares; it was just a more advanced position (see, George Knight, *A User-Friendly Guide to the 1888 Message*, p. 74).

44. Woodrow Whidden has gone to great lengths in misrepresenting Waggoner on the issue of the divinity of Christ: "Ellen White's hearty support of Jones and Waggoner is unquestioned. The key issue, however, seems to be whether this strong support meant *total* support for all their theological positions. For instance, did she support their view that Christ was a created god (Arianism)?" (*Ellen White on Salvation*, p. 90). Whidden took this same view into the Primacy of the Gospel Committee (a committee setup by Robert Folkenberg in 1994, while serving as General Conference President, for the purpose of considering the doctrine of righteousness by faith): "We began our

committee with Dr. Whidden trying to force me [Robert Wieland] to confess that E. J. Waggoner was an Arian. An Arian is one who doesn't believe that Christ is eternal, divine, He was created. I said, 'I can't do that.' [Whidden said], 'Brother Wieland, everybody believes that.' [Wieland said] 'I'm sorry I can't agree with that.' [Whidden] pressed me hard: 'You mean to say that you are the only one here that is going to say that Waggoner was not an Arian?' I said, 'I cannot agree with that'" (Robert J. Wieland, "Third Angel's Message & Corporate Repentance," March 24, 1996). George Knight misrepresents history as well, as he seeks to force Waggoner into an Arian view with a semi-Arian label: "[N]ot everything that Waggoner, Jones and Prescott taught about Jesus was clearsighted, even in the immediate post-Minneapolis period. … [I]n *Christ and His Righteousness* (1890) [Waggoner] put forth semi-Arian views of Christ when he wrote that 'there was a time when Christ proceeded forth and came from God.' That semi-Arianism, which taught that Christ *was not equal with God*, had been prominent in Adventist theology from its inception in the 1840s. Just because *Waggoner taught such views* in the late 1880s and early 1890s, however, did not make them truth. Ellen White and most of the church would reject both views along with others during the 1890s" (*From 1888 to Apostasy*, pp. 132-133, emphasis supplied). But Waggoner never once said that Christ "was not equal to God." David McMahon ultimately misrepresents Waggoner as well, stating: "Waggoner tried to boldly confess Christ's divinity. He denied that Christ is a created being. He said that Christ is God, both Creator and Lawgiver. … Nevertheless, Waggoner *was still Arian in the classical sense*" (*Ellet Joseph Waggoner: The Myth and the Man*, p. 102, emphasis supplied). But why such an agenda to misrepresent Waggoner on the divinity of Christ? In biographical critiques that often seem cynical, Knight and Whidden, slander Jones and Waggoner, while promoting their own Fordian theology; a theology that seeks to promote the Evangelical view of the nature of Christ made popular by *Questions on Doctrine*, and Desmond Ford. So the issue is really not over the divinity of Christ. Knight and Whidden build a straw man in regard to Waggoner's view on the divine nature of Christ, then often move to the subject of the human nature of Christ. This is a classic example of a bait-and-switch tactic that is as old as sin itself. The point being, *if* Waggoner was nothing short of an Arian regarding his views on the divine nature of Christ—jesus "was a created god"—how can Waggoner possibly be trusted regarding his views on the human nature of Christ? Such a viewpoint can only be taken, however, when doing violence to historical facts.

45. Jones' and Waggoner's view on the human nature of Christ was that which the Church held for nearly 100 years; from the Church's very inception until the early 1950s. This view, sometimes called postlapsarian or post–Fall, teaches that Jesus took fallen human nature, the nature of Adam *after* the Fall. Consequently, Christ's flesh is considered like that of all human beings, not only in a physical sense, but also carrying within it

inherent tendencies to sin-tendencies to which Jesus, however, never succumbed. Although Christ was "in all points tempted as we are," the Bible says He was "yet without sin" (Heb. 4:15). Thus, Christ not only "condemned sin in the flesh," He also made it possible "that the righteousness of the law might be fulfilled in us, who walk not after the flesh but after the Spirit" (Rom. 8:3, 4). This teaching, though based on the Bible, was and is contrary to the beliefs of mainline Christianity (although it must be said that some eminent Protestant theologians are coming to believe the post-Fall view). The Prelapsarian position, sometimes called the pre-Fall view, argues that Christ took Adam's sinless human nature; that which Adam had *before* the Fall. Christ was tempted in all things, but it was not from within since He inherited from Adam *none* of our *propensities* or our *tendencies* to sin. Whatever Christ bore, whether the burden and penalty of our iniquities, or the diseases and frailties of our human nature, all was taken and borne *vicariously*. This particular view, which is essentially the view of Roman Catholicism via the Immaculate Conception, and mainline Protestantism via the doctrine of Original Sin, was adapted and promoted amongst Seventh-day Adventists through the book *Questions on Doctrines* in the early 1950s. A third view, sometimes called the Alternative Christology, is a synthesis between the post–Fall and pre–Fall views, and is the most recent and probably the most widespread view among Seventh-day Adventist leadership in North America since the early 1980s. This view declares that Christ inherited from Adam only "innocent infirmities," such as hunger, pain, weakness, sorrow and death. But unlike all other fallen human beings born into this world since the Fall, Jesus inherited none of the inclinations to evil associated with fallen human nature. Thus He was neither exactly like Adam before the Fall nor exactly like Adam after the Fall. For a thorough presentation on the history of Adventist thought on the human nature of Christ, and from which the above summary was taken, see: J. R. Zurcher, *Touched with Our Feelings*, pp. 271-274. As mentioned above, the change from the accepted post-Fall view of the human nature of Christ in 1888 to the view held by many in the church today dates back to the 1950s and the book *Questions on Doctrine*. But the prevalence today of the pre-Fall view is best attributed to Desmond Ford and his Reformationist challenge, which advocated four concepts (including his support of the new pre-Fall view): "Advocated first in Australia by Brinsmead and Ford during the early 1970s and, following a period of insemination by way of Brinsmead's *Present Truth*, this view has been vigorously promoted in the U. S. by Ford; the primary Reformationist charge is that the doctrine of righteousness by faith has been confused in the SDA church by the denial of the doctrine of original sin. This, they hold, has given rise to three related heresies: a) that the gospel includes sanctification as well as justification; b) that Christ took the fallen nature of Adam; and c) a 'final generation' must develop perfect characters before Christ's return" (A. Leroy Moore, *Theology in Crisis*, p. 23). In his book, *The Shaking of Adventism*, Geoffrey

Paxton, an Australian Anglican Minister, expressed support for the Evangelical gospel coming into the Seventh-day Adventist church with the same four concepts: "Belief that both the destiny of the Church and its preparation of the world for Christ's long-delayed second advent hinge upon a true conception of righteousness by faith, demands the commitment of every effort to expose what is seen as serious confusion regarding this heart of the gospel. Affirmation of the doctrine of original sin underlies each of the three primary challenges to traditional Adventist theology: 1) repudiation of perfectionism, 2) denial of Christ's assumption of sinful flesh, and 3) restriction of the doctrine of justification by faith to strictly forensic, objective factors" (p. 29). In David McMahon's *E. J. Waggoner: The Myth and the Man* (published through Desmond Ford's Verdict Publications), the author challenges Waggoner's theology both pre and post 1888, in support of the Evangelical gospel with the same four basic concepts: "All four basic Reformationist charges against contemporary SDA theology are aimed [by David McMahon] at the theology Waggoner enunciated in the months following Minneapolis" (stated by, A. Leroy Moore, *op cit.*, p. 419). In an interview with Julius Nam (professor of religion at Loma Linda University, and co-organizer of *Questions on Doctrine* 50th Anniversary Conference), Woodrow Whidden expresses support for the same four concepts made popular by Desmond Ford: "But when one really hones in on the meaning of the atonement and the humanity of Christ, we see that sin mainly has to do with the profound derangement of sinful [*sic*], the human depravity that we are all born with (Christ excepted). ... And the reason that both of these earnest groups [Historic SDAs and 1888 Study Committee] are off the mark is because they have failed to fully come to terms with the meaning of the atonement and the radical nature of human sin. ... [T]hey have zeroed in on issues which were not a part of Ellen White's emphasis on the meaning of 1888. Here I have special reference to . . . the sinful human nature of Christ, a perfectionist emphasis that seems undergirded by a mostly 'behavioristic' definition of sin, final generation vindication of God and their misapplication of Ellen White's support for Jones and Waggoner. ... In my estimation, both need to shed themselves of all of these emphases which have scant support in the Bible and the writings of Ellen G. White. ... Both the 'historic' and the '1888 Study Committee' folks need . . . to pay more attention to issues which surround the meaning of the Atonement, the sinlessness of Christ's human nature, radical human sin, and justification by grace through faith alone. ... And once again, what undergirded [Andreasen's] defective views on the humanity of Christ was a defective view of the nature of sin" ("Progressive Adventism: Re-Imagining the Adventist Vision. Interlogue #18~Woodrow Whidden," An interview with Julius Nam, posted Feb. 16, 2007; http://progressiveadventism.com/2007/02/16/interlogue-18-woodrow-whidden/, accessed April 8, 2010). In regard to those who hold the post-Fall view, Whidden bemoans the fact several times: "I am dismayed at . . . their almost total neglect of Ellen White's counsels regarding the authority of the 'brethren of experience.'. . . Here is where I think such conservative [progressive], Bible believing and Ellen White affirming Adventists such as the Adventist Theological Society and the conservative [progressive] Adventist scholarship in many of our academic institutions and the Biblical Research Institute of the General Conference can be of help (if the 'historics' and the '1888 Study Committee' believers will give them a good hearing). . . . Both 'historic' and the '1888 Study Committee' folks need a deeper respect for these scholarly 'brethren of experience.'. . . And here lies the great divide between what you call a 'big chunk of mainstream conservative [progressive]' Adventists (especially the majority of Scholars in our institutions of higher learning the world over, the Adventist Theological Society, and the *BRI*) and the so-called conservative 'historics' and '1888 Study Committee' Seventh-day Adventists. . . . I have been a fully elected member of BRICOM (Biblical Research Institute Committee) since the summer of 2006. . . . The major work of this committee is to give theological interpretive input to the leadership of the General Conference" (*Ibid.*). Although we would agree with the biblical concept of submitting to the "brethren of experience," we would suggest there is another, just as important concept in regard to the doctrine of Jesus. It's the one that Peter and the other apostles expressed to the highly educated, Greek influenced, progressive Sadducees of his day: "We ought to obey God rather than men" (Acts 5:29). Whidden's optimism of the "brethren of experience," however, is somewhat misplaced. There are many who do not hold to his and Desmond Ford's theological positions. That said, there is perhaps still need for concern. In the same interview, Whidden speaks of his future goals: "When I finish this project [biography on Waggoner], my next goal will be to produce a new SDA undergraduate textbook. The BRI wants to sponsor such a project, but it has not yet been settled if I will be their author. I am probably going to do this, even if the BRI goes another direction. I hope to co-author this with a seasoned colleague in undergraduate education. As to the future of SDA historiography: I would hope that we will continue to seek greater clarity on our key understandings of how our historic views on soteriology, the nature of the Atonement, and the person of Christ can be brought to further maturity and redemptive clarity. I would hope to be a part of the writing of a history of the Ford/Rea Crisis of the late 1970s and the early 1980s. I sense that enough time has passed that we can more candidly deal with this hot button topic. The issues still very much hang over us and I think we are now more clearly positioned to get some further clarification about them" (*Ibid.*). The question, however, is whether our church, and especially our young people, really need more of Ford's theology foisted on them through the writings of progressive, modern day historians and theologians.

46. E. J. Waggoner, "Condemned and Justified," *Signs of the Times*, July 3, 1884, p. 409.

47. E. J. Waggoner, "A New Creature in Christ," *Signs of the Times*, July 17, 1884, p. 424.

48. E. J. Waggoner, "Under the Law," *Signs of the Times*, Sept. 18, 1884, p. 569.

49. E. J. Waggoner, "Thoughts on Galatians 3, No. 8," *Signs of the Times*, Aug. 26, 1886, p. 518.

50. G. I. Butler, *The Law in the Book of Galatians: Is it the Moral Law, or Does it Refer to That System of Laws Peculiarly Jewish?* (Battle Creek Mich.: Review and Herald Pub. House, 1886), p. 57.

51. The fact that Christ took upon His sinless nature our sinful nature was to Waggoner "one of the most encouraging things." For Waggoner, the nature of Christ was more than just a creedal doctrine; it was part of the everlasting gospel, which included the good news of the covenants, and was understood in the context of justification by faith in the righteousness of Christ. Unfortunately, some historic Adventists representing various independent ministries have sometimes presented the human nature of Christ as a legalistic doctrine void of good news, and thus made it a message that discourages rather then encourages. This, of course, has not only "turned many against the post-Fall view of the human nature of Christ," but has also given ammunition to the leading brethren who hold to the "new" pre-Fall view (see: Herbert E. Douglass, *A Fork in the Road*, pp. 16, 33, 85; Jack Sequeira, *Saviour of the World*, pp. 11-12; Roy Adams, *The Nature of Christ*, p. 11).

52. E. J. Waggoner, *The Gospel in the Book of Galatians*, pp. 60-61. Waggoner was quoting from Hebrews 2:17—"*in all things*"—in his book *Gospel in Galatians*. Once again George Knight misquotes historic evidence stating of Waggoner: "Concerning the human nature of Christ, in 1887 Waggoner wrote that 'if Christ had not been made *in all ways* like unto his brethren, then his sinless life would be no encouragement to us.'. . . Once again Ellen White took a different track" (*A User-Friendly Guide to the 1888 Message*, p. 75, emphasis in original). Knight changes Waggoner's phrase from "*in all things*," to "*in all ways*," and makes no mention that Waggoner was quoting from the book of Hebrews.

53. W. C. White to Dan T. Jones, April 8, 1890; in *Manuscripts and Memories*, pp. 167-168.

54. A. G. Daniells to W. C. White, April 14, 1902; in *Manuscripts and Memories*, p. 318.

55. W. C. White, "Notes Made at the Minneapolis Meetings 1888," Oct. 17, 1888, and "Diary of R. Dewitt Hottel, 1888," Oct. 17, 1888; in *Manuscripts and Memories*, pp. 423, 506.

56. LeRoy E. Froom, *Movement of Destiny*, pp. 200, 201; E. J. Waggoner, "The Divinity of Christ," March 25, April 1, 8, 15, 22, May 6, 1889.

57. Ellen G. White, "The Work of the Minister," *Review and Herald*, Sept. 11, 1888, p. 578, emphasis supplied.

58. Ellen G. White, "Harmony with Apostate Powers A Sign of Enmity of God," *Signs of the Times*, June 18, 1894, p. 500, emphasis supplied.

59. Ellen G. White, "No Caste in Christ," *Review and Herald*, Dec. 22, 1891, p. 785, emphasis supplied.

60. Ellen G. White, "Spiritual Weakness Inexcusable," *Review and Herald*, July 1, 1890, p. 402, emphasis supplied.

61. Ellen G. White to H. Miller, Letter 5, June 2, 1889; in *1888 Materials*, p. 332, emphasis supplied.

62. Ellen G. White, "The Work of the Minister," *Review and Herald*, Sept. 11, 1888, p. 578.

63. Ellen G. White Manuscript 5, "Sermon," June 19, 1889; in *1888 Materials*, p. 349.

64. Ellen G. White, "The Perils and Privileges of the Last Days," *Review and Herald*, Nov. 22, 1892, p. 722; in *1888 Materials*, p. 1073, emphasis supplied.

65. Ellen G. White to O. A. Olsen, Letter 57, May 1, 1895; in *1888 Materials*, p. 1336, emphasis supplied.

66. Ellen G. White Manuscript 8, "Sabbath Talk," Oct. 20, 1888; in *1888 Materials*, pp. 122, 125.

67. E. J. Waggoner, "God Manifest in the Flesh," *The Signs of the Times*, Jan. 21, 1889, p. 39. Ellen White stated the same: "It is a mystery that is left unexplained to mortals that Christ could be tempted in all points like as we are, and yet be without sin" (to W. L. Baker, Letter 8, Feb. 9, 1895; *Manuscript Releases*, vol. 13, p. 19).

68. E. J. Waggoner, "God Manifest in the Flesh," *The Signs of the Times*, Jan. 21, 1889, p. 39.

69. *Ibid.*, emphasis supplied. It seems that the point Waggoner was seeking to make is what Ellen White stated a few years before: "It is impossible for man to be tempted above that he is able to bear while he relies upon Jesus" ("Christ Triumphant in Our Behalf," *The Signs of the Times*, Aug. 4, 1887, p. 465). Waggoner was also speaking without the benefit of Ellen White's later statement: "Many claim that it was impossible for Christ to be overcome by temptation. Then He could not have been placed in Adam's position; He could not have gained the victory that Adam failed to gain. If we have in any sense a more trying conflict than had Christ, then He would not be able to succor us. But our Saviour took humanity, with all its liabilities. He took the nature of man, with the possibility of yielding to temptation. We have nothing to bear which He has not endured" (*The Desire of Ages*, p. 117). Notice Ellen White's point that the truth that Christ could have fallen was required in order to reach man where he was at, and this could be done only by taking our sinful fallen nature.

70. Dan T. Jones to J. H. Morrison, March 17, 1890, p. 4, archives of the General Conference of Seventh-day Adventists.

71. Ellen G. White to Brethren Ballenger and Leon Smith, Letter 53, Jan. 17, 1890; in *1888 Materials*, pp. 528-532.

72. *Ibid.*, pp. 530, 529.

73. Dan T. Jones to J. H. Morrison, March 17, 1890, p. 4, archives of the General Conference of Seventh-day Adventists.

74. Ellen G. White, "How to Meet a Controverted Point of Doctrine," *Review and Herald*, Feb. 18, 1890, p. 97, "Morning Talk," Jan. 29, 1890; in *1888 Materials*, p. 533.

75. Some have tried to separate the subject of the human nature of Christ from the "1888 message," and from the controversy that surrounded Jones and Waggoner in the late 1880s and 1890s. George Knight states that Jones and Waggoner's "view of Christ's nature created *no* controversy in the Adventism of the 1890s. It was a generally accepted theological non-issue. ... Major controversies over Jones's position on the nature of Christ did not arise until long after his death. ... As noted earlier, the nature of Christ did not become a divisive issue in Adventist circles until the 1950s" (*From 1888 to Apostasy*, pp. 133, 135, 140, emphasis supplied). Knight does admit, however, "that does not mean that the topic never surfaced. After all, we do have at least *one* statement on the topic [in] Waggoner's *Gospel in Galatians*" (*A User-Friendly Guide to the 1888 Message*, p. 153). Woodrow Whidden, on the other hand, in trying to distance the subject of the human nature of Christ from the "1888 message" takes a different stance. He seeks to substantiate the idea that Jones' and Waggoner's view on the nature of Christ could not have been part of the 1888 message Ellen White endorsed, because their view received "provocative opposition." He places Jones' and Waggoner's view with the "numerous theological wrecks lying on the Adventist doctrinal highway" that have not withstood "the test of time and theological scrutiny." Whidden states emphatically: "While Ralph Larson has demonstrated (in *The Word Was Made Flesh*) that a rather strong consensus on a post-Fall view existed until the middle of 1950s, George Knight has also shown that there was provocative opposition to the post-Fall view of none other than A. T. Jones in the mid-1890s (Knight [*From 1888 to Apostasy*] 132–150)" (*Ellen White on the Humanity of Christ*, p. 79). But reading the pages listed by Whidden, the reader will find that Knight wrote no such statement. Thus it would be best in deciding this issue, to let history speak for itself. The point is that the post-Fall view of the nature of Christ was part of Jones' and Waggoner's message, both before and after 1888, and was, for the most part, the accepted view. However, when Jones and Waggoner presented it in the context of justification by faith through the righteousness of Christ, the covenants, and the perfection of character of the final generation, many opposed their teaching. The same is true today.

76.  Dr. D. H. Kress was present at the Ministerial Institute and recalls this event some 42 years later: "Whenever meetings of this kind are held, there is always danger that some teachings will be carried to extremes. Elder Waggoner began to teach that Jesus, being God in the flesh, could not sin; that it was impossible for Him to sin... Elder Uriah Smith, in teaching, took the position that God did not know when He created man that he would sin; that, being God, He could choose to know or not to know." Kress states that Ellen White "appeared" at the early morning meeting the next day with "a special message." She "began by referring to the blessings that were ours at such gatherings for Bible study and consecration. Then she referred to the danger of receiving error, and referred to the teaching of righteousness by faith, and said, 'Truth often lies very close to error.' This led her to the theory many had been rejoicing in, that it was impossible for Christ to sin. She said that God risked something when He gave His only begotten Son to this world; that it was possible for Christ to sin. This made prayer on His part a necessity... Elder Smith's theory was next shown to be wrong." Kress explains that Ellen White then began to speak to those who had taken "a position against Elders Waggoner and Jones" at Minneapolis in regard to the "doctrine of righteousness by faith." As she began to call some of the men by name, Dr. Kress, perhaps feeling guilty himself, fully expected to "be the next one whose sins would be pointed out." But, sitting near a pillar he "managed to keep hidden from her view" (Lauretta and Daniel Kress, *Under the Guiding Hand: Life Experiences of Doctors Kress* [Washington, D. C.: College Press, 1932], pp. 113-115). Dr. Kress's account, however, is not totally reliable. He includes events from the 1891 General Conference as if being part of the 1890 Ministerial Institute.

77.  Ellen G. White, "Morning Talk," Jan. 29, 1890, *Review and Herald*, Feb. 18, 1890, p. 98; in *1888 Materials*, p. 534.

78.  E. J. Waggoner, *Christ and His Righteousness* (Oakland, Cal.: Pacific Press Pub. Co., 1890), pp. 24-31. There is no evidence that Waggoner stated that "Christ could not sin" after this Ministerial Institute. In a short response found in the *Signs* a few months later, Waggoner clarifies his point on Christ not being capable of sinning: "The fact that Christ 'did no sin'—that he 'knew no sin,' although subjected to the severest assaults of Satan, is sufficient to show that he could not be induced to sin. This is the idea intended to be conveyed in the note referred to [that Christ could not sin]. In one sense, it was possible for Christ to sin, provided he had wished to, for the nature which he took was a nature subject to sin. Yet it was impossible for him to sin, because 'God was in Christ, and that in perfect fullness... He demonstrated in his own person the power of divinity to prevail against the power of Satan working through human weakness" ("Christ, the Sinless One," *Signs of the Times*, June 9, 1890, p. 342). This was in line with what Ellen White had written just one year before, with her added emphasis on the importance of understanding this in order to stand at the end of time: "Christ

could have done nothing during His earthly ministry in saving fallen man if the divine had not been blended with the human. The limited capacity of man cannot define this wonderful mystery—the blending the two natures, the divine and the human. It can never be explained. Man must wonder and be silent. And yet man is privileged to be a partaker of the divine nature, and in this way he can to some degree enter into the mystery. This wonderful exhibition of God's love was made on the cross of Calvary. Divinity took the nature of humanity, and for what purpose?—That through the righteousness of Christ humanity might partake of the divine nature. This union of divinity and humanity, which was possible with Christ, is incomprehensible to human minds. The wonderful things to take place in our world—the greatest events of all ages—are incomprehensible to worldly minds; they cannot be explained by human sciences. The powers of heaven shall be shaken. Christ is coming in power and great glory, but His coming is not such a mystery as the things to take place before that event. Man must be a partaker of the divine nature in order to stand in this evil time, when the mysteries of satanic agencies are at work. Only by the divine power united with the human can souls endure through these times of trial. Says Christ, 'Without me ye can do nothing.' Then there must be far less of self and more of Jesus" (Letter 5, June 19, 1889; in *1888 Materials*, p. 332).

79. George Knight lists this incident as one of seven items that reveal that Jones' and Waggoner's teachings were out of harmony with Ellen White, and this representing "only a sample of those differences." Yet, the full story of this incident is not told. At the same time the reader is reminded over a dozen times throughout his book that Ellen White "*repeatedly asserted that she didn't agree with all of their teachings.*" And, "she had serious disagreements with some of their assertions, even in areas related to salvation." It seems that the thrust of all these comments is ultimately to lead the reader to think that "*Jones and Waggoner had developed a theology* [on the nature of Christ] *built on a concept that directly contradicted Ellen White*" (*A User-Friendly Guide to the 1888 Message*, pp. 74, 69, 76, 163, emphasis in original; see also, 55, 72-74, 76, 79, 165, 166, 179, 180). Woodrow Whidden also mentions this incident, suggesting that it was Waggoner's views on the human nature of Christ, which led him to "draw some most curious theological conclusions." Whidden mentions nothing about the meetings held at the Ministerial Institute, but states rather: "While the issue of Christ not being able to sin because of His inherent deity will not receive much further development, the fact that [Waggoner] speaks of the indwelling Christ in believers, giving them the same victory over sin, is one of the factors that will receive increasing accent for the rest of his ministry." This thesis, we are told by Whidden, not only "provides a key to understanding [Waggoner's] perfectionistic optimism, but a possible clue to his later aberrant tendencies" (*E. J. Waggoner*, pp. 196). In a footnote, Whidden suggests that "the book *Christ and His Righteousness* . . . repeats essentially the same thought that

because divine power dwelled in Christ, He could resist inherent weakness of the flesh" (*Ibid.*, p. 211 fn. 15). In summarizing the incident, Whidden reveals an interesting point about his biography on Waggoner: "Undoubtedly the most significant and portentous theological trend of the early post-Minneapolis period . . . was Waggoner's early 1889 emphasis on the indwelling Christ. ... In light of the above-mentioned concept, *the working theological thesis for the rest of this biography is that it would become the source for almost all of the errant theological and practical paths that Waggoner would tread for the balance of his life*" (*Ibid.*, p. 210, emphasis supplied). True to his word, Whidden spends not just the rest of his biography, but almost the entire biography, seeking to force Adventist 1888 history into his "theological thesis" which has become so popular among Evangelical and Reformationist Adventists (see Chapter 13, footnote 33). But Waggoner *did* remove his idea that Christ "could not sin," when he published *Christ and His Righteousness*. Yet he kept the concepts that were true, and that which Ellen White would also clearly state herself: "In Christ dwelt the fullness of the Godhead bodily. This is why, although He was tempted in all points like as we are, He stood before the world, from His first entrance into it, untainted by corruption, though surrounded by it. Are we not also to become partakers of that fullness, and is it not thus, and thus only, that we can overcome as He overcame? We lose much by not dwelling constantly upon the character of Christ" (Manuscript 16, Oct. 1, 1890; "Draw from the Source of Strength," *Signs of the Times*, Oct. 10, 1892).

80. Dan T. Jones to J. H. Morrison, March 17, 1890, p. 4, archives of the General Conference of Seventh-day Adventists.

81. Ellen G. White Manuscript 4, March 8, 1890, "Sermon"; in *1888 Materials*, pp. 594-595. George Knight also proclaims that the message was not "theological or doctrinal, but attitudinal." His support for such a view is based on the letters of none other than Dan Jones (*Angry Saints*, pp. 93-94).

82. As mentioned above in footnote 75, some have suggested that Jones' and Waggoner's teaching on the nature of Christ was not part of the 1888 message. They suggest, rather, that it was an erroneous doctrine that "evolved" shortly after the Minneapolis Conference and therefore should not be included with the real "1888 message" that Ellen White endorsed. Those with this understanding seek to promote the idea that the 1888 message is only that message which was preached in the year 1888 at the Minneapolis Conference. Thus, anytime Jones and Waggoner presented only that which they presented at Minneapolis, they were giving the real 1888 message. Added to this understanding is the idea that all of Ellen White's endorsements of Jones and Waggoner, even into the latter part of the 1890s, applied only to that part of their message which they had presented at Minneapolis. But alas, they say, we don't have any transcript of Jones' and Waggoner's message at Minneapolis, and therefore we cannot really

know what Ellen White specifically endorsed. The conclusion then, is that Ellen White endorsed Jones' and Waggoner's teaching in regard to *basic Christianity*, but not their teaching on any distinctively Adventists doctrines, which they taught. Of course the term "*basic Christianity*," is often defined as the Evangelical gospel. Desmond Ford expressed many of these ideas in the 1970s: "One of the most glaring examples of poor scholarship . . . is the use made of the writings of Waggoner and Jones. The writers have concluded that because Ellen White endorsed the emphasis of these brethren at Minneapolis when they presented Christ and Christ alone as the basis for a believer's salvation that therefore she endorsed all that these men taught. Nothing could be further from the truth" ("Observations on *Conflicting Conceptions on Righteousness by Faith*," Adventist Heritage Center, Andrews University, Berrien Springs, MI., [1970s], p. 18). Ford also states: "The question naturally comes up—If Ellen White on the one hand takes the Reformation stand, how can she support Waggoner on the other hand when he has elements which are more Catholic in theology than Reformation? How can this be reconciled? 1. Waggoner's teachings were not fully developed at Minneapolis. As the years went on, probably because of a gradually changed emphasis on the inward work of Christ on the heart, he defected into a type of pantheism, which is really a version of perfectionism. 2. The emphasis of his teaching at Minneapolis that Ellen White supported was the uplifting of Christ as the only hope of mankind; and the utter worthlessness of human merit to effect salvation" (*The Doctrinal Decline of Dr. E. J. Waggoner: Its Relationship to the Omega Apostasy*, [1970s], p. 30). George Knight has presented these ideas throughout his writings on 1888: "The truth is that *for Ellen White the 1888 message is the message of 1888 rather than the message of 1893 or 1895.*" "It is not the particular interpretation that they placed upon the gospel that is all important, but the gospel itself." "[T]he human nature of Christ had an extremely small role at the Minneapolis meetings. Mrs. White would later commend the 1888 message for uplifting the 'divine person' of Jesus (*Testimonies to Ministers*, p. 92), but we find no such commendation or mention of any discussion of Christ's human nature at Minneapolis" (*A User-Friendly Guide to the 1888 Message*, pp. 165, 152-153, emphasis in original). "None of these records demonstrate that the divinity of Christ, the human nature of Christ, or 'sinless living' were topics of emphasis or discussion at the 1888 meetings. Persons holding that those topics were central to the theology of the meetings generally read subsequent developments in Jones and Waggoner's treatment of righteousness by faith back into the 1888 meetings" (*From 1888 to Apostasy*, pp. 133, 37). In his biography on Waggoner, David McMahon takes the same view: "There is no evidence that Waggoner's teaching on the humanity of Christ was part of his message in 1888. This is one of the Waggoner myths demolished by an investigation of the original sources. However, in the 1889-1891 period Waggoner began giving great prominence to the humanity of Christ. ... Waggoner did not enunciate a new heresy in his unfortunate theological development. ... [It] logically leads to the abandonment of justification by an imputed righteousness on the one hand and to the development of pantheism on the other" (*The Myth and the Man*, pp. 104, 108). Woodrow Whidden also supports these views: "George Knight is right on target when he contends that none of the records of Minneapolis 'demonstrate that the divinity of Christ, the human nature of Christ ... were topics of emphasis or discussion at the 1888 meetings'" (*Ellen White on Salvation*, p. 89). Roy Adams follows the same line of reasoning in his book that "relied heavily on George Knight's well-documented historical-theological assessment of A. T. Jones." Adams' conclusions are therefore the same: "As already indicated, the actual messages of both Jones and Waggoner at the 1888 session were never recorded. (Some Adventist's today see this as providential—'one of the best things that happened to the 1888 message,' says Knight [*From 1888 to Apostasy*, p. 70].) This means that there is no way of discovering what Jones and Waggoner actually said and therefore, we cannot be sure about what precisely was included in Ellen White's endorsement" (*The Nature of Christ*, p. 32). In answer to such statements it must be said that Ellen White never used the words "the 1888 message." This term, of modern origin, has been used correctly to identify the General Conference in which that message *began*. During all the years that followed the 1888 Conference, Ellen White never gave the impression that her support of Jones and Waggoner was for only that which they had presented specifically at the 1888 Conference. Nor did she give the impression that any part of that message expressed in greater detail was somehow not part of the 1888 message. To the contrary, many of her numerous endorsements of Jones and Waggoner speak of "advancing truth," "new light," "increased light," "increasing light," "truths that are entirely new," "new forms," "a new frame work," "more light," etc. (*1888 Materials*, pp. 547, 463, 806, 219, 1651, 498, 259, 86). As to the nature of Christ, it should be self-evident from this chapter that indeed the nature of Christ, as Waggoner presented it before and shortly after the Minneapolis Conference, was part of that 1888 message. This was part of his "basic Christianity." We can be thankful that Roman Catholics hold many *basic Christian beliefs*, such as a belief in the inspiration of the Bible, God the Father, Jesus Christ His Son, the Holy Spirit, Christ's death on the Cross, Jesus love for man, confession and forgiveness, justification by faith, sanctification, baptism, the second coming, and a final dealing with sin in hell. They even believe that the Virgin Mary gave birth to Christ in human flesh. But someone might rightly suggest that there is a vast difference between the "basic Christianity" of Roman Catholicism and the "basic Christianity" that makes up the third angel's message that is yet to lighten the earth with its glory. We will take a second look at this topic in Vol. 2 of *The Return of the Latter Rain*.

83. Ellen G. White to Bro. Olsen, Letter 116, Aug. 27, 1890; in *1888 Materials*, p. 703.

# CHAPTER 12

# *Faulty Promises*
## *Differing Views on the Two Covenants*

Being deeply impressed with the events of the past year, Ellen White wrote several articles to be printed in the *Review* in early 1890. Repeatedly she drew attention to the time in which the Church was living—the day of atonement. She had recognized the message sent through Jones and Waggoner as the law and gospel combined. She saw them presenting the great truths of justification by faith combined with the cleansing of the sanctuary. God was seeking not only to forgive His people for their sins, but also to cleanse them from their sins by blotting them out, and thus prepare them to stand in the day of His coming. This preparation required a heart work, an individual cooperation with the great High Priest, which would be accomplished if the light shining upon them were fully accepted and brought into their experience. But if light was refused, the showers of the latter rain would be withdrawn:

> We are in the day of atonement, and we are to work in harmony with Christ's work of cleansing the sanctuary from the sins of the people. Let no man who desires to be found with the wedding garment on, resist our Lord in his office work. As he is, so will his followers be in this world. We must now set before the people the work which by faith we see our great High-priest accomplishing in the heavenly sanctuary. Those who do not sympathize with Jesus in his work in the heavenly courts... are joining with the enemy of God and man in leading minds away from the truth and work for this time.[1]

> Christ is in the heavenly sanctuary, and he is there to make an atonement for the people. He is there to present his wounded side and pierced hands to his Father. He is there to plead for his Church that is upon the earth. He is cleansing the sanctuary from the sins of the people. What is our work? It is our work to be in harmony with the work of Christ. By faith we are to work with him, to be in union with him.[2]

The mediatorial work of Christ, the grand and holy mysteries of redemption, are not studied or comprehended by the people who claim to have light in advance of every other people on the face of the earth. Were Jesus personally upon earth, he would address a large number who claim to believe present truth, with the words he addressed to the Pharisees: "Ye do err, not knowing the Scriptures, nor the power of God." The most learned of the Jewish scribes did not discern the relation of Christ to the law; they did not comprehend the salvation which was offered. ... As long as we are content with our limited knowledge, we are disqualified to obtain rich views of truth. We cannot comprehend the facts connected with the atonement, and the high and holy character of God's law. The church to whom God has entrusted the treasures of truth needs to be converted. If we are blessed, we can bless others; but if we do not receive the Holy Spirit in our hearts, we cannot give forth light to others.[3]

Christ is cleansing the temple in heaven from the sins of the people, and we must work in harmony with him upon the earth, cleansing the soul temple from its moral defilement.[4]

The people have not entered into the holy place, where Jesus has gone to make an atonement for his children. We need the Holy Spirit in order to understand the truths for this time; but there is spiritual drought in the churches,...

Meetings should be held in every church for solemn prayer and earnest searching of the word to know what is truth. Take the promises of God, and ask God in living faith for the outpouring of his Holy Spirit. When the Holy Spirit is shed upon us, marrow and fatness will be drawn from the word of God. ... Men must advance in the path of duty from light to a greater light, for light unimproved becomes darkness, and a means of treasuring up wrath for themselves against the day of wrath. ...

When the churches become living, working churches, the Holy Spirit will be given in answer to their sincere request. ... The Bible will be regarded as a charter from heaven. ... Then the windows of heaven will be open for the showers of the latter rain. The followers of Christ will be united in love. ...

God has given to his people the light of great and solemn truths. He has opened to their understanding the mysteries of salvation; and if these truths are not improved, the favor of God will be withdrawn.[5]

Ellen White sensed the urgency of the times. Unfortunately, while all heaven was busy seeking to prepare the church to give the loud cry to the world, the brethren at the heart of the work were embroiled in controversy over what they felt was dangerous doctrine. As a result of a deeper understanding of the cleansing of the sanctuary, Jones and Waggoner had come to see the two covenants in a light that differed from the common view.[6] This gave rise for great concern among many of the brethren.

The Ministerial Institute that started in November 1889 with A. T. Jones teaching Bible and history for the first two-month term had just ended. As Waggoner took up the work for the second three-month term, teaching Bible classes, church history and Hebrew, controversy erupted again.[7] Waggoner had been teaching on the book of Isaiah, but decided to take up the issue of the covenants. His change in plans may have resulted from questions arising on the topic of the covenants due to the Sabbath School lesson quarterly, which he had authored. At any rate, Waggoner's change in plans was quickly altered.

## *The Two Covenants*

Although much has been written about the controversy over the law in Galatians that took place at the Minneapolis General Conference, the controversy over the covenants was perhaps of greater significance. For both parties involved, the law in Galatians and the two covenants were closely connected, and thus the acceptance of a particular view on the one issue required the acceptance of the same view on the other issue.

Waggoner had mentioned the covenants in his series of articles in the *Signs* that ran for nine weeks during the summer of 1886. Butler responded with his book, *The Law in the Book of Galatians*, resulting in increased controversy at the 1886 General Conference. Waggoner's response, *The Gospel in the Book of Galatians*, was distributed at the Minneapolis Conference. The main issue, at that point, was the identification of the law spoken of in Galatians chapter 3, but, the underlying arguments reveal that both men were dealing with the issue of the covenants as well.

During the course of Waggoner's presentations at Minneapolis, he spent some time covering the covenants. On Friday, October 19, 1888, he compared passages of scripture in Acts, Romans and in the second and third chapters of Galatians. According to the *Daily Bulletin* "his purpose was to show that the real point of controversy was justification by faith in Christ, which faith is reckoned to us as to Abraham, for righteousness. The covenant and promises to Abraham are the covenant and promises to us."[8] W. C. White noted that Waggoner compared "the covenant with Abraham with the Second [or New] Covenant. They are the same."[9] On the following Sunday morning, Waggoner's eighth lecture was titled: "Two Covenants, and Their Relation to the Law."[10] It is quite possible, based on J. H. Morrison's response, that Waggoner took up Galatians chapter 4 and spoke on the allegory of Sarah and Hagar, maintaining that the old covenant, symbolized by Hagar, is a condition of salvation by works, which was not limited to an Old Testament dispensation. For the same reason the new covenant, symbolized by Sarah, represents salvation by faith in Christ alone, and was just as accessible in Old Testament times as it is today. Waggoner was always clear that there were not two dispensations (saved by works in the Old Testament and saved by faith in the New Testament), but that salvation has always been by faith in Christ. The issue is not a time period, but the condition of the heart.

J. H. Morrison responded to Waggoner's lectures claiming "we had always believed in 'Justification by faith' and were children of the free woman." This was clearly an allusion to the covenant allegory of Galatians.[11]

Although we do not have a transcript of Waggoner's presentations at Minneapolis, we do know what his position was on the covenants. His book *Glad Tidings* was based on notes of his sremons that his wife had taken down of his sermons at the 1888 Conference.[12]* He also published his views in both *Bible Readings* and the *Senior Sabbath School Quarterly* in the early part of 1889, and he presented extensively on the covenants at the 1890 Ministerial Institute, which according to Dan Jones was "similar to what he presented at Minneapolis."[13]

Ellen White noted that during the spring of 1889 she attended a meeting "where the subject of the two covenants was presented by Elder A. T. Jones." It is clear that there were brethren who were in disagreement with Jones' view, for she adds: "I could not be pleased with the spirit that was manifested by Elder Underwood. He seemed to ask questions not for the sake of obtaining light, but of bringing in confusion and perplexity by questions he did not believe himself."[14]

Neither are we left with any doubt as to where G. I. Butler, Uriah Smith, R. C. Porter, and Dan Jones stood in regard to the covenants either. All these men disagreed with Jones and Waggoner on certain points and made it clear

R.C. PORTER

publicly.[15] Smith had run two series of articles on the covenants in 1887; one in the *Review*, and the other in the *Bible Echo*.[16] Smith also published the book *The Two Covenants* during this same time period.[17] Both Porter and Smith gave public talks at the 1890 Ministerial Institute, which were written down and are extant today. Dan Jones also had much to say about the covenants in his correspondence during the early part of 1890.[18]*

But why so much contention? What were the differences in the views that were held on this topic? As mentioned before, Jones and Waggoner understood that the law in Galatians was connected to the covenants, that in turn were an intrinsic part of the doctrine of justification by faith. Those who opposed Jones and Waggoner saw little connection between the covenants and justification by faith. They all claimed to believe in justification by faith and felt that Jones and Waggoner were over-emphasizing it, using the "much-vaunted doctrine" as a front to push their ideas on the law in Galatians, and the covenant questions.[19]

## *Points of Agreement*

First, it is important to establish on what points there was mutual agreement. Both parties believed that man was to be a keeper of all the commandments of God, including the Seventh-day Sabbath, and that the terms under both covenants required this. The question had more to do with *how* man was to keep the commandments. Neither party disagreed that God had made a covenant with Abraham which defined the terms of salvation to the end of time. Both saw that the covenants had been made with Israel, and not with the Gentiles. Neither stated that God had made a mistake in making any covenant. Both parties believed that God desired a people who would rightly represent Him on this earth and be the basis for the evangelism of all nations. As Waggoner put it: "But will there ever be any people on the earth who will have attained to that perfection of character? Indeed there will be. ... When the Lord comes there will be a company who will be found 'complete in Him'... To perfect this work in the hearts of individuals, and to prepare such a company, is the work of the Third Angel's Message."[20]

Although it can be said that there was mutual agreement on these points, according to both parties' statements, opponents often questioned whether Jones and Waggoner really believed what they taught, and whether their doctrine did not, in fact, undermine the very positions they claimed to support. Many of the brethren felt that Jones and Waggoner were teaching doctrines that led to the same conclusion as Dispensationalists—that the ten commandments had been done away with and Sunday, therefore, was the new day of worship. Jones and Waggoner, on the other hand, suggested that the brethren had formed their doctrine, not on sound biblical exegesis, but on a line of reasoning formed only to try to counter the positions taken by Dispensationalists. It is clear that this was in fact the case, as we read Uriah Smith's introductory remarks found in his work, *The Two Covenants*:

> The subject of the covenants is becoming a theme of particular interest to Seventh-day Adventists at the present time, because it is just now considered a favorite point of attack by some of those who oppose the doctrine of the perpetuity of the ten commandments, and the still binding obligation of the original Sabbath. Having exhausted every other source of theoretical opposition to the Sabbath in their futile efforts to overthrow it, they now claim that in the doctrine of the covenants they find conclusive evidence that the ten commandments have been superceded by something better. ... Briefly stated, then, their claim is this: That the ten commandments constituted the first or old covenant; that that covenant was faulty and has been done away.[21]

Galatians 3:19 was often quoted by Dispensationalists to prove that the ten commandments were added at Mt. Sinai and were binding only until Christ (the seed) was to come: "Wherefore then serveth the law? It was added because of transgressions, till the seed should come to whom the promise was made." Galatians 3:24 was then quoted as a final proof-text asserting that the commandments were no longer binding since Christ's death: "Wherefore the law was our schoolmaster to bring us unto Christ that we might be justified by faith." It was claimed that Christians were now justified by faith and not by the law.

## *Old View*

In response to such teachings, Adventists, under the leadership of Uriah Smith, G. I. Butler and others, taught a view on the covenants that they felt answered all the objections coming from the Christian world.[22]* Smith taught that there was really only one plan, only one covenant that God had made with Abraham which He carried out in two phases, the old and the new covenant: "In the accomplishment of that promise which He gave to Abraham there were two stages, two dispensations, and by each of these He was carrying on the same idea."[23]* The first stage or dispensation was that of the old covenant; when God entered into a covenant with Israel at Mount Sinai. Here the people promised to keep the ten commandments and whatever else the Lord was to require: "They, in other words, signed in blank all that the Lord should give them, and the Lord could fill in what He pleased; and whatever He did fill in it that would be a part of the covenant to which they had agreed." Thus God instituted the ceremonial law and the sanctuary service "that sin might abound." This was the only law referred to in Galatians, especially the schoolmaster that led to Christ, the very core and essence of the old covenant.[24]

Uriah Smith defined the term "covenant" by quoting from Webster's dictionary which stated that a covenant was "'a mutual agreement of two or more persons or parties, in writing and under seal, to do or to refrain from, some act or thing; a contract; stipulation.'" Thus the old covenant made at Sinai was a "formal and mutual agreement between God and [Israel], based upon mutual promises. ... The people said, We will keep God's law [both moral and ceremonial]. God said, Then I will make you a kingdom of priests. ... This was the agreement or covenant made between them." Webster's secondary definition of the term covenant—"'a writing containing the terms of agreement between two parties'"—was used to explain why the ten commandments are called a covenant; "they were simply the basis of that agreement," but not the actual covenant itself.[25]*

Uriah Smith saw that there were "three things to be accomplished by God in making this [old] covenant." First, "to carry out as it pertained to that time the promise of Abraham." That is, that the promise to Abraham was that his "literal seed" the children of Israel, would occupy Canaan. Second, that God might have a "holy people through whom He might manifest His name." And third, that through the "system of ceremonies, and that system of worship which confined them to one place," the people would be hedged in "from the nations of the world around them" and thus "when the seed, Christ, should come, His genealogy could be traced back, without any spirit of doubt from those Jews, to Abraham." Smith taught that the promises made to Abraham, pertaining to what Smith called the first stage, were "secured through this [old] covenant" when "Israel were put in possession of that land as God had promised."[26]

Uriah Smith maintained that the fault with the old covenant lay not with God or necessarily with the people, but with the promises, for they "were the best promises that God could make at that time." The problem was that the old covenant "was not able to carry out the matter to the final consummation" because "it did not have the right sacrifices, only the blood of animals." Thus when Christ came to earth, the old covenant of ceremonial laws were done away with, and the new covenant was put into place by the sacrifice of Christ who was the seed to come. The new covenant supplied the deficiency of the old by providing a sacrifice that would take away sin. Smith explained Paul's allegory in Galatians chapter 4, by suggesting that the old covenant "gendered to bondage" only when the Jews desired to continue practicing circumcision and keeping the ceremonial law. Because "they disbelieved on Christ... the Jewish people, the literal seed, corresponded to Ishmael; that Christ, the true seed, corresponded to Isaac."[27]

Most of Smith's explanations had virtually one goal in mind, to convince the Christian world that the old covenant was the ceremonial law—the only law to which the book of Galatians was speaking—and that the ten commandments were still binding, including the Sabbath.

## *Jones' and Waggoner's View*

In contrast, Jones' and Waggoner's understanding of the covenants was not based on opinions formed in an attempt to defend against false accusations from the Christian world—that the ten commandments were done away with—but rather based on an understanding of the everlasting gospel which permeates the entire Bible. They saw the two covenants not as representing two dispensations or matters of time—the Old and New Testament, but *rather representing the condition of the heart*, regardless of what time period in which a person had lived. Man can today be just as much under the old covenant as were the people who stood at Mt Sinai. Waggoner taught that the second or new covenant "existed before the covenant was made at Sinai," and in fact "the second covenant existed in every feature long before the first [or old], even from the days of Adam." It was then that the "plan of salvation was developed."[28]

The covenant and the promise to Abraham were one and the same. God promised Abraham and all nations through him ("all families of the earth"), that He would give men the whole earth made new after having made them free from the curse. This promise included everlasting life and the making righteous of all who believe, for one must be righteous to inherit that land. This everlasting covenant "God confirmed in Christ, Gal. 3:17… by an oath, in addition to the promise. These 'two immutable things, in which it was impossible for God to lie,' made the sacrifice of Christ as efficacious in the days of Abraham and Moses as it is now." God had pledged Himself, and His own existence, to our salvation in Jesus Christ. His life for ours, if we are lost while believing in Him.[29]

Unlike Smith and Butler, who defined the word "covenant" by going to Webster's dictionary alone, Jones and Waggoner saw that "neither of [Webster's] definitions is extensive enough to cover all the uses of the word in the Bible. … It is only another instance of the impossibility of a perfect comparison between divine and human things." The "main point is to understand just what is meant in each instance, and this the Scriptures themselves enable us readily to do." Thus, Jones and Waggoner allowed the Bible to define its own terms. For example, "In Gen. 9:9-16 the word 'covenant' is used with reference to a promise of God [made to every beast of the earth], given without any condition expressed or implied."[30]*

In the same way, the "everlasting covenant" made with Abraham was not a *contract*, in the sense of two equal parties making an agreement—it was the promise of God to Abraham and his response of faith. Abraham believed God and it was counted to him for righteousness. Abraham gave more than a mental assent. He appreciated and treasured the promises of God, and in this sense *kept* the covenant with God, thus becoming the father of all them that believe (Romans 4:11). The "new covenant" or "second covenant" was really the *same* covenant that God had already made with Abraham. It was called such only because it was the second covenant made with Israel as a nation, and new to them in contrast to the old covenant. "There is no blessing that can be gained by virtue of the second covenant that was not promised to Abraham. And we, with whom the second covenant is made, can share the inheritance which it promises only by being children of Abraham (Galatians 3:29); all who are of faith are the children of Abraham."[31]

But what about the first covenant? Why did God enter into a different covenant with Israel than he had with Abraham? Waggoner explained that according to Exodus 6:2-8, God purposed to set Israel free from their Egyptian bondage in fulfillment of His covenant with Abraham. When He brought them to the foot of Mount Sinai, He reminded them of what He had done to the Egyptians and how He had borne them on eagle's wings. God desired the people to enter into the same covenant of faith that He had made with Abraham, but the people had failed to trust Him at the Red Sea, in the giving of manna, and at the waters of Meribah (Psalms 106). Now, at Mount Sinai, the Lord tested them again, referring to the covenant given to Abraham long before, and He exhorted them to keep it, assuring them of the results. The covenant with Abraham was a covenant of *faith*, and they could keep it simply by *keeping the faith*. God did not ask them to enter into another covenant with Him, but only to accept His covenant of peace.

The proper response of the people therefore would have been: "Amen, even so, O Lord, let it be done unto us according to thy will." Instead the people responded by making a promise themselves: "All that the Lord has spoken we will do" (Exodus 19:8).[32]

Waggoner made it clear several times that "in the first covenant the people promised to keep all the commandments of God, so as to be worthy of a place in His kingdom. This was a virtual promise to make themselves righteous; for God did not promise to help them."[33] "The first covenant was simply this: A promise on the part of the people to keep His holy law, and a statement on the part of God, of the result to them if they should obey Him." Again, "the promises in the old covenant were really all on the part of the people. ... [T]he first covenant was a promise on the part of the people that they would *make themselves* holy. But this they could not do."[34] The people assumed the responsibility of working the works of God, showing a lack of appreciation of His greatness and holiness. It is only when men are ignorant of God's righteousness that they go about to establish their own righteousness, and refuse to submit themselves to the righteousness of God. Their promises were worthless because they did not have the power to fulfill them, yet Israel repeated the promise twice (Ex. 24:3, 7).

As a result of Israel's unbelief, the Lord followed an alternate plan and came down to the level of the people. He descended on Mount Sinai in the midst of fire, lightning, and an earthquake, causing the people to tremble as He spoke the words of the ten commandments—none of which had he done for Abraham, on whose heart He had written those same ten precepts. Although the moral law "had been known since the creation," Waggoner saw it as the "added" law and the "schoolmaster" that was to bring us to Christ, as spoken of in Galatians 3:19, 24.[35]

Waggoner recognized that "God's law—called His covenant—was the basis of the [old] covenant between Him and Israel." Yet, Waggoner made it clear that the ten commandments "antedated," or already existed before being spoken at Sinai, and were thus "entirely distinct from the transaction at Horeb." Although the desired outcome of both covenants was the same—the keeping of God's commandments—this could never be the case when the covenant was based on man's promises. Consequently, the purpose for the giving of the ten commandments was to direct "the minds of the people to the Abrahamic covenant, which God confirmed in Christ." This was the purpose of the law for all time: "God's plan of salvation of sinners, whether now or in the days of Moses, is: The law sent home emphatically to the individual, to produce conviction of sin, and thus to drive the sinner to seek freedom… which was extended long before, but which the sinner would not listen to,… and the living of a life of righteousness by faith in Christ."[36]

In contrast to Smith and Butler, who taught that the ceremonial law *was* the old covenant, Waggoner believed that the "'ordinances of divine service' formed no part of the first covenant. If they had, they must have been mentioned in the making of that covenant; but they were not. They were connected with it, but not a part of it. They were simply the means by which the people acknowledged the justice of their condemnation to death for the violation of the law which they had covenanted to keep, and their faith in the Mediator of the new covenant."[37]

Waggoner felt that Butler's position seemed to "imply that before the first advent men approached God by means of the ceremonial law, and that after that they approached Him through the Messiah." Butler had expressed the idea that "in the so–called Jewish dispensation forgiveness of sins was only *figurative*. … there was no real forgiveness of sins until Christ, the real Sacrifice, was offered." He had also made the provisions of Christ exclusive to the Jews, who were under the ceremonial law.[38]

Waggoner, on the other hand, believed that "all transgressions committed under that covenant, that were pardoned, were pardoned by virtue of the second covenant, of which Christ is mediator. Even though Christ's blood was not shed until hundreds of years after the first covenant was made, sins were forgiven whenever they were confessed" on account of the "Abrahamic covenant, which God confirmed in Christ," who had been slain from the foundation of the world. "If the first covenant had contained pardon, and promise of divine assistance, there would have been no necessity of any other covenant."[39]

Waggoner also protested against the exclusiveness of Butler's view: "[Christ] redeems none who were not in the condition which He was made. And since only the Jews were subject to the ceremonial law, your theory would make it that He came to save only the Jews. I am glad that the proper interpretation does not oblige us to limit the plan of salvation in this way. Christ died for all men; all men were under the condemnation of the law of God; and so He was made under its condemnation. By the grace of God He tasted death for every man [Heb. 2:9]."[40]

Waggoner did not believe, as Smith did, that the old covenant was faulty because the promises referred to the *ceremonial system*, but because the promises of that covenant were those of the people. Israel had lightly esteemed the everlasting covenant that God had made with Abraham, and in the face of all that God had done for them, they presumptuously took upon themselves the responsibility of their own salvation. By doing so they entered into a covenant that "gendereth to bondage," of which the allegory of Sarah and Hagar in Galatians 4 speaks: "It is a vivid contrast between the old covenant, with its ministration of death, and the new covenant, with its ministration of the Spirit of life. … We are not directed to Mount Sinai, to trust in the law for righteousness, when it has for us only curses, nor to the old covenant, with its ministration of death, but to Mount Zion, where we may find the law of the Spirit of life in Christ Jesus, the mediator of the new covenant, and may find peace and help 'exceeding abundantly above all that we ask or think.'"[41]

Finally, unlike Smith and Butler—who believed that the promises to Abraham and his "seed," referred to in Genesis 15 and 17, were fulfilled in the old covenant dispensation by Israel coming into possession of Canaan—Waggoner saw that the everlasting promise to Abraham was for the earth made new. This promise would not be ultimately fulfilled until his seed, which was Christ, came into possession of the promised inheritance at the second coming. Galatians 3:19 states: "Wherefore then serveth the law? It was added because of transgression, till the seed should come to whom the promise was made." Waggoner's view was that "at the coming referred to, the seed will inherit the promise. ... Christ has not received it, for we are joint heirs with him; and when he receives it, Abraham and all those who are his children through faith, will likewise receive it. ... [T]here are not many promises referred to in this nineteenth verse, but only the one promise, the inheritance, and that promised inheritance will be received at the second coming of Christ and not before."[42]*

When comparing these two views on the covenants, it is not hard to see how tension could easily arise. The Ministerial Institute became the next battleground where advancing light met the darkness of tradition and unbelief.

# CHAPTER 12 FOOTNOTES

1. Ellen G. White, "The Need of Complete Consecration," *Review and Herald*, Jan. 21, 1890, p. 33.

2. Ellen G. White, "The Lord Must be Our Light," *Review and Herald*, Jan. 28, 1890, p. 49.

3. Ellen G. White, "The Relation of Christ to the Law is not Understood," *Review and Herald*, Feb. 4, 1890, pp. 65, 66.

4. Ellen G. White, "The Danger of Talking Doubt," *Review and Herald*, Feb. 11, 1890, p. 81.

5. Ellen G. White, "Need of Earnestness in the Cause of God," *Review and Herald,* Feb. 25, 1890, pp. 113, 114.

6. Robert Van Ornam, *The Doctrine of the Everlasting Covenant in the Writings of Ellet J. Waggoner*, (Graduate Thesis Loma Linda University, 1985) pp. 12, 38.

7. Arthur L. White, *The Lonely Years*, p. 454.

8. "Third Day's Proceedings," *General Conference Daily Bulletin*, Oct. 21, 1888; in *Manuscripts and Memories*, p. 361.

9. W. C. White, "Notes Made at the Minneapolis Meetings 1888," Oct. 15, 1888; in *Manuscripts and Memories*, p. 424.

10. "Sabbath Disclosures," St. Paul *Pioneer Press*, Oct. 22, 1888, p. 6; in *Manuscripts and Memories*, p. 582.

11. R. T. Nash, "An Eye Witness Account," p. 2; in *Manuscripts and Memories*, p. 352.

12. Jessie F. Moser-Waggoner to L. E. Froom, April 16, 1930, found in LeRoy E. Froom, *Movement of Destiny*, pp. 189, 200-201, 243, 260. See: Chapter 4, footnote 4.

13. Dan T. Jones to S. N. Haskell, [March] 1890 (letter book, p. 910). See also: Tim Crosby, "Ellen G. White and the Law in Galatians: A Study in the Dynamics of Present Truth" (unpublished manuscript; Ellen G. White Estate Document file, 61a); Clinton Wahlen, "What Did E. J. Waggoner Say at Minneapolis?" (*Adventist Heritage*, Winter 1988) pp. 22-37.

14. Ellen G. White Manuscript 19, "Diary Entries," March 5, 1889; in *1888 Materials*, p. 272.

15. Uriah Smith to Ellen G. White, Feb. 17, 1890; Uriah Smith to L. F. Trubey, Feb. 11, 1902; in *Manuscripts and Memories*, pp. 154, 312.

16. Uriah Smith, "God's Covenants with Men," *Review and Herald*, Sept. 13, 20, 27, Oct. 11, 25, Nov. 1, 20, 1887, pp. 584, 600-601, 617-618, 632-633, 664-665, 680; "The Two Covenants," *Bible Echo and Signs of the Times*, Nov., Dec., 1887, pp. 162-163, 178-179, Jan., Feb., Mar., 1888, pp. 2-3, 22, 34-35.

17. Uriah Smith, *The Two Covenants* (Battle Creek, MI: Review and Herald, n.d.),

18. "Remarks of Eld. R. C. Porter at the Ministers' Bible School," Feb. 24, 1890, and "Remarks of Eld. Uriah Smith, Bible School," Feb. 19, 1890, archives of the General Conference of Seventh-day Adventists. Dan Jones' comments will be documented throughout the rest of this chapter.

19. E. J. Waggoner, *The Gospel in Galatians*, p. 70; and A. T. Jones to C. E. Holmes, May 12, 1921; in *Manuscripts and Memories*, pp. 65, 327.

20. E. J. Waggoner, "Truth and its Importance," *Signs of the Times*, Dec. 28, 1888, p. 790.

21. Uriah Smith, *The Two Covenants*, p. 3.

22. Strangely enough, however, Waggoner rightly "'charged the leading men in the General Conference with having [implicitly] endorsed [D. M.] Canright's view on the covenants.'" Canright had recently separated from the church and "'no longer believed that the Ten Commandments were binding upon Christians and had given up the law, the Sabbath, the messages, the sanctuary, our position upon [the] United States in prophecy, the testimonies, health reform, the ordinances of humility. ... [H]e did not believe the Papacy had changed the Sabbath'" (Dan T. Jones to G. I. Butler, Feb. 13, 1890; see also, Arthur L. White, *The Lonely* Years, p. 360).

23. R. C. Porter agreed with Smith. No less than ten times in a sermon on the covenants he stated that the Abrahamic covenant embraced both the old and new covenant: "The Abrahamic covenant is the everlasting covenant; and the two covenants are but the means in the different ages for the carrying out of that plan." He also believed that the old covenant fulfilled the promises to Abraham through his literal seed (Israel) in the land of Canaan, and the new covenant would be fulfilled in a spiritual sense and the heavenly Canaan through the literal seed, Christ (Remarks of Eld. R. C. Porter at the Ministers' Bible School, Feb. 24, 1890).

24. "Remarks of Eld. Uriah Smith, Bible School," Feb. 19, 1890, pp. 5, 10.

25. Uriah Smith, *The Two Covenants*, pp. 5-9. This explanation on Smith's part seems to fall short of discounting the claim that the ten commandments were the old covenant and thus done away with at the cross.

26. "Remarks of Eld. Uriah Smith, Bible School," Feb. 19, 1890, pp. 15, 16.

27. *Ibid.*, pp. 16, 22.

28. E. J. Waggoner, "The Two Covenants," *Bible Readings for the Home Circle* (Battle Creek, MI.: Review and Herald Pub. Co., 1889), pp. 316.

29. E. J. Waggoner, *Sabbath-School Lessons on the Letter to the Hebrews, for Senior Classes January 4 to March 29, 1890*, (Oakland, Calif.: Pacific Press Pub. Co., 1889), p. 26; also "Lesson 20—Hebrews 9:8-14 (Sabbath, Feb. 15)," *Review and Herald*, Feb. 4, 1890, p. 78.

30. *Ibid.*, pp. 8-9; also "Lesson 15—Hebrews 8:2-6 (Sabbath, Jan. 11)," *Review and Herald*, Jan. 7, 1890, p. 14. The 1888 edition of *Bible Readings* lists Smith's and Butler's view of the old covenant, using Webster's Dictionary to define the term. When Waggoner edited the 1889 edition of *Bible Readings*, he did not remove Webster's definition, but he did make it clear with his other notes and references that he based his understanding on the Bible and not Webster. When he rewrote the 1889 Sabbath School lessons, Waggoner again left both of Webster's two principle definitions in the lesson, but made it clear that neither definition was extensive enough to cover all the uses of the word in the Bible. Never once would Waggoner, when writing his own articles, use Webster to define the word "covenant."

31. *Ibid.*, pp. 20; also "Lesson 18—Hebrews 8:6-13 (Sabbath, Feb. 1)," *Review and Herald*, Jan. 21, 1890, p. 45.

32. E. J. Waggoner, "The Promises to Israel: The Covenant of Promise," *Present Truth*, Dec. 10, 1896, p. 789.

33. E. J. Waggoner, "The Two Covenants," *Bible Readings for the Home Circle*, p. 314.

34. E. J. Waggoner, *Sabbath-School Lessons on the Letter to the Hebrews*, pp. 9, 11; also "Lesson 15—Hebrews 8:2-6 (Sabbath, Jan. 11)," and "Lesson 16—Hebrews 8:8-13 (Sabbath, Jan 18)," *Review and Herald*, Jan. 7, 1890, p. 14.

35. E. J. Waggoner, *The Gospel in the Book of Galatians*, pp. 24-26, 43-48.

36. E. J. Waggoner, *Sabbath-School Lessons on the Letter to the Hebrews*, pp. 9, 26, 24; also "Lesson 15—Hebrews 8:2-6 (Sabbath, Jan. 11)," *Review and Herald*, Jan. 7, 1890, p. 14; and "Lesson 20—Hebrews 9:8-14 (Sabbath, Feb. 15)," *Review and Herald*, Feb. 4, 1890, p. 78; and "Lesson 19—Hebrews 9:1-7 (Sabbath, Feb. 8)," *Review and Herald*, Jan. 28, 1890, p. 61.

37. *Ibid.*, pp. 23-24; also "Lesson 19—Hebrews 9:1-7 (Sabbath, Feb. 8)," *Review and Herald*, Jan. 28, 1890, p. 61.

38. E. J. Waggoner, *The Gospel in the Book of Galatians*, pp. 12, 58-61.

39. E. J. Waggoner, *Sabbath-School Lessons on the Letter to the Hebrews*, pp. 25-26, 12, 63; also "Lesson 20—Hebrews 9:8-14 (Sabbath, Feb. 15)," *Review and Herald*, Feb. 4, 1890, p. 78; and "Lesson 16—Hebrews 8:8-13 (Sabbath, Jan. 18)," *Review and Herald*, Jan. 7, 1890, p. 14.

40. E. J. Waggoner, The Gospel in the Book of Galatians, p. 63.

41. E. J. Waggoner, *Sabbath-School Lessons on the Letter to the Hebrews, for Senior Classes April 5 to June 28, 1890*, (Oakland, Calif.: Pacific Press Pub. Co., 1890), p. 33; also "Lesson 33—Hebrews 12:18-39 (Sabbath, June 21)," *Review and Herald*, June 10, 1890, p. 366.

42. E. J. Waggoner, *The Gospel in Galatians*, p. 39. G. I. Butler misrepresented Waggoner on this point by suggesting that Waggoner had claimed "that 'the seed' has not yet come, and will not come till the second advent of Christ. It would be hard for the writer to really think that any believer in Christ would take that position, had we not read it in our own beloved *Signs of the Times* of July 29, 1886" (G. I. Butler, *The Law in Galatians*, p. 46). Waggoner responded by saying: "If this had been written by some men I should think it was deliberate misrepresentation; for it certainly does woefully misrepresent the view which I take and have published. ... It is true that I held, and still hold, that the coming of the seed spoken of in Gal. 3:19, means the second coming of Christ; but that does not imply that Christ has not already come, or that he is not now the seed" (*The Gospel in the Book of Galatians*, p. 37). It would seem that E. J. Waggoner's position on the *seed* as well as on the *law* referred to in Galatians 3:19 would give a valid answer to those who felt the ten commandments were done away with at the cross. It would be understood that the ten commandment law was a schoolmaster as it were, leading people to Christ, until He should come the second time to receive His inheritance. No reference can be found to Galatians 3:19 in Ellen White's published writings, but G. B. Starr tells of an experience he had with Ellen White while working with her in Australia: "I explained to her that I understood that the law [in Gal. 3:19] was spoken at Mount Sinai to reveal transgression, and I understood the 'seed' referred to Jesus, who was the heir to whom the new earth was promised, as stated in verses 16-18, and that the coming referred to in verse 19 was His second coming to claim his inheritance. To this she seemed to consent" (G. B. Starr, *Fifty years with One of God's Seers*, unpublished manuscript, pp. 26-27).

# CHAPTER 13

# *Faulty Guideposts*

## *The Solemn Responsibility Resting upon Those in Leadership Positions*

In 1884, the *Review and Herald* began printing a monthly periodical called the *Bible Reading Gazette*, which contained Bible studies written by many different ministers and lay evangelists. At the end of the year the 12 volumes contained a total of 162 lessons, which were bound in book form and sold by colporteurs around the country with a large degree of success. As a result, the *Review*

prepared a similar series of studies, again written by various authors, and sold under the name *Bible Readings for the Home Circle.* In the first edition published in 1888, under the section "The Two Covenants," twenty-eight questions and answers eloquently expressed the views held by Uriah Smith, G. I. Butler, and others, including their definition of the old covenant and the idea of two dispensations.[1]

At the 1888 General Conference, E. J. Waggoner and several others were asked to prepare new "Bible Readings." Waggoner prepared a new "Reading" on the subject of the covenants and submitted it to the *Review and Herald* publishing board. Interestingly enough, his new "Reading" was accepted, and placed in the new 1889 edition, "circulating it by the tens of thousand everywhere."[2] The new edition still had twenty-eight questions and answers, but they were very different from the previous edition. Waggoner had removed the idea of the two dispensations and he made it clear that the old covenant was based upon the promises of the people "to make themselves righteous."[3] He also removed the concluding statement of the 1888 edition: "When we partake of the bread and wine, to what do we pledge ourselves?— To be true to our covenant relation with God."[4] Waggoner did not speak against entering into a covenant with God, only that it be the new covenant based on faith and not on man's promises.

In the spring of 1889, E. J. Waggoner was asked to finish writing the *Senior Sabbath School Quarterly* on the book of Hebrews, which would run for three quarters—October 1889 through June 1890. His father, J. H. Waggoner, had not completed the task before his death in April 1889. Because some of the original lessons had been lost, and because E. J. Waggoner did not agree with his father on some of the ideas concerning the covenants, he rewrote five or six of the lessons, having been given the freedom to write his own views instead. The book of Hebrews, having much to do with the sanctuary and the covenants, afforded Waggoner an opportunity to write out more fully his views on the subject.

When Waggoner finished, the lessons were hastily sent to the different editorial committee members for critique. Unfortunately, Uriah Smith's name had been accidentally left off the list of committee members. To atone for the mistake, C. H. Jones, manager of Pacific Press, sent a set of lessons to Smith with all the changes and additions. But Smith, seeing the name of J. H. Waggoner in the introduction to the lessons, passed them on for publication, not noticing C. H. Jones' explanation of the changes and additions that E. J. Waggoner had made to the lessons for the first and second quarter of 1890. This oversight, perhaps providential, would cause Smith a great deal of trouble and add to the controversy that soon followed.[5]

By January 11, 1890, the Sabbath School lessons had progressed to Hebrews chapter 8, where Paul writes of the new covenant in connection with Christ and His priestly ministry in the heavenly sanctuary. As church members around the country opened their new Sabbath School lessons, they found Waggoner's teaching on the covenants. For many in Battle Creek, this was not a welcome sight. For Dan Jones, Sabbath school teacher at the Battle Creek Tabernacle and school board member overseeing the Ministerial Institute, this was cause for concern. Upon seeing the new lessons, which had "a good deal in them that I could not indorse on the subject of the covenant question," Dan Jones "resigned as teacher in the Sabbath school, and stayed away from the [Ministerial] school a couple weeks."[6]

Others followed Dan Jones' example, some staying away from the Ministerial Institute where Waggoner was teaching, and others making objections during Sabbath School class. But this was only the beginning of trouble, for Waggoner announced on Friday, January 17, that he would "take up the covenant question the next Monday morning" during one of his classes at the Ministerial Institute. When Dan Jones caught wind of Waggoner's plans, he set out immediately to try to stop them.[7]

## *Underhanded Dealings*

Although many have never heard of Dan Jones, he was perhaps one of the most influential men in the Adventist Church during the late 1800s. Jones held many job titles including secretary of the General Conference, member of the powerful General Conference executive committee, one of the General Conference Association Trustees, vice president of the International Tract Society, vice president and executive committee member for the National Religious Liberty Association, chairman of the Committee of Twenty-one formed at the 1889 Conference, and a member of many other subcommittees.[8]* Unfortunately, he used his position of authority to influence others in opposition to both Jones and Waggoner. During the Ministerial Institute he was in continual correspondence with other church leaders on the various committees seeking support for his plan of action.

Dan Jones was so concerned over Waggoner's views on the covenants that he would later write: "I have been worrying and fretting over this thing until it has hurt me worse than a half year's work."[9] In order to understand why this was the case, we need to understand a few facts about the Adventist Church at that time. Church membership worldwide was just slightly over 28,000, of which nearly 26,000 lived in the United States. Only 207 ordained ministers, and 158 "licentiates," or licensed ministers, labored for the 895 churches scattered across the country.[10] Of these 365 laborers, the majority held responsibilities on the local Conference and/or General Conference level as well.

Since the first Adventist college at Battle Creek had not been established until 1875, most laborers had not received any formal ministerial training. Most had come from "various backgrounds—professions, businesses, the workbench, and the farm," and had not had an opportunity for more education.[11] Of those who had attended Adventist colleges, few had received any specific, or substantial ministerial training. For instance, "none of the contemporary Adventist schools offered anything in the way of systematic theological study. Up until 1888, for example, the only Bible study classes scheduled at Battle Creek College were a ninth- and tenth-grade class in Old and New Testament history, and a two-term, twice-weekly lecture by Uriah Smith on church doctrines. Attendance was purely voluntary."

In an attempt to revise Adventist education, W. W. Prescott, Educational Secretary and President of Battle Creek College, had devised the plan for the Ministerial Institutes to be "'entirely separate from the College,'" for the specific purpose of giving further education to those ministers already in the field. The curriculum "featured Christian Evidences, Church History, Greek, Hebrew, Church Government, Logic, Civics, Biblical Studies, and Bible Doctrines." After Prescott had confessed his opposition to Jones and Waggoner in December of 1888, he sought to give them more opportunities to present the message laid upon their hearts. But when "a surprising 157 ministerial students" showed up for the Ministerial Institute, representing nearly half the entire Adventist ministerial work force, Dan Jones could not help but be distressed. There was a great possibility that whatever Waggoner presented in his classes would have a noticeable effect upon Adventist thinking and its worldwide work.[12]

Upon hearing of Waggoner's plans to begin teaching on the subject of the covenants early Monday morning, Dan Jones decided to "go and have a talk with Bro. White and the Dr. [Waggoner] in reference to the matter." He wished to "prevail on them to lay over that question, at least until Prof. Prescott and Eld. Olsen" returned to campus. Rather than talk with Waggoner first, Dan Jones went to W. C. White "and told him how [he] felt." But White would not commit himself, telling Jones to go "talk with the Dr." himself. Finally, late Friday evening, Dan Jones went and talked with Waggoner for almost two hours, but Waggoner was "firm in his decision to go on with the work he had laid out" for the class. So far Jones' efforts were in vain.

Not one to give up easily, Dan Jones went Sabbath morning to have a talk with Ellen White. According to him, after he "laid the matter before her" and told her how he "felt about it," she expressed the "thought that the question ought to be investigated by the leading brethren… before it was brought in the school." Dan Jones told Ellen White that he had attempted this very thing, but that Waggoner was "disinclined to make any change in his plan." Ellen White suggested again, according to Jones, that the brethren get together with Waggoner first before the classes started on Monday.[13]

Dan Jones now went back to Waggoner and shared "what Sister White had said." But one might rightly wonder how much of the story he really shared, for according to him, Waggoner "was immovable." Dan Jones then spoke to Waggoner about having an investigation to which Waggoner "seemed perfectly willing." Waggoner said, "he wanted both sides of the question fully brought out." At this, Dan Jones set about to schedule a meeting for Sunday evening with Uriah Smith, R. C. Porter and several others.

At seven o'clock Sunday evening, in the General Conference room, a meeting was held with Waggoner to investigate the covenant question. Dan Jones was elected chairman of the meeting, which turned out to be more of an *interrogation* session than an *investigation*. After "stating what the object of the meeting was" Jones asked how they should proceed. Smith "suggested that we take up the points of difference in the covenant question and consider them." Because Dan Jones was the one who had called the meeting, it was decided that he should state the points of difference:

After thinking a moment, I said that if it was placed on me to state the points of difference, I could do no better than to take the Sabbath-school lessons, and refer to some points that were made in them which were questionable to my mind, and I thought they were questionable to the minds of others present. So I commenced with note 1 on page 11, the first sentence of which reads as follows: "Let the student note that the terms of the old covenant were really all on the part of the people." I told them that I could not agree with that statement, and asked if all the others present agreed with it. Bro. Smith said that he did not; Bro Porter also dissented. I asked Bro Smith's reasons for disagreeing. He read Deut. 26:17-19, and asked if that referred to the old covenant. No one answered; but Bro. White raised the question as to what it took to constitute a covenant, whether we should take Webster's definition or not. ... Bro. Smith again very quietly asked if the verses he had read referred to the old covenant. Another question was raised. ... When that was over Bro. Smith again asked if the verses that he had read referred to the old covenant. Dr. Waggoner then said that he objected to that way of investigating the covenant question; said that he did not understand that he had come to this meeting to have the Sabbath-school lessons picked to pieces, but to investigate the covenant question, and he did not think it could be satisfactorily investigated in that way. He went on at some length; stated that he had understood that all agreed with his position on the covenant question. He considered that the REVIEW & HERALD Publishing Board were committed to his position as they had accepted a "Reading" which he had prepared on that subject, and put it in the [1889] "Bible-Readings" in place of the one that was in the first edition of that book, and have been circulating it by the tens of thousands everywhere. He also intimated very deicdedly [*sic*] that Eld. Smith had practically committed himself in favor of his position [by publishing the Sabbath-school lessons].[14]

The biggest concern some of the brethren had was over Waggoner's definition of the old covenant. However, Dan Jones "read a few more points in the lessons where [he] considered there was difference of opinion":

Then I stated what the object of the investigation was for; that Dr. Waggoner had announced that he would take up the subject in the school the next week, and that it seemed to me wrong to take up a controverted subject, and teach it in a General Conference school… where there were members of the faculty and members of the managing board that did not agree with the doctrines taught. … I did not think [Waggoner] ought to bring anything into the school that they would not endorse, or bring in any new doctrine until he had consulted with them in reference to it. … If they all thought it was the right thing for him to go on and teach the covenant question in the school as he had in the Sabbath-school lessons, I would say nothing more about it; though I could not see the propriety of it. Bro Smith then said he would rather it would not be taught in the school. Br. Waggoner made the plea that he understood when he came here that he was to teach his own views, and that he would not have come on any other conditions; said that he did not want to come in the first place, and only consented to teach when he was pressed to do so.[15]

At this point "Eld. McCoy and Prof. Miller both spoke rather favorably toward allowing the Dr. to go on and teach the covenant question in the school, as it had already come out in the Sabbath-school lessons." W. C. White also "favored his doing so, and referred to some things that he had heard his mother say that he interpreted to mean that it was right for him to do so." At this Dan Jones unabashedly stated that "it might be alright to do so; but I could not see the propriety of it, and that as far as I was concerned I wanted to put myself on record as opposed to its being done." [16]*

M.B. MILLER

The meeting dragged on till midnight, "when it was adjourned without coming to any decision." According to Dan Jones, "everything passed off pleasantly. There was not a harsh or unkind word spoken, and I think not a hard feeling on the part of anyone." Apparently Waggoner did not feel the same; the very next day he turned in his resignation for that class.[17]*

Waggoner's resignation created a problem that Dan Jones had not thought about; who would teach that class period for all the students at the Ministerial School? Jones set out to try to make "satisfactory arrangement" with W. C. White and Waggoner to cover the class period. But, Jones stated, "I could not see my way clear to give up the principle that seemed to me to be so just and right, and give my consent for" Waggoner's views to be presented in the school. It is no wonder, with Dan Jones' attitude, that Waggoner was "inexorable," and refused to teach the class. White suggested that Uriah Smith be asked to take the class since "the Dr. was doing too much anyway and needed more time for his editorial work and rest." Smith agreed to take the class, and Dan Jones "arranged to make a smooth matter of it before the class… by stating that it had been thought best for Bro. Smith to come in… for the present, as Dr. Waggoner was overworked and needed rest." A few minutes before Waggoner closed his first class period, Dan Jones arrived with Uriah Smith to give his announcement. Later he described what took place:

> After [Waggoner] had closed, he said: "Sometimes the unexpected happens, and something very unexpected has happened to me. There have been objections made to my teaching the covenant question in this school, very much to my surprise, and I will not take it up for the present. Bro. [Dan] Jones will explain to you the change that has been made." That upset my little speech completely that I had fixed up to make; so I could only say that it had been thought best to postpone the presentation of the covenant question for the present at least.[18]

Waggoner had unwittingly exposed Dan Jones' questionable dealings. For the time being, though, the covenant question was on hold. Some of the students were not at all pleased "at being deprived of the instruction of Bro. Waggoner." The very next day, one student wrote to O. A. Olsen, General Conference president and school board member, expressing his thoughts that he "was hoping that we might have a candid investigation" of the covenant question. It would be several weeks before that request was granted. In the meantime opposition to both A. T. Jones and E. J. Waggoner grew increasingly bold.[19]

## The Discrediting of God's Messengers

Dan Jones did not stop after he effectively terminated Waggoner's presentations on the covenants. During the days and weeks ahead, he was in continual correspondence with other leaders across the country, sharing with them his prejudices. To receive such a letter from the Secretary of the General Conference, and member of the Executive Committee, was of no small consequence. Only a few days after Waggoner resigned his class, Dan Jones sent off a letter to A. W. Allee, a church leader in Missouri, giving him counsel for an upcoming Institute to be held in that State:

I think an Institute in Missouri would be a splendid thing; but I believe an Institute on a quiet plan will be just as valuable to you as to make a great parade over it and get in… Eld. A. T. Jones, and E. J. Waggoner. To tell you the truth, I do not have very much confidence in some of their ways of presenting things. They try to drive everything before them, and will not admit that their position can possibly be subject to the least criticism. They say, "It is truth; and all you need to do is to study it as long as I have, and you will see it;"[20]* and simply laugh at any ideas that may be presented by others that will disagree in the least with their own. But our more thoughtful men,—Bro. Smith, Bro. Littlejohn, Bro. Corliss, Bro. Gage, and others,—do not agree with them on many positions which they take on National Reform, and on some theological questions,—like the covenants, the law in Galatians, etc. But these things they make prominent wherever they go; and in fact, do not dwell upon any other subjects scarcely than those upon which there is a difference of opinion among our leading brethren. I do not think you want to bring that spirit into the Missouri Conference. If you could get Bro. Gates and Bro. Farnsworth, and have a ministerial institute for the study of the Bible and of plans of work, and then depend largely upon yourselves to dig out the principles of truth and plans adapted to your work in Missouri, it would be worth more to you than a high-falutin theory that never has worked and never will work anywhere.[21]

This is how Dan Jones used his influence in an underhanded way to keep, what he called "a high-falutin theory," from going any farther than it had. He was not the only one that was sharing his opinions openly. Uriah Smith, feeling that Waggoner's temporary resignation was not enough to stop the progress of his false theories, wrote a disclaimer in the *Review*. He made it clear that he did not support the current Sabbath School lessons with Waggoner's view of the covenants:

To the many inquirers who are writing us concerning the new theological departure in the Sabbath-school lessons, we would say that, according to the profession we make, the Bible and the Bible alone, is our only rule of faith and practice; and any view presented should be tested and decided by that Word. None need feel bound to accept any doctrine simply because it appears in the S. S. Lessons or REVIEW. The lessons are sent out under the auspices of the General S. S. Association: and it is not necessarily to be understood that the REVIEW, in any acting part in spreading them before the people, indorses all that they may contain; especially, in view of the fact that when it was decided by the REVIEW and HERALD Board to open a Sabbath-school department in the REVIEW, and publish the lessons therein, it was not known what the lessons would be. It would, of course, be greatly to be desired that all propositions advanced should be such as would commend themselves to the acceptance of all thoughtful Bible students as in accordance with both reason and Scripture; but if in any case they do not seem to be such, it is not only the privilege but the duty of those who detect their disagreement with the Scriptures, to reject them without scruple and without reserve.[22]

Uriah Smith called on all to take the "Bible and the Bible alone" as their rule of faith. He stated this ever so sincerely, feeling that the Bible supported his positions, and refuted the "new theological departure" of Waggoner's Sabbath School lessons.[23]* Ellen White would soon answer such premises, but it would not be until after Waggoner was given a chance to present the covenants during the latter part of February. The decision to let him present the subject was left hanging until O. A. Olsen and W. W. Prescott returned to Battle Creek. In the meantime, Waggoner continued to teach several classes at the Ministerial Institute. His underlying theme remained the same; justification by faith and the righteousness of Christ. Unfortunately, this did nothing to stop the controversy already brewing.

As Ellen White saw tension growing at the Ministerial Institute over the issue of the covenants, she feared the Minneapolis episode was about to be repeated. She began to attend many of the meetings, speaking every day for three weeks with but one or two exceptions.[24] As was the case with the law in Galatians question, the real issue at the heart of the covenant question was how the law and the gospel are combined; how mankind is saved. A failure to have a clear understanding on this point would affect one's entire Christian experience and bring confusion into the work.

### *Responsibility Resting on the Leadership*

The responsibility for the poor condition of the churches rested upon the ministers who were to break the bread of life to their congregations. The whole purpose of the Ministerial Institute was to better equip the ministers to fulfill their God-given responsibilities. With nearly half the Church's laborers gathered in Battle Creek, Ellen White realized the great possibilities if everyone went forth from the Institute truly converted and with the message of Christ's righteousness. She also realized that Satan was seeking to prevent such a thing from happening: "I am convinced that Satan saw that there was very much at stake here, and he did not want to lose his hold on our ministering brethren. And if the full victory comes, there will go forth from this meeting many ministers with an experience of the highest value."[25] Ellen White was also led to realize the dire results if victory did not come, if the brethren refused to walk in the light shining upon their pathway.

In her morning talks, Ellen White spoke decidedly against the prevailing spirit, even comparing her "testimony" with that of "Moses in his farewell address: 'I call heaven and earth to record this day against you, that I have set before you life and death, blessing and cursing: therefore choose life, *that both you and thy seed may live* [Deut. 30:19].'" Truly the decisions being made at the heart of the work would affect many generations to come. Her diary gives an account of what was taking place: "I entreated them to search the Scriptures for themselves. ... In the days of Christ the scribes and Pharisees searched the Old Testament Scriptures. But they interpreted what they read to sustain their traditions. ... Divided on most points, they were united on one point,—opposition to Christ. And today it seems that men have united to make of no effect the message that the Lord has sent. ... They change the meaning of God's Word to suit their own opinions. ... God has a controversy with those who wrest the Scriptures, making them conform to their preconceived ideas." It was in this context that she warned the "brethren standing in positions of responsibility not to grieve the Spirit of God away from their hearts. ... Do not turn away from the messages that God sends, as you did at Minneapolis." With an aching heart she could ask: "Why do they not arise and shine, because their light has come, and the glory of the Lord has risen upon them?"[26]

On February 3, Ellen White stood before the brethren and pleaded with them to accept the light that was being presented to them. She knew that there had "been efforts—a contrary influence—to throw back the light, the light which God has been forcing in here upon us in regard to the righteousness of Christ." She could unabashedly state: "If God has ever spoken by me, it is the truth, brethren. It is the truth that every soul of you will receive, or your soul will be left in darkness as barren as the hills of Gilboa." God was giving them precious opportunities:

> Now, I want to say, brethren, there is a door open, and no man can close it to you—no matter whether it is those in the highest position or the lowest position—they cannot close it. But you can. You can close the door of your heart that the light which God has sent you for the last year-and-a-half—or nearly that—shall not have its influence and its effect upon your life, nor be brought into your religious experience. This is what God sends His messengers for. [27]

She reminded the brethren that after John the Baptist had come with a message that agitated and stirred the hearts of his listeners, Christ came in "with a healing balm, a message which, with the heart broken up, the seed [could] fall into prepared soil." Yet "John's disciples became jealous of Christ." In the same manner, she continued, "God has workmen. They carry the work so far and they can carry it no further. … Now God calls upon another workman to come right in and advance that work. The one that was working becomes circumscribed. He cannot see that the very line of work that he is working in is not to be pursued to the very close of time. There has to be more light and power infused into the work than we have had." [28]*

## A Promise Kept

As Ellen White continued her discourse, she carried her listeners back in time; past the previous year's many campmeetings, past the 1888 Minneapolis Conference with all its conflict, all the way back to the time when she sat at the side of her dying husband in 1881. It was here, she recalled, that God had made a promise:

> This work is to be carried upward and forward, and the building is to go up. Thus God has worked with His workmen; He buried the workmen, but the work progresses still.

> When I sat with the hand of my dying husband in my own, I knew that God was at work. While I sat there on the bed by his side, he in such feverness, it was there, like a clear chain of light presented before me: The workmen are buried, but the work shall go on. *I have workmen that shall take hold of this work.* Fear not; be not discouraged; it shall go forward.

It was there I understood that I was to take the work and a burden stronger than I had ever borne before. It was there that I promised the Lord that I would stand at my post of duty, and I have tried to do it. I do, as far as possible, the work that God has given me to do, with the understanding that God *was to bring an element in this work that we have not had yet.*[29]*

There was no question in Ellen White's mind that God had fulfilled His promise. He had not only miraculously healed her less than a year after her husband's death as she lay "a candidate for the grave," but God had also given Waggoner his divine calling only a few days later while Ellen White spoke at the Healdsburg campmeeting during the fall of 1882.[30] Not long after, God again fulfilled His promise by calling A. T. Jones to join in the expanding work. Now in the year 1890, according to Ellen White, their message had brought "an element in this work that we have not had yet."

Immediately after speaking of her husband's death, Ellen White reminded her listeners how those in responsible positions were treating the new light of that message which God had promised to send. What were the results of the meetings that had been held the previous summer when she stood side-by-side with God's chosen messengers?

A TYPICAL CAMPMEETING TENT

Our young men look at the older men that stand still as a stick and will not move to accept any new light that is brought in; they [younger men] will laugh and ridicule what these men say [Jones and Waggoner] and what they do as of no consequence. Who carries the burden of that laugh, and of that contempt, I ask you? It is the very ones that have interposed themselves between the light that God has given, that it shall not go to the people who should have it. ...

Now, brethren, I say, clear the King's highway, for your soul's sake. If you have interposed between the people and the light, get out of the way, or God will move you out of the way. ...

Now it is just exactly as in the days of the Jews. When a message came in, why all the power of the leaders was put against it, that it should not have access to the people. ... If God sends us light, let it come to us, and let no man close the door, or try to close it. Don't close it yourselves. Open the door of your heart and let the brilliant rays of light shine into your heart and into your mind. I pray you, let the Sun of Righteousness in. ...

How long is the grace of God to come to this people in vain? I plead with you, for Christ's sake, clear the King's highway, and trifle not with the Spirit of God.

We have traveled all through to the different places of the meetings that I might stand side by side with the messengers of God that I knew were His messengers, that I knew had a message for His people. I gave my message with them right in harmony with the very message they were bearing. What did we see? We saw a power attending the message. ...

I try to present it to you, that you may see the evidence that I saw, but it seems that the words go as into empty air. How long is it to be thus? How long will the people at the heart of the work hold themselves against God?[31]

Ellen White could not have made it clearer. The young men who laughed and ridiculed the message presented by Jones and Waggoner were doing so as a result of the example set by the older men in leadership positions. Consequently it was the older men who would carry the "burden" of that laugh. Yes, the older men as *individuals* were committing sin, but the effects of their sins were far-reaching in their influence. Ellen White was warning them against following in the steps of the Jewish leaders; the results would be fearful.[32]*

When Ellen White published her morning talk a few weeks later in the *Review*, she added several paragraphs reaffirming her support for Jones and Waggoner, and the very message, "as it has been presented." She admonished those standing in the way:

> How long will it be before you will believe the testimonies of God's Spirit? When is the truth for this time to find access to your hearts? Will you wait till Christ comes? How long will God permit the way to be hedged up? Clear the King's highway, I beseech you, and make his paths straight.

> I have traveled from place to place, attending meetings where the message of the righteousness of Christ was preached. I considered it a privilege to stand by the side of my brethren, and give my testimony with the message for the time; and I saw that power attended the message wherever it was spoken. You could not make the people believe in South Lancaster that it was not a message of light that came to them. The people confessed their sins, and appropriated the righteousness of Christ. God has set his hand to do this work. We labored in Chicago; it was a week before there was a break in the meetings. But like a wave of glory, the blessing of God swept over us as we pointed men to the Lamb of God that taketh away the sin of the world. The Lord revealed his glory, and we felt the deep movings of his Spirit. Everywhere the message led to the confession of sin, and to the putting away of iniquity. …

> Suppose that you blot out the testimony that has been going during these last two years proclaiming the righteousness of Christ, who can you point to as bringing out special light for the people? *This message as it has been presented*, should go to every church that claims to believe the truth, and bring our people up to a higher stand-point. …[33]*

> Every worker has his place; but God does not want any man to think that no other message is to be heard but that which he may have given. We want the past message and the fresh message.[34]

On Wednesday, February 5, Ellen White spoke once again to those gathered at the meetings in Battle Creek. She pled with the brethren to draw nigh to God and to one another. She tried to encourage them that God was seeking to bless them with "light flashing from the throne of God... that the people might be able to stand in the day of God." Churches were "ready to die" due to a lack of "spiritual food." The ministers were to present to these churches truths "not from another man's brain, but from the light you have received by diligent search of the Word of God." She encouraged her listeners once again with the wonderful results in South Lancaster where she had worked alongside A. T. Jones in sharing this message:

> Nearly every student was swept in by the heavenly current, and living testimonies were given that were not surpassed even by the testimonies of 1844 before the disappointment. Many learned at South Lancaster what it meant to surrender their hearts to God—what it meant to be converted. Many said, "I have for years professed to be a follower of Jesus, but I never knew before what it meant to know Jesus or the Father. I have learned from this experience what it means to be a Christian."…
>
> Brethren, there is light for us; there is light for the people of God, "and the light shineth in darkness; and the darkness comprehended it not." The reason men do not understand is because they fasten themselves in a position of questioning and doubt. They do not cultivate faith. If God gives light, you must walk in the light, and follow the light. Light is flashing from the throne of God, and what is this for?—It is that a people may be prepared to stand in the day of God.[35]

Notwithstanding these events, the brethren still cautioned others not to attend classes given by Jones and Waggoner, and some attended only to ask questions for the sake of discrediting their presentations. Ellen White warned them that it was "too late in the day to cry out against men for manifesting too much earnestness in the service of God; to say 'You are excited; you are too intense, too positive.' It is too late to caution your brethren in studying the Bible for themselves, [for fear] they may be deceived by error." She felt a great sense of urgency to warn the brethren against repeating the mistake of the Jews:

> As I am writing on the "Life of Christ [*The Desire of Ages*]," I lift up my heart in prayer to God that light may come to His people. As I see something of the loveliness of Christ, my heart ascends to God, 'O, let this glory be revealed to thy servants! Let prejudice and unbelief vanish from their hearts.' Every line I trace about the condition of the people in the time of Christ, about their attitude toward the Light of the world, in which I see danger that we shall take the same position, I offer up a prayer to God: 'O let not this be the condition of thy people. Forbid that thy people shall make this mistake. Increase their faith.'. . . We shall have to meet unbelief in every form in the world, but it is when we meet *unbelief in those who should be leaders of the people*, that our souls are wounded. This is that which grieves us, and *that which grieves the Spirit of God.*[36*]

The Holy Spirit was being grieved away by the unbelief of those primarily in leadership positions. They were blocking the light from coming to the people, and their influence was affecting the entire church.

The very next morning when Ellen White spoke to the leading brethren, she wondered why "a good many" men, including Uriah Smith, were not attending the meetings. Was it for fear they would be "won?" They were staying away and "all the time firing in the dark against [Jones and Waggoner]." She stated that the ministers "should understand where the Spirit of God is," that they "might know the impressions that the Lord is making upon His people." These were, Ellen White stated, "the very men that ought to be here to feel their interest of having the truth for their positions of trust... to be fitting for these positions, [but] they are not here at all; they do not come near." Instead of quibbling and trying to find hooks on which to hang their doubts, these ministers needed to go to their "knees in prayer; for Christ's sake see the error and mistake of the Jews."[37]

Ellen White told of how she awoke the morning before with such a heavy burden. She felt such a responsibility knowing that men were "not walking in the light." She entreated the brethren: "When you go from this place, Oh be so full of the message that it is like fire shut up in your bones, that you cannot hold your peace. It is true men will say, 'You are too excited; you are making too much of this matter, and you do not think enough of the law; now, you must think more of the law; don't be all the time reaching for this righteousness of Christ, but build up the law.' Let the law take care of itself. We have been at work on the law until we get as dry as the hills of Gilboa, without dew or rain. Let us trust in the merits of Jesus Christ of Nazareth." Would they heed the admonition?[38]

The following morning, Ellen White continued along the same lines. The brethren were making a mistake in "considering men infallible." The people were looking to the "ministers to take care of them" as if they had no personal work to do themselves. But, regardless of a man's position, whether he was an old leader in the work or a newcomer, the people were to study the Bible for themselves to see what was truth. The people were to put their trust in God and not man, for "there are not any of us infallible."[39]* But the fallibility of man did not negate the fact that God had more light for His people which was to be given through His appointed messengers: "There is power for this people. I know it. God has been revealing it to me for years, and the time has come. We want to know that that living faith should be inspired in our hearts, and that we shall be reaching out for more light and more knowledge."[40]

Ellen White was not called to be a prophet who settled every difference of opinion, telling people what they must or must not believe. She had not been the *easy way out* in the past, neither would she be the *easy way out* during the conflict over the covenants. In the early days when the pioneers discovered truths about the Sabbath and the heavenly Sanctuary, the Lord confirmed these truths through Ellen White's prophetic gift only after they had earnestly studied the Bible. This would also be the case with the law in Galatians and the covenants. The Lord did not reveal all the light on these points of controversy at once. As Ellen White saw opposition rising against that light, she pointed the people to the Bible. The purpose for such study was not only to determine if what Jones and Waggoner presented was truth; it was also to lead the people to a personal *experience* in that truth. The Church was already dealing with the lukewarm results of a mere mental assent to a list of creedal truths; justification by faith being one of them. Furthermore, Ellen White's authority as a prophet of God was being greatly questioned by many church leaders because she supported Jones and Waggoner and the message they presented. She knew that if the people would go to the Bible for themselves they would see that God was indeed sending showers of blessings upon His Church:

> Now, here you are in this school. Brother Waggoner may present the truth before you. You may say that the matter that he presents is truth. But then what will you do? You must go to the Scriptures for yourselves. You must search them with humble hearts. If you are just full of prejudice and your own preconceived opinions, and if you entertain the idea that there is nothing for you to know, and that you know all that is worth knowing, you will not get any benefit here. But if you come like children, you want to learn all there is for you. ... The Lord of Heaven has led the mind of man to make a specialty of studying the Scripture and when those Scriptures are presented, He has given

[us] reasoning powers… [to] see the evidence just as well as he [the presenter] can see it; I can find the evidence as he finds it. I can go out and speak the truth because I know it is the truth. …

I believe without a doubt that God has given precious truth at the right time to Brother Jones and Brother Waggoner. Do I place them as infallible? Do I say that they will not make a statement or have an idea that cannot be questioned or that cannot be error? Do I say so? No, I do not say any such thing. Nor do I say that of any man in the world. But I do say God has sent light, and do be careful how you treat it.[41]

At that particular point in time, the Lord had not specifically revealed to Ellen White that Jones and Waggoner's position on the covenants was correct. He had, however, made it clear that He was sending light and precious truth, howbeit through fallible men. The important question was not whether Jones and Waggoner were infallible, but how the brethren were treating the light that God had sent. Instead of looking for flaws in the messengers and the message, they were to study as if looking for light. Instead of telling the people to stay away from the meetings, they were to encourage investigation:

I speak of these men [ministers] that they may know, that they may understand, what is truth; and if they will not hear, if they will keep away, just as the ministers tell the congregations, the stay-away argument, don't go to hear. Now, you want to hear everything. If he [Waggoner] has got error we want to know it, we want to understand it… and then we want to investigate for ourselves. We want to know that it is truth; and if it is truth, brethren, those children in the Sabbath School class want it, and every soul of them need it. … Those that are in responsible positions, I say you are under obligation to God to know what is going on here. …

This has given me such a sadness and grief to know that there are those who have just had their hearts filled with prejudice. And they listen for every word they can catch. … Who says they [Jones and Waggoner] are perfect? Who claims it? We claim God has given us light in the right time. And now we should receive the truth of God—receive it as of heavenly origin. … When a point is proven, Oh, they [the brethren] will not acknowledge a word. Why, they see no light, but pour it in, question after question. Well, not one point is settled. They do not acknowledge they have met that point; but pour in a whole list of questions. Now, brethren, we want to know what it is to examine the Scriptures, as those who want light, and not those who want to shut out the light.[42]

Such was the state of things at the Ministerial Institute before Waggoner even had an opportunity to present on the two covenants. An environment was set in place conducive to rejecting all the light that God was seeking to pour upon His people. Those gathered there were ministers and leaders in the church. And although their acceptance or rejection of the light sent from heaven was an individual choice, the consequences would affect the entire church; their sin would be corporate, like that of the Jews. Men had become "guide–posts pointing in the wrong direction." For their sins, the "whole church stands accountable."[43]*

# CHAPTER 13 FOOTNOTES

1. "The Two Covenants," *Bible Readings for the Home Circle* (Battle Creek, MI.: Review and Herald Pub. House, 1888), pp. 214-219.

2. Dan T. Jones to E. W. Farnsworth, Feb. 9, 1890, p. 5, archives of the General Conference of Seventh-day Adventists.

3. E. J. Waggoner, "The Two Covenants," *Bible Readings for the Home Circle* (1889), pp. 312-317.

4. "The Two Covenants," *Bible Readings for the Home Circle* (1888), p. 219.

5. Robert Van Ornam, *The Doctrine of the Everlasting Covenant in the Writings of Ellet J. Waggoner*, (Graduate Thesis Loma Linda University, 1985) p. 23.

6. Dan T. Jones to E. W. Farnsworth, Feb. 9, 1890, archives of the General Conference of Seventh-day Adventists.

7. *Ibid.*

8. The General Conference Executive Committee is the administrative body or governing body that in essence runs the church: "The powers of the Executive Committee between sessions are quite broad. As a part of its responsibilities the committee votes the annual appropriations to the world divisions... adopts the policies that regulate the operation of the worldwide work, sends missionaries to overseas fields, and in general carries out the objective of the General Conference. ... It fills vacancies in any office, board, or committee of the General Conference; issues credentials and licenses to workers" (*SDA Encyclopedia*, vol. 10, p. 500). This committee was made up of five members until 1888, when it was expanded to seven members. At the 1889 General Conference, two more members were added bringing the total to nine: "O. A. Olsen, S. N. Haskell, W. C. White, D. T. Jones, R. A. Underwood, R. M. Kilgore, E. W. Farnsworth, E. H. Gates, A. R. Henry" (*General Conference Daily Bulletin*, Nov. 6, 1889, p. 140). Of those nine members who were responsible for the goals, plans, and ultimately the direction the church would go, at least six were openly opposed to Jones and Waggoner and the message they were presenting.

9. Dan T. Jones to George I. Butler, Feb. 13, 1890, p. 10.

10. General Conference Daily Bulletin, Nov. 6, 1889, p. 153.

11. "Minister," *SDA Encyclopedia*, vol. 10, p. 901.

12. Gilbert M. Valentine, *The Shaping of Adventism*, pp. 49-50.

13. Dan T. Jones to E. W. Farnsworth, Feb. 9, 1890, archives of the General Conference of Seventh-day Adventists.

14. *Ibid.*

15. *Ibid.*

16. *Ibid.* So much for Dan Jones' statement shortly before, that if all felt it was okay for Waggoner to teach he "would say nothing more about it." Perhaps he was not aware that just like Minneapolis, "the history of that meeting has passed into eternity with its burden of record and when the judgment shall sit and the books shall be opened there will be found registered a history that many who were at that meeting will not be pleased to meet" (Ellen G. White, Letter 67, Sept. 17, 1890; in *1888 Materials*, p. 706).

17. Dan T. Jones to E. W. Farnsworth, Feb. 9, 1890, archives of the General Conference of Seventh-day Adventists. In Dan Jones' mind, only brotherly kindness was shown at the meeting. Ellen White exposed his concept as false: "Some may say, 'I do not hate my brother; I am not so bad as that.' But how little they understand their own hearts. They may think they have a zeal for God in their feelings against their brother,

if his ideas seem in any way to conflict with theirs; feelings are brought to the surface that have no kinship with love. They show no disposition to harmonize with him. They would as lief [gladly] be at swords' point with their brother as not. And yet he may be bearing a message from God to the people—just the light they need for this time" (Ellen G. White, Letter 19d, Sept. 1, 1892; in *1888 Materials*, p. 1022).

18. Dan T. Jones to E. W. Farnsworth, Feb. 9, 1890, archives of the General Conference of Seventh-day Adventists.

19. S. A. Whittier to O. A. Olsen, Jan. 22, 1890, archives of the General Conference of Seventh-day Adventists.

20. This alleged statement by A. T. Jones was circulated by Uriah Smith, and even interjected into a letter Smith wrote to Ellen White (Feb. 17, 1890; in *Manuscripts and Memories*, p. 152). Ellen White responded by writing to Jones and confronting him with the alleged statements (Letter 55, March 17, 1890, unpublished). Jones responded to the allegations in a letter written to Ellen White (a letter which is not extant), and also had a chance to explain his side of the story at a ministers' meeting held in the Conference office (Ellen G. White to W. C. White, Letter 83, March 13, 1890; in *1888 Materials*, p. 627). As a result Ellen White wrote to Uriah Smith stating that he "had accused [Jones] wrongfully" (Letter 73, Nov. 25, 1890; in *1888 Materials*, p. 734). The damage had been done, however. It is much easier to start a rumor than it is to stop one. In a letter to Uriah Smith, Ellen White explained how this happened: "You have strengthened the hands and minds of such men as Larson, Porter, Dan Jones, Eldridge and Morrison and Nicola and a vast number through them. All quote you, and the enemy of righteousness looks on pleased" (Letter 59, March 8, 1890; in *1888 Materials*, p. 599).

21. Dan T. Jones to A. W. Allee, Jan. 23, 1890, archives of the General Conference of Seventh-day Adventists.

22. Uriah Smith, "Editorial Notes," *Review and Herald*, Jan. 28, 1890, p. 64.

23. This point cannot be missed. The opponents of Jones and Waggoner were claiming the Bible and the Bible only as their rule of faith. This was exactly what the Scribes and Pharisees had done with Christ; quoting from the books of Moses to prove that they were right and He was wrong. Yet Jones and Waggoner had come with a message that called people back to the Bible *and* to the beautiful truths found in its pages. Ellen White supported this approach, and in answer to those opposing Jones and Waggoner invited them back numerous times to study the Scriptures that they might believe what was being presented. But her calls to a deeper study of the Scriptures do not invalidate her statements of support for what Jones and Waggoner were teaching *from the Scriptures*. Would it not seem a little strange for the "Lord in His great

mercy" to "send a most precious message through Elders Waggoner and Jones," that included a call for deeper Bible study, if what they presented as a result of their deeper Bible study was in fact full of fatal errors? This is, however, exactly the type of accusations that were being leveled against them over 120 years ago. The leading brethren claimed to believe in the Bible and the doctrine of justification by faith, they just didn't believe in Jones' and Waggoner's "new theological departure." This same mind-set is alive today among those who disagree with Jones and Waggoner in regard to the nature of Christ, righteousness by faith, the final generation, the latter rain, and the covenants. George Knight states: "The church needs to read the Bible through the eyes of Moses, John, Paul, and other Bible writers rather than through the eyes of any other source. ... Some today would have us read the Bible through the eyes of Jones and Waggoner. Such a practice may be the most perilous mistake. ... Ellen White upheld both men because they were leading Adventism back to Christ and the Bible, not because they had the final word on theology or even had a theology with which she fully agreed." (*A User–Friendly Guide*, p. 179). But Ellen White also warned of the subtle deception that was unsettling people's faith in the Spirit of Prophecy, brought about by the very men that were fighting against the message sent through Jones and Waggoner, while they were claiming to uphold the Bible themselves: "The enemy has made his masterly efforts to unsettle the faith of our own people in the Testimonies, and when these errors come in they claim to prove all the positions by the Bible, but they misinterpret the Scripture. ... This is just as Satan designed it should be, and those who have been preparing the way for the people to pay no heed to the warnings and reproofs of the Testimonies of the Spirit of God will see that a tide of errors of all kinds will spring into life" (Ellen G. White to W. C. White, Letter 109, Dec. 6, 1890; in *1888 Materials*, p. 739).

24. Ellen G. White Manuscript 22, April 24, 1890, "Diary"; in *1888 Materials*, p. 579; Dan T. Jones to E. W. Farnsworth, Feb. 9, 1890.

25. Ellen G. White to Willie and Mary White, Letter 83, March 13, 1890; in *1888 Materials*, p. 635.

26. Ellen G. White Manuscript 22, Jan. 10, 1890, "Diary"; in *1888 Materials*, pp. 570-575, emphasis supplied.

27. Ellen G. White Manuscript 9, Feb. 3, 1890, "Responding to New Light"; in *1888 Materials*, pp. 537, 538.

28. *Ibid.*, pp. 539-540. Ellen White's comments to this point must be understood in the light of her next statements. She was likely referring to the work that even her husband had done.

29. *Ibid.*, p. 540, emphasis supplied. When Ellen White edited this sermon for the *Review and Herald* she rephrased this sentence to read: "He would bring a large measure of

His Holy Spirit into the work. ..." ("The Present Message," *Review and Herald*, March 18, 1890, p. 161; in *1888 Materials*, p. 545).

30. Ellen G. White, "My Health Restored," *Review and Herald*, Nov. 2, 1882, p. 484; E. J. Waggoner to Ellen G. White, Nov. 3, 1903. See Chapter 2.

31. *Ibid.*, pp. 540-543.

32. "For the rejection of Christ, with the results that followed, they [the Scribes and Pharisees] were responsible. A nation's sin and a nation's ruin were due to the religious leaders" (Ellen G. White, *Christ's Object Lessons*, p. 305). Could the same principle hold true today? This gives no license to laity, nor to off-shoot groups that point to the church as Babylon. But it does show the awesome responsibility that leadership carries, and is one good reason we should uphold and join those in leadership positions in seeking the Lord.

33. It is a sad fact that many today condemn the very message ("as it has been presented"), that Ellen White so highly endorsed. Is the situation any different now? Desmond Ford states: "Preachers Waggoner and Jones at the famous Minneapolis Conference of 1888 had the first gleamings of the light which irradiated the Roman world in the first century, Europe in the sixteenth, and which is to envelop the whole world just prior to Christ's return. ... Unfortunately, neither man was clear on other important points such as the distinction between justification and sanctification... [and] the nature of Christ. ... Possibly this faulty theology was responsible for Waggoner and Jones both becoming tainted with pantheistic sentiments" (Australian *Signs of the Times*, Feb. 1978, p. 30). Robert Brinsmead wrote: "At special periods in our history the gospel has struggled to break through to the Adventist community. The year 1888 marked such a period. But even here we must keep a proper perspective. ... Waggoner had light on justification for the Adventist community. But better material on justification by faith could be found among Protestant scholars of his day." (*Judge by the Gospel: A Review of Adventism* [1980], pp. 14-15). Geoffrey J. Paxton concludes: "The problem of the 1888 renewal was twofold. First, although Waggoner and Jones moved in the direction of the Reformation in stressing the necessity of the doing and dying of the God-man in order to stand in the judgment, they did not possess enough light to see this in a completely Reformational *Christ alone* perspective" (*The Shaking of Adventism*, [1977], p. 67). David P. McMahon claims: "Waggoner was one of Adventism's greatest gospel preachers. But he did not compare with the great Protestant preachers of the time." "In these articles [1889] Waggoner began to adopt an 'effective' justification. ... This Roman principle quickly displaces the Protestant element. ... This was a fatal mistake." "Waggoner had not yet developed his pantheism by February, 1889. But he possessed a logical mind that followed his premises through to their final end." "For Waggoner, however, it seemed that a little leaven of Roman Catholic justification soon

leavened the whole lump. If his articles on justification in 1890 were disappointing, his lectures on Romans at the General Conference of 1891 were terrible. ... Waggoner's concept of justification in these lectures was wholly Roman Catholic. Justification was understood as an inward work of sanctifying the believer" (*The Myth and the Man*, [1979], pp. 64, 94-95, 99). Burt Haloviak asserts: "The author hopes in this chapter to suggest that the roots to the aberrant theology that were confronted in 1903 [holy flesh and pantheism] were consistently present in the theological system of Jones and Waggoner because they lacked objective views of justification. Those roots of aberration are visible in the presentations on justification by faith given by A T Jones in May of 1889 at the Ottawa, Kansas, campmeeting." "Analysis of those meetings allows us not only to identify the nature of the 1888 message, but also to see the elements waiting to develop into the holy flesh and *Living Temple* apostasies [*sic*]" ("From Righteousness to Holy Flesh: Judgement at Minneapolis," [1988], chapter 9, pp. 2, 41). Roy Adams contends: "As we have seen, the perfectionistic agitation within the Seventh-day Adventist Church today had its genesis in the post-1888 teachings of A. T. Jones and E. J. Waggoner" (*The Nature of Christ* [1994], p. 37). George Knight insists: "In his Ottawa, Kansas, sermons of May 1889, for example, Jones pointed out that the indwelling of Christ's divine nature and power would enable individuals eventually to keep God's commandments. ... This teaching... became a major root for the spread of sinless perfectionism among Seventh-day Adventists—a root that produced some prolific branches in the 1890s. There is, for example a fairly direct line from Jones in the post-Minneapolis period to the holy flesh movement in Indiana in 1900." "The holy flesh excitement erupted in Indiana in 1899. ... The key Indiana doctrines of 'translation faith' and 'the power to overcome every tendency to sin,' for example he had preached beginning at least as early as 1889. ..." (*From 1888 to Apostasy*, [1987], pp. 56, 57). Woodrow Whidden's "working theological thesis" for his biography on Waggoner, from cover to cover, seeks to substantiate the ideas listed above: "Undoubtedly the most significant and portentous theological trend of the early post-Minneapolis period (1888 to mid-1892) was Waggoner's early 1889 emphasis on the indwelling Christ. ... [I]t would become the source for almost all of the errant theological and practical paths that Waggoner would tread for the balance of his life." "In the years following 1888, however, there began a subtle slide into an unhealthy subjectivism that never seemed to halt. The critical developments came in the years 1889 and 1892." "Can it be justly said that Waggoner's mystical, subjective views of the justifying work of the immanent Christ led him into the mazes of panentheism? And we would suggest that it most likely did" (*E. J. Waggoner* [2008], pp. 210, 358, 363). Leroy Moore does a nice job of summarizing the views listed above, and gives insight as to why there is such a desperate attempt to condemn the real 1888 message: "Reformationists hold that Jones and Waggoner, acknowledged 1888 exponents of that message [in 1888], embedded four heresies in SDA doctrine [soon after 1888]: rejection of the historic doctrine of original sin; inclusion of *sanctification* in righteousness by faith; claiming that Christ connected sinful flesh with His own sinless nature; and holding the doctrine of perfection. [Ellen] White's unusual endorsement of Jones and Waggoner, whose earliest printed works reflect the above concepts [as truth not heresy], requires overwhelming evidence to prove that she recognized their theological errors immediately after Minneapolis, reflecting Roman Catholic heresy. Developments before, during and after Minneapolis deny such claims" (*Theology in Crisis*, p. 294).

34. "The Present Message," *Review and Herald*, March 18, 1890, p. 161; in *1888 Materials*, p. 545, emphasis supplied.

35. Ellen G. White, "Draw Nigh to God," Morning Talk Feb. 5, 1890, *Review and Herald*, March 4, 1890, p. 129.

36. *Ibid.*, pp. 129, 130. All the while Ellen White was writing material for *The Desire of Ages* (from 1890 through 1898), she was impressed with the parallels between the leaders of the Jewish nation and that of the Seventh-day Adventist church. "Over 100 times" she gave warning that we not repeat the mistake of the Jews. When reading *The Desire of Ages* with this in mind, one can readily see the parallels in *Ellen G. White 1888 Materials* ("Ellen White's Hidden Message in *The Desire of Ages*," 1888 Message Newsletter, Jan.-Feb., 1997, pp. 3-5). It is also interesting to note what Ellen White penned in her diary the day she gave this morning talk: "I attended the early morning meeting. We had a good social meeting, and I then bore a decided testimony. How earnestly I am moved by the Spirit of God. Before I stand on my feet, I have no thought of speaking as plainly as I do. But the Spirit of God rests upon me with power, and I can not but speak the words given me. I dare not withhold one word of the testimony. If the solemn call to repentance is not heeded, if false statements are made in regard to it, I may be cast down, I may feel sad, but I have no retraction to make. I speak the words given me by a power higher than human power, and I can not, if I would, recall one sentence. In the night season the Lord gives me instruction in symbols, and then explains their meaning. He gives me the word, and I dare not refuse to give it to the people. The love of Christ, and, I venture to add, the love of souls, constrains me, and I can not hold my peace. If evil is done by the word spoken, it is because those to whom the message is given have no place in their hearts for the word of God" (Manuscript 22, 1890, "Diary, Entries," Feb. 5, 1890; in *1888 Materials*, pp. 578-579).

37. Ellen G. White Manuscript 10, Feb. 6, 1890, "Who Will Accept the Light From Heaven?"; in *1888 Materials*, pp. 549, 555.

38. *Ibid.*, p. 557.

39. We must be clear that "there are not any of us infallible," including Jones and Waggoner. They did make mistakes and had some incorrect views in their theological understanding, which Ellen White corrected. Yet, we must be careful that we do not continue the same rebellion in which the leading brethren participated in by rejecting Ellen White's counsel and by always seeking to find hooks on which to hang our doubts in regard to the most precious message. In 1892 Ellen White stated: "It is quite possible that Elder Jones or Waggoner may be overthrown by the temptations of the enemy; but if they should be, this would not prove that they had had no message from God, or that the work that they had done was all a mistake. But should this happen, *how many would take this position, and enter into a fatal delusion because they are not under the control of the Spirit of God.* They walk in the sparks of their own kindling, and cannot distinguish between the fire they have kindled and the light which God has given, and they walk in blindness as did the Jews" (Ellen G. White to Uriah Smith, Letter 24, Sept. 19, 1892; in *1888 Materials*, pp. 1044-1045, emphasis supplied, with the italicized words being a statement of fact, not a question in the original source). Sadly, both Jones and Waggoner made mistakes after 1892, and were both "overthrown by the temptations of the enemy," in the late 1890s. But the important point for us to remember today is that we do not "enter into a fatal delusion," as Ellen White predicted would happen, and through our teaching and writing make 1888 history fit a new theology. See footnote 32.

40. Ellen G. White Manuscript 56, Feb. 7, 1890, "Lessons From the Vine"; in *1888 Materials*, pp. 562, 564.

41. *Ibid.*, pp. 562-567.

42. *Ibid.*, pp. 566, 567.

43. Ellen G. White Manuscript 30, March 12, 1890, and "Be Zealous and Repent," *Review and Herald*, Dec. 23, 1890; in *1888 Materials*, pp. 916, and 764. A look through the first two volumes of *Ellen G. White's 1888 Materials* explains how this could be the case (all emphasis supplied): The people were looking "in a large degree to the men they have set before them in the place of God" (p. 354). They were following their "*example* far more than they have looked to God and sought His counsel" (p. 793). Ellen White described this putting "man where God should be," as "idolatry" (p. 886). The brethren could "never lead the people to an experience of which [they were] not partakers" (p. 512). The people "will go no farther then you will go" (p. 793). The brethren were to respect the light God had given, not only for their "own safety, but also for the *safety of the church* of God" (p. 956). When Uriah Smith rejected the message of Jones and Waggoner, he became "the stumbling block of *many others*" (p. 733). He "strengthened the hands and minds of such men as Larson, Porter, Dan Jones, Eldridge and Morrison and Nicola and

a *vast number through them*" (p. 599). He *had "quite a number* fully engaged with [him] in the work, men in responsible positions, presidents of conferences, ministers and workers, that formed a *confederacy* to question, to criticize. ... The *position* these men have occupied and the *influence this position* has given them *has caused many to doubt*, who will never be settled again and the deceptions and delusions of these last days will overcome them... for they have decided *from the example given them*" (p. 797). These "representative men" (p. 779), walking in darkness could "not discern light from heaven" which was affecting "the *whole tenor of their thoughts*, their decisions, their propositions, their counsels" (p. 727). "Yet," Ellen White stated, "Elder Smith is placed in positions as teacher to *mold and fashion the minds of students* when it is a well known fact that he is not standing in the light" (p. 714). Ellen White realized that "the work [was] being *swayed* in wrong lines" (p. 888). "The position and work of Elders Butler, Farnsworth, Smith, and *numerous others*, is to unsettle the faith of the people of God by things which they say but which they ought not to say, and things left unsaid which they ought to say. And this state of things—unbelief, prejudice, and Pharisaism—*is leavening the church*" (p. 717). The "spirit manifested at Battle Creek has been the spirit in *many churches*" (p. 746). As a result "sinners in our borders have become hardened and have been fearfully established in unbelief" (p. 867). Because Ellen White supported the "Bible truth" presented by Jones and Waggoner—"from the source which the Lord chose to send it"—these men in prominent positions doubted her calling. They were "scattering the seeds of doubt and unsettling the *confidence of the churches* in the testimonies" (p. 677, 676). Ellen White stated: "I hear every where I go objections to the testimonies, quoting Elders Smith and Butler" (p. 715). "Those who have been reproved fasten upon this doubting, unbelieving position of our *leading men* and feel at liberty to say the testimonies given for them were not true" (p. 684). As a result, the blood of other souls would "rest upon those who have been blinded by the enemy" (p. 853). Ellen White could rightly ask: "Shall we repeat the history of the Jews in our work?" (p. 545). "Had the common people of the Jewish nation been allowed to receive His message... they would not have rejected Jesus" (p. 906). Yet, she stated, "the *leaders of the people of to-day* pursue the same course of action that the Jews pursued" (p. 911). As a result "God withholds His Spirit from them and darkness envelopes them as it did the Jewish nation" (p. 718). "The men in *responsible positions* have disappointed Jesus. ... The Spirit of God is grieved," but "they are so dull of comprehension that they know it not" (pp. 519, 717). It is no wonder that Ellen White stated that unless these evils which "bring the displeasure of God" are corrected, "the whole church stands accountable for them" (p. 764).

# CHAPTER 14

# *Convincing Evidence*

## *Don't Waste Your Time Coming up with a View Different From Waggoner's*

"The trouble we have been having on the covenant question for the last three weeks has seemed to wear me more military than ordinary work." So said Dan Jones in his letter to E. W. Farnsworth, February 18, 1890. Although Waggoner had been prevented from teaching on the subject in late January at the Ministerial Institute, the topic had by no means been laid to rest. When O. A. Olsen and W. W. Prescott returned to Battle Creek, they found that all was not well at the heart of the work. Before the week was over, arrangements had been made "to investigate the covenant question before the minister's school, and such others as may wish to come in." Prescott chose to chair the meetings that would begin the very next week. Waggoner would finally be "allowed the floor to present his views." He would not, however, be able to present his views without objections; others would "be permitted to ask questions or present *counter-arguments* if they chose to do so." No doubt there were many objections, for according to Dan Jones, it was "evident that this question has stirred the people all over the country, and has met with much opposition." Much of that opposition was coming from Dan Jones himself, which he readily shared in his correspondence with others around the country.[1]*

On Sunday morning, February 16, Waggoner began the first of 10 two-hour sessions that would be held during the next two weeks on the topic of the covenants. Of the ten sessions Waggoner presented six, while Uriah Smith, R. C. Porter, and Bro. Bourdeau—evangelist and General Conference worker—presented one and a half each. According to Dan Jones, "two distinct views of the covenants" were presented, "one favoring the position that has been held

in the past by our people, which was presented by
Eld. Smith and Bro. Porter; and another party in
favor of the advanced views held by Dr. Waggoner,
supported by Eld. Bourdeau." There is no question
that Waggoner presented the covenants as he had
in the *Bible Readings* and *Senior Sabbath School*
lessons,[2] which Dan Jones said was "similar to what
he presented at Minneapolis." The presentations of
Smith and Porter confirm this, for their presentations
were meant as a rebuttal to Waggoner's teaching.[3]*

D.T. BOURDEAU

During his second presentation, Waggoner
compared the old and new covenants, "showing that each had three objective
points: first, righteousness; second, inheritance of the earth; and third, kingdom
of priests." God had promised man righteousness that would qualify him for
everlasting life in the earth made new, and through this living experience
man would become a witness to the character of God. It was at *this point* in
Waggoner's presentation that he shared concepts with which the brethren
strongly disagreed: "Nothing was presented that Eld. Smith or anyone else...
could object to, until near the close... when Dr. Waggoner drew a parallel
between the old and new covenants." What was it that the brethren strongly
disagreed with? According to Dan Jones, it was because Waggoner had stated
that in the first, or old covenant, "it all depended upon the obedience of the
people; in the second, or new covenant, God does it for the people."[4]

Because of the objections raised by many of the brethren, and to "show perfect
fairness to all concerned in the investigation," W. W. Prescott decided to allow
Uriah Smith to take up the third session and present the traditional view.[5]

### Uriah Smith and R. C. Porter Respond

For well over a year, Uriah Smith had been carrying a burden of concern
for what he felt was taking place in the church he had helped to pioneer. Even
before the Minneapolis Conference he had felt that there was a decided effort,
a conspiracy as it were, by Jones and Waggoner to urge new doctrines upon

God's last day people. In his mind, the church already believed in the doctrine of justification by faith. As for the new ideas on the law in Galatians and the covenants, he felt these were only false side issues being pawned off as new light and that they had no connection with justification by faith. Even worse for Smith was the fact that Ellen White supported these men which, in his mind, damaged her credibility.

Smith had never sat down and talked with Ellen White to understand her positions, neither had he responded to her several letters over the past year. He found it very disturbing that Waggoner be allowed to present the covenants before the Ministerial Institute. He had supported Dan Jones' attempt to ban Waggoner from presenting and had written a disclaimer in the *Review*.[6] After receiving another letter from Ellen White written February 16 (not extant), and listening to both of Waggoner's presentations on the covenants, Smith could take it no longer. He fired off a response to Ellen White, letting her know how he felt about the whole ordeal. Smith's six-page letter clearly expresses his deep and sincere concern. He desired to be in the "fullest union" with her, but he could not get around "some of the perplexities."[7]

Smith assured Ellen White: "It is not my wish that anyone should allow my position on any question to decide his belief on that subject." He reminded Ellen White that unlike A. T. Jones, who allegedly stated, "'I have got the truth and you will have to come to the same position in the end,'" he always said to one and all, "'Examine the question and take only such a position as to you seems satisfactory.'"[8]* Smith traced some events beginning with 1886, to explain his side of the story. "Next to the death of Brother White, the greatest calamity that ever befell our cause was when Dr. Waggoner put his articles on the book of Galatians through the *Signs*." As far as he was concerned, E. J. Waggoner's views were the same as his father's, J. H. Waggoner, which Ellen White, as far as he understood, had condemned back in 1856. If Smith were under "oath at a court of justice," he would be "obliged to testify" that the "only point then at issue" was whether the law in Galatians represented the moral or ceremonial law.

Smith could not see how E. J. Waggoner's views went beyond his father's; neither could he understand that Ellen White's counsel to J. H. Waggoner was that he not make prominent his view at that time. For this reason Smith felt Ellen White had changed: "When you apparently endorsed his [E. J. Waggoner's] position as a whole… it was a great surprise to many. And when they asked me what that meant, and how I could account for it, really, Sister White, I did not know what to say, and I do not know what yet."[9]

"The next unfortunate move," Smith went on, "was when the brethren in California met, just before the [Minneapolis] Conference, and laid their plans to post up, and bring their views on the ten horns and the law in Galatians into that Conference. … [A]nd so they were introduced, and nearly ruined the Conference as I feared it would." Smith felt that "a settled plan has been formed to urge these changes of doctrine upon our people till they shall come to be considered the views of the body." Why wouldn't he feel that way when "at all the camp–meetings, at institutes, schools, ministers' meetings, etc.," these views were "kept to the front, and put in at every possible place and opportunity":

> So you see two reasons why I can but look upon it with distrust; namely, because, first, it seems to me contrary to the Scriptures, and secondly, contrary to what you have previously seen. I do not mean his [Waggoner's] views on justification by faith, and righteousness through Christ, for those we have always believed; but his view on the law in Galatians, which he deduces as a conclusion from his premises on those other points.

> The real point at issue at that Conference was the law in Galatians; but Brother Waggoner's six preliminary discourses on righteousness we could all agree to; and I should have enjoyed them first rate, had I not known all the while that he designed them to pave the way for his position on Galatians, which I deem as erroneous. I of course do not believe there is any necessary and logical connection between the two, but you know a truth may be used in such a way and with such an apparent purpose, as to spoil the pleasure we would otherwise feel in listening to it. …

> I believe I am willing to receive light at any time, from anybody. But what claims to be light must, for me, show itself to be according to the Scripture and based on good solid reasons which convince the judgment, before it appears light to me. And when anyone presents something which I have long known and believed, it is impossible for me to call that new light.[10]

Smith's point cannot be overlooked. He claimed to believe in justification by faith; to him this was not new light. He just disagreed with Jones' and Waggoner's views on the covenants and the law in Galatians. He rejected their position based on his understanding of the Scripture and what he felt Ellen White had been shown in the past. On both accounts he was mistaken. He could not see, as did Ellen White, that indeed what Jones and Waggoner presented on the covenants and the law in Galatians was "new light" which placed justification by faith in a "new setting." This was the "third angel's message in verity" that, if accepted, would lighten the earth with its glory.[11]

Near the end of his letter, Smith related to Ellen White what he was "told that Brother A. T. Jones has taught here in the class this winter." He had been told that Jones was undermining prophetic dates familiar to Adventists and supporting others who were doing the same. Smith informed Ellen White that he "might mention many other points, but will not take the time. It is these things that trouble me. These are the things that I am opposing." He warned her that these false views, "if they are carried out, will utterly undermine your work, and shake the faith in the message." Yet, "because I venture a word of caution on some of these points, I am held up in public as one who is shooting in the dark, and does not know what he is opposing. I think I do know to some degree what I am opposing."[12] Smith could not see that it was he, not Jones and Waggoner, who was undermining the work of Ellen White. Within a few days it was clearly shown that Smith accused Jones "wrongfully."[13]

After sending his letter to Ellen White, Smith had opportunity to present similar views publicly. On February 19, he presented his views on the covenants in contrast to what Waggoner had already presented in the two previous meetings. Smith desired not to present "anything in a controversial way," but only to present "what the Bible teaches." If something he said was not "in accordance with the ideas already presented" by Waggoner, it was "simply because it seems to me to be the better view, a better position." Smith was thankful that "in regard to the subject of justification by faith and righteousness in Christ… there is harmony." He was "not aware that there has ever been, or is, or ever can be, any difference of opinion among Seventh-day Adventists on this point. But on this subject of the covenants; there are some points, some scriptures, where there seems to be a difference of opinion." Thus, Smith saw little connection between justification by faith and the covenants, whereas Jones and Waggoner connected the two; viewing justification by faith in the light of the two covenants.[14]

Throughout his presentation, Smith objected to what he felt were Waggoner's heretical views. He spoke of the two covenants as "two stages, two dispensations" of the Abrahamic covenant. The first stage was fulfilled to the literal seed of Abraham when they inherited the promised land. The second stage would be fulfilled at the resurrection and the earth made new. Smith understood the old covenant as a contract or transaction the people made with God. They promised to keep the ten commandments and whatever else the Lord would add. The Lord then added the ceremonial law and the sanctuary service, "that sin might abound." But alas, the old covenant was faulty because "it was not able to carry out the matter to the final consummation." Why? Because "it did not have the right sacrifices—only the blood of animals." After the cross and the sacrifice of Christ, the new covenant was made, representing a new dispensation. Now the people were to enter into the same type of contract as under the old—promising to keep God's commandments. The reason the "old covenant could gender to bondage" in Paul's day was because "certain teachers had come down from Jerusalem troubling their minds and saying they must be circumcised." This was Paul's only point in his allegory in the book of Galatians chapter 4. Smith hoped his explanation would convince others of Waggoner's erroneous views.[15]

Over the next several days, Waggoner continued his presentations on the covenants and their relation to righteousness by faith. There was "much interruption," as objections and questions were raised for the sole purpose of proving his position wrong.[16] Dan Jones felt Waggoner deserved such treatment. "It is that disposition to crowd in and take advantage, that seems to be so manifest in both Dr. Waggoner and Eld. A. T. Jones that makes their labors unpleasant to some of the brethren here at Battle Creek, I think; and we can readily account for its being so." Dan Jones was sure that Jones and Waggoner had presented their "new theories… in our denominational schools and ministerial institutes, and run them through the sabbath-school lessons" without going through the brethren who had "done much to formulate the doctrines." This was "altogether out of place" and "hereafter more care would be taken that the sabbath-school lessons should be thoroughly examined and approved before being sent out all over the country."[17]

On February 24, R. C. Porter took up the subject of the covenants during one of the two-hour sessions. He was even less amiable than Smith, telling the ministers: "I hope to present something that I think is more in harmony with the truth on the point… which, it seems to me, is the better view." Porter, like Smith, saw that the "Abrahamic covenant embraced both the old and the new covenant." The "two covenants are but the means in the different ages for the carrying out" of God's plan—two dispensations. More than a half dozen times Porter reiterated this point, seeking to make a contrast with Waggoner's view. To R. C. Porter the old covenant did not differ from the new covenant, only as to the matter of time in which it was instigated. "Under every covenant the conditions must be the same: they must be obedience [*sic*], positive obedience." And besides, Porter stated, the "Lord promised the people" just as much help "under the old covenant" as under the new, for "it surely was not made unless there was help to enable man to keep the covenant." Porter also believed that promises made to Abraham were fulfilled in the old covenant to the children of Israel; God "accomplished all He designed to."[18]

Through all these arguments Porter was trying to establish that the old covenant: was based on time, was based on the mutual agreement of God and the people, was fulfilled to Abraham's literal seed, was done away with at the Cross, and was thus not a covenant that could be entered into under the new dispensation. It is clear that for Porter, Smith, and many other brethren, their biggest objection to Waggoner's views was his position that neither covenant represented a dispensation or time period during the plan of salvation, but rather the condition of men's hearts regardless of when they lived on earth, and second, that the old covenant was based on the promises of the people, whereas the new or everlasting covenant was based on the promises of God.[19]*

Waggoner believed that instead of responding in faith as Abraham their father had done, Israel had manifested pride and self–sufficiency, vainly promising "all that the Lord has spoken we will do" (Ex. 19:8). Thus God had come down on Sinai and spoke the ten commandments with thunder and lightning. This was primarily that schoolmaster, or added law which was to bring them to Christ. To this view the brethren could never concede, and for this reason they rose up in opposition against God's appointed messenger.

During the last week of February, the final presentation of the covenants was given. "At the close it was plain to be seen that there were two distinct views of the covenants as it had been presented,—one favoring the position that has been held in the past by our people… and another party in favor of the advanced views held by Dr. Waggoner." Although no official action was taken, Dan Jones hints that some sort of summary statement or resolution was made: "No expression was taken that would in any way draw the lines between the parties *stronger than necessary*." Dan Jones suggests the covenant question was then "dropped, and the school is going on with its regular work."[20] This hardly meant, however, that the issue had been resolved. A few days later, Dan Jones admitted "the investigation on the covenant question closed up with no better satisfaction than before it began."[21] In fact, Jones stated, "the result has not been to bring the brethren together and unite them in working for the upbuilding of the cause of God, but has rather been to create party spirit and party feelings, and to magnify the differences and views that existed between them."[22] Sad to say, Dan Jones himself was responsible to a large degree for that "party spirit" that was leading many of the younger ministers to reject Waggoner and the views he was presenting.

But what about Ellen White? What was her opinion on the covenants? Was it of any concern to her? If it was, why did she remain silent while Waggoner was presenting on the topic?

### Ellen White Takes Her Stand

During the later part of January and early February, Ellen White participated in the Ministerial Institute, speaking "every day, with one or two exceptions" for "three weeks."[23] However, during the two-week investigation of the covenants, we find her strangely silent. One reason for such silence was the investigations themselves. These two-hour classes on the covenants most likely took the place of the morning meeting where Ellen White usually spoke. But Ellen White herself gives the main reason for her silence: "I have been watching to see what course these men would take, how much light would come into their souls. I have been watching to see." It was her desire that the brethren recognize for themselves the light being presented. In fact, when Dan Jones came to her during the investigations and asked her opinion, she pointedly replied: "I will not tell you my opinion; my faith. Dig in the Bible. Sink the shaft of truth to find out what is truth." It was not because she was without an opinion on the subject that she refused to answer Jones' question, but because she wanted the brethren to accept the light based on their own study of the Bible. Besides, many of them doubted her inspiration and authority, and it would have done little good for her to declare her position prematurely.[24]

Ellen White was not in the dark on the subject of the covenants, nor about the opposition that was taking place: "while I have been keeping in silence, the Lord has been revealing night after night, the position of individual cases before me."[25] It was not long before the Lord urged her to give her testimony, and to ardently state: "No more will my lips be sealed."[26] When the covenant investigation ended during the last week of February, other meetings took their place, running "from half past seven to nine." Ellen White began attending the meetings, and speaking "quite freely."[27]

On Sabbath morning, March 1, Ellen White wrote solemn thoughts in her diary: "I have been shown that love for Christ and for God has well-nigh died out of our churches. And because we do not love God, we are lacking in love for one another." She wrote of the men "binding themselves together in unsanctified confederacies," framing "resolutions" and laying "plans that do not bear the endorsement of God."[28] In her Sabbath sermon, she preached on "Christ's riding into Jerusalem" which made a "solemn impression upon the full house." In the afternoon she spoke again, saying "just as straight things as God ever gave me to speak." On Sunday as she attended the morning meeting held in the east vestry of the Tabernacle, "there were but few" who attended. By midweek, however, the room was well filled with ministers and other brethren and sisters from Battle Creek; the number swelling to over three hundred.[29]*

All week Ellen White spoke very directly with the brethren gathered before her. She found it a "difficult problem" to know how to deal with their "strong spirits."[30]* On Friday morning, March 7, she "went into the ministers' meeting" with her soul "greatly distressed." In the night season her soul had been in "agony" as the Lord had once again "laid it all open again before me, just the influence that was at work, and just where it would lead." She "did not know what to expect, or how long this thing was going to persevere." She reminded the large group of ministers how she had warned them after Minneapolis "that every one of them that laid that hardness into their hearts... they never would see a ray of light till they confessed it."[31] That was exactly what was taking place. On Sabbath morning, still burdened with what the Lord had revealed to her the day before, Ellen White wrote once again to Uriah Smith. She knew the effect he was having upon others and could not let him go on oblivious to the fact:

> Night before last, the Lord opened many things to my mind. It was plainly revealed what your influence has been, what it was at Minneapolis. ... You will not only have in the day of final accounts to meet your own course of action but the result of your influence upon other minds. You have refused my testimonies... you have labored to make them of none effect as did Korah, Dathan and Abiram. ...

> You have strengthened the hands and minds of such men as Larson, Porter, Dan Jones, Eldridge and Morrison and Nicola and a vast number through them. All quote you, and the enemy of righteousness looks on pleased. ...

> After your course of action has unsettled the minds and faith in the testimonies, what have you gained? If you should recover your faith, how can you remove the impressions of unbelief you have sown in other minds? Do not labor so hard to do the very work Satan is doing. This work was done in Minneapolis. Satan triumphed. This work has been done here [too].[32]

As Ellen White continued to write, she made it clear where she stood on the covenant question. It was more than just her own opinion, for it had been revealed to her from heaven itself. She described Waggoner's presentations of the covenants as "true light," and Smith's as a twisting of the Scriptures:[33]*

> Night before last I was shown that evidences in regard to the covenants were clear and convincing. Yourself, Brother Dan Jones, Brother Porter and others

are spending your investigative powers for naught to produce a position on the covenants to vary from the position that Brother Waggoner has presented, when had you received the true light which shineth, you would have not imitated or gone over the same manner of interpretation and misconstruing the Scriptures as did the Jews. What made them so zealous? Why did they hang on the words of Christ? Why did spies follow him to mark His words that they could repeat and misinterpret and twist in a way to mean that which their own unsanctified minds would make them to mean? In this way, they deceived the people. They made false issues. ...

The covenant question is a clear question and would be received by every candid, unprejudiced mind, but I was brought where the Lord gave me an insight into this matter. You have turned from plain light because you were afraid that the law question in Galatians would have to be accepted. As to the law in Galatians, I have no burden and never have had and know Brother Smith, Porter, [Dan] Jones or anyone will never be prepared to receive light... until every one of you are converted. ...

I would not now depend upon your knowledge or interpretation of Scriptures. ... If you turn from one ray of light fearing it will necessitate an acceptance of positions you do not wish to receive, that light becomes to you darkness.[34]

Later that morning E. J. Waggoner gave "a most powerful discourse" to all those gathered in the Battle Creek Tabernacle. Ellen White heard from "many who were present, and their testimony was unanimous that God spoke through him." In the afternoon, "Elders Olsen and Waggoner led the meeting" held in the office chapel where a "large number were present." Ellen White rose up to speak and "all knew that the Spirit and power of God were upon" her. She spoke with "earnestness and decision," repeating some of the same things she had written to Uriah Smith earlier that day.[35] She wanted everyone to know where she stood on the covenant question and how she viewed it in connection with the third angel's message:

[T]he light that came to me night before last laid it all open again before me, just the influence that was at work, and just where it would lead. I want to tell you brethren, whoever you are, I want to tell you, that you are just going over the very same ground that they went over in the days of Christ. You have had their experience; But God deliver us from having the come-out-of-it as they had. ... May God have mercy upon your souls, because you need it. You have stood right in the way of God. The earth is to be lighted with His glory, and if you stand where you stand today, you might just as quick say that the Spirit of God was the spirit of the devil. You have said it now in your actions, in your attitudes, that it is the spirit of the devil. ...

Why do you not hear the words of Christ that are presented to you? Why will you have darkness? They are so afraid to see that there is another ray of light. ... Do not hang on to Brother Smith. In the name of God, I tell you, he is not in the light. He has not been in the light since he was at Minneapolis. ... [Y]ou have tried in every way to resist the Spirit of God. May God have compassion on your souls. ...

But if Jesus, when He was upon earth, with all His power and miracles could not break down that prejudice that was in the heart of the people, what can we do?... Let the truth of God come into your hearts; open the door. Now I tell you here before God, that the covenant question, as it has been presented, is the truth.[36]* It is the light. In clear lines it has been laid before me. And those who have been resisting light, I ask you whether they have been working for God, or for the devil. It is the clear light of heaven, and it means much to us. It means to show us that you cannot depend upon your own smartness and your criticism, but you must hang your helpless soul upon Jesus Christ, and upon Him alone. God help you to see. God help you to understand.[37]

Following Ellen White's earnest appeal, "many bore testimony and some confessions were made; but," according to Ellen White, "the break was not complete, and we did not have that complete victory I desired." Sunday morning Ellen White spoke again, pouring out her "testimony in warnings, reproof, and encouragement."[38] She started the meeting by reading the story of Pentecost from the book of Acts. Then, speaking to the leaders before her, she readily exclaimed: "Now, brethren, the blessing that is here spoken of we may receive when we come to God with our whole heart, when we empty it of every kind of prejudice and all this doubting and unbelief; then we can expect the Spirit of God." Ellen White reminded her listeners of Jesus' dedication in the temple while He was yet an infant. The priest "that was there officiating did not know Him," but Simeon "recognized Him because he was where he could discern spiritual things... he recognized the Spirit of God." In one of her strongest appeals, Ellen White cautioned the brethren that in their present condition they were incapable of recognizing the movings of the Spirit, and of the fourth angel spoken of in Revelation chapter 18:

And how is it with us individually? We know that the Spirit of God has been with us. We know that it has been with us time and again in the meetings. We have not a doubt but that the Lord was with Elder Waggoner as he spoke yesterday.[39]* We have not a doubt of that. I have not a doubt that the power of God in rich measure was hanging over us, and everything was light in the Lord to me yesterday afternoon in the minister's meeting. Now, if there had been a throwing open the door of the heart and letting Jesus in, we would have had a precious season there yesterday. I have not a doubt of it.

If we place ourselves in a position that we will not recognize the light God sends or His messages to us, then we are in danger of sinning against the Holy Ghost. Then [it is dangerous] for us to turn and see if we can find some little thing that is done that we can hang some of our doubts upon and begin to question! The question is, has God sent the truth? Has God raised up these men to proclaim the truth? I say, yes, *God has sent men to bring us the truth that we should not have had unless God had sent somebody to bring it to us.* God has let me have a light of what His Spirit is, and therefore I accept it, and I no more dare to lift my hand against these persons, because it would be against Jesus Christ, who is to be recognized in His messengers.

Now, brethren, God wants us to take our position with the man that carries the lantern; we want to take our position where the light is, and where God has given the trumpet a certain sound. … We have been in perplexity, and we have been in doubt, and the churches are ready to die. But now here we read: "And after these things I saw another angel come down from heaven, having great power; and the earth was lightened with his glory. …" Well now, how are we going to know anything about that message if we are not in a position to recognize anything of the light of heaven when it comes to us? And we will just as soon pick up the darkest deception when it comes to us from somebody that agrees with us. … [T]hat is just the work that has been going on here ever since the meeting at Minneapolis. Because God sends a message in His name that does not agree with your ideas, therefore [you conclude] it cannot be a message from God.[40]

## *Backbone of Rebellion is Broken*

Ellen White's strong appeals were not without effect. Many began to see the whole situation in a different light and realized that they had been wrongly influenced. Ellen White felt that "this had been the hardest, long and persistent resistance" she had ever had. "Some confessions were made and quite a number who had been in darkness made confessions of their finding Jesus and being free in the Lord." More freedom was coming into the meetings and the darkness was "no longer a controlling element." Yet Ellen White hoped for "more of God's Spirit," and to see "these ministers free in the Lord and joyful in their God."[41]

Monday, March 10, brought Ellen White more good news that she shared with her son W. C. White: "I am much pleased to learn that Professor Prescott is giving the same lessons in his class to the students that Brother Waggoner has been giving. He is presenting the covenants. John [Froom] thinks it is presented in a clear and convincing manner. Since I made the statement last Sabbath that the view of the covenants as it had been taught by Brother Waggoner was truth, it seems that great relief has come to many minds. I am inclined to think Brother Prescott receives the testimony, although he was not present when I made this statement. I thought it time to take my position, and I am glad that the Lord urged me to give the testimony that I did."

Ellen White also felt she no longer carried the load of not being able to express herself freely: "I am free and talk as the Spirit of God giveth me utterance." She stated that as a result, the "men who have held things have no power now." The "largest number present" were now receiving her testimony. There were also many others who "with tears confessed" how tried they felt "because they could not have the privilege of listening to Elder Waggoner's teaching without so much interruption." Thus, those who had been "shedding darkness on the class" began to see the results of their rebellion.[42]

The following day, Ellen White shared again with the brethren. She told them how the believers had to meet with "prejudice and with ridicule and with sneers and with criticism" in 1844, and this was "the very same character that we have had to meet here in this conference." Thus it was their "duty—without revealing the spirit that the churches manifested, which was so unlike Christ"—to go to the Word of God for themselves. "The great error with churches in all ages has been to reach a certain point in their understanding of Bible truth and there stop. ... and they refuse light." Yet God had "greater light," "more or increased light" that would "shine in greater clearness and more abundantly upon all who have improved the light given." They were to "expect light" to "continue to shine from the Word of God," and to "reveal more and more distinctly the truth as it is in Jesus."[43]

While encouraging deeper Bible study, Ellen White also warned that "as a people we are certainly in great danger… of considering our ideas, because long cherished, to be Bible doctrines and on every point infallible, and measuring everyone by the rule of our interpretation of Bible truth. This is our danger, and this would be the greatest evil that could ever come to us as a people." The tendency to put "entire dependence upon the leaders" and not study for oneself, was after the manner of the "church of Rome." With solemn earnestness Ellen White warned of the results of such a stance:

> We have seen in our experience that when the Lord sends rays of light from the open door of the sanctuary to His people, Satan stirs up the minds of many. But the end is not yet. There will be those who will resist the light and crowd down those whom God has made His channels to communicate light. … The watchmen have not kept pace with the opening providence of God, and the real heaven-sent message and messengers are scorned.
>
> There will go from this meeting men who claim to know the truth who are gathering about their souls the garments not woven in the loom of heaven. The spirit that they have received here will be carried with them. I tremble for the future of our cause. Those who do not in this place yield to the evidence God has given will war against their brethren whom God is using. They will make it very hard. … These men will have opportunities to be convinced that they have been warring against the Holy Spirit of God. Some will be convinced; others will hold firmly their own spirit. They will not die to self and let the Lord Jesus come into their hearts. They will be more and still more deceived until they cannot discern truth and righteousness. They will, under another spirit, seek to place upon the work a mold that God shall not approve; and they will endeavor to act out the attributes of Satan in assuming control of human minds and thus control the work and cause of God.[44]

Following Ellen White's morning talk many testimonies were given and confessions made. Brother Larsen "confessed that his feelings had not been right." Brother Porter, who had opposed Waggoner during the covenant investigation, stood "all broken up so that he could say nothing for a few moments." He confessed the wrong he had done Ellen White and Elder Waggoner, and humbly asked them "to forgive him." Brother Prescott "wept like a baby when Brother L[arsen] and P[orter] were making their confessions." In fact, "the whole room was sobbing and praising God for there was a revealing of His power." Men "so strong and high-headed" began to feel that they had been "working against the Spirit of God." At this, Ellen White could write to W. C. White that "the backbone of the rebellion is broken *in those who have come in from other places.*"[45]* God was indeed seeking to pour out His Spirit on a languishing church. Oh, that all would have recognized it and confessed.

## *Two Special Meetings*

On Wednesday afternoon, March 12, Ellen White called for a "meeting of the prominent ones." Recognizing that the Holy Spirit was working on many hearts, Ellen White wanted the key leaders in Battle Creek to meet together and seek to clear up the controversy that had existed since Minneapolis. For the first time, Ellen White and E. J. Waggoner would be able to give an answer to many of the false accusations that had been afloat since before the Minneapolis Conference. After prayer, Ellen White "said that Brother Waggoner had some things to say" which she "wished them to hear, which would disabuse some minds." Waggoner, with the help of C. H. Jones (manager of Pacific Press and president of the International Sabbath School Assn.), was able to take up "the Sabbath School lessons," explaining that nothing underhanded had been done in introducing his views on the covenants. He explained that he had been asked by the General Conference to rewrite the two lessons that were missing, but upon examination he found that he would have to rewrite several of the other lessons as well. None of this was done, however, without obtaining permission from the Sabbath School Association. Waggoner made it clear that at every step he had run the lessons through the proper channels, and that the lessons were not published without first receiving the approval of all the committee members, including Eld. Smith. All had "liberty to speak as they saw fit, asking any questions. All these things seemed satisfactory." Ellen White felt that Waggoner "spoke well," leaving a "favorable impression… upon minds, and there was no rising up, no spirit of opposition" to what he had to say.[46]*

Ellen White then shared what her experience was before and during the Minneapolis Conference, and how she had labored "to get the messengers and message to have a fair chance." She "told freely" of the "prejudice existing in minds," and what the Lord had revealed to her during that time. She spoke of how her "testimony had been made of none effect" since Minneapolis, and how men had not even come for an interview to see if the accusations were correct. She asked how Uriah Smith could treat her as he did; what was the cause for all this? "It was finally simmered down to this—that a letter had come from California to Brother Butler, telling them that plans were all made to drive the law in Galatians." This was "met and explained" by herself and Waggoner; "there were no plans laid."[47]

The meeting, which lasted for several hours, "was very much a success." Ellen White thought, "those who had made so much out of so very little, were much surprised at the outcome or showing up of the matter." With all this progress, however, Ellen White felt "almost hopeless in reference to expecting a general breaking up of the soul under the influence of the Spirit and power of God." She was sick and exhausted for the remainder of the week. When asked to speak on Sabbath, she refused, for she "had not the strength." She sent word to Dan Jones to have Waggoner speak, and with a "little reluctance" he was "finally invited." Waggoner "gave a most precious discourse on the message to the Laodicean church,—just what was needed. This was another rich blessing to the church."

In the afternoon "another meeting was held in the office chapel." Sick as she was, Ellen White attended and spoke up several times. Many shared their testimonies, "but there was no decided break." Brother Porter talked, "but was not free." Ellen White reminded them that when "the Lord sends us light and food that all the churches need, we may well expect that the enemy of all righteousness will do his utmost to prevent that light coming in its native heavenly bearings to the people." Those whose minds were "full of unbelief and doubts" Satan would use to "intercept the light that God means shall come to His chosen ones."[48]

On Sunday morning, March 16, "weary and almost discouraged," Ellen White ventured into the meeting. When it was about to close she "made some very close remarks. I kept before them what they had done to make of none effect that which the Lord was trying to do and why. The law in Galatians was their only plea." After such a talk, R. C. Porter "made humble confession with tears," telling Ellen White, "we will sustain you as you go forth to your trying work." Would he live up to his word? [49]

In another meeting that same day, Ellen White continued her appeal. She repeated many of the same warnings. Unless true confessions were made "everyone who has taken a position similar to the one they took in Minneapolis would go into the darkest unbelief." This would place them "where there is no reserve power that God has to reach them with. Every arrow in His quiver is exhausted." In every meeting that she attended she "felt that there is a pressure of unbelief." She could go among those that had "never heard of the truth and their hearts are more susceptible than those that have been in the truth." When God "manifests His power as He has manifested it," she declared, "it is very nigh unto the sin of the Holy Ghost to disbelieve it":

> If ever a people needed to be removed, it is those that took their position in Minneapolis at that time on the wrong side. …

> Let no soul go out from here with darkness, for he will be a body of darkness wherever he goes. He scatters the seeds of darkness everywhere. He carries all these seeds and he begins to sow them, and it unsettles the confidence of the people in the very truths that God wants to come to His people. …

> I know that He has a blessing for us. He had it at Minneapolis, and He had it for us at the time of the General Conference here [1889]. But there was no reception. …

> It is something beyond anything I ever saw in all my experience since I first started in the work. The people of God who have had light and evidences have stood where God would not let His blessing fall upon them. In the chapel hall [yesterday] the power of God was all ready to fall upon us. I felt for a little time as though I could look right into glory; but the spirit that was there drove it away. …

> One brother thinks that Sister White doesn't understand her own testimonies. Heard that in Minneapolis. Why? Because the brethren did not agree with

them. Well, there are some things that I understand. I understand enough to acknowledge the Spirit of God and to follow the voice of the Shepherd. I understand that much.[50]

In a letter to Uriah Smith, Ellen White confirmed her earlier statement. In the "meeting on the Sabbath in the office chapel… the Spirit of the Lord came nigh to us. Christ knocked for entrance but no room was made for Him, the door was not opened and the light of His glory, so nigh, was withdrawn."[51] Thus, exactly as had happened at the 1888 and 1889 General Conference, the outpouring of the Holy Spirit had been pushed away.

Ellen White wanted "to know why the enemy is having such power upon human minds as he has here." She wanted to know why the brethren had "been standing here and questioning, and just about ready to give up the Testimonies." She asked that the leading brethren might "assemble again… and if anything can be taken out of the way, God help us to do it!"[52] Because A. T. Jones was unable to attend the first special meeting, having been in Tennessee, Ellen White wanted him to have an opportunity to answer "all the objections that have been created." She wanted to get the "snags out of the way and make those who have talked of these things bury them if possible, never to be resurrected."[53]*

On Wednesday, March 19, the second special meeting was held. A. T. Jones "talked very plainly, yet tenderly in regard to their crediting hearsay and not, in brotherly love, taking the matter to the one talked about." Earlier in the ministerial meetings, Uriah Smith had responded to Ellen White's "letter of appeal by writing [her] a letter accusing Elder Jones of tearing up the pillars of our faith." A. T. Jones' explanation revealed that Uriah Smith had "accused him wrongfully."[54] Dan Jones was "surprised to see some things that look inexplicable, vanish away into thin air when a few explanations were made. Some reports that had gone out in reference to points Eld. [A. T.] Jones had taught here in the school, which was supposed to rest on indisputable evidence, all vanished away until there was nothing at all of it. The reports proved to be utterly false."[55] Unfortunately, Uriah Smith did not confess the wrong he had committed nor seek to revoke the false rumors he had spread around; it is much easier to tell a lie about someone than it is to retract it.

Ellen White then spoke to the brethren as straight as she knew how. Writing her son later that day she stated: "Willie, I talked as they had never heard me talk before. I went over again the transactions at Minneapolis and since that time." It was, she exclaimed, "as solemn a meeting as I had ever seen." Ellen White "addressed plain remarks to Elder Smith," exclaiming that although "it was not surprising" that the brethren "who had known but little of the work the Lord had given [her] to do should have temptations," but Elder Smith "was not excusable." She "had reason to expect [her] brethren would act like sensible men, weigh evidence, give credence to evidence, and not turn aside from light and facts of truth and give credence to tidbits of hearsay and suppositions."

As a result of this meeting and the explanations given, Ellen White could declare: "the whole atmosphere is changed." Many were subdued, realizing how foolish their opposition had been. At last a break had come, and the final week of the Institute did indeed exhibit a different spirit.[56]

Tired and exhausted, Ellen White left Battle Creek before the last weekend of the Institute. Having "spoken for the last time" she felt her "duty was discharged." She "had no more to say to the church or to [her] ministering brethren."[57] As she headed for Chicago and then Colorado before returning to California, she hoped that the progress made in the final days of the Institute would continue moving forward. Unfortunately that hope was never realized.

# CHAPTER 14 FOOTNOTES

1.  Dan T. Jones to E. W. Farnsworth, Feb. 14, 1890, emphasis supplied, archives of the General Conference of Seventh-day Adventists. For other detailed narratives of the covenants topic, see: Paul E. Penno, *Calvary at Sinai*, especially chapters 12 through 17; Clinton Wahlen, *Selected Aspects of Ellet J. Waggoner's Eschatology and Their Relation to His Understanding of Righteousness by Faith, 1882-1895*, pp. 107-111, 162-177; Robert Van Ornam, *The Doctrine of the Everlasting Covenant in the Writings of Ellet J. Waggoner*.

2.  E. J. Waggoner, "The Two Covenants," Bible Readings for the Home Circle (1889); Sabbath School Lessons on the Letter to the Hebrews, for Senior Classes, January 4 to March 29, 1890. See also chapter 12.

3.  Dan Jones to S. N. Haskell, [March] 1890, archives of the General Conference of Seventh-day Adventists. At this point in time, we have not been able to obtain copies of Waggoner's presentations at the 1890 Ministerial Institute. However, the fact that Uriah Smith and R. C. Porter's presentations were recorded leads one to believe that Waggoner's were probably recorded as well. Nonetheless, in the absence of Waggoner's presentations, it is still clear from other available materials what he believed regarding the covenants and with which points the brethren disagreed with him.

4.  Dan T. Jones to E. W. Farnsworth, Feb. 18, 1890, archives of the General Conference of Seventh-day Adventists.

5.  Dan T. Jones to R. A. Underwood, Feb. 18, 1890, archives of the General Conference of Seventh-day Adventists.

6.  Uriah Smith, "Editorial Note," *Review and Herald*, Jan. 28, 1890, p. 64.

7.  Uriah Smith to Ellen White, Feb. 17, 1890; in *Manuscripts and Memories*, p. 156.

8.  Smith felt he was allowing others freedom to choose which position they should take while Jones, he felt, was using coercion and rash statements to promote his "erroneous" views. Ellen White later proved that Jones never made such a rash statement and that Smith's suppositions were false. See footnote 54 and 55, and Chapter 13, footnote 20.

9.  *Ibid.*, pp. 152-155.

10. *Ibid.*, pp. 154-157.

11. Ellen G. White, "Repentance the Gift of God," *Review and Herald*, April 1, 1890, p. 193.

12. Uriah Smith to Ellen White, Feb. 17, 1890; in *Manuscripts and Memories*, p. 156-157.

13. Ellen G. White to W. C. White, Letter 83, March 13, 1890, and Ellen G. White to Uriah Smith, Letter 73, Nov. 25, 1890; in *1888 Materials*, pp. 627, 734. See also footnote 8.

14. "Remarks of Eld. Uriah Smith, Bible School," Feb. 19, 1890, archives of the General Conference of Seventh-day Adventists.

15. *Ibid*.

16. Ellen G. White to W. C. White, Letter 30, March 10, 1890, in *1888 Materials*, p. 624.

17. Dan Jones to C. H. Jones, [Feb.] 1890, archives of the General Conference of Seventh-day Adventists.

18. "Remarks of Eld. R. C. Porter at the Ministers' Bible School," Feb. 24, 1890, archives of the General Conference of Seventh-day Adventists.

19. The very same arguments and objections brought against Jones and Waggoner over a hundred and twenty years ago are being repeated today. See: Ken LeBrun, *Two Covenants or One?* (unpublished manuscript, n.d.); Biblical Research Institute to Ken LeBrun, March 15, 1988.

20. Dan Jones to S. N. Haskell, [March], 1890, emphasis supplied, archives of the General Conference of Seventh-day Adventists.

21. Dan Jones to R. M. Kilgore, March 16, 1890, archives of the General Conference of Seventh-day Adventists.

22. Dan Jones to J. D. Pegg, March 17, 1890, archives of the General Conference of Seventh-day Adventists.

23. Ellen G. White Manuscript 22, "Diary Entries," Feb. 8, 1890; in *1888 Materials*, p. 579.

24. Ellen G. White Manuscript 4, "Sermon," March 8, 1890; in *1888 Materials*, p. 597.

25. *Ibid*.

26. Ellen G. White to W. C. White, Letter 30, March 10, 1890; in *1888 Materials*, p. 623.

27. Dan T. Jones to R. A. Underwood, March 14, 1890, and Dan T. Jones to R. M. Kilgore, March 16, 1890, archives of the General Conference of Seventh-day Adventists.

28. Ellen G. White Manuscript 22, "Diary Entries," March 1, 1890; in *1888 Materials*, pp. 580-581.

29. Ellen G. White to W. C. White, Letter 80, March 7, 1890; in *1888 Materials*, pp. 590-592. Dan Jones reported in the *Review* that Eld. Olsen "took charge" of the early morning meetings where Ellen White "bore her testimony." "As the news of the good meetings went out, many came in from the Battle Creek church, the office, the college,

and the sanitarium, till the east vestry of the Tabernacle, which will seat about 300, was filled to overflowing each morning" (Dan. T. Jones "The Work in Battle Creek," *Review and Herald*, April 1, 1890, pp. 204-205. See also O. A. Olsen, "The Ministers' School," *Review and Herald*, April 1, 1890, pp. 200-201; and Dan T. Jones to R. A. Underwood, March 14, 1890).

30. Ellen G. White to W. C. White, Letter 80, March 7, 1890; in *1888 Materials*, pp. 591. Early in the week when Ellen White was "making an illustration very pointed, [Matthew] Larson [had] on the broad grin." She asked him twice "the reason of such demonstrations. He finally said it was because he appreciated the illustration." Ellen White responded: "'Very well... If it fits you, take it and I hope all will do this.'" A couple days later Ellen White received a letter from Larson in which he asked her "to set him right before the people, because of [her] sharp rebuke—that is, confess [she] had wronged him." Larson was a minister from Iowa, a debater who turned "light into darkness." Ellen White stated that she was afraid of him, for he "put a false interpretation upon" her words (*1888 Materials*, pp. 591, 594). He continued to have a hatred for Jones and Waggoner and the message of the covenants they taught (A. G. Daniells to W. C. White, April 14, 1902; in *Manuscripts and Memories*, p. 320). After Ellen White's death, Larson wrote a pamphlet against Jones and Waggoner and the position on covenants presented in Waggoner's *Glad Tidings* (1900). As was his habit, Larson used Ellen White's writings, putting a "false interpretation upon" them, to try to prove Jones' and Waggoner's position wrong (*The Law in Galatians: Is it the Moral Law?* [n.p. 1919]; E. A. Jones to R. L. Odom, Jan. 5, 1961).

31. Ellen G. White Manuscript 4, "Sermon," March 8, 1890; in *1888 Materials*, p. 593.

32. Ellen G. White to Uriah Smith, Letter 59, March 8, 1890; in *1888 Materials*, pp. 599, 604-605.

33. This point should not be overlooked. Jones and Waggoner encouraged people to go to their Bibles and find the very truths that they were presenting. Ellen White not only supported their emphasis on the Bible, but *also the truths presented from the Bible*. The opposition Jones and Waggoner received was not because they presented from the Bible, but because *what* they presented differed from that of the brethren. The same kind of opposition against the *message* of Jones and Waggoner exists today: "We must always remember that God's 1888 spokesmen got their message from the Word. *The imperative is not to fixate on the words of Jones and Waggoner, but on those of Jesus and the apostles.* Jones and Waggoner had error mixed in their message, but the Bible is always a safe guide" (George R. Knight, *From 1888 to Apostasy*, p. 69, emphasis in original). Although we would not question that the Bible is a safe guide, it is also true that Jones and Waggoner were sent with a message *from* the Bible. Ellen White supported that message. Those who rejected it then, and now, claim their message was not in line with the Bible. See also, Chapter 13, footnote 23.

34. Ellen G. White to Uriah Smith, Letter 59, March 8, 1890; in *1888 Materials*, pp. 604-605.

35. Ellen G. White to W. C. White, Letter 82, March 9, 1890; in *1888 Materials*, p. 617.

36. In a letter to W. C. White the following day, Ellen White said she had told the brethren "yesterday that the position of the covenants I believed as presented in my Volume I. If that was Dr. Waggoner's position then he had the truth" (*Ibid.*, p. 617). This raises an interesting question. *Spirit of Prophecy*, Volume I, was originally published in 1870, but made no mention of or differentiation between the old and new covenants. In 1886, Ellen White had begun the task of enlarging Volume I, and adapting it for the "reading of the general public" (Arthur L. White, *The Lonely Years*, p. 435). In early 1887, however, she turned her attention to *Spirit of Prophecy*, Volume 4, which was published in 1888 under the title, *The Great Controversy*. It was not until after the 1889 General Conference session that she once again took up the work of revising Volume I, which she continued during the Ministerial Institute. Four days after she publicly expressed her support of Waggoner's view on the covenants, she wrote to W. C. White stating simply: "I think the change in Volume I will be well" (Letter 83, March 13, 1890; in *1888 Materials*, p. 635). On June 21, she wrote to O. A. Olsen: "Vol. 1 is coming out nearly completed, after a long tedious delay for want of corrections" (Letter 115; in *1888 Materials*, p. 680). It was not until August 26 that the *Review and Herald* announced the availability of the new edition titled *Patriarchs and Prophets*. Among the many changes found in the revision was an eleven page chapter "The Law and the Covenants," which presented the covenants as Waggoner had presented them. This led many to question the new edition, one brother even asking Ellen White if a particular statement was "dictated by the Spirit of inspiration or has the idea been *suggested* by investigation?" (E. P. Dexter to Ellen G. White, March 11, 1891, emphasis supplied). The question arises, when did Ellen White add the view of the covenants? Was it after she heard Waggoner present on the subject and received confirmation from God on March 7, 1890? This would be in harmony with how the Lord used her in the early years when landmarks were laid (See: Herbert E. Douglass, *Messenger of the Lord*, Review and Herald 1998, pp. 156-158). Following is a summary of Ellen White's view on the covenants as found in *Patriarchs and Prophets*, chapter 32, "The Law and the Covenants": "As the Bible presents two laws, one changeless and eternal, the other provisional and temporary, so there are two covenants. The covenant of grace was first made with man in Eden. ... This same covenant was renewed to Abraham in the promise, 'In thy seed shall all the nations of the earth be blessed.' Genesis 22:18. This promise pointed to Christ. So Abraham understood it (see Galatians 3:8, 16), and he trusted in Christ for the forgiveness of sins. It was this faith that was accounted unto him for

righteousness. ... And the Lord declared to him, 'I will establish My covenant between Me and thee and thy seed after thee in their generations, for an everlasting covenant, to be a God unto thee and to thy seed after thee.' Genesis 17:7. ... Though this covenant was made with Adam and renewed to Abraham, it could not be ratified until the death of Christ. It had existed by the promise of God since the first intimation of redemption had been given; it had been accepted by faith; yet when ratified by Christ, it is called a new covenant. The law of God was the basis of this covenant, which was simply an arrangement for bringing men again into harmony with the divine will, placing them where they could obey God's law. Another compact—called in Scripture the 'old' covenant—was formed between God and Israel at Sinai, and was then ratified by the blood of a sacrifice. The Abrahamic covenant was ratified by the blood of Christ, and it is called the 'second,' or 'new,' covenant, because the blood by which it was sealed was shed after the blood of the first [or old] covenant. That the new covenant was valid in the days of Abraham is evident from the fact that it was then confirmed both by the promise and by the oath of God—the 'two immutable things, in which it was impossible for God to lie.' Hebrews 6:18. But if the Abrahamic covenant contained the promise of redemption, why was another covenant formed at Sinai? In their bondage the people had to a great extent lost the knowledge of God and of the principles of the Abrahamic covenant. In delivering them from Egypt, God sought to reveal to them His power and His mercy, that they might be led to love and trust Him. He brought them down to the Red Sea—where, pursued by the Egyptians, escape seemed impossible—that they might realize their utter helplessness, their need of divine aid; and then He wrought deliverance for them. Thus they were filled with love and gratitude to God and with confidence in His power to help them. He had bound them to Himself as their deliverer from temporal bondage. But there was a still greater truth to be impressed upon their minds. Living in the midst of idolatry and corruption, they had no true conception of the holiness of God, of the exceeding sinfulness of their own hearts, their utter inability, in themselves, to render obedience to God's law, and their need of a Saviour. All this they must be taught. ... The people did not realize the sinfulness of their own hearts, and that without Christ it was impossible for them to keep God's law; and they readily entered into covenant with God. Feeling that they were able to establish their own righteousness, they declared, 'All that the Lord hath said will we do, and be obedient.' Exodus 24:7. ... [A]nd yet only a few weeks passed before they broke their covenant with God, and bowed down to worship a graven image. They could not hope for the favor of God through a covenant which they had broken; and now, seeing their sinfulness and their need of pardon, they were brought to feel their need of the Saviour revealed in the Abrahamic covenant and shadowed forth in the sacrificial offerings. Now by faith and love they were bound to God as their deliverer from the bondage of sin. Now they were prepared to appreciate the blessings of the new covenant. The terms of the 'old covenant' were, Obey and live: 'If a man do, he shall even live in them' (Ezekiel 20:11; Leviticus 18:5); but 'cursed be he that confirmeth not all the words of this law to do them.' Deuteronomy 27:26. The 'new covenant' was established upon 'better promises'—the promise of forgiveness of sins and of the grace of God to renew the heart and bring it into harmony with the principles of God's law. 'This shall be the covenant that I will make with the house of Israel; After those days, saith the Lord, *I will put my law* in their inward parts, *and write it in their hearts.* … I will *forgive* their iniquity, and will remember their sin no more.' Jeremiah 31:33, 34. The same law that was engraved upon the tables of stone is written by the Holy Spirit upon the tables of the heart. Instead of going about to establish our own righteousness we accept the righteousness of Christ. His blood atones for our sins. His obedience is accepted for us. Then the heart renewed by the Holy Spirit will bring forth 'the fruits of the Spirit.' Through the grace of Christ we shall live in obedience to the law of God written upon our hearts. Having the Spirit of Christ, we shall walk even as He walked. Through the prophet He declared of Himself, 'I delight to do Thy will, O My God: yea, Thy law is within My heart.' Psalm 40:8. … The apostle Paul clearly presents the relation between faith and the law under the new covenant. He says: 'Being *justified by faith*, we have peace with God through our Lord Jesus Christ.' 'Do we then make void the law through faith? God forbid: yea, we establish the law.' 'For what the law could not do, in that it was weak through the flesh'—it could not justify man, because in his sinful nature he could not keep the law—'God sending His own Son in the likeness of sinful flesh, and for sin, condemned sin in the flesh: that *the righteousness of the law* might be fulfilled in us, who walk not after the flesh, but after the Spirit.' Romans 5:1, 3:31, 8:3, 4" (*Patriarchs and Prophets*, pp. 370-373, emphasis in original).

37. Ellen G. White Manuscript 4, "Sermon," March 8, 1890; in *1888 Materials*, pp. 593-597.

38. Ellen G. White to W. C. White, Letter 82, March 9, 1890; in *1888 Materials*, p. 617.

39. The manifestation of the Spirit of God at that meeting made an impression on many minds that never was effaced. G. B. Starr, Luther Warren, Dr. D. H. Kress, and Dr. John E. Froom all remembered the event: Ellen White "declared that an angel of God stood at Brother Waggoner's side that morning as he presented the 'message of truth'" (Quoted in LeRoy E. Froom, *Movement of Destiny*, p. 263). Dr. Kress remembered that while presenting "Waggoner broke down and wept. Sister White, who was present, followed him with some remarks after he took his seat. She began by saying, 'The Spirit of God rested upon Elder Waggoner while he was speaking,' and then she gave her message. … It is impossible to describe the spirit which rested upon us" (Daniel H. Kress, *Under the Guiding Hand*, p. 113).

40. Ellen G. White Manuscript 2, March 9, 1890; in *1888 Materials*, pp. 606-609, emphasis supplied.

41. Ellen G. White to W. A. Colcord, Letter 60, March 10, 1890, and Ellen G. White to W. C. White, Letter 30, March 10, 1890; in *1888 Materials*, pp. 620, 622.

42. Ellen G. White to W. C. White, Letter 30, March 10, 1890; in *1888 Materials*, pp. 623-624.

43. Ellen G. White Manuscript 37, "Light in God's Word," n.d. 1890; in *1888 Materials*, pp. 830, 826-827.

44. *Ibid.*, pp. 830-831.

45. Ellen G. White to W. C. White, Letter 30, March 10, 1890; in *1888 Materials*, pp. 625-626, emphasis supplied. We must not misinterpret Ellen White's statement. She saw that the backbone of rebellion was broken up "in those who have come in from other places." The opposition no longer had a monopoly upon the entire gathering at the Ministerial Institute. But this in no way stopped the opposition against Jones and Waggoner. As we will see in the chapters ahead, many of those who confessed, including Larsen and Porter, were found once again fighting against the light. Many of the confessions made were in regard to the validity of Ellen White's testimonies. In the same way, Israel confessed for rebelling against the twelve spies on the borders of Canaan, yet they were unchanged in heart. Likewise, many at the Ministerial Institute confessed that they were in the wrong but did not abandon their rebellious course. The tendency of modern historians has been to quote Ellen White's statement of the "backbone of rebellion" being broken, as proof that opposition to that message soon ceased: "[I]t must be evident to the reader that within a few months or a few years of the Minneapolis meeting, the majority of the persons concerned in the opposition to the light of righteousness by faith repented of their wrong course and took their stand for truth and right" (A. V. Olson, *Through Crisis to Victory*, pp. 71, 104-112). George Knight states: "With the alleged California conspiracy removed as an issue, Ellen White began to think about new work and plans. On March 19, O. A. Olsen... surmised that she would soon be sailing for [Australia] now that the back bone of the conspiracy theory was broken" (*Angry Saints*, p. 92. See also: A. L White, *The Lonely Years*, p. 456; *From 1888 to Apostasy*, p. 52). But history records a different and more accurate view, as we shall see in the chapters ahead. We summarize here by quoting from A. T. Jones, who said that the tide was turned "with the people, and apparently with most of the leading men. But this later was only apparent; it was never real, for all the time in the General Conference Committee and amongst others there was a secret antagonism always carried on" (A. T. Jones to C. E. Holmes, May 12, 1921; in *Manuscripts and Memories* 329).

46. Ellen G. White to W. C. White, Letter 83, March 13, 1890; in *1888 Materials*, pp. 627-628. See also Dan T. Jones to R. A. Underwood, March 21, 1890, archives of the General Conference of Seventh-day Adventists. W. C. White reported to O. A. Olsen

that "as a member of the committee," he remembered "that there were three copies of matter which Dr. Waggoner had added to the lessons as we examined them last July [1889] under the apple tree. I remember hearing Dr. Waggoner and Mrs. Jones plan that the first copy should be sent to Oakland and one placed in the hands of Eld. Smith, and I was afterwards told that this had been done. ... In all my connection with the lesson writers and lesson committees, I have never seen any disposition or apparent desire to have the lessons passed to the printer without a most thorough examination by Eld. Smith and his associates" (W. C. White to O. A. Olsen, March 17, 1890, archives of the General Conference of Seventh-day Adventists). This gives a credible answer to the assertions by George Knight that suggest there would not have been a Minneapolis episode if only Jones and Waggoner had humbly come to the older men and submitted their ideas to them (see *From 1888 to Apostasy*, p. 74; *A User-Friendly Guide to the 1888 Message*, pp. 176-178). To the contrary, neither Jones' nor Waggoner's personality, nor supposed inappropriate actions on their part, were responsible for the rejection that took place. See Chapter 4, footnote 41.

47. Ellen G. White to W. C. White, Letter 83, March 13, 1890; in *1888 Materials*, pp. 627-628.

48. *Ibid.*, pp. 628-631.

49. *Ibid.*, pp. 631, 633.

50. Ellen G. White Manuscript 2, March 16, 1890; in *1888 Materials*, pp. 613-616.

51. Ellen G. White to Uriah Smith, Letter 73, Nov. 25, 1890; in *1888 Materials*, p. 734.

52. Ellen G. White Manuscript 2, "Sermon," March 9, 1890; in *1888 Materials*, p. 615.

53. Ellen G. White to W. C. White, Letter 83, March 13, 1890; in *1888 Materials*, p. 634. Jones had been defending R. M. King, a fellow Seventh-day Adventist, against accusations of Sunday law violations in Tennessee. For more information on this case see: Eric Syme, *A History of SDA Church-State Relations in the United States*, pp. 36, 37; A. T. Jones, *"Due Process of Law" and the Divine Right to Dissent* (New York: National Religious Liberty Assn., 1892). This volume is Jones' review of the King case.

54. Ellen G. White to Uriah Smith, Letter 73, Nov. 25, 1890; in *1888 Materials*, p. 734.

55. Dan T. Jones to E. W. Farnsworth, March 21, 1890, archives of the General Conference of Seventh-day Adventists.

56. Ellen G. White to W. C. White, Letter 84, March 19, 1890; in *1888 Materials*, pp. 642-643.

57. Ellen G. White to J. S. Washburn, Letter 36a, Sept. 18, 1890; in *1888 Materials*, p. 708.

# CHAPTER 15

# *Stand by the Landmarks*

## *"The Law in Galatians Was Their Only Plea"*

After an exhausting three weeks of labor during the latter part of the 1890 Ministerial Institute, Ellen White returned to California. She had spoken every day, with but few exceptions, and "sometimes twice each day." Her labors were not all in vain, for a great change had come in the atmosphere at the meetings. Most of this was the result of the two special meetings that had taken place with the prominent leaders in Battle Creek. A. T. Jones and E. J. Waggoner had finally been given an opportunity to explain their side of the story and give answer to all the false accusations that had been perpetuated since before the Minneapolis conference. This made a "deep impression" on many that had been warring against them, and many confessions were made. Many saw the validity of the Testimonies once again and took their stand as supporters of them.[1]*

Dan Jones felt that it "would have been lamentable to leave Battle Creek without these two special meetings and the definite explanations made." He now felt like "a changed man." When some asked why these meetings had not been held sooner, Ellen White "explained that the state of their impressions and feelings was of such a character that we could not reach them, for they had ears, but they were dull of hearing; hearts had they, but they were hard and unimpressible."[2]* Nonetheless, Ellen White could state, "thank God, victory has come."[3] "The backbone of the rebellion is broken in those who have come in from other places."[4] God had not forsaken His people.

Ellen White was not the only one who was grateful: "Brother Olsen is so glad and feels so relieved, he scarcely knows what to do with himself. Brother Waggoner feels so thankful."[5] This was very encouraging, considering that only a few days before O. A. Olsen had grieved over the poor condition of the ministry:

"I feel sadly over our ministry. When I look out upon our men from a general standpoint, we are not very well prepared to meet the emergency before us." Olsen realized that unless God came "with greater power" and granted "special blessings and special favors we shall be far behind our opportunities."[6] He could see that "while on the one hand God's providence is opening the way as never before, on the other hand it seems that the enemy is working with a vengeance."[7]

Now Olsen could attest to the progress made at the Ministerial Institute, and he wrote accordingly in an article published in the *Review*: "One important feature of the Bible school was the labors of Sister White.... These were seasons of special interest, and will be long remembered by those who were present. Sister White enjoyed great freedom, and on several occasions the power of the Lord was manifest in a large measure.... [W]e feel very thankful for the blessing of God and the success that has attended the present effort."[8] Dan Jones supported Olsen's observation in a similar article in the same *Review*:

> Sister White attended many of the meetings, and bore her testimony with much freedom and power. The restraint which had existed on the part of some connected with the school was removed by explanations that were made, and a tender spirit came in.... All were greatly benefited, and many who had been cold and formal in their work in the past, received such an experience in the things of God as to give them new courage and hope for the future. At the morning meeting on the last day of the school nearly all spoke, and their unanimous testimony was that they had been greatly benefited by the school and by their associations together, and that they could go to their fields of labor with better courage and greater hopes of success than ever before.[9]

Before the Institute closed, Ellen White was "convinced that Satan saw that there was very much at stake here, and he did not want to lose his hold on our ministering brethren. And *if the full victory comes*, there will go forth from this meeting many ministers with an experience of the highest value."[10] For all practical purposes it appeared that final victory had indeed come, and if history did not speak otherwise, we could come to no other conclusion. But just as in the case of the 1889 revivals and the 1889 General Conference, the 1890 Ministerial Institute turned out to be much less than a great victory. Only a few weeks later, we find Ellen White in great financial straits, suffering from poor health and discouragement, and the Testimonies being questioned again by many of the leading brethren. In order to understand what led up to this state of affairs, we must take an honest second look at Dan Jones and the positions he took during and shortly after the 1890 Ministerial Institute in regard to both the law in Galatians and the covenants.[11]*

## *Inopportune Absence*

When Dan Jones approached Ellen White during the covenant presentations at the Ministerial Institute and asked her opinion, she had frankly responded: "I will not tell you my opinion, my faith. Dig in the Bible."[12] A few days later, however, Ellen White *did* give her opinion, both in writing and through speaking publicly. Unfortunately for Dan Jones, he could not be present. On Sunday, March 2, he left Battle Creek for Tennessee in order to help defend R. M. King in one of the most important Sunday law cases thus far, and would not return to Battle Creek until Monday, March 10, some eight days later.[13]*

Thus Dan Jones missed an entire week of early morning meetings where Ellen White spoke very directly with the brethren in regard to what was taking place. He was not present the Sabbath morning when Ellen White so clearly stated: "Now I tell you here before God, that the covenant question, as it has been presented [by Waggoner], is the truth. It is the light. In clear lines it has been laid before me. And those who have been resisting light, I ask you whether they have been working for God, or for the devil?"[14] Chances are that Dan Jones also did not receive a copy of the letter Ellen White wrote Uriah Smith that same Sabbath morning where she stated most emphatically: "Night before last I was shown that evidences in regard to the covenants were clear and convincing. Yourself, Brother Dan Jones, Brother Porter and others are spending your investigative powers for naught to produce a position on the covenants to vary from the position that Brother Waggoner has presented.... The Covenant question is a clear question and would be received by every candid, unprejudiced mind."[15] Dan Jones also missed the following Sunday morning meeting where Ellen White asked those present: "Has God raised up these men [Jones and Waggoner] to proclaim the truth? I say, yes, God has sent men to bring us the truth that we should not have had unless God had sent somebody to bring it to us."[16]

It is obvious that Dan Jones had quite a surprise awaiting him when he returned to Battle Creek. Monday morning, the very day he returned, Ellen White wrote to W. C. White stating: "I am much pleased to learn that Professor Prescott is giving the same lessons in his class to his students that Brother Waggoner has been giving. He is presenting the covenants.... Since I made the statement last Sabbath that the view of the covenants as it had been taught by Waggoner was truth, it seems that great relief has come to many minds."[17] It did not take long for the report to come to Dan Jones that Ellen White "fully endorsed Dr. Waggoner's position on the covenant question," which brought anything but relief to his mind.[18]

Tuesday morning, Dan Jones attended his first morning meeting in more than a week. The "room was full" as Ellen White, O. A. Olsen, E. J. Waggoner and W. W. Prescott spoke. Here many confessions were made including one by R. C. Porter. Although Porter "could not see clearly on all points in regard to the covenants" he "confessed the wrong that he had done [Ellen White] and Elder Waggoner." As a result of such confessions, the "whole room was sobbing and praising God for there was a revealing of His power." It is no wonder that Ellen White could declare that "the backbone of the rebellion is broken in those who have come in from other places." This must have made an impression on Dan Jones for he "kept his head bowed upon the seat all the time. Did not lift it up once till the meeting closed."[19]

It was Wednesday, March 12, that Ellen White had called for the first of the two special meetings with all the prominent church leaders in Battle Creek, including Dan Jones. For the first time, Ellen White and E. J. Waggoner were able to give an answer to many of the false accusations that had been afloat since before the Minneapolis Conference. What had been the basis for all these accusations? "It was finally simmered down to this—that a letter had come from California to Brother Butler, telling them that plans were all made to drive the law in Galatians." This was "met and explained, that there were no plans laid." There had been no such conspiracy. Although much good resulted from this five hour meeting, there was not "a general breaking up of the soul under the influence of the Spirit and power of God" as Ellen White had hoped for.[20]

When Ellen White sent word to Dan Jones to invite Waggoner to speak on Sabbath "there seemed to be a little reluctance, but finally [Waggoner] was invited and gave a most precious discourse." The afternoon meeting was held in the office chapel where the "Spirit of the Lord came nigh to us. Christ knocked for entrance but no room was made for Him, the door was not opened and the light of His glory, so nigh, was withdrawn." Confessions had been made but not as "clearly and to the point" as Ellen White had expected. It was here that Dan Jones spoke of his terrible temptations "to give up the testimonies." Ellen White mused at how hard it was "for these men to die" to self.[21]

Finally, on Sunday morning, March 16, Ellen White, "weary and almost discouraged," ventured into the meeting and made some "very close remarks." She kept before them "what they had done to make of none effect that which the Lord was trying to do and why. *The law in Galatians was their only plea.*" Wasting no more time, Ellen White spoke of the root problem that kept them from accepting new light:

> Why, I asked, is your interpretation of the law in Galatians more dear to you, and you more zealous to maintain your ideas on this point, than to acknowledge the workings of the Spirit of God? You have been weighing every precious heaven-sent testimony by your own scales as you interpreted the law in Galatians. Nothing could come to you in regard to the truth and the power of God unless it should bear your imprint, the precious ideas you had idolized on the law of Galatians.
>
> These testimonies of the Spirit of God, the fruits of the Spirit of God, have no weight unless they are stamped with your ideas of the law in Galatians. I am afraid of you and I am afraid of your interpretation of any scripture which has revealed itself in such an unchristlike spirit as you have manifested and has cost me so much unnecessary labor.... Let your caution be exercised in the line of fear lest you are committing the sin against the Holy Ghost.... I say if your views on the law in Galatians, and the fruits, are of the character I have seen in Minneapolis and ever since up to this time, my prayer is that I may be as far from your understanding and interpretation of the Scriptures as it is possible for me to be.... You could not have given a better refutation of your own theories than you have done.
>
> Now brethren, I have nothing to say, no burden in regard to the law in Galatians. This matter looks to me of minor consequence in comparison with the spirit you have brought into your faith. It is exactly of the same piece that was manifested by the Jews in reference to the work and mission of Jesus Christ.[22]

The leading brethren were rejecting advancing light because they realized it was contrary to their "pet theories" on the law in Galatians. Their old views must be put aside in order to accept the message the Lord had graciously sent through Jones and Waggoner. The spirit manifested by so many was one of the greatest evidences that their interpretation of Scripture was indeed wrong. Ellen White pressed the point further. Rather than being one of the landmarks, their theory on the law in Galatians had become, of all things, Baal worship:

> The gospel of Christ, His lessons, His teachings, have had but very little place in the experience and the discourses of those who claim to believe the truth. Any pet theory, any human idea, becomes of gravest importance and as sacred as an idol to which everything must bow. This has verily been the case in the theory of the law in Galatians. Anything that becomes such a hobby as to usurp the place of Christ, any idea so exalted as to be placed where nothing of light or evidence can find a lodgement [sic]in the mind, takes the form of an idol, to which everything is sacrificed. The law in Galatians is not a vital question and never has been. Those who have called it one of the old landmarks simply do not know what they are talking about. It never was an old landmark, and it never will become such....

> I say, through the word given me of God, Those who have stood so firmly to defend their ideas and positions on the law in Galatians have need to search their hearts as with a lighted candle, to see what manner of spirit has actuated them. With Paul I would say, "Who hath bewitched you, that you should not obey the truth?" Gal. 3:1. What satanic persistency and obstinacy has been evidenced! I have had no anxiety about the law in Galatians, but I have had anxiety that our leading brethren should not go over the same ground of resistance to light and the manifest testimonies of the Spirit of God, and reject everything to idolize their own supposed ideas and pet theories. I am forced, by the attitude my brethren have taken and the spirit evidenced, to say, God deliver me from your ideas of the law in Galatians.[23]

It is just as important that *we* understand today what Ellen White was seeking to get across to the brethren as it was for *them* to understand. More than a dozen times, Ellen White referred to the commonly held view of the law in Galatians as "your ideas," "your understanding," "your interpretation," "your theories" and "your views," which they were clinging to as if it were a landmark of faith that could never be understood another way. They were willing to sacrifice the very outpouring of the Spirit of Christ in order to hold on to their "pet theories." Their "unchristlike spirit" and "satanic persistency" led Ellen White to desire to be as far away from their "understanding and interpretation" as she could possibly be. It was in this context that Ellen White stated she "had no anxiety," "no burden in regard to the law in Galatians," as they had interpreted it. It was not a "vital question," but of "minor consequence" *compared* to the spirit they manifested. She would not herself reject the plain light on the covenant question over their cherished ideas of the law in Galatians.[24]

Ellen White was in no way suggesting that doctrine was immaterial and that her only concern was that the brethren treat one another kindly in their disagreements. Contrarily, she had clearly been shown that Waggoner's view on the covenants was truth, and she, unlike so many of the brethren, would not reject it even if it meant giving up the common view on the law in Galatians. She had made this evident in her letter to Smith only one week before: "The covenant question is a clear question and would be received by every candid, unprejudiced mind, but I was brought where the Lord gave me an insight into this matter. You have turned from plain light because you were afraid that the law question in Galatians would have to be accepted. As to the law in Galatians, I have no burden and never have had."[25]

The fact that Ellen White had no burden for the law in Galatians does not mean she was denying a clearer revelation. At Minneapolis she stated that Waggoner's views "in reference to the law in Galatians, if I fully understand his position, do not harmonize with the understanding *I have had*." Yet, she was "willing to be instructed as a child," for truth would "lose nothing by investigation."[26] She had included herself with the brethren by stating that Jones and Waggoner may "differ with *us*."[27] And by the end of the conference she began to wonder "for the first time" if "it might be *we* did not hold correct views after all upon the law in Galatians, for the truth required no such spirit to sustain it."[28] She was sure that "if *we* have had the truth on this subject our brethren have failed to be sanctified through it."[29]

As demonstrated above, by the time of the 1890 Ministerial Institute Ellen White did not identify herself with the common view, but spoke of it numerous times as "your view." Less than a year later she could state that "by taking *wrong* positions in the controversy over the law in Galatians—a question that many have not fully understood before taking a *wrong* position—the church has sustained a sad loss."[30] Several years later Ellen White underscored this idea and clearly endorsed Jones and Waggoner's position stating: "'The law was our school master. . .' In this Scripture [Gal 3:24], the Holy Spirit through the apostle is speaking *especially of the moral law*.... An unwillingness to yield up preconceived opinions, and to accept *this truth*, lay at the foundation of a large share of the opposition manifested at Minneapolis against the Lord's message through Brethren Waggoner and Jones. By exciting *that* opposition, Satan succeeded in shutting away from our people, in a great measure, the special power of the Holy Spirit that God longed to impart to them.... The *light* that is to lighten the whole earth with its glory was resisted."[31] All this must be kept in mind while reviewing the aftermath of the 1890 Ministerial Institute, otherwise we might walk away with false premises in regard to the great truths of the covenants presented there.

## *Mental Gymnastics*

By looking at the correspondence of Dan Jones during and after the Ministerial Institute, we are able to get an inside look at the personal struggle that he and his colleagues went through. It's obvious they did not agree with Jones and Waggoner's view of the law in Galatians or the covenants, which were so closely connected. They claimed to believe in justification by faith, but felt that Jones' and Waggoner's view undermined the Sabbath, the law, and the third angel's message. When Ellen White strongly supported Jones and Waggoner and their views, the Testimonies were called into question; perhaps she had *changed*. Yet the temptation to give up the Testimonies brought only darkness and discouragement, for they were tied in with the third angel's message, and to give them up meant, "to yield everything."[32] It is easy to see that in this state of mind something had to give; something must be laid aside.

On March 14, following the first of the "two special meetings," Dan Jones wrote of his understanding of the situation thus far. Writing to D. T. Shireman—self-supporting evangelist from Kansas—about the experience they were having in Battle Creek, Dan Jones reveals some of the inner struggle he was going through: "I have been led to see the danger of trusting to outward appearances, and trying to make things go as I thought they ought to.... [W]hen light from Him shines in upon our hearts and reveals the motives and purposes that have prompted us, in their true light, the sight is anything but encouraging."[33]* Writing the same day to R. A. Underwood, Jones shares more of his personal thoughts about the meeting that took place:

> It seems from what has been said that brethren [W. C.] White, Waggoner and Jones did not have any preconcerted plan when they came over from the Pacific Coast to the Minneapolis meeting to lay their views before the brethren at that time, and have not been attempting to carry through any such plans since. Sister White has come out a little stronger in favor of Dr. Waggoner, but yet has not committed herself definitely as to the points of doctrine in his exposition of the two covenants. She says that she has been shown that he had light on the covenant question, but was not shown as to what that light was. *At least that is the way I understand it at the present time.*[34]*

Dan Jones was grappling with accepting what had been revealed to Ellen White in support of Waggoner views on the covenants. How could he comprehend what he had heard in one of the "two special meetings," along with the reports of Ellen White's statements made during his absence from the Institute, without acknowledging Waggoner's positions as truth? It is understandable that the following morning he shared his great struggle of doubting the Testimonies. He was questioning how Ellen White could truly support Waggoner's views. It is apparent that the "pressure of unbelief," which Ellen White said she felt in "every meeting," was present in the experience of Dan Jones, and would drive away the power of God that was ready to fall upon him.[35]

Then, on Sunday morning when Ellen White laid out the root cause of the rejection that was taking place—"their interpretation of the law in Galatians"—Dan Jones formulated evidence in his own mind that allowed him to make "some acknowledgements" and also take his "position on the testimonies." Unfortunately it was not an acceptance of the truths taught by Jones and Waggoner that led Dan Jones to make his acknowledgements, but a case of mental gymnastics which enabled him to accept Ellen White as a prophet, yet at the same time reject heaven's endorsement. His inner struggle must have been great, for Ellen White stated that "he looked as if he had had a spell of sickness" as he spoke.[36] That afternoon Dan Jones revealed to R. M. Kilgore what had taken place:

> The investigation on the covenant question closed up with no better satisfaction than before it began.... For a time it was thought that [Ellen White] fully endorsed Dr. Waggoner's position on the covenant question, and was so reported to be when I returned from Tennessee... but later developments show that such was not the case. It turns out now that the doctrinal points in the matter have [not] been the real points at issue. It is the spirit alone that has been manifested to which she objected, and to which Eld. Waggoner takes exceptions. Both Sister White and Dr. Waggoner stated that the doctrinal points were not the points at issue. So that removes the real point that was in my mind all the time. I understood that it was the bringing in of new doctrines that were not approved by the denomination, that was the real point at issue. But if I have been mistaken in that matter I am glad to be corrected. I have thought all the time that Sister White did not mean to say that Dr. Waggoner was correct in his position on the covenant question as far as doctrine is concerned; because it was so manifestly wrong that I could not at all be reconciled to the idea that she would give it her unqualified approval.... As far as I am concerned I am willing to drop the whole question, if others will do the same, and put my thought and labor toward the advancement of the truth.... Perhaps both parties will respect each other more than they have in the past, and there will be more counsel in reference to introducing any points of doctrine in the future, than there has been in the past.[37]

All the initial conviction Dan Jones had that Ellen White had indeed been urged by the Lord to support Jones' and Waggoner's views on the covenants was now set aside for a more pleasing opinion. In the days that followed, Dan Jones shared his new understanding with many other leaders who were not able to attend the ministerial meetings. The more he shared his views, the more his views developed, and the more settled in his mind was the idea that doctrines were not the issue, *only* one's attitude. Yet it is interesting to note that Dan Jones' attitude did not change; he still would not allow A. T. Jones and E. J. Waggoner the freedom to hold a different view than his own. It was not long before he began to express the same old attitudes as he sought to justify his convictions against their views. On Monday, March 17, Dan Jones sent at least two more letters:

We have had a pretty stormy time here this winter, especially since you was [sic] here, in reference to the bringing in of the two covenants into the ministers school.... The result has not been to bring the brethren together and unite them in working for the upbuilding of the cause of God, but has rather been to create party spirit and party feelings.... Sister White... says it is not what we believe that she feels exercised about; it is not that we should all hold just the same view in reference to the covenants, in reference to the law in Galatians, or in reference to any point of doctrine; but that we should all have the spirit of Christ, and should all be united in building up and pushing forward the third angel's message. It seems to me that her position is evidently the correct one, and the principle will apply to other matters with just as much force as it applies to the covenant question, or the law in Galatians.... I was just as certain as I could be that certain plans and purposes were being carried out by Dr. Waggoner and others and that certain motives were behind these plans and purposes; but it now appears that I was altogether mistaken in both. It seems strange how it could be so. Every circumstance seemed to add to the evidence to prove the things true; but regardless of all this, they have been proven untrue. This brought to my mind that we can not rely upon circumstantial evidence.[38]

Well, we have had quite a hassel [sic] here this winter over bringing the covenant question into the bible school for ministers. I objected to it. It caused quite a stir.... I am willing to confess that in my opposition to this work I have not always been as free from personal feelings as I should have been.... It seemed for awhile that Sister White would come out and endorse Dr. Waggoner's position on the covenant question fully, and it was a great perplexity to me to know how to look upon the matter; for it seemed clear to my mind that his positions were not all correct. But later it is stated that the matter of doctrine was not the important point in the issue at all. Sister White and Dr. Waggoner said they did not care what we believed on the law in Galatians or on the covenants; what they wanted to see was that we might all accept the doctrine of justification by faith; that we may get the benefit of it ourselves and teach it to others. With this I am perfectly in harmony. I believe in the doctrine of justification by faith, and I am also willing to concede that it has not been given the prominence in the past that its importance demands.... Another thing that has been brought out by these meetings is the fact that no plan had been laid by the brethren who came from California, to teach their peculiar views in the institute in Minneapolis.... I understood that there was considerable importance attached to the points of doctrine involved in the questions of the law in Galatians and the two covenants. I had also thought that these brethren had laid their plans to get their views before the people, and that it was being accomplished step by step through institutes, workers' meetings, and bible-schools. Now if this is not true, then I say again, I have been laboring under a mistake, and will have to acknowledge that I have been under a mistake in these matters.[39]

With each passing letter, Dan Jones expressed more conviction in his changing opinion. He now concluded that Jones' and Waggoner's "peculiar views" were not of importance, only that justification by faith—to which everyone agreed—be accepted by the brethren as they worked together in unity. Dan Jones had found a way to preserve his old views, his personal experience and his belief in the Testimonies, while at the same time rejecting advancing light which he so despised. He wrote as one with authority, yet misrepresented what had been said at the meetings, even falsely reporting that Waggoner had "given up the position that in the old covenant the promises were all on the part of the people"[40]* Dan Jones was willing to admit that he had not had the right spirit, but seemed to justify it by reason of his sincerity. Although he felt like a new man because of the relief at the explanations made, he still seemed to question their validity.

Writing to W. C. White the following morning, Dan Jones took on a more conciliatory attitude. He had laid the greatest blame on W. C. White for what he felt was "using your mother to give influence and power to your work." He admitted that he "had not stayed clear of all feeling" against those "specially connected with pushing forward the law in Galatians, the covenant question, etc.," and now asked for White's "pardon." Matters in regard to Waggoner's Sabbath School lessons had been cleared up "to some extent," though he admitted, "it is not as clear yet as I would like to see it." Dan Jones then shared his perception of the explanations given:

> I had supposed in the past that a few doctrinal points… were the question at issue, and that the object of certain ones… was to bring in those doctrines and establish them as the belief of the denomination. I thought the doctrine of justification by faith, with which I have agreed theoretically, and with which all our leading brethren have agreed, was only a rider, so to speak, to carry through these other things that were more subject to criticism [law in Galatians and covenants]; and by connecting the two together,—one with which no one found objection [justification by faith],—that rather than reject those that were objectionable, our people would be led to accept that which they could not (fully)

endorse.[41]* Your mother and Dr. Waggoner both say that the points of doctrine are not the matters at issue at all, but it is the spirit shown by our people in opposition to these questions which they object to. I am perfectly free to acknowledge that the spirit has not been the Spirit of Christ.... [T]he point in your mother's mind and in the mind of Dr. Waggoner, was not to bring in these questions and force them upon all, but to bring in the doctrine of justification by faith and the spirit of Christ and try to get the people converted to God. This I most heartily endorse.[42]*

We should recall what Ellen White told J. S. Washburn, in the spring of 1889; that the real underlying issue at Minneapolis was over "righteousness by faith," not the law in Galatians.[43] Jones and Waggoner had come not to force some abstract doctrine, but to share the message of righteousness by faith. It just so happens that this most precious message—because it was the epitome of Jones' and Waggoner's view of the law in Galatians and the covenants—differed from the ideas of the leading brethren. Thus, the law in Galatians and the covenants became a stumbling block over which the brethren rejected the genuine "third angel's message in verity." At the 1889 General Conference, Ellen White stated that "Baal" would be the religion of many who had "slighted, spoken against and ridiculed" the "only true religion" of justification by faith.[44] It was true that Jones and Waggoner had not come with a preconceived plan to push their views and that justification by faith was their real burden. But Dan Jones misinterpreted this explanation, thinking he could reject their Heaven-sent message as long as he had the right spirit. After all, he already believed "theoretically" in justification by faith.

After the second "special meeting" held on March 19—the last meeting that Ellen White attended before heading west—Dan Jones felt like a changed man. It was here that A. T. Jones was able to give an answer for the false rumors that had been spread around in regard to his teaching. Many confessions followed this explanation and a new atmosphere seemed to come in. Unfortunately, in the days that followed the meeting, Dan Jones became less accurate in his evaluation of the whole situation and yet more confident that his observations were correct. With each letter he expressed more certainty that, although he might have had a wrong spirit and even "made a fool of himself," he had not done wrong in stopping Waggoner's presentations.[45] In fact, he felt Waggoner was really the one to blame:

There has been no concession made with reference to the points of doctrine, or the interpretation of the scripture, but only the spirit that was shown and the way in which the work was done.... I have not yet seen that I did wrong in asking Dr. Waggoner to postpone the presentation of the covenant question in the school until Eld. Olsen and Prof. Prescott should return first. From what Eld. Olsen has said to me, I think they did not consider that I am at fault in that matter at all. But when the Dr. [Waggoner] refused to do so, it brought on a complication of circumstances that left the way open for suspicions of his work to arise, and they did arise.[46]

Dan Jones communication with others about Jones and Waggoner and their views grew less and less supportive as time went on. When he returned from his eight-day trip to Tennessee, he was afraid Ellen White "fully endorsed Dr. Waggoner's position." Within a few days, he expressed that she had only been shown Waggoner had "light... but was not shown as to what that light was." Then he wrote that there was no inducement, "that all hold just the same view in reference to the covenants." Later he stated that "the matter of doctrine was not the important point," and still later, that "no concessions" were made in favor of Waggoner's views.[47] Dan Jones finally concluded that Ellen White "has not endorsed Dr. Waggoner's position," nor expects to.

Dan Jones' description of Waggoner's views took a similar course. What he first described simply as "their views" he soon referred to as "their peculiar views." Then he described it as blatant "error," stating that although Waggoner might not be blamed for the printing of the Sabbath School lessons, the Lesson Committee certainly should have "rejected" them.

On March 21, 1890, two days after the second special meeting with Ellen White and other leaders, Dan Jones wrote to R. M. Kilgore and R. A. Underwood, grossly misrepresenting what Ellen White had said:

Sister White says she has not endorsed Dr. Waggoner's position on the law in Galatians, and expected it would be a long time before she should; her mind is not exercised on that matter at all. They said it was not the question of points of doctrine that they cared for; *all could believe what they pleased*; but they wanted to see the spirit of Christ come in more.... We could all endorse this of course, and did.[48]

They did not ask any of us to concede any point of doctrine on the covenants, or the law in Galatians; on the contrary they said that *matters of doctrine were not the questions at issue; that they cared nothing about what we believed*: it was the spirit manifested that they thought was wrong and wished to have corrected.... *Sister White stated that she had not endorsed the position of Dr. Waggoner on the law in Galatians, or the covenant question, did not expect to do so*; her mind is not exercised in that direction.... Dr. Waggoner explained how the Sabbath-school lessons were prepared... and submitted to the Lesson Committee for examination before being published. This being true, I do not see that he was to blame for anything that the lessons might have contained.... Of course it would not follow that what he taught in these lessons was correct by any means; but men are expected to write as they believe, to interpret scripture as they understand it.... [H]is errors ought to have been detected by the Lesson Committee, and the lessons either refused or rejected. But when they passed through the hands of that Committee and were published by the Sabbath-school Association, it seems to me that the Lesson Committee is as much responsible for the theology that the lessons contained as the writer of the lessons himself.[49]

Less than a week later, Dan Jones made it clear that he had not changed in his understanding of the doctrinal issues, but his confidence in the explanations shared during the two "special meetings" was beginning to wane. He had been willing to admit his mistake in judging Jones' and Waggoner's motives but felt it was their responsibility not to act in such a way as to invite judgments:

Perhaps we have been mistaken in some of our opinions that we have held.... I do not see now what can be done but to accept the explanations that have been made, and act upon them.... While I hold the same position on the law in Galatians, and the covenant question that I have always held, I am glad to have my mind relieved in reference to the motive and plans of some of the brethren.... Let us hope that in the future our brethren will not act in such a way as to lay the foundation for unjust judgement on their plans and purposes.[50]

Only a few days passed before Dan Jones was again questioning the validity of the Testimonies. In a letter to R. C. Porter, he expressed sympathy with Uriah Smith who could not "understand why... Sister White spoke at one time positively against a certain thing, as she did against the law in Galatians, to Elder [J. H.] Waggoner several years ago, then turn around and practically give her support to the same thing when it comes up in a little different way." To this, Dan Jones confessed he was "trying to think as little about it as possible."[51]

Uriah Smith had obviously not changed his views either, and the letter he had written to Ellen White only a few weeks before appears to have been passed around for Dan Jones to consider. Smith was still strengthening the "hands and minds" of others, which Ellen White had warned against.[52] In a *Review* article published the very next week, Smith himself showed he had not changed his views, even in light of the clear statements made at the Ministerial Institute.[53*]

As for Dan Jones, he continued his spiral, not only intimating doubt in the honesty of Jones' and Waggoner's testimony, but hoping they had learned a good lesson from his own design. Only a few days before, he had rejoiced that "all could believe what they pleased." Now he was unwilling to extend this same courtesy:

> I know it is a little difficult in the fact of the circumstantial [sic] evidence that has surrounded this matter for a year and a half, for us to come to the conclusion now that those matters that transpired in Minneapolis were all done in lamb-like innocence. But if Dr. Waggoner says that he did not have any plan when he came there, and Brother Jones says the same, and Sister White sustains them, what can we do but accept it as a fact?... You may think that we have kicked a little up here, and then have been roped in, and swallowed whole. Such is not the case by any means. I consider that we gained every point that we were holding for, and think the other side was glad enough to be let down a little easy; and I was willing that it should be, if they have learned the lessons that we designed they should learn. I feel confident now that Dr. Waggoner will be very cautious about throwing his peculiar views before the people until they have been carefully examined by the leading brethren; and I think the leading brethren will be much more careful in their examinations of these peculiar views than they have been in the past.[54]

## Darkness the Result

"If you turn from one ray of light fearing it will necessitate an acceptance of positions you do not wish to receive, that light becomes to you darkness.... I speak what I know."[55] So wrote Ellen White to Uriah Smith in regard to his rejection of the "true light" on the covenant question that he was not willing to accept. Many times during the same year Ellen White warned against such darkness and lamented its presence in the church.[56*]

No greater evidence could be given that Ellen White's prognosis was correct than the experience of Dan Jones following the 1890 Ministerial Institute. On almost every point, he misunderstood what Ellen White said during her final week at the Institute. Ellen White had clearly endorsed Waggoner's view on the covenants, warning the brethren that their own view on the law in Galatians was preventing many from receiving light. She herself was not exercised over the matter, for it was not an issue to keep her from accepting advancing light. This Dan Jones had interpreted as evidence that she did not endorse Jones and Waggoner, and that all could believe what they wanted. Ellen White had stated that the spirit manifested by the brethren should be of bigger concern than their pet ideas. To this Dan Jones suggested that doctrine was not the important point, but only the spirit one had. Yet in the end he allowed only for his own view.

Ellen White had stated that there was no organized plan to push the law in Galatians and the covenants, but that the real message was justification by faith. This Dan Jones twisted to mean that a mere assent to justification by faith, which he already espoused, was sufficient without accepting Jones' and Waggoner's message. What Dan Jones endorsed were ideas similar to that of the ecumenical movement, which suggests unity and fellowship in a common understanding—laying aside differences—yet persecuting those who do not hold their same views.

Ellen White recognized a better way: "'If we walk in the light as he is in the light, we have fellowship with one another,'" but if you "'walk in the sparks ye have kindled... ye shall lie down in sorrow.'"[57]*

When the Lord "urged" Ellen White to stand before her brethren that fateful Sabbath morning and take her "position" on the covenant question, she was "in perfect freedom, calling light, light, and darkness, darkness." Yet numerous times she warned the brethren that if they turned "from one ray of light... that light becomes to you darkness." That prediction had come true.[58]*

Did the long-hoped for victory come as a result of the 1890 Ministerial Institute? The sad fact of the matter is that the situation only grew more serious. Not only were many rejecting heaven-sent light, but many were told Ellen White herself did not endorse that light. It is unfortunate that over 120 years later the 1890 Ministerial Institute is looked upon as a great turning point for the good.[59]* But what is perhaps even sadder is the fact that many sparks of Dan Jones' own kindling are today still burning out of control.[60]*

# CHAPTER 15 FOOTNOTES

1. Ellen G. White to W. C. White, Letter 84, March 19, 1890; in *1888 Materials*, p. 643. For other detailed narratives of the covenants topic see chapter 14, footnote 1.

2. *Ibid.*, p. 642-643. In a letter to W. C. White, O. A. Olsen stated that "Bro. Dan T. Jones *feels* like another man, and I am glad it is so. Still he has been pretty slow to make acknowledgements" (W. C. White to O. A. Olsen, March 20, 1890, emphasis supplied, archives of the General Conference of Seventh-day Adventists). From subsequent evidence it seems that the assessment that Dan Jones was a changed man was as much, if not more, his own idea than it was Ellen White's: "Brother Dan Jones *says* it would have been lamentable to leave Battle Creek without these two special meetings [March 12 &19] and the definite explanations made. He is a changed man" (*1888* p. 643; emphasis supplied).

3. Ellen G. White to W. A. Colcord, Letter 60, March 10, 1890; in *1888 Materials*, p. 620.

4. Ellen G. White to W. C. White, Letter 30, March 10, 1890; in *1888 Materials*, p. 625.

5. *Ibid.*, p. 626.

6. O. A. Olsen to G. C. Tenny, March 20, 1890, archives of the General Conference of Seventh-day Adventists.

7. O. A. Olsen to C. H. Jones, [March], 1890, archives of the General Conference of Seventh-day Adventists.

8. O. A. Olsen, "The Ministers' School," *Review and Herald*, April 4, 1890, p. 201.

9. Dan T. Jones, "The Work in Battle Creek," *Review and Herald*, April 4, 1890, pp. 204-205.

10. Ellen G. White to W. C. White, Letter 83, March 13, 1890; in *1888 Materials*, p. 635, emphasis supplied.

11. In order to take a closer look at the struggle that Dan Jones went through in regard to Jones and Waggoner and the law in Galatians and covenant questions—and the ultimate affect it had on the Church—we will cover some of the same material found in earlier chapters.

12. Ellen G. White Manuscript 4, "Sermon," March 8, 1890; in *1888 Materials*, p. 596, emphasis supplied.

13. Dan T. Jones to E. W. Farnsworth, March 21, 1890, archives of the General Conference of Seventh-day Adventists; and Ellen G. White to W. C. White, Letter 30, March 10, 1890; in *1888 Materials*, p. 623. R. M. King was one of many Seventh-day Adventists arrested for violation of Sunday laws. For a summary of his case before the Supreme court of Tennessee on March 6, 1890, see: William A. Blakely, *American State Papers Bearing on Sunday Legislation* (1911), pp. 676-694.

14. Ellen G. White Manuscript 4, "Sermon," March 8, 1890; in *1888 Materials*, p. 596.

15. Ellen G. White to Uriah Smith, Letter 59, March 8, 1890; in *1888 Materials*, p. 604.

16. Ellen G. White Manuscript 2, "Sermon," March 9, 1890; in *1888 Materials*, p. 608.

17. Ellen G. White to W. C. White, Letter 30, March 10, 1890; in *1888 Materials*, p. 623.

18. Dan Jones to R. M. Kilgore, March 16, 1890, archives of the General Conference of Seventh-day Adventists.

19. Ellen G. White to W. C. White, Letter 30, March 10, 1890; in *1888 Materials*, pp. 625-626.

20. Ellen G. White to W. C. White, Letter 83, March 13, 1890; in *1888 Materials*, pp. 627-629.

21. *Ibid.*, p. 629; and Ellen G. White to Uriah Smith, Letter 73, Nov. 25, 1890; in *1888 Materials*, p. 734.

22. Ellen G. White to W. C. White, Letter 83, March 13-16, 1890; in *1888 Materials*, pp. 631-632.

23. Ellen G. White Manuscript 55, [March 16], 1890; in *1888 Materials*, p. 841.

24. See for example: *1888 Materials*, pp. 631, 842, 632, 700, 702, 841, 273, 631, 841, 632, 220.

25. Ellen G. White to Uriah Smith, Letter 59, March 8, 1890; in *1888 Materials*, p. 604.

26. Ellen G. White Manuscript 15, "To Brethren Assembled at General Conference," Nov., 1888; in *1888 Materials*, p. 163, emphasis supplied.

27. Ellen G. White to G. I. Butler, Letter 21, Oct. 14, 1888; in *1888 Materials*, p. 88, emphasis supplied.

28. Ellen G. White Manuscript 24, "Looking Back at Minneapolis," Dec., 1888; in *1888 Materials*, p. 221, emphasis supplied.

29. Ellen G. White to W. M. Healey, Letter 7, Dec. 9, 1888; in *1888 Materials*, p. 189, emphasis supplied.

30. Ellen G. White Manuscript 21, "Diary Entry," Feb. 27, 1891; in *1888 Materials*, p. 894, emphasis supplied.

31. Ellen G. White to Uriah Smith, Letter 96, June 6, 1896; in *1888 Materials*, p. 1575, emphasis supplied.

32. Ellen G. White to W. C. White, Letter 83, March 13, 1890; in *1888 Materials*, p. 629.

33. Dan T. Jones to D. T. Shireman, March 14, 1890, archives of the General Conference of Seventh-day Adventists. See Chapter 13 for more details on the "two special meetings."

34. Dan T. Jones to R. A. Underwood, March 14, 1890, archives of the General Conference of Seventh-day Adventists: (emphasis supplied). Dan Jones believed that Ellen White had been shown Waggoner had light, but strangely she didn't know what it was. This is echoed today by those who seek to deal with Ellen White's endorsements, yet still reject what Jones and Waggoner taught that disagrees with their Evangelical Reformationist gospel. See, chapter 4, footnote 3.

35. Ellen G. White Manuscript 2, "Sermon," March 9, 1890, and Manuscript 2, "Sermon," March 16, 1890; in *1888 Materials*, pp. 611, 641.

36. Ellen G. White to W. C. White, Letter 83, March 13, 1890; in *1888 Materials*, p. 633.

37. Dan T. Jones to R. M. Kilgore, March 16, 1890, archives of the General Conference of Seventh-day Adventists.

38. Dan T. Jones to J. D. Pegg, March 17, 1890, archives of the General Conference of Seventh-day Adventists.

39. Dan T. Jones to J. H. Morrison, March 16, 1890, archives of the General Conference of Seventh-day Adventists.

40. *Ibid*. The position that promises of the old covenant were all based on the part of the people was one of the major contentions that Dan Jones and the others had with Waggoner's view (Dan T. Jones to E. W. Farnsworth, Feb. 9, 18, 1890). It was also the position that Ellen White said Dan Jones and others were wasting their investigative powers trying to refute (*1888 Materials*, p. 604), and the position she took in her new book *Patriarchs and Prophets* (p. 372; see Chapter 14, footnote 36). O. A. Olsen contradicted Dan Jones assessment the following day in a letter written to R. A. Underwood. He admitted that it was "evident that we have misunderstood some things," and that there was "more to this covenant question than we are aware of.... Sr. White has come out very pointedly" (O. A. Olsen to R. A. Underwood, March 18, 1890). Other evidence proves Waggoner did not change his view. Only a few months after the Ministerial Institute, the Review and Herald office canceled an order of 1000 new books from Pacific Press because Waggoner's view "that the promises were all on the part of the people" was present (Dan T. Jones to R. C. Porter, June 2, 1890). In every major work that Waggoner produced in the years that followed, he continued to present the same view (*The Present Truth*, Dec. 10, 1896, p. 788; *The Everlasting Covenant* [1900], p. 327; *The Glad Tidings*, [1900], pp. 71, 100). It would be well for the reader to closely compare Ellen White's March 16

sermon and Dan Jones interpretation of it in the days that followed. Jones not only *misinterpreted* what she said, he also began *putting words in her mouth* that she never said.

41. Uriah Smith took a similar view: "The real point at issue at that Conference [1888] was the law in Galatians; but Brother Waggoner's six preliminary discourses on righteousness we could all agree to; and I should have enjoyed them first rate, had I not known all the while that he designed them to pave the way for his position on Galatians, which I deem as erroneous. I of course do not believe there is any necessary and logical connection between the two, but know a truth may be used in such a way and with such an apparent purpose, as to spoil the pleasure we would otherwise feel in listening to it (Uriah Smith to Ellen G. White, Feb. 17, 1890; in *Manuscripts and Memories*, p. 154). A. T. Jones later wrote of this fatal attitude: "In that… conference the tide of things was indicated by what one of the Battle Creek leaders said one day to a cluster of men after one of Bro. Waggoner's studies. He said, 'Now we could say Amen to all of that if that is all there were to it. But away down yonder there is still something to come. And this is to lead us to that. And if we say Amen to this we will have to say Amen to that and then we are caught.' Thus they would not say Amen to what they knew was true for fear of what was to come after, to which they would not say Amen anyhow—and which never came either, for there was no such thing, and so robbed themselves of what their own hearts told them was the truth; and by fighting what they only imagined, they fastened themselves in opposition to what they knew that they should have said Amen to" (A. T. Jones to C. E. Holmes, May 12, 1921; *Manuscripts and Memories*, p. 329).

42. Dan T. Jones to W. C. White, March 18, 1890, archives of the General Conference of Seventh-day Adventists. Within six months Dan Jones was in a state of "spiritual leanness," and ready to concede that the doctrine of justification by faith had not been accepted perhaps as much as he thought: "We all believe it and claim to endorse it fully; but, as you say, we have not felt in sympathy with those who have been making a specialty of presenting this subject to the people, and it has really been almost mortifying to us to see the hungry people take it in as it has been presented to them. I am free to confess that I have not felt just right on this matter" (Dan T. Jones to E. W. Farnsworth, Sept. 19, 1890, archives of the General Conference of Seventh-day Adventists).

43. "Interview with J. S. Washburn, at Hagerstown, Md., June 4, 1950," p. 2.

44. Ellen G. White to General Conference, Letter 24, Oct., 1889; in *1888 Materials*, p. 444.

45. Ellen G. White to W. C. White, Letter 84, March 19, 1890; in *1888 Materials*, p. 643.

46. Dan T. Jones to E. W. Farnsworth, March 21, 1890, archives of the General Conference of Seventh-day Adventists.

47. References to this summary of Dan Jones statements are listed above in this chapter.

48. Dan T. Jones to R. M. Kilgore, March 21, 1890, archives of the General Conference of Seventh-day Adventists, emphasis supplied.

49. Dan T. Jones to R. A. Underwood, March 21, 1890, archives of the General Conference of Seventh-day Adventists, emphasis supplied.

50. Dan T. Jones to G. I. Butler, March 27, 1890, archives of the General Conference of Seventh-day Adventists.

51. Dan T. Jones to R. C. Porter, April 1, 1890, archives of the General Conference of Seventh-day Adventists.

52. Uriah Smith to Ellen G. White, Feb. 17, 1890; in *Manuscripts and Memories*, p. 152-157; and Ellen G. White to Uriah Smith, Letter 59, March 8, 1890; in *1888 Materials*, p. 599.

53. Uriah Smith, "The Ark and the Law," *Review and Herald*, April 8, 1890, p. 216. One only has to read Smith's entire article to realize that the justification by faith he believed in was far different from the "most precious message" Jones and Waggoner were presenting: "God can never approach man with offers of blessing through Jesus Christ, without putting in the very forefront of every such transaction his own law, the transcript of his will, harmony with which is the indispensable condition of every favor to be bestowed; for what blessings could God confer, or promise to confer, upon men as individuals, families, or nations who would not yield to him their hearts, and seek to obey him? (The blessings which the wicked receive in this life do not militate against this rule; for these are given simply on account of the few righteous who are in the world.) In the formation of the covenant, this condition must therefore first appear, as it does; 'If ye will obey my voice indeed, and keep my covenant' Ex. 19:5. When the people assented to this, then God could proceed to enter upon the covenant proper. And the outward symbol of that covenant... must consist of its terms... including the promise of the people to obey God's law on the moral plan of action, and such other regulations of a civil and ceremonial nature as he might see fit to ordain" (*Ibid.*). In contrast to Smith, Ellen White expressed God's active love for all men: "To the death of Christ we owe even this earthly life. The bread we eat is the purchase of His broken body. The water we drink is bought by His spilled blood. Never one, saint or sinner, eats his daily food, but he is nourished by the body and the blood of Christ. The cross of Calvary is stamped on every loaf" (*Desire of Ages*, p. 660).

54. Dan T. Jones to G. I. Butler, April 14, 1890, archives of the General Conference of Seventh-day Adventists.

55. Ellen G. White to Uriah Smith, Letter 59, March 8, 1890; in *1888 Materials*, p. 605.

56. Ellen White would repeat this theme many times in the years following Minneapolis: "The reason why I felt so at Minneapolis was that I have seen that everyone who has taken a position similar... would go into the darkest unbelief" (*1888 Materials*, p. 610). "Those who opposed... the message that had come to us for more than a year, had not the spirit of labor, but were sinking down into darkness" (*Ibid.*, p. 633). "Brother Irwin says that the spirituality is at a very low ebb all through the conference" (*Ibid.*, p. 678). "The efforts that have been made for the few years past tend to put out the eyes that Israel shall not discern their defections, and God withholds His Spirit from them and darkness envelopes them as it did the Jewish nation" (*Ibid.*, p. 718). "The Lord has presented before me that those who have been in any measure blinded by the enemy... will be in peril because they can not discern light from heaven, and will be inclined to accept a falsehood.... The evidences that God has given are no evidence to them, because they have blinded their own eyes by choosing darkness rather than light. Then they will originate something they call light, which the Lord calls 'sparks of their own kindling'" (*Ibid.*, p. 727). "The enemy has made his masterly efforts to unsettle the faith of our own people in the Testimonies, and when these errors come in they claim to prove all the positions by the Bible, but they misinterpret the Scripture.... This is just as Satan designed it should be, and those who have been preparing the way for the people to pay no heed to the warnings and reproofs of the testimonies of the Spirit of God will see that a tide of errors of all kinds will spring into life" (*Ibid.*, p. 739).

57. Ellen G. White to Uriah Smith, Letter 25b, Aug. 30, 1892; in *1888 Materials*, p. 1008. Ellen White mentioned many times the "sparks" that were the result of rejecting light: "At the time of the loud cry of the third angel those who have been in any measure blinded by the enemy... will be inclined to accept falsehood.... After rejecting light, they will originate theories which they will call 'light,' but which the Lord calls, 'Sparks of their own kindling'" (*1888 Materials*, p. 1079). "If we neglect to walk in the light given, it becomes darkness to us; and the darkness is proportionate to the light and privileges which we have not improved" (*Ibid.*, p. 143). "When I have been made to pass over the history of the Jewish nation and have seen where they stumbled because they did not walk in the light, I have been led to realize where we as a people would be led if we refuse the light God would give us" (*Ibid.*, p. 152). "The Lord will no more excuse the rejection of light in any one of those who claim to believe in the truth in our day than He excused the Jews for their rejecting light that came from the Lord's appointed agencies. In this our day the refusal to walk in the light leaves men in darkness always" (*Ibid.*, p. 301). "O, it is the hardest place in the world to speak where great light has come to men in responsible positions. They have been enlightened, but have chosen darkness rather than light.... Their blindness of mind is correspondingly great as the light was great that shone upon them. What will be the end of this stubborn unblief [sic] we have yet to learn" (*Ibid.*, p. 710). "Many will not be convinced, because

they are not inclined to confess. To resist and reject even one ray of light from heaven because of pride and stubbornness of heart, makes it easier to refuse light the second time. Thus men form a habit of rejecting light" (*Ibid.*, p. 895).

58. Ellen G. White to W. C. White, Letter 82, March 9, 1890; in *1888 Materials*, p. 617. Ellen White repeated these thoughts many times: "I would show them that unless they were imbued with the Spirit of God they could do no good in their work.... They must walk in Christ's light or Satan would put his blinder before their eyes and they would call light darkness and darkness light" (*Ibid.*, p. 504). "Satan was roused to oppose [Jesus], for had he not put forth every effort since the fall to make light appear darkness, and darkness light? As Christ sought to place truth before the people in its proper relation to their salvation, Satan worked through the Jewish leaders, and inspired them with enmity against the Redeemer of the world. They determined to do all in their power to prevent him from making an impression upon the people" (*Ibid.*, p. 533). "Those who have had every evidence God saw fit to give them, that His spirit and power was with me, and yet turned from it all to walk in the sparks of their own kindling, and have shown a wonderful blindness, want of perception and knowing the things that be of God, and in their resistance to light and evidence in their choosing the darkness rather than the light, have virtually said, "We do not want God's ways, but we want our own ways" (*Ibid.*, p. 649). "'Sister White's testimonies are no longer reliable.'. . . These men have sown the seed and the harvest will surely follow. Now the churches have a stumblingblock placed before their feet not easily removed, and if the ones who have been engaged in this do not see and realize where they have grieved the Spirit of God and make confession of their wrongs, darkness will surely gather more densely about their souls. They will be blinded and call light darkness and darkness light, truth error and error truth, and they will not discern the light when it shall come, and will fight against it" (*Ibid.*, p. 704).

59. We would all wish that 1891 was a total victory, but writing this over 120 later, we might wonder if such optimism has only delayed our acceptance of the Laodicean message. A. V. Olson stated: "The battle had been long and hard. The victory was not won in a day or a month. No, not even in a year!... The enemy of souls made a desperate effort to wreck the Advent Movement, but, thank God, he failed. Through the mighty workings of the Spirit of God upon human hearts, the enemy was defeated" (*Through Crisis to Victory 1888-1901*, p. 113). LeRoy Froom said: "It is consequently neither accurate nor honest to maintain that Mrs. White's early statement as to the 'some' who rejected the Message in 1888 continued to be a static figure... when the proportions definitely changed in favor of acceptance. It is surely deceptive to seek to maintain that the *leadership*, or even a majority... rejected the message... much less that they maintained that attitude irrespective, in subsequent years. Such contravenes the incontrovertible facts of history" (*Movement of Destiny*, pp. 369-370). George

Knight concludes: "Those explanations [of Dan Jones] proved to be a major turning point in the post Minneapolis conflict.... From that time on the heat of the controversy significantly subsided, even though the battle over the law in Galatians and animosity toward Jones, Waggoner, and Mrs. White continued to simmer in the minds of a portion of the denomination's leaders" (*Angry Saints*, p. 93).

60. It would seem that many of George Knight's main positions on 1888 are taken from Dan Jones, and found scattered throughout his books on the topic. Knight states: "In a subsequent meeting, Ellen White came to grips with the obsession over doctrinal issues. 'She says,' Dan Jones reported, '*it is not what we believe that she feels exercised about*; it is not that we should all hold just the same view in reference to the covenants, in reference to the law in Galatians, *or in reference to any other point of doctrine; but that we should all have the spirit of Christ*, and should be united in building up and pushing forward the third angel's message' [DTJ to J. D. Pegg, Mar 17, 1890]. *That quotation takes on much more meaning when we realize that a week earlier Ellen White had publicly told the ministers, including Dan Jones, that she had been shown that Waggoner had the truth on the covenants....* In the light of that clear stand she was still more concerned with their attitudes than with their acceptance of her and Waggoner's theological position. It was that fact that had so surprised Dan Jones and opened him up to reconciliation. The next day... Dan Jones wrote to W. C. White. His letter again highlights the nature of the Minneapolis conflict [DTJ to WCW, Mar 18, 1890]." Knight continues by stating that according to Dan Jones, "those explanations [of Ellen White] proved to be a major turning point in the post Minneapolis conflict.... The spirited interchange that led to the breakthrough in March 1890 illustrates Mrs. White's point that the real crisis at Minneapolis was not theological or doctrinal, but attitudinal.... The breakthrough on the California conspiracy lessened the animosity of the spirit of Minneapolis.... One result was a renewed confidence in Ellen White" (*Angry Saints*, pp. 93-94). This same concept is presented in Knight's biography of A. T. Jones: "The message as Ellen White viewed it, is not doctrinal. We do not find her concerned with the law in Galatians, the covenants, or the Trinity. Nor do we find her expounding upon the human or divine nature of Christ or sinless living as key elements of the message. She was not even obsessed with the doctrine of righteousness by faith. Her special interest was Jesus Christ" (*From 1888 to Apostasy*, pp. 69, 52). One might rightly ask why George Knight quotes Dan Jones as an authority even though Ellen White intimated Dan Jones was at that time "working... for the devil" (*1888 Materials*, p. 596). Yet Knight rejects outright G. B. Starr's statement—"'Sister White says that we have been in the time of the latter rain since the Minneapolis meeting'" (1893 *GCB* 377)—because the "source" of that information was "not Ellen White but G. B. Starr" (*A User-Friendly Guide to the 1888 Message*, p. 112).

# CHAPTER 16

# *Confused Ideas of Salvation*

## *"I am often referred to the parable of the ten virgins"*

News travels fast even in an age before telecommunication. Following the close of the 1890 Ministerial Institute, participants who had come from across the country returned to their homes to once again take up their labors. Despite the glowing reports published in the *Review,* many sensed from the reports of the participants themselves that all had not gone well. J. S. Washburn, who was unable to attend the meetings because of "sickness in the family," was one minister who felt a deep concern for the condition of the church. He had been richly blessed the year before during the campmeeting revival at Ottawa, Kansas, and was still living under that blessing. As reports came back from Battle Creek, he began to "think it was in a measure 'Minneapolis' over again." In a desire to find out the truth about the matter and to inquire what exactly the Lord was seeking to do for His people, Washburn sent a letter to Ellen White:

> Dear Sister White… I was in the Ottawa Kansas last May attending the Institute there and I was most deeply impressed by the sermons of Eld. A. T. Jones on the righteousness of Christ and by the talks I had with you. I have been thinking since that time… that among our people before the end of time a special work on true holiness would be brought out. I have thought that now in fear of the counterfeit holiness [we] have missed very much of God's special blessing in fact have failed to experience true holiness…. It seems to me God is just holding over our heads a great blessing, but is waiting for us to be ready for it before bestowing it upon us. And that this blessing is true holiness and that when we shall come up to our duties and privileges in this matter then our work shall go with the "loud cry." Is this true or is it a mistake?… I am straining my eyes into the future for light on this subject. Is there light for us? It does seem to me as I never realized it before that we are in the condition spoken of in Rev. 3:14-17

and that our experience at Minneapolis and other places and times is evidence that we did not know it. And that there and since Christ is counseling us to buy the gold and white raiment and anoint our eyes with the eye salve, Is this so?... If out of the multitude of your cares and burdens you can find time to answer these questions your answer will be most gratefully received.[1]

Although Ellen White was still suffering exhaustion from the stressful Ministerial Institute and from carrying a heavy workload, she took the time to respond to Washburn's letter.[2]* It was with pleasure that she read his letter, "for the thought that the work of the Spirit of God wrought upon your heart at the Kansas meeting has so far not been effaced, is of great satisfaction." Washburn had received "a glimpse of the righteousness of Christ" which he had not lost as "others did when they came in contact with those who did not appreciate this blessed truth." Ellen White challenged Washburn that if he had "been permitted to stand in the presence of the Sun of Righteousness" it was not that he might "absorb and conceal the bright beams," but that he might "become a light to others." Then in page after page, Ellen White poured out her concern for the church she loved:

> When the third angel's message is preached as it should be, power attends its proclamation, and it becomes an abiding influence.... I am often referred to the parable of the ten virgins, five of whom were wise, and five foolish. This parable has been and will be fulfilled to the very letter, for it has a special application to this time....
>
> The enemy has men in our ranks through whom he works, that the light which God has permitted to shine upon the heart and illuminate the chambers of the mind may be darkened. There are persons who have received the precious light of the righteousness of Christ, but they do not act upon it; they are foolish virgins.... Satan uses those who claim to believe the truth, but whose light has become darkness, as his mediums to utter his falsehoods and transmit his darkness. They are foolish virgins indeed choosing darkness rather than light and dishonoring God.... Those who have despised the divine grace that is at their command, that would have qualified them to be the inhabitants of heaven, will be the foolish virgins....
>
> The state of the church represented by the foolish virgins, is also spoken of as the Laodicean state.... Since the time of the Minneapolis meeting, I have seen the state of the Laodicean Church as never before. I have heard the rebuke of God spoken to those who feel so well satisfied, who know not their spiritual

destitution.… Like the Jews, many have closed their eyes lest they should see; but there is as great [a] peril now… as there was when He was upon earth.…[3]*

Those who realize their need of repentance toward God, and faith toward our Lord Jesus Christ, will have contrition of soul, will repent for their resistance of the Spirit of the Lord. They will confess their sin in refusing the light that Heaven has so graciously sent them, and they will forsake the sin that grieved and insulted the Spirit of the Lord.[4]

The new 1888 edition of *The Great Controversy* contained several chapters mentioning the parable of the ten virgins and its prophetic fulfillment in the midnight cry of 1844—"behold the Bridegroom cometh." In the summer of 1844 "the two classes represented by the wise and foolish virgins were… developed." The wise virgins "had received the grace of God, the regenerating, enlightening power of the Holy Spirit, which renders His word a lamp to the feet and a light to the path." Through earnest study following the great disappointment, those with the heavenly oil came to realize that Christ had begun his work in the most holy place where the marriage was to take place, and they "went in with Him."[5]*

Just prior to the 1888 General Conference, Ellen White was informed through a dream that "the time had come when the temple and its worshipers had to be measured;" all heaven was in activity.[6] Time and again since the Minneapolis conference Ellen White had tried to help the brethren understand that God was seeking to prepare a people to stand in that day when He would return "from the wedding" (Luke 12:36). God was seeking their cooperation in the final work of atonement and sent a "most precious message" that "invited the people to receive the righteousness of Christ, which is manifest in obedience to all the commandments of God."[7] God desired to impart that heavenly oil which is not only a "symbol of the Holy Spirit;" that "oil is the righteousness of Christ. It represents character."[8]

But alas, that very message was being despised and rejected. It is no wonder that Ellen White stated that the parable of the ten virgins had been and would be fulfilled to the very letter, for it had special application to *that very time*.[9]* Those who "have despised the divine grace," who "claim to believe the truth, but whose light has become darkness," and those who "received the precious light of the righteousness of Christ, but… do not act upon it," are all alike "foolish virgins." They were responsible for bringing about the Laodicean condition.[10]*

Ellen White warned Washburn that Satan was seeking to bring in confusion through false ideas of salvation. Even the "gospel of truth" was being "contaminated":

> Are we wise virgins, or must we be classed among the foolish?… That which passes with many for the religion of Christ, is made up of ideas and theories, a mixture of truth and error. Some are trying to become good enough to be saved.… Penances, mortifications of the flesh, constant confession of sin, without sincere repentance; fasts, festivals, and outward observances, unaccompanied by true devotion,—all these are of no value whatever. The sacrifice of Christ is sufficient.… A failure to appreciate the value of the offering of Christ, has a debasing influence… it leads us to receive unsound and perilous theories concerning the salvation that has been purchased for us at infinite cost.[11]

> The reason why the churches are weak and sickly and ready to die, is that the enemy has brought influences of a discouraging nature to bear upon trembling souls. He has sought to shut Jesus from their view as the Comforter, as one who reproves, who warns, who admonishes them saying, 'This is the way, walk ye in it.'… Satan has achieved his greatest success through interposing himself between the soul and the Saviour.[12]

## *Confusion Nothing New*

Conflicting views on salvation and the resulting confusion were nothing new to Ellen White. Soon after Waggoner was prevented from presenting on the covenants during the earlier part of the 1890 Ministerial Institute, Ellen White realized the Minneapolis episode was about to be repeated. As was the case with the law in Galatians question, the real issue at the heart of the covenant question was how mankind is saved. She began to attend many of the meetings, speaking every day for three weeks with but one or two exceptions.[13]

Were Jones and Waggoner teaching some kind of heresy? Did not man have a part to play in his salvation? For several days Ellen White addressed this important issue during her morning talks. She wasted no time getting to the heart of the question—what are the conditions of salvation?

The question will come up, How is it? Is it by conditions that we receive salvation? Never by conditions do we come to Christ. And if we come to Christ, then what is the condition? The condition is that by living faith we lay hold wholly and entirely upon the merits of the blood of a crucified and risen Saviour. When we do that, then we work the works of righteousness. But when God is calling the sinner in our world, and inviting him, there is no condition there; he is drawn by the invitation of Christ and it is not, "Now you have got to respond in order to come to God." The sinner comes, and as he comes and views Christ elevated upon that cross of Calvary, which God impresses upon his mind, there is a love beyond anything that is imagined that he has taken hold of. And what then?... And there is repentance toward God; and what then?—why, faith toward our Lord and Saviour Jesus Christ that can speak pardon to the transgressor....

The devil has been working for a year to obliterate these ideas—the whole of them. And it takes hard work to change their old opinions. They think they have to trust in their own righteousness, and in their own works, and keep looking at themselves, and not appropriating the righteousness of Christ and bringing it into their life, and into their character.[14]

Yes, man has a part to play in his salvation. He is not to fight off the drawing invitation of the cross of Calvary. By beholding he is to become changed, and by a living faith he takes hold "wholly and entirely" upon the merits of Jesus Christ. Instead of looking for merit in his own righteousness, man is to look to the merits of Christ.

It was during this same time that Ellen White wrote her Manuscript 36, 1890. This manuscript was most likely based on her morning talks given to the ministers gathered in Battle Creek during the Ministerial Institute. Her heart ached as she realized that the majority of the laborers "sent forth to labor" did not themselves "understand the plan of salvation and what true conversion is; in fact they need to be converted." The ministers needed to be "enlightened" and "educated to dwell more particularly upon subjects which explain true conversion." The problem was that "unconverted men have stood in the pulpits sermonizing." They were trying to present truths that "their own hearts have never experienced." And yet, when God sent a message that contained the divine remedy for the poor condition among the ministry, the brethren were responding with "trivial" remarks, and speaking "so unguardedly of the true ideas" of Jones and Waggoner. Ellen White could "but weep" as she thought of those under the "spell of Satan."[15]*

Ellen White admonished those in a "fog of bewilderment" to heed the counsel of the true Witness: "they need the divine love represented by gold tried in the fire; they need the white raiment of Christ's pure character; and they need the heavenly eyesalve that they might discern with astonishment the utter worthlessness of creature merit to earn the wages of eternal life." The general state of the ministry was keeping the church from completing its task:

The danger has been presented to me again and again of entertaining, as a people, false ideas of justification by faith. I have been shown for years that Satan would work in a special manner to confuse the mind on this point. The law of God has been largely dwelt upon, and has been presented to congregations, almost as destitute of the knowledge of Jesus Christ and His relation to the law as was the offering of Cain. I have been shown that many have been kept from the faith because of the mixed, confused ideas of salvation, because the ministers have worked in a wrong manner to reach hearts. The point which has been urged upon my mind for years is the imputed righteousness of Christ....

There is not a point that needs to be dwelt upon more earnestly, repeated more frequently, or established more firmly in the minds of all, than the impossibility of fallen man meriting anything by his own best good works. Salvation is through faith in Jesus Christ alone....

Let the subject be made distinct and plain that it is not possible to effect anything in our standing before God or in the gift of God to us through creature merit.... Here is an opportunity for falsehood to be accepted as truth. If any man can merit salvation by anything he may do, then he is in the same position as the Catholic to do penance for his sins. Salvation, then, is partly of debt, that may be earned as wages. If man cannot, by any of his good works, merit salvation, then it must be wholly of grace, received by man as a sinner because he receives and believes in Jesus.... And all this controversy is ended, as soon as the matter is settled that the merits of fallen man in his good works can never procure eternal life for him....

Discussions may be entered into by mortals strenuously advocating creature merit, and each man striving for the supremacy, but they simply do not know that all the time, in principle and character, they are misrepresenting the truth as it is in Jesus....

I ask, How can I present this matter as it is? The Lord Jesus imparts all the powers, all the grace, all the penitence, all the inclination, all the pardon of sins, in presenting His righteousness for man to grasp by living faith—which is also the gift of God. If you would gather together everything that is good and holy and noble and lovely in man, and then present the subject to the angels of God as acting a part in the salvation of the human soul or in merit, the proposition would be rejected as treason.[16]

In order for the world to be lightened with the glory of Christ and His righteousness, there must first be an *experiential knowledge on the part of those who would share that message.* Yet, Ellen White said, "we hear so many things preached in regard to the conversion of the soul that are not the truth." It was not the message presented by Jones and Waggoner that was the cause of the trouble, for "solid faith will not lead any one away into fanaticism or into acting the slothful servant. It is the bewitching power of Satan that leads men to look to themselves in the place of looking to Jesus":

> Men are educated to think that if a man repents he shall be pardoned, supposing that repentance is the way, the door, into heaven; that there is a certain assured value in repentance to buy for him forgiveness. Can man repent of himself? No more than he can pardon himself....
>
> There is danger in regarding justification by faith as placing merit on faith. When you take the righteousness of Christ as a free gift you are justified freely through the redemption of Christ.... [W]ho gave the understanding, who moved on the heart, who first drew the mind to view Christ on the cross of Calvary. Faith is rendering to God the intellectual powers, abandonment of the mind and will to God, and making Christ the only door to enter into the kingdom of heaven.
>
> When men learn they cannot earn righteousness by their own merit of works, and they look with firm and entire reliance upon Jesus Christ as their only hope, there will not be so much of self and so little of Jesus. Souls and bodies are defiled and polluted by sin, the heart is estranged from God, yet many are struggling in their own finite strength to win salvation by good works. Jesus, they think, will do some of the saving; they must do the rest. They need to see by faith the righteousness of Christ as their only hope for time and for eternity.[17]

Ellen White elaborated on these ideas in a *Review* article published shortly after the Ministerial Institute. Many had "erroneous ideas in regard to the nature of repentance." They were under the impression that one "cannot come to Christ unless they first repent, and that repentance prepares them for the forgiveness of their sins." Only those who have a "broken and contrite heart" will "feel the need of a Saviour. But must the sinner wait until he has repented before he can come to Jesus? Is repentance to be made an obstacle between the sinner and the Saviour?" Repentance is as much a gift to be received as is forgiveness. It is Christ who is "constantly drawing men to Himself, while Satan is as diligently seeking by every imaginable device to draw men away from their Redeemer." This is exactly what Satan was seeking to do to the message that was to lighten the earth with its glory:

> Some of our brethren have expressed fears that we shall dwell too much upon the subject of justification by faith, but I hope and pray that none will be needlessly alarmed; for there is no danger in presenting this doctrine as it is set forth in the Scriptures.... Some of our brethren are not receiving the message of God upon this subject. They appear to be anxious that none of our ministers shall depart from their former manner of teaching the good old doctrines. We inquire, Is it not time that fresh light should come to the people of God, to awaken them to greater earnestness and zeal?... [Satan] has cast his own dark shadow between us and our God, that we may not see the true character of God....
>
> Several have written to me, inquiring if the message of justification by faith is the third angel's message, and I have answered, "It is the third angel's message in verity." The prophet declares, "And after these things I saw another angel come down from heaven, having great power; and the earth was lightened with his glory." Brightness, glory, and power are to be connected with the third angel's message, and conviction will follow wherever it is preached in demonstration of the Spirit. How will any of our brethren know when this light shall come to the people of God? As yet, we certainly have not seen the light that answers to this description. God has light for his people, and all who will accept it will see the sinfulness of remaining in a lukewarm condition; they will heed the counsel of the True Witness.[18]

The message of justification by faith presented by Jones and Waggoner was the "third angel's message in verity" that was to be attended with "brightness, glory, and power" from that angel of Revelation 18 and lighten the earth with glory. But how would the brethren recognize this light if they continued in a "lukewarm condition"? They were in such a state that they could not see "the light that answers to this description." As a result, Ellen White could solemnly state: "This I do know, that our churches are dying for the want of teaching on the subject of righteousness by faith in Christ, and for kindred truths."[19]

## *Law and Gospel Combined*

One of the greatest concerns the brethren had with what Jones and Waggoner were teaching was that the moral law was being undermined, thus doing away with the Sabbath, the third angel's message, and the very reason for the Church's existence. Ellen White, however, was just as sure that the message of Jones and Waggoner was not doing away with the law, but rather combined the law and the gospel in a way that if understood would "lighten the earth with its glory."[20]* Many times she referred to this vital combination as the answer to all the confusion and extremes both inside and outside of the church. In Ellen White's Manuscript 36, mentioned earlier, she addressed this important issue. The "absence of devotion, piety, and sanctification of the outer man," came not as a result of Jones' and Waggoner's teaching, but "through denying Jesus Christ our righteousness":

> While one class pervert the doctrine of justification by faith and neglect to comply with the conditions laid down in the Word of God—"If ye love Me, keep My commandments"—there is fully as great an error on the part of those who claim to believe and obey the commandments of God but who place themselves in opposition to the precious rays of light—new to them—reflected from the cross of Calvary. The first class do not see the wondrous things in the law of God for all who are doers of His Word. The others cavil over trivialities and neglect the weightier matters, mercy and the love of God....

> On the one hand, religionists generally have divorced the law and the gospel, while we have, on the other hand, almost done the same from another standpoint. We have not held up before the people the righteousness of Christ and the full significance of His great plan of redemption. We have left out Christ and His matchless love, brought in theories and reasoning, and preached argumentative discourses.[21]

Ellen White penned similar words in her *Review* article of May 27, 1890. "The relation of Christ to the law" was but "faintly comprehended." The brethren were shrinking "from the presentation of justification by faith." Yet Ellen White added, "just as soon as Christ is discovered in His true position in relation to the law, the misconception that has existed on this important matter will be removed. The law and the gospel are so blended that the truth cannot be presented as it is in Jesus, without blending these subjects in perfect agreement. The law is the gospel of Christ veiled; the gospel of Jesus is nothing more or less than the law defined, showing its far-reaching principles."[22]

These thoughts were not only shared publicly, but Ellen White contemplated their significance in her diary: "The law and the gospel go hand in hand. The one is the complement of the other. The law without faith in the gospel of Christ cannot save the transgressor of law. The gospel without the law is inefficient and powerless. The law and the gospel are a perfect whole.... The two blended... produce the love and faith unfeigned."[23]

In a diary entry written just prior to the 1891 General Conference, Ellen White again emphasized these important points. There was a fear "that there was danger of carrying the subject of justification by faith altogether too far, and of not dwelling enough on the law." Yet she herself saw "no cause for alarm," when the subject was based "not on the ideas and opinions of men, but on a plain 'Thus saith the Lord:'"

> Many remarks have been made to the effect that in our campmeetings the speakers have dwelt upon the law, the law, and not on Jesus. This statement is not strictly true, but have not the people had some reason for making these remarks?... Many of our ministers have merely sermonized, presenting subjects in an argumentative way and scarcely mentioning the saving power of the Redeemer.... Why is not He presented to the people as the Living Bread?— Because He is not abiding in the hearts of many of those who think it their duty to preach the law....

> The law and the gospel, revealed in the Word, are to be preached to the people; for the law and the gospel, blended, will convict of sin. God's law, while condemning sin, points to the gospel, revealing Jesus Christ.... In no discourse are they to be divorced....

> Many have been teaching the binding claims of God's law, but have not been able to see to the end of that which was abolished. They have not seen that Jesus Christ is the glory of the law.... Many of our brethren and sisters do not discern the wondrous things that are seen in God's law....

> The religion of many is very much like an icicle—freezing cold.... They cannot touch the hearts of others, because their own hearts are not surcharged with the blessed love that flows from the heart of Christ.... They dwell upon stern duty as if it were a master ruling with a scepter of iron—a master, stern, inflexible, and powerful—devoid of the sweet, melting love and tender compassion of Christ. Still others go to the opposite extreme, making religious emotions prominent, and on special occasions manifesting intense zeal....

Many commit the error of trying to define minutely the fine points of distinction between justification and sanctification.[24]* Into the definitions of these two terms they often bring their own ideas and speculations. Why try to be more minute than inspiration on the vital question of righteousness by faith? Why try to work out every minute point, as if the salvation of the soul depended upon all having exactly your understanding of this matter?... You are making a world of an atom, and an atom of a world.[25]

Only a few weeks later Ellen White spoke before the General Conference and those who were "indulging skepticism and infidelity," refusing the message God had sent: "When we speak of the grace of God, of Jesus and His love, speak of the Saviour as one who is able to keep us from sin, and to save to the uttermost all who come unto Him, many will say, 'O, I am afraid you are going where the holiness people go. I am afraid you are going after the Salvation Army.' Brethren, you need not be afraid of the plain teachings of the Bible.... Do not let any man or woman, or any council or party, lead you to suppress the precious light that God has permitted to shine from heaven in regard to the commandments of God and the testimony of Jesus."[26]*

The result of divorcing the law and the gospel always brings extremes and false doctrine. The "religionists," or "holiness people," or dispensationalists, had separated the law from the gospel, failing to recognize "the wondrous things in the law of God." Yet their understanding of the gospel was not correct either. They claimed with "great zeal... 'Only believe in Christ, and be saved; but away with the law of God'" and just as zealously proclaimed they were "holy" and "sinless."[27] Many Adventists, "on the other hand, [had] almost done the same from another standpoint." They had failed to see the full significance of the "righteousness of Christ and... His great plan of redemption." Neither had they understood the immensity of the law; otherwise they would not have "thought that their own merits were of considerable value."[28] Both extremes had a false idea of what constituted true holiness.

The "most precious message" sent through Jones and Waggoner was not a combination of two false extremes but *the truth* of the law and the gospel combined: "There is *much light* yet to shine forth *from the law of God and the gospel of righteousness*. This message, understood in its true character, and proclaimed in the Spirit, will lighten the earth with its glory."[29] Those who turned away from the message often gave conflicting views; some attributing it to perfectionism, others to antinomianism. Notwithstanding, the true message was a clearer understanding of both the *law* and the *gospel* and their great power when combined. This was a complete message which was to be grasped by a genuine living faith that would inevitably work by love. The message led neither to liberalism or legalism, to antinomianism or perfectionism.

## *Misplacing the Blame*

Ellen White was clear that the confusion coming into the church was the result of refusing heaven-sent blessings. Others, however, were not so sure. The week that Washburn wrote to Ellen White inquiring about what was taking place, Dan Jones was attending a Minister's Institute in Kansas City, some sixty miles north from where the revival meetings took place in Ottawa Kansas the year before. He found that "some of the best ministers in the state" were under "a cloud and going into discouragement." Dan Jones attributed the cause for such discouragement to the "exaggerated ideas they had received of what our brethren [Jones and Waggoner] taught on the subject of justification by faith." The brethren had "got the idea that the position is now taken that we should stand in a position where we do not sin, that all sin should be put away entirely."[30]

Strangely enough, not only were some confused on the genuine results of true faith that works by love, others "had got the idea some way that the doctrine of justification by faith practically did away with the law." Of course, Dan Jones stated that he "explained the position that we do take on the subject of justification" with the endorsement of Bro. Covert and Eld. Farnsworth, which made the brethren feel "much better."[31] Reporting to R. C. Porter a few days later, Dan Jones shared more of his concerns and whom he felt was to blame:

> There is a rumor afloat,—how much credit to give to it I can not tell,—that Sister White is coming out in a testimony against Bro. Smith and Bro. Butler, that stirs up the Captain [Eldridge]. I hope this may prove to be only a rumor, and that everything will conspire to let this matter of the covenant question and the Minneapolis matter rest for awhile until it dies out of the minds of the people.

From what I can learn, there has been a great deal of discouragement all over the field, especially on the part of ministers (It may be just as extensive among lay brethren, but we have not had opportunity to ascertain that yet), that has grown out of the Sabbath school lessons, and the discussions that have been had on the covenant question, and the law in Galatians. Some of our best ministers do not seem to know what to believe, and they are all broken up.… [T]he reason for the discouragement was that new doctrines were coming in, and our people were becoming unsettled as to the old landmarks, and they did not know what to preach as they went out to the field.… [A]s they were throwing away old and accepted doctrines, and taking up new ones, they thought there was not much assurance that those which we now hold might not be thrown away in the future, and new theories accepted in their place. I find the agitation on the covenant question and justification by faith has lost none of its force as it has gone out to different parts of the field, but has rather gathered strength and taken on objectionable features, until they see it now in a much worse light than it really is. How I wish our leading brethren could get together and settle all these things among themselves, and not bring them before the public where the influence will go out and discourage the brethren in all parts of the field, and weaken their hands in the work which God has given them to do.[32]

Rather than hope the brethren would repent, Dan Jones hoped the Testimonies would remain silent. He wished they could get together and settle the matter not realizing that the two special meetings held in Battle Creek would have done so if hearts were open to receive the evidence. Dan Jones had clear enough vision to see that there were problems throughout the field, but darkness created by the sparks of his own kindling blinded him to the real cause. He felt there was a "marked contrast" between the second quarter Sabbath school lessons (written by J. H. Waggoner) and those they had used during the winter (by E. J. Waggoner): "The lessons now [by J. H. Waggoner] are full of hope and faith and courage. I enjoy them exceedingly, and know that they contain meat for our people everywhere. How unfortunate, it seems to me, that the others [by E. J. Waggoner] should not have been of the same character… What we get in this world is a mixture of good and evil, usually with the evil very much predominating. I have come to the conclusion that even among Seventh-day Adventists it is necessary for us to heed the injunction of the Apostle, 'Try all things; hold fast that which is good.'… [I]f it does not stand the test, it should be rejected."[33]

By late summer, Dan Jones was willing to admit to E. W. Farnsworth that although every man claimed to believe in justification by faith, many were in fact fighting against it. He was also honest enough to admit that feelings of jealousy had cropped up as a result of seeing so many hungry people take in a special message they had never fully heard or understood before:

> I too have thought a good deal about this matter and my mind has been exercised much the same as your own. I have thought it over and over and have come to the conclusion that the position held by those that did not fully indorse the view on justification by faith, while they claim to believe fully in that doctrine, has been practically one of opposition to it. I know there is not a man that would say that he did not believe in justification by faith. We all believe it and claim to endorse it fully; but, as you say, we have not felt in sympathy with those who have been making a specialty of presenting this subject to the people, and it has really been almost mortifying to us to see the hungry people take it in as it has been presented to them. I am free to confess that I have not felt just right on this matter.[34]

No sooner had Dan Jones made this confession, however, than he began to make excuses for his own feelings and actions. He was "not ready to say yet" that he had done "wrong, and that Dr. Waggoner did right" in the matter of the covenant question: "What I have criticized most in the course of those who have pushed the subject of justification and some other questions, is the spirit in which it has been done. I cannot believe that it is done in the spirit of Christ. All along I have had more objection to that than to the matter itself. But… perhaps we have looked more at the men that were doing the work and the manner in which it was done, than at the work itself."[35]

## *No Heresy, No Fanaticism!*

Many of those who opposed the message presented by Jones and Waggoner vacillated on the reasons for their opposition. At times the content of the message was the focus of their objections, while on other occasions the spirit of the messengers was held up as the reason for opposition. To both of these objections Ellen White gave an answer. In a *Review* article printed soon after the 1890 Ministerial Institute, Ellen White exposed the thinking of those who were objecting. Because many felt they could not accept the message of truth presented, they would turn to the messengers seeking to find flaws in order to excuse their doubts. To this Ellen White gave one of her strongest warnings; the loud cry would not be comprehended, the latter rain would be called a false light:

> Do not stand as many of you have done, apparently wavering between dependence upon the righteousness of Christ, and dependence upon your own righteousness. Deception has come upon some minds until they have thought that their own merits were of considerable value....

> All will come to a decision wholly for God or for Baal. God has sent to His people testimonies of truth and righteousness, and they are called to lift up Jesus, and to exalt his righteousness. Those whom God has sent with a message are only men, but what is the character of the message which they bear? Will you dare to turn from, or make light of, the warnings, because God did not consult you as to what would be preferred? God calls men who will speak, who will cry aloud and spare not. God has raised up His messengers to do his work for this time. Some have turned from the message of the righteousness of Christ to criticize the men and their imperfections, because they do not speak the message of truth with all the grace and polish desirable. They have too much zeal, are too much in earnest, speak with too much positiveness, and the message that would bring healing and life and comfort to many weary and oppressed souls, is, in a measure, excluded.... Christ has registered all the hard, proud, sneering speeches spoken against his servants as against Himself.

> The third angel's message will not be comprehended, the light which will lighten the earth with its glory will be called a false light, by those who refuse to walk in its advancing glory. The work that might have been done, will be left undone by the rejecters of truth, because of their unbelief. We entreat of you who oppose the light of truth, to stand out of the way of God's people.... Messages bearing the divine credentials have been sent to God's people.... We know that God has wrought among us.... [D]o not think that you have caught all the rays of light, that there is no increased illumination to come to our world.[36]

Exactly three months later, Ellen White again clarified the reason for the confusion coming into the Church. It was not the message or the spirit of the messengers, but the spirit of those who were resisting:

> The spirit of resistance that has been exhibited in presenting the righteousness of Christ as our only hope has grieved the Spirit of God, and the result of this opposition has required the delivery of this matter the more earnestly and decidedly, causing deeper searching into the subject and calling out an array

of arguments that the messenger himself did not know was so firm, so full, so thorough upon this subject of justification by faith and the righteousness of Christ as our only hope....

It has caused me great sadness of heart to see that those who ought to be giving the trumpet a certain sound... to prepare a people to stand in the day of the Lord, are in darkness and have stood as sentinels to bar the way that the confusion they create would bring confusion and misunderstanding. Satan sees it is his time to make a strike. Fanaticism and errors will prevail, and the men who ought to have stood in the light... were exercised on the wrong side to oppose that which was of God.... Their position [Jones and Waggoner] is seen to be wrong by very many, and they cry, "Danger, fanaticism," when there is no heresy and fanaticism....

Now the churches have a stumblingblock placed before their feet not easily removed, and if the ones who have been engaged in this do not see and realize where they have grieved the Spirit of God and make confession of their wrongs, darkness will surely gather more densely about their souls. They will be blinded and call light darkness and darkness light, truth error and error truth, and they will not discern the light when it shall come, and will fight against it.[37]

In the book *The Great Controversy*, printed in the summer of 1888, Ellen White described the darkness that came into the Protestant churches who rejected the light of the first and second angel's messages. Here a clear warning was given: "The spiritual darkness which falls upon nations, upon churches and individuals, is due, not to an arbitrary withdrawal of the succors of divine grace on the part of God, but to the neglect or rejection of divine light on the part of men....

Where the message of divine truth is spurned or slighted, there the church will be enshrouded in darkness; faith and love will grow cold, and estrangement and dissension enter. Church members center their interest and energies in worldly pursuits, and sinners become hardened in their impenitence."[38]

The darkness that was settling upon many in the Seventh-day Adventist Church in 1890 was not the result of the *message* given by Jones and Waggoner, nor was it the result of an offensive *spirit* on their part, it was rather the direct result of spurning and slighting divine truth. Not only had "estrangement and dissension" entered the work, but also as we shall see in the next chapter, worldly policies were creeping in, blurring the vision and the message that was to be given to the world.

# CHAPTER 16 FOOTNOTES

1. J. S. Washburn to Ellen G. White, April 17, 1890; in *Manuscripts and Memories*, p. 174.

2. Unfortunately Washburn never received Ellen White's reply. By early June, following his mother's death, Washburn was in a very "discouraged condition." J. H. Durland reported that Washburn "said he had felt like giving up everything.... He spoke freely of the unfavorable influence of the leading ministers in the Conf. on the Testimonies." Thankfully after Durland spent "nearly half a day" with Washburn, "he began to see light and... came back to the tent rejoicing" (J. H. Durland to O. A. Olsen, June 2, 1890). Finally in September, Washburn wrote a second letter to Ellen White. She responded that very day, explaining what had taken place: "The article in the paper [*Review and Herald*, Aug. 19 and 26, 1890] was an answer to your letter. I wrote it as a private letter long before it appeared in the *Review*; but as I read it to a few of our brethren, they urged me to put it in the paper, that others might be benefited by it, and I consented." Ellen White agreed to this, but "the delay [she] could not interpret," for there was to be "no delay in printing the matter." Not only had Washburn never received a copy, but the letter was not published in the *Review* until August 19 and 26, 1890, four months after Ellen White wrote it (Ellen G. White to J. S. Washburn, Letter 36a, Sept. 18, 1890; in *1888 Materials*, p. 708).

3. Ellen G. White, "The Righteousness of Christ," *Review and Herald*, Aug. 19, 1890, p. 497. The opening remarks of the Aug. 19, 1890 *Review* article make it clear that it was originally a personal letter written in response to Washburn's inquiry. The concluding article of Aug. 26, 1890, does not repeat this information, but is the only portion of the letter included in the *Ellen G. White 1888 Materials*.

4. Ellen G. White, "The Righteousness of Christ (concluded)," *Review and Herald*, Aug. 26, 1890, p. 513; in *1888 Materials*, pp. 695-696.

5. Ellen G. White, *The Great Controversy*, p. 427, 1888 ed., see also pp. 391-432.

6. Ellen G. White Manuscript 26, Oct. 1888; in *1888 Materials*, p. 157.

7. Ellen G. White, *Testimonies to Ministers*, pp. 92, 234.

8. Ellen G. White, *Christ's Object Lessons*, p. 407.

9. This would not be the last time Ellen White was impressed that this parable was being fulfilled: "We see that the professed believers will be represented by the ten virgins, five of whom were wise, and five were foolish. I fear this is the average the Lord saw of those that would be unready.... Those who, since the Minneapolis meeting have had the privilege of listening to the words spoken by the messengers of God... have had the invitation, 'Come, for all things are now ready....' Those who have made their various excuses for neglecting to respond to the call; have lost much. The light has been shining upon justification by faith and the imputed righteousness of Christ" (Ellen G. White to J. E. White, Letter 86, Sept. 26, 1895; in *1888 Materials*, pp. 1455-1456).

10. Once again this refutes the idea that the 1888 message was accepted because many believed it "theoretically" or assented to it (see chapter 6). What was the remedy? "The message given us by A. T. Jones, and E. J. Waggoner is the message of God to the Laodicean church, and woe unto anyone who professes to believe the truth and yet does not reflect to others the God-given rays" (Ellen G. White to Uriah Smith, Letter 24, Sept. 19, 1892; in *1888 Materials*, p. 1052).

11. Ellen G. White, "The Righteousness of Christ," *Review and Herald*, Aug. 19, 1890, p. 497.

12. Ellen G. White, "The Righteousness of Christ (concluded)," *Review and Herald*, Aug. 26, 1890, p. 513; in *1888 Materials*, p. 696.

13. Ellen G. White Manuscript 22, "Diary Entries," Feb. 8, 1890; in *1888 Materials*, p. 579; and Dan Jones to E. W. Farnsworth, Feb. 9, 1890, archives of the General Conference of Seventh-day Adventists.

14. Ellen G. White Manuscript 9, Feb. 3, 1890; in *1888 Materials*, pp. 537, 542.

15. Ellen G. White Manuscript 36, n.d., 1890; in *1888 Materials*, pp. 811, 821-822 (This same manuscript is published in *Faith and Works*, pp. 15-28. However, the order of the paragraphs is different than that found in *1888 Materials*, which gives it a slightly different emphasis). Sadly, the plight of the theology promoted by Butler, Smith, Dan Jones and many others was epitomized in the *Way of Life* engraving first commissioned by James White in 1876. While seeking to uplift the downtrodden law by making it the center focus of their theology—as seen in the large "law tree" at the center of the picture—they inadvertently made it impossible for believers to be law-keepers in the fullest sense by taking the focus off Christ. The second *Way of Life* picture, based on James White's revisions, illustrated appropriately the very element that God was bringing into the work through the message of Jones and Waggoner—**Christ** *the Way of Life*. See chapter 1 (*Preach Christ More*), footnote 33.

16. *Ibid.*, pp. 810-816.

17. *Ibid.*, pp. 810-816.

18. Ellen G. White, "Repentance the Gift of God," *Review and Herald*, April 1, 1890, pp. 193-194.

19. Ellen G. White, "Morning Talk," Feb. 6, 1890, *Review and Herald*, March 25, 1890; in *1888 Materials*, p. 548.

20. Ellen G. White Manuscript 15, Nov. 1888; in *1888 Materials*, p. 166. In his book, *The 1888 Message for the Year 2000*, Steve Wohlberg focuses largely on this aspect of the 1888 message, bringing out many interesting and helpful insights (pp. 17-25, 28-105). It must be remembered, however, that this aspect is not the sum total of that message, nor is it sufficient in itself in explaining what took place at Minneapolis and the years that followed.

21. Ellen G. White Manuscript 36, n.d., 1890; in *1888 Materials*, p. 822, and *Faith and Works*, pp. 15-16.

22. Ellen G. White, "Living Channels of Light," *Review and Herald*, May 27, 1890; in *1888 Materials*, p. 674.

23. Ellen G. White Manuscript 53, "Diary Entries," Dec. 1890; in *1888 Materials*, p. 783.

24. The context of this paragraph in Ellen White's diary must be understood in the light of the entire entry. She was writing of those who were afraid of "carrying the subject of justification by faith altogether too far;" those who "merely sermonized" and gave "argumentative" discourses; those who had divorced the gospel from the law; those who took "wrong positions in the controversy over the law in Galatians." It was in this context that she stated; "many commit the error of trying to define minutely the fine points of distinction." George Knight has taken this paragraph to mean that Ellen White was writing a "disclaimer to the position that a theological understanding of righteousness by faith is all-important.... The message of 1888, as Ellen White viewed it, is not doctrinal" (*From 1888 to Apostasy*, p. 69). But throughout her diary entry, Ellen White expressed just the opposite. The law and the gospel blended was the answer to all the false ideas that resulted from separating the two grand truths. This was that message, "rightly understood" that would lighten the earth with its glory (*1888 Materials*, p. 166).

25. Ellen G. White Manuscript 21, Feb. 27, 1891; in *1888 Materials*, pp. 890-898.

26. Ellen G. White, "Our Present Danger," Evening Talk, March 24, 1891, *General Conference Daily Bulletin*, April 13, 1891; in *1888 Materials*, p. 904. W. A. Spicer, long time missionary, editor and administrator, shared an experience that sheds some light on Ellen White's comment about going after the Salvation Army: "The sound of that call from Minneapolis went out over the land, and over all lands where we had workers. We heard it over in England, where I was at the time [1888].... It was a call to preach the only gospel that ever has been. Yet, somehow, brethren—good brethren—stumbled over the way the call had come, it seemed. The first time I met an old layman friend and worker on my return from Europe, he said to me: 'Ah, you won't know yourself here. Now it is all Salvation Army, glory hallelujah, you will find.' But a few years of service in Europe, trying to win men to Christ, I had learned not to be afraid of telling out our joy in Christ's salvation" ("The General Conference of 1888—Blessings and Trails," *Review and Herald*, March 9, 1944, pp. 6, 7).

27. Ellen G. White, *Faith and Works*, pp. 15-16; "Campmeeting at Williamsport, Pa," *Review and Herald*, Aug. 13, 1889, p. 514; "Hearing and Doing," March 7, 1885, *Sermons and Talks*, vol. 1, p. 18.

28. Ellen G. White, *Faith and Works*, pp. 15-16; "Living Channels of Light," *Review and Herald*, May 27, 1890, p. 321; in *1888 Materials*, p. 673.

29. Ellen G. White Manuscript 15, Nov. 1888; in *1888 Materials*, p. 166, emphasis supplied. See also, Chapter 9, footnote 16.

30. Dan T. Jones to O. A. Olsen, April 27, 1890, archives of the General Conference of Seventh-day Adventists.

31. *Ibid*.

32. Dan T. Jones to R. C. Porter, May 5, 1890, archives of the General Conference of Seventh-day Adventists.

33. *Ibid*.

34. Dan T. Jones to E. W. Farnsworth, Sept. 19, 1890, archives of the General Conference of Seventh-day Adventists.

35. *Ibid*.

36. Ellen G. White, "Living Channels of Light," *Review and Herald*, May 27, 1890, pp. 321-322; in *1888 Materials*, pp. 673-674.

37. Ellen G. White to O. A. Olsen, Letter 116, Aug. 27, 1890; in *1888 Materials*, pp. 703-704.

38. Ellen G. White, *The Great Controversy*, pp. 377, 378.

# CHAPTER 17

# *Religious Liberty*

## *"Take Not the First Steps in This Road That Leads to the Inquisition"*

If Dan Jones seemed harsh in regard to Waggoner's Sabbath School lessons, he was more so in regard to A. T. Jones' work for religious liberty. In 1887, the General Conference appointed a Religious Liberty Committee to help direct in the momentous work, electing A. T. Jones as president. With increasing legislation seeking to instigate Sunday laws, the need to publicize the religious liberty issue became more urgent. At the request of E. J. Waggoner, the General Conference appointed A. T. Jones as a delegate

to appear before the Senate to speak against the Blair bill.[1] In July 1889, the National Religious Liberty Association (NRLA) replaced the Religious Liberty Committee; Captain Eldridge replaced A. T. Jones as president and Dan Jones became vice president. The *American Sentinel*, although not officially connected with the NRLA, was the church's official religious liberty paper. With both A. T. Jones and E. J. Waggoner as editors, the *Sentinel* had reached a yearly circulation of more than 260,000 by 1889, and played a major role in alerting U. S. citizens to the impending Sunday-law crisis.[2]

SENATOR HENRY W. BLAIR

437

Because Jones and Waggoner had spent so much time back east since 1889, C. P. Bollman became local managing editor of the *Sentinel* in California. But not all appreciated his work nor that of the editors of the *Sentinel* through whom so much had been done.

As early as December, 1888, Ellen White declared that the *Sentinel* had been "in God's order, one of the voices sounding the alarm, that the people might hear, and realize their danger, and do the work required at the present time." Yet, she grieved that "much might have been done with the *Sentinel*, if counter-influences [inside the church] had not been at work to hinder it,… to make of none effect the warnings [given]."[3]

At the 1889 General Conference, the newly formed NRLA passed bylaws that would attempt to hinder the work of the *Sentinel* even more. Although the *Sentinel* was not officially under the NRLA's jurisdiction, many of its officers, including Dan Jones and Captain Eldridge, sought complete control over the paper's content.[4]

Even though A. T. Jones had been most successful in his work for religious liberty, speaking twice before the U. S. Senate against the Blair bill, Dan Jones and many others did not appreciate what they felt were "extravagant positions." This all came to a head in early 1890, about the same time the newest Sunday legislation was introduced to Congress.

Writing to A. W. Allee in late January, Dan Jones gave counsel against inviting Jones and Waggoner, "champion anti–national Reform men," to an Institute held in Missouri. He did not "have very much confidence in some of their ways of presenting things. They try to drive everything before them, and will not admit that their position can possibly be subject to the least criticism." Dan Jones also conceded that "our more thoughtful men,—Bro. Smith, Bro. Littlejohn, Bro. Corliss, Bro. Gage, and others,—do not agree with them on many positions which they take on National Reform, and on some theological questions." For this reason he felt Allee would "not want to bring that spirit into the Missouri Conference" along with all the "high–falutin theory that never has worked and never will work anywhere."[5] Dan Jones expressed similar feelings to others during the time of the Ministerial Institute.

C. H. JONES

He told C. H. Jones, manager of Pacific Press, that it was "that disposition, to crowd in and take advantage, that seems to be so manifest in both Dr. Waggoner and Eld. A. T. Jones that makes their labors unpleasant to some of the brethren here in Battle Creek, I think: and we can readily account for its being so."[6]*

Early in 1890, the brethren decided to move the *Sentinel* back to the Pacific Press branch office in New York City. This would bring the *Sentinel* closer to the heart of the religious liberty work and to where A. T. Jones could more closely oversee its production. When C. P. Bollman, local managing editor for the *Sentinel*, came from San Francisco on his way to New York, he stopped in Battle Creek for a few days. He wished to speak to Captain Eldridge, president of the NRLA, about "the position the *Sentinel* should hold in relation to the NRLAssociation." In Eldridge's absence, vice president Dan Jones responded to Bollman's inquiry. He talked "to him straight about the *Sentinel* and its extravagant positions and unnecessary personalities; told him plainly that [he] did not take any stock in it either." Later A. T. Jones, W. C. White and some others were called in to "talk the matter over again." Dan Jones shared his views telling them "that until there could be some change in the tone of the paper, I should oppose connecting it in any way with the NRL Association." Although "no promises" were made, Dan Jones conceded there was "considerable improvement" three months after the paper moved to New York. Still he was not completely satisfied and continued "private correspondence" trying to get the paper improved further: "Some of their hairsplitting, so called logical reasoning is ridiculous, and should not enter into such a paper."[7]

W. C. White, on the other hand, was not of the same mind. Writing to tell A. T. Jones he had just received the "proofs" for the next *Sentinel*, White unabashedly stated: "We are doing all we can to increase the circulation of the *Sentinel*." Although, he too, felt there was an improvement in the paper in regard to "sharp thrusts and hard sayings" since it had moved to New York, he did not consider the paper in the same light that Dan Jones did: "I beg of you to do all you can to secure for us at an early date such tracts [as] are needed for our present work."[8]

Ellen White, who was in Battle Creek at the time, said nothing in regard to the *Sentinel*, notwithstanding that time would soon come. It was not until the end of 1890 that she specifically voiced again her strong support for A. T. Jones' work for religious liberty through the pages of the *Sentinel*. Although Jones and Waggoner were only men and subject to human weakness, Ellen White had warned the brethren repeatedly against seeking to find fault in them in order to excuse their rejection of the present message: "Do not catch at every objection, however small, and make it as large as possible, and preserve it for future use. No one has said that we shall find perfection in any man's investigations."[9] She sternly admonished the unbelieving brethren: "Now, I want you to be careful, everyone of you, what position you take, whether you enshroud yourselves in the clouds of unbelief because you see imperfections; you see a word or a little item, perhaps, that may take place, and judge them from that. You are to see what God is doing with them. You are to see whether God is working with them, and then you are to acknowledge the Spirit of God that is revealed in them. And if you choose to resist it you will be acting just as the Jews acted."[10]

## *Accomplishments Speak for Themselves*

On January 6, 1890, Representative W. C. P. Breckenridge of Kentucky introduced a bill designed to "prevent anyone from being forced to labor on Sunday" within the District of Columbia. Seventh-day Adventists held that the bill was deceptive since no one was being compelled to labor on Sunday. Its actual purpose was to force people to rest on Sunday. The bill appeared to be just an initial step on the pathway of religious legislation toward complete Sunday laws.[11]

Emotions ran high at a well-advertised Sunday Law Convention held in Washington, D.C. early that year in Washington, D. C. Reverend Wilber F. Crafts, National Sunday law advocate, spoke very critically of Seventh-day Adventists, whom he said were ardently fighting the bill even with its "liberal provisions." A second speaker denounced Adventists as "'an insignificant sect of narrow-minded bigots'" who joined with atheists, secularists, and socialists to oppose the bill. A third speaker launched a "personal attack on Alonzo Jones… for his efforts to defeat the bill." This emotional state of mind continued throughout the bill's initial hearing.[12]

Finally on February 18, 1890, a hearing was held before the House Committee on the Breckenridge bill. A. T. Jones, along with two other Seventh-day Adventists, stood before the Committee speaking against the bill. Jones not only argued very powerfully against the bill's unconstitutionality, but he also used arguments from one of Rev. Crafts' own books to prove there was no need for this legislation. "After the hearing, members of the Congressional Committee grasped the hands" of A. T. Jones and the other Adventist "representatives… and congratulated them on the strength of their position, while the advocates of the Sunday bill 'silently stole away.'" The House Committee apparently satisfied itself that the measure was religious and in violation of the First Amendment, and the Breckenridge Bill went down in defeat.[13]

Returning to Battle Creek after the hearings, A. T. Jones gave a talk at the Minister's devotional meeting on the morning of March 20, 1890. O. A. Olsen reported that it was "deeply interesting to note how the providence of God has gone out before us." The Lord had "directed it" so that certain people were in the right place at the right time, and "things fitted in so exactly and so properly" that it was obvious He was leading:

> Bro. Jones also stated that he had never realized the blessing of God in such a measure as when he spoke before the committee of the house in the last hearing. He said, it seemed as though the sentences he should speak were written on the wall, or suspended in the air before him; and it was not only they themselves that felt that they had a blessing, but all who were present could appreciate and realize that the power of God was there in a most remarkable manner. All these things are encouraging indications.[14]*

Dan Jones reported that "it was very impressive to hear [A. T. Jones] tell of it, and how the Spirit of God worked for them there." At times "during his speech it seemed that the words and sentences were just before his eyes as plainly as if they were written, and that he seemed to be reading them off as if they were held up before him in large letters." Indeed the Lord had picked the right man for the job and had blessed him with His Spirit.[15]*

But even with all this evidence that the Lord was using A. T. Jones to do a grand work, Dan Jones was as a man convinced against his will and thus of the same opinion still. No sooner had he finished reporting on A. T. Jones' providential experience in Washington than he took up his complaint about the "very bad shape" of things that resulted from Jones and Waggoner bringing in the law in Galatians and covenant questions.[16]

Ellen White was rightly troubled by the disposition of the brethren toward Jones and Waggoner. By turning from all the evidence that "God is working *with* them" and failing to "acknowledge the Spirit of God that is revealed *in* them," the brethren were "acting just as the Jews acted."[17] It was during this time that Ellen White penned the words in *Patriarchs and Prophets*: "It is hardly possible for men to offer greater insult to God than to despise and reject the instrumentalities He would use for their salvation."[18]

But Ellen White's concern was for more than just the leading brethren. She was concerned for the "young men" who were "watching to see in what spirit the ministers come to the investigation of the Scriptures; whether they have a teachable spirit, and are humble enough to accept evidence, and receive light from the messengers whom God chooses to send." This led her to admonish: "Young men should search the Scriptures for themselves…. The Jews perished as a nation because they were drawn from the truth of the Bible by their rulers, priests, and elders. Had they heeded the lessons of Jesus, and searched the Scriptures for themselves, they would not have perished."[19] Writing in *The Signs of the Times*, Ellen White underscored this crucial point:

> Should the Lord reveal light after His own plan, many would not respect or comprehend it; they would ridicule the bearer of God's message as one who set himself up above those who were better qualified to teach. The papal

authorities first ridiculed the reformers, and when this did not quench the spirit of investigation, they placed them behind prison walls.... We should be very cautious lest we take the first steps in this road that leads to the Inquisition. The truth of God is progressive; it is always onward, going from strength to greater strength, from light to greater light. We have much reason to believe that the Lord will send us increased truth, for a great work is yet to be done... Much has been lost because our ministers and people have concluded that we have had all the truth essential for us as a people; but such a conclusion is erroneous and in harmony with the deceptions of Satan; for truth will be constantly unfolding.

The greatest care should be exercised lest we do despite to the Spirit of God by treating with indifference and scorn the messenger, and the messages, God sends to His people, and so reject light because our hearts are not in harmony with God.[20]

## *1890-1891 Ministerial School*

By midsummer 1890, plans were already being laid for a second Ministerial Institute to be held in Battle Creek. The school would start Friday, October 31, and run for 16 weeks, finishing on Friday, February 27, 1891, just a few days before the start of the General Conference session. O. A. Olsen and W. C. White spoke with A. T. Jones about teaching once again at the school, along with E. J. Waggoner. Upon hearing of these plans C. H. Jones said he was "somewhat surprised" that Jones and Waggoner would be "selected to teach any school of this kind when their theology has been so severely criticized." Besides, as manager of Pacific Press, he wanted to "know something a little more definite," since plans "would affect them very materially." Waggoner did a work, stated C. H. Jones, "which but very few individuals can do as well as he. He not only has charge of the *Signs*, but is chairman of the editorial committee for *Young People's Library*, and this in itself is quite an important publication. Then his long residence here has made him familiar with all branches of our work, and he can take hold to advantage almost anywhere." Whatever plans were to be made "someone should communicate with Dr. Waggoner at once. It could not be expected that he can pull up and leave home in a moment."[21]

When Ellen White heard the news that Waggoner was to be "called to the east to attend the Ministerial Institutes, and to teach the school" she was torn: "I wish Dr. Waggoner could be teacher… and think it is his place, but could you see the pitiful condition of things here!" Already Ellen White could describe the conditions in California as "certainly deplorable." On the Pacific Coast, there was "scarcely a man who carries a weight of influence." When "A. T. Jones went east, then Dr. Waggoner and Charlie Jones, it was too much to take away at one time."[22] Yet, Ellen White added, don't send R. A. Underwood to fill the position. If he "is still in his opposition state, at war in feelings against A. T. Jones and E. J. Waggoner, keep him east, do not let him have a wide territory where he can circulate and sow broadcast the seed of envy, jealousy, and rebellion."[23]

By September, Dan Jones was speaking more positively of the upcoming Institute: "The prospect seems quite favorable for a good attendance at the Ministers' School. With Prof. Prescott as principal and one of the leading teachers, and Eld Smith to come in also as one of the leading teachers, and Dr. Waggoner to connect with it with his energy and zeal, I think the school will be one of real value to all who attend." One reason for Dan Jones' acceptance of Jones and Waggoner being teachers at the school may have been due to his own feelings of "spiritual leanness." He felt that since the last Ministerial Institute, and the way things erupted, that he had "been losing ground spiritually." Yet, he was not "ready to say" that he "did wrong, and that Dr. Waggoner did right in that matter." Dan Jones was honest enough, however, to recognize the spirit of God at work: "Bro. A. T. Jones made us a short visit here, day before yesterday, on his way to the Pacific Coast. He is full of zeal and energy. No one can talk with or hear him talk without being impressed that he is in earnest, and that he has the spirit of God with him."[24]

With about sixty ministers present and "still more to come," the Ministerial Institute began its opening exercises. W. W. Prescott, E. J. Waggoner, and W. A. Colcord would be the main presenters, with Uriah Smith and others filling in. After the opening weekend, many felt the meetings began on a positive note, "as though we had begun just where we left off last spring." There were great hopes that as a result of these meetings there would be "advancement not only in our knowledge of the Bible, and in how to apply ourselves to study, but also in spiritual experience."[25] Because of anxiety on Dan Jones' part about a repeat of the previous year, Prescott agreed to "assign" Waggoner his teaching area rather than allowing him to choose his own. Prescott would teach the sensitive class on the book of Galatians himself.[26] Ellen White, on the other hand, had anxiety over Uriah Smith teaching in the school:

> Smith is placed in positions as teacher to mold and fashion the minds of students when it is a well known fact that he is not standing in the light; he is not working in God's order. He is sowing seeds of unbelief that spring up and bear fruit for some souls to harvest....

> I consider the position and work of Elders Butler, Farnsworth, Smith, and *numerous others*, is to unsettle the faith of the people of God by things which they say but which they ought not to say, and things left unsaid which they ought to say. And this state of things—unbelief, prejudice, and Pharisaism—is leavening the church.... They have had all the evidence that will ever be given them in the manifestation of the fruit of the Spirit of God attending the messages given, but they have closed their eyes lest they shall see, and hardened their hearts lest they shall feel. The Spirit of God has been grieved, and they are so dull of comprehension that they know it not....

> There is much loose work done everywhere, and the efforts that have been made for the few years past tend to put out the eyes that Israel shall not discern their defections, and God withholds His Spirit from them and darkness envelopes [*sic*] them as it did the Jewish nation.[27]

Ellen White's concerns proved to be legitimate. When word got around to G. I. Butler that W. W. Prescott was teaching Waggoner's "absurd position" on the book in Galatians, he responded with disgust: "Great Scott, has it come to this that such things are to be indoctrinated into the minds of our young people?"[28] Most ministers attending the school felt differently however, profiting by their study and enjoying participation in the fieldwork provided. This seems to summarize the Ministerial Institute in general. Those who attended the meetings received a great blessing, while those who stayed away found only something to criticize.

By the end of November "nearly 100" were present with "still more to come." Reports of the meetings were still very positive: "The best of interest is manifested. Teachers and students are enjoying much of the Spirit of God.... We long to see our people everywhere drink deeper draughts from the well of salvation."[29]

Even E. J. Waggoner gave a positive report to Ellen White with less than a month to go in the Institute: "He rejoiced that there was an entirely different atmosphere pervading the meetings than was in the ministerial institute last year." Ellen White could "thank the Lord for this testimony."[30] Following the close of the Ministerial Institute, O. A. Olsen reported to the General Conference that "the amount of good accomplished by these schools it is impossible for us to estimate. The blessing of God has been present in a large measure."[31] Once again, if this was all there was to report on the meetings it would be well, but history does not lie.

Ellen White, although thankful for the blessings that had been gained, was still very concerned over the general state of the ministry. Some who attended meetings were giving suggestions and asking questions "full of unbelief." There had been "a multiplying of expressions with little substantial knowledge, little increase of solid principles."[32] Moreover, some of the brethren connected with the work would not "attend meetings" and were fearful of what was being taught.[33] During the closing meeting of the Ministerial Institute, Ellen White spoke in regard "to matters that were deeply impressing [her] mind":

> I referred to the fear that had been expressed by some who were not members of the ministerial institute, and who had not been present at all the Bible classes of the school—a fear that there was danger of carrying the subject of justification by faith altogether too far, and of not dwelling enough on the law. Judging from the meetings that I have been privileged to attend, I could see no cause for alarm; and so I felt called upon to say that this fear was cherished by those who had not heard all the precious lessons given, and that therefore they were not warranted in coming to such a conclusion....
>
> When precious rays of light from the Sun of Righteousness have shone upon our pathway, some have opened wide the door of the heart, welcoming the heaven-sent light.... Others have needed the divine anointing to improve their

spiritual eyesight, in order that they may distinguish the light of truth from the darkness of error. Because of their blindness, they have lost an experience that would have been more precious to them than silver and gold. Some, I fear, will never recover that which they have lost.[34]

## *Under Fire Again*

There were other concerns on Ellen White's mind during the Ministerial Institute, which she was eager to resolve. Since early November 1890, she had had several experiences in which a great burden was placed upon her in regard to the publishing work, specifically in regard to the *American Sentinel*. On October 8, 1890, Ellen White left Battle Creek with W. C. White and her secretary-nurse, Sara McEnterfer, for nearly three months of travel

and labor in the Eastern states. Ellen White was scheduled to attend important meetings in the New England Conference, Atlantic Conference, Virginia Conference and the state of Pennsylvania. After several weeks of labor, Ellen White arrived in Salamanca, New York, on Thursday night, October 31, with a severe head cold as the result of her travels in chilly winter weather. By the end of the weekend, she was so ill and thoroughly exhausted that Sara McEnterfer urged her to return to her home in Battle Creek and receive treatment at the Sanitarium. After a long hard day on Monday, November 3, Ellen White returned to her guestroom weary, weak and perplexed.

SARA MCENTERFER

She desired to rest, pray and decide whether she should continue with her scheduled appointments or return to Battle Creek.[35]*

Back in Battle Creek *that very day*, the "second annual session of the National Religious Liberty Association convened in the Tabernacle… at 5 o'clock p. m., with President C. Eldridge in the chair." Twenty-six committee members listened as Secretary W. H. McKee reported on the labor of the

Association for the past year. A detailed description was given of all the work done countering the Breckinridge bill and the influence of Rev. Crafts, the defending of Mr. King in Tennessee, and the circulating of petitions against Sunday legislation. The report included a description of all the material the NRLA had circulated that year. Over four million pages of pamphlets and tracts, ten thousand manuals, thirty thousand petition blanks, and other assorted material had been circulated. A close reading of the report shows that although thirty thousand copies of the *American Sentinel* were given out December of 1889, only ten thousand more copies were circulated the following year. It was stated that in one particular incident, the NRLA did not have "time to order an edition of the *American Sentinel*" so they "made up" their own paper to distribute. But there were other reasons given why the *Sentinel* was not being used by the NRLA; it took too much of a "sectarian" position.[36]

Dan Jones had stirred up opposition against the *Sentinel* earlier in the year over what he considered "sharp thrusts." Now there was a growing concern that the paper wrote too directly of Seventh-day Adventist's peculiar doctrines. This concern was largely due to the fact that during 1890 many of the leaders of the NRLA had found an open door to present the principles of religious liberty they were advocating before large audiences of secular and non-Christian people. It appeared to them that it would be a wise plan to improve these opportunities and clearly present the principles of religious liberty, especially if unassociated with the teachings of the Scripture regarding the sacredness of the Sabbath and the nearness of the second advent of Christ.[37]

Pressure from other non–Christian groups had been brought to bear upon the Executive Committee of the NRLA to engage "unconsecrated persons, even infidels," in its work against Sunday legislation in order to have a wider influence.[38] Many in the NRLA felt this was the direction they should follow in order to accomplish a greater work.[39]* In fact, the NRLA's president, C. Eldridge, reported to the Association in his November 3 talk that there was "wisdom of the organization of the National Religious Liberty Association, because, under the Association name, its members could do far more in behalf of Religious Liberty, than under any sectarian name;" i.e., as Seventh-day Adventists.[40]

A. T. Jones, on the other hand, would have totally disagreed. Although he was on the NRLA's Executive Committee, he could not attend this annual meeting, and thus was unable to voice his apprehension.[41]* But there was no question where he stood. He stated openly at the 1891 General Conference that he was "willing to bear the blame" because he would not print in the *Sentinel* just any speech that was delivered "in the interest of religious liberty." He knew "that there is a good deal more to the question of religious liberty than simply talking about religious liberty":

> Outside of the third angel's message, there is no religious liberty in this world at this time.... [I]f we would know the real principles of religious liberty—know them properly, and hold them all the time—we must get them from the third angel's message; we must get them from God in the way he is giving them to the world at this time, and put them where they belong....
>
> Now there are some people outside of the Seventh-day Adventist church who understand the principles of religious liberty so far as they know them; but they don't understand them far enough. And it is the purpose of the third angel's message, to hold before the world and everybody in it, the true principles of religious liberty.... The truth is that, were it not for the third angel's message, every soul of us would be in favor of religious legislation. Every soul of us, because we are just the kind of people who, without the blessing and influence of the Spirit of God, would be in that very business.[42]

A. T. Jones' stance brought criticism against him, which would soon come to a head at the final Association meeting held December 7, 1890, where new officers were voted for the following year. Being absent from the meeting, A. T. Jones was removed from the Executive Committee, while C. Eldridge, Dan Jones, W. A. Colcord and A. F. Ballenger were all reelected. Both A. T. Jones and E. J. Waggoner were once again placed on the Editorial Committee, but resolutions were passed which would limit their ability to give any input.[43]* At the 1889 General Conference the Association had voted to "have an organ, through which to advocate its principles and advertise and mould its work."[44] The *American Sentinel* had been the church's religious liberty "organ" up to that time. Now a resolution was passed "that the distribution of literature by the Association be done through the International Tract Society, and that the [NRLA] keep the society supplied with sufficient quantities of this literature." Although the *American Sentinel* would be part of that literature, the Association voted that "plans for local NRLA work be published in the Religious Liberty department of the *Home Missionary*" located in Battle Creek.

The Association also voted that "through its Executive Committee," on which A. T. Jones no longer served, instead of its Editorial Committee, on which A. T. Jones and E. J. Waggoner both served, the *American Sentinel* was to be "supplied each week with enough interesting and well-edited matter, to fill three columns of that journal." It is clear that the Association was systematically seeking to control or phase out the *Sentinel* as its religious liberty "organ." In another resolution which reflected the plans for the coming year, the Association voted that its members "affiliate with… other Christian associations, in distributing literature, in holding monthly meetings, and in all their efforts in behalf of Religious Liberty."[45]* Although these plans were not faulty in every regard, great danger lay ahead.

## *Salamanca Vision*

Back in Salamanca, New York, on the evening of November 3, 1890—the date of the second annual session of the NRLA meeting in Battle Creek—Ellen White knelt beside her bed to pray, weary, weak, and perplexed. Should she continue her travels and try to keep her speaking appointments or should she return to Battle Creek?

> Before the first word of petition had been offered she felt that the room was filled with the fragrance of roses. Looking up to see whence the fragrance came, she saw the room flooded with soft, silvery light. Instantly her pain and weariness disappeared. The perplexity and discouragement of mind vanished, and hope and comfort and peace filled her heart. Then losing all consciousness regarding her surroundings, she was shown in vision many things relating to the progress of the cause in different parts of the world, and the conditions which were helping or hindering the work. Among the many views presented to her, were several showing the *conditions existing in Battle Creek*. In a very full and striking manner, these were laid out before her.[46]

Tuesday morning, November 4, when W. C. White and A. T. Robinson called on Ellen White to see what she had decided to do, they found her dressed and well. She told them of her experience the evening before and the peace and joy she felt through the night. She had been unable to sleep, not because of sickness, but on account her heart was filled with joy and gladness. Now she would continue her work in the East. Ellen White started telling her son and A. T. Robinson what was revealed to her during the night: "'In the vision I seemed to be in Battle Creek, and the angel messenger bade me, "Follow me."'" She hesitated, for the scene had gone from her; she could not call it to mind. After visiting for a time with the two men, Ellen White sought once again to tell them what had been revealed to her in regard to the work in Battle Creek, but just as before, she could not call it to mind.[47]

A. T. ROBINSON

In her November 4 diary entry, Ellen White wrote a few short words: "I longed to be where I could write out the things that were opened before me the past night. It was the Lord...."[48] Her sentence was left unfinished, perhaps to be finished at a later time. A few weeks later she was again visited by a heavenly messenger and brought to see what was taking place in Battle Creek. What she was unable to tell others in person, she was able to write down in her diary:

> During the night I have been in communion with God. I have been brought by my guide into the councils in Battle Creek, and I have a message to bear to you whether you will hear or not, whether you will receive it or reject it. The people must know that they are not moving in the order of God. They have left Christ out of their councils. Leading men are giving a mold to the work that will result in the loss of many souls.... Many come here from foreign countries, thinking that Battle Creek, from whence come the publications of truth, will be next to heaven. How disappointed they feel when they hear in this place the message of God spoken of lightly, when they hear the messengers of God, by some in responsible places, made a subject of ridicule.[49]

Nine days later, and before the report of NRLA's annual meeting made its way into the *Review*, Ellen White once again wrote in her diary giving more details of what she had been shown in vision. The people of the world were trying to induce Adventists to soften our message; to suppress one of its more distinctive features:

> They say: "Why do you in your teaching make the seventh–day Sabbath so prominent? This seems to be always thrust before us; we should harmonize with you if you would not say so much on this point; keep the seventh–day Sabbath out of the *Sentinel*, and we will give it our influence and support." And there has been a disposition on the part of some of our workers to adopt this policy.
>
> I am bidden to warn you that deceptive sentiments are entertained, a false modesty and caution, a disposition to withhold the profession of our faith. In the night season, matters have been presented before me that have greatly troubled my mind. I have seemed to be in meetings for counsel where these subjects were discussed, and written documents were presented, advocating concession. Brethren, shall we permit the world to shape the message that God has given us to bear to them?…
>
> Shall we, for the sake of policy, betray a sacred trust? If the world is in error and delusion, breaking the law of God, is it not our duty to show them their sin and danger? We must proclaim the third angel's message.
>
> What is the *Sentinel* for, but to be the voice of the watchmen on the walls of Zion, to sound the danger signal. We care not to cringe and beg pardon of the world for telling them the truth: we should scorn concealment…. Let it be understood that Seventh-day Adventists can make no compromise. In your opinions and faith there must not be the least appearance of wavering; the world has a right to know what to expect from us, and will look upon us as dishonest… if we carry even the semblance of being uncommitted.[50]

With only a few days remaining before Ellen White returned to Battle Creek, she penned the following words in her diary: "My mind has been in painful exercise during the night. I was in a meeting in Battle Creek, and heard many suggestions made and saw a spirit manifested not of God. They were having a storm of words. How my heart ached."[51] Upon returning to Battle Creek December 30, Ellen White soon became involved in the final weeks of the Ministerial Institute. It was at some point in time following her return that she filled in her diary entry for November 21, 1890.[52]*

> In the night season I was present in several councils, and there I heard words repeated by influential men to the effect that if the *American Sentinel* would drop

the words "Seventh-day Adventists" from its columns, and would say nothing about the Sabbath, the great men of the world would patronize it. It would become popular and do a larger work. This looked very pleasing. These men could not see why we could not affiliate with unbelievers and non-professors to make the *American Sentinel* a great success. I saw their countenances brighten, and they began to work on a policy to make the *Sentinel* a popular success.

This policy is the first step in a succession of wrong steps. The principles which have been advocated in the *American Sentinel* are the very sum and substance of the advocacy of the Sabbath, and when men begin to talk of changing these principles, they are doing a work which it does not belong to them to do. Like Uzzah, they are attempting to steady the ark which belongs to God and is under His special supervision. Said my guide to those in these councils, "Who of the men among you have felt the burden of the cause from the first, and have accepted responsibilities under the trying circumstances? Who has carried the burden of the work during the years of its existence? Who has practiced self-denial and self-sacrifice? The Lord made a place for His staunch servants, whose voices have been heard in warning. He carried forward His work before any of you put your hands to it, and He can and will find a place for the truth you would suppress. In the *American Sentinel* has been published the truth for this time. Take heed what you do. 'Except the Lord build the house, they labor in vain that build it.'"[53]

Ellen White had observed more than one council meeting taking place; she was "present in several." Clearly more had gone on during the NRLA's annual meeting than was reported in the *Review*. It was Ellen White's angel guide who asked such penetrating questions of those who were criticizing the Lord's "staunch servants." E. J. Waggoner and A. T. Jones had "carried the burden of the work" of religious liberty "during the years of its existence." They had "practiced self-denial and self-sacrifice" while Dan Jones and others sought only to ridicule their work. Ellen White's guide offered not one word of censure against Jones and Waggoner, but stated simply that God would find a place for "the truth" the *American Sentinel* had published.

A few days later Ellen White penned more words in her diary in regard to what she had been shown. She "was in Battle Creek, and in a council assembled there were ministers and responsible men from the Review office. There were sentiments advanced and with no very gentle spirit urged to be adopted, which filled me with surprise and apprehension and distress.... They would adopt plans which appeared wise, but Satan was the instigator of these measures."[54] It is no wonder she was carrying a heavy burden for what was taking place.

## 1891 General Conference

The twenty-ninth session of the Seventh-day Adventist General Conference convened in the Tabernacle at Battle Creek, Michigan on March 5, 1891. Credentials were presented by 102 delegates, representing twenty-nine Conferences and four mission fields. When the conference opened, Ellen White was asked to speak to the workers each morning of the week at half–past five. She was also scheduled to speak for the first Sabbath, March 7, at the afternoon service beginning at 2:30. As Ellen White stood before four thousand of her fellow workers and believers, her heart was impressed with the seriousness of the hour. All that had been impressed upon her mind in the months prior to the conference seemed to present itself with new significance. Her discourse was a powerful appeal for Seventh-day Adventists to hold forth the distinctive features of their faith. Then she said in substance:

> "While at Salamanca, New York matters of importance were revealed to me. In a vision of the night I seemed to be here in Battle Creek, and the angel messenger bade me, 'Follow me.'" She hesitated; the scene was gone. She could not call it to mind. She continued to speak of how we must hold forth the distinctive features of our faith. Then she said, "I must tell you of the vision which was given to me at Salamanca; for in that vision important matters were revealed to me. In the vision I seemed to be in Battle Creek. I was taken to the Review and Herald office, and the angel messenger bade me, 'Follow me.'" Again she faltered; it had gone from her. She went on with her sermon, and a third time that afternoon she attempted to recount that vision, but she was not allowed to tell it. Finally she said, "Of this, I shall have more to say later." She rounded out her sermon in about an hour's time, and the meeting was dismissed. Everyone had noticed that she was unable to call the vision to mind.[55]

Later in the afternoon a ministers' meeting was held in the east vestry of the Tabernacle. Ellen White was present and pleaded for a deeper consecration. At the close of this special meeting, Elder O. A. Olsen asked her if she would attend the ministers' meeting in the morning. She replied that she had done her part and would leave the burden with him. Thus it was planned that Olsen and Prescott lead the meeting.[56]

That Sabbath evening, March 7, after sundown, and after Ellen White had retired to her room, a special closed-door meeting was held in the Review and Herald's office chapel. About 30 to 40 people were present, the majority representing the National Religious Liberty Association, and a few representing the Pacific Press, publishers of the *American Sentinel*. The meeting was opened and conducted by Dan Jones, vice president of the NRLA. He stated in a very strong way that the Association could not continue to use the *American Sentinel* as the organ of the Association, unless it would modify its attitude toward some of what was termed the more objectionable features of our denominational views. A. T. Jones responded, stating that as long as he had anything to do with the editorship of the paper, there would be no such change as suggested. The meeting assumed the form of a very warm discussion between those who took opposite sides of the question. At that point someone locked the door, proposing that it should not be opened until the question was settled.

At some point during the meeting, A. F. Ballenger, NRLA Executive Committee member, stood to his feet and held up the most recent copy of the

A. F. BALLENGER

*Sentinel,* pointing out certain articles that should be omitted.[57]* A. T. Jones and C. P. Bowman had been running pointed articles through the paper on the Sabbath question and the Second Advent and their relation to religious liberty. Many from the NRLA ardently disapproved, feeling the articles were too "strong." They didn't want anything sectarian by appeal to the Scriptures to be found in the *Sentinel*, but wanted the paper to advocate the broad principles of civil and religious liberty, carefully avoiding any church affiliation. They argued that the paper was read and approved by men of influence in state and church, and now to offend their senses by declaring in a strong way the seventh-day Sabbath and the end of the world, would be suicidal to the interests of the *American Sentinel* and the NRLA.

The meeting dragged on for hours in apparent deadlock, with the assertion on the part of the NRLA men that unless the Pacific Press would accede to their demands and drop the strong articles along with the terms "Seventh-day Adventist" and "the Sabbath" from the columns of the paper, they would no longer use it as the organ of the Association. That meant killing the paper. Finally, a little before three o'clock early Sunday morning, a vote was taken.[58]* The majority voted to drop the *Sentinel* and start another paper as the organ of the Religious Liberty Association. The door was now unlocked and the men went off to their rooms to sleep, having only a few short hours before the 5:30 morning meeting.[59]

One can only imagine how A. T. Jones might have felt as he walked out into the cool morning air and headed to his room. The real religious liberty cause, for which he had fought so hard, seemed destined for defeat. Those who should have given their support had treated his diligent work with scorn and ridicule. One can only wonder what prayers went up from him that early morning. Did he sleep at all that night before having to be up for the 5:30 morning meeting? God, who does not slumber or sleep, was fully aware of what had taken place. He well knew the monumental times in which those on earth were living. He knew it was the time of the latter rain and that the message He was sending was to lighten the earth with His glory.

No sooner had the meeting closed than an angel was commissioned to wake Ellen White; it was time for her to share what she had been shown in Salamanca four months before. Arising from her bed, Ellen White went to her bureau and took out the diaries in which she had made the record of what she had been shown. As the scenes came once again clearly to her mind, she wrote out in more detail what she had been unable to share many times before.

A few hours later, as W. C. White and two other brethren passed by Ellen White's residence on their way to the early morning meeting, they noticed her light on. Knowing that his mother had not planned to attend the early morning meeting, W. C. White went in to inquire if she were alright. He found her busily engaged in writing. She told him that an angel of God had wakened her about three o'clock and had bidden her go to the ministers' meeting and relate some things shown her at Salamanca. She said that she arose quickly and had been writing for about two hours.[60]*

At the minister's meeting, opening prayer had just been offered when Ellen White entered with a package of manuscripts under her arm. With evident surprise Elder Olsen said: "We are glad to see you, Sister White. Have you a message for us this morning?" "Indeed I have," was her reply, as she stepped to the front. Then she began where she had left off the day before. She told the brethren how she had been awakened that very morning and urged to share what she had been shown while in Salamanca four months before. She told how she had seen herself "bearing a message to an assembly which seemed to be the General Conference":[61]

> I was moved by the Spirit of God to say many things, to make most earnest appeals, for the truth was urged upon me that great danger lay before those at the heart of the work.... The words were to be in earnest. "Speak the word that I shall give thee, to prevent their doing things which would separate God from the publishing house and sacrifice pure and holy principles which must be maintained."... Many things were unfolded to me. The eyes which once wept over impenitent Jerusalem—for their impenitence, their ignorance of God and of Jesus Christ, their Redeemer—were bent upon the great heart of the work in Battle Creek....
>
> Witticisms and your sharp criticisms, after the infidel style, please the devil but not the Lord. The Spirit of God has not been controlling in your councils. There have been misstatements of messengers and of the messages they bring. How dare you do it?... No confidence should be placed in the judgment of those who do this thing, no weight attached to their advice or resolutions.... Accusing the workmen and the work of the ones whom God is using is accusing Jesus Christ in the person of His saints.... The prejudices and opinions that prevailed at Minneapolis are not dead by any means. The seeds there sown are ready to spring into life and bear a like harvest, because the roots are still left. The tops have been cut off, but the roots are not dead, and will bear their unholy fruit, to poison the perception and blind the understanding of those you connect with, in regard to the messengers and messages that God sends.[62]*

Those who had criticized A. T. Jones for his work in the *Sentinel* had faulty judgment. Many of them had repented a year before at the 1890 Ministerial Institute, but their repentance was not genuine; only the "tops" had been cut off, leaving the roots to spring again to life. Continuing on, Ellen White spoke specifically of a meeting she had observed:

> I was present in one of your councils. One arose, and in a very earnest, decided manner, held up a paper. I could read the heading plainly—*American Sentinel*. There were criticisms made upon the articles published therein. It was declared that this must be cut out, and that must be changed. Strong words were uttered and a strong unchristlike spirit prevailed. My guide gave me words to speak to the ones who were present who were not slow to make their accusations. In substance I will state the reproof given: That there was a spirit of strife in the midst of the council. The Lord had not presided in their councils and their minds and hearts were not under the controlling influence of the Spirit of God. Let the adversaries of our faith be the ones to instigate and develop plans which are being formed.... The light which the Lord has given should be respected for your own safety, as well as for the safety of the church of God....

> You will need to make straight paths for your feet, lest they be turned out of the way.... I know a work must be done for the people or many will not receive the light of the angel which is sent from heaven to fill the whole earth with his glory. Do not think that when the latter rain comes you will be a vessel unto honor to receive the showers of blessing—even the glory of God—when you have been lifting up your souls unto vanity, speaking perverse thing, secretly cherishing the roots of bitterness you brought to Minneapolis, which you have carefully cultivated and watered ever since.[63]

Ellen White went on to tell the brethren that she had been shown the *Sentinel* was being widely read and favorably received. It had gathered the confidence of people to whom the full light of truth was due. These articles, instead of lessening the list of subscribers, would increase its circulation and demand. Ellen White solemnly asked: "Are our people now to cut out the Sabbath message from the *Sentinel* and heed the advice and counsel of worldly men, keeping the *Sentinel* from carrying this most important truth to the world?"[64] Several times throughout Ellen White's lengthy talk, she mentioned Israel and the rebellion that led to the judgments of God. She specifically mentioned the experience of Elijah—the trials he endured and the message he gave.

She clearly compared this not only to her own experience, but also to the experience of Jones and Waggoner who had been so maligned for their work in behalf of religious liberty through the *Sentinel*:

> Let a Christian walk with the Lord in all humility of mind and he is called narrow, bigoted, exclusive. If he is zealous, the world will call him a fanatic. Let him speak the truth decidedly with pen and voice and go forth in the spirit and power of Elijah to proclaim the day of the Lord, and he is called by the world excitable; they say he is denouncing everything but that which he believes. Let the Christian be whatever grace can make him, and the world cannot understand it....
>
> Let us look at the case of Elijah.... The king accuses Elijah, "Art thou he that troubleth Israel?" 1 Kings 18:17 Does he betray sacred trusts because Israel has perverted her faith and disowned her allegiance to her God? Does he prophesy smooth things to please and pacify the king and secure his favor?... No, no! Elijah is a man who proclaims the truth, just such truth that the occasion demands.... The answer came from Elijah, "I have not troubled Israel; but thou, and thy father's house, in that ye have forsaken the commandments of the Lord, and thou hast followed Baalim." 1 Kings 18:18. This is the very course men will take who are now in office.... I have a warning to give to this body assembled in this house in General Conference. There is danger of our institutions creating plans and ways and means that mean not success, but defeat....
>
> There has been a departure from God, and there has not as yet been zealous work in repenting and coming back to the first love.... Baal will be the purpose, the faith, the religion of a sorrowful number among us, because they choose their own way instead of God's way. The true religion, the only religion of the Bible—believing in the forgiveness of sins, the righteousness of Christ, and the blood of the Lamb—has been not only slighted and spoken against, ridiculed, and criticized, but suspicions and jealousies have been created, leading into fanaticism and atheism.[65]

The ministers' morning meeting which usually closed at 6:30 a.m., continued on into the forenoon. After Ellen White finished her reading and speaking, she sat down, and the room was wrapped in silence. Many who had not been at the meeting the night before sat in bewilderment. Elder Olsen was in deep perplexity, as he had known nothing of the meeting the evening before.[66] He was so surprised, and the things Ellen White presented seemed so unreasonable, that he was quite nonplused in his mind as to what this meant.

Finally the silence was broken by the weeping voice of A. F. Ballenger. Holding up the current issue of the *American Sentinel*, Ballenger pointed to the front-page article and said: "'I was in the meeting last night, and I am the man who made the remarks about the articles in the paper.'" "'This is the article on the Sabbath referred to by Sister White, and I am the man who said such strong articles should not appear in the *Sentinel*.'"[67] Ballenger went on to confess his error: "'I am sorry to say that I was on the wrong side, but I take this opportunity to place myself on the right side.'"[68]

Ellen White, who for the first time laid eyes upon the current issue of the *Sentinel*—the same one she had seen only in her dream—sat with a look of perplexity on her face. She turned to Brother Ballenger and exclaimed in amazement: "Last night! the meeting was last night?" One by one, the men who had attended the meeting the night before rose to their feet and confessed their part in what had taken place. Even those who had defended the *Sentinel* gave testimonies of thanksgiving. C. H. Jones stated that Ellen White had described the meeting correctly in every particular. He was so thankful for the light that had come, for it had become a serious situation. At some point during the morning meeting, Dan Jones, who had led out in seeking to kill the *Sentinel* the night before, stood and confessed: "'Sister White, I thought I was right. Now I know I was wrong.'" A. T. Jones, who had watched as the *Sentinel* suffered apparent defeat, answered in humility and self-forgetfulness: "'You are right—now, anyhow.'"[69]* The Holy Spirit had been powerfully manifested and a different spirit came into the meeting.

Because of the sequence of events that led up to the morning meeting, Ellen White stated later that "the excuse could not possibly be used, 'someone told her.' No one had an opportunity to see me or speak with me between the evening meeting and the morning meeting that I attended."[70] As a result, not only was the cause of God spared for a time from a serious mistake, but the experience provided unimpeachable evidence to not a few, of the reliability and integrity of the Spirit of Prophecy:

> The relation of this vision made a profound and solemn impression upon that large congregation of Seventh-day Adventist ministers present at that early morning meeting. When they heard those who had been reproved for the wrong

course taken in that council confess that all Mrs. White had said about them was true in every particular, they saw that the seal of divine inspiration had been set upon that vision and testimony. The power and solemnity of that meeting made an impression upon the minds of those present not soon to be forgotten.[71]

But the very incident which proved to many, beyond a shadow of a doubt, that Ellen White was inspired and led by God, also brought the conviction that they could not escape her ever-present, authoritative Testimonies. Within three weeks, the Board of Foreign Missions would vote to send Ellen White, along with her workers and W.C. White to Australia.[72]* Years later, Ellen White would make it clear that the Lord was not in their leaving America. But powerful forces at the heart of the work were very willing to have them leave. As is always the case, the Lord did not force His hand but allowed His people to choose their own way:

> The Lord was not in our leaving America. He did not reveal that it was his will that I should leave Battle Creek. The Lord did not plan this, but he let you all move after your own imaginings. The Lord would have had W. C. White, his mother, and her workers remain in America. We were needed at the heart of the work, and had your spiritual perception discerned the true situation, you would never have consented to the movements made. But the Lord read the hearts of all. There was so great a willingness to have us leave, that the Lord permitted this thing to take place. Those who were weary of the testimonies borne were left without the persons who bore them. Our separation from Battle Creek was to let men have their own will and way, which they thought superior to the way of the Lord....
>
> There we should have stood shoulder to shoulder, creating a healthful atmosphere to be felt in all our conferences. It was not the Lord who devised this matter. I could not get one ray of light to leave America. But when the Lord presented this matter to me as it really was, I opened my lips to no one, because I knew that no one would discern the matter in all its bearings. When we left, relief was felt by many, but not so much by yourself, and the Lord was displeased; for he had set us to stand at the wheels of the moving machinery at Battle Creek.
>
> Such great responsibilities call for the continual counsel of God, that they may be carried forward in a right way. But this counsel was not considered a necessity. That the people of Battle Creek should feel that they could have us leave at the time we did, was the result of man's devising, and not the Lord's.[73]

A month following the General Conference session the *Review* reprinted a sermon delivered by Ellen White at a worker's meetings in September, 1887. Her monumental words remain poignant today: "The latter rain is to fall upon the people of God. A mighty angel is to come down from heaven, and the whole earth is to be lighted with his glory. Are we ready to take part in the glorious work of the third angel? Are our vessels ready to receive the heavenly dew? Have we defilement and sin in the heart? If so, let us cleanse the soul temple, and prepare for the showers of the latter rain. The refreshing from the presence of the Lord will never come to hearts filled with impurity. May God help us to die to self, that Christ, the hope of glory, may be formed within!"[74] We will continue our study in *The Return of the Latter Rain*, volume 2.

## [To Be Continued]

*A list of chapter titles for volume 2
follows the endnotes for this chapter.*

# CHAPTER 17 FOOTNOTES

1. E. J. Waggoner, "Eleventh Day's Preceedings," *Review and Herald*, Nov. 13, 1888, p. 712; in *Manuscripts and Memories*, p. 408.

2. See: Eric Syme, *A History of SDA Church-State Relations*, pp. 20-35; "Public Affairs and Religious Liberty, Dept. of," *SDA Encyclopedia*, vol. 10, pp. 1158-1164.

3. Ellen G. White, "The 'American Sentinel' and its Mission," *Review and Herald*, Dec. 18, 1888, p. 791.

4. "National Religious Liberty Association," *General Conference Daily Bulletin*, Nov. 5, 1889, p. 148.

5. Dan T. Jones to A. W. Allee, Jan. 23, 1890, archives of the General Conference of Seventh-day Adventists.

6. Dan T. Jones to C. H. Jones, [Feb] 1890, archives of the General Conference of Seventh-day Adventists. We have repeated this information here as found in Chapter 13, to give a fuller context to the opposition Jones and Waggoner received in regard to their work for religious liberty.

7. Dan T. Jones to J. H. Morrison, March 17, 1890, archives of the General Conference of Seventh-day Adventists.

8. W. C. White to A. T. Jones, Feb. 14, 1890.

9. Ellen G. White, " Morning Talk," Feb. 6, 1890, *Review and Herald*, March 25, 1890; in *1888 Materials*, p. 548.

10. Ellen G. White Manuscript 2, "Sermon," March 9, 1890; in *1888 Materials*, pp. 608-609.

11. Eric Syme, *A History of SDA Church-State Relations*, p. 35.

12. *Ibid.*, pp. 35-36.

13. Eric Syme, *A History of SDA Church-state Relations*, pp. 34-36; William A. Blakely, *American State Papers Bearing on Sunday Legislation* (1911), pp. 367-370; J. O. Corliss, "The Hearing on the Sunday Rest Bill," *Review and Herald*, Feb. 25, 1890, pp. 124-125, and "The Second Annual Session of the National Religious Liberty Association," *Review and Herald*, Dec. 16, 1890, p. 779; A. T. Jones, "Arguments on the Breckinridge Sunday Bill," *Sentinel Library*, No. 28, April, 1890.

14. O. A. Olsen to G. C. Tenny, March 20, 1890, copy received from George R. Knight's personal collection. A. T. Jones' speech before the House Committee can be found in *The Sentinel Library*, April 1890, pp. 25-51. This periodical was produced from semi–monthly to quarterly by Pacific Press during the years 1889 to 1894 as a series of pamphlets on religious liberty issues. The May 1891 issue listed, in 126 pages, all the Sunday laws at that time for 45 States and Territories. These would be a valuable resource to have reprinted today.

15. Sanford Edwards observed the following: "A. T. Jones: A tall awkward man with the features of a frontiersman; self-educated, a tenor voice, a wonderful gift of language, a wonderful scholar in history and Bible. As a public speaker he had no equal in the denomination up to his time. He could quote whole chapters from Romans and Galatians, and Hebrews and Revelation in a way to give you a new vision of the beauty of the Bible. At the close of one sermon he quoted the lovely hymn, 'There's a Wideness in God's Mercy' all through to the end. It was the most wonderful elocutionary effort I have ever heard. The audience (1500) was so deeply moved that for 2 hours they stood up and made confessions and reconsecrations. It was not a mass movement but an individual movement. God spoke thru Jones mightily in those days" (Sanford P. S. Edwards to Emmett K. Vande Vere, April 27, 1956, quoted in: *Windows* [Nashville, Tenn.: Southern Pub. Assn., 1975], pp. 209-210).

16. Dan T. Jones to R. A. Underwood, March 21, 1890, archives of the General Conference of Seventh-day Adventists.

17. Ellen G. White Manuscript 2, "Sermon," March 9, 1890; in *1888 Materials*, p. 609.

18. Ellen G. White, *Patriarchs and Prophets*, p. 402.

19. Ellen G. White, *Gospel Workers*, pp. 128-129, 1893 ed., taken from writings up to 1890.

20. Ellen G. White, "Candid Investigation Necessary to an Understanding of the Truth," *Signs of the Times*, May 26, 1890, pp. 305-306.

21. C. H. Jones to O. A. Olsen, August 13, 1890, archives of the General Conference of Seventh-day Adventists.

22. Ellen G. White to O. A. Olsen, Letter 46, May 8, 1890; in *1888 Materials*, pp. 645-648.

23. Ellen G. White to W. C. White, Letter 103, Aug. 19, 1890; in *1888 Materials*, p. 688.

24. Dan T. Jones to E. W. Farnsworth, Sept. 19, 1890, archives of the General Conference of Seventh-day Adventists.

25. O. A. Olsen, "The Opening of the Minister's School," *Review and Herald*, Nov. 4, 1890, p. 688; see also "The Week of Prayer," Dec. 2, 1890, pp. 745-746.

26. Gilbert M. Valentine, "W. W. Prescott—SDA Educator," p. 127. Prescott actually taught only the first three chapters and then let Waggoner teach the rest. Dan T. Jones to R. C. Porter, Oct. 23, 1890, archives of the General Conference of Seventh-day Adventists.

27. Ellen G. White to O. A. Olsen, Letter 20, Oct. 7, 1890; in *1888 Materials*, pp. 714-716, emphasis supplied.

28. G. I. Butler to Dan Jones, Feb. 16, 1891; in Gilbert M. Valentine, "W. W. Prescott—SDA Educator," p. 127.

29. O. A. Olsen, "The Week of Prayer," Dec. 2, 1890, p. 746.

30. Ellen G. White Manuscript 40, "Diary Entries," Jan. 13, 1891; in *1888 Materials*, p. 876.

31. O. A. Olsen, "Ministers School," *General Conference Daily Bulletin*, March 6, 1891, p. 4.

32. Ellen G. White Manuscript 40, "Diary Entries," Jan. 14, 1891; in *1888 Materials*, p. 879.

33. Ellen G. White Manuscript 40, "Salamanca Vision," 1890, March 1891; in *1888 Materials*, p. 929.

34. Ellen G. White Manuscript 21, Feb. 27, 1891; in *1888 Materials*, pp. 890, 895.

35. Detailed accounts of Ellen White's travels and the Salamanca experience are recorded in: Robert W. Olson, "The Salamanca Vision and the 1890 Diary," (Ellen G. White Estate 1983); A. L. White in, *A Prophet Among You* (Mountain View, Ca.: Pacific Press, 1955), pp. 471-480; A. L. White, *The Lonely Years*, pp. 463-483; C. C. Crisler in, *Life Sketches of Ellen G. White*, pp. 309-318. In the "Preface" of the 1915 edition of *Life Sketches*, produced after Ellen White's death, the following statement is found: "With chapter forty-two, on page 255, her life-story is continued by C. C. Crisler, who, with the assistance of her son, W. C. White and D. E. Robinson, has completed the sketch" (p. 6).

36. "The Second Annual Session of the National Religious Liberty Association," *Review and Herald*, Dec. 16, 1890, pp. 779-780.

37. C. C. Crisler, *Life Sketches*, p. 312.

38. "General Conference Proceedings," *General Conference Daily Bulletin*, March 22, 1891, p. 192.

39. At the 1891 General Conference Dan Jones denied that this was the case. But it goes directly against all the other evidence, including the testimony of Ellen White (*Ibid.*).

40. "The Second Annual Session of the National Religious Liberty Association," *Review and Herald*, Dec. 16, 1890, p. 780.

41. "Editorial Note" *Review and Herald*, Dec. 23, 1890, p. 800. Jones was in California at the time, and would pass through Battle Creek in December before heading to the East Coast.

42. A. T. Jones, "Religious Liberty," *General Conference Daily Bulletin*, March 15, 1891, p. 105.

43. Belonging to a specific Committee was sometimes only a token. Both E. J. Waggoner and A. T. Jones were voted to serve on the General Conference Book Committee at the 1889 and 1891 General Conference sessions, with eleven other members (1889 *General Conference Daily Bulletin*, p. 124; 1891 *General Conference Daily Bulletin*, p. 219). In September of 1891, E. J. Waggoner wrote to O. A. Olsen expressing no personal complaint, but concern for the good of the cause. He had read a report stating the "Book Committee," without his knowledge, had voted to have the Review and Herald publish G. I. Butler's book for the colored people. Yet, Waggoner stated, "as a member of the Book Committee, I would like to see the manuscript." He felt "quite sure that there is good prospect that the book will be as much in need of examination as any other book. If it is put through without examination except by a committee of three, I am sure there will be dissatisfaction.... Certainly every member has the right to examine any manuscript that properly comes before the committee at all" (E. J. Waggoner to O. A. Olsen, Sept 15, 1891). With only three out of thirteen voting on the book, it is clear that Jones and Waggoner were not included. In a similar way to that in which Butler's book was approved without any examination on Jones' or Waggoner's part, some of Jones' and Waggoner's manuscripts were voted down without any examination on the committee's part (see O. A. Tate to W. C. White, Oct. 7, 1895; in *Manuscripts and Memories*, p. 294).

44. "National Religious Liberty Association," *General Conference Daily Bulletin*, Nov. 5, 1889, p. 148.

45. "The Second Annual Session of the National Religious Liberty Association," *Review and Herald*, Dec. 16, 1890, p. 781. It is interesting to note that W. C. White was elected to serve on the Association's Plans and Future Labor Committee, and his name appears in the *Review* as having supported all these resolutions which were passed on November 3 and 7. Yet he was not present at these meetings in Battle Creek, being with his mother in Salamanca, New York.

46. C. C. Crisler in, *Life Sketches*, p. 310, emphasis supplied.

47. A. L. White in, *A Prophet Among You*, p. 474.

48. Ellen G. White Manuscript 44, "Diary" Nov. 4, 1890; in "Manuscript Releases No. 1033, The Salamanca Vision and the 1890 Diary," p. 20.

49. Ellen G. White Manuscript 6, Nov. 25, 1890; in "Manuscript Releases No. 1033, The Salamanca Vision and the 1890 Diary," pp. 31-32.

50. Ellen G. White Manuscript 16, Dec. 4, 1890; in "Manuscript Releases No. 1033, The Salamanca Vision and the 1890 Diary," p. 37.

51. Ellen G. White Manuscript 53, Dec. 25, 1890; in "Manuscript Releases No. 1033, The Salamanca Vision and the 1890 Diary," p. 52.

52. It seems evident that Ellen White's comments found in MS 29, and MS 44, 1890, were written after her return to Battle Creek. See: Robert W. Olson, "The Salamanca Vision and the 1890 Diary," (Washington, D.C.: Ellen G. White Estates, 1983), p. 58. Olson suggests that Ellen White's comments "seem to include descriptions of not one, but two, night visions."

53. Ellen G. White Manuscript 29, 1890; in "Manuscript Releases No. 1033, The Salamanca Vision and the 1890 Diary," pp. 59-60.

54. Ellen G. White Manuscript 44, "Diary" Nov. 4, 1890; in "Manuscript Releases No. 1033, The Salamanca Vision and the 1890 Diary," p. 61.

55. A. L. White in; *A Prophet Among You* (Mountain View, CA: Pacific Press, 1955) p. 476.

56. Details for this section are gleaned from: Robert W. Olson, "The Salamanca Vision and the 1890 Diary"; C. C. Crisler in *Life Sketches of Ellen G. White*, pp. 309-318; A. L. White in *A Prophet Among You*, pp. 471-480; A. L. White, *The Lonely Years*, pp. 463-483.

57. The front-page article in the March 5, 1891 *Sentinel* was written by A. T. Jones and titled: "What Does the Bible Teach about the Sabbath?" This article was like many others A. T. Jones had written, and which Dan Jones had criticized so ardently the year before. The article set out to prove from the writings of Mr. Crafts himself—the most prominent Sunday-law advocate—that the Sabbath was religious in nature and not civil. Thus, A. T. Jones concluded, "no civil government on earth can ever of right, have anything whatever to do with" the Sabbath. And the American Sabbath Union "know that their plea for a 'civil' Sabbath is a fraud" (p. 1).

58. Robert W. Olson, "The Salamanca Vision and the 1890 Diary," p. 77. C. Eldridge stated that, "'We remained in that room till three o'clock'" before the vote was taken and the door was opened. See footnote 60.

59. See footnote 56 for supporting references.

60. C. C. Crisler in, *Life Sketches of Ellen G. White*, p. 315. W. C. White found Ellen White "busily engaged in writing. She then told him that an angel of God had wakened her about three o'clock." Was God on time?

61. *Ibid.*, pp. 315-316.

62. Ellen G. White Manuscript 40, 1890; in *1888 Materials*, pp. 917, 941-942. Robert Olson, former director of the Ellen G. White Estates, suggests that at least part of this MS 40 found in Ellen White's diary was written early Sunday morning, March 8, 1891. There is no question that she read from it at the Sunday morning meeting ("The Salamanca Vision and the 1890 Diary," p. 63).

63. *Ibid.*, pp. 942-943, 946.

64. Ellen G. White Manuscript 59, May 20, 1905; in "Manuscript Releases No. 1033, The Salamanca Vision and the 1890 Diary," p. 69.

65. Ellen G. White Manuscript 40, 1890; in *1888 Materials*, pp. 928, 944-945, 948.

66. This is only one of many incidents that prove that O. A. Olsen was unaware of the deep bitterness and hatred being carried out against Jones and Waggoner. It was just such events which finally led Ellen White to exclaim: "Elder Olsen has acted as did Aaron" (*1888 Materials*, p. 1608).

67. Robert W. Olson, "The Salamanca Vision and the 1890 Diary," pp. 85, 83.

68. C. C. Crisler in, *Life Sketches of Ellen G. White*, p. 317.

69. Robert Olson, "The Salamanca Vision and the 1890 Diary," p. 75. This eyewitness account of A. T. Robinson differs widely from many modern portrayals of A. T. Jones. It would be well to note that Ellen White and her heavenly messenger never mentioned one word of censure against A. T. Jones and the *Sentinel* during this 1890-1891 confrontation, nor did they side with Dan Jones and his associates. George Knight, however, not only takes Dan Jones' side in this confrontation, but spends two entire chapters seeking to paint A. T. Jones as "aggressive," "brutal," "radical," and "extreme," in his "positions" of religious liberty. Knight states that Jones "consistently held to a doctrinaire [impractical theorist, fanatical, dogmatic] polar extreme. His mind did not possess much ability for flexible interpretation." He "imbibed of the spirit of Minneapolis," a problem which he found "impossible to overcome" (*From 1888 to Apostasy*, pp. 75-88, 117-131). It is not difficult to understand how Knight could go to such lengths to discredit Jones when one realizes what he openly stated after writing Jones' biography: "I must have failed to communicate effectively. I was doing my best to demonstrate that Jones was aberrant from beginning to end.

In the late 1880s and early 1890s this is demonstrated by his harshness and failure to demonstrate Christian courtesy.... [H]is extreme use of language that seemingly led some toward the holy flesh excitement, his extremes in nearly every area of religious liberty... and so on. The point that I was attempting to communicate was that throughout Jones's 'hero' period, he was beset by serious character traits, in spite of Ellen White's endorsement of him" ("A Spark in the Dark: A Reply to a Sermonette Masquerading as a Critique, George Knight answers Dennis Hokama," *Adventist Currents*, April 1988, p.43). But it was not just Ellen White's endorsement that suggests that Jones had a message to bear, it was the heavenly guide who stated: "In the *American Sentinel* has been published the truth for this time" (Ellen G. White Manuscript 29, 1890; in "Manuscript Releases No. 1033" p. 60).

70. Ellen G. White Manuscript 59, May 20, 1905; in "Manuscript Releases No. 1033, The Salamanca Vision and the 1890 Diary," p. 70.

71. Robert W. Olson, "The Salamanca Vision and the 1890 Diary," p. 86.

72. "Proceedings of the Board of Foreign Missions," *General Conference Daily Bulletin*, April 13, 1891, p. 56. The General Conference session lasted from March 5 through March 25, with a number of meetings held ten days following the close of the session (*Ibid.*, p. 52). The morning meeting where Ellen White shared the Salamanca vision took place Sunday, March 8, 1891.

73. Ellen G. White to O. A. Olsen, Letter 127, Dec. 1, 1896; in *1888 Materials*, pp. 1622-1624.

74. Ellen G. White, "What Shall We do that We Might Work the Works of God," April 21, 1890, p. 241.

## *Future Chapters titles of* The Return of the Latter Rain, *Volume 2, will include:*

Chapter 18
**Prophet Without Honor**
*"The Lord Was Not in Our Leaving America"*

Chapter 19
**Arise and Shine**
*"The Light is Shining Now!"*

Chapter 20
**1893 General Conference Session**
*"The Lord was Pouring out His Spirit Upon the People."*

Chapter 21
**The False Loud Cry**
*"If You are Teaching That the Seventh-day Adventist Church is Babylon, You Are Wrong."*

Chapter 22
**The Darkness That Followed**
They Said: *"The Working of the Holy Spirit was Fanaticism."*

Chapter 23
**Anna Rice: The Greatest Evidence the Latter Rain Began**
*"I Have More Confidence in Them Today Than I Have Had in the Past."*

Chapter 24
**Armadale 1895**
*"Savior of All Men"* because *"He Was Made Like Unto His Brethren."*

Chapter 25
**Continued Rejection**
*"They Said . . . It is Not Showers From Heaven of the Latter Rain."*

Chapter 26
**1901: What Might Have Been**
*"We May Have to Remain Here . . . Many More Years."*

# Come!  Buy Gold!

After all He's done for you and me,
Why are we afraid to be His Bride?
Won't we let Him come inside?
He's knocking at the door.

We're "rich" we say, "we don't need more,
In need of nothing at all!"
We grieved Him before; will He bear it once more,
Will His heart break again?

Come! Buy gold, refined by fire,
Garments, whiter than snow,
Eyesalve, for your eyes that you may see–
That you may see your need!

One hundred years ago, He came knocking at our door,
But we wouldn't let Him in.
We were too proud to admit our sin,
We grieved and disappointed Him.

Repent! Look on Him whom you have pierced,
Mourn for Him, weep bitterly.
It was your sins that wounded Him,
Yet these things He still offers you,

Come! Buy gold, refined by fire,
Garments, whiter than snow,
Eyesalve for your eyes that you may see–
That you may see your need!

A fountain will be opened to cleanse every soul,
Come! Quench your thirst.
Those whom I love I rebuke and chasten,
Be zealous, repent.
Whoever hears My voice and opens the door,
With him I will come in and dine!

He who overcomes will I
Grant to sit on My throne.
Just as I overcame
And sat on My Father's throne!

The whole earth will be lightened with Thy Glory,
Nations will come to Thy light!
Your sons and your daughters will come from afar,
The harvest will be ripe!

Come! Buy gold refined by fire,
Garments, whiter than snow,
Eyesalve for your eyes that you may see–
That you may see your need.

*(Words and Music by Cherie Duffield)*

## APPENDIX A

# *The Heart of the 1888 Message*

The beautiful aspects of the 1888 message which the Lord sent over 120 years ago are best described in Ellen White's 1896 statement as found in the book *Testimonies to Ministers*:

> The Lord in his great mercy sent a most precious message to his people through Elders Waggoner and Jones. This message was to bring more prominently before the world the uplifted Saviour, the sacrifice for the sins of the whole world. It presented justification through faith in the Surety; it invited the people to receive the righteousness of Christ, which is made manifest in obedience to all the commandments of God. Many had lost sight of Jesus. They needed to have their eyes directed to his divine person, his merits, and his changeless love for the human family. All power is given into his hands, that he may dispense rich gifts unto men, imparting the priceless gift of his own righteousness to the helpless human agent. This is the message that God commanded to be given to the world. It is the third angel's message, which is to be proclaimed with a loud voice, and attended with the outpouring of his Spirit in a large measure.

> The uplifted Saviour is to appear ... sitting upon the throne, to dispense the priceless covenant blessings. ... Christ is pleading for the church in the heavenly courts above. ...

> Notwithstanding our unworthiness, we are ever to bear in mind that there is One that can take away sin and save the sinner. ...

> God gave to His servants a testimony that presented the truth as it is in Jesus, which is the third angel's message, in clear, distinct lines. ...

> This ... testimony ... presents the law and the gospel, binding up the two in a perfect whole. (See Romans 5 and 1 John 3:9 to the close of the chapter). These precious scriptures will be impressed upon every heart that is opened to receive them.

> This is the very work which the Lord designs that the message He has given His servant shall perform in the heart and mind of every human agent. It is the perpetual life of the church to love God supremely and to love others as they love themselves. ...

> Neglect this great salvation, kept before you for years, despise this glorious offer of justification through the blood of Christ, and sanctification through the cleansing power of the Holy Spirit, and there remaineth no more sacrifice for sins, but a certain fearful looking for of judgment and fiery indignation. …

> I entreat you now to humble yourselves and cease your stubborn resistance of light and evidence.[1]

At least ten great gospel truths that make the 1888 message "most precious" can be found in this statement. We will look briefly at ten of them here:

**(1)** As mentioned previously, Jones and Waggoner presented truth "as it is in Jesus." Every truth came from a correct understanding of who He was and what He came to this earth to accomplish. This included a deeper understanding of the height from which Christ had come and the depth to which he stooped in order to save mankind. Many Adventist pioneers had Arian roots and saw Christ as a created being, or as having a beginning. Even Uriah Smith in 1865 wrote of Christ as the "first created being."[2] But Jones and Waggoner exalted Christ's divinity. They saw Him as "self existent," having "life in Himself," possessing "by nature all the attributes of Divinity." Waggoner unequivocally proclaimed at the 1888 General Conference: "We believe in [the] Divinity of Christ. He is God."[3]

Speaking of the message sent through Jones and Waggoner, Ellen White exclaimed: "Messages bearing the divine credentials have been sent to God's people… The fullness of the Godhead in Jesus Christ has been set forth among us with beauty and loveliness, to charm all whose hearts were not closed with prejudice."[4] In her well-known statement about the "most precious message," she put it this way: "This message was to bring more prominently before the world the uplifted Saviour. … [T]he people… needed to have their eyes directed to His divine person, His merits."[5] In lifting up Christ, however, Jones and Waggoner didn't go to the other extreme and teach that the Father, Son, and Holy Spirit were "identical" who only role-played three assignments in the plan of salvation. With but few exceptions they believed and consistently taught the truth of the Godhead in the same terms as the Bible and Ellen White.

Closely connected with their understanding of the divine nature of Christ was their understanding of His human nature. Christ came all the way to where we are, taking upon Himself "the likeness of sinful flesh." He took upon his sinless nature our sinful human nature, and yet was without sin. To Jones and Waggoner Christ "was in the same condition that the men are in whom He died to save. ... I am not implying Christ was a sinner. ... If Christ had not been made *in all thing*s like unto His brethren, then his sinless life would be no encouragement to us."[6]

To Ellen White this was "presenting Christ as a Saviour who was not afar off, but night at hand."[7] It was bringing "more prominently before the world the uplifted Saviour,"[8] both in his divine and human nature which had not been done.[9] This was "humanity inhabited by Deity, the revelation of God in human nature,—this was God's gift to our world. ... God in human flesh,—God in our tried and tempted nature."[10] Not all were happy with this teaching. Letters came to Ellen White "affirming that Christ could not have had the same nature as man, for if he had, he would have fallen under similar temptations." She responded: "If he did not have man's nature, he could not be our example... he could not have been tempted as man has been... he could not be our helper."[11]

**(2)** Thus God took the initiative in salvation, and continues to take the initiative. He is the good Shepherd who is seeking His lost sheep even though they have not sought Him. He is constantly drawing all men to repentance. God's agape love is unlike man's love, for His love is changeless—not based on conditions—seeking good for His enemies. Waggoner wrote that "God does not wait for sinners to desire pardon, before he makes an effort to save them."[12] "Not only does He call us, but He draws us. No one can come to Him without being drawn, and so Christ is lifted up to draw all to God."[13]

Jones stated that "God's mind concerning human nature is never fulfilled until He finds us at His own right hand, glorified. ... He comes and calls us into this, let us go where He will lead us. ... Here the heavenly Shepherd is leading us."[14]

Ellen White described this part of the message stating; "it invited the people to receive the righteousness of Christ. ... They needed to have their eyes directed to His… changeless love for the human family."[15] "In the parable of the lost sheep, Christ teaches that salvation does not come through our seeking after God but through God's seeking after us."[16] "None will ever come to Christ, save those who respond to the drawing of the Father's love. But God is drawing all hearts unto Him, and only those who resist His drawing will refuse to come to Christ."[17]

**(3)** By Christ coming all the way down to be with men, He became the second Adam and *accomplished* something for every human being without any choice on their part. He was not *offered* to the world from the foundation of the world, He was *given* to the world. He died the second death for every man, which gave a verdict of acquittal, by satisfying the demands of justice. In Him the human race is accepted. Thus Christ literally saved the world from premature destruction and has elected all men to be eternally saved. He has given life to all men and brought immortality to light. And to each person He has given a measure of faith.

Jones stated that "He chose every soul in the world; He chose him in Christ before the foundation of the world, predestined him unto the adoption of children and made him accepted in the Beloved."[18]

As Waggoner put it: "This faith is dealt to every man, even as Christ gave himself to every man. Do you ask what then can prevent every man from being saved? The answer is nothing, except the fact that all men will not keep the faith. If all would keep all that God gives them, all would be saved." "There is no exception here. As the condemnation came upon all, so the justification comes upon all. Christ has tasted death for every man."[19]

Ellen White described this part of their message as bringing "more prominently before the world the uplifted Saviour, the sacrifice for the sins of the whole world. … (See Romans 5 and 1John 3:9 to the close of the chapter)."[20] Thus it is that Christ's death actually did something for everyone without his or her choice, both temporal and eternal, but the fullness of this great Gift will never be fully realized or experienced without a response. Rather than taking away mankind's choice, the cross of Christ is that which gives them a choice. It is the cross of Christ that elicits or draws out a response from everyone: "What will you do with the Gift I have given you?" It is upon this response, this choice, that everyone's eternal destiny hangs. "There are only two classes in the whole universe,—those who believe in Christ and whose faith leads them to keep God's commandments, and those who do not believe in him, and are disobedient."[21] "There always have been and always will be two classes… the believers in Jesus, and those who reject him… and refuse to believe the truth."[22] "Thus every one will be condemned or acquitted out of his own mouth, and the righteousness of God will be vindicated."[23]

(**4**) So it is that God will not force anyone into heaven. He has purchased for mankind freedom of choice. The sinner must persistently resist His love in order to be lost. Waggoner made it clear: "God has wrought out salvation for every man, and has given it to him, but the majority spurn it and throw it away. The judgment will reveal the fact that full salvation was given to every man and that the lost have deliberately thrown away their birthright possession."[24] "God had implanted in the soul of every man some knowledge of right and wrong, and some natural desires for the right; and whenever a man gives himself wholly to sin, he does so only by resisting the strivings of the Spirit."[25] "His death has secured pardon and life for all. Nothing can keep them from salvation except their own perverse will. Men must take themselves out of the hand of God, in order to be lost."[26]

Jones agreed: "All the grace of God is given freely to every one, bringing salvation to all. … Having given it all, he is clear, even though men may reject it."[27] "The Lord will not compel any one to take it. … No man will die the second death who has not chosen sin rather than righteousness, death rather than life."[28]

Ellen White, writing during this time period, put it this way: "The sinner may resist this love, may refuse to be drawn to Christ, but if he does not resist he will be drawn to Jesus."[29] "The blessings of salvation are for every soul. Nothing but his own choice can prevent any man from becoming a partaker of the promise in Christ by the gospel."[30] Speaking of that "most precious message" she specifically stated: "I entreat you now to humble yourselves and cease your stubborn resistance of light and evidence."[31] "Jesus died for the whole world, but in stubborn unbelief men refuse to be fashioned after the divine pattern."[32] "Christ has made an ample sacrifice for all! What justice required, Christ had rendered in the offering of Himself. ... Those who reject the gift of life will be without excuse [John 3:16 quoted]."[33] "The wrath of God is not declared against men merely because of the sins which they have committed, but for choosing to continue in a state of resistance."[34] Since Christ has already paid the penalty for every man's sin, the only reason anyone can be condemned at last is continued unbelief, and the disobedience which is an inevitable result—a refusal to appreciate the redemption achieved by Christ on His cross and the atonement ministered by Him as High Priest that would cleanse us from all sin. It is in this sense that sin is (or sin is the result of) a constant resisting of His grace, which always leads to transgression of the law.

(5) The only other possible response is that of faith; genuine faith which works by love. But this is more than a mere mental assent to doctrinal truth, it is a realization of the height and depth of the love (agape) of God for the human race. "You may say that you believe in Jesus, when you have an appreciation of the cost of salvation."[35] By looking at the cross men see the law and the gospel—love and justice—perfectly blended. The heart is gripped with the magnitude of the sacrifice required by a broken law, the transcript of God's character. It is more than the letter of the law that brings us to Christ, but the Spirit of the law as revealed in the life and death of Christ which brings conviction of sin and a desire for forgiveness and restoration. "His love will call forth a response... and [our] lives will show to those around [us] that the Spirit of God is controlling [us]." In proportion to our realization of the great sacrifice—"the length of the chain let down from heaven to draw us up"—is our realization of the extent to which God's holy law reaches.[36] "God reaches for the hand of faith in us to direct it to lay fast hold upon the divinity of Christ, that we may attain to perfection of character."[37] Our desire will be for that perfect righteousness which is found only in Christ.

Thus it is that *justification by faith* is much more than the appreciating and receiving a legal declaration of acquittal; *it changes the heart*. The sinner has now received the atonement, which is reconciliation with God. Since it is impossible to be truly reconciled to Him and not also be reconciled to His holy law, it follows that true *justification by faith* makes the believer obedient to all the commandments of God. "Here we have the love of the Father in giving His son to die for fallen man, that he might keep the law of Jehovah. Now Jesus stands in our world, His divinity clothed with humanity, and man must be clothed with Christ's righteousness. Then he can, through the righteousness of Christ, stand acquitted before God."[38]

Waggoner expressed it this way: "We are saved by faith in Jesus Christ; but Christ saves us from our sins, and not in them."[39] "We have the most positive evidence that the keeping of the commandments of God and the faith of Jesus are inseparably connected. No one can keep the commandments without faith in Jesus, and no one ever has real faith in Jesus except as he is driven to it by the terms of the violated law, and by a sincere desire to have the righteousness of the law fulfilled in him. ... [A]nd none can obey it except as they yield to the striving of the Holy Spirit, and come to Christ."[40] "It is not that God gives a man righteousness as a reward for believing certain dogmas; the gospel is something entirely different from that. It is this, that true faith has Christ alone as its object, and it brings Christ's life actually into the heart; and therefore it must bring righteousness."[41]

Jones stated the same: "Faith is 'the gift of God' (Eph. 2:8); and that it is given to everybody is plainly stated in Scriptures [Rom. 12:3 quoted]. This measure of faith which 'God hath dealt to every man' is the capital with which God endows and starts 'every man that cometh into the world;' and every man is expected to trade upon this capital—cultivate it—to the salvation of his soul."[42] "Do you want to be like Jesus? Then receive the grace that he has so fully and so freely given. Receive it in the measure in which *He has given it*, not in the measure in which you think you deserve it. Yield yourself to it. ... It will make you like Jesus."[43]

Ellen White described this part of that "most precious message," stating: "It presented justification through faith in the Surety; it invited the people to receive the righteousness of Christ, which is made manifest in obedience to all the commandments of God."[44] "The heart needs the presence of the heavenly Guest,—Christ abiding in the soul. We are to dwell in Christ, and Christ is to dwell in us by faith."[45] "Let Christ, the divine Life dwell in you and through you reveal the heaven-born love that will inspire hope in the hopeless and bring heaven's peace to the sin-stricken heart."[46]

(**6**) This marvelous work is accomplished through the ministry of the new covenant wherein the Lord actually writes His law *in the heart* of the believer. Obedience is loved and sin hated. The old and new covenants are not primarily a matter of time but of condition. Abraham's faith enabled him to live under the new covenant, while multitudes of Christians today live under the old covenant. The new covenant is God's one-way promise to write His law in our hearts, and to give us everlasting salvation as a free gift in Christ. The old covenant is the vain promise of the people to be faithful and obey, which gives birth to bondage (Gal. 4:24). So it is that under the new covenant salvation comes by believing God's promises to enable us to obey, not by our making promises to Him, which we cannot obey. This new covenant truth was an essential element of the 1888 message and was also at the heart of the controversy over the law in Galatians.

Waggoner expressed it this way: "These two covenants exist today. The two covenants are not matters of time, but of condition. ... So the covenant from Sinai holds all who adhere to it in bondage 'under the law,' while the covenant from above gives freedom, not freedom from obedience to the law, but freedom from disobedience to it. ... The difference between the two covenants may be put briefly thus: In the covenant from Sinai we ourselves have to do with the law alone, while in the covenant from above we have the law in Christ."[47]

Jones' view was the same: "The first [old] covenant rested upon the promises of the people, and depended solely upon the efforts of the people. The second [new] covenant consists solely of the promise of God, and depends upon the power and work of God."[48]

Ellen White supported Jones and Waggoner in this view of the covenants and also proclaimed the same good news: "All power is given into His hands, that He may dispense rich gifts unto men, imparting the priceless gift of His own righteousness to the helpless human agent. … The uplifted Saviour is to appear… sitting upon the throne, to dispense the priceless covenant blessings."[49] "The terms of the 'old covenant' were, obey and live. … The 'new covenant' was established upon 'better promises'—the promise of forgiveness of sins and of the grace of God to renew the heart and bring it into harmony with the principles of God's law."[50] "Your promises and resolutions are like ropes of sand. You cannot control your thoughts, your impulses, your affections. The knowledge of your broken promises and forfeited pledges weakens your confidence in your own sincerity, and causes you to feel that God cannot accept you. … What you need to understand is the true force of the will."[51]

(7) The validity of God's promises can be seen in the fact that our Savior "condemned sin in the flesh" of fallen mankind, and conquered the sin problem for the human race. This means that He has outlawed sin. In the light of the cross, the devil cannot force anyone to sin. Because of Him, there is now no reason for any human being to go on living under the frightful "dominion" of sin. Righteousness is by faith; sin is by unbelief. Sinful addictions lose their grip if one has "the faith of Jesus" (Rev. 14:12).

Waggoner stated it this way: "To do this as the Bible enjoins, to consider Christ continually and intelligently, just as He is, will transform one into a perfect Christian."[52] Jones made it clear as well: "[Christ] has made and consecrated a way by which, in Him, every believer can in this world, and for a whole lifetime, live a life holy, harmless, undefiled, separate from sinners, and as a consequence be made with Him higher than the heavens. … Christ attained it in human flesh in this world, and thus made and consecrated a way by which, in Him, every believer can attain it."[53]

Ellen White supported Jones and Waggoner on this teaching: "God was manifested in the flesh to condemn sin in the flesh. … No man can say that he is hopelessly subject to the bondage of sin and Satan. Christ has assumed the responsibilities of the human race. ... He testifies that through this imputed righteousness the believing soul shall obey the commandments of God."[54] Speaking of that most precious message, she stated: "The efficacy of the blood of Christ was to be presented to the people with freshness and power, that their faith might lay hold upon its merits. ... Notwithstanding our unworthiness, we are ever to bear in mind that there is One that can take away sin and save the sinner. ... Those who received the message were greatly blessed, for they saw the bright rays of the Sun of Righteousness, and life and hope sprang up in their hearts."[55]

(8) The desire to see sin and sorrow come to an end is therefore not based on selfish motivations. A higher motivation will be realized in the closing years of time than has prevailed in the church in past ages. There is a concern for Christ that He receive His reward and find His rest in the final eradication of sin. This new motivation transcends fear of being lost or hope of reward in being saved; obedience is loved. The higher motivation is symbolized in the climax of Scripture— the Bride of Christ making herself ready. This takes place when believers really appreciate the love (agape) of God manifested to all men. This constrains them to live for Him and the "marriage of the Lamb" can finally take place (Rev. 19:7).

Waggoner expressed the final vindication of God's character this way: "God is now accused by Satan of injustice and indifference, and even of cruelty. Thousands of men have echoed the charge. But the judgment will declare the righteousness of God. His character, as well as that of man, is on trial. In the judgment every act, both of God and man, that has been done since creation, will be seen by all in all its bearings. And when every thing is seen in that perfect light, God will be acquitted of all wrongdoing, even by His enemies."[56]

Jones wrote of it in this way: "When Jesus comes, it is to take His people unto Himself. It is to present to Himself His glorious church, 'not having spot, or wrinkle, or any such thing,' but that it is 'holy and without blemish.' It is to see Himself perfectly reflected in all His saints. And before He comes thus, His people must be in that condition. ... And this state of perfection, this developing in each believer the complete image of Jesus—this is the finishing of the mystery of God, which is Christ in you the hope of glory. This consummation is accomplished in the cleansing of the sanctuary."[57]

Ellen White expressed this theme often in her writings: "It is not the fear of punishment, or the hope of everlasting reward, that leads the disciples of Christ to follow Him. They behold the Saviour's matchless love, revealed throughout His pilgrimage on earth, from the manger of Bethlehem to Calvary's cross, and the sight of Him attracts, it softens and subdues the soul. Love awakens in the heart of the beholders. They hear His voice, and they follow Him."[58] "Christ is waiting with longing desire for the manifestation of Himself in His church. When the character of Christ shall be perfectly reproduced in His people, then He will come to claim them as His own. It is the privilege of every Christian not only to look for but to hasten the coming of our Lord Jesus Christ."[59] "Few give thought to the suffering that sin has caused our Creator. All heaven suffered in Christ's agony; but that suffering did not begin or end with His manifestation in humanity. The cross is a revelation to our dull senses of the pain that, from its very inception, sin has brought to the heart of God."[60] Of that "most precious message," she wrote: "This is the very work which the Lord designs that the message He has given His servant shall perform in the heart and mind of every human agent. It is the perpetual life of the church to love God supremely and to love others as they love themselves."[61]

(9) The 1888 message is especially precious because it joins together the true biblical truth of justification by faith with the unique biblical idea of the cleansing of the heavenly sanctuary. This is true righteousness by faith. This work is contingent on the full cleansing of the hearts of God's people on earth, which the High Priest will accomplish with all who let Him. This is Bible truth that the world is waiting to discover. It is "the third angel's message in verity,"[62] which is centered in the Most Holy Apartment ministry of Christ since 1844.[63] It forms the essential element of truth that will yet lighten the earth with the glory of a final, fully developed presentation of "the everlasting gospel" of Revelation 14 and 18.

Waggoner expressed this view right after the 1888 General Conference stating: "But will there ever be any people on the earth who will have attained to that perfection of character? Indeed there will be [Zeph. 3:13 quoted]. When the Lord comes there will be a company who will be found 'complete in him,' having not their own righteousness, but that perfect righteousness of God, which comes by faith of Jesus Christ. To perfect this work in the hearts of individuals, and to prepare such a company, is the work of the Third Angel's Message. That message, therefore, is not a mass of dry theories, but is a living practical reality."[64] Years later Waggoner was still writing about this very important message: "That God has a sanctuary in the heavens, and that Christ is priest there, cannot be doubted by anyone who reads the Scriptures. … Therefore it follows that the cleansing of the sanctuary—a work which is set forth in the Scriptures as immediately preceding the coming of the Lord— is coincident with complete cleansing of the people of God on earth, and preparing them for translation when the Lord comes."[65]

Jones wrote with the same urgency: "This special message of justification which God has been sending us is to prepare us for glorification at the coming of the Lord. In this, God is giving to us the strongest sign that it is possible for Him to give, that the next thing is the coming of the Lord."[66] Years later he had the same emphasis: "Though I preach the finishing of transgression in the lives of individuals; and though I preach the making an end of sins, and the making of reconciliation for iniquity, and the bringing in of everlasting righteousness, in the life of the individual; and yet do not preach with it the sanctuary and its cleansing, that is not the third angel's message. That great day can not come till the sanctuary is cleansed. The sanctuary can not be cleansed until transgression is finished in your life and mine; till an end of sins is made in your life and mine; and reconciliation made for the sins that have been committed; and then, oh, then, in place of it all, everlasting righteousness brought in, to hold us steady in the path of righteousness."[67]

Ellen White speaking of what took place in 1844, shows the connection between the third angel's message and the cleansing of the sanctuary: "Those who rejected the first message could not be benefited by the second, and were not benefited by the midnight cry, which was to prepare them to enter with

Jesus by faith into the Most Holy place of the heavenly Sanctuary. And by rejecting the two former messages, they can see no light in the third angel's message, which shows the way into the Most Holy place."[68] In 1888 she saw that Christ was still in the sanctuary seeking to prepare a people for His Second Coming. Jones and Waggoner had been sent with a message for this very reason: "Now Christ is in the heavenly sanctuary. And what is He doing? Making atonement for us, cleansing the sanctuary from the sins of the people. Then we must enter by faith into the sanctuary with Him. … The closing work of the third angel's message will be attended with a power that will send the rays of the Sun of Righteousness into all the highways and byways of life."[69] In 1890 she wrote several articles about the relationship between this message and the cleansing of the Sanctuary: "We are in the day of atonement, and we are to work in harmony with Christ's work of cleansing of the sanctuary from the sins of the people. Let no man who desires to be found with the wedding garment on, resist our Lord in his office work."[70] Speaking of that "most precious message" she wrote: "Christ is pleading for the church in the heavenly courts above. … As the priest sprinkled the warm blood upon the mercy seat… so while we confess our sins and plead the efficacy of Christ's atoning blood, our prayers are to ascend to heaven. … God gave to His servants a testimony that presented the truth as it is in Jesus, which is the third angel's message, in clear, distinct lines."[71]

(10) Since Christ has already paid the penalty for every man's sin, and is constantly drawing man to repentance, the only reason anyone can be condemned at last is continued unbelief, a refusal to appreciate the redemption achieved by Christ on His cross and ministered by Him as High Priest. It follows then that *if one understands and believes* how good the good news of salvation really is, then it is actual*ly easier* to be saved then it is to be lost. Christ's yoke is easy, and His burden light, and to resist is the hard downward road to destruction. Light is stronger than darkness, grace is stronger than sin, and the Holy Spirit is stronger than the flesh when the heart is surrendered to Christ. But to resist the Holy Spirit's conviction of

good news is to "kick against the goads." Those who *refuse* to believe will find it easy to follow their own natural tendencies to do evil. The true gospel exposes this unbelief and leads to an effective repentance that prepares the believer for the return of Christ if man will only choose Him. Any difficulty is the result of failing to believe the gospel, to believe that "God reaches for the hand of faith in us to direct it to lay fast hold upon the divinity of Christ, that we may attain to perfection of character."[72] Christ will hold our hand more firmly than we can possibly hold His.

Jones expressed it this way: "When grace reigns, it is easier to do right than it is to do wrong. That is the comparison [Rom. 5:21]. … So it is as literally true that under the reign of grace it is easier to do right than to do wrong, as it is true that under the reign of sin it is easier to do wrong than it is to do right."[73] "Salvation from sin certainly depends upon there being more power in grace than there is in sin. … Because man naturally is enslaved to a power—the power of sin—that is absolute in its reign. And so long as that power has sway, it is not only difficult, but impossible to do the good that he knows and that he would. But let a mightier power than that have sway, then is it not plain enough that it will be just as easy to serve the will of the mightier power, when it reigns, as it was to serve the will of the other power when it reigned?"[74]

Waggoner agreed: "Many people have the notion that it is impossible for them to believe. That is grave error. Faith is just as easy and natural as breathing. It is the common inheritance of all men, and the one thing wherein all are equal. It is only when men build up a barrier of pride about themselves (Ps. 73:6) that they find it difficult to believe. … The question is, In what measure has God given every man faith?… [T]he faith which he gives is the faith of Jesus. The faith of Jesus is given in the gift of Jesus Himself, and Christ is given in His fullness to every man."[75] "We need not try to improve on the Scriptures, and say that the goodness of God *tends* to lead men to repentance. The Bible says that it *does* lead them to repentance. … But not all repent? Why? Because they despise the riches of the goodness and forbearance and long-suffering of God, and break away from the merciful leading of the Lord. But whoever does not resist the Lord, will surely be brought to repentance and salvation."[76]

Ellen White expressed the same things: "For fifty years I have borne Christ's yoke, and I can testify that his yoke is easy, and His burden is light. I have never found any difficulty except when I manufactured a yoke of my own, and laid aside the yoke of Christ."[77] "Tell the people in clear, hopeful language how they may escape the heritage of shame which is our deserved portion. But for Christ's sake do not present before them ideas that will discourage them, that will make the way to heaven seem very difficult."[78] "But the way to life is narrow and the entrance strait. If you cling to any besetting sin you will find the way too narrow for you to enter. … Yet do not therefore conclude that the upward path is the hard and the downward road the easy way. All along the road that leads to death there are pains and penalties, there are sorrows and disappointments, there are warnings not to go on. God's love has made it hard for the heedless and headstrong to destroy themselves."[79] "Christ will hold our hand more firmly than we can possibly hold His."[80]

Speaking of those who were rejecting that "most precious message" she warned: "If you reject Christ's delegated messengers, you reject Christ. Neglect this great salvation, kept before you for years, despise this glorious offer of justification through the blood of Christ, and sanctification through the cleansing power of the Holy Spirit, and there remaineth no more sacrifice for sins, but a certain fearful looking for of judgment and fiery indignation."[81]

Granted, there are other aspects of the 1888 message that influenced the work of the church for years to come, such as religious liberty, education, medical work, and reforms in health; but the heart of that message, as recognized by Ellen White, was righteousness by faith. Many other books have been printed that deal more specifically with the aspects of the message as mentioned above. We will deal more specifically with many of these aspects of the message in *The Return of the Latter Rain*, volume 2.[82]*

# APPENDIX A FOOTNOTES

1. Ellen G. White to O. A. Olsen, Letter 57, May 1, 1895; in *1888 Materials*, p. 1336-1342, and *Testimonies to Ministers*, p. 92-98.

2. Uriah Smith, *Thoughts on Revelation*, (Battle Creek, MI: Review and Herald, 1865), p. 59.

3. "Notes of W. C. White Taken at Minneapolis," Oct. 16, 1888; in *Manuscripts and Memories*, p. 421.

4. Ellen G. White, "Living Channels of Light," *Review and Herald*, May 27, 1890, p. 321.

5. Ellen G. White, *Testimonies to Ministers*, pp. 91-92.

6. E. J. Waggoner, *Gospel in Galatians*, pp. 60-61.

7. Ellen G. White, *1888 Materials*, p. 267.

8. Ellen G. White, *Testimonies to Ministers*, p. 91.

9. Ellen G. White, *1888 Materials*, p. 1076.

10. Ellen G. White, Letter 77, Nov. 14, 1895, unpublished.

11. Ellen G. White, *1888 Materials*, p. 533.

12. E. J. Waggoner, *Signs of the Times*, Jan. 27, 1888, p. 56.

13. E. J. Waggoner, *Waggoner on Romans*, p. 140.

14. A. T. Jones, *General Conference Daily Bulletin*, Feb. 27, 1895, p. 366.

15. Ellen G. White, *Testimonies to Ministers*, p. 92.

16. Ellen G. White, *Christ's Object Lessons*, p. 189.

17. Ellen G. White, *Desire of Ages*, p. 387.

18. A. T. Jones, *General Conference Daily Bulletin*, Feb. 26, 1893, p. 401.

19. E. J. Waggoner, *Waggoner on Romans*, pp. 69, 101.

20. Ellen G. White, *Testimonies to Ministers*, pp. 91, 94.

21. Ellen G. White, "Believe on the Lord Jesus Christ," *Review and Herald*, June 23, 1896, p. 386.

22. Ellen G. White, "Principle Never to be Sacrificed for Peace," *Review and Herald*, July 24, 1894, p. 465.

23. Ellen G. White, "Notes of Travel," *Review and Herald*, Nov. 4, 1884, p. 690.

24. E. J. Waggoner, *The Glad Tidings*, p. 14.

25. E. J. Waggoner, *Signs of the Times*, Nov. 30, 1888, p. 726.

26. E. J. Waggoner, *Waggoner on Romans*, p. 144.

27. A. T. Jones, *Review and Herald*, April 17, 1894, p. 248.

28. A. T. Jones, *General Conference Daily Bulletin*, Feb. 21, 1895, p. 269.

29. Ellen G. White, *Steps to Christ*, p. 27.

30. Ellen G. White, *Desire of Ages*, p. 403.

31. Ellen G. White, *Testimonies to Ministers*, p. 98.

32. Ellen G. White, "The Beatitudes," *Signs of the Times*, May 30, 1892, p. 455.

33. Ellen G. White, "Chosen in Christ," *Signs of the Times*, Jan. 2, 1893, p. 134.

34. Ellen G. White, *Testimonies to Ministers*, p. 74.

35. Ellen G. White, "How do We Stand?" *Review and Herald*, July 24, 1888, p. 466.

36. Ellen G. White, *1888 Materials*, p. 131.

37. Ellen G. White, *Desire of Ages*, p. 123.

38. Ellen G. White, Manuscript 5, "Christ and the Law, June 19, 1889, p. 9; in *1888 Materials*, p. 345.

39. E. J. Waggoner, *Signs of the Times*, June 15, 1888, p. 358.

40. E. J. Waggoner, *Signs of the Times*, Dec. 28, 1888, p. 790.

41. E. J. Waggoner, *Waggoner on Romans*, p. 74.

42. A. T. Jones, *Lessons on Faith*, p. 21.

43. A. T. Jones, *Lessons on Faith*, p. 81.

44. Ellen G. White, *Testimonies to Ministers*, p. 92.

45. Ellen G. White, *1888 Materials*, p. 1537.

46. Ellen G. White, *Thoughts From the Mount of Blessings*, p. 114-115.

47. E. J. Waggoner, *The Glad Tidings*, pp. 100-101.

48. A. T. Jones, *Review and Herald*, July 24, 1900, p. 472.

49. Ellen G. White, *Testimonies to Ministers*, p. 92.

50. Ellen G. White, *Patriarchs and Prophets*, p. 372.

51. Ellen G. White, *Steps to Christ*, p. 47.

52. E. J. Waggoner, *Christ and His Righteousness*, p. 5.

53. A. T. Jones, *The Consecrated Way to Christian Perfection*, p. 83.

54. Ellen G. White, "Work for God," *Signs of the Times*, Jan. 16, 1896, p. 37.

55. Ellen G. White, *Testimonies to Ministers*, pp. 92-95.

56. E. J. Waggoner, *Present Truth*, Aug. 16, 1894, p. 516.

57. A. T. Jones, *The Consecrated Way to Christian Perfection*, p. 88.

58. Ellen G. White, *Desire of Ages*, p. 480.

59. Ellen G. White, *Christ's Object Lessons*, p. 69.

60. Ellen G. White, *Education*, p. 263.

61. Ellen G. White, *Testimonies to Ministers*, p. 95.

62. Ellen G. White, "Repentance the Gift of God," *Review and Herald*, April 1, 1890, p. 193.

63. Ellen G. White, *Early Writings*, p. 254.

64. E. J. Waggoner, *Signs of the Times*, Dec. 28, 1888, p. 790.

65. E. J. Waggoner, *Present Truth*, Dec. 8, 1898, p. 773.

66. A. T. Jones, *General Conference Daily Bulletin*, Feb. 27, 1895, p. 367.

67. A. T. Jones, *General Conference Daily Bulletin*, April 1, 1903, p. 43.

68. Ellen G. White, *Spiritual Gifts*, book 1, p. 171.

69. Ellen G. White, *1888 Material*, pp. 127, 166.

70. Ellen G. White, "The Need of Complete Consecration," *Review and Herald*, Jan. 21, 1890, p. 34.

71. Ellen G. White, *Testimonies to Ministers*, pp. 92-93.

72. Ellen G. White, *Desire of Ages*, p. 123.

73. A. T. Jones, *Review and Herald*, July 25, 1899, p. 471.

74. A. T. Jones, *Review and Herald*, Sept. 1, 1896, p. 557.

75. E. J. Waggoner, *Waggoner on Romans*, p. 179.

76. E. J. Waggoner, *Waggoner on Romans*, p. 42.

77. Ellen G. White, "Christ's Yoke is Easy," *Signs of the Times*, July 8, 1889, p. 402.

78. Ellen G. White, Letter 15a 1890; in *Selected Messages* book 1, p. 182.

79. Ellen G. White, *Mount of Blessings*, p. 139.

80. Ellen G. White Manuscript 20, "Diary," Dec. 28, 1891, p. 7, unpublished.

81. Ellen G. White, *Testimonies to Ministers*, p. 97.

82. I am indebted to Robert Wieland and Donald Short for the conception of the thoughts above. See: *1888 Re-examined*, pp. ii-iii. However, the author takes full responsibility for adjustments and wording as laid out here.

## APPENDIX B

# *Saviour of All Men*

One subject that has brought about much discussion in the last few years has to do with the sacrifice of Christ and what it accomplished in the past and accomplishes today. Often much of the contention centers on Romans 5, particularly verse 18. What did Christ's death accomplish for all men? In 1895, Ellen White wrote her well known statement of the "most precious message" sent to the Seventh-day Adventist Church through "Elders Waggoner and Jones." She described it as the message that was to go to the world and be "attended by the outpouring of His Spirit in a large measure." A few paragraphs later, and still speaking of this message, Ellen White proclaimed: "It presents the law and the gospel, binding up the two in a perfect whole. (See Romans 5, and 1 John 3:9-24.) These precious scriptures will be impressed upon every heart that is opened to receive them."[1]

Romans 5 was a chapter that Waggoner, Jones, and Prescott all preached and wrote about prior to Ellen White's May 1, 1895 statement in *Testimonies to Ministers*.[2] This Scripture represents the very heart of the gospel—what Adam's sin did to the whole human race, and what Christ's sacrifice did for the whole human race. 1 John 3 is a chapter of practical godliness—love in action, keeping the law—demonstrated by loving one's brethren. According to Ellen White these two Scriptures present the law and the gospel bound as a perfect whole. God has said that he will impress these Scriptures upon every heart that is open to receive them.

There are two aspects of Romans 5: What Adam's sin and what Christ's sacrifice did for all men without our choice, and what Adam's sin and what Christ's sacrifice do that requires our choice. Thus, the truths found in Romans 5 do not do away with justification by faith—they explain the foundation for it.

Christ's death actually did something for every man, both temporal and eternal, but the fullness of this great Gift will never be fully realized or experienced without a response. However, the cross of Christ elicits or draws out a response from every man: "What will you do with the Gift I have given you?" It is upon this response that each man's eternal destiny is decided. Unfortunately, "the majority spurn" their birthright of eternal life, "and throw it away."[3]

Just as the sin of Adam brought a "verdict of condemnation" upon all men,[4] "even so" on His cross, Christ the second Adam, brought on "all men" a "verdict of acquittal" (Rom. 5:12-18, NEB). This is the temporary, or corporate, "justification of life" that has been given to all men (Rom. 5:18, KJV). Thus men are now born free from the condemnation of Adam and given the ability to choose.

But the "very essence of the gospel is restoration," to be saved from sin, not in sin.[5] One can only begin to realize the magnitude of the plan of salvation when it is understood in light of the great controversy between Christ and Satan. As mankind is brought face to face with the sacrifice on Calvary he begins "to realize the value of salvation ... to understand what it cost."[6] Real faith comes from a heart that has an "appreciation of the cost of salvation."[7] The justification by faith that results from the surrender of the will to Christ, is more than just a legal pardon for past sins—the law is written on the heart so the sinner can and will stop sinning. This is the purpose of justification by faith, and yet it could never have taken place if Christ had not stepped in and paid the sinner's debt (both Adam's and ours), from the foundation of the world. Thus justification and sanctification by faith in their entirety constitute true righteousness by faith.

The Bible presents two aspects of the plan of salvation throughout, but most clearly in Romans 5; the gift of "justification of life" for all men, and justification by faith for all who believe. Ellen White presents these two aspects throughout her writings as well, but a failure to clearly see and keep a balanced view can lead to errors and falling into a theological ditch. One aspect of salvation does not do away with the other, but separated they can be dangerous. Christ's corporate sacrifice for all men, misrepresented or presented on its own, can lead to cheap grace. But misrepresenting or presenting the sinner's required response by faith without the presentation of what God has already done for all men can lead to a legalism void of true love for God and man. Both of these problems make up a lukewarm Laodicean Church. Not until we see and comprehend (judge) the love of God as "One died for all, then all died," will we be "constrained" to love God supremely and our neighbor as ourselves (2 Cor. 5:14).

Following are some of Ellen White's statements where she uses different words to describe what Christ has done, or what He is to all men.[8]* The purpose of this compilation is to show just some of Ellen White's statements on this aspect of salvation. It is not the purpose of this compilation, however, to do away with her other statements which speak of man's response.

For instance, speaking in a corporate sense, Ellen White clearly states: "The human race is accepted in the Beloved."[9] But in other places Ellen White presents balancing statements in regard to man's response of faith, saying: "Those who do the works of Christ are accepted in the Beloved."[10] Both these statements are inspired and true; we don't have to throw one or the other away. "As the Sacrifice in our behalf was complete, so our restoration from the defilement of sin is to be complete."[11]

Many times Ellen White includes both aspects of the plan of salvation in the same statement: "Christ has made an ample sacrifice for all! What justice required, Christ had rendered in the offering of Himself,...." Here we see the corporate aspect, but Ellen White continues: "and 'how shall we escape if we neglect so great salvation?' Those who reject the gift of life will be without excuse... [John 3:16 quoted]."[12] Thus she beautifully presents the two aspects together. Another example: "Jesus has purchased redemption for us. It is ours [the whole world's]; but we are placed here on probation to see if we will prove worthy of eternal life."[13] One more example: "The Son of God suffered the penalty of sin, reconciling the world unto Himself. He who knew no sin became a sin-offering...." But Ellen White continues: "that fallen, sinful human beings, through repentance and confession, might receive pardon."[14] Again, we see that both aspects of the plan of salvation presented here together. In other places Ellen White speaks to only one of these aspects, but none of these statements, either singularly or in compilation form, should be used to disprove or misrepresent the plan of salvation in its totality.

I would encourage the reader to look up the following statements and see how these complimentary aspects of the plan of salvation are clearly presented together. Because we often look for and see only one aspect—justification by faith, man's response—I have listed below only the portion of her statements that expresses the corporate aspect—that which justification by faith is built upon—for the purpose of drawing more attention to this aspect.

"He redeemed Adam's disgraceful fall, and **saved the world**."[15]

"The **Saviour of the world** became sin for the race."[16]

"He has paid the **ransom** money for **the whole world**."[17]

"The Jews saw in the sacrificial offerings the symbol of Christ whose blood was shed for the **salvation of the world**."[18]

"The **world's Redeemer** estimates the value of the human soul by the price which He has paid for it on Calvary."[19]

"The entire plan of sacrificial worship was a foreshadowing of the Saviour's death to **redeem the world**."[20]

"Satan knows that Christ has purchased **redemption for the whole world**, and is determined to wrest from the hand of Christ every soul that he can possibly influence."[21]

"He is the Maker of all mankind. All men are of **one family by creation**, and all are **one through redemption**."[22]
"He has signed the **emancipation papers of the race**."[23]

"Christ, the **surety of the human race**, works with uninterrupted activity."[24]

"The words spoken in indignation, 'To what purpose is this waste?' brought vividly before Christ the greatest sacrifice ever made,—the gift of Himself as the **propitiation for a lost world**."[25]

"On the cross of Christ the Saviour made an **atonement for the fallen race**."[26]

"Christ, the great Antitype, both **Sacrifice and High Priest** ... for the sins of the **world**."[27]

"Before the coming of Christ to the world evidences abundant had been given that God loved the **human race**. But in the **gift of Christ to a race** so undeserving was demonstrated the love of God beyond all dispute."[28]

"We should cultivate true Christian courtesy and tender sympathy, even for the **roughest, hardest cases of humanity** ... who are still **subjects of grace** and precious in the sight of the Lord."[29]

"Yes, Christ gave **His life for the life of the world**."[30]

"Thus Christ gave **humanity an existence out of Himself**."[31]

"With his long human arm the Son of God **encircled the whole human family**, while with his divine arm he grasped the throne of the Infinite."[32]

"By the lost sheep Christ represents **not only the individual sinner but the one world** that has apostatized and has been ruined by sin.... **this little fallen world—the one lost sheep**—is more precious in His sight than are the ninety and nine that went not astray from the fold. Christ, the loved Commander in the heavenly courts, stooped from His high estate, laid aside the glory that He had with the Father, in order to **save the one lost world**."[33]

"By dying for man, Jesus **exalted humanity in the scale of moral value with God**."[34]

"Through the victory of Christ, the **human race was elevated in moral value**, not because of anything they had done, but because of the great work that had been wrought out for them through the only begotten Son of God."[35]

"As man's substitute and surety, in human nature through divine power, **Christ placed man on vantage ground**."[36]
"The **human race is accepted in the Beloved**."[37]

"And when in His dying agony the Saviour cried out, 'It is finished,' **He drew the world back into favor with God**."[38]

"Those who claim to be descendants of Abraham have attempted to number Israel, as though the gift of eternal life belonged to a select few. They would have the benefits of salvation limited to their own nation. **But God has placed every individual of our race under divine favor**."[39]

"'This is my beloved Son, in whom I am well pleased.' How many have read over this relation, and **have not had their hearts stirred by its significant truths**! Many have **thought that it did not concern mankind**; but it is of the greatest importance to **each one of them**. Jesus was accepted of Heaven as a representative of the human race. With all our sin and weakness, we are not cast aside as worthless; **we are accepted in the Beloved**."[40]

"The religion of Christ uplifts **the receiver** to a higher plane of thought and action, **while at the same time** it presents **the whole human race** as alike the objects of the love of God, being **purchased** by the sacrifice of his Son."[41]

"**Every blessing, whether temporal or spiritual**, comes to us as the purchase of his blood."[42]

"**All men have been bought** with this infinite price. ...God has purchased the will, the affections, the mind, the soul, of every human being. Whether believers or unbelievers, all men are the Lord's property."[43]

"**Jesus has purchased redemption for us. It is ours**."[44]

"The Son of God suffered the penalty of sin, **reconciling the world** unto Himself."[45]

"His mission was to exalt the Father's law and make it honorable, and to justify its claims by paying with his own life the penalty of its transgression. It was thus that he made **reconciliation between God and man**."[46]

"Christ came not **confessing** His own sins; but guilt was imputed to him as the sinner's substitute. He came not to repent on His own account; but in behalf of the sinner."[47]

"**His perfection of character was placed in man's behalf**. The curse of the law Christ took upon Himself."[48]

"After Christ had taken the necessary steps in repentance, conversion, and faith in **behalf of the human race**, He went to John to be baptized of him in Jordan."[49]

"He proclaims Himself the **Advocate of the sinful human family**."[50]

"Christ had cast up the immeasurable sum of guilt to be canceled because of sin, and he gathered to his dying soul this vast responsibility, **taking the sins of the whole world upon himself**."[51]

"The guilt of fallen humanity He must bear. Upon Him who knew no sin must be laid the **iniquity of us all**."[52]

"When the **whole world** was under condemnation, Christ **took upon himself the guilt** of the sinner; he bore the wrath of God for the transgressor, and thus suffering the penalty of sin, he ransoms the sinner."[53]

"Christ **became sin for the fallen race**, in **taking upon himself the condemnation** resting upon the sinner for his transgression of the law of God. Christ stood at the head of the human family as their representative. He had taken upon himself the **sins of the world**. In the likeness of sinful flesh he condemned sin in the flesh."[54]

"**Justification is the opposite of condemnation**."[55]

"Justice demands that **sin be not merely pardoned, but the death penalty must be executed**. God, in the gift of His only-begotten Son, **met both these requirements**. By dying in man's stead, **Christ exhausted the penalty and provided a pardon**."[56]

"He was the surety for man, the ambassador for God—the surety for man to **satisfy** by His righteousness in man's behalf the **demands of the law**, and the representative of God to make manifest His character to a **fallen race**."[57]

"Christ **satisfied the demands of the law** in His human nature."[58]

# Appendix B Footnotes

1. Ellen G. White, *Testimonies to Ministers*, pp. 91, 94.

2. We will deal more fully with this subject in chapter 24, to be published in volume 2

3. E. J. Waggoner, *The Glad Tidings*, p. 14.

4. For Ellen White statements on the results of Adam's sin on the whole race see: *Review and Herald*, Feb. 24, 1874; *Manuscript Releases*, vol. 9, p. 229; *Spirit of Prophecy*, vol. 4, pp. 49-50; *Great Controversy*, p. 180; *Manuscript Releases*, vol. 9, p. 236; *Spiritual Gifts*, vol. 3, p. 46; *Spalding and Magan*, p. 146; *Youth Instructor*, April 1, 1897.

5. Ellen G. White, *Desire of Ages*, p. 824.

6. *Testimonies*, vol. 2, p. 200.

7. *Review and Herald*, July 24, 1888.

8. I have compiled a collection which, without editing, has more than 160 pages of Ellen White statements that include both aspects of the plan of salvation. **All the following references are from Ellen G. White:**

9. *1888 Materials*, p. 124.

10. *Signs of the Times*, Sept. 19, 1895.

11. *Testimonies*, vol. 8, p. 312.

12. *Signs of the Times*, Jan. 2, 1893.

13. *Signs of the Times*, Nov. 26, 1886.

14. *Manuscript Releases*, vol. 11, p. 365.

15. *Youth Instructor*, June 2, 1898.

16. *Review and Herald*, Sept. 18, 1874.

17. *Home Missionary*, July 1, 1897.

18. *Selected Messages*, book 1, pp. 106-107.

19. *Bible Echo*, Jan. 8, 1894.

20. *Desire of Ages*, p. 165.

21. *Review and Herald*, May 19, 1896.

22. *Christ's Object Lessons*, p. 386.

23. *Ministry of Healing*, p. 89.

24. *Review and Herald*, March 5, 1901.

25. *Desire of Ages*, p. 565.

26. *Signs of the Times*, Dec. 17, 1902.

27. *Signs of the Times*, Sept. 19, 1892.

28. *Signs of the Times,* Feb. 5, 1894.

29. *Testimonies*, vol. 3, p. 422.

30. *Review and Herald*, May 1, 1900.

31. *Selected Messages*, book 1, p. 251.

32. *Youth Instructor*, July 29, 1895.

33. *Christ's Object Lessons*, p. 190.

34. *Notebook Leaflets*, vol. 1, p. 82.

35. *Bible Echo*, Dec. 1, 1893.

36. *Review and Herald*, April 24, 1894.

37. *1888 Materials*, p. 124.

38. *Signs of the Times*, Feb. 14, 1900.

39. *Youth Instructor*, Aug. 5, 1897.

40. *Signs of the Times*, July 28, 1890.

41. *Signs of the Times*, Aug. 17, 1891.

42. *Review and Herald*, Nov. 24, 1896.

43. *Christ's Object Lessons*, p. 326.

44. *Youth Instructor*, Nov. 4, 1897.

45. *Steps to Christ*, p. 35.

46. *Signs of the Times*, Aug. 25, 1887.

47. *Review and Herald*, Jan. 21, 1873.

48. *Manuscript Releases*, vol. 6, p. 233.

49. 1901*General Conference Bulletin*, p. 36.

50. *Manuscript Releases*, vol. 17, p. 213.

51. *Signs of the Times*, Aug. 17, 1891.

52. *Desire of Ages*, p. 685.

53. *Review and Herald* Sept. 1, 1891.

54. *Review and Herald*, May 6, 1875.

55. *1888 Materials*, p. 899.

56. *Selected Messages*, book 1, pp. 339-340.

57. *Selected Messages*, book 1, p. 257.

58. *Faith and Works*, p. 93.

# More publications from 4th Angel Publishers...

### *The Third Angel's Message; 1893 &1897*

The 1893 and 1897 sermons that AT Jones gave at the General Conferences Ellen White described in this way: "I have been instructed to use those discourses of yours printed in the General Conference bulletins of 1893, 1897... I was shown that many would be helped by the articles... which were of the Holy Spirits framing." In these sermons you will see for yourself Christ and His righteousness exalted.

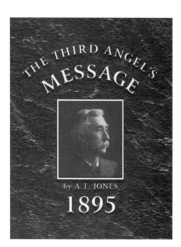

### *The Third Angel's Message; 1895*

Just after the 1895 General Conference ended in April, in May of that year Ellen White wrote, "The Lord in His great mercy sent a most precious message to His people through Eld. Waggoner and Jones."

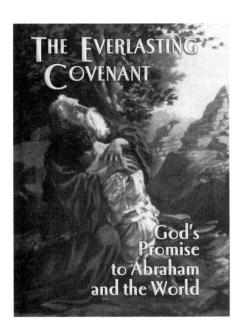

### The Everlasting Covenant

Ellen White wrote to those who were opposing Waggoner on the Convenants "...night before last I was shown that evidences in regard to the covenants were clear and convincing youself (and others) are spending your investigative powers for naught to produce a position on the convenants to vary from the position that Brother Waggoner has presented..."

### Ellen White and the Lord Cry

Read for yourself what Ellen White wrote about the message that came to us in 1888 as well as what she said about the messengers. It will bless your heart and give you confidence in the movement of God.

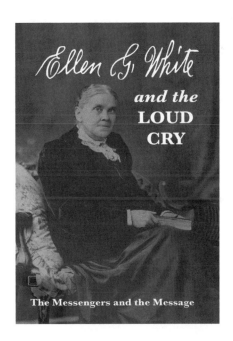

### For more information or to inquire about purchasing these books see the following page.

**Amazon Books**: www.amazon.com

**Light Bearers Ministry:** www.lbm.org

**Orion Publishing:** www.orion-publishing.org

**Glad Tidings Publishers**: www.gtpublishers.org

**Teach Services**: www.teachservices.com

*Or contact your local*
**ABC: 1-800-765-6955**

**For bulk orders, questions or comments: (866) 546-6469**